Kirby 108   Research Paper
                   1000-1500 words
MWF-2   footnotes 10 minim
                   sources 5 minim
T Th - 10   outline
                   footnote
                   Bibliography
Mon. 1/30 Baker 253-267   note cards
Tues. 1/31 "   269 - 281   Bibliography Cards
thur 2/2   "   289 - 296   4x6 cards
                            MLA

LITERARY REFLECTIONS

LITERARY Third Edition
REFLECTIONS

William R. Elkins
Emporia Kansas State College

Jack L. Kendall
*University of Oklahoma

John R. Willingham
University of Kansas

McGraw-Hill Book Company

New York   St. Louis   San Francisco   Auckland   Düsseldorf
Johannesburg   Kuala Lumpur   London   Mexico   Montreal   New Delhi
Panama   Paris   São Paulo   Singapore   Sydney   Tokyo   Toronto

For
EILEEN, CHARLYCE, AND YVONNE

This book was set in Vega by Rocappi, Inc.
The editors were Ellen B. Fuchs and Barry Benjamin;
the designer was J. E. O'Connor;
the production supervisor was Charles Hess.
Kingsport Press, Inc., was printer and binder.

LITERARY REFLECTIONS

2 3 4 5 6 7 8 9 0   KPKP   7 9 8 7 6

LIBRARY OF CONGRESS CATALOGING IN PUBLICATION DATA

Elkins, William R.   comp.
    Literary reflections.

    Includes indexes.
    1.   College readers.   I.   Kendall, Jack L., joint comp.
II.   Willingham, John R., joint comp.   III.   Title.
PE1122.E4   1976   808'.04275   75-19195
ISBN 0-07-019182-4

Photo Credits:

Cover, Parts I and III
David Strickler, Monkmeyer Press Photo

Parts II and V
Paul Conklin, Monkmeyer Press Photo

Part IV
George Martin, Design Photo International

Part VI
Hugh Rogers, Monkmeyer Press Photo

ACKNOWLEDGMENTS

Jean Anouilh, "Antigone," adapted and translated by Lewis Galantière. Copyright 1946 by Random House, Inc. Reprinted by permission of Random House, Inc.

W. H. Auden, "The Unknown Citizen," "A Summer Night," and "Schoolchildren," from *Collected Shorter Poems 1927-1957* by W. H. Auden. Copyright 1940 by W. H. Auden. Reprinted in the United States by permission of Random House, Inc., and in Canada by permission of Faber and Faber, Ltd.

James Baldwin, "Faulkner and Desegregation," from *Nobody Knows My Name* by James Baldwin. Copyright © 1954, 1956, 1958, 1959, 1960, 1961 by James Baldwin. Used with permission of The Dial Press, Inc.

John Barth, "Night-Sea Journey," from *Lost in the Funhouse* by John Barth. Copyright © 1966 by John Barth. Reprinted by permission of Doubleday & Company, Inc.

Philip Booth, "Cold-Water Flat," from *Letter from a Distant Land* by Philip Booth. Copyright 1953 by Philip Booth. Reprinted by permission of The Viking Press, Inc.

Ivan Bunin, "The Gentleman from San Francisco," from *The Gentleman from San Francisco and Other Stories* by Ivan Bunin. Copyright 1923, 1951 by Alfred A. Knopf, Inc. Reprinted by permission of Random House, Inc.

Gray Burr, "A Skater's Waltz," reprinted from *A Choice of Attitudes* by Gray Burr. Copyright © 1965 by Gray Burr. Reprinted by permission of Wesleyan University Press.

Mervyn Cadwallader, "Marriage as a Wretched Institution." Copyright © 1966 by The Atlantic Monthly Company, Boston, Mass. Reprinted with permission.

E. E. Cummings, "since feeling is first." Copyright 1926 by Horace Liveright; copyright 1954 by E. E. Cummings. "pity this busy monster, manunkind." Copyright 1944 by E. E. Cummings. Both reprinted from *Poems 1923-1954* by E. E. Cummings. Reprinted by permission of Harcourt Brace Jovanovich, Inc.

Barbara Davis, "Elevators," from *New American Poetry,* edited by Richard Monaco. Copyright © 1973 by McGraw-Hill, Inc. Used with permission of McGraw-Hill Book Company.

James Dickey, "In the Tree House at Night," from *Poems 1957-1967* by James Dickey. Copyright 1961 by James Dickey. Reprinted by permission of Wesleyan University Press. "In the Tree House at Night" first appeared in *The New Yorker.*

Emily Dickinson, "She Rose to His Requirement," from *The Poems of Emily Dickinson*, Thomas H. Johnson, Editor. Reprinted by permission of the publishers and the Trustees of Amherst College, Cambridge, Mass.: The Belknap Press of Harvard University. Copyright 1951, 1955 by The President and Fellows of Harvard College.

Ernest Dowson, "Vitae Summa Brevis Spem Nos Vetat Incohare Longam," from *The Poetical Works of Ernest Dowson,* edited by Desmond Flower. Reprinted by permission of Associated University Presses, Inc.

William Faulkner, "Letter to the North," from *Essays, Speeches and Public Letters* by William Faulkner. Copyright © 1956 by William Faulkner. Reprinted by permission of Random House, Inc.

Lawrence Ferlinghetti, "Christ climbed down . . . ," from *A Coney Island of the Mind* by Lawrence Ferlinghetti. Copyright © 1958 by Lawrence Ferlinghetti. Reprinted by permission of New Directions Publishing Corporation.

Edward Field, "Unwanted," from *Stand up, Friend, with Me.* Copyright 1963 by Edward Field. Reprinted by permission of Grove Press, Inc.

Erich Fromm, "The Theory of Love," excerpt from pp. 20-31, from *The Art of Loving* by Erich Fromm. Copyright © 1956 by Erich Fromm. Reprinted by permission of Harper and Row, Publishers, Inc.

Robert Frost, "The Death of the Hired Man" and "After Apple-Picking," from *The Poetry of Robert Frost,* edited by Edward Connery Lathem. Copyright 1930, 1939, © 1969 by Holt, Rinehart and Winston, Inc. Copyright © 1958 by Robert Frost. Copyright © 1967 by Lesley Frost Ballantine. Reprinted by permission of Holt, Rinehart and Winston, Inc.

Mary Gordon, "The Dead Ladies," from *New American Poetry,* edited by Richard Monaco. Copyright © 1973 by McGraw-Hill, Inc. Used with permission of McGraw-Hill Book Company.

Thom Gunn, "On the Move," from *The Sense of Movement* by Thom Gunn. Reprinted by permission of Faber & Faber, Ltd.

Thomas Hardy, "Neutral Tones" and "Friends Beyond," from *Collected Poems* by Thomas Hardy. Copyright 1925 by Macmillan Publishing Company, Inc. Reprinted by permission of Macmillan

Publishing Company, Inc., The Macmillan Co. of Canada, Limited, Macmillan London and Basingstoke, and the Trustees of the Hardy Estate.

Ernest Hemingway, "A Clean, Well-Lighted Place," from *Winner Take Nothing* by Ernest Hemingway. Copyright 1933 by Charles Scribner's Sons. Reprinted by permission of Charles Scribner's Sons.

Gerard Manley Hopkins, "God's Grandeur" and "The Caged Skylark," from *Poems of Gerard Manley Hopkins,* third edition, edited by W. H. Gardner. Copyright 1948 by Oxford University Press, Inc. Reprinted by permission of Oxford University Press, Inc.

Robinson Jeffers, "Hurt Hawks" and "Shine Perishing Republic," from *The Selected Poetry of Robinson Jeffers.* Copyright 1928 and renewed 1956 by Robinson Jeffers. Reprinted by permission of Random House, Inc.

Elizabeth Jennings, "One Flesh," from *Collected Poems* by Elizabeth Jennings. Reprinted by permission of Macmillan London and Basingstoke.

LeRoi Jones, "Expressive Language," from *Home: Social Essays* by LeRoi Jones. Copyright © 1963, 1966 by LeRoi Jones. Reprinted by permission of William Morrow & Company, Inc.

Robert Kastenbaum, "The Kingdom Where Nobody Dies," from *Saturday Review Science,* January 1973. Reprinted with permission.

Søren Kierkegaard, "Despair Is 'the Sickness Unto Death.'" Reprinted from *The Sickness Unto Death* by Søren Kierkegaard. Translated by Walter Lowrie. Copyright 1941. Reprinted by permission of Princeton University Press.

Martin Luther King, Jr., "I Have a Dream." Copyright © 1963 by Martin Luther King, Jr. Reprinted by permission of Joan Daves.

Jules Laforgue, "Apotheosis." Translated by Vernon Watkins from *An Anthology of French Poetry from Nevale to Valery in English Translation.* Edited by Angel Flores. Copyright © 1958 by Angel Flores, Doubleday Anchor. Reprinted by permission of Doubleday Anchor.

Philip Larkin, "Wires" and "Wedding Wind," from *The Less Deceived.* Copyright © 1955, 1970 by The Marvell Press. By permission of The Marvell Press, Hessle, Yorkshire, England.

D. H. Lawrence, "Terra Incognita," from *The Complete Poems of D. H. Lawrence,* edited by Vivian de Sola Pinto and F. Warren Roberts. Copyright © 1964, 1971 by Angelo Ravagli. All rights reserved. "The Rocking Horse Winner" from *The Complete Short Stories of D. H. Lawrence,* volume III. Copyright 1933 by the Estate of D. H. Lawrence. Copyright © renewed 1961 by Angelo Ravagli and C. M. Weekley, Executors of the Estate of Frieda Lawrence Ravagli. "The Spirit Of The Place" from *Studies in Classic American Literature* by D. H. Lawrence. Copyright 1923. Renewed 1951 by D. H. Lawrence. All rights reserved. All three works are reprinted by permission of The Viking Press, Inc.

C. Day Lewis, "The Poet," from *Short Is the Time: Poems 1936–1943.* Copyright 1940, 1943. Reprinted by permission of the Executors of the Estate of C. Day Lewis, Jonathan Cape, Ltd., and the Hogarth Press.

Edward Lueders, "Your Poem, Man . . . ," from *Some Haystacks Don't Even Have Any Needle and Other Complete Modern Poems* by Stephen Dunning, Edward Lueders, and Hugh Smith. Copyright © 1969 by Scott, Foresman and Company. Reprinted by permission of the publisher.

Archibald MacLeish, "Hypocrite Auteur," from *The Collected Poems of Archibald MacLeish.* Copyright © 1962 by Archibald MacLeish. Reprinted by permission of the publisher, Houghton Mifflin Company.

Bryan MacMahon, "Chestnut and Jet," from *The Lion-Tamer and Other Stories* by Bryan MacMahon. Copyright 1949 by Bryan MacMahon. Reprinted by permission of the publishers, E. P. Dutton & Co., Inc.

Thomas Mann, "Little Herr Friedemann," from *Stories of Three Decades* by Thomas Mann. Copyright 1936 by Alfred A. Knopf, Inc. Reprinted by permission of Random House, Inc.

Vassar Miller, "In Consolation." Reprinted from *Wage War on Silence* by Vassar Miller. Copyright © 1960 by Vassar Miller. By permission of Wesleyan University Press.

Marianne Moore, "Poetry," from *Collected Poems* by Marianne Moore. Copyright © 1935 by Marianne Moore. Renewed 1963 by Marianne Moore and T. S. Eliot. Reprinted by permission of Macmillan Publishing Co., Inc.

Howard Nemerov, "Boom!" from *New and Selected Poems* by Howard Nemerov. Copyright the University of Chicago, 1960. Reprinted by permission of the Margot Johnson Agency.

Joyce Carol Oates, "An Interior Monologue," from *The Wheel of Love and Other Stories* by Joyce Carol Oates. Copyright © 1969, 1970 by Joyce Carol Oates. Reprinted by permission of the publisher, Vanguard Press, Inc.

Flannery O'Connor, "The Life You Save May Be Your Own." Reprinted from her volume, *A Good Man Is Hard to Find and Other Stories.* Copyright © 1953, by Flannery O'Connor. Reprinted by permission of Harcourt Brace Jovanovich, Inc.

Eugene O'Neill, "Bound East For Cardiff," from *The Plays of Eugene O'Neill,* volume I, copyright 1955. Reprinted by permission of Random House, Inc.

Robert Pack, "A Bird in Search of a Cage," from *Poets of Today, II; The Irony of Joy: Poems* by Robert Pack. Copyright 1955 by Robert Pack. Reprinted by permission of Charles Scribner's Sons.

Vance Packard, "The Growing Power of Admen." Copyright © 1957 by the Atlantic Monthly Company, Boston, Mass.

Kenneth Patchen, "The New Being," from *Collected Poems* by Kenneth Patchen. Copyright 1949 by Kenneth Patchen. Reprinted by permission of New Directions Publishing Corporation.

Sylvia Plath, "Point Shirley" and "Sculptor," from *The Colossus and Other Poems* by Sylvia Plath. Copyright 1959, 1960, 1963; 1967 by Ted Hughes. By permission of Miss Olwyn Hughes and Random House, Inc.

Ezra Pound, "Commission," from *Personae* by Ezra Pound. Copyright 1926 by Ezra Pound. Reprinted by permission of New Directions Publishing Corporation.

Adrienne Rich, "The Stranger," from *Necessities of Life: Poems 1962–1965* by Adrienne Rich. Copyright © 1966 by W. W. Norton & Company, Inc. By permission of W. W. Norton & Company, Inc.

Theodore Roethke, "The Far Field," from *The Collected Poems of Theodore Roethke.* Copyright © 1962 by Beatrice Roethke, Administratrix of the estate of Theodore Roethke. Reprinted by permission of Doubleday & Company, Inc.

Philip Roth, "The Conversion of the Jews," from *Goodbye Columbus* by Philip Roth. Copyright © 1959 by Philip Roth. Reprinted by permission of the publisher, Houghton Mifflin Company.

William Saroyan, "Hello Out There," from *Razzle-Dazzle* by William Saroyan. Copyright by William Saroyan. Published by Harcourt, Brace and World, Company. Reprinted by permission of the author. All rights reserved.

Karl Shapiro, "Drug Store," from *Poems 1940–1953* by Karl Shapiro. Copyright 1941 by Karl Shapiro. Reprinted by permission of Random House, Inc.

Irwin Shaw, "The Girls in Their Summer Dresses," from *Selected Short Stories of Irwin Shaw.* Copyright 1939, renewed 1967 by Irwin Shaw. Reprinted by permission of Random House, Inc.

Joel Sloman, "Blueprint." By permission of the author.

Alexander Solzhenitsyn, "Zakhar-the-Pouch," from *Stories and Prose Poems* by Alexander Solzhenitsyn, translated by Michael Glenny. Translation copyright © 1970, 1971 by Michael Glenny. Published by The Bodley Head Ltd. Reprinted by permission of Farrar, Straus, and Giroux, Inc. and The Bodley Head Ltd.

Wallace Stevens, "Of Modern Poetry," from *The Collected Poems of Wallace Stevens* by Wallace Stevens. Copyright 1942 by Wallace Stevens. Reprinted by permission of Random House, Inc.

Melvin G. Storm, translator of "The Wanderer" from Old English, especially for this edition of *Literary Reflections.*

Karen Swenson, "The Price of Women." Copyright © 1973 from the book *An Attic of Ideals* by Karen Swenson. Reprinted by permission of Doubleday & Company, Inc.

A. C. Swinburne, "The Garden of Proserpine," from *Complete Works of Algernon* by Charles Swinburne, William Heinemann, Ltd., 1925.

John Updike, "Ex-Basketball Player," from *The Carpentered Hen and Other Tame Creatures* by John Updike. Copyright © 1957 by John Updike. Reprinted by permission of Harper & Row, Publishers, Inc.

John Wain, "Poem Feigned to Have Been Written by an Electronic Brain," from *Word Carved on a Sill* by John Wain. Reprinted by permission of Curtis Brown Ltd., London.

Robert Penn Warren, "Goodwood Comes Back," from his volume *The Circus in the Attic.* Copyright © 1941, 1969 by Robert Penn Warren. By permission of Harcourt Brace Jovanovich, Inc. "Pondy Woods" from *Selected Poems: New and Old 1923–1966* by Robert Penn Warren. Copyright 1944 by Robert Penn Warren. Reprinted by permission of Random House, Inc.

Eudora Welty, "Powerhouse." Reprinted from her volume *A Curtain of Green and Other Stories.* Copyright 1941, 1969 by Eudora Welty. Reprinted by permission of Harcourt Brace Jovanovich, Inc.

Leslie A. White, "The Symbol: The Origin and Basis of Human Behavior," from *The Science of Culture* by Leslie A. White. Copyright 1949 by Leslie A. White. Reprinted by permission of Farrar, Straus and Giroux, Inc.

Richard Wilbur, "Junk," from his volume *Advice to a Prophet and Other Poems.* Copyright © 1961 by Richard Wilbur. Reprinted by permission of Harcourt Brace Jovanovich, Inc.

Thornton Wilder, "Pullman Car Hiawatha," from *The Long Christmas Dinner and Other One Act Plays in One Act* by Thornton Wilder. Copyright 1931 by Yale University Press and Coward-McCann, Inc. Copyright 1959 by Thornton Wilder. Reprinted by permission of Harper & Row, Inc. Caution: *The Long Christmas Dinner and Other Plays in One Act* is the sole property of the author and is fully protected by copyright. The plays herein may not be acted by professionals or amateurs without formal permission and the payment of royalty. All rights, including professional, amateur, stock, radio and television, broadcasting, motion picture, recitation, lecturing, public reading, and the rights of translation into foreign languages are reserved. All professional inquiries and all requests for amateur rights should be addressed to Samuel French, 25 West 45 Street, New York, New York 10019.

William Carlos Williams, "Tract," from *Collected Earlier Poems* by William Carlos Williams. Copyright 1938 by New Directions Publishing Corporation. Reprinted by permission of New Directions Publishing Corporation.

William Butler Yeats, "The Leaders Of The Crowd," from *Later Poems* by William Butler Yeats. Copyright 1924 by Macmillan Publishing Co., Inc. Renewed 1952 by Bertha Georgie Yeats. "Sailing to Byzantium" from *Collected Poems* by William Butler Yeats. Copyright 1928 by Macmillan Publishing Co., Inc. Renewed 1956 by Bertha Georgie Yeats. Both reprinted in the United States with permission of The Macmillan Company. Canadian rights granted by permission of William Butler Yeats, Miss Anne Yeats, and Macmillan Co. of Canada.

CONTENTS

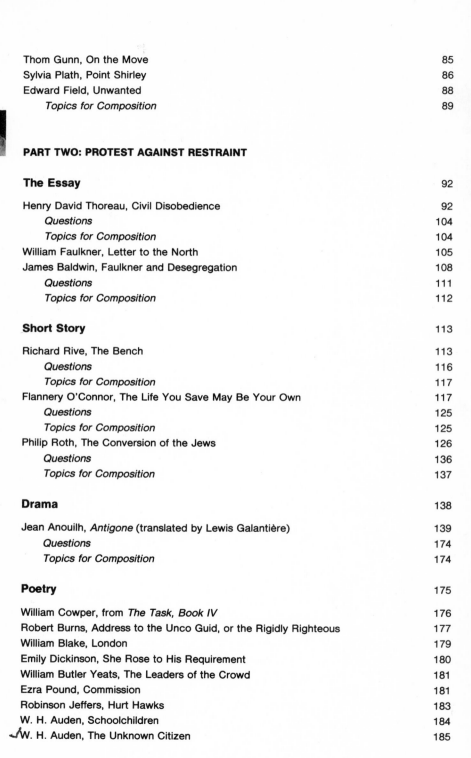

PART THREE: THE MEANING OF LOVE

The Essay   196

Short Story   207

Poetry   227

PART FIVE: THE SEARCH FOR MODES OF EXPRESSION

PART SIX: IN VIEW OF DEATH

PREFACE

By relating literature to thematic headings which suggest the most compelling aspects of the human condition. *Literary Reflections* gives students an immediate and meaningful reason for reading, which stimulates their ability to make comparisons among attitudes, among the distinctive characteristics of each literary type, and, equally important, among the formal strategies of individual authors. Much recent attention given to students' reading capabilities or, more properly, the lack of them emphasizes the validity of our approach. And it is axiomatic that students' abilities to write well depend on their abilities to read well. For these important reasons, we have retained the format of the preceding editions. We have added selections in order to broaden the student's participation in the variety of attitudes and techniques that writers evidence as they reflect upon human experience.

Our text thus serves three separate but overlapping purposes. It offers a stimulating insight into the history of ideas. It provides a viable means of identifying, comparing, and contrasting modes of expression. And it challenges students to come to grips with universally relevant ideas and problems, as they recur in literature, and encourages them to work out, carefully and imaginatively, their own formulations of them.

To accomplish our objectives, we have arranged the selections in six thematic units. Each unit is internally structured to present (1) essays that introduce in a relatively familiar prose form the thematic emphasis of the unit; (2) short stories as a logical step from the essay to more imaginative writing; (3) four plays (three of them have only one act) that share some features with fiction but add the impact of visual presentation or imagined production on a stage; and (4) selected poetry that carries students to the most intricate, most compressed, hence most intense form of literary expression. In effect, that movement from type to type within each unit enhances both the understanding of technique and the interest in ideas.

In addition, we have provided brief introductory discussions for each thematic heading to support and guide students' reading. For each selection, we have appended appropriate headnotes, provocative study questions, and suggestions for composition. All these devices are intended simply to challenge students without in any way preempting their critical judgments. The book, then, contains ample material for a rich encounter with literature and adds, for those who wish it, a framework for purposeful writing about literature. And the thematic organization, keeping faith with each author's general intent and vision, should not hamper the perceptive instructor who chooses his or her own alignment of selections.

We are very much aware of our continuing debt to those many colleagues and students whose comments and advice have helped shape this book. We are especially grateful to Ellen B. Fuchs, McGraw-Hill English Editor, for her patient guidance and cheerful cooperation. And we once again express our thanks to Yvonne Willingham of the University Press of Kansas for her editorial expertise in preparing the manuscript.

William R. Elkins
Jack L. Kendall
John R. Willingham

INTRODUCTION
TO LITERARY TYPES

Critics and scholars have speculated endlessly from the days of Aristotle about the nature and analysis of literature. *Literary Reflections* demonstrates not only the vital relationship between human experience and literary expression but it also directs the reader's attention to the apparently unlimited variety of uses of language in effecting techniques and forms. For any generalization about literature must include statements about the artist's use of words in a certain way to achieve a certain effect. And such statements necessarily must recognize the existence of conventional categories—literary genres or types. In this volume, we encounter four major genres—the essay, the short story, the drama, and the poem. Although the resources of any one of these may be present in the others, we can make some statements which are generally true only for each of the four types.

THE ESSAY

The term essay, as the designation for a type of literary composition, first appeared in English toward the end of the sixteenth century. To the Elizabethans the word meant a kind of literary exploration, an attempt (cf. the French verb *essayer,* "to try") to state something—perhaps a serious argument, sometimes a more or less random reflection upon experience. However or whenever it originally appeared, the essay has always involved exposition of an idea. The author may be relatively uninterested in aesthetic effects, but he or she is always attempting an orderly arrangement of thought. The characteristic mode of the essay, then, is "man thinking" in relatively formal structures. In a well-developed essay, the reader looks for a central idea or thesis, either explicit or implicit. The rest is mainly the arrangement of evidence, of reasons, of illustrations, or whatever amplification the thesis requires. If the author's literary bent permits, he or she may in addition utilize figurative language, narration, description, or dramatic incident as important elements of his thought. The "literary essay," distinguished by its conscious display of style and rhetorical virtuosity, does not enjoy in the twentieth century the favor it enjoyed up through the nineteenth century. Far more familiar today is the "article" which we find in newspapers and magazines, with the writer's ideas set forth in relatively familiar terms. The journalist, such as Vance Packard, with his characteristically simple language and short paragraphs, fills for our day the role which brought honor to such men as Richard Steele, Joseph Addison, Jonathan Swift, Thomas Carlyle, Thomas Babington Macaulay, Ralph Waldo Emerson, and James Russell Lowell. Nevertheless such twentieth-century stylists as George Orwell, Virginia Woolf, Loren Eisley, and Alfred Kazin keep alive the tradition of the essay as a creative literary medium. For discriminating readers, the journey with such representatives of "man thinking" (as Emerson called his ideal "American scholar") can be stimulating and fruitful, whether the author presents himself as an analyst of juvenile delinquency, as a professional sociologist probing the difficulties of love in the modern world, as a scientist advancing his hypothesis about life on Mars, or as a "personal essayist" simply detailing his reactions to old china or recalling his memories of a Creole courtyard in old New Orleans.

THE SHORT STORY

Relatively new as a recognized literary genre, the short story utilizes the mode of narrative. That is, someone recounts for us a plausible, sequential experience. Gertrude Stein may have simplified outrageously the formula for narration. "And after that what changes what changes after that, after that what changes and what changes after that and after that and what changes and after that and what changes after that"; but she emphasized rightly the importance of progression and the relationship of events within imagined time. The writer of fiction further imposes upon his or her narrative a deliberate design by the kind of characters created, the quality and outcome of the situation in which those characters are involved, and the establishment of a viewpoint toward those characters and their situations. Whether the story is told ostensibly by a character deeply involved in the events of the plot, by an outside observer, or even frankly by the author, the method of fiction establishes some meaningful order of events, reveals what of significance the characters did and said, and brings the sequence to a conclusion that implies an attitude toward experience. The order of events may be as straightforward as that outlined by Miss Stein; on the other hand, the narrative may leap backward and forward in time, as it does in Joyce Carol Oates' "An Interior Monologue," making strategic use of what in the movies is called the "flashback." But even when straight chronological order is violated, fiction creates for us a world more or less like the one we have known: the big difference between fiction and life arises from the writer's prerogative to impose upon his or her fictional "world" the kind of order and control the writer desires.

Whereas the essayist restricts his statement to facts, to a report of what he has thought and observed, to his beliefs and an invitation to the reader to accept or at least understand those beliefs, the writer of fiction, particularly in our day, characteristically does not intervene in his narrative with direct, editorial statement. He merely tells his story as artfully as possible and allows the combination of characterization, plot, theme, imagery, dramatic situation, and condensed narrative to imply as much about his world view as it can. Ivan Bunin does not have to state directly his attitude toward the materialistic values of his nameless "Gentleman from San Francisco"; every juxtaposition of scene and every exchange of dialogue forcibly conveys to us Bunin's judgments. The difference between the "pulp" magazine story or the saccharine tale in a woman's magazine, on the one hand, and the memorable fictional illumination of human experience, on the other, is simply one of insight and artistry, which together distinguish good fiction from escape fiction.

Every student has heard of the pyramid design for plot—in which generating circumstances rise through conflict to *denouement* (literally, the "untying of the knot," or the solution). And ordinarily the pyramid design fits the typical short story rather well. In one way or another, the author of a short story quickly establishes a situation containing the seeds of conflict which rises to a point of crisis or "climax" before descending, perhaps very abruptly, to the resolution or *denouement*. Although the sequence of events may not end happily, it must satisfy the reader's sense of appropriateness in terms of the kind of conflict narrated.

THE DRAMA

Drama, an ancient literary form, was explained by the Greeks with considerable sophistication. Aristotle analyzed the various elements—plot, diction, spectacle—which the dramatist utilizes; and his successors have elaborated endlessly upon theories of the drama. Although much of what we have said about the short story is equally true of the drama (both relate stories, both ask the reader to accept as plausible the sequence of events, and both have a plot design), the writer of fiction tells us in his or her own way *about* certain characters in a certain situation, whereas the dramatist conjures up a world to be created by stage designers and actors and brought to life by actors.

In "Hello Out There," William Saroyan allows considerable leeway for stage design: for the setting, he tells us only, "There is a fellow in a small-town prison cell. . . ." On the other hand, Jean Anouilh offers relatively precise, often suggestive directions for the stark setting of *Antigone,* for the kind of atmosphere he expects, for the aura of character and incident he envisions. In any of Shakespeare's plays poetry is the only clue to character interpretation, but an imaginative director can find ways to refine those clues. Hamlet can be made as morosely meditative as the director wishes; Macbeth can be made as passive or as aggressive as the vision of actors and production planners can contrive. Beyond an occasional direction like "suddenly" or "almost to himself," Saroyan interferes very little with the possibilities for an actor's interpretation of the Young Man's role. Anouilh, however, specifies the tone and effect he desires from gestures, facial expressions, and speeches.

In any play the characters are interpreted, with the help of such notes and stage directions as the dramatist provides, by directors and by actors who move on and off a stage, speak to each other or to themselves as the script of the play dictates, and seem with the help of lighting, makeup, stage properties, costumes, and gestures to be real people who undergo a span of experience before an audience. One important distinction between drama and fiction is that those segments of imagined experience selected by the playwright as most important are acted out before an audience; moreover, those segments, whether or not divided into acts and scenes, occupy exactly the same time span spent by the audience in watching those segments. To read a play successfully, we must supply through the imagination the staging, the lighting, the direction, the sound effects, and, with such help as we may get from the stage directions, the movements of the actors. Reading a play may be a relatively poor substitute for watching a performance of it, but the reading can be both exciting and profitable nevertheless. We can pause to consider the possible implications of a character's speech, or we may backtrack as often as we wish in order to fathom the emerging form of the drama. And to the extent that drama forces us to attend to each word a character speaks, it requires something of the close reading that we give to poetry.

THE POEM

Like the short story and the novel, the poem may relate a narrative. Or, as in Browning's "The Bishop Orders His Tomb at St. Praxed's Church" or Frost's "The Death of the Hired Man," the poem may be a drama in miniature: though it is not intended for a performance, its characters simply speak aloud and reveal a dramatic situation. Although it is the most ancient and exalted literary type, poetry is harder than any of the other types to define. We know that poems look different: the poet dictates how his or her work will appear upon the printed page. Its lines, unlike those of prose, tend to be symmetrical, though sentence units are not always completed within the line. Even the poems of an idiosyncratic modern poet like E. E. Cummings, with unconventional uses of typography, have a more formal appearance than any work of prose. But quantitative measures like typography, stanzaic pattern, or meter do not really help much to define poetry. For greeting card "verse" exhibits many of the physical properties of poetry. Qualitative standards, on the other hand, discover for us the presence of poetry. The essential point is that in poetry language is compressed and elevated beyond that of ordinary discourse. Poetry may not always be, as William Wordsworth said, "emotion recollected in tranquillity"; but at least, whether in conventionally metrical or "free" verse or even "prose poems," the conscious ordering of language is all-important. In its compulsion toward rhythmic patterns and selective word sounds, poetry suggests strong relationships to music; in its typical drive to evoke images, poetry suggests comparisons with painting. Perhaps Emerson's witty definition of a poem as a "metre-making argument" comes close enough to a formal definition; but in its combined appeals to emotion and thought through the artful arrangement of words, even the relatively short poem, if it is successful, brings to the reader a sudden illumination of the human condition and a "deliverance" that cannot be obtained through any other literary type. In the twentieth century, poetry probably does not enjoy the prestige it commanded in other ages; on the other hand, more poets write and more experimentation takes place than in any other century.

LITERARY REFLECTIONS

PART ONE

THE SEARCH
FOR A PLACE
IN SOCIETY

When we speak of man's search for a place in society, we touch upon that side of man's nature that he almost always conceals from others and often conceals from himself. Obviously, the search for a place is both a search for a physical place and a search for an inner sense of identity. In this dual function, only the physical place manifests itself; yet the search is primarily an inner one. Each man, whether or not he admits it, carries within him an ideal image of himself. This self-image is a primary consideration in his attempts to place himself physically within society. In short, the search for a place becomes an attempt of each man to reconcile that ideal image he has of himself not only with his position in society but, also, with the treatment that society accords him. Consequently, writers have found the inner conflict between the *what ought to be* and the *what is,* a theme so basic, yet so diverse, that its treatment lends itself to all types of literature.

D. H. Lawrence's essay, "The Spirit of Place," is the first chapter of his book, *Studies in Classic American Literature.* In this essay, Lawrence considers place as a dominant factor in the development of a national character and a national literature. But, in keeping with the dual function of place, Lawrence has much to say about man's inner search for identity and its control of his actions, and the physical place in which he chooses to exercise his actions. Lawrence says, "Men are only free when they are doing what the deepest self likes."

Martin Luther King, Jr., in his famous speech, "I Have a Dream," offers a contemporary statement about the black man's place in American society. Like Lawrence, King sees a potential for the emergence of an American democracy which will destroy the old masters and create equality. But unlike Lawrence, who writes as an observer from a foreign land, King speaks as one who vibrates with a sense of place which, though partially denied, is nevertheless American.

Stephen Crane's short story, "An Experiment in Misery," fictionalizes the plight of the wanderer, the social outcast, whose sense of displacement is only ironically placated when he finds companionship of a kind with those like him. Crane's story, set in nineteenth-century America, offers additional comments by contrasting the emergence of a mighty and wealthy nation with the degradation and deprivation of human dignity.

The second short story, Thomas Mann's "Little Herr Friedemann," takes another turn within this theme. Herr Friedemann, crippled from birth, has created a world of compromise, suppressing his normal desires in recognition that society cannot accept abnormality. When, however, he forgets the limitations of his place in society, he finds the disparity between the *what is* and the *what ought to be* too great to allow a return to the world of compromise.

Alexander Solzhenitsyn's "Zakhar-the-Pouch" deals with many of the same points found in Lawrence's essay. The main character, Zakhar, is the physical expression of the "spirit of place" as he officially guards a Russian monument, a monument which in its treatment by others juxtaposed with its importance to "Mother Russia" becomes the focal point for the contrarities and inequities that mark man's efforts to capture place and time.

William Saroyan's "Hello Out There" becomes very quickly a dialogue about "here," "there," and "somewhere." Its specific setting in a dusty West Texas town is, of course, relatively incidental, though the constant wind and aimless dust of the plains appropriately mirror the constant frustrations and aimless lives of people who have not found a "place" that answers to the yearning of the homeless heart. The "rape" that precedes but generates the situation of the play and the looming "lynching bee" that closes it hint at the forces which oppose the life that would be liberated for escape to "Frisco," or wherever the imaginative individual places the location of hope for and fulfillment of life's possibilities. Significantly and appropriately this first play in a book thematically structured around important literary avenues for exploring the human condition acknowledges somewhere within its brief scope not only the compulsion to find and possess a "place" but also all the other five basic motifs—abhorrence of restraint, the possibilities of love, the ubiquity of materialism, the need for adequate expression, and the inexorable threat of death.

THE ESSAY

The essay that follows points up the fact that literary classifications should be flexible enough to accommodate the creative talents of the writer. Lawrence's informal approach to what is generally considered a formal area (literary criticism) in essay writing illustrates that the writer of the essay need not be limited by dictates of form in his attempt to reach his reader. Lawrence disarms his reader with a wide variety of unexpected techniques. We should be alert, however, and weigh carefully our reaction to the following:

1 The conversational, bantering tone
2 The use of charged, colorful, idiosyncratic speech forms more characteristic of the orated diatribe than the essay
3 The highly subjective point of view—Lawrence's experience becomes authority for every man's experience
4 The name-calling, blatantly revealing Lawrence's prejudices in such a way as to suggest that they should rightly be every man's prejudices

THE SPIRIT OF PLACE

D. H. Lawrence

We like to think of the old-fashioned American classics as children's books. Just childishness, on our part. The old American art-speech contains an alien quality, which belongs to the American continent and to nowhere else. But, of course, so long as we insist on reading the books as children's tales, we miss all that.

One wonders what the proper high-brow Romans of the third and fourth or later centuries read into the strange utterances of Lucretius or Apuleius or Tertullian, Augustine or Athanasius. The uncanny voice of Iberian Spain, the weirdness of old Carthage, the passion of Libya and North Africa; you may bet the proper old Romans never heard these at all. They read old Latin inference over the top of it, as we read old European inference over the top of Poe or Hawthorne.

It is hard to hear a new voice, as hard as it is to listen to an unknown language. We just don't listen. There is a new voice in the old American classics. The world has declined to hear it, and has babbled about children's stories.

Why?—Out of fear. The world fears a new experience more than it fears anything. Because a new experience displaces so many old experiences. And it is like trying to use muscles that have perhaps never been used, or that have been going stiff for ages. It hurts horribly.

The world doesn't fear a new idea. It can pigeon-hole any idea. But it can't pigeon-hole a real new experience. It can only dodge. The world is a great dodger, and the Americans the greatest. Because they dodge their own very selves.

There is a new feeling in the old American books, far more than there is in the modern American books, which are pretty empty of any feeling, and proud of it. There is a "different" feeling in the old American classics. It is the shifting over from the old

5

psyche to something new, a displacement. And displacements hurt. This hurts. So we try to tie it up, like a cut finger. Put a rag round it.

It is a cut too. Cutting away the old emotions and consciousness. Don't ask what is left.

Art-speech is the only truth. An artist is usually a damned liar, but his art, if it be art, will tell you the truth of his day. And that is all that matters. Away with eternal truth. Truth lives from day to day, and the marvellous Plato of yesterday is chiefly bosh to-day.

The old American artists were hopeless liars. But they were artists, in spite of themselves. Which is more than you can say of most living practitioners.

And you can please yourself, when you read *The Scarlet Letter,* whether you accept what that sugary, blue-eyed little darling of a Hawthorne has to say for himself, false as all darlings are, or whether you read the impeccable truth of his art-speech.

The curious thing about art-speech is that it prevaricates so terribly, I mean it tells such lies. I suppose because we always all the time tell ourselves lies. And out of a pattern of lies art weaves the truth. Like Dostoevsky posing as a sort of Jesus, but most truthfully revealing himself all the while as a little horror.

Truly art is a sort of subterfuge. But thank God for it, we can see through the subterfuge if we choose. Art has two great functions. First, it provides an emotional experience. And then, if we have the courage of our own feelings, it becomes a mine of practical truth. We have had the feelings *ad nauseam.* But we've never dared dig the actual truth out of them, the truth that concerns us, whether it concerns our grandchildren or not.

The artist usually sets out—or used to—to point a moral and adorn a tale. The tale, however, points the other way, as a rule. Two blankly opposing morals, the artist's and the tale's. Never trust the artist. Trust the tale. The proper function of a critic is to save the tale from the artist who created it.

Now we know our business in these studies: saving the American tale from the American artist.

Let us look at this American artist first. How did he ever get to America, to start with? Why isn't he a European still, like his father before him?

Now listen to me, don't listen to him. He'll tell you the lie you expect. Which is partly your fault for expecting it.

He didn't come in search of freedom of worship. England had more freedom of worship in the year 1700 than America had. Won by Englishmen who wanted freedom, and so stopped at home and fought for it. And got it. Freedom of worship? Read the history of New England during the first century of its existence.

Freedom anyhow? The land of the free! This the land of the free! Why, if I say anything that displeases them, the free mob will lynch me, and that's my freedom. Free? Why, I have never been in any country where the individual has such an abject fear of his fellow countrymen. Because, as I say, they are free to lynch him the moment he shows he is not one of them.

No, no, if you're so fond of the truth about Queen Victoria, try a little about yourself.

Those Pilgrim Fathers and their successors never came here for freedom of worship. What did they set up when they got here? Freedom, would you call it?

They didn't come for freedom. Or if they did, they sadly went back on themselves.

All right then, what did they come for? For lots of reasons. Perhaps least of all in search of freedom of any sort: positive freedom, that is.

They came largely to get *away*—that most simple of motives. To get away. Away from what? In the long run, away from themselves. Away from everything. That's why most people have come to America, and still do come. To get away from everything they are and have been.

"Henceforth be masterless."

Which is all very well, but it isn't freedom. Rather the reverse. A hopeless sort of constraint. It is never freedom till you find something you really *positively want to be*. And people in America have always been shouting about the things they are *not*. Unless, of course, they are millionaires, made or in the making.

And after all there is a positive side to the movement. All that vast flood of human life that has flowed over the Atlantic in ships from Europe to America has not flowed over simply on a tide of revulsion from Europe and from the confinements of the European ways of life. This revulsion was, and still is, I believe, the prime motive in emigration. But there was some cause, even for the revulsion.

It seems as if at times man had a frenzy for getting away from any control of any sort. In Europe the old Christianity was the real master. The Church and the true aristocracy bore the responsibility for the working out of the Christian ideals: a little irregularly, maybe, but responsible nevertheless.

Mastery, kingship, fatherhood had their power destroyed at the time of the Renaissance.

And it was precisely at this moment that the great drift over the Atlantic started. What were men drifting away from? The old authority of Europe? Were they breaking the bonds of authority, and escaping to a new more absolute unrestrainedness? Maybe. But there was more to it.

Liberty is all very well, but men cannot live without masters. There is always a master. And men either live in glad obedience to the master they believe in, or they live in a frictional oppostion to the master they wish to undermine. In America this frictional opposition has been the vital factor. It has given the Yankee his kick. Only the continual influx of more servile Europeans has provided America with an obedient labouring class. The true obedience never outlasting the first generation.

But there sits the old master, over in Europe. Like a parent. Somewhere deep in every American heart lies a rebellion against the old parenthood of Europe. Yet no American feels he has completely escaped its mastery. Hence the slow, smouldering patience of American opposition. The slow, smouldering, corrosive obedience to the old master Europe, the unwilling subject, the unremitting opposition.

Whatever else you are, be masterless.

Ca Ca Caliban
Get a new master, be a new man.

Escaped slaves, we might say, people the republics of Liberia or Haiti. Liberia enough! Are we to look at America in the same way? A vast republic of escaped slaves. When you consider the hordes from eastern Europe, you might well say it: a vast republic of escaped slaves. But one dare not say this of the Pilgrim Fathers, and the great old body of idealist Americans, the modern Americans tortured with thought. A vast republic of escaped slaves. Look out, America! And a minority of earnest, self-tortured people.

The masterless.

Ca Ca Caliban
Get a new master, be a new man.

What did the Pilgrim Fathers come for, then, when they came so gruesomely over the black sea? Oh, it was in a black spirit. A black revulsion from Europe, from the old authority of Europe, from kings and bishops and popes. And more. When you look into it, more. They were black, masterful men, they wanted something else. No kings, no bishops maybe. Even no God Almighty. But also, no more of this new "humanity" which followed the Renaissance. None of this new liberty which was to be so pretty in Europe. Something grimmer, by no means free-and-easy.

America has never been easy, and is not easy to-day. Americans have always been at a certain tension. Their liberty is a thing of sheer will, sheer tension: a liberty of <u>Thou shalt not.</u> And it has been so from the first. The land of <u>Thou shalt not.</u> Only the first commandment is: <u>Thou shalt not presume to be a master.</u> Hence democracy.

"We are the masterless." That is what the American Eagle shrieks. It's a Hen-Eagle.

The Spaniards refused the post-Renaissance liberty of Europe. And the Spaniards filled most of America. The Yankees, too, refused, refused the post-Renaissance humanism of Europe. First and foremost, they hated masters. But under that, they hated the flowing ease of humour in Europe. At the bottom of the American soul was always a dark suspense, at the bottom of the Spanish-American soul the same. And this dark suspense hated and hates the old European spontaneity, watches it collapse with satisfaction.

Every continent has its own great spirit of place. Every people is polarized in some particular locality, which is home, the homeland. Different places on the face of the earth have different vital effluence, different vibration, different chemical exhalation, different polarity with different stars: call it what you like. But the spirit of place is a great reality. The Nile valley produced not only the corn, but the terrific religions of Egypt. China produces the Chinese, and will go on doing so. The Chinese in San Francisco will in time cease to be Chinese, for America is a great melting-pot.

There was a tremendous polarity in Italy, in the city of Rome. And this seems to have died. For even places die. The Island of Great Britain had a wonderful terrestrial magnetism or polarity of its own, which made the British people. For the moment, this polarity seems to be breaking. Can England die? And what if England dies?

Men are less free than they imagine; ah, far less free. The freest are perhaps least free.

Men are free when they are in a living homeland, not when they are straying and breaking away. Men are free when they are obeying some deep, inward voice of religious belief. Obeying from within. Men are free when they belong to a living, organic, *believing* community, active in fulfilling some unfulfilled, perhaps unrealized purpose. Not when they are escaping to some wild west. The most unfree souls go west, and shout of freedom. Men are freest when they are most unconscious of freedom. The shout is a rattling of chains, always was.

Men are not free when they are doing just what they like. The moment you can do just what you like, there is nothing you care about doing. Men are only free when they are doing what the deepest self likes.

And there is getting down to the deepest self! It takes some diving.

Because the deepest self is way down, and the conscious self is an obstinate monkey. But of one thing we may be sure. If one wants to be free, one has to give up the illusion of doing what one likes, and seek what it wishes done.

But before you can do what it likes, you must first break the spell of the old mastery, the old it.

Perhaps at the Renaissance, when kingship and fatherhood fell, Europe drifted into a very dangerous half-truth: of liberty and equality. Perhaps the men who went to America felt this, and so repudiated the old world together. Went one better than Europe. Liberty in America has meant so far the breaking away from *all* dominion. The true liberty will only begin when Americans discover it, and proceed possibly to fulfil it. It being the deepest whole self of man, the self in its wholeness, not idealistic halfness.

That's why the Pilgrim Fathers came to America, then; and that's why we come. Driven by it. We cannot see that invisible winds carry us, as they carry swarms of locusts, that invisible magnetism brings us as it brings the migrating birds to their unforeknown goal. But it is so. We are not the marvellous choosers and deciders we think we are. It chooses for us, and decides for us. Unless, of course, we are just escaped slaves, vulgarly cocksure of our ready-made destiny. But if we are living people, in touch with the source, it drives us and decides us. We are free only so long as we obey. When we run counter, and think we will do as we like, we just flee around like Orestes pursued by the Eumenides.

And still, when the great day begins, when Americans have at last discovered America and their own wholeness, still there will be the vast number of escaped slaves to reckon with, those who have no cocksure, ready-made destinies.

Which will win in America, the escaped slaves, or the new whole men?

The real American day hasn't begun yet. Or at least not yet sunrise. So far it has been the false dawn. That is, in the progressive American consciousness there has been the one dominant desire, to do away with the old thing. Do away with masters, exalt the will of the people. The will of the people being nothing but a figment, the exalting doesn't count for much. So, in the name of the will of the people, get rid of masters. When you have got rid of masters, you are left with this mere phrase of the will of the people. Then you pause and bethink yourself, and try to recover your own wholeness.

So much for the conscious American motive, and for democracy over here. Democracy in America is just the tool with which the old master of Europe, the European spirit, is undermined. Europe destroyed, potentially, American democracy will evaporate. America will begin.

American consciousness has so far been a false dawn. The negative ideal of democracy. But underneath, and contrary to this open ideal, the first hints and revelations, of it. It, the American whole soul.

You have got to pull the democratic and idealistic clothes off American utterance, and see what you can of the dusky body of it underneath.

"Henceforth be masterless."

Henceforth be mastered.

QUESTIONS

1 Why does Lawrence say that the world finds it hard to hear a new voice? In what way does he draw a parallel between the "new voice" and a new experience?

2 How does Lawrence view the intent of the artist in respect to the art that he creates?

3 Lawrence sees the story of America's founding as a myth. What theory does he offer to replace the myth? Is his definition of freedom valid?

4 What does he mean by "Henceforth be masterless"?

5 If we separate Lawrence's hysteria from his subject matter, what three main ideas emerge?

TOPICS FOR COMPOSITION

1 Lawrence's style may obscure many interesting ideas. Write a summary of this essay.

2 The author speaks of a tension in the American idea of freedom. He literally means that Americans constantly work to preserve their concept of freedom. Support this idea by focusing on current events.

3 Investigate the possibilities of complete freedom—the idea of "Henceforth be masterless."

☐

"I Have a Dream" is oratory. As such it provides many insights into techniques of persuasive rhetoric. Although a certain amount of emotionalism is part of an effective appeal, a highly successful work, such as King's speech, relies mainly on carefully chosen appeals that will hold the audience by relating to issues well-known to them. As you read this speech, note how King uses:

1 History to provide initial support and as a springboard for his appeal

2 Urgency to add relevancy to his appeal

3 A warning, couched in reasoned terms, to give added emphasis to his statement

4 A prophecy to encompass a vision of hope

"I HAVE A DREAM . . ."

Martin Luther King, Jr.

Five score years ago, a great American, in whose symbolic shadow we stand, signed the Emancipation Proclamation. This momentous decree came as a great beacon light of hope to millions of Negro slaves who had been seared in the flames of withering injustice. It came as a joyous daybreak to end the long night of captivity.

But one hundred years later, we must face the tragic fact that the Negro is still not free. One hundred years later, the life of the Negro is still sadly crippled by the manacles of segregation and the chains of discrimination. One hundred years later, the Negro lives on a lonely island of poverty in the midst of a vast ocean of material prosperity. One hundred years later, the Negro is still languished in the corners of American society and finds himself an exile in his own land. So we have come here today to dramatize an appalling condition.

In a sense we have come to our nation's Capital to cash a check. When the architects of our republic wrote the magnificent words of the Constitution and the Declaration of Independence, they were signing a promissory note to which every American was to fall heir. This note was a promise that all men would be guaranteed the unalienable rights of life, liberty, and the pursuit of happiness.

It is obvious today that America has defaulted on this promissory note insofar as her citizens of color are concerned. Instead of honoring this sacred obligation, America has given the Negro people a bad check; a check which has come back marked "insufficient funds." But we refuse to believe that the bank of justice is bankrupt. We refuse to believe that there are insufficient funds in the great vaults of opportunity of this nation. So we have come to cash this check—a check that will give us upon demand the riches of freedom and the security of justice. We have also come to this hallowed spot to remind America and the fierce urgency of *now*. This is no time to engage in the luxury of cooling off or to take the tranquilizing of gradualism. *Now* is the time to make real the promises of Democracy. *Now* is the time to rise from the dark and desolate valley of segregation to the sunlit path of racial justice. *Now* is the time to open the doors of opportunity to all of God's children. *Now* is the time to lift our nation from the quicksands of racial injustice to the solid rock of brotherhood.

It would be fatal for the nation to overlook the urgency of the moment and to underestimate the determination of the Negro. This sweltering summer of the Negro's legitimate discontent will not pass until there is an invigorating autumn of freedom and equality. 1963 is not an end, but a beginning. Those who hope that the Negro needed to blow off steam and will now be content will have a rude awakening if the nation returns to business as usual. There will be neither rest nor tranquillity in America until the Negro is granted his citizenship rights. The whirlwinds of revolt will continue to shake the foundation of our nation until the bright day of justice emerges.

But there is something that I must say to my people who stand on the warm threshold which leads into the palace of justice. In the process of gaining our rightful place we must not be guilty of wrongful deeds. Let us not seek to satisfy our thirst for freedom by drinking from the cup of bitterness and hatred. We must forever conduct our struggle on the high plane of dignity and discipline. We must not allow our creative protest to degenerate into physical violence. Again and again we must rise to the majestic heights of meeting physical force with soul force. The marvelous new militancy which has engulfed the Negro community must not lead us to a distrust of all white people, for many of our white brothers, as evidenced by their presence here today, have come to realize that their destiny is tied up with our destiny and their freedom is inextricably bound to our freedom. We cannot walk alone.

And as we walk, we must make the pledge that we shall march ahead. We cannot turn back. There are those who are asking the devotees of civil rights, "When will you be satisfied?" We can never be satisfied as long as the Negro is the victim of the unspeakable horrors of police brutality. We can never be satisfied as long as our bodies, heavy with the fatigue of travel, cannot gain lodging in the motels of the highways and the hotels of the cities. We cannot be satisfied as long as the Negro's basic mobility is from a smaller ghetto to a larger one. We can never be satisfied as long as a Negro in Mississippi cannot vote and a Negro in New York believes he has nothing for which to vote. No, no, we are not satisfied, and we will not be satisfied until justice rolls down like waters and righteousness like a mighty stream.

I am not unmindful that some of you have come here out of great trials and tribulations. Some of you have come fresh from narrow jail cells. Some of you have come from areas where your quest for freedom left you battered by the storms of persecution and staggered by the winds of police brutality. You have been the veterans of creative suffering. Continue to work with the faith that unearned suffering is redemptive.

Go back to Mississippi, go back to Alabama, go back to South Carolina, go back to Georgia, go back to Louisiana, go back to the slums and ghettos of our northern cities, knowing that somehow this situation can and will be changed. Let us not wallow in the valley of despair.

I say to you today, my friends, that in spite of the difficulties and frustrations of the moment I still have a dream. It is a dream deeply rooted in the American dream.

I have a dream that one day this nation will rise up and live out the true meaning of its creed: "We hold these truths to be self-evident; that all men are created equal."

I have a dream that one day on the red hills of Georgia the sons of former slaves and the sons of former slaveowners will be able to sit down together at the table of brotherhood.

I have a dream that one day even the state of Mississippi, a desert state sweltering with the heat of injustice and oppression, will be transformed into an oasis of freedom and justice.

I have a dream that my four little children will one day live in a nation where they will not be judged by the color of their skin but by the content of their character.

I have a dream today.

I have a dream that one day the state of Alabama, whose governor's lips are presently dripping with the words of interposition and nullification, will be transformed into a situation where little black boys and black girls will be able to join hands with little white boys and white girls and walk together as sisters and brothers.

I have a dream today.

I have a dream that one day every valley shall be exalted, every hill and mountain shall be made low, the rough places will be made plain, and the crooked places will be made straight, and the glory of the Lord shall be revealed, and all flesh shall see it together.

This is our hope. This is the faith with which I return to the South. With this faith we will be able to hew out of the mountain of despair a stone of hope. With this faith we will be able to transform the jangling discords of our nation into a beautiful symphony of brotherhood. With this faith we will be able to work together, to pray together, to struggle together, to go to jail together, to stand up for freedom together, knowing that we will be free one day.

This will be the day when all of God's children will be able to sing with new meaning

> My country, 'tis of thee,
> Sweet land of liberty,
>   Of thee I sing:
> Land where my fathers died,
> Land of the pilgrims' pride.
> From every mountain-side
>   Let freedom ring.

And if America is to be a great nation this must become true. So let freedom ring from the prodigious hilltops of New Hampshire. Let freedom ring from the mighty mountains of New York. Let freedom ring from the heightening Alleghenies of Pennsylvania!

Let freedom ring from the snowcapped Rockies of Colorado!

Let freedom ring from the curvacious peaks of California!

But not only that; let freedom ring from Stone Mountain of Georgia!

Let freedom ring from Lookout Mountain of Tennessee!

Let freedom ring from every hill and molehill of Mississippi. From every mountain-side, let freedom ring.

When we let freedom ring, when we let it ring from every village and every hamlet, from every state and every city, we will be able to speed up that day when all of God's children, black men and white men, Jews and Gentiles, Protestants and Catholics, will be able to join hands and sing in the words of the old Negro spiritual, "Free at last! free at last! thank God almighty, we are free at last!"

QUESTIONS

1 Granting that King knew well his audience, examine the appropriateness of his word choice, his sentence structure, his use of metaphor and analogy.
2 What is the most prominent structural feature in this speech?

TOPICS FOR COMPOSITION

1 Freedom is an often-used word in both Lawrence's essay and King's speech. Write an essay in which you compare and contrast King's and Lawrence's use of the word in an attempt to arrive at each man's definition of freedom.
2 Write an essay examining King's position in light of today's events.

SHORT STORY

Crane's title, "An Experiment in Misery," is his initial effort to draw the reader into his story, to touch within us those common responses that give its title and its tale meanings broader than its characters, time, and place. Indeed, as the story progresses, it becomes evident that our participation is necessary to the "experiment." Note the following techniques:

1   The forbidding details of the setting: the late night, the cold and storm, and the artificiality of the lighting and the machinery of the city
2   The description of the young man and the response that it brings until he finds those with whom he can superficially identify
3   The progressive pattern of initiation, perhaps only unconsciously understood by the young man, but more fully comprehensible to us

AN EXPERIMENT IN MISERY

Stephen Crane

It was late at night, and a fine rain was swirling softly down, causing the pavements to glisten with hue of steel and blue and yellow in the rays of the innumerable lights. A youth was trudging slowly, without enthusiasm, with his hands buried deep in his trousers' pockets, toward the downtown places where beds can be hired for coppers. He was clothed in an aged and tattered suit, and his derby was a marvel of dust-covered crown and torn rim. He was going forth to eat as the wanderer may eat, and sleep as the homeless sleep. By the time he had reached City Hall Park he was so completely plastered with yells of "bum" and "hobo," and with various unholy epithets that small boys had applied to him at intervals, that he was in a state of the most profound dejection. The sifting rain saturated the old velvet collar of his overcoat, and as the wet cloth pressed against his neck, he felt that there no longer could be pleasure in life. He looked about him searching for an outcast of highest degree that they too might share miseries, but the lights threw a quivering glare over rows and circles of deserted benches that glistened damply, showing patches of wet sod behind them. It seemed that their usual freights had fled on this night to better things. There were only squads of well-dressed Brooklyn people who swarmed towards the bridge.

The young man loitered about for a time and then went shuffling off down Park Row. In the sudden descent in style of the dress of the crowd he felt relief, and as if he were at last in his own country. He began to see tatters that matched his tatters. In Chatham Square there were aimless men strewn in front of saloons and lodging-houses, standing sadly, patiently, reminding one vaguely of the attitudes of chickens in a storm. He aligned himself with these men, and turned slowly to occupy himself with the flowing life of the great street.

Through the mists of the cold and storming night, the cable cars went in silent procession, great affairs shining with red and brass, moving with formidable power, calm and irresistible, dangerful and gloomy, breaking silence only by the loud fierce cry

14

of the gong. Two rivers of people swarmed along the sidewalks, spattered with black mud, which made each shoe leave a scarlike impression. Overhead elevated trains with a shrill grinding of the wheels stopped at the station, which upon its leglike pillars seemed to resemble some monstrous kind of crab squatting over the street. The quick fat puffings of the engines could be heard. Down an alley there were somber curtains of purple and black, on which street lamps dully glittered like embroidered flowers.

A saloon stood with a voracious air on a corner. A sign leaning against the front of the door-post announced "Free hot soup to-night!" The swing doors, snapping to and fro like ravenous lips, made gratified smacks as the saloon gorged itself with plump men, eating with astounding and endless appetite, smiling in some indescribable manner as the men came from all directions like sacrifices to a heathenish superstition.

Caught by the delectable sign the young man allowed himself to be swallowed. A bartender placed a schooner of dark and portentous beer on the bar. Its monumental form upreared until the froth a-top was above the crown of the young man's brown derby.

"Soup over there, gents," said the bartender affably. A little yellow man in rags and the youth grasped their schooners and went with speed toward a lunch counter, where a man with oily but imposing whiskers ladled genially from a kettle until he had furnished his two mendicants with a soup that was steaming hot, and in which there were little floating suggestions of chicken. The young man, sipping his broth, felt the cordiality expressed by the warmth of the mixture, and he beamed at the man with oily but imposing whiskers, who was presiding like a priest behind an altar. "Have some more, gents?" he inquired of the two sorry figures before him. The little yellow man accepted with a swift gesture, but the youth shook his head and went out, following a man whose wondrous seediness promised that he would have a knowledge of cheap lodging-houses.

On the sidewalk he accosted the seedy man. "Say, do you know a cheap place to sleep?"

The other hesitated for a time, gazing sideways. Finally he nodded in the direction of the street, "I sleep up there," he said, "when I've got the price."

"How much?"

"Ten cents."

The young man shook his head dolefully. "That's too rich for me."

At that moment there approached the two a reeling man in strange garments. His head was a fuddle of bushy hair and whiskers, from which his eyes peered with a guilty slant. In a close scrutiny it was possible to distinguish the cruel lines of a mouth which looked as if its lips had just closed with satisfaction over some tender and piteous morsel. He appeared like an assassin steeped in crimes performed awkwardly.

But at this time his voice was tuned to the coaxing key of an affectionate puppy. He looked at the men with wheedling eyes, and began to sing a little melody for charity.

"Say, gents, can't yeh give a poor feller a couple of cents t' git a bed? I got five, and I gits anudder two I gits me a bed. Now, on th' square, gents, can't yeh jest gimme two cents t' git a bed? Now, yeh know how a respecter'ble gentlem'n feels when he's down on his luck, an' I——"

The seedy man, staring with imperturbable countenance at a train which clattered overhead, interrupted in an expressionless voice—"Ah, go t' h——!"

But the youth spoke to the prayerful assassin in tones of astonishment and inquiry. "Say, you must be crazy! Why don't yeh strike somebody that looks as if they had money?"

The assassin, tottering about on his uncertain legs, and at intervals brushing imaginary obstacles from before his nose, entered into a long explanation of the psychology of the situation. It was so profound that it was unintelligible.

When he had exhausted the subject, the young man said to him:

"Let's see th' five cents."

The assassin wore an expression of drunken woe at this sentence, filled with suspicion of him. With a deeply pained air he began to fumble in his clothing, his red hands trembling. Presently he announced in a voice of bitter grief, as if he had been betrayed—"There's on'y four."

"Four," said the young man thoughtfully. "Well, look here, I'm a stranger here, an' if ye'll steer me to your cheap joint I'll find the other three."

The assassin's countenance became instantly radiant with joy. His whiskers quivered with the wealth of his alleged emotions. He seized the young man's hand in a transport of delight and friendliness.

"B' Gawd," he cried, "if ye'll do that, b' Gawd, I'd say yeh was a damned good fellow, I would, an' I'd remember yeh all m' life, I would, b' Gawd, an' if I ever got a chance I'd return the compliment"—he spoke with drunken dignity—"b' Gawd, I'd treat yeh white, I would, an' I'd allus remember yeh."

The young man drew back, looking at the assassin coldly. "Oh, that's all right," he said. "You show me th' joint—that's all you've got t' do."

The assassin, gesticulating gratitude, led the young man along a dark street. Finally he stopped before a little dusty door. He raised his hand impressively. "Look-a-here," he said, and there was a thrill of deep and ancient wisdom upon his face, "I've brought yeh here, an' that's my part, ain't it? If th' place don't suit yeh, yeh needn't git mad at me, need yeh? There won't be no bad feelin', will there?"

"No," said the young man.

The assassin waved his arm tragically, and led the march up the steep stairway. On the way the young man furnished the assassin with three pennies. At the top a man with benevolent spectacles looked at them through a hole in a board. He collected their money, wrote some names on a register, and speedily was leading the two men along a gloom-shrouded corridor.

Shortly after the beginning of this journey the young man felt his liver turn white, for from the dark and secret places of the building there suddenly came to his nostrils strange and unspeakable odors, that assailed him like malignant diseases with wings. They seemed to be from human bodies closely packed in dens; the exhalations from a hundred pairs of reeking lips; the fumes from a thousand bygone debauches: the expression of a thousand present miseries.

A man, naked save for a little snuff-colored undershirt, was parading sleepily along the corridor. He rubbed his eyes, and, giving vent to a prodigious yawn, demanded to be told the time.

"Half-past one."

The man yawned again. He opened a door, and for a moment his form was out-lined against a black, opaque interior. To this door came the three men, and as it was again opened the unholy odors rushed out like fiends, so that the young man was obliged to struggle as against an overpowering wind.

It was some time before the youth's eyes were good in the intense gloom within, but the man with benevolent spectacles led him skilfully, pausing but a moment to deposit the limp assassin upon a cot. He took the youth to a cot that lay tranquilly by the window, and showing him a tall locker for clothes that stood near the head with the ominous air of a tombstone, left him.

The youth sat on his cot and peered about him. There was a gas-jet in a distant part of the room, that burned a small flickering orange-hued flame. It caused vast masses of tumbled shadows in all parts of the place, save where, immediately about it, there was a little grey haze. As the young man's eyes became used to the darkness, he could see upon the cots that thickly littered the floor the forms of men sprawled out, lying in deathlike silence, or heaving and snoring with tremendous effort, like stabbed fish.

The youth locked his derby and his shoes in the mummy case near him, and then lay down with an old and familiar coat around his shoulders. A blanket he handed gingerly, drawing it over part of the coat. The cot was covered with leather, and as cold as melting snow. The youth was obliged to shiver for some time on this affair, which was like a slab. Presently, however, his chill gave him peace, and during this period of leisure from it he turned his head to stare at his friend the assassin, whom he could dimly discern where he lay sprawled on a cot in the abandon of a man filled with drink. He was snoring with incredible vigor. His wet hair and beard dimly glistened, and his inflamed nose shone with subdued lustre like a red light in a fog.

Within reach of the youth's hand was one who lay with yellow breast and shoul-ders bare to the cold drafts. One arm hung over the side of the cot, and the fingers lay full length upon the wet cement floor of the room. Beneath the inky brows could be seen the eyes of the man exposed by the partly opened lids. To the youth it seemed that he and this corpse-like being were exchanging a prolonged stare, and that the other threatened with his eyes. He drew back, watching his neighbor from the shadows of his blanket edge. The man did not move once through the night, but lay in this stillness as of death like a body stretched out expectant of the surgeon's knife.

And all through the room could be seen the tawny hues of naked flesh, limbs thrust into the darkness, projecting beyond the cots; upreared knees, arms hanging long and thin over the cot edges. For the most part they were statuesque, carven, dead. With the curious lockers standing all about like tombstones, there was a strange effect of a graveyard where bodies were merely flung.

Yet occasionally could be seen limbs wildly tossing in fantastic nightmare ges-tures, accompanied by guttural cries, grunts, oaths. And there was one fellow off in a gloomy corner, who in his dreams was oppressed by some frightful calamity, for of a sudden he began to utter long wails that went almost like yells from a hound, echoing wailfully and weird through this chill place of tombstones where men lay like the dead.

The sound in its high piercing beginnings, that dwindled to final melancholy moans, expressed a red and grim tragedy of the unfathomable possibilities of the man's dreams. But to the youth these were not merely the shrieks of a vision-pierced man: they were an utterance of the meaning of the room and its occupants. It was to him the protest of the wretch who feels the touch of the imperturbable granite wheels, and who then cries with an impersonal eloquence, with a strength not from him, giving voice to the wail of a whole section, a class, a people. This, weaving into the young man's brain, and mingling with his views of the vast and sombre shadows that, like mighty black fingers, curled around the naked bodies, made the young man so that he did not sleep, but lay carving the biographies for these men from his meagre experience. At times the fellow in the corner howled in a writhing agony of his imaginations.

Finally a long lance-point of grey light shot through the dusty panes of the window. Without, the young man could see roofs drearily white in the dawning. The point of light yellowed and grew brighter, until the golden rays of the morning sun came in bravely and strong. They touched with radiant color the form of a small fat man, who snored in stuttering fashion. His round and shiny bald head glowed suddenly with the valor of a decoration. He sat up, blinked at the sun, swore fretfully, and pulled his blanket over the ornamental splendors of his head.

The youth contentedly watched this rout of the shadows before the bright spears of the sun, and presently he slumbered. When he awoke he heard the voice of the assassin raised in valiant curses. Putting up his head, he perceived his comrade seated on the side of the cot engaged in scratching his neck with long finger-nails that rasped like files.

"Hully Jee, dis is a new breed. They've got can-openers on their feet." He continued in a violent tirade.

The young man hastily unlocked his closet and took out his shoes and hat. As he sat on the side of the cot lacing his shoes, he glanced about and saw that daylight had made the room comparatively commonplace and uninteresting. The men, whose faces seemed stolid, serene or absent, were engaged in dressing, while a great crackle of bantering conversation arose.

A few were parading in unconcerned nakedness. Here and there were men of brawn, whose skins shone clear and ruddy. They took splendid poses, standing massively like chiefs. When they had dressed in their ungainly garments there was an extraordinary change. They then showed bumps and deficiencies of all kinds.

There were others who exhibited many deformities. Shoulders were slanting, humped, pulled this way and pulled that way. And notable among these latter men was the little fat man who had refused to allow his head to be glorified. His pudgy form, builded like a pear, bustled to and fro, while he swore in fishwife fashion. It appeared that some article of his apparel had vanished.

The young man attired speedily, and went to his friend the assassin. At first the latter looked dazed at the sight of the youth. This face seemed to be appealing to him through the cloud wastes of his memory. He scratched his neck and reflected. At last he grinned, a broad smile gradually spreading until his countenance was a round illumination. "Hello, Willie," he cried cheerily.

"Hello," said the young man. "Are yeh ready t' fly?"

"Sure." The assassin tied his shoe carefully with some twine and came ambling.

When he reached the street the young man experienced no sudden relief from unholy atmospheres. He had forgotten all about them, and had been breathing naturally, and with no sensation of discomfort or distress.

He was thinking of these things as he walked along the street, when he was suddenly startled by feeling the assassin's hand, trembling with excitement, clutching his arm, and when the assassin spoke, his voice went into quavers from a supreme agitation.

"I'll be hully, bloomin' blowed if there wasn't a feller with a nightshirt on up there in that joint."

The youth was bewildered for a moment, but presently he turned to smile indulgently at the assassin's humor.

"Oh, you're a d——d liar," he merely said.

Whereupon the assassin began to gesture extravagantly, and take oath by strange gods. He frantically placed himself at the mercy of remarkable fates if his tale were not true.

"Yes, he did! I cross m' heart thousan' times!" he protested, and at the moment his eyes were large with amazement, his mouth wrinkled in unnatural glee.

"Yessir! A nightshirt! A hully white nightshirt!"

"You lie!"

"No, sir! I hope ter die b'fore I kin git anudder ball if there wasn't a jay wid a hully, bloomin' white nightshirt!"

His face was filled with the infinite wonder of it. "A hully white nightshirt," he continually repeated.

The young man saw the dark entrance to a basement restaurant. There was a sign which read "No mystery about our hash"! and there were other age-stained and world-battered legends which told him that the place was within his means. He stopped before it and spoke to the assassin. "I guess I'll git somethin' t' eat."

At this the assassin, for some reason, appeared to be quite embarrassed. He gazed at the seductive front of the eating place for a moment. Then he started slowly up the street. "Well, good-bye, Willie," he said bravely.

For an instant the youth studied the departing figure. Then he called out, "Hol' on a minnet." As they came together he spoke in a certain fierce way, as if he feared that the other would think him to be charitable. "Look-a-here, if yeh wanta git some breakfas' I'll lend yeh three cents t' do it with. But say, look-a-here, you've gota git out an' hustle. I ain't goin' t' support yeh, or I'll go broke b'fore night. I ain't no millionaire."

"I take me oath, Willie," said the assassin earnestly, "th' on'y thing I really needs is a ball. Me t'roat feels like a fryin'-pan. But as I can't get a ball, why, th' next bes' thing is breakfast, an' if yeh do that for me, b' Gawd, I say yeh was th' whitest lad I ever see."

They spent a few moments in dexterous exchanges of phrases, in which they each protested that the other was, as the assassin had originally said, "a respecter'ble gentlem'n." And they concluded with mutual assurances that they were the souls of intelligence and virtue. Then they went into the restaurant.

There was a long counter, dimly lighted from hidden sources. Two or three men in soiled white aprons rushed here and there.

The youth bought a bowl of coffee for two cents and a roll for one cent. The assassin purchased the same. The bowls were webbed with brown seams, and the tin spoons wore an air of having emerged from the first pyramid. Upon them were black mosslike encrustations of age, and they were bent and scarred from the attacks of long-forgotten teeth. But over their repast the wanderers waxed warm and mellow. The assassin grew affable as the hot mixture went soothingly down his parched throat, and the young man felt courage flow in his veins.

Memories began to throng in on the assassin, and he brought forth long tales, intricate, incoherent, delivered with a chattering swiftness as from an old woman. "——great job out'n Orange. Boss keep yeh hustlin' though all time. I was there three days, and then I went an' ask 'im t' lend me a dollar. 'G-g-go ter the devil,' he ses, an' I lose me job."

"South no good. Damn niggers work for twenty-five an' thirty cents a day. Run white man out. Good grub, though. Easy livin'.''

"Yas; useter work little in Toledo, raftin' logs. Make two or three dollars er day in the spring. Lived high. Cold as ice, though, in the winter."

"I was raised in northern N'York. O-a-ah, yeh jest oughto live there. No beer ner whisky, though, way off in the woods. But all th' good hot grub yeh can eat. B'Gawd, I hung around there long as I could till th' ol' man fired me. 'Git t' hell outa here, yeh wuthless skunk, git t' hell outa here, an' go die,' he ses. 'You're a hell of a father,' I ses, 'you are,' an' I quit 'im.''

As they were passing from the dim eating place, they encountered an old man who was trying to steal forth with a tiny package of food, but a tall man with an indomitable moustache stood dragon fashion, barring the way of escape. They heard the old man raise a plaintive protest. "Ah, you always want to know what I take out, and you never see that I usually bring a package in here from my place of business."

As the wanderers trudged slowly along Park Row, the assassin began to expand and grow blithe. "B'Gawd, we've been livin' like kings," he said, smacking appreciative lips.

"Look out, or we'll have t' pay fer it t'night," said the youth with gloomy warning.

But the assassin refused to turn his gaze toward the future. He went with a limping step, into which he injected a suggestion of lamblike gambols. His mouth was wreathed in a red grin.

In the City Hall Park the two wanderers sat down in the little circle of benches sanctified by traditions of their class. They huddled in their old garments, slumbrously conscious of the march of the hours which for them had no meaning.

The people of the street hurrying hither and thither made a blend of black figures changing yet frieze-like. They walked in their good clothes as upon important missions, giving no gaze to the two wanderers seated upon the benches. They expressed to the young man his infinite distance from all that he valued. Social position, comfort, the pleasures of living, were unconquerable kingdoms. He felt a sudden awe.

And in the background a multitude of buildings, of pitiless hues and sternly high, were to him emblematic of a nation forcing its regal head into the clouds, throwing no downward glances; in the sublimity of its aspirations ignoring the wretches who may flounder at its feet. The roar of the city in his ear was to him the confusion of strange tongues, babbling heedlessly; it was the clink of coin, the voice of the city's hopes which were to him no hopes.

He confessed himself an outcast, and his eyes from under the lowered rim of his hat began to glance guiltily, wearing the criminal expression that comes with certain convictions.

QUESTIONS

1 An experiment is scientific, thereby objective. How does Crane maintain an objective viewpoint?
2 What instinctual drives motivate the actions of his characters?
3 What realization does the main character reach? What does this realization mean in respect to man's ability to direct his life?

TOPICS FOR COMPOSITION

1 Martin Luther King, Jr. would most likely disagree with Crane's deterministic philosophy. Write an essay in which you examine the precepts of deterministic naturalism in relation to Crane's story and King's speech.
2 If Crane's story is truly universal, "the wanderer" is to some degree a part of our world. Write an essay in which you identify the modern wanderer and his influence on society.

☐

To more fully understand Thomas Mann's investigation into the psychology of human action, we should recognize that the author explicitly and implicitly frees his main character from most of the responsibility for his own actions. Mann primarily accomplishes this by the way in which he portrays the characters who surround Herr Friedemann. As you read this story, give careful attention to the attendant characters; especially note Mann's portrayal of the following:

1 The nurse, who symbolizes mankind's weaknesses and absorbs the initial responsibility for Friedemann's misfortune
2 The mother and the sisters, whose passive natures contribute to Friedemann's early development
3 Friedemann's classmates and associates, whose compassionate attitudes, paradoxically, increase his isolation
4 Frau von Rinnlingen, whose alien qualities disrupt the tranquillity of Friedemann's existence

LITTLE HERR FRIEDEMANN

Thomas Mann

It was the nurse's fault. When they first suspected, Frau Consul Friedemann had spoken to her very gravely about the need of controlling her weakness. But what good did that do? Or the glass of red wine which she got daily besides the beer which was needed for the milk? For they suddenly discovered that she even sank so low as to drink the methylated spirit which was kept for the spirit lamp. Before they could send her away and get someone to take her place, the mischief was done. One day the mother and sisters came home to find that little Johannes, then about a month old, had fallen from the couch and lay on the floor, uttering a appallingly faint little cry, while the nurse stood beside him quite stupefied.

The doctor came and with firm, gentle hands tested the little creature's contracted and twitching limbs. He made a very serious face. The three girls stood sobbing in a corner and the Frau Consul in the anguish of her heart prayed aloud.

The poor mother, just before the child's birth, had already suffered a crushing blow: her husband, the Dutch Consul, had been snatched away from her by sudden and violent illness, and now she was too broken to cherish any hope that little Johannes would be spared to her. But by the second day the doctor had given her hand an encouraging squeeze and told her that all immediate danger was over. There was no longer any sign that the brain was affected. The facial expression was altered, it had lost the fixed and staring look. . . . Of course, they must see how things went on—and hope for the best, hope for the best.

The grey gabled house in which Johannes Friedemann grew up stood by the north gate of the little old commercial city. The front door led into a large flag-paved entry, out of which a stair with a white wooden balustrade led up into the second storey. The faded wall-paper in the living-room had a landscape pattern, and straight-backed chairs and sofas in dark-red plush stood round the heavy mahogany table.

Often in his childhood Johannes sat here at the window, which always had a fine showing of flowers, on a small footstool at his mother's feet, listening to some fairy-tale she told him, gazing at her smooth grey head, her mild and gentle face, and breathing in the faint scent she exhaled. She showed him the picture of his father, a kindly man with grey side-whiskers—he was now in heaven, she said, and awaiting them there.

Behind the house was a small garden where in summer they spent much of their time, despite the smell of burnt sugar which came over from the refinery close by. There was a gnarled old walnut tree in whose shade little Johannes would sit, on a low wooden stool, cracking walnuts, while Frau Friedemann and her three daughters, now grown women, took refuge from the sun under a grey canvas tent. The mother's gaze often strayed from her embroidery to look with sad and loving eyes at her child.

He was not beautiful, little Johannes, as he crouched on his stool industriously cracking his nuts. In fact, he was a strange sight, with his pigeon breast, humped back, and disproportionately long arms. But his hands and feet were delicately formed, he had soft red-brown eyes like a doe's, a sensitive mouth, and fine, light-brown hair. His head, had it not sat so deep between his shoulders, might almost have been called pretty.

When he was seven he went to school, where time passed swiftly and uniformly. He walked every day, with the strut deformed people often have, past the quaint gabled houses and shops to the old schoolhouse with the vaulted arcades. When he had done his preparation he would read in his books with the lovely title-page illustrations in colour, or else work in the garden, while his sisters kept house for their invalid mother. They went out too, for they belonged to the best society of the town; but unfortunately they had not married, for they had not much money nor any looks to recommend them.

Johannes too was now and then invited out by his schoolmates, but it is not likely that he enjoyed it. He could not take part in their games, and they were always embarrassed in his company, so there was no feeling of good fellowship.

There came a time when he began to hear certain matters talked about, in the courtyard at school. He listened wide-eyed and large-eared, quite silent, to his companions' raving over this or that little girl. Such things, though they entirely engrossed the attention of these others, were not, he felt, for him; they belonged in the same category as the ball games and gymnastics. At times he felt a little sad. But at length he had become quite used to standing on one side and not taking part.

But after all it came about—when he was sixteen—that he felt suddenly drawn to a girl of his own age. She was the sister of a classmate of his, a blonde, hilarious hoyden, and he met her when calling at her brother's house. He felt strangely embarrassed in her neighbourhood; she too was embarrassed and treated him with such artificial cordiality that it made him sad.

One summer afternoon as he was walking by himself on the wall outside the town, he heard a whispering behind a jasmine bush and peeped cautiously through the branches. There she sat on a bench beside a long-legged, red-haired youth of his acquaintance. They had their arms about each other and he was imprinting on her lips a kiss, which she returned amid giggles. Johannes looked, turned round, and went softly away.

His head was sunk deeper than ever between his shoulders, his hands trembled, and a sharp pain shot upwards from his chest to his throat. But he choked it down, straightening himself as well as he could. "Good," said he to himself. "That is over. Never again will I let myself in for any of it. To the others it brings joy and happiness, for me it can only mean sadness and pain. I am done with it. For me that is all over. Never again."

The resolution did him good. He had renounced, renounced forever. He went home, took up a book, or else played on his violin, which despite his deformed chest he had learned to do.

At seventeen Johannes left school to go into business, like everybody else he knew. He was apprenticed to the big lumber firm of Herr Schlievogt down on the river-bank. They were kind and considerate, he on his side was responsive and friendly, time passed with peaceful regularity. But in his twenty-first year his mother died, after a lingering illness.

This was a sore blow for Johannes Friedemann, and the pain of it endured. He cherished this grief, he gave himself up to it as one gives oneself to a great joy, he fed it with a thousand childhood memories; it was the first important event in his life and he made the most of it.

Is not life in and for itself a good, regardless of whether we may call its content "happiness"? Johannes Friedemann felt that it was so, and he loved life. He, who had renounced the greatest joy it can bring us, taught himself with infinite, incredible care to take pleasure in what it had still to offer. A walk in the springtime in the parks surrounding the town; the fragrance of a flower; the song of a bird—might not one feel grateful for such things as these?

And that we need to be taught how to enjoy, yes, that our education is always and only equal to our capacity for enjoyment—he knew that too, and he trained himself. Music he loved, and attended all the concerts that were given in the town. He came to play the violin not so badly himself, no matter what a figure of fun he made when he did it; and took delight in every beautiful soft tone he succeeded in producing. Also, by much reading he came in time to possess a literary taste the like of which did not exist in the place. He kept up with the new books, even the foreign ones; he knew how to savour the seductive rhythm of a lyric or the ultimate flavour of a subtly told tale—yes, one might almost call him a connoisseur.

He learned to understand that to everything belongs its own enjoyment and that it is absurd to distinguish between an experience which is "happy" and one which is not. With a right good will he accepted each emotion as it came, each mood, whether sad or gay. Even he cherished the unfulfilled desires, the longings. He loved them for their own sakes and told himself that with fulfillment the best of them would be past. The vague, sweet, painful yearning and hope of quiet spring evenings—are they not richer in joy than all the fruition the summer can bring? Yes, he was a connoisseur, our little Herr Friedemann.

But of course they did not know that, the people whom he met on the street, who bowed to him with the kindly, compassionate air he knew so well. They could not know that this unhappy cripple, strutting comically along in his light overcoat and shiny top hat—strange to say, he was a little vain—they could not know how tenderly he loved the mild flow of his life, charged with no great emotions, it is true, but full of a quiet and tranquil happiness which was his own creation.

But Herr Friedemann's great preference, his real passion, was for the theatre. He possessed a dramatic sense which was unusually strong; at a telling theatrical effect or the catastrophe of a tragedy his whole small frame would shake with emotion. He had his regular seat in the first row of boxes at the opera-house; was an assiduous frequenter and often took his sisters with him. Since their mother's death they kept house for their brother in the old home which they all owned together.

It was a pity they were unmarried still; but with the decline of hope had come resignation—Friederike, the eldest, was seventeen years further on than Herr Friedemann. She and her sister Henriette were over-tall and thin, whereas Pfiffi, the youngest, was too short and stout. She had a funny way, too, of shaking herself as she talked, and water came in the corners of her mouth.

Little Herr Friedemann did not trouble himself overmuch about his three sisters. But they stuck together loyally and were always of one mind. Whenever an engagement was announced in their circle they with one voice said how very gratifying that was.

Their brother continued to live with them even after he became independent, as he did by leaving Herr Schlievogt's firm and going into business for himself, in an agency of sorts, which was no great tax on his time. His offices were in a couple of rooms on the ground floor of the house so that at mealtimes he had but the pair of stairs to mount—for he suffered now and then from asthma.

His thirtieth birthday fell on a fine warm June day, and after dinner he sat out in the grey canvas tent, with a new head-rest embroidered by Henriette. He had a good cigar in his mouth and a good book in his hand. But sometimes he would put the latter down to listen to the sparrows chirping blithely in the old nut tree and look at the clean gravel path leading up to the house between lawns bright with summer flowers.

Little Herr Friedemann wore no beard, and his face had scarcely changed at all, save that the features were slightly sharper. He wore his fine light-brown hair parted on one side.

Once, as he let the book fall on his knee and looked up into the sunny blue sky, he said to himself: "Well, so that is thirty years. Perhaps there may be ten or even twenty more, God knows. They will mount up without a sound or a stir and pass by like those that are gone; and I look forward to them with peace in my heart."

Now, it happened in July of the same year that a new appointment to the office of District Commandant had set the whole town talking. The stout and jolly gentleman who had for many years occupied the post had been very popular in social circles and they saw him go with great regret. It was in compliance with goodness knows what regulations that Herr von Rinnlingen and no other was sent thither from the capital.

In any case the exchange was not such a bad one. The new Commandant was married but childless. He rented a spacious villa in the southern suburbs of the city and seemed to intend to set up an establishment. There was a report that he was very rich—which received confirmation in the fact that he brought with him four servants, five riding and carriage horses, a landau and a light hunting-cart.

Soon after their arrival the husband and wife left cards on all the best society, and their names were on every tongue. But it was not Herr von Rinnlingen, it was his wife who was the centre of interest. All the men were dazed, for the moment too dazed to pass judgment; but their wives were quite prompt and definite in the view that Gerda von Rinnlingen was not their sort.

"Of course, she comes from the metropolis, her ways would naturally be different," Frau Hagenström, the lawyer's wife, said, in conversation with Henriette Friedemann. "She smokes, and she rides. That is of course. But it is her manners—they are not only free, they are positively brusque, or even worse. You see, no one could call her ugly, one might even say she is pretty; but she has not a trace of feminine charm in her looks or gestures or her laugh—they completely lack everything that makes a man fall in love with a woman. She is not a flirt—and goodness knows I would be the last to disparage her for that. But it is strange to see so young a woman—she is only twenty-four—so entirely wanting in natural charm. I am not expressing myself very well, my dear, but I know what I mean. All the men are simply bewildered. In a few weeks, you will see, they will be disgusted.''

"Well," Fräulein Friedemann said, "she certainly has everything she wants.''

"Yes," cried Frau Hagenström, "look at her husband! And how does she treat him? You ought to see it—you will see it! I would be the first to approve of a married woman behaving with a certain reserve towards the other sex. But how does she behave to her own husband? She has a way of fixing him with an ice-cold stare and saying 'My dear friend!' with a pitying expression that drives me mad. For when you look at him—upright, correct, gallant, a brilliant officer and a splendidly preserved man of forty! They have been married four years, my dear.''

Herr Friedemann was first vouchsafed a glimpse of Frau von Rinnlingen in the main street of the town, among all the rows of shops, at midday, when he was coming from the Bourse, where he had done a little bidding.

He was strolling along beside Herr Stephens, looking tiny and important, as usual. Herr Stephens was in the wholesale trade, a huge stocky man with round side-whiskers and bushy eyebrows. Both of them wore top hats; their overcoats were unbuttoned on account of the heat. They tapped their canes along the pavement and talked of the political situation; but half-way down the street Stephens suddenly said:

"Deuce take it if there isn't the Rinnlingen driving along.''

"Good," answered Herr Friedemann in his high, rather sharp voice, looking expectantly ahead. "Because I have never yet set eyes on her. And here we have the yellow cart we hear so much about.''

It was in fact the hunting-cart which Frau von Rinnlingen was herself driving today with a pair of thoroughbreds; a groom sat behind her, with folded arms. She wore a loose beige coat and skirt and a small round straw hat with a brown leather band, beneath which her well-waved red-blonde hair, a good, thick crop, was drawn into a knot at the nape of her neck. Her face was oval, with a dead-white skin and faint bluish shadows lurking under the close-set eyes. Her nose was short but well-shaped, with a becoming little saddle of freckles; whether her mouth was as good or no could not be told, for she kept it in continual motion, sucking the lower and biting the upper lip.

Herr Stephens, as the cart came abreast of them, greeted her with a great show of deference; little Herr Friedemann lifted his hat too and looked at her with wide-eyed attention. She lowered her whip, nodded slightly, and drove slowly past, looking at the houses and shop-windows.

After a few paces Herr Stephens said:

"She has been taking a drive and was on her way home.''

Little Herr Friedemann made no answer, but stared before him at the pavement. Presently he started, looked at his companion, and asked: "What did you say?''

And Herr Stephens repeated his acute remark.

Three days after that Johannes Friedemann came home at midday from his usual walk. Dinner was at half past twelve, and he would spend the interval in his office at the right of the entrance door. But the maid came across the entry and told him that there were visitors.

"In my office?" he asked.

"No, upstairs with the mistresses."

"Who are they?"

"Herr and Frau Colonel von Rinnlingen."

"Ah," said Johannes Friedemann. "Then I will—"

And he mounted the stairs. He crossed the lobby and laid his hand on the knob of the high white door leading into the "landscape room." And then he drew back, turned round, and slowly returned as he had come. And spoke to himself, for there was no one else there, and said: "No, better not."

He went into his office, sat down at his desk, and took up the paper. But after a little he dropped it again and sat looking to one side out of the window. Thus he sat until the maid came to say that luncheon was ready; then he went up into the dining-room where his sisters were already waiting, and sat down in his chair, in which there were three music-books.

As she ladled the soup Henriette said:

"Johannes, do you know who were here?"

"Well?" he asked.

"The new Commandant and his wife."

"Indeed? That was friendly of them."

"Yes," said Pfiffi, a little water coming in the corners of her mouth. "I found them both very agreeable."

"And we must lose no time in returning the call," said Friederike. "I suggest that we go next Sunday, the day after tomorrow."

"Sunday," Henriette and Pfiffi said.

"You will go with us, Johannes?" asked Friederike.

"Of course he will," said Pfiffi, and gave herself a little shake. Herr Friedemann had not heard her at all; he was eating his soup, with a hushed and troubled air. It was as though he were listening to some strange noise he heard.

Next evening *Lohengrin* was being given at the opera, and everybody in society was present. The small auditorium was crowded, humming with voices and smelling of gas and perfumery. And every eye-glass in the stalls was directed towards box thirteen, next to the stage; for this was the first appearance of Herr and Frau von Rinnlingen and one could give them a good looking-over.

When little Herr Friedemann, in flawless dress clothes and glistening white pigeon-breasted shirt-front, entered his box, which was number thirteen, he started back at the door, making a gesture with his hand towards his brow. His nostrils dilated feverishly. Then he took his seat, which was next to Frau von Rinnlingen's.

She contemplated him for a little while, with her under lip stuck out; then she turned to exchange a few words with her husband, a tall, broad-shouldered gentleman with a brown, good-natured face and turned-up moustaches.

When the overture began and Frau von Rinnlingen leaned over the balustrade Herr Friedemann gave her a quick, searching side glance. She wore a light-coloured evening frock, the only one in the theatre which was slightly low in the neck. Her sleeves were full and her white gloves came up to her elbows. Her figure was statelier than it had looked under the loose coat; her full bosom slowly rose and fell and the knot of red-blonde hair hung low and heavy at the nape of her neck.

Herr Friedemann was pale, much paler than usual, and little beads of perspiration stood on his brow beneath the smoothly parted brown hair. He could see Frau von Rinnlingen's left arm, which lay upon the balustrade. She had taken off her glove and the rounded, dead-white arm and ringless hand, both of them shot with pale blue veins, were directly under his eye—he could not help seeing them.

The fiddles sang, the trombones crashed, Telramund was slain, general jubilation reigned in the orchestra, and little Herr Friedemann sat there motionless and pallid, his head drawn in between his shoulders, his forefinger to his lips and one hand thrust into the opening of his waistcoat.

As the curtain fell, Frau von Rinnlingen got up to leave the box with her husband. Johannes Friedemann saw her without looking, wiped his handkerchief across his brow, then rose suddenly and went as far as the door into the foyer, where he turned, came back to his chair, and sat down in the same posture as before.

When the bell rang and his neighbours re-entered the box he felt Frau von Rinnlingen's eyes upon him, so that finally against his will he raised his head. As their eyes met, hers did not swerve aside; she continued to gaze without embarrassment until he himself, deeply humiliated, was forced to look away. He turned a shade paler and felt a strange, sweet pang of anger and scorn. The music began again.

Towards the end of the act Frau von Rinnlingen chanced to drop her fan; it fell at Herr Friedemann's feet. They both stooped at the same time, but she reached it first and gave a little mocking smile as she said: "Thank you."

Their heads were quite close together and just for a second he got the warm scent of her breast. His face was drawn, his whole body twitched, and his heart thumped so horribly that he lost his breath. He sat without moving for half a minute, then he pushed back his chair, got up quietly, and went out.

He crossed the lobby, pursued by the music; got his top hat from the cloak-room, his light overcoat and his stick, went down the stairs and out of doors.

It was a warm, still evening. In the gas-lit street the gabled houses towered towards a sky where stars were softly beaming. The pavement echoed the steps of a few passers-by. Someone spoke to him, but he heard and saw nothing; his head was bowed and his deformed chest shook with the violence of his breathing. Now and then he murmured to himself:

"My God, my God!"

He was gazing horror-struck within himself, beholding the havoc which had been wrought with his tenderly cherished, scrupulously managed feelings. Suddenly he was quite overpowered by the strength of his tortured longing. Giddy and drunken he leaned against a lamp-post and his quivering lips uttered the one word: "Gerda!"

The stillness was complete. Far and wide not a soul was to be seen. Little Herr Friedemann pulled himself together and went on, up the street in which the opera-house stood and which ran steeply down to the river, then along the main street northwards to his home.

How she had looked at him! She had forced him, actually, to cast down his eyes! She had humiliated him with her glance. But was she not a woman and he a man? And those strange brown eyes of hers—had they not positively glittered with unholy joy?

Again he felt the same surge of sensual, impotent hatred mount up in him; then he relived the moment when her head had touched his, when he had breathed in the fragrance of her body—and for the second time he halted, bent his deformed torso backwards, drew in the air through clenched teeth, and murmured helplessly, desperately, uncontrollably:

"My God, my God!"

Then went on again, slowly, mechanically, through the heavy evening air, through the empty echoing streets until he stood before his own house. He paused a minute in the entry, breathing the cool, dank inside air; then he went into his office.

He sat down at his desk by the open window and stared straight ahead of him at a large yellow rose which somebody had set there in a glass of water. He took it up and smelt it with his eyes closed, then put it down with a gesture of weary sadness. No, no. That was all over. What was even that fragrance to him now? What any of all those things that up to now had been the well-springs of his joy?

He turned away and gazed into the quiet street. At intervals steps passed and the sound died away. The stars stood still and glittered. He felt so weak, so utterly tired to death. His head was quite vacant, and suddenly his despair began to melt into a gentle, pervading melancholy. A few lines of a poem flickered through his head, he heard the *Lohengrin* music in his ears, he saw Frau von Rinnlingen's face and her round white arm on the red velvet—then he fell into a heavy fever-burdened sleep.

Often he was near waking, but feared to do so and managed to sink back into forgetfulness again. But when it had grown quite light, he opened his eyes and looked round him with a wide and painful gaze. He remembered everything, it was as though the anguish had never been intermitted by sleep.

His head was heavy and his eyes burned. But when he had washed up and bathed his head with cologne he felt better and sat down in his place by the still open window. It was early, perhaps only five o'clock. Now and then a baker's boy passed; otherwise there was no one to be seen. In the opposite house the blinds were down. But birds were twittering and the sky was luminously blue. A wonderfully beautiful Sunday morning.

A feeling of comfort and confidence came over little Herr Friedemann. Why had he been distressing himself? Was not everything just as it had been? The attack of yesterday had been a bad one. Granted. But it should be the last. It was not too late, he could still escape destruction. He must avoid every occasion of a fresh seizure; he felt sure he could do this. He felt the strength to conquer and suppress his weakness.

It struck half past seven and Friederike came in with the coffee, setting it on the round table in front of the leather sofa against the rear wall.

"Good morning, Johannes," said she; "here is your breakfast."

"Thanks," said little Herr Friedemann. And then: "Dear Friederike, I am sorry, but you will have to pay your call without me, I do not feel well enough to go. I have slept badly and have a headache—in short, I must ask you—"

"What a pity!" answered Friederike. "You must go another time. But you do look ill. Shall I lend you my menthol pencil?"

"Thanks," said Herr Friedemann. "It will pass." And Friederike went out.

Standing at the table he slowly drank his coffee and ate a croisant. He felt satisfied with himself and proud of his firmness. When he had finished he sat down again by the open window, with a cigar. The food had done him good and he felt happy and hopeful. He took a book and sat reading and smoking and blinking into the sunlight.

Morning had fully come, wagons rattled past, there were many voices and the sound of the bells on passing trams. With and among it all was woven the twittering and chirping; there was a radiant blue sky, a soft mild air.

At ten o'clock he heard his sisters cross the entry; the front door creaked, and he idly noticed that they passed his window. An hour went by. He felt more and more happy.

A sort of hubris mounted in him. What a heavenly air—and how the birds were singing! He felt like taking a little walk. Then suddenly, without any transition, yet accompanied by a terror namelessly sweet came the thought: "Suppose I were to go to her!" And suppressing, as though by actual muscular effort, every warning voice within him, he added with blissful resolution: "I will go to her!"

He changed into his Sunday clothes, took his top hat and his stock, and hurried with quickened breath through the town and into the southern suburbs. Without looking at a soul he kept raising and dropping his head with each eager step, completely rapt in his exalted state until he arrived at the avenue of chestnut trees and the red brick villa with the name of Commandant von Rinnlingen on the gate-post.

But here he was seized by a tremor, his heart throbbed and pounded in his breast. He went across the vestibule and rang at the inside door. The die was cast, there was no retreating now. "Come what come may," thought he, and felt the stillness of death within him.

The door suddenly opened and the maid came toward him across the vestibule; she took his card and hurried away up the red-carpeted stair. Herr Friedemann gazed fixedly at the bright colour until she came back and said that her mistress would like him to come up.

He put down his stick beside the door leading into the salon and stole a look at himself in the glass. His face was pale, the eyes red, his hair was sticking to his brow, the hand that held his top hat kept on shaking.

The maid opened the door and he went in. He found himself in a rather large, half-darkened room, with drawn curtains. At his right was a piano, and about the round table in the centre stood several arm-chairs covered in brown silk. The sofa stood along the left-hand wall, with a landscape painting in a heavy gilt frame hanging above it. The wall-paper too was dark in tone. There was an alcove filled with potted palms.

A minute passed, then Frau von Rinnlingen opened the portières on the right and approached him noiselessly over the thick brown carpet. She wore a simply cut frock of red and black plaid. A ray of light, with motes dancing in it, streamed from the alcove and fell upon her heavy red hair so that it shone like gold. She kept her strange eyes fixed upon him with a searching gaze and as usual stuck out her under lip.

"Good morning, Frau Commandant," began little Herr Friedemann, and looked up at her, for he came only as high as her chest. "I wished to pay you my respects too. When my sisters did so I was unfortunately out . . . I regretted sincerely . . ."

He had no idea at all what else he should say; and there she stood and gazed ruthlessly at him as though she would force him to go on. The blood rushed to his head. "She sees through me," he thought, "she will torture and despise me. Her eyes keep flickering. . . ."

But at last she said, in a very high, clear voice:

"It is kind of you to have come. I have also been sorry not to see you before. Will you please sit down?"

She took her seat close beside him, leaned back, and put her arm along the arm of the chair. He sat bent over, holding his hat between his knees. She went on:

"Did you know that your sisters were here a quarter of an hour ago? They told me you were ill."

"Yes," he answered, "I did not feel well enough to go out, I thought I should not be able to. That is why I am late."

"You do not look very well even now," said she tranquilly, not shifting her gaze. "You are pale and your eyes are inflamed. You are not very strong, perhaps?"

"Oh," said Herr Friedemann, stammering, "I've not much to complain of, as a rule."

"I am ailing a good deal too," she went on, still not turning her eyes from him, "but nobody notices it. I am nervous, and sometimes I have the strangest feelings."

She paused, lowered her chin to her breast, and looked up expectantly at him. He made no reply, simply sat with his dreamy gaze directed upon her. How strangely she spoke, and how her clear and thrilling voice affected him! His heart beat more quietly and he felt as though he were in a dream. She began again:

"I am not wrong in thinking that you left the opera last night before it was over?"

"Yes, madam."

"I was sorry to see that. You listened like a music-lover—though the performance was only tolerable. You are fond of music, I am sure. Do you play the piano?"

"I play the violin, a little," said Herr Friedemann. "That is, really not very much—"

"You play the violin?" she asked, and looked past him consideringly. "But we might play together," she suddenly said. "I can accompany a little. It would be a pleasure to find somebody here—would you come?"

"I am quite at your service—with pleasure," said he, stiffly. He was still as though in a dream. A pause ensued. Then suddenly her expression changed. He saw it alter for one of cruel, though hardly perceptible mockery, and again she fixed him with that same searching, uncannily flickering gaze. His face burned, he knew not where to turn; drawing his head down between his shoulders he stared confusedly at the carpet, while there shot through him once more that strangely sweet and torturing sense of impotent rage.

He made a desperate effort and raised his eyes. She was looking over his head at the door. With the utmost difficulty he fetched out a few words:

"And you are so far not too dissatisfied with your stay in our city?"

"Oh, no," said Frau Rinnlingen indifferently. "No, certainly not; why should I not be satisfied? To be sure, I feel a little hampered, as though everybody's eyes were upon me, but—oh, before I forget it," she went on quickly, "we are entertaining a few people next week, a small, informal company. A little music, perhaps, and conversation. . . . There is a charming garden at the back, it runs down to the river. You and your sisters will be receiving an invitation in due course, but perhaps I may ask you now to give us the pleasure of your company?"

Herr Friedemann was just expressing his gratitude for the invitation when the door-knob was seized energetically from without and the Commandant entered. They both rose and Frau von Rinnlingen introduced the two men to each other. Her husband bowed to them both with equal courtesy. His bronze face glistened with the heat.

He drew off his gloves, addressing Herr Friedemann in a powerful, rather sharp-edged voice. The latter looked up at him with large vacant eyes and had the feeling that he would presently be clapped benevolently on the shoulder. Heels together, inclining from the waist, the Commandant turned to his wife and asked, in a much gentler tone;

"Have you asked Herr Friedemann if he will give us the pleasure of his company at our little party, my love? If you are willing I should like to fix the date for next week and I hope that the weather will remain fine so that we can enjoy ourselves in the garden."

"Just as you say," answered Frau von Rinnlingen, and gazed past him.

Two minutes later Herr Friedemann got up to go. At the door he turned and bowed to her once more, meeting her expressionless gaze still fixed upon him.

He went away, but he did not go back to the town; unconsciously he struck into a path that led away from the avenue towards the old ruined fort by the river, among well-kept lawns and shady avenues with benches.

He walked quickly and absently, with bent head. He felt intolerably hot, as though aware of flames leaping and sinking within him, and his head throbbed with fatigue.

It was as though her gaze still rested on him—not vacantly as it had at the end, but with that flickering cruelty which went with the strange still way she spoke. Did it give her pleasure to put him beside himself, to see him helpless? Looking through and through him like that, could she not feel a little pity?

He had gone along the river-bank under the moss-grown wall; he sat down on a bench within a half-circle of blossoming jasmine. The sweet, heavy scent was all about him, the sun brooded upon the dimpling water.

He was weary, he was worn out; and yet within him all was tumult and anguish. Were it not better to take one last look and then to go down into that quiet water; after a brief struggle to be free and safe and at peace? Ah, peace, peace—that was what he wanted! Not peace in an empty and soundless void, but a gentle, sunlit peace, full of good, of tranquil thoughts.

All his tender love of life thrilled through him in that moment, all his profound yearning for his vanished "happiness." But then he looked about him into the silent, endlessly indifferent peace of nature, saw how the river went its own way in the sun, how the grasses quivered and the flowers stood up where they blossomed, only to fade and be blown away; saw how all that was bent submissively to the will of life; and there came over him all at once that sense of acquaintance and understanding with the inevitable which can make those who know it superior to the blows of fate.

He remembered the afternoon of his thirtieth birthday and the peaceful happiness with which he, untroubled by fears or hopes, had looked forward to what was left of his life. He had seen no light and no shadow there, only a mild twilight radiance gently declining into the dark. With what a calm and superior smile had he contemplated the years still to come—how long ago was that?

Then this woman had come, she had to come, it was his fate that she should, for she herself was his fate and she alone. He had known it from the first moment. She had come—and though he had tried his best to defend his peace, her coming had roused in him all those forces which from his youth up he had sought to suppress, feeling, as he did, that they spelled torture and destruction. They had seized upon him with frightful, irresistible power and flung him to the earth.

They were his destruction, well he knew it. But why struggle, then, and why torture himself? Let everything take its course. He would go his appointed way, closing his eyes before the yawning void, bowing to his fate, bowing to the overwhelming, anguishingly sweet, irresistible power.

The water glittered, the jasmine gave out its strong, pungent scent, the birds chattered in the tree-tops that gave glimpses among them of a heavy, velvety-blue sky. Little hump-backed Herr Friedemann sat long upon his bench; he sat bent over, holding his head in his hands.

Everybody agreed that the Rinnlingens entertained very well. Some thirty guests sat in the spacious dining-room, at the long, prettily decorated table, and the butler and two hired waiters were already handing round the ices. Dishes clattered, glasses rang, there was a warm aroma of food and perfumes. Here were comfortable merchants with their wives and daughters; most of the officers of the garrison; a few professional men, lawyers and the popular old family doctor—in short, all the best society.

A nephew of the Commandant, on a visit, a student of mathematics, sat deep in conversation with Fräulein Hagenström, whose place was directly opposite Herr Friedemann's, at the lower end of the table. Johannes Friedemann sat there on a rich velvet cushion, beside the unbeautiful wife of the Colonial Director and not far off Frau von Rinnlingen, who had been escorted to table by Consul Stephens. It was astonishing, the change which had taken place in little Herr Friedemann in these few days. Perhaps the incandescent lighting in the room was partly to blame; but his cheeks looked sunken, he made a more crippled impression even than usual, and his inflamed eyes, with their dark rings, glowed with an inexpressibly tragic light. He drank a great deal of wine and now and then addressed a remark to his neighbour.

Frau von Rinnlingen had not so far spoken to him at all; but now she leaned over and called out:

"I have been expecting you in vain these days, you and your fiddle."

He looked vacantly at her for a while before he replied. She wore a light-coloured frock with a low neck that left the white throat bare; a Maréchal Niel rose in full bloom was fastened in her shining hair. Her cheeks were a little flushed, but the same bluish shadows lurked in the corners of her eyes.

Herr Friedemann looked at his plate and forced himself to make some sort of reply; after which the school superintendent's wife asked him if he did not love Beethoven and he had to answer that too. But at this point the Commandant, sitting at the head of the table, caught his wife's eye, tapped on his glass and said:

"Ladies and gentlemen, I suggest that we drink our coffee in the next room. It must be fairly decent out in the garden too, and whoever wants a little fresh air, I am for him."

Lieutenant von Deidesheim made a tactful little joke to cover the ensuing pause, and the table rose in the midst of laughter. Herr Friedemann and his partner were among the last to quit the room; he escorted her through the "old German" smoking-room to the dim and pleasant living-room, where he took his leave.

He was dressed with great care: his evening clothes were irreproachable, his shirt was dazzlingly white, his slender, well-shaped feet were encased in patent-leather pumps, which now and then betrayed the fact that he wore red silk stockings.

He looked out into the corridor and saw a good many people descending the steps into the garden. But he took up a position at the door of the smoking-room, with his cigar and coffee, where he could see into the living-room.

Some of the men stood talking in this room, and at the right of the door a little knot had formed round a small table, the centre of which was the mathematics student, who was eagerly talking. He had made the assertion that one could draw through a given point more than one parallel to a straight line; Frau Hagenström had cried that this was impossible, and he had gone on to prove it so conclusively that his hearers were constrained to behave as though they understood.

At the rear of the room, on the sofa beside the red-shaded lamp, Gerda von Rinnlingen sat in conversation with young Fräulein Stephens. She leaned back among the yellow silk cushions with one knee slung over the other, slowly smoking a cigarette, breathing out the smoke through her nose and sticking out her lower lip. Fräulein Stephens sat stiff as a graven image beside her, answering her questions with an assiduous smile.

Nobody was looking at little Herr Friedemann, so nobody saw that his large eyes were constantly directed upon Frau von Rinnlingen. He sat rather droopingly and looked at her. There was no passion in his gaze nor scarcely any pain. But there was something dull and heavy there, a dead weight of impotent, involuntary adoration.

Some ten minutes went by. Then as though she had been secretly watching him the whole time, Frau von Rinnlingen approached and paused in front of him. He got up as he heard her say:

"Would you care to go into the garden with me, Herr Friedemann?"

He answered:

"With pleasure, madam."

"You have never seen our garden?" she asked him as they went down the steps. "It is fairly large. I hope that there are not too many people in it; I should like to get a breath of fresh air. I got a headache during supper; perhaps the red wine was too strong for me. Let us go this way." They passed through a glass door, the vestibule, and a cool little courtyard, whence they gained the open air by descending a couple more steps.

The scent of all the flower-beds rose into the wonderful, warm, starry night. The garden lay in full moonlight and the guests were strolling up and down the white gravel paths, smoking and talking as they went. A group had gathered round the old fountain, where the much-loved old doctor was making them laugh by sailing paper boats.

With a little nod Frau von Rinnlingen passed them by, and pointed ahead of her, where the fragrant and well-cared-for garden blended into the darker park.

"Shall we go down this middle path?" asked she. At the beginning of it stood two low, squat obelisks.

In the vista at the end of the chestnut alley they could see the river shining green and bright in the moonlight. All about them was darkness and coolness. Here and there side paths branched off, all of them probably curving down to the river. For a long time there was not a sound.

"Down by the water," she said, "there is a pretty spot where I often sit. We could stop and talk a little. See the stars glittering here and there through the trees."

He did not answer, gazing, as they approached it, at the river's shimmering green surface. You could see the other bank and the park along the city wall. They left the alley and came out on the grassy slope down to the river, and she said:

"Here is our place, a little to the right, and there is no one there."

The bench stood facing the water, some six paces away, with its back to the trees. It was warmer here in the open. Crickets chirped among the grass, which at the river's edge gave way to sparse reeds. The moonlit water gave off a soft light.

For a while they both looked in silence. Then he heard her voice; it thrilled him to recognize the same low, gentle, pensive tone of a week ago, which now as then moved him so strangely:

"How long have you had your infirmity, Herr Friedemann? Were you born so?"

He swallowed before he replied, for his throat felt as though he were choking. Then he said, politely and gently:

"No, *gnädige Frau.* It comes from their having let me fall, when I was an infant."

"And how old are you now?" she asked again.

"Thirty years old."

"Thirty years old," she repeated. "And these thirty years were not happy ones?"

Little Herr Friedemann shook his head, his lips quivered.

"No," he said, "that was all lies and my imagination."

"Then you have thought that you were happy?" she asked.

"I have tried to be," he replied, and she responded:

"That was brave of you."

A minute passed. The crickets chirped and behind them the boughs rustled lightly.

"I understand a good deal about unhappiness," she told him. "These summer nights by the water are the best thing for it."

He made no direct answer, but gestured feebly across the water, at the opposite bank, lying peaceful in the darkness.

"I was sitting over there not long ago," he said.

"When you came from me?" she asked. He only nodded.

Then suddenly he started up from his seat, trembling all over; he sobbed and gave vent to a sound, a wail which yet seemed like a release from strain, and sank slowly to the ground before her. He had touched her hand with his as it lay beside him on the bench, and clung to it now, seizing the other as he knelt before her, this little cripple, trembling and shuddering; he buried his face in her lap and stammered between his gasps in a voice which was scarcely human:

"You know, you understand . . . let me . . . I can no longer . . . my God, oh, my God!"

She did not repulse him, neither did she bend her face towards him. She sat erect, leaning a little away, and her close-set eyes, wherein the liquid shimmer of the water seemed to be mirrored, stared beyond him into space.

Then she gave him an abrupt push and uttered a short, scornful laugh. She tore her hands from his burning fingers, clutched his arm, and flung him sidewise upon the ground. Then she sprang up and vanished down the wooded avenue.

He lay there with his face in the grass, stunned, unmanned, shudders coursing swiftly through his frame. He pulled himself together, got up somehow, took two steps, and fell again, close to the water. What were his sensations at this moment? Perhaps he was feeling that same luxury of hate which he had felt before when she had humiliated him with her glance, degenerated now, when he lay before her on the ground and she had treated him like a dog, into an insane rage which must at all costs find expression even against himself—a disgust, perhaps of himself, which filled him with a thirst to destroy himself, to tear himself to pieces, to blot himself utterly out.

On his belly he dragged his body a little further, lifted its upper part, and let it fall into the water. He did not raise his head nor move his legs, which still lay on the bank.

The crickets stopped chirping a moment at the noise of the little splash. Then they went on as before, the boughs lightly rustled, and down the long alley came the faint sound of laughter.

QUESTIONS

1 What is the significance of Herr Friedemann's proficiency in artistic endeavors in relation to the search theme?

2 Frau von Rinnlingen's actions appear difficult to understand. How can you explain her motivation in cultivating Friedemann? How can you explain her final rejection?

3 What are the outward manifestations of Friedemann's "image of himself"?

4 From all viewpoints—the author's, Friedemann's, and ours—the story could only end with the death of Friedemann. Explain why.

TOPICS FOR COMPOSITION

1 Mann's story, among those selections read thus far, probes more deeply into the inner feelings of man. Using question 3 above as your beginning point, write an essay showing how Mann develops and parallels the outward manifestations of the search with the inner image of himself that Friedemann displays.

2   Obviously, Mann's story illustrates a theme that we might classify as "the social outcast." Write an essay dealing with the "social outcast" in our society. In other words, for what reason or reasons are groups and individuals ostracized by society? Your possible range here is broad: select from minority groups, criminals, social misfits, physical and mental defectives, and others of that kind.

☐

Alexander Solzhenitsyn, Nobel prize winner and Russian exile, finds the immediacy of the past within the present a significant theme in many of his works. "Zakhar-the-Pouch" is an excellent example of this kind of collapse of time creating an overpowering sense of place. For Solzhenitsyn, it is the spirit of the people and their fierce loyalty to the land and its history that denotes place. Zakhar and the contents of his pouch make up that sort of character. As you read the story, take note of the interaction of immediate events, Zakhar's response to them, and the historical importance of the events of September 7, 1380.

ZAKHAR-THE-POUCH

Alexander Solzhenitsyn

You asked me to tell you something about my cycling holiday last summer. Well, if it's not too boring, listen to this one about Kulikovo Field.

We had been meaning to go there for a long time, but it was somehow a difficult place to reach. There are no brightly painted notices or signposts to show you the way, and you won't find it on a single map, even though this battle cost more Russian lives in the fourteenth century than Borodino did in the nineteenth. There has been only one such encounter for fifteen hundred years, not only in Russia but in all Europe. It was a battle not merely between principalities or nation-states, but between continents.

Perhaps we chose a rather roundabout way to get there: from Epiphania through Kazanovka and Monastirshchina. It was only because there had been no rain till then that we were able to ride instead of pushing our bikes; to cross the Don, which was not yet in full spate, and its tributary, the Nepriadva, we wheeled them over narrow, two-plank footbridges.

After a long trek, we stood on a hill and caught sight of what looked like a needle pointing into the sky from a distant flat-topped rise. We went downhill and lost sight of it. Then we started to climb again, and the grey needle reappeared, this time more distinct, and next to it we saw what looked like a church. There seemed to be something uniquely strange about its design, something never seen except in fairy tales: its domes looked transparent and fluid; they shimmered deceptively in the cascading sunlight of the hot August day—one minute they were there and the next they were gone.

We guessed rightly that we would be able to quench our thirst and fill our water bottles at the well in the valley, which proved to be invaluable later on. But the peasant who handed us the bucket, in reply to our question: "Where's Kulikovo Field?" just stared at us as if we were idiots.

"You don't say Kulikóko, you say Kulíkovo. The village of Kulíkovka is right next to the battlefield, but Kulikóvka's over there, on the other side of the Don."

After our meeting with this man, we travelled along deserted country lanes, and until we reached the monument several kilometres away, we did not come across a single person. It must have been because no one happened to be around on that particular day, for we could see the wheel of a combine harvester flailing somewhere in the distance. People obviously frequented this place and would do so again, because all the land had been planted with crops as far as the eye could see, and the harvest was almost ready—buckwheat, clover, sugar beet, rye, and peas (we had shelled some of those young peas); yet we saw no one that day and we passed through what seemed like the blessed calm of a reservation. Nothing disturbed us from musing on the fate of those fair-haired warriors, nine out of every ten of whom lay seven feet beneath the present topsoil, and whose bones had now dissolved into the earth, in order that Holy Russia might rid herself of the heathen Mussulman.

The features of the land—this wide slope gradually ascending to Mamai Hill—could not have greatly changed over six centuries, except that the forest had disappeared. Spread out before us was the very place where they had crossed the Don in the evening and the night of September 7, 1380, then settled down to feed their horses (though the majority were foot soldiers), sharpen their swords, restore their morale, pray, and hope—almost a quarter of a million Russians, certainly more than two hundred thousand. The population of Russia then was barely a seventh of what it is now, so that an army of that size staggers the imagination.

And for nine out of every ten warriors, that was to be their last morning on earth.

On that occasion our men had not crossed the Don from choice, for what army would want to stand and fight with its retreat blocked by a river? The truth of history is bitter but it is better to admit it: Mamai had as allies not only Circassians, Genoese, and Lithuanians but also Prince Oleg of Ryazan. (One must understand Oleg's motives also: he had no other way of protecting his territory from the Tartars, as it lay right across their path. His land had been ravaged by fire three times in the preceding seven years.) That is why the Russians had crossed the Don—to protect their rear from their own people, the men of Ryazan: in any other circumstances, Orthodox Christians would not have attacked them.

The needle loomed up in front of us, though it was no longer a needle but an imposing tower, unlike anything I had ever seen. We could not reach it directly: the tracks had come to an end and we were confronted by standing crops. We wheeled our bicycles round the edges of the fields and, finally, starting nowhere in particular, there emerged from the ground an old, neglected, abandoned road, overgrown with weeds, which grew more distinct as it drew nearer to the monument and even had ditches on either side of it.

Suddenly the crops came to an end and the hillside became even more like a reservation, a piece of fallow land overgrown with tough rye-grass instead of the usual feather-grass. We paid homage to this ancient place in the best way possible—just by breathing the pure air. One look around, and behold!—there in the light of sunrise the

Mongol chief Telebei is engaged in single combat with Prince Peresvet, the two lean- ing against each other like two sheaves of wheat; the Mongolian cavalry are shooting their arrows and brandishing their spears; with faces contorted with blood lust, they trample on the Russian infantry, breaking through the core of their formation and driving them back to where a milky cloud of mist has risen from the Nepriadva and the Don.

Our men were mown down like wheat, and we were trampled to death beneath their hoofs.

Here, at the very axis of the bloody carnage, provided that the person who guessed the spot did so correctly, are the monument and the church with the unearthly domes which had so amazed us from afar. There turned out to be a simple solution to the puzzle: the local inhabitants have ripped off the metal from all five domes for their own requirements, so the domes have become transparent; their delicate structure is still intact, except that it now consists of nothing but the framework, and from a dis- tance it looks like a mirage.

The monument, too, is remarkable at close quarters. Unless you go right up to it and touch it, you will not understand how it was made. Although it was built in the last century, in fact well over a hundred years ago, the idea—of piecing the monument together from sections of cast iron—is entirely modern, except that nowadays it would not be cast in iron. It is made up of two square platforms, one on top of another, then a twelve-sided structure which gradually becomes round; the lower part is decorated in relief with iron shields, swords, helmets, and Slavonic inscriptions. Farther up, it rises in the shape of a fourfold cylinder cast so that it looks like four massive organ pipes welded together. Then comes a capping piece with an incised pattern, and above it all a gilded cross triumphing over a crescent. The whole tower—fully thirty metres high— is made up of figured slabs so tightly bolted together that not a single rivet or seam is visible, just as if the monument had been cast in a single piece—at least until time, or more likely the sons and grandsons of the men who put it up, had begun to knock holes in it.

After the long route to the monument through empty fields, we had assumed that the place would be deserted. As we walked along, we were wondering why it was in this state. This was, after all, a historic spot. What happened here was a turning point in the fate of Russia. For our invaders have not always come from the West . . . Yet this place is spurned, forgotten.

How glad we were to be mistaken! At once, not far from the monument, we caught sight of a grey-haired old man and two young boys. They had thrown down their rucksacks and were lying in the grass, writing something in a large book the size of a class register. When we approached, we found that he was a literature teacher who had met the boys somewhere nearby, and that the book was not a school exercise book, but none other than the Visitors' Comments Book. But there was no museum here; where, then, in all this wild field was the book kept?

Suddenly a massive shadow blotted out the sun. We turned. It was the Keeper of Kulikovo Field—the man whose duty it was to guard our glorious heritage.

We did not have time to focus the camera, and in any case it was impossible to take a snapshot into the sun. What is more, the Keeper would have refused to be photographed (he knew what he was worth and refused to let himself be photographed all day). How shall I set about describing him? Should I begin with the man himself? Or start with his sack? (He was carrying an ordinary peasant's sack, only half full and evidently not very heavy since he was holding it without effort.)

The Keeper was a hot-tempered muzhik who looked something of a ruffian. His arms and legs were hefty, and his shirt was dashingly unbuttoned. Red hair stuck out from under the cap planted sideways on his head, and although it was obviously a week since he had shaved, a fresh reddish scratch ran right across his cheek.

"Ah!" he greeted us in a disapproving voice as he loomed over us. "You've just arrived, have you? How did you get here?"

He seemed puzzled, as if the place were completely fenced in and we had found a hole to crawl through. We nodded towards the bicycles, which we had propped up in the bushes. Although he was holding the sack as though about to board a train, he looked as if he would demand to see our passports. His face was haggard, with a pointed chin and a determined expression.

"I'm warning you! Don't damage the grass with your bicycles!"

With this, he let us know immediately that here, on Kulikovo Field, you were not free to do as you liked.

The Keeper's unbuttoned coat was long-skirted and enveloped him like a parka; it was patched in a few places and was the colour you read about in folk tales—somewhere between grey, brown, red, and purple. A star glinted in the lapel of his jacket; at first we thought it was a medal, but then we realised it was just the ordinary little badge, with Lenin's head in a circle, that everyone buys on Revolution Day. A long blue-and-white-striped linen shirt, obviously home-made, was hanging out from underneath his jacket and was gathered at the waist by an army belt with a five-pointed star on the buckle. His second-hand officer's breeches were tucked into the frayed tops of his canvas boots.

"Well?" he asked the teacher, in a much gentler tone of voice. "How's the writing going?"

"Fine, Zakhar Dmitrich," he replied, calling him by name. "We've nearly finished."

"Will *you*"—more sternly again—"be writing too?"

"Later on." We tried to escape from his insistent questions by cutting in: "Do you know when this monument was built?"

"Of course I do!" he snapped, offended, coughing and spluttering at the insult. "What do you think I'm here for?"

And carefully lowering his sack (which clinked with what sounded like bottles), the Keeper pulled a document out of his pocket and unfolded it; it was a page of an exercise book on which was written, in capital letters and in complete disregard of the ruled lines, a copy of the monument's dedication to Dmitry Donskoi and the year—1848.

"What is that?"

"Well, comrades," sighed Zakhar Dmitrich, revealing by his frankness that he was not quite the tyrant that he had at first pretended to be, "it's like this. I copied it myself from the plaque because everyone asks when it was built. I'll show you where the plaque was, if you like."

"What became of it?"

"Some rogue from our village pinched it—and we can't do anything about it."

"Do you know who it was?"

"Of course I know. I scared off some of his gang of louts, I dealt with them all right, but he and the rest got away. I'd like to lay my hands on all those vandals, I'd show 'em."

"But why did he steal the plaque?"

"For his house."

"Can't you take it back?"

"Ha, ha!" Zakhar threw back his head in reply to our foolish question. "That's the problem! I don't have any authority. They won't give me a gun. I need a machine gun in a job like this."

Looking at the scratch across his cheek, we thought to ourselves it was just as well they didn't give him a gun.

Then the teacher finished what he was writing and handed back the Comments Book. We thought that Zakhar Dmitrich would put it under his arm or into his sack, but we were wrong. He opened the flap of his dirty jacket and revealed, sewn inside, a sort of pocket or bag made of sacking (in fact, it was more like a pouch than anything else), the exact size of the Comments Book, which fitted neatly into it. Also attached to the pouch was a slot for the blunt indelible pencil which he lent to visitors.

Convinced that we were now suitably intimidated, Zakhar-the-Pouch picked up his sack (the clinking *was* glass) and went off with his long, loping stride into the bushes. Here the brusque forcefulness with which he had first met us vanished. Hunching himself miserably, he sat down, lit a cigarette, and smoked with such unalleviated grief, with such despair, that one might have thought all those who had perished on this battlefield had died only yesterday and had been his closest relatives, and that now he did not know how to go on living.

We decided to spend the whole day and night here: to see whether nighttime at Kulikovo really was as Blok described it in his poem. Without hurrying, we walked over to the monument, inspected the abandoned church, and wandered over the field, trying to imagine the dispositions of the battlefield on that eighth of September; then we clambered up onto the iron surface of the monument.

Plenty of people had been here before us. It would be quite wrong to say that the monument had been forgotten. People had been busy carving the iron surface of the monument with chisels and scratching it with nails, while those with less energy had written more faintly on the church walls with charcoal: "Maria Polyneyeva and Nikolai Lazarev were here from 8/5/50 to 24/5 . . ." "Delegates of the regional conference were here . . ." "Workers from the Kimovskaya Postal Administration were here 23/6/52 . . ." And so on and so on.

Then three young working lads from Novomoskovsk drove up on motorbikes. Jumping off lightly onto the iron surface, they started to examine the warm grey-black body of the monument and slapped it affectionately; they were surprised at how well made it was and explained to us how it had been done. In return, from the top platform we pointed out everything we knew about the battle.

But who can know nowadays exactly where and how it took place? According to the manuscripts, the Mongol-Tartar cavalry cut into our infantry regiments, decimated them, and drove them back towards the crossings over the Don, thus turning the Don from a protective moat against Oleg into a possible death trap. If the worst had happened, Dmitry would have been called "Donskoi" for the opposite reason. But he had taken everything into careful account and stood his ground, something of which not every grand duke was capable. He left a boyar dressed in his, Dmitry's, attire, fighting beneath his flag, while he himself fought as an ordinary foot soldier, and he was once seen taking on four Tartars at once. But the grand-ducal standard was chopped down and Dmitry, his armour severely battered, barely managed to crawl to the wood, when the Mongols broke through the Russian lines and drove them back. But then another Dmitry, Volinsky-Bobrok, the governor of Moscow, who had been lying in ambush with his army, attacked the ferocious Tartars from the rear. He drove them back, harrying them as they galloped away. Then he wheeled sharply and forced them into the river Nepriadva. From that moment the Russians took heart: they re-formed and turned on the Tartars, rose from the ground and drove all the khans, the enemy commanders, even Mamai himself, forty versts away across the river Ptan as far as Krasivaya Mech. (But here one legend contradicts another. An old man from the neighbouring village of Ivanovka had his own version: the mist, he said, had not lifted, and in the mist Mamai, thinking a broad oak tree beside him was a Russian warrior, took fright—"Ah, mighty is the Christian God!"—and so fled.)

Afterwards the Russians cleared the field of battle and buried the dead: it took them eight days.

"There's one they didn't pick up—they left him behind!" the cheerful fitter from Novomoskovsk said accusingly.

We turned around and could not help but burst out laughing. Yes!—one fallen warrior was lying there this very day, not far from the monument, face down on mother earth—his native land. His bold head had dropped to the ground and his valiant limbs were spread-eagled; he was without his shield or sword and, in place of his helmet, wore a threadbare cap, and near his hand lay a sack. (All the same, he was careful not to crush the edge of his jacket with the pouch in it, where he kept the Comments Book; he had pulled it out from undernearth his stomach and it lay on the grass beside him.) Perhaps he was just lying there in a drunken stupor, but if he was sleeping or thinking, then the way he was sprawled across the ground was very touching. He went perfectly with the field. They should cast an iron figure like that and place it here.

However, for all his height, Zakhar was too skinny to be a warrior.

"He doesn't want to work on the kolkhoz, so he found himself a soft government job where he can get a suntan," one of the lads growled.

What we disliked most of all was the way Zakhar flew at all the new arrivals, especially those who looked as if they might cause him trouble. During the day a few more people arrived; when he heard their cars he would get up, shake himself, and pounce on them with threats, as if they, not he, were responsible for the monument. Before they had time to be annoyed, Zakhar himself would give vent to violent indignation about the desolation of the place. It seemed incredible that he could harbour such passion.

"Don't you think it's a disgrace?" he said, waving his arms aggressively, to four people who got out of a Zaporozhetz car. "I'll bide my time, then I'll walk right through the regional department of culture." (With those long legs he could easily have done it.) "I'll take leave and I'll go to Moscow, right to Furtseva, the Minister of Culture herself. I'll tell her everything."

Then, as soon as he noticed that the visitors were intimidated and were not standing up to him, he picked up his sack with an air of importance, as an official picks up his briefcase, and went off to have a smoke and a nap.

Wandering here and there, we met Zakhar several times during the day. We noticed that when he walked he limped in one leg, and we asked him what had caused this.

He replied proudly: "It's a souvenir from the war!"

Again we did not believe him: he was just a practised liar.

We had drunk our water bottles dry, so we went up to Zakhar and asked him where we could get some water. Wa-ater? The whole trouble was, he explained, that there was no well here and they wouldn't allocate any money to dig one. The only source of drinking water in the whole field was the puddles. The well was in the village.

After that, he no longer bothered to get up to talk to us, as if we were old friends.

When we complained about the inscriptions having been hacked away or scratched over, Zakhar retorted: "Have a look and see if you can read any of the dates. If you find any new damage, then you can blame me. All this vandalism was done before my time; they don't dare try it when I'm around! Well, perhaps some scoundrel hid in the church and then scribbled on the walls—I've only got one pair of legs, you know!"

The church, dedicated to St. Sergei of Radonezh, who united the Russian forces and brought them to battle and soon afterwards effected the reconciliation between Dmitry Donskoi and Oleg of Ryazan, was a sturdy fortress-like building with tightly interlocking limbs: the truncated pyramid of the nave, a cloister surmounted by a watchtower, and two round castellated towers. There were a few windows like loopholes.

Inside it, everything had been stripped and there wasn't even a floor—you walked over sand. We asked Zakhar about it.

"Ha, ha, ha! It was all pinched!" He gloated over us. "It was during the war. Our people in Kulikovo tore up all the slabs from the floors and paved their yards, so they wouldn't have to walk in the muck. I made a list of who took the slabs . . . Then the war ended, but they still went on pinching the stuff. Even before that, our troops had used all the ikon screens to put round the edges of dugouts and for heating their stoves."

As the hours passed and he got used to us, Zakhar was no longer embarrassed to delve into his sack in front of us, and we gradually found out exactly what was inside it. It contained empty bottles (twelve kopecks) and jam jars (five kopecks) left behind by visitors—he picked them up in the bushes after their picnics—and also a full bottle of water, because he had no other access to drinking water during the day. He carried two loaves of rye bread, which he broke bits off now and again and chewed for his frugal meals.

"People come here in crowds all day long. I don't have any time to go off to the village for a meal."

On some days he probably carried a precious half bottle of vodka in there or some canned fish; then he would clutch the sack tightly, afraid to leave it anywhere. That day, when the sun had already begun to set, a friend on a motorbike came to see him; they sat in the bushes for an hour and a half. Then the friend went away and Zakhar came back without his sack. He talked rather more loudly, waved his arms more vigorously, and, noticing that I was writing something, warned us: "I'm in charge here, let me tell you! In '57 they decided to put a building up here. See those posts over there, planted round the monument? They've been here since then. They were cast in Tula. They were supposed to join up the posts with chains, but the chains never came. So they gave me this job and they pay me for it. Without me, the whole place would be in ruins!"

"How much do you get paid, Zakhar Dmitrich?"

After a sigh like a blacksmith's bellows, he was speechless for a moment. He mumbled something, then said quietly: "Twenty-seven roubles."

"What? The minimum's thirty."

"Well, maybe it is . . . And I don't get any days off, either. Morning to dusk I'm on the job without a break, and I even have to come back late at night too."

What an incorrigible old liar he is, we thought.

"Why do you have to be here at night?"

"Why d'you think?" he said in an offended voice. "How can I leave the place at night? Someone's got to watch it all the time. If a car comes, I have to make a note of its number."

"Why the number?"

"Well, they won't let me have a gun. They say I might shoot the visitors. The only authority I've got is to take their number. And supposing they do some damage?"

"What do you do with the number afterwards?"

"Nothing. I just keep it . . . Now they've built a house for tourists, have you seen it? I have to guard that too."

We had, of course, seen the house. Single-story, with several rooms, it was near completion but was still kept locked. The windows had been put in, and several were already broken; the floors were laid, but the plastering was not yet finished.

"Will you let us stay the night there?" (Towards sunset, it had begun to get cold; it was going to be a bitter night.)

"In the tourist house? No, it's impossible."

"Then who's it for?"

"No, it can't be done. Anyway, I haven't got the keys. So you needn't bother to ask. You can sleep in my shed."

His low shed with its sloping roof was designed for a half a dozen sheep. Bending down, we peered inside. Broken, trampled straw was scattered around; on the floor there was a cooking pot with some leftovers in it, a few more empty bottles, and a desiccated piece of bread. However, there was room for our bikes, and we could lie down and still leave enough space for Zakhar to stretch out.

He made use of our stay to take some time off.

"I'm off to Kulikovo to have supper at home. Grab a bite of something hot. Leave the door on the hook."

"Knock when you want to come in," we said, laughingly.

"O.K."

Zakhar-the-Pouch turned back the other flap of his miraculous jacket, to reveal two loops sewn into it. Out of his inexhaustible sack he drew an axe with a shortened handle and placed it firmly in the loops.

"Well," he said gloomily, "that's all I have for protection. They won't allow me anything else."

He said this in a tone of the deepest doom, as if he were expecting a horde of infidels to gallop up one of these nights and overthrow the monument, and he would have to face them alone with his little hatchet. We even shuddered at his voice as we sat there in the half light. Perhaps he wasn't a buffoon at all? Perhaps he really believed that if he didn't stand guard every night the battlefield and the monument were doomed?

Weakened by drink and a day of noisy activity, stooping and barely managing to hobble, Zakhar went off to his village and we laughed at him once more.

As had been our wish, we were left alone on Kulikovo Field. Night set in, with a full moon. The tower of the monument and the fortress-like church were silhouetted against it like great black screens. The distant lights of Kulikovka and Ivanovka competed faintly with the light of the moon. Not one aeroplane flew overhead; no motorcar rumbled by, no train rattled past in the distance. By moonlight the pattern of the nearby fields was no longer visible. Earth, grass, and moonlit solitude were as they had been in 1380. The centuries stood still, and as we wandered over the field we could evoke the whole scene—the campfires and the troops of dark horses. From the river Nepriadva came the sound of swans, just as Blok had described.

We wanted to understand the battle of Kulikovo in its entirety, grasp its inevitability, ignore the infuriating ambiguities of the chronicles: nothing had been as simple or as straightforward as it seemed; history had repeated itself after a long time-lag, and when it did, the result was disastrous. After the victory, the warriors of Russia faded away. Tokhtamysh immediately replaced Mamai, and two years after Kulikovo, he crushed the power of Muscovy; Dmitry Donskoi fled to Kostroma, while Tokhtamysh again destroyed both Ryazan and Moscow, took the Kremlin by ruse, plundered it, set it afire, chopped off heads, and dragged his prisoners back in chains to the Golden Horde, the Tartar capital.

Centuries pass and the devious path of history is simplified for the distant spectator until it looks as straight as a road drawn by a cartographer.

The night turned bitterly cold, but we shut ourselves in the shed and slept soundly right through it. We had decided to leave early in the morning. It was hardly light when we pushed our bicycles out and, with chattering teeth, started to load up.

The grass was white with hoarfrost; wisps of fog stretched from the hollow in which Kulikovka village lay and across the fields, dotted with haycocks. Just as we emerged from the shed to mount our bicycles and leave, we heard a loud, ferocious bark coming from one of the haycocks, and a shaggy grey dog ran out and made straight for us. As it bounded out, the haycock collapsed behind it; wakened by the barking, a tall figure arose from beneath it, called for the dog, and began to shake off the straw. It was already light enough for us to recognise him as our Zakhar-the-Pouch, still wearing his curious short-sleeved overcoat.

He had spent the night in the haycock, in the bone-chilling cold. Why? Was it anxiety or was it devotion to the place that had made him do it?

Immediately our previous attitude of amused condescension vanished. Rising out of the haycock on that frosty morning, he was no longer the ridiculous Keeper but rather the Spirit of the Field, a kind of guardian angel who never left the place.

He came towards us, still shaking himself and rubbing his hands together, and with his cap pushed back on his head, he seemed like a dear old friend.

"Why didn't you knock, Zakhar Dmitrich?"

"I didn't want to disturb you." He shrugged his shoulders and yawned. He was covered all over in straw and fluff. As he unbuttoned his coat to shake himself, we caught sight of both the Comments Book and his sole legal weapon, the hatchet, in their respective places.

The grey dog by his side was baring its teeth.

We said goodbye warmly and were already pedalling off as he stood there with his long arm raised, calling out: "Don't worry! I'll see to it! I'll go right to Furtseva! To Furtseva herself!"

That was two years ago. Perhaps the place is tidier now and better cared for. I have been a bit slow about writing this, but I haven't forgotten the Field of Kulikovo, or its Keeper, its red-haired tutelary spirit.

And let it be said that we Russians would be very foolish to neglect that place.

QUESTIONS

1. Why are the details of the monument's construction important?
2. How does Zakhar's sense of his position and the way in which he performs it contribute to the ambiguity of the historical details?
3. How do the interests of the narrator, the writer and the boy, and the motorcyclists combine to emphasize the importance of place?

TOPICS FOR COMPOSITION

1. Neither Crane's young man nor Solzhenitsyn's Zakhar is an attractive character. Write an essay in which you compare and contrast the two in order to show why we sympathize with both.
2. Solzhenitsyn's story comments on the role of government in the creation of a sense of place. Argue the effectiveness and ineffectiveness of government's attempts to legislate a sense of national loyalty.
3. Describe a visit to a national monument. Attempt to capture not only the sense of place but its impact on you.

DRAMA

In "Hello Out There" two lonely people together postulate a place—San Francisco—where the individual is no longer alone or exploited ("raped"). The very title and its recurrence in the dialogue insist upon the urgency of establishing a place beyond the emptiness of Wheeling and Matador, Texas—beyond the Young Man's prison cell and The Girl's equally desolate prison of hopelessness, ridicule, and exploitation. San Francisco becomes, in their mutually stirred imaginations, the *locus* of the ideal—a place of "Cool fog and seagulls," where more people "love somebody" than a town like Matador, where there is "Nothing . . . but the lonesome wind all the time, lifting the dirt and blowing out to the prairie." In the play's inevitable *dénouement,* the horror of life in a meaningless place is forced upon an indignant husband as well as upon The Girl.

1 The exchanges between the Young Man and The Girl move gradually but insistently from mere banality toward a kind of visionary eloquence. The Girl confesses, "I'm nobody here"; and the Young Man sees his past in terms of "going from one poor little town to another, trying to get in on something good somewhere."
2 The inescapable contrasts between the "Frisco" of the charged imagination, on the one hand, and Wheeling and Matador, Texas, or a jail cell of stark reality, on the other, point up Saroyan's theme of the imperative call of the unfettered life.
3 Everything in the play's context that conspires against the achievement of "place"— including The Woman—reveals itself as an enemy of love and life.

HELLO OUT THERE

William Saroyan

For George Bernard Shaw

CHARACTERS

A YOUNG MAN   TWO OTHER MEN
A GIRL   A WOMAN
A MAN

> Scene: There is a fellow in a small-town prison cell, tapping slowly on the floor with a spoon. After tapping half a minute, as if he were trying to telegraph words, he gets up and begins walking around the cell. At last he stops, stands at the center of the cell, and doesn't move for a long time. He feels his head, as if it were wounded. Then he looks around. Then he calls out dramatically, kidding the world.

YOUNG MAN   Hello—out there! *(Pause)* Hello—out there! Hello—out there! *(Long pause)* Nobody out there. *(Still more dramatically, but more comically, too)* Hello—out there! Hello—out there!

(A GIRL'S VOICE is heard, very sweet and soft)

THE VOICE   Hello.

YOUNG MAN   Hello—out there.

THE VOICE   Hello.

YOUNG MAN   Is that you, Katey?

THE VOICE   No—this here is Emily.

YOUNG MAN   Who? *(Swiftly)* Hello out there.

THE VOICE   Emily.

YOUNG MAN   Emily who? I don't know anybody named Emily. Are you that girl I met at Sam's in Salinas about three years ago?

THE VOICE   No—I'm the girl who cooks here. I'm the cook. I've never been in Salinas. I don't even know where it is.

YOUNG MAN   Hello out there. You say you cook here?

THE VOICE   Yes.

YOUNG MAN   Well, why don't you study up and learn to cook? How come I don't get no jello or anything good?

THE VOICE   I just cook what they tell me to. *(Pause)* You lonesome?

YOUNG MAN   Lonesome as a coyote. Hear me hollering? Hello out there!

THE VOICE   Who you hollering to?

YOUNG MAN   Well—nobody, I guess. I been trying to think of somebody to write a letter to, but I can't think of anybody.

THE VOICE   What about Katey?

YOUNG MAN   I don't know anybody named Katey.

THE VOICE   Then why did you say, Is that you, Katey?

YOUNG MAN   Katey's a good name. I always did like a name like Katey. I never *knew* anybody named Katey, though.

THE VOICE   *I* did.

YOUNG MAN   Yeah? What was she like? Tall girl, or little one?

THE VOICE   Kind of medium.

YOUNG MAN   Hello out there. What sort of a looking girl are *you*?

THE VOICE   Oh, I don't know.

YOUNG MAN   Didn't anybody ever tell you? Didn't anybody ever talk to you that way?

THE VOICE   What way?

YOUNG MAN   You know. Didn't they?

THE VOICE   No, they didn't.

YOUNG MAN   Ah, the fools—they should have. I can tell from your voice you're O.K.

THE VOICE   Maybe I am and maybe I ain't.

YOUNG MAN   I never missed yet.

THE VOICE   Yeah, I know. That's why you're in jail.

YOUNG MAN   The whole thing was a mistake.

THE VOICE   They claim it was rape.

YOUNG MAN   No—it wasn't.

THE VOICE   That's what they claim it was.

YOUNG MAN   They're a lot of fools.

THE VOICE   Well, you sure are in trouble. Are you scared?

YOUNG MAN   Scared to death. *(Suddenly)* Hello out there!

THE VOICE   What do you keep saying that for all the time?

YOUNG MAN   I'm lonesome. I'm as lonesome as a coyote. *(A long one)* Hello—out there!

(THE GIRL appears, over to one side. She is a plain girl in plain clothes.)

THE GIRL   I'm kind of lonesome, too.

YOUNG MAN *(Turning and looking at her)*   Hey—No fooling? Are you?

THE GIRL   Yeah—I'm almost as lonesome as a coyote myself.

YOUNG MAN   Who *you* lonesome for?

THE GIRL   I don't know.

YOUNG MAN   It's the same with me. The minute they put you in a place like this you remember all the girls you ever knew, and all the girls you didn't get to know, and it sure gets lonesome.

THE GIRL   I bet it does.

YOUNG MAN   Ah, it's awful. *(Pause)* You're a pretty kid, you know that?

THE GIRL   You're just talking.

YOUNG MAN   No, I'm not just talking—you *are* pretty. Any fool could see that. You're just about the prettiest kid in the whole world.

THE GIRL   I'm not—and you know it.

YOUNG MAN   No—you are. I never saw anyone prettier in all my born days; in all my travels. I knew Texas would bring me luck.

THE GIRL   Luck? You're in jail, aren't you? You've got a whole gang of people all worked up, haven't you?

YOUNG MAN   Ah, that's nothing. I'll get out of this.

THE GIRL   Maybe.

YOUNG MAN   No, I'll be all right—*now.*

THE GIRL   What do you mean—now?

YOUNG MAN   I mean after seeing you. I got something now. You know for a while there I didn't care one way or another. Tired. *(Pause)* Tired of trying for the best all the time and never getting it. *(Suddenly)* Hello out there!

THE GIRL   Who you calling now?

YOUNG MAN   You.

THE GIRL   Why, I'm right here.

YOUNG MAN   I know. *(Calling)* Hello out there!

THE GIRL   Hello.

YOUNG MAN   Ah, you're sweet. *(Pause)* I'm going to marry you. I'm going away with you. I'm going to take you to San Francisco or some place like that. I *am,* now. I'm going to win myself some real money, too. I'm going to study 'em real careful and pick myself some winners, and we're going to have a lot of money.

THE GIRL   Yeah?

YOUNG MAN   Yeah. Tell me your name and all that stuff.

THE GIRL   Emily.

YOUNG MAN   I know that. What's the rest of it? Where were you born? Come on, tell me the whole thing.

THE GIRL   Emily Smith.

YOUNG MAN   Honest to God?

THE GIRL   Honest. That's my name—Emily Smith.

YOUNG MAN   Ah, you're the sweetest girl in the whole world.

THE GIRL   Why?

YOUNG MAN   I don't know why, but you are, that's all. Where were you born?

THE GIRL   Matador, Texas.

YOUNG MAN   Where's that?

THE GIRL   Right here.

YOUNG MAN   Is this Matador, Texas?

THE GIRL   Yeah, it's Matador. They brought you here from Wheeling.

YOUNG MAN   Is that where I was—Wheeling?

THE GIRL   Didn't you even know what town you were in?

YOUNG MAN   All towns are alike. You don't go up and ask somebody what town you're in. It doesn't make any difference. How far away is Wheeling?

THE GIRL   Sixteen or seventeen miles. Didn't you know they moved you?

YOUNG MAN   How could I know, when I was out—cold? Somebody hit me over the head with a lead pipe or something. What'd they hit me for?

THE GIRL   Rape—that's what they *said.*

YOUNG MAN   Ah, that's a lie. *(Amazed, almost to himself)* She wanted me to give her money.

THE GIRL   Money?

YOUNG MAN   Yeah, if I'd have known she was a woman like that—well, by God, I'd have gone on down the street and stretched out in a park somewhere and gone to sleep.

THE GIRL   Is that what she wanted—money?

YOUNG MAN   Yeah. A fellow like me hopping freights all over the country, trying to break his bad luck, going from one poor little town to another, trying to get in on something good somewhere, and she asks for money. I thought she was lonesome. She *said* she was.

THE GIRL   Maybe she was.

YOUNG MAN   She was *something.*

THE GIRL   I guess I'd never see you, if it didn't happen, though.

YOUNG MAN   Oh, I don't know—maybe I'd just mosey along this way and see you in this town somewhere. I'd recognize you, too.

THE GIRL   Recognize me?

YOUNG MAN   Sure, I'd recognize you the minute I laid eyes on you.

THE GIRL   Well, who would I be?

YOUNG MAN   Mine, that's who.

THE GIRL   Honest?

YOUNG MAN   Honest to God.

THE GIRL   You just say that because you're in jail.

YOUNG MAN No, I mean it. You just pack up and wait for me. We'll high-roll the hell out of here to Frisco.

THE GIRL You're just lonesome.

YOUNG MAN I been lonesome all my life—there's no cure for that—but you and me— we can have a lot of fun hanging around together. You'll bring me luck. I know it.

THE GIRL What are you looking for luck for all the time?

YOUNG MAN I'm a gambler. I don't work. I've *got* to have luck, or I'm a bum. I haven't had any decent luck in years. Two whole years now—one place to another. Bad luck all the time. That's why I got in trouble back there in Wheeling, too. That was no accident. That was my bad luck following me around. So here I am, with my head half busted. I guess it was her old man that did it.

THE GIRL You mean her father?

YOUNG MAN No, her husband. If I had an old lady like that, I'd throw her out.

THE GIRL Do you think you'll have better luck, if I go with you?

YOUNG MAN It's a cinch. I'm a good handicapper. All I need is somebody good like you with me. It's no good always walking around in the streets for anything that might be there at the time. You got to have somebody staying with you all the time— through winters when it's cold, and springtime when it's pretty, and summertime when it's nice and hot and you can go swimming—through *all* the times—rain and snow and all the different kinds of weather a man's got to go through before he dies. You got to have somebody who's right. Somebody who knows you, from away back. You got to have somebody who even knows you're wrong but likes you just the same. I know I'm wrong, but I just don't want anything the hard way, working like a dog, or the *easy* way, working like a dog—working's the hard way and the easy way both. All I got to do is beat the price, always—and then I don't feel lousy and don't hate anybody. If you go along with me, I'll be the finest guy anybody ever saw. I won't be wrong any more. You know when you get enough of that money, you *can't* be wrong any more—you're right because the money says so. I'll have a lot of money and you'll be just about the prettiest, most wonderful kid in the whole world. I'll be proud walking around Frisco with you on my arm and people turning around to look at us.

THE GIRL Do you think they will?

YOUNG MAN Sure they will. When I get back in some decent clothes, and you're on my arm—well, Katey, they'll turn around and look, and they'll see something, too.

THE GIRL Katey?

YOUNG MAN Yeah—that's your name from now on. You're the first girl I ever called Katey. I've been saving it for you. O.K.?

THE GIRL O.K.

YOUNG MAN How long have I been here?

THE GIRL Since last night. You didn't wake up until late this morning, though.

YOUNG MAN What time is it now? About nine?

THE GIRL About ten.

YOUNG MAN Have you got the key to this lousy cell?

THE GIRL No. They don't let me fool with any keys.

YOUNG MAN   Well, can you get it?

THE GIRL   No.

YOUNG MAN   Can you *try*?

THE GIRL   They wouldn't let me get near any keys. I cook for this jail, when they've got somebody in it. I clean up and things like that.

YOUNG MAN   Well, I want to get out of here. Don't you know the guy that runs this joint?

THE GIRL   I know him, but he wouldn't let you out. They were talking of taking you to another jail in another town.

YOUNG MAN   Yeah? Why?

THE GIRL   Because they're afraid.

YOUNG MAN   What are they afraid of?

THE GIRL   They're afraid these people from Wheeling will come over in the middle of the night and break in.

YOUNG MAN   Yeah? What do they want to do that for?

THE GIRL   Don't *you* know what they want to do it for?

YOUNG MAN   Yeah, I know all right.

THE GIRL   Are you scared?

YOUNG MAN   Sure I'm scared. Nothing scares a man more than ignorance. You can argue with people who ain't fools, but you can't argue with fools—they just go to work and do what they're set on doing. Get me out of here.

THE GIRL   How?

YOUNG MAN   Well, go get the guy with the key, and let me talk to him.

THE GIRL   He's gone home. Everybody's gone home.

YOUNG MAN   You mean I'm in this little jail all alone?

THE GIRL   Well—yeah—except me.

YOUNG MAN   Well, what's the big idea—doesn't anybody stay here all the time?

THE GIRL   No, they go home every night. I clean up and then I go, too. I hung around tonight.

YOUNG MAN   What made you do that?

THE GIRL   I wanted to talk to you.

YOUNG MAN   Honest? What did you want to talk about?

THE GIRL   Oh, I don't know. I took care of you last night. You were talking in your sleep. You liked me, too. I didn't think you'd like me when you woke up, though.

YOUNG MAN   Yeah? Why not?

THE GIRL   I don't know.

YOUNG MAN   Yeah? Well, you're wonderful, see?

THE GIRL   Nobody ever talked to me that way. All the fellows in town—*(Pause)*

YOUNG MAN   What about 'em? *(Pause)* Well, what about 'em? Come on—tell me.

THE GIRL   They laugh at me.

YOUNG MAN   Laugh at *you*? They're fools. What do they know about anything? You go get your things and come back here. I'll take you with me to Frisco. How old are you?

THE GIRL   Oh, I'm of age.

YOUNG MAN   How old are you?—Don't lie to me! Sixteen?

THE GIRL   I'm seventeen.

YOUNG MAN   Well, bring your father and mother. We'll get married before we go.

THE GIRL   They wouldn't let me go.

YOUNG MAN   Why not?

THE GIRL   I don't know, but they wouldn't. I know they wouldn't.

YOUNG MAN   You go tell your father not to be a fool, see? What is he, a farmer?

THE GIRL   No—nothing. He gets a little relief from the government because he's supposed to be hurt or something—his side hurts, he says. I don't know what it is.

YOUNG MAN   Ah, he's a liar. Well, I'm taking you with me, see?

THE GIRL   He takes the money I earn, too.

YOUNG MAN   He's got no right to do that.

THE GIRL   I know it, but he does it.

YOUNG MAN *(Almost to himself)*   This world stinks. You shouldn't have been born in this town, anyway, and you shouldn't have had a man like that for a father, either.

THE GIRL   Sometimes I feel sorry for him.

YOUNG MAN   Never mind feeling sorry for him. *(Pointing a finger)* I'm going to talk to your father some day. I've got a few things to tell that guy.

THE GIRL   I know you have.

YOUNG MAN *(Suddenly)*   Hello—out there! See if you can get that fellow with the keys to come down and let me out.

THE GIRL   Oh, I couldn't.

YOUNG MAN   Why not?

THE GIRL   I'm nobody here—they give me fifty cents every day I work.

YOUNG MAN   How much?

THE GIRL   Fifty cents.

YOUNG MAN *(To the world)*   You see? They ought to pay money to *look* at you. To breathe the *air* you breathe. I don't know. Sometimes I figure it never is going to make sense. Hello—out there! I'm scared. You try to get me out of here. I'm scared them fools are going to come here from Wheeling and go crazy, thinking they're heroes. Get me out of here, Katey.

THE GIRL   I don't know what to do. Maybe I could break the door down.

YOUNG MAN   No, you couldn't do that. Is there a hammer out there or anything?

THE GIRL   Only a broom. Maybe they've locked the broom up, too.

YOUNG MAN   Go see if you can find anything.

THE GIRL   All right. *(She goes)*

YOUNG MAN   Hello—out there! Hello—out there! *(Pause)* Hello—out there! Hello—out there! *(Pause)* Putting me in jail. *(With contempt)* Rape! Rape? *They* rape everything good that was ever born. His side hurts. They laugh at her. Fifty cents a day. Little punk people. Hurting the only good thing that ever came their way. *(Suddenly)* Hello—out there!

THE GIRL *(Returning)*   There isn't a thing out there. They've locked everything up for the night.

YOUNG MAN   Any cigarettes?

THE GIRL   Everything's locked up—all the drawers of the desk, all the closet doors—everything.

YOUNG MAN   I ought to have a cigarette.

THE GIRL   I could get you a package maybe, somewhere. I guess the drug store's open. It's about a mile.

YOUNG MAN   A mile? I don't want to be alone that long.

THE GIRL   I could run all the way, and all the way back.

YOUNG MAN   You're the sweetest girl that ever lived.

THE GIRL   What kind do you want?

YOUNG MAN   Oh, any kind—Chesterfields or Camels or Lucky Strikes—any kind at all.

THE GIRL   I'll go get a package. *(She turns to go)*

YOUNG MAN   What about the money?

THE GIRL   I've got some money. I've got a quarter I been saving. I'll run all the way. *(She is about to go.)*

YOUNG MAN   Come here.

THE GIRL   *(Going to him)*   What?

YOUNG MAN   Give me your hand. *(He takes her hand and looks at it, smiling. He lifts it and kisses it.)* I'm scared to death.

THE GIRL   I am, too.

YOUNG MAN   I'm not lying—I don't care what happens to me, but I'm scared nobody will ever come out here to this God-forsaken broken-down town and find you. I'm scared you'll get used to it and not mind. I'm scared you'll never get to Frisco and have 'em all turning around to look at you. Listen—go get me a gun, because if they come, I'll kill 'em! They don't understand. Get me a gun!

THE GIRL   I could get my father's gun. I know where he hides it.

YOUNG MAN   Go get it. Never mind the cigarettes. Run all the way. *(Pause, smiling but seriously)* Hello, Katey.

THE GIRL   Hello. What's your name?

YOUNG MAN   Photo-Finish is what they *call* me. My races are always photo-finish races. You don't know what that means, but it means they're very close. So close the only way they can tell which horse wins is to look at a photograph after the race is over. Well, every race I bet turns out to be a photo-finish race, and my horse never wins. It's my bad luck, all the time. That's why they call me Photo-Finish. Say it before you go.

THE GIRL   Photo-Finish.

YOUNG MAN   Come here. *(THE GIRL moves close and he kisses her.)* Now, hurry. Run all the way.

THE GIRL   I'll run. *(THE GIRL turns and runs. The YOUNG MAN stands at the center of the cell a long time. THE GIRL comes running back in. Almost crying)* I'm afraid. I'm afraid I won't see you again. If I come back and you're not here, I—

YOUNG MAN   Hello—out there!

THE GIRL   It's so lonely in this town. Nothing here but the lonesome wind all the time, lifting the dirt and blowing out to the prairie. I'll stay *here.* I won't *let* them take you away.

YOUNG MAN   Listen, Katey. Do what I tell you. Go get that gun and come back. Maybe they won't come tonight. Maybe they won't come at all. I'll hide the gun and when they let me out you can take it back and put it where you found it. And then we'll go away. But if they come, I'll kill 'em! Now, hurry—

THE GIRL   All right. *(Pause)* I want to tell you something.

YOUNG MAN   O.K.

THE GIRL *(Very softly)*   If you're not here when I come back, well, I'll have the gun and I'll know what to do with it.

YOUNG MAN   You know how to handle a gun?

THE GIRL   I know how.

YOUNG MAN   Don't be a fool. *(Takes off his shoe, brings out some currency)* Don't be a fool, see? Here's some money. Eighty dollars. Take it and go to Frisco. Look around and find somebody. Find somebody alive and halfway human, see? Promise me —if I'm not here when you come back, just throw the gun away and get the hell to Frisco. Look around and find somebody.

THE GIRL   I don't *want* to find anybody.

YOUNG MAN *(Swiftly, desperately)*   Listen, if I'm not here when you come back, how do you know I haven't gotten away? Now, do what I tell you. I'll meet you in Frisco. I've got a couple of dollars in my other shoe. I'll see you in San Francisco.

THE GIRL *(With wonder)*   San Francisco?

YOUNG MAN   That's right—San Francisco. That's where you and me belong.

THE GIRL   I've always wanted to go to *some* place like San Francisco—but how could I go alone?

YOUNG MAN   Well, you're not alone any more, see?

THE GIRL   Tell me a little what it's like.

YOUNG MAN *(Very swiftly, almost impatiently at first, but gradually slower and with remembrance, smiling, and* THE GIRL *moving closer to him as he speaks)*   Well, it's on the Pacific to begin with—ocean water all around. Cool fog and sea-gulls. Ships from all over the world. It's got seven hills. The little streets go up and down, around and all over. Every night the fog-horns bawl. But they won't be bawling for you and me.

THE GIRL   What else?

YOUNG MAN   That's about all, I guess.

THE GIRL   Are people different in San Francisco?

YOUNG MAN   People are the same everywhere. They're different only when they love somebody. That's the only thing that makes 'em different. More people in Frisco love somebody, that's all.

THE GIRL   Nobody anywhere loves anybody as much as I love you.

YOUNG MAN *(Shouting, as if to the world)*   You see? Hearing you say that, a man could die and still be ahead of the game. Now, hurry. And don't forget, if I'm not here when you come back, get the hell to San Francisco where you'll have a chance. Do you hear me? *(*THE GIRL *stands a moment looking at him, then backs away, turns and runs. The* YOUNG MAN *stares after her, troubled and smiling. Then he turns away from the image of her and walks about like a lion in a cage. After a while he sits down suddenly and buries his head in his hands. From a distance the sound of several automobiles approaching is heard. He listens a moment, then ignores the implications of the sound, whatever they may be. Several automobile doors are slammed. He ignores this also. A wooden door is opened with a key and closed, and footsteps are heard in a hall. Walking easily, almost casually and yet* *arrogantly, a* MAN *comes in. The* YOUNG MAN *jumps up suddenly and shouts at the man, almost scaring him)* What the hell kind of jail-keeper are you, anyway? Why don't you attend to your business? You get paid for it, don't you? Now, get me out of here.

THE MAN   But I'm *not* the jail-keeper.

YOUNG MAN   Yeah, Well, who are you, then?

THE MAN   I'm the husband.

YOUNG MAN   What husband you talking about?

THE MAN   You know what husband.

YOUNG MAN   Hey! *(Pause, looking at* THE MAN*)* Are you the guy that hit me over the head last night?

THE MAN   I am.

YOUNG MAN *(With righteous indignation)*   What do you mean going around hitting people over the head?

THE MAN   Oh, I don't know. What do you *mean* going around—the way you do?

YOUNG MAN *(Rubbing his head)*   You hurt my head. You got no right to hit anybody over the head.

THE MAN *(Suddenly angry, shouting)*   Answer my question! What do you mean?

YOUNG MAN   Listen, you—don't be hollering at me just because I'm locked up.

THE MAN *(With contempt, slowly)*   You're a dog!

YOUNG MAN   Yeah? Well, let me tell you something. You *think* you're the husband. You're the husband of nothing. *(Slowly)* What's more, your wife—if you want to call her that—is a tramp. Why don't you throw her out in the street where she belongs?

THE MAN *(Draws a pistol)*   Shut up!

YOUNG MAN   Yeah? Go ahead, shoot—*(Softly)* and spoil the fun. What'll your pals think? They'll be disappointed, won't they? What's the fun hanging a man who's already dead? *(*THE MAN *puts the gun away.)* That's right, because now you can have some fun yourself, telling me what you're going to do. That's what you came here for, isn't it? Well, you don't need to tell me. I *know* what you're going to do. I've read the papers and I know. They have fun. A mob of 'em fall on one man and beat him, don't they? They tear off his clothes and kick him, don't they? And women and little children stand around watching, don't they? Well, before you go on *this* picnic, I'm going to tell you a few things. Not that that's going to send you home with your pals—the other heroes. No. You've been outraged. A stranger has come to town and violated your women. Your pure, innocent, virtuous women. You fellows have got to set this thing right. You're men, not mice. You're homemakers, and you beat your children. *(Suddenly)* Listen, you—I didn't know she was your wife. I didn't know she was anybody's wife.

THE MAN   You're a liar!

YOUNG MAN   Sometimes—when it'll do somebody some good—but not this time. Do you want to hear about it? *(*THE MAN *doesn't answer.)* All right, I'll tell you. I met her at a lunch counter. She came in and sat next to me. There was plenty of room, but she sat next to me. Somebody had put a nickel in the phonograph and a fellow was singing *New San Antonio Rose*. Well, she got to talking about the song. I thought she was talking to the waiter, but *he* didn't answer her, so after a while *I* answered her. That's how I met her. I didn't think anything of it. We left the place together and started walking. The first thing I knew she said, This is where I live.

THE MAN You're a dirty liar!

YOUNG MAN Do you want to hear it? Or not? (THE MAN *does not answer*.) O.K. She asked me to come in. Maybe she had something in mind, maybe she didn't. Didn't make any difference to me, one way or the other. If she was lonely, all right. If not, all right.

THE MAN You're telling a lot of dirty lies!

YOUNG MAN I'm telling the truth. Maybe your wife's out there with your pals. Well, call her in. I got nothing against her, or you—or any of you. Call her in, and ask her a few questions. Are you in love with her? (THE MAN *doesn't answer*.) Well, that's too bad.

THE MAN What do you mean, too bad?

YOUNG MAN I mean this may not be the first time something like this has happened.

THE MAN *(Swiftly)* Shut up!

YOUNG MAN Oh, you know it. You've always known it. You're afraid of your pals, that's all. She asked me for money. That's all she wanted. I wouldn't be here now if I had given her the money.

THE MAN *(Slowly)* How much did she ask for?

YOUNG MAN I didn't ask her how much. I told her I'd made a mistake. She said she would make trouble if I didn't give her money. Well, I don't like bargaining, and I don't like being threatened, either. I told her to get the hell away from me. The next thing I knew she'd run out of the house and was hollering. *(Pause)* Now, why don't you go out there and tell 'em they took me to another jail—go home and pack up and leave her. You're a pretty good guy, you're just afraid of your pals. (THE MAN *draws his gun again. He is very frightened. He moves a step toward the* YOUNG MAN *then fires three times. The* YOUNG MAN *falls to his knees.* THE MAN *turns and runs, horrified)* Hello—out there! *(He is bent forward.* THE GIRL *comes running in, and halts suddenly, looking at him)*

THE GIRL There were some people in the street, men and women and kids—so I came in through the back, through a window. I couldn't find the gun. I looked all over but I couldn't find it. What's the matter?

YOUNG MAN Nothing—nothing. Everything's all right. Listen. Listen, kid. Get the hell out of here. Go out the same way you came in and run—run like hell—run all night. Get to another town and get on a train. Do you hear me?

THE GIRL What's happened?

YOUNG MAN Get away—just get away from here. Take any train that's going—you can get to Frisco later.

THE GIRL *(Almost sobbing)* I don't want to go any place without you.

YOUNG MAN I can't go. Something's happened. *(He looks at her)* But I'll be with you always—God damn it. Always!

(He falls forward. THE GIRL stands near him, then begins to sob softly, walking away. She stands over to one side, stops sobbing, and stares out. The excitement of the mob outside increases. THE MAN, with two of his pals, comes running in. THE GIRL watches, unseen)

THE MAN   Here's the son of a bitch!
ANOTHER MAN   O.K. Open the cell, Harry.

(The THIRD MAN goes to the cell door, unlocks it, and swings it open.)

(A WOMAN comes running in.)

THE WOMAN   Where is he? I want to see him. Is he dead? *(Looking down at him, as the MEN pick him up)* There he is. *(Pause)* Yeah, that's him. *(Her husband looks at her with contempt, then at the dead man.)*

THE MAN *(Trying to laugh)*   All right—let's get it over with.
THIRD MAN   Right you are, George. Give me a hand, Harry. *(They lift the body)*
THE GIRL *(Suddenly, fiercely)*   Put him down!
THE MAN   What's this?
SECOND MAN   What are you doing here? Why aren't you out in the street?
THE GIRL   Put him down and go away. *(She runs toward the MEN. THE WOMAN grabs her.)*
THE WOMAN   Here—where do you think *you're* going?
THE GIRL   Let me go. You've got no right to take him away.
THE WOMAN   Well, listen to her, will you? *(She slaps THE GIRL and pushes her to the floor.)* Listen to the little slut, will you?

(They all go, carrying the YOUNG MAN's body. THE GIRL gets up slowly, no longer sobbing. She looks around at everything, then looks straight out, and whispers.)

THE GIRL   Hello—out—there! Hello—out there!

QUESTIONS

1   Why does the Young Man compulsively reiterate "Hello out there" not only at the beginning of, but also throughout the play? Do you think The Girl has been waiting for such a seemingly cryptic communication?

2   How do you interpret the Young Man's quickly informing The Girl that she is "a pretty kid" (though Saroyan informs us that "She is a plain girl in plain clothes"), proposing marriage, and promising to take her to "San Francisco or some place like that"? Can these seemingly hasty developments be interpreted as his imaginative perception that neither her native Matador nor his jail cell adequately defines the possibilities of their being?

3   How is the dialogue between the outraged husband (The Man) and the Young Man related to the earlier dialogue of the Young Man and The Girl? Is The Man also a "displaced" person? And does his shooting of the Young Man suggest that he too has gained insight into the inadequacies of "place"?

4   Is the ending of the play, in your opinion, the only really satisfactory solution to the conflict of values? Are the mob also trying to assert their sense of "a place in society"?

TOPICS FOR COMPOSITION

1 Collect all the references to "place" in the play and analyze their relationships and contrasts. Try to find a scheme of classification that will link all the characters to a "place"—not only two small towns in Texas or a celebrated city in California but also more abstract, perhaps even nebulous, human associations with a sense of "place."

2 Compare and contrast the situations of the Young Man and The Girl. Are both the prisoners of a society that tries to circumscribe or to legislate the individual's "search for a place"?

3 Argue for or against the possible proposition that Saroyan suggests symbolic identification of geographical locations with human experience and aspiration.

POETRY

The need for a place in society, because it is part of a larger, very complex need for orientation, finds expression in many ways, as the poems that follow will amply demonstrate. It is indeed not easy to generalize about a group of works that vary as much in perspective as these do; yet, it is possible to make comparisons among them which will illuminate their common theme—and at the same time illustrate the range of poetic vision. It is admittedly a far cry, for example, from Alexander Pope's reflections on social principles to E. A. Robinson's description of old Mr. Flood conversing drunkenly with himself in the moonlight; and a far cry, perhaps, from either of these to Robert Pack's little fantasy about a bird in search of a cage. Yet the larger perspective offered by Pope's discourse should make it easier to grasp and respond fully to the symbolic implications of Robinson's vignette: that loneliness is to some extent a universal human condition and that we are all more or less vulnerable to the forces within and without that have Mr. Flood talking to himself. And our emotional response to these implications should in turn make us more receptive to Pope's earnest philosophizing. In fact, it might lead us to accept too uncritically his assertion (best viewed, perhaps, as a possibly self-fulfilling prophecy) that social harmony must prevail because self-love and social love, rightly viewed, will always be the same. But then we have Robert Pack's poem to remind us that the problem is not so simple, since there must be taken into account a desire for freedom that transcends ordinary selfishness. Thus comparison leads us to look more deeply into the meaning of each of the poems and also into the ways in which we can clarify in writing our own views on the general subject.

Comparison of poems from different periods, moreover, will provide useful historical perspective and food for thought about the effects of changing social conditions. The passage from Shakespeare, for example, reflects almost implicit belief in the necessity of a stable, hierarchical social structure; Pope speaks for the so-called Age of Reason, when faith in rational control of the self and society was in the ascendant; Whitman's "Crossing Brooklyn Ferry" voices the later romantic hope that imaginative sympathy or a mystical sense of the vital unity of all things would make possible a feeling of free participation that reason alone could not give; and Arnold's poem marks the decline of romantic optimism and the beginning of a feeling of alienation that has persisted in some quarters up to the present time. The several contemporary poems, then, will help us to compare our general outlook with those of past eras and so enable us to analyze in some depth the special conditions that nowadays affect the search for self-fulfillment through social participation.

Once again, it must not be forgotten that these poems can provide not only ideas to be developed or analyzed but also much insight into the nature of language and effective communication. As writers, we would do well to compare carefully the ways in which these poets achieve perspective, emphasis, and unity of thought and tone.

THE WANDERER

Anonymous—translated by Melvin G. Storm

The lonely man ever longs for kindness,
For the mercy of God, but, sorrowing at heart,
He long must row over the rime-cold sea,
He must follow the exile's path, for his fate is firm.
Mindful of woes, remembering cruel slaughters,   5
Bereft of his kinsmen, thus said the Wanderer:
"I am bound in the cold of the mornings to lament
My cares alone. No one now lives
To hold in common trust the thoughts of my heart.
I have found it a truth that the noblest warrior   10
Binds fast his feelings, veils his pains,
Locks his sorrows secret in his soul.
"The soul that is weary is slave to fate;
Fate holds the troubled heart in thrall:
Therefore men eager for glory—though often mournful—   15
Sorrow in silence, conceal their cares.
So then must I, wretched and homeless
And far from kinsmen, fetter my mood;
For long ago, to the grave's dark keeping
I lost my lord, my treasure-giver   20
And set out, sorrowful as winter
To seek the hearth of a friendly chief,
One whose mead-hall would offer me haven,
Whose folk would comfort my heart with friendship.
But cruel sorrow ever walks with the exile,   25
His only mate when his loved friends are gone.
He is held by the turns of the trail he wanders
And not by the twistings of bright wound gold;
He knows but the frost in his heart, not the fruits of the earth.
Often he remembers jolly companions, the joy of gifts,   30
Remembers his fallow boyhood, when his lord taught him to feast:
All fallen away! He who has long been lonely knows
How often sorrow and sleep join to deceive
And bind in dreams the grieving lone-dweller:
In his mind then he sees his master; he imagines   35
The embrace of happy greeting—sits at his feet
Before the gift-seat in a summer of gladness.
But then the friendless, lordless warrior wakes,
Sees before him only the winter sea-ways—
The sea-birds fold their feathers, dive, and soar again   40
And the hard sky mingles snow with hail.

Then he feels the heart's heavy wound,
Pressed by longing for love, renew its pain
When memories of kinsmen tease his mind.
He smiles at imagined faces, 45
Eagerly greets with joyful welcoming words
The mist-made friends that ever float away
And speak no words in answer. Sorrow is full
To him who sends too often soaring
His weary heart back over the sea in dreams. 50
　　"No wonder, then, if I should grieve,
If my spirit should bow to bitter darkness,
When I consider the sad lives of the most courageous—
How quickly they desert the hall in death.
This earth decays: daily it further dies and wastes away. 55
But the wise man needs his winters;
Weary, he barters seasons of pain for wisdom.
He learns the price of patience: learns he must be
Neither too hot of heart nor too hasty of speech,
Nor too frail in battle, nor too overbold, 60
Nor too much a coward, nor too glad, nor too greedy,
Nor too eager to speak in boast before knowing success,
Before seeing the thoughts of his heart take shape in deeds.
　　"The wise man finds how fleeting is the world,
Knows how the wealth of earth will waste, 65
As even now throughout this freezing land
Walls stand wind-blown,
Storm-beaten dead dwellings in shrouds of frost.
The wine-halls crumble, lords sleep
In dreamless death; the war-troops have fallen 70
Brave by the wall: battle took many;
One was borne off in pieces by birds
Over the high waves; one fell prey
To the grey wolf's plunder; a sad-faced friend
Covered one in a cave of earth. 75
Thus the Creator of men laid waste his creation,
Relentlessly silenced the sounds of its people,
Made the works of the giants of old stand empty.
　　"The one who wisely sees these foundations, wasted walls,
Remembers from distant days cruel deaths, 80
Deeply considers this dark life, and says,
'Where is the horse? Where is the man? Where is the chief?
Where are the feast-seats? Where are the joys of the feasting?
Alas the bright cup! Alas the warrior brilliant in armor!
Alas the prince's power! Those times have passed, 85
Grown dark under night's cloud, as if they never were.

Where stood loved warriors stand now walls alone,
Wondrously high, adorned with serpent shapes.
Ashen spears, ravenous for slaughter,
Took off the earls: hard fate felled them.   90
And now storms beat these cliffs,
Snow binds the earth;
Night shadows darken, and dread winter
Sends from the north fierce hail-showers against men.
   "'Earth's kingdom teems with hardship;   95
Fate changes always the world under heaven.
Here goods vanish, here friends die,
Here men and kinsmen forever pass away,
And fate drains empty the world itself.' "
Thus spoke the man wise in soul, who sat musing apart.   100
He is good who keeps faith and binds fast his distress,
Who reveals not his pain unless he know remedy.
Men longing for mercy must look from the world
And seek help in our heavenly Father, in whom is all strength.

Ca. eighth century

1: The speaker was, in the days whose passing he laments, a thane, a member of the bodyguard of a lord or king; no social relationship was more highly valued in Anglo-Saxon culture. *23 meadhall:* the meeting places of the lords and their thanes. Mead is wine made from honey. *90 earls:* warriors.

QUESTIONS

1 This dramatic monologue underscores some of the advantages and disadvantages of a small, tightly knit society. What are some of these?
2 Are there in our time any groups that offer social relationships comparable to those described in this poem?
3 Does there appear to be, in the culture represented here, a close causal relationship between social values and religious belief? Would you want to make any generalizations on this subject?

ULYSSES' SPEECH ON DEGREE
FROM
TROILUS AND CRESSIDA, I, iii, 75–137
William Shakespeare

Troy, yet upon his basis, had been down,
And the great Hector's sword had lacked a master,
But for these instances.
The specialty of rule hath been neglected.
And look how many Grecian tents do stand   5
Hollow upon this plain, so many hollow factions.
When that the general is not like the hive
To whom the foragers shall all repair,
What honey is expected? Degree being vizarded,
The unworthiest shows as fairly in the mask.   10
The heavens themselves, the planets and this center,
Observe degree, priority, and place,
Insisture, course, proportion, season, form,
Office and custom, in all line of order.
And therefore is the glorious planet Sol   15
In noble eminence enthroned and sphered
Amidst the other, whose medicinable eye
Corrects the ill aspects of planets evil,
And posts like the commandment of a king,
Sans check to good and bad. But when the planets   20
In evil mixture to disorder wander,
What plagues and what portents, what mutiny,
What raging of the sea, shaking of earth,
Commotion in the winds, frights, changes, horrors,
Divert and crack, rend and deracinate,   25
The unity and married calm of states
Quite from their fixture! Oh, when degree is shaked,
Which is the ladder to all high designs,
The enterprise is sick! How could communities
Degrees in schools and brotherhoods in cities,   30
Peaceful commerce from dividable shores,
The primogenitive and due of birth,
Prerogative of age, crowns, scepters, laurels,
But by degree, stand in authentic place?
Take but degree away, untune that string,   35
And hark what discord follows! Each thing meets
In mere oppugnancy. The bounded waters
Should lift their bosoms higher than the shores,
And make a sop of all this solid globe.
Strength should be lord of imbecility,   40
And the rude son should strike his father dead.

Force should be right, or rather, right and wrong,
Between whose endless jar justice resides,
Should lose their names, and so should justice too.
Then everything includes itself in power, 45
Power into will, will into appetite,
And appetite, a universal wolf,
So doubly seconded with will and power,
Must make perforce a universal prey,
And last eat up himself. Great Agamemnon, 50
This chaos, when degree is suffocate,
Follows the choking.

1630

1: Ulysses is explaining to the Greeks that they have failed to capture Troy because their leader, Agamemnon, has lost his authority. *3 instances:* reasons. *4 rule:* discipline. *9 Degree being vizarded:* rank being obscured, as by a mask. *11 center:* the earth. *13 Insisture:* regularity. *14 Office:* function; *in all line of order:* according to degree of importance. *18:* controls their positions, upon which their influence depended. *25 deracinate:* uproot. *27 fixture:* established place. *32 primogenitive:* the right of the oldest son to inheritance. *37 oppugnancy:* complete opposition. *40 imbecility:* weakness.

QUESTIONS

1 What forces, according to Ulysses, come into play when "degree" is neglected?
2 Note the examples of degree mentioned by Ulysses. What kinds of rank or authority are most important in our time?
3 Ulysses urges that hierarchical order is the law of nature. How does our conception of rightful authority differ?
4 Would people feel more secure if various kinds of authority or distinction were more closely defined? Would they be more ambitious, assuming that it was possible to rise to higher "places"? Would they be happier, on the whole?

AN ESSAY ON MAN, EPISTLE III, 269–319

Alexander Pope

So drives self-love, through just and through unjust,
To one man's power, ambition, lucre, lust:
The same self-love, in all, becomes the cause
Of what restrains him, government and laws.
For, what one likes if others like as well, 5
What serves one will, when many wills rebel?
How shall he keep, what, sleeping or awake,
A weaker may surprise, a stronger take?
His safety must his liberty restrain;

All join to guard what each desires to gain.   10
Forced into virtue thus by self-defence,
Even kings learned justice and benevolence;
Self-love forsook the path it first pursued,
And found the private in the public good.
        'Twas then the studious head or generous mind,   15
Follower of God or friend of humankind,
Poet or patriot, rose but to restore
The faith and moral nature gave before;
Re-lumed her ancient light, not kindled new;
If not God's image, yet his shadow drew;   20
Taught power's due use to people and to kings
Taught nor to slack, nor strain its tender strings;
The less, or greater, set so justly true,
That touching one must strike the other too;
Till jarring interests of themselves create   25
The according music of a well-mixed state.
Such is the world's great harmony, that springs
From order, union, full consent of things;
Where small and great, where weak and mighty, made
To serve, not suffer, strengthen, not invade—   30
More powerful each as needful to the rest,
And, in proportion as it blesses, blessed—
Draw to one point, and to one centre bring
Beast, man, or angel, servant, lord, or king.
        For forms of government let fools contest;   35
Whate'er is best administered is best:
For modes of faith let graceless zealots fight;
His can't be wrong whose life is in the right:
In faith and hope the world will disagree,
But all mankind's concern is charity: 40
All must be false that thwart this one great end
And all of God, that bless mankind or mend.
        Man, like the generous vine, supported lives;
The strength he gains is from the embrace he gives.
On their own axis as the planets run,   45
Yet make at once their circle round the sun;
So two consistent motions act the soul,
And one regards itself, and one the whole.
        Thus God and nature linked the general frame,
And bade self-love and social be the same.   50
                    1733–1734

1-2: The poet has explained that when reason is obscured by fear, self-love leads to tyranny and conflict, despite the lesson of interdependence taught by nature.

QUESTIONS

1 Pope's subject here is social love. What is his thesis? What is his argument?
2 Does Pope indicate precisely enough how social love will express itself? Do you find his definition of love adequate?
3 Consider the structure of this passage. What is the function of the paragraphing? Does each paragraph have a new idea to present? Does each paragraph have a special purpose?
4 Are there any features of Pope's style that might be effective in prose writing? Be able to point out at least one.

A SUMMER NIGHT

Matthew Arnold

In the deserted, moon-blanched street,
How lonely rings the echo of my feet!
Those windows, which I gaze at, frown,
Silent and white, unopening down,
Repellent as the world—but see,   5
A break between the housetops shows
The moon! and, lost behind her, fading dim
Into the dewy dark obscurity
Down at the far horizon's rim,
Doth a whole tract of heaven disclose!   10

And to my mind the thought
Is on a sudden brought
Of a past night, and a far different scene.
Headlands stood out into the moonlit deep
As clearly as at noon;   15
The spring-tide's brimming flow
Heaved dazzlingly between;
Houses, with long white sweep,
Girdled the glistening bay;
Behind, through the soft air,   20
The blue haze-cradled mountains spread away.
That night was far more fair—
But the same restless pacings to and fro,
And the same vainly throbbing heart was there,
And the same bright, calm moon.   25

And the calm moonlight seems to say:
Hast thou then still the old unquiet breast,
Which neither deadens into rest,

Nor ever feels the fiery glow
That whirls the spirit from itself away,   30
But fluctuates to and fro,
Never by passion quite possessed
And never quite benumbed by the world's sway?—
And I, I know not if to pray
Still to be what I am, or yield and be   35
Like all the other men I see.

For most men in a brazen prison live,
Where, in the sun's hot eye,
With heads bent o'er their toil, they languidly
Their lives to some unmeaning taskwork give,   40
Dreaming of naught beyond their prison-wall.
And as, year after year,
Fresh products of their barren labor fall
From their tired hands, and rest
Never yet comes more near,   45
Gloom settles slowly down over their breast;
And while they try to stem
The waves of mournful thought by which they are prest
Death in their prison reaches them,
Unfreed, having seen nothing, still unblest.   50

And the rest, a few,
Escape their prison and depart
On the wide ocean of life anew.
There the freed prisoner, where'er his heart
Listeth, will sail;   55
Nor doth he know how there prevail,
Despotic on that sea,
Trade-winds which cross it from eternity.
Awhile he holds some false way, undebarred
By thwarting signs, and braves   60
The freshening wind and blackening waves,
And then the tempest strikes him; and between
The lightning-bursts is seen
Only a driving wreck,
And the pale master on his spar-strewn deck   65
With anguished face and flying hair
Grasping the rudder hard,
Still bent to make some port he knows not where,
Still standing for some false, impossible shore.
And sterner comes the roar   70
Of sea and wind, and through the deepening gloom

Fainter and fainter wreck and helmsman loom,
And he too disappears, and comes no more.

Is there no life, but these alone?
Madman or slave, must man be one?   75

Plainness and clearness without shadow of stain!
Clearness divine!
Ye heavens, whose pure dark regions have no sign
Of languor, though so calm, and, though so great,
Are yet untroubled and unpassionate;   80
Who, though so noble, share in the world's toil,
And, though so tasked, keep free from dust and soil!
I will not say that your mild deeps retain
A tinge, it may be, of their silent pain
Who have longed deeply once, and longed in vain—   85
But I will rather say that you remain
A world above man's head, to let him see
How boundless might his soul's horizons be,
How vast, yet of what clear transparency!
How it were good to abide there, and breathe free;   90
How fair a lot to fill
Is left to each man still!

                                   1852

33 sway: control.

QUESTIONS

1   The reflections in this poem might be said to revolve around the poet's idea of "the
    world's sway"—the effect upon the individual spirit of submission to the control of
    society. This effect is described metaphorically in lines 51–73. Is there anything in
    your experience of society that would help you if you were asked to explain what
    the poet is talking about?
2   What, in the poet's view, are the alternatives to submission to the world's sway?
    What is his own position?
3   Why does the poet use so much sky imagery? What effect does his contemplation
    of celestial bodies have finally upon his state of mind?

CROSSING BROOKLYN FERRY

Walt Whitman

1

Flood-tide below me! I see you face to face!
Clouds of the west—sun there half an hour high—I see you also face to face.

Crowds of men and women attired in the usual costumes, how curious you
    are to me!
On the ferry-boats the hundreds and hundreds that cross, returning home, are
    more curious to me than you suppose,
And you that shall cross from shore to shore years hence are more to me,
    and more in my meditations, than you might suppose.   5

2

The impalpable sustenance of me from all things at all hours of the day,
The simple, compact, well-join'd scheme, myself disintegrated, every one
    disintegrated yet part of the scheme.
The similitudes of the past and those of the future,
The glories strung like beads on my smallest sights and hearings, on the walk
    in the street and the passage over the river,
The current rushing so swiftly and swimming with me far away,   10
The others that are to follow me, the ties between me and them,
The certainty of others, the life, love, sight, hearing of others.

Others will enter the gates of the ferry and cross from shore to shore,
Others will watch the run of the flood-tide,
Others will see the shipping of Manhattan north and west, and the heights of
    Brooklyn to the south and east,   15
Others will see the islands large and small;
Fifty years hence, others will see them as they cross, the sun half an hour high,
A hundred years hence, or ever so many hundred years hence, others will
    see them,
Will enjoy the sunset, the pouring-in of the flood-tide, the falling-back to the
    sea of the ebb-tide.

3

It avails not, time nor place—distance avails not,   20
I am with you, you men and women of a generation, or ever so many
    generations hence,
Just as you feel when you look on the river and sky, so I felt,
Just as any of you is one of a living crowd, I was one of a crowd,
Just as you are refresh'd by the gladness of the river and the bright flow, I was
    refresh'd,

Just as you stand and lean on the rail, yet hurry with the swift current, I stood
    yet was hurried,   25
Just as you look on the numberless masts of ships and the thick-stemm'd
    pipes of steamboats, I look'd.

I too many and many a time cross'd the river of old,
Watched the Twelfth-month sea-gulls, saw them high in the air floating with
    motionless wings, oscillating their bodies,
Saw how the glistening yellow lit up parts of their bodies and left the rest
    in strong shadow,
Saw the slow-wheeling circles and the gradual edging toward the south,   30
Saw the reflection of the summer sky in the water,
Had my eyes dazzled by the shimmering track of beams,
Look'd at the fine centrifugal spokes of light round the shape of my head in
    the sunlit water,
Look'd on the haze on the hills southward and south-westward,
Look'd on the vapor as it flew in fleeces tinged with violet,   35
Look'd toward the lower bay to notice the vessels arriving,
Saw their approach, saw aboard those that were near me,
Saw the white sails of schooners and sloops, saw the ships at anchor,
The sailors at work in the rigging or out astride the spars,
The round masts, the swinging motion of the hulls, the slender serpentine
    pennants,   40
The large and small steamers in motion, the pilots in their pilot-houses,
The white wake left by the passage, the quick tremulous whirl of the wheels,
The flags of all nations, the falling of them at sunset,
The scallop-edged waves in the twilight, the ladled cups, the frolicsome crests
    and glistening,
The stretch afar growing dimmer and dimmer, the gray walls of the granite
    storehouses by the docks,   45
On the river the shadowy group, the big steam-tug closely flank'd on each side
    by the barges, the hay-boat, the belated lighter,
On the neighboring shore the fires from the foundry chimneys burning high and
    glaringly into the night,
Casting their flicker of black contrasted with wild red and yellow light over
    the tops of houses and down into the clefts of streets.

4
These and all else were to me the same as they are to you,
I loved well those cities, loved well the stately and rapid river,   50
The men and women I saw were all near to me,
Others the same—others who look back on me because I look'd forward
    to them,
(The time will come, though I stop here to-day and to-night.)

5

What is it then between us?
What is the count of the scores or hundreds of years between us?   55

Whatever it is, it avails not—distance avails not, and place avails not,
I too lived, Brooklyn of ample hills was mine,
I too walk'd the streets of Manhattan island, and bathed in the waters around
    it,
I too felt the curious abrupt questionings stir within me,
In the day among crowds of people sometimes they came upon me   60
In my walks home late at night or as I lay in my bed they came upon me,
I too had been struck from the float forever held in solution,
I too had receiv'd identity by my body,
That I was I knew was of my body, and what I should be I knew I should be
    of my body.

6

It is not upon you alone the dark patches fall,   65
The dark threw its patches down upon me also,
The best I had done seem'd to me blank and suspicious,
My great thoughts as I supposed them, were they not in reality meagre?
Nor is it you alone who knew what it is to be evil,
I am he who knew what it was to be evil,   70
I too knitted the old knot of contrariety,
Blabb'd, blush'd, resented, lied, stole, grudg'd,
Had guile, anger, lust, hot wishes I dared not speak,
Was wayward, vain, greedy, shallow, sly, cowardly, malignant,
The wolf, the snake, the hog, not wanting in me,   75
The cheating look, the frivolous word, the adulterous wish, not wanting,
Refusals, hates, postponements, meanness, laziness, none of these wanting,
Was one with the rest, the days and haps of the rest,
Was call'd my nighest name by clear loud voices of young men as they saw
    me approaching or passing,
Felt their arms on my neck as I stood, or the negligent leaning of their flesh
    against me as I sat,   80
Saw many I loved in the street or ferry-boat or public assembly, yet never told
    them a word,
Lived the same life with the rest, the same old laughing, gnawing, sleeping,
Play'd the part that still looks back on the actor or actress,
The same old role, the role that is what we make it, as great as we like,
Or as small as we like, or both great and small.   85

7

Closer yet I approach you,
What thought you have of me now, I had as much of you—I laid in my stores
    in advance,

I consider'd long and seriously of you before you were born.
Who was to know what should come home to me?
Who knows but I am enjoying this?   90
Who knows, for all the distance, but I am as good as looking at you now, for
    all you cannot see me?

8

Ah, what can ever be more stately and admirable to me than mast-hemm'd
    Manhattan?
River and sunset and scallop-edg'd waves of flood-tide?
The sea-gulls oscillating their bodies, the hay-boat in the twilight, and the
    belated lighter?

What gods can exceed these that clasp me by the hand, and with voices I love
    call me promptly and loudly by my nighest name as I approach?   95

What is more subtle than this which ties me to the woman or man that looks
    in my face?

Which fuses me into you now, and pours my meaning into you?

We understand then do we not?
What I promis'd without mentioning it, have you not accepted?
What the study could not teach—what the preaching could not accomplish
    is accomplish'd, is it not?   100

9

Flow on, river! flow with the flood-tide, and ebb with the ebb-tide!
Frolic on, crested and scallop-edg'd waves!
Gorgeous clouds of the sunset! drench with your splendor me, or the men and
    women generations after me!
Cross from shore to shore, countless crowds of passengers!
Stand up, tall masts of Mannahatta! stand up, beautiful hills of Brooklyn!   105
Throb, baffled and curious brain! throw out questions and answers!
Suspend here and everywhere, eternal float of solution!
Gaze, loving and thirsting eyes, in the house or street or public assembly!
Sound out, voices of young men! loudly and musically call me by my nighest
    name!
Live, old life! play the part that looks back on the actor or actress!   110
Play the old role, the role that is great or small according as one makes it!
Consider, you who peruse me, whether I may not in unknown ways be looking
    upon you;
Be firm, rail over the river, to support those who lean idly, yet haste with the
    hasting current;
Fly on, sea-birds! fly sideways, or wheel in large circles high in the air;
Receive the summer sky, you water, and faithfully hold it till all downcast eyes
    have time to take it from you!   115

Diverge, fine spokes of light, from the shape of my head, or any one's head,
    in the sunlit water!
Come on, ships from the lower bay! pass up or down, white-sail'd schooners,
    sloops, lighters!
Flaunt away, flags of all nations! be duly lower'd at sunset!
Burn high your fires, foundry chimneys! cast black shadows at nightfall! cast
    red and yellow light over the tops of the houses!
Appearances, now or henceforth, indicate what you are,   120
You necessary film, continue to envelop the soul,
About my body for me, and your body for you, be hung our divinest aromas,
Thrive, cities—bring your freight, bring your shows, ample and sufficient rivers,
Expand, being than which none else is perhaps more spiritual,
Keep your places, objects than which none else is more lasting.   125

You have waited, you always wait, you dumb, beautiful ministers,
We receive you with free sense at last, and are insatiate henceforward,
Not you any more shall be able to foil us, or withhold yourselves from us,
We use you,—and do not cast you aside—we plant you permanently within us,
We fathom you not—we love you—there is perfection in you also,   130
You furnish your parts toward eternity,
Great or small, you furnish your parts toward the soul.

                    1856–1881

62 float: dissolved substance.   *78 haps:* happenings.

QUESTIONS

1   To whom is the poet speaking?
2   What are the bonds that unite the speaker to other people?
3   What are the two principal metaphors used to describe individual existence? What
    do they mean? How are they related?
4   What is the speaker's view of the relation between the human spirit and the things
    of nature?
5   Why does the poet use so much repetition in the last part of the poem?

THE DEATH OF THE HIRED MAN

Robert Frost

Mary sat musing on the lamp-flame at the table,
Waiting for Warren. When she heard his step,
She ran on tiptoe down the darkened passage
To meet him in the doorway with the news
And put him on his guard. "Silas is back."   5

She pushed him outward with her through the door
And shut it after her. "Be kind," she said.
She took the market things from Warren's arms
And set them on the porch, then drew him down
To sit beside her on the wooden steps.   10

"When was I ever anything but kind to him?
But I'll not have the fellow back," he said.
"I told him so last haying, didn't I?
If he left then, I said, that ended it.
What good is he? Who else will harbor him   15
At his age for the little he can do?
What help he is there's no depending on.
Off he goes always when I need him most.
He thinks he ought to earn a little pay,
Enough at least to buy tobacco with,   20
So he won't have to beg and be beholden.
'All right,' I say, 'I can't afford to pay
Any fixed wages, though I wish I could.'
'Someone else can.' 'Then someone else will have to.'
I shouldn't mind his bettering himself   25
If that was what it was. You can be certain,
When he begins like that, there's someone at him
Trying to coax him off with pocket money—
In haying time, when any help is scarce.
In winter he comes back to us. I'm done."   30

"Sh! not so loud: he'll hear you," Mary said.

"I want him to: he'll have to soon or late."

"He's worn out. He's asleep beside the stove.
When I came up from Rowe's I found him here,
Huddled against the barn door fast asleep,   35
A miserable sight, and frightening, too—
You needn't smile—I didn't recognize him—
I wasn't looking for him—and he's changed.
Wait till you see."

              "Where did you say he'd been?"

"He didn't say. I dragged him to the house,   40
And gave him tea and tried to make him smoke.
I tried to make him talk about his travels.
Nothing would do: he just kept nodding off."

"What did he say? Did he say anything?"

"But little."

       "Anything? Mary, confess   45
He said he'd come to ditch the meadow for me."

"Warren!"

       "But did he? I just want to know."

"Of course he did. What would you have him say?
Surely you wouldn't grudge the poor old man
Some humble way to save his self-respect.   50
He added, if you really care to know,
He meant to clear the upper pasture, too.
That sounds like something you have heard before?
Warren, I wish you could have heard the way
He jumbled everything. I stopped to look   55
Two or three times—he made me feel so queer—
To see if he was talking in his sleep.
He ran on Harold Wilson—you remember—
The boy you had in haying four years since.
He's finished school, and teaching in his college.   60
Silas declares you'll have to get him back.
He says they two will make a team for work:
Between them they will lay this farm as smooth!
The way he mixed that in with other things.
He thinks young Wilson a likely lad, though daft   65
On education—you know how they fought
All through July under the blazing sun,
Silas up on the cart to build the load,
Harold along beside to pitch it on."

"Yes, I took care to keep well out of earshot."   70

"Well, those days trouble Silas like a dream.
You wouldn't think they would. How some things linger!
Harold's young college-boy's assurance piqued him.
After so many years he still keeps finding
Good arguments he sees he might have used.   75
I sympathize. I know just how it feels
To think of the right thing to say too late.
Harold's associated in his mind with Latin.
He asked me what I thought of Harold's saying
He studied Latin, like the violin,   80
Because he liked it—that an argument!
He said he couldn't make the boy believe

He could find water with a hazel prong—
Which showed how much good school had ever done him.
He wanted to go over that. But most of all   85
He thinks if he could have another chance
To teach him how to build a load of hay——"

"I know, that's Silas' one accomplishment.
He bundles every forkful in its place,
And tags and numbers it for future reference,   90
So he can find and easily dislodge it
In the unloading. Silas does that well.
He takes it out in bunches like big birds' nests.
You never see him standing on the hay
He's trying to lift, straining to lift himself."   95

"He thinks if he could teach him that, he'd be
Some good perhaps to someone in the world.
He hates to see a boy the fool of books.
Poor Silas, so concerned for other folk,
And nothing to look backward to with pride,   100
And nothing to look forward to with hope,
So now and never any different."

Part of a moon was falling down the west,
Dragging the whole sky with it to the hills.
Its light poured softly in her lap. She saw it   105
And spread her apron to it. She put out her hand
Among the harplike morning-glory strings,
Taut with the dew from garden bed to eaves,
As if she played unheard some tenderness
That wrought on him beside her in the night.   110
"Warren," she said, "he has come home to die:
You needn't be afraid he'll leave you this time."

"Home," he mocked gently.

                    "Yes, what else but home?
It all depends on what you mean by home.
Of course he's nothing to us, any more   115
Than was the hound that came a stranger to us
Out of the woods, worn out upon the trail."

"Home is the place where, when you have to go there,
They have to take you in,"

                    "I should have called it
Something you somehow haven't to deserve."   120

Warren leaned out and took a step or two,
Picked up a little stick, and brought it back
And broke it in his hand and tossed it by.
"Silas has better claim on us you think
Than on his brother? Thirteen little miles   125
As the road winds would bring him to his door.
Silas has walked that far no doubt today.
Why doesn't he go there? His brother's rich,
A somebody—director in the bank."

"He never told us that."

                      "We know it, though."   130

"I think his brother ought to help, of course.
I'll see to that if there is need. He ought of right
To take him in, and might be willing to—
He may be better than appearances.
But have some pity on Silas. Do you think   135
If he had any pride in claiming kin
Or anything he looked for from his brother,
He'd keep so still about him all this time?"

"I wonder what's between them."

                    "I can tell you.
Silas is what he is—we wouldn't mind him—   140
But just the kind that kinsfolk can't abide.
He never did a thing so very bad.
He don't know why he isn't quite as good
As anybody. Worthless though he is,
He won't be made ashamed to please his brother."   145

"*I* can't think Si ever hurt anyone."

"No, but he hurt my heart the way he lay
And rolled his old head on that sharp-edged chair-back.
He wouldn't let me put him on the lounge.
You must go in and see what you can do.   150
I made the bed up for him there tonight.
You'll be surprised at him—how much he's broken.
His working days are done; I'm sure of it."

"I'd not be in a hurry to say that."

"I haven't been. Go, look, see for yourself.   155
But, Warren, please remember how it is:
He's come to help you ditch the meadow.
He has a plan. You mustn't laugh at him.
He may not speak of it, and then he may.
I'll sit and see if that small sailing cloud   160

Will hit or miss the moon."

           It hit the moon.
Then there were three there, making a dim row,
The moon, the little silver cloud, and she.

Warren returned—too soon, it seemed to her—
Slipped to her side, caught up her hand and waited.   165

"Warren?" she questioned.

           "Dead," was all he answered.

QUESTIONS

1 Would you say that Silas is a man who has failed to find a place for himself in society? What is his view of the matter? Why does he "run on" about Harold Wilson?
2 What is Warren's view of the relation between the individual and society? To what extent does Mary disagree with him?
3 What is the significance of lines 105–112? Do they have anything to do with social harmony?
4 Does Mary prevail over Warren? How do we know?

A SUMMER NIGHT, 1933

W. H. Auden

(To Geoffrey Hoyland)

Out on the lawn I lie in bed,
Vega conspicuous overhead
   In the windless nights of June,
As congregated leaves complete
Their day's activity; my feet   5
   Point to the rising moon.

Lucky, this point in time and space
Is chosen as my working-place,
    Where the sexy airs of summer,
The bathing hours and the bare arms,   10
The leisured drives through a land of farms
    Are good to the newcomer.

Equal with colleagues in a ring
I sit on each calm evening
    Enchanted as the flowers   15
The opening light draws out of hiding
With all its gradual dove-like pleading,
    Its logic and its powers

That later we, though parted then,
May still recall these evenings when   20
    Fear gave his watch no look;
The lion griefs loped from the shade
And on our knees their muzzles laid,
    And Death put down his book

Now north and south and east and west   25
Those I love lie down to rest;
    The moon looks on them all,
The healers and the brilliant talkers
The eccentrics and the silent walkers,
    The dumpy and the tall.   30

She climbs the European sky,
Churches and power-station lie
    Alike among earth's fixtures:
Into the galleries she peers
And blankly as a butcher stares   35
    Upon the marvellous pictures

To gravity attentive, she
Can notice nothing here, though we
    Whom hunger does not move,
From gardens where we feel secure   40
Look up and with a sigh endure
    The tyrannies of love:

And, gentle, do not care to know,
Where Poland draws her eastern bow,
    What violence is done,   45

Nor ask what doubtful act allows
Our freedom in this English house,
   Our picnics in the sun.

Soon, soon, through dykes of our content
The crumpling flood will force a rent   50
   And, taller than a tree,
Hold sudden death before our eyes
Whose river dreams long hid the size
   And vigours of the sea.

But when the waters make retreat   55
And through the black mud first the wheat
   In shy green stalks appears,
When stranded monsters gasping lie,
And sounds of riveting terrify
   Their whorled unsubtle ears,   60

May these delights we dread to lose,
This privacy, need no excuse
   But to that strength belong,
As through a child's rash happy cries
The drowned parental voices rise   65
   In unlamenting song.

After discharges of alarm
All unpredicted let them calm
   The pulse of nervous nations,
Forgive the murderer in his glass,   70
Tough in their patience to surpass
   The tigress her swift motions.

            1936

2 Vega: the brightest star in the constellation Lyra.   *44* Poland was in 1933 a focal point of the international tensions that finally were resolved by World War II.   *70* The phrase "the murderer in his glass" probably has reference to lines 34–36.

QUESTIONS

1 This poem, of course, is pervaded by an awareness of impending large-scale social catastrophe such as many people still dread; yet the speaker, as it seems, manages to reconcile himself to this terrible circumstance. Would you call him an escapist, or not?

2 The poet here uses an almost chaotic variety of metaphors. Can you think of any reason for his doing so?

COLD-WATER FLAT

Philip Booth

    Come to conquer
  this living labyrinth of rock,
    young Theseus of Dubuque
finds he is mazed without a minotaur,
without his Ariadne in the dark.   5

    He dreams beyond
  his steelwalled fear to fields grown
    vertical with corn
and hope. Home to this heroic end:
imprisoned in the city of alone;   10

    here smog obscures
  his visionary victor's world
    and street sounds dulled
with rain reverberate in airshaft hours
where braver conquerors have been felled.   15

    Amazed at night,
  stalking the seven maids no sword
    can save, he is devoured
in passageways of reinforced concrete,
trapped by his beast, and overpowered   20

    in sleepless dead-
  end dreams. How now, Theseus? How send
    word home you are confined
with neither wings nor lover's thread
in the city that a murderer designed?   25

1955

Cold-Water Flat: The poet alludes repeatedly to the following mythic story of the encounter between the Athenian hero Theseus and a monster called the Minotaur. Minos, the ruler of Crete, whose son had perished in an expedition undertaken while he, as a guest of Aegeus, King of Athens, had conquered Athens and demanded that a tribute of seven Athenian maids and seven youths be sent to him every nine years. When the young people reached Crete, they were placed in an inescapable labyrinth, built by the great inventor Daedalus, there to be devoured by the fabulous Minotaur, who was half human, half bull. When he was old enough, Theseus, who was the son of Aegeus, volunteered to be one of the victims, intending to slay the Minotaur by one means or another. By good fortune, Ariadne, the daughter of Minos, saw Theseus when he and the others were paraded toward the labyrinth, and fell in love with him. She sent for him and promised that she would help him escape from the labyrinth if he would promise to take her to Athens and marry her. Upon his readily agreeing, she gave him a device which she had procured from Daedalus himself, a ball of thread. As he was instructed, Theseus fastened one end of the thread by the inside of the door and unwound the ball as he went boldly into the maze to seek out the Minotaur. He found the monster asleep, fell upon him, and battered him to death with his fists. Then he retraced his steps with the aid of the thread, the other intended victims following him. Once outside, they fled quickly to their ship, taking Ariadne with them, and set sail for Athens.

QUESTIONS

1 Reconstruct the story upon which this poem is based. Who is "young Theseus of Dubuque"? Why did he leave Dubuque? What has happened to him?
2 What is the general purpose of the comparison between the young man from Dubuque and Theseus? Do any of the details of that comparison have a special significance?

A BIRD IN SEARCH OF A CAGE

Robert Pack

Said the bird in search of a cage,
This world is even large for wings,
The mindless seasons drive me down
Tormenting me with changing things.

A cage is not escape, but need,   5
And though once in all travel's done,
I'll sing so every bird will know
My wanderings in moon and sun,

And all the crickets will be stilled,
And stilled the summer air and grass,   10
And hushed the secrets of the wind,
For when my final callings pass.

And if a friend should stop to talk,
Reminding me of what is past,
And ask the meaning of my song,   15
I'd say that only cages last.

               1955

QUESTIONS

1 This poem, obviously, has something to say about freedom, and it is not, of course, about the nature of birds. What kind of freedom is the poet talking about? What does the cage stand for? Is the poem an allegory?
2 Is there any irony in this poem?
3 What does this poem say about the problem of finding a place in the scheme of things?

EX-BASKETBALL PLAYER

John Updike

Pearl Avenue runs past the high-school lot.
Bends with the trolley tracks, and stops, cut off
Before it has a chance to go two blocks,
At Colonel McComsky Plaza. Berth's Garage
Is on the corner facing west, and there,   5
Most days, you'll find Flick Webb, who helps Berth out.

Flick stands tall among the idiot pumps—
Five on a side, the old bubble-head style,
Their rubber elbows hanging loose and low.
One's nostrils are two S's, and his eyes   10
An E and O. And one is squat, without
A head at all—more of a football type.

Once Flick played for the high-school team, the Wizards.
He was good: in fact, the best. In '46,
He bucketed three hundred ninety points,   15
A county record still. The ball loved Flick.
I saw him rack up thirty-eight of forty
In one home game. His hands were like wild birds.

He never learned a trade, he just sells gas,
Checks oil, and changes flats. Once in a while,   20
As a gag, he dribbles an inner tube,
But most of us remember anyway.
His hands are fine and nervous on the lug wrench.
It makes no difference to the lung wrench, though.

Off work, he hangs around Mae's Luncheonette.   25
Grease-grey and kind of coiled, he plays pinball,
Sips lemon cokes, and smokes those thin cigars;
Flick seldom speaks to Mae, just sits and nods
Beyond her face towards bright applauding tiers
Of Necco Wafers, Nibs and Juju Beads.   30

                                        1957

30 Nibs, Juju Beads: packaged candies.

QUESTIONS

1   What purpose does the brief description of Pearl Avenue serve? Is there any special
    significance in the selection of the details? Does the description help set the tone of
    the poem?
2   Does the ex-basketball player really dribble inner tubes just as a gag?

ON THE MOVE

'Man, you gotta Go.'

Thom Gunn

The blue jay scuffling in the bushes follows
Some hidden purpose, and the gust of birds
That spurts across the field, the wheeling swallows,
Have nested in the trees and undergrowth.
Seeking their instinct, or their poise, or both,   5
One moves with an uncertain violence
Under the dust thrown by a baffled sense
Or the dull thunder of approximate words.

On motorcycles, up the road, they come:
Small, black, as flies hanging in heat, the Boys,   10
Until the distance throws them forth, their hum
Bulges to thunder held by calf and thigh.
In goggles, donned impersonality,
In gleaming jackets trophied with the dust,
They strap in doubt—by hiding it, robust—   15
And almost hear a meaning in their noise.

Exact conclusion of their hardiness
Has no shape yet, but from known whereabouts
They ride, direction where the tires press.
They scare a flight of birds across the field: 20
Much that is natural, to the will must yield.
Men manufacture both machine and soul,
And use what they imperfectly control
To dare a future from the taken routes.

It is a part solution, after all.   25
One is not necessarily discord
On earth; or damned because, half animal,
One lacks direct instinct, because one wakes
Afloat on movement that divides and breaks.
One joins the movement in a valueless world,   30
Choosing it, till, both hurler and the hurled,
One moves as well, always toward, toward.

A minute holds them, who have come to go:
The self-defined, astride the created will
They burst away; the towns they travel through   35
Are home for neither bird nor holiness,

For birds and saints complete their purposes.
At worst, one is in motion; and at best,
Reaching no absolute, in which to rest,
One is always nearer by not keeping still.   40

1957

6 One: a person. "Their," in the preceding line, refers, of course, to the birds.

QUESTIONS

1   Note again the metaphors in lines 7 and 8. Why did the poet choose these particular images?
2   Does the metaphor in line 10 serve any purpose aside from that of helping the reader visualize the scene?
3   What does this poem have to say about seeking a place in society?

POINT SHIRLEY

Sylvia Plath

From Water-Tower Hill to the brick prison
The shingle booms, bickering under
The sea's collapse.
Snowcakes break and welter. This year
The gritted wave leaps   5
The seawall and drops onto a bier
Of quahog chips,
Leaving a salty mash of ice to whiten

In my grandmother's sand yard. She is dead,
Whose laundry snapped and froze here, who   10
Kept house against
What the sluttish, rutted sea could do.
Squall waves once danced
Ship timbers in through the cellar window;
A thresh-tailed, lanced   15
Shark littered in the geranium bed—

Such collusion of mulish elements
She wore her broom straws to the nub.
Twenty years out
Of her hand, the house still hugs in each drab   20
Stucco socket

The purple egg-stones: from Great Head's knob
To the filled-in Gut
The sea in its cold gizzard ground those rounds.

Nobody wintering now behind   25
The planked-up windows where she set
Her wheat loaves
And apple cakes to cool. What is it
Survives, grieves
So, over this battered, obstinate spit   30
Of gravel? The waves'
Spewed relics clicker masses in the wind,

Gray waves the stub-necked eiders ride.
A labor of love, and that labor lost.
Steadily the sea   35
East at Point Shirley. She died blessed,
And I come by
Bones, bones only, pawed and tossed,
A dog-faced sea.
The sun sinks under Boston, bloody red.   40

I would get from these dry-papped stones
The milk your love instilled in them.
The black ducks dive.
And though your graciousness might stream,
And I contrive,   45
Grandmother, stones are nothing of home
To that spumiest dove.
Against both bar and tower the black sea runs.
                                        1960

2 shingle: coarse gravel.   *7 quahog:* a kind of clam.

QUESTIONS

1   What does her grandmother's former home stand for in the mind of the speaker?
    The answer or answers to this question should lead to some comprehension of
    other symbolic implications.
2   This poem seems to be highly personal even in its symbolism. Can you find any
    justification for such an approach to the general theme of this section?
3   Do you find any ambivalence here?

UNWANTED

Edward Field

The poster with my picture on it
Is hanging on the bulletin board in the Post Office.

I stand by it hoping to be recognized
Posing first full face and then profile

But everybody passes by and I have to admit   5
The photograph was taken some years ago.

I was unwanted then and I'm unwanted now
Ah guess ah'll go up echo mountain and crah.

I wish someone would find my fingerprints somewhere
Maybe on a corpse and say, You're it.   10

Description: Male, or reasonably so
White, but not lily-white and usually deep-red

Thirty-fivish, and looks it lately
Five-feet-nine and one-hundred-thirty pounds: no physique

Black hair going gray, hairline receding fast   15
What used to be curly, now fuzzy

Brown eyes starey under beetling brow
Mole on chin, probably will become a wen

It is perfectly obvious that he was not popular at school
No good at baseball, and wet his bed.   20

His aliases tell his history: Dumbell, Good-for-nothing,
Jewboy, Fieldinsky, Skinny, Fierce Face, Greaseball, Sissy.

Warning: This man is not dangerous, answers to any name
Responds to love, don't call him or he will come.

1963

QUESTIONS

1   What characteristic of our society is reflected in this poem? Why and in what way
    has the speaker been rejected by his fellow men?
2   What is the tone of this self-portrait? In other words, what kind of emotional re-
    sponse does the speaker want to evoke? What kind does he expect? Is he partly
    speaking to himself or for his own benefit?

TOPICS FOR COMPOSITION

1 Make a case for the argument that there are people in our own time who might well feel much as the speaker in "The Wanderer" does. For this purpose you might wish to attempt a kind of paraphrase.

2 Is Pope's conception of social love adequate to explain all social conduct and feeling? If you think so, write an essay of 500 or 600 words defending the thesis that self-love and social love are the same. Use Pope's ideas if you wish, but try to draw upon your own knowledge and experience for illustration. If you disagree with Pope, write an essay explaining why. Other poems in this section may provide material for your argument.

3 Write a commentary on the relevance of Arnold's "A Summer Night" to modern society—that is, if you find any.

4 Write a short essay comparing Walt Whitman's response to life in a large city with that of Philip Booth. Limit your comparison so that you will have only two or three points to make. You might approach the matter by regarding "Cold-Water Flat" as an answer to Whitman, who, after all, addresses himself to people of the future—or simply by explaining why you are more inclined to agree with one of the poets than the other. If you would like to engage in further analysis, concentrate on the basic reason or reasons for the differences in attitude. You might even wish to dwell on the significance of certain differences in the use of imagery.

5 Using Auden's "A Summer Night, 1933" as an aid to reflection on the subject, write a commentary on the effect of the threat of nuclear war upon social attitudes.

6 "Cold-Water Flat" has to do with the decline of heroism. Have we lost faith in the possibility of heroic living, outside of rather special circumstances such as a war temporarily provides? Write an essay on some point or points that might be raised in a discussion of the matter. For example, you might address yourself to the question, "Are our modern heroes authentic?" and give a tentative answer by examining a typical kind of hero worship.

7 Use either Warren's or Mary's definition of home ("The Death of the Hired Man," lines 121–122) as the thesis for an essay. If you prefer, write an essay explaining what Warren means and why Mary disagrees with him.

8 Do the ideas expressed in Pope's "An Essay on Man" have any applicability to the problem posed in "The Death of the Hired Man"? Explain your view in an essay.

9 Drawing upon an interpretation of Robert Pack's "A Bird in Search of a Cage," write an essay on the thesis that "a cage is not escape, but need."

10 We see that John Updike's "ex-basketball player," though he does not know it, has been exploited. Are our schools being used unintentionally in other ways to exploit students? Do schools tend to have closed societies that isolate students from the larger society they are about to enter? Write a commentary on one of these subjects.

11 Comment upon the principal symbolic implications of the descriptive details in John Updike's "Ex-Basketball Player."

12 Write a commentary on "On the Move" as an existentialist poem.

13 Write an analysis of the personality and/or background of the speaker in "Point Shirley."

14 Drawing upon your own experience of patterns of social acceptance, write an essay with the title "The Unwanted."

PART TWO

PROTEST AGAINST RESTRAINT

When we approach the problem of protest, we recognize that our problem is neither new nor unique; for, certainly, our world is one where protest is constantly with us. Moreover, man's need to protest the restraint that society places on his individuality takes many forms. The protest may be private, concerned only with an issue one man considers vital to his individuality, remaining hidden from all but the most perceptive observer. Or the protest may be public, concerned with a social or political alignment, involving a kindred segment of mankind and, of course, the public view. The following selections, the products of various times and places, show some of the different ways in which man has responded to threats against his individuality.

Since we live during a time when the question of civil rights is a major issue, we would be hard pressed to find a better introductory selection than Henry David Thoreau's "Civil Disobedience." Thoreau's major point, that a good citizen, when oppressed by a bad law, has a duty to break that law, has become the guiding principle of today's civil protests. But equally important to Thoreau's philosophy is the fact that the citizen's protest must remain passive: nowhere in his essay does Thoreau advocate violent overthrow of existing authority. Thoreau's view, radical during his time, is now considered by some as restraining for its insistence on nonviolence. William Faulkner's "Letter to the North" and James Baldwin's "Faulkner and Desegregation" provide a contemporary view of the current civil rights conflict. On the one hand, Faulkner speaks out for restraint, stating that time and the Southern conscience will bring about an end to inequality. On the other hand, James Baldwin, noted Negro essayist and spokesman for his race in the civil rights controversy, says that the time for restraint has passed, pointing to almost two hundred years of stagnation alleviated only by the pressure of protest.

Richard Rive, a South African black, in his short story, "The Bench," protests the imposed restraint of apartheid. Rive's main character, existing as he does under a system that denies civil liberties to nonwhites, makes an individual bid for human dignity and personal freedom.

"The Life You Save May Be Your Own," by Flannery O'Connor, presents a harsh view of the extent to which individual restraint is a part of everyday life. Her main character uses and abuses personal restraint within the context of relationships where characters struggle to find freedom though they do not fully understand the web of forces that motivate their actions.

"The Conversion of the Jews," by Philip Roth, also concerns an individual protest, by a young Jewish boy, against not only the dogma of his religion, but the insistence by the older generation that he accept the dogma without question. Ozzie's real protest then, as Roth states in the story, is that "what he wanted to know was different."

In *Antigone,* Jean Anouilh, by juxtaposing ancient mythical material and numerous "modern touches," tries to establish the universal implications of a strong contest between individual imperatives and social denials. Antigone tries to explain to Creon and to all the others the necessity of her civil disobedience—that, if we may substitute Thoreau's words, she cannot "keep pace with [her] companions" because she "hears a different drummer." Society seemingly requires an order and decorum which exact the sacrifice of conscience and even genuine individuality. And Creon makes a strong case for the kind of "happiness" which civil obedience guarantees. But Antigone and Anouilh profoundly question the worth of such "happiness" against the equally strong case to be made for the ultimate value of an individual's full assertion of his own life's mandate. Presumably in such assertion, even at the expense of giving up life, lies the only possibility of gaining that life.

THE ESSAY

Although this essay is probably longer and more involved than those you will write, we can use its length to advantage to illustrate techniques that are common to effective persuasive writing. As you read, notice the abundant variety of support that Thoreau provides. In particular, observe how he supports his controlling techniques of personal observation, personal experience, and appeal to authority with methods of analogy; cause-to-effect relationship; comparison and contrast; narration; definition; description.

CIVIL DISOBEDIENCE

Henry David Thoreau

I heartily accept the motto,—"That government is best which governs least;" and I should like to see it acted up to more rapidly and systematically. Carried out, it finally amounts to this, which also I believe,—"That government is best which governs not at all;" and when men are prepared for it, that will be the kind of government which they will have. Government is at best but an expedient; but most governments are usually, and all governments are sometimes, inexpedient. The objections which have been brought against a standing army, and they are many and weighty, and deserve to prevail, may also at last be brought against a standing government. The standing army is only an arm of the standing government. The government itself, which is only the mode which the people have chosen to execute their will, is equally liable to be abused and perverted before the people can act through it. Witness the present Mexican war, the work of comparatively a few individuals using the standing government as their tool; for, in the outset, the people would not have consented to this measure.

This American government,—what is it but a tradition, though a recent one, endeavoring to transmit itself unimpaired to posterity, but each instant losing some of its integrity? It has not the vitality and force of a single living man; for a single man can bend it to his will. It is a sort of wooden gun to the people themselves. But it is not the less necessary for this; for the people must have some complicated machinery or other, and hear its din, to satisfy that idea of government which they have. Governments show thus how successfully men can be imposed on, even impose on themselves, for their own advantage. It is excellent, we must all allow. Yet this government never of itself furthered any enterprise, but by the alacrity with which it got out of its way. *It* does not keep the country free. *It* does not settle the West. *It* does not educate. The character inherent in the American people has done all that has been accomplished; it would have done somewhat more, if the government had not sometimes got in its way. For government is an expedient by which men would fain succeed in letting one another alone; and, as has been said, when it is most expedient, the governed are most let alone by it. Trade and commerce, if they were not made of India-rubber, would never manage to bounce over the obstacles which legislators are continually putting in their way; and, if one were to judge these men wholly by the effects of their actions and not partly by their intensions, they would deserve to be classed and punished with those mischievous persons who put obstructions on the railroads.

But, to speak practically and as a citizen, unlike those who call themselves no-government men, I ask for, not *at once* no government, but *at once* a better government. Let every man make known what kind of government would command his respect, and that will be one step toward obtaining it.

After all, the practical reason why, when the power is once in the hands of the people, a majority are permitted, and for a long period continue, to rule is not because they are most likely to be in the right, nor because this seems fairest to the minority, but because they are physically the strongest. But a government in which the majority rule in all cases cannot be based on justice, even as far as men understand it. Can there be a government in which majorities do not virtually decide right and wrong, but conscience?—in which majorities decide only those questions to which the rule of expediency is applicable? Must the citizen ever for a moment, or in the least degree, resign his conscience to the legislator? Why has every man a conscience, then? I think that we should be men first, and subjects afterward. It is not desirable to cultivate a respect for the law, so much as for the right. The only obligation which I have a right to assume is to do at any time what I think right. It is truly enough said, that a corporation has no conscience; but a corporation of conscientious men is a corporation *with* a conscience. Law never made men a whit more just; and, by means of their respect for it, even the well-disposed are daily made the agents of injustice. A common and natural result of an undue respect for law is, that you may see a file of soldiers, colonel, captain corporal, privates, powder-monkeys, and all, marching in admirable-order over hill and dale to the wars, against their wills, ay, against their common sense and consciences, which makes it very steep marching indeed, and produces a palpitation of the heart. They have no doubt that it is a damnable business in which they are concerned; they are all peaceably inclined. Now, what are they? Men at all? or small movable forts and magazines, at the service of some unscrupulous man in power? Visit the Navy-Yard, and behold a marine, such a man as an American government can make, or such as it can make a man with its black arts,—a mere shadow and reminiscence of humanity, a man laid out alive and standing, and already, as one may say, buried under arms with funeral accompaniments, though it may be,—

> Not a drum was heard, not a funeral note,
>   As his course to the rampart we hurried;
> Not a soldier discharged his farewell shot
>   O'er the grave where our hero we buried.

The mass of men serve the state thus, not as men mainly, but as machines, with their bodies. They are the standing army, and the militia, jailers, constables, posse comitatus, etc. In most cases there is no free exercise whatever of the judgment or of the moral sense; but they put themselves on a level with wood and earth and stones; and wooden men can perhaps be manufactured that will serve the purpose as well. Such command no more respect than men of straw or a lump of dirt. They have the same sort of worth only as horses and dogs. Yet such as these even are commonly esteemed good citizens. Others—as most legislators, politicians, lawyers, ministers, and office-holders—serve the state chiefly with their heads; and, as they rarely make any moral distinctions, they are as likely to serve the Devil, without *intending* it, as God. A very few, as heroes, patriots, martyrs, reformers in the great sense, and *men,* serve the state with their consciences also, and so necessarily resist it for the most part; and they are commonly treated as enemies by it. A wise man will only be useful as a man, and will not submit to be "clay," and "stop a hole to keep the wind away," but leave that office to his dust at least:—

> I am too high-born to be propertied,
> To be a secondary at control,
> Or useful serving-man and instrument
> To any sovereign state throughout the world.

He who gives himself entirely to his fellowmen appears to them useless and selfish; but he who gives himself partially to them is pronounced a benefactor and philanthropist.

How does it become a man to behave toward this American government to-day? I answer, that he cannot without disgrace be associated with it. I cannot for an instant recognize the political organization as *my* government which is the *slave's* government also.

All men recognize the right of revolution; that is, the right to refuse allegiance to, and to resist, the government, when its tyranny or its inefficiency are great and unendurable. But almost all say that such is not the case now. But such was the case, they think, in the Revolution of '75. If one were to tell me that this was a bad government because it taxed certain foreign commodities brought to its ports, it is most probable that I should not make an ado about it, for I can do without them. All machines have their friction; and possibly this does enough good to counterbalance the evil. At any rate, it is a great evil to make a stir about it. But when the friction comes to have its machine, and oppression and robbery are organized, I say, let us not have such a machine any longer. In other words, when a sixth of the population of a nation which has undertaken to be the refuge of liberty are slaves, and a whole country is unjustly overrun and conquered by a foreign army, and subjected to military law, I think that it is not too soon for honest men to rebel and revolutionize. What makes this duty the more urgent is the fact that the country so overrun is not our own, but ours is the invading army. . . .

> A drab of state, a cloth-o'-silver slut,
> To have her train borne up, and her soul trail in the dirt.

Practically speaking, the opponents to a reform in Massachusetts are not a hundred thousand politicians at the South, but a hundred thousand merchants and farmers here, who are more interested in commerce and agriculture than they are in humanity, and are not prepared to do justice to the slave and to Mexico, *cost what it may.* I quarrel not with far-off foes, but with those who, near at home, coöperate with, and do the bidding of, those far away, and without whom the latter would be harmless. We are accustomed to say, that the mass of men are unprepared; but improvement is slow, because the few are not materially wiser or better than the many. It is not so important that many should be as good as you, as that there be some absolute goodness some-where; for that will leaven the whole lump. There are thousands who are *in opinion* opposed to slavery and to the war, who yet in effect do nothing to put an end to them; who, esteeming themselves children of Washington and Franklin, sit down with their hands in their pockets, and say that they know not what to do, and do nothing; who even postpone the question of freedom to the question of free-trade, and quietly read the prices-current along with the latest advices from Mexico, after dinner, and, it may be, fall asleep over them both. What is the price-current of an honest man and patriot to-day? They hesitate, and they regret, and sometimes they petition; but they do noth-ing in earnest and with effect. They will wait, well disposed, for others to remedy the evil, that they may no longer have it to regret. At most, they give only a cheap vote, and a feeble countenance and God-speed, to the right, as it goes by them. There are nine hundred and ninety-nine patrons of virtue to one virtuous man. But it is easier to deal with the real possessor of a thing than with the temporary guardian of it.

All voting is a sort of gaming, like checkers or backgammon, with a slight moral tinge to it, a playing with right and wrong, with moral questions; and betting naturally accompanies it. The character of the voters is not staked. I cast my vote, perchance, as I think right; but I am not vitally concerned that that right should prevail. I am willing to leave it to the majority. Its obligation, therefore, never exceeds that of expediency. Even voting *for the right* is *doing* nothing for it. It is only expressing to men feebly your desire that it should prevail. A wise man will not leave the right to the mercy of chance, nor wish it to prevail through the power of the majority. There is but little virtue in the action of masses of men. When the majority shall at length vote for the abolition of slavery, it will be because they are indifferent to slavery, or because there is but little slavery left to be abolished by their vote. *They* will then be the only slaves. Only *his* vote can hasten the abolition of slavery who asserts his own freedom by his vote.

I hear of a convention to be held at Baltimore, or elsewhere, for the selection of a candidate for the Presidency, made up chiefly of editors, and men who are politicians by profession; but I think, what is it to any independent, intelligent, and respectable man what decision they may come to? Shall we not have the advantage of his wisdom and honesty, nevertheless? Can we not count upon some independent votes? Are there not many individuals in the country who do not attend conventions? But no: I find that the respectable man, so called, has immediately drifted from his position, and despairs of his country, when his country has more reason to despair of him. He forthwith adopts one of the candidates thus selected as the only *available* one, thus proving that he is himself *available* for any purposes of the demagogue. His vote is of no more worth than that of any unprincipled foreigner or hireling native, who may have been bought. O for a man who is a *man,* and, as my neighbor says, has a bone in his back which you cannot pass your hand through! Our statistics are at fault: the popula-tion has been returned too large. How many *men* are there to a square thousand miles in this country? Hardly one. Does not America offer any inducement for men to settle here? The American has dwindled into an Odd Fellow,—one who may be known by the development of his organ of gregariousness, and a manifest lack of intellect and cheerful self-reliance; whose first and chief concern, on coming into the world, is to see that the Alms-houses are in good repair; and, before yet he has lawfully donned the virile garb, to collect a fund for the support of the widows and orphans that may be; who, in short, ventures to live only by the aid of the Mutual Insurance company, which has promised to bury him decently.

It is not a man's duty, as a matter of course, to devote himself to the eradication of any, even the most enormous wrong; he may still properly have other concerns to engage him; but it is his duty, at least to wash his hands of it, and, if he gives it no thought longer, not to give it practically his support. If I devote myself to other pursuits and contemplations, I must first see, at least, that I do not pursue them sitting upon another man's shoulders. I must get off him first, that he may pursue his contemplations too. See what gross inconsistency is tolerated. I have heard some of my townsmen say, "I should like to have them order me out to help put down an insurrection of the slaves, or to march to Mexico;—see if I would go;" and yet these very men have each, directly by their allegiance, and so indirectly, at least, by their money, furnished a substitute. The soldier is applauded who refuses to serve in an unjust war by those who do not refuse to sustain the unjust government which makes the war; is applauded by those whose own act and authority he disregards and sets at naught; as if the state were penitent to that degree that it hired one to scourge it while it sinned, but not to that degree that it left off sinning for a moment. Thus, under the name of Order and Civil Government, we are all made at last to pay homage to and support our own meanness. After the first blush of sin comes its indifference; and from immoral it becomes, as it were, *un*moral, and not quite unnecessary to that life which we have made.

The broadest and most prevalent error requires the most disinterested virtue to sustain it. The slight reproach to which the virtue of patriotism is commonly liable, the noble are most likely to incur. Those who, while they disapprove of the character and measures of a government, yield to it their allegiance and support are undoubtedly its most conscientious supporters, and so frequently the most serious obstacles to reform. Some are petitioning the state to dissolve the Union, to disregard the requisitions of the President. Why do they not dissolve it themselves,—the union between themselves and the state,—and refuse to pay their quota into its treasury? Do not they stand in the same relation to the state that the state does to the Union? And have not the same reasons prevented the state from resisting the Union which have prevented them from resisting the state?

How can a man be satisfied to entertain an opinion merely, and enjoy *it*? Is there any enjoyment in it, if his opinion is that he is aggrieved? If you are cheated out of a single dollar by your neighbor, you do not rest satisfied with knowing that you are cheated, or with saying that you are cheated, or even with petitioning him to pay you your due; but you take effectual steps at once to obtain the full amount, and see that you are never cheated again. Action from principle, the perception and the performance of right, changes things and relations; it is essentially revolutionary, and does not consist wholly with anything which was. It not only divides states and churches, it divides families; ay, it divides the *individual,* separating the diabolical in him from the divine.

Unjust laws exist: shall we be content to obey them, or shall we endeavor to amend them, and obey them until we have succeeded, or shall we transgress them at once? Men generally, under such a government as this, think that they ought to wait until they have persuaded the majority to alter them. They think that, if they should resist, the remedy would be worse than the evil. But it is the fault of the government itself that the remedy *is* worse than the evil. *It* makes it worse. Why is it not more apt to anticipate and provide for reform? Why does it not cherish its wise minority? Why does it cry and resist before it is hurt? Why does it not encourage its citizens to be on the alert to point out its faults, and *do* better than it would have them? Why does it always crucify Christ, and excommunicate Copernicus and Luther, and pronounce Washington and Franklin rebels?

One would think, that a deliberate and practical denial of its authority was the only offense never contemplated by government; else, why has it not assigned its definite, its suitable and proportionate penalty? If a man who has no property refuses but once to earn nine shillings for the state, he is put in prison for a period unlimited by any law that I know, and determined only by the discretion of those who placed him there; but if he should steal ninety times nine shillings from the state, he is soon permitted to go at large again.

If the injustice is part of the necessary friction of the machine of government, let it go, let it go: perchance it will wear smooth,—certainly the machine will wear out. If the injustice has a spring, or a pulley, or a rope, or a crank, exclusively for itself, then perhaps you may consider whether the remedy will not be worse than the evil; but if it is of such a nature that it requires you to be the agent of injustice to another, then, I say, break the law. Let your life be a counter friction to stop the machine. What I have to do is to see, at any rate, that I do not lend myself to the wrong which I condemn.

As for adopting the ways which the state has provided for remedying the evil, I know not of such ways. They take too much time, and a man's life will be gone. I have other affairs to attend to. I came into this world, not chiefly to make this a good place to live in, but to live in it, be it good or bad. A man has not everything to do, but something; and because he cannot do *everything,* it is not necessary that he should do *something* wrong. It is not my business to be petitioning the Governor or the Legislature any more than it is theirs to petition me; and if they should not hear my petition, what should I do then? But in this case the state has provided no way: its very Constitution is the evil. This may seem to be harsh and stubborn and unconciliatory; but it is to treat with the utmost kindness and consideration the only spirit that can appreciate or deserve it. So is all change for the better, like birth and death, which convulse the body.

I do not hesitate to say, that those who call themselves Abolitionists should at once effectually withdraw their support, both in person and property, from the government of Massachusetts, and not wait till they constitute a majority of one, before they suffer the right to prevail through them. I think that it is enough if they have God on their side, without waiting for that other one. Moreover, any man more right than his neighbors constitutes a majority of one already.

I meet this American government, or its representative, the state government, directly, and face to face, once a year—no more—in the person of its tax-gatherer; this is the only mode in which a man situated as I am necessarily meets it; and it then says distinctly, Recognize me; and the simplest, the most effectual, and, in the present posture of affairs, the indispensablest mode of treating with it on this head, of express-ing your little satisfaction with and love for it, is to deny it then. My civil neighbor, the tax-gatherer, is the very man I have to deal with,—for it is, after all, with men and not with parchment that I quarrel,—and he has voluntarily chosen to be an agent for the government. How shall he ever know well what he is and does as an officer of the government, or as a man, until he is obliged to consider whether he shall treat me, his neighbor, for whom he has respect, as a neighbor and well-disposed man, or as a maniac and disturber of the peace, and see if he can get over this obstruction to his neighborliness without a ruder and more impetuous thought or speech corresponding with his action. I know this well, that if one thousand, if one hundred, if ten men whom I could name,—if ten *honest* men only,—ay, if *one* honest man, in this State of Massa-chusetts, *ceasing to hold slaves,* were actually to withdraw from this copartnership, and be locked up in the county jail therefor, it would be the abolition of slavery in America. For it matters not how small the beginning may seem to be: what is once well done is done forever. But we love better to talk about it: that we say is our mission. Reform keeps many scores of newspapers in its service, but not one man. If my es-teemed neighbor, the State's ambassador, who will devote his days to the settlement of the question of human rights in the Council Chamber, instead of being threatened with the prisons of Carolina, were to sit down the prisoner of Massachusetts, that State which is so anxious to foist the sin of slavery upon her sister,—though at present she can discover only an act of inhospitality to be the ground of a quarrel with her,—the Legislature would not wholly waive the subject the following winter.

Under a government which imprisons any unjustly, the true place for a just man is also a prison. The proper place to-day, the only place which Massachusetts has pro-vided for her freer and less desponding spirits, is in her prisons, to be put out and locked out of the State by her own act, as they have already put themselves out by their principles. It is there that the fugitive slave, and the Mexican prisoner on parole, and the Indian come to plead the wrongs of his race should find them; on that sepa-rate, but more free and honorable ground, where the State places those who are not *with* her, but *against* her,—the only house in a slave State in which a free man can abide with honor. If any think that their influence would be lost there, and their voices no longer afflict the ear of the State, that they would not be as an enemy within its walls, they do not know by how much truth is stronger than error, nor how much more eloquently and effectively he can combat injustice who has experienced a little in his own person. Cast your whole vote, not a strip of paper merely, but your whole influ-ence. A minority is powerless while it conforms to the majority; it is not even a minority then; but it is irresistible when it clogs by its whole weight. If the alternative is to keep all just men in prison, or give up war and slavery, the State will not hesitate which to choose. If a thousand men were not to pay their tax-bills this year, that would not be a violent and bloody measure, as it would be to pay them, and enable the State to commit violence and shed innocent blood. This is, in fact, the definition of a peaceable revolution, if any such is possible. If the tax-gatherer, or any other public officer, asks me, as one has done, "But what shall I do?" my answer is, "If you really wish to do anything, resign your office." When the subject has refused allegiance, and the officer has resigned his office, then the revolution is accomplished. But even suppose blood should flow. Is there not a sort of blood shed when the conscience is wounded? Through this wound a man's real manhood and immortality flow out, and he bleeds to an everlasting death. I see this blood flowing now.

I have contemplated the imprisonment of the offender, rather than the seizure of his goods,—though both will serve the same purpose,—because they who assert the purest right, and consequently are most dangerous to a corrupt State, commonly have not spent much time in accumulating property. To such the State renders comparatively small service, and a slight tax is wont to appear exorbitant, particularly if they are obliged to earn it by special labor with their hands. If there were one who lived wholly without the use of money, the State itself would hesitate to demand it of him. But the rich man—not to make any invidious comparison—is always sold to the institution which makes him rich. Absolutely speaking, the more money, the less virtue; for money comes between a man and his objects, and obtains them for him; and it was certainly no great virtue to obtain it. It puts to rest many questions which he would otherwise be taxed to answer; while the only new question which it puts is the hard but superfluous one, how to spend it. Thus his moral ground is taken from under his feet. The opportunities of living are diminished in proportion as what are called the "means" are increased. The best thing a man can do for his culture when he is rich is to endeavor to carry out those schemes which he entertained when he was poor. Christ answered the Herodians according to their condition. "Show me the tribute-money," said he;—and one took a penny out of his pocket;—if you use money which has the image of Cæsar on it, and which he has made current and valuable, that is, *if you are men of the State,* and gladly enjoy the advantages of Cæsar's government, then pay him back some of his own when he demands it. "Render therefore to Cæsar that which is Cæsar's, and to God those things which are God's"—leaving them no wiser than before as to which was which; for they did not wish to know. . . .

I have paid no poll-tax for six years. I was put into a jail once on this account, for one night; and, as I stood considering the walls of solid stone, two or three feet thick, the door of wood and iron, a foot thick, and the iron grating which strained the light, I could not help being struck with the foolishness of that institution which treated me as if I were mere flesh and blood and bones, to be locked up. I wondered that it should have concluded at length that this was the best use it could put me to, and had never thought to avail itself of my services in some way. I saw that, if there was a wall of stone between me and my townsmen, there was a still more difficult one to climb or break through before they could get to be as free as I was. I did not for a moment feel confined, and the walls seemed a great waste of stone and mortar. I felt as if I alone of all my townsmen had paid my tax. They plainly did not know how to treat me, but behaved like persons who are underbred. In every threat and in every compliment there was a blunder; for they thought that my chief desire was to stand the other side of that stone wall. I could not but smile to see how industriously they locked the door of my meditations, which followed them out again without let or hindrance, and *they* were really all that was dangerous. As they could not reach me, they had resolved to punish my body; just as boys, if they cannot come at some person against whom they have a spite, will abuse his dog. I saw that the State was half-witted, that it was timid as a lone woman with her silver spoons, and that it did not know its friends from its foes, and I lost all my remaining respect for it, and pitied it.

Thus the State never intentionally confronts a man's sense, intellectual or moral, but only his body, his senses. It is not armed with superior wit or honesty, but with superior physical strength. I was not born to be forced. I will breathe after my own fashion. Let us see who is the strongest. What force has a multitude? They only can force me who obey a higher law than I. They force me to become like themselves. I do not hear of *men* being *forced* to live this way or that by masses of men. What sort of life were that to live? When I meet a government which says to me, "Your money or your life," why should I be in haste to give it my money? It may be in a great strait, and not know what to do: I cannot help that. It must help itself; do as I do. It is not worth the while to snivel about it. I am not responsible for the successful working of the machinery of society. I am not the son of the engineer. I perceive that, when an acorn and a chestnut fall side by side, the one does not remain inert to make way for the other, but both obey their own laws, and spring and grow and flourish as best they can, till one, perchance, overshadows and destroys the other. If a plant cannot live according to its nature, it dies; and so a man. . . .

When I came out of prison,—for some one interfered, and paid that tax,—I did not perceive that great changes had taken place on the common, such as he observed who went in a youth and emerged a tottering and gray-headed man; and yet a change had to my eyes come over the scene,—the town, and State, and country,—greater than any that mere time could effect. I saw yet more distinctly the State in which I lived. I saw to what extent the people among whom I lived could be trusted as good neighbors and friends; that their friendship was for summer weather only; that they did not greatly propose to do right; that they were a distinct race from me by their prejudices and superstitions, as the Chinamen and Malays are; that in their sacrifices to humanity they ran no risks, not even to their property; that after all they were not so noble but they treated the thief as he had treated them, and hoped, by a certain outward observance and a few prayers, and by walking in a particular straight though useless path from time to time, to save their souls. This may be to judge my neighbors harshly; for I believe that many of them are not aware that they have such an institution as the jail in their village.

It was formerly the custom in our village, when a poor debtor came out of jail, for his acquaintances to salute him, looking through their fingers, which were crossed to represent the grating of a jail window, "How do ye do?" My neighbors did not thus salute me, but first looked at me, and then at one another, as if I had returned from a long journey. I was put into jail as I was going to the shoemaker's to get a shoe which was mended. When I was let out the next morning, I proceeded to finish my errand, and, having put on my mended shoe, joined a huckleberry party, who were impatient to put themselves under my conduct; and in half an hour,—for the horse was soon tackled,—was in the midst of a huckleberry field, on one of our highest hills, two miles off, and then the State was nowhere to be seen. . . .

I have never declined paying the highway tax, because I am as desirous of being a good neighbor as I am of being a bad subject; and as for supporting schools, I am doing my part to educate my fellow-countrymen now. It is for no particular item in the tax-bill that I refuse to pay it. I simply wish to refuse allegiance to the State, to withdraw and stand aloof from it effectually. I do not care to trace the course of my dollar, if I could, till it buys a man or a musket to shoot one with,—the dollar is innocent,—but I am concerned to trace the effects of my allegiance. In fact, I quietly declare war with the State, after my fashion, though I will still make what use and get what advantage of her I can, as is usual in such cases.

If others pay the tax which is demanded of me, from a sympathy with the State, they do but what they have already done in their own case, or rather they abet injustice to a greater extent than the State requires. If they pay the tax from a mistaken interest in the individual taxed, to save his property, or prevent his going to jail, it is because they have not considered wisely how far they let their private feelings interfere with the public good.

This, then, is my position at present. But one cannot be too much on his guard in such a case, lest his action be biased by obstinacy or an undue regard for the opinions of men. Let him see that he does only what belongs to himself and to the hour.

I think sometimes, Why, this people mean well, they are only ignorant; they would do better if they knew how: why give your neighbors this pain to treat you as they are not inclined to? But I think again, This is no reason why I should do as they do, or permit others to suffer much greater pain of a different kind. Again, I sometimes say to myself, When many millions of men, without heat, without ill will, without personal feeling of any kind, demand of you a few shillings only, without the possibility, such is their constitution, of retracting or altering their present demand, and without the possibility, on your side, of appeal to any other millions, why expose yourself to this overwhelming brute force? You do not resist cold and hunger, the winds and the waves, thus obstinately; you quietly submit to a thousand similar necessities. You do not put your head into the fire. But just in proportion as I regard this as not wholly a brute force, but partly a human force, and consider that I have relations to those millions as to so many millions of men, and not of mere brute or inanimate things, I see that appeal is possible, first and instantaneously, from them to the Maker of them, and, secondly, from them to themselves. But if I put my head deliberately into the fire, there is no appeal to fire or to the Maker of fire, and I have only myself to blame. If I could convince myself that I have any right to be satisfied with men as they are, and to treat them accordingly, and not according, in some respects, to my requisitions and expectations of what they and I ought to be, then, like a good Mussulman and fatalist, I should endeavor to be satisfied with things as they are, and say it is the will of God. And, above all, there is this difference between resisting this and a purely brute or natural force, that I can resist this with some effect; but I cannot expect, like Orpheus, to change the nature of the rocks and trees and beasts.

I do not wish to quarrel with any man or nation. I do not wish to split hairs, to make fine distinctions, or set myself up as better than my neighbors. I seek rather, I may say, even an excuse for conforming to the laws of the land. I am but too ready to conform to them. Indeed, I have reason to suspect myself on this head; and each year, as the tax-gatherer comes round, I find myself disposed to review the acts and position of the general and State governments, and the spirit of the people, to discover a pretext for conformity. . . .

I believe that the State will soon be able to take all my work of this sort out of my hands, and then I shall be no better a patriot than my fellow-countrymen. Seen from a lower point of view, the Constitution, with all its faults, is very good; the law and the courts are very respectable; even this State and this American government are, in many respects, very admirable, and rare things, to be thankful for, such as a great many have described them; but seen from a point of view a little higher, they are what I have described them; seen from a higher still, and the highest, who shall say what they are, or that they are worth looking at or thinking of at all?

However, the government does not concern me much, and I shall bestow the fewest possible thoughts on it. It is not many moments that I live under a government, even in this world. If a man is thought-free, fancy-free, imagination-free, that which *is not* never for a long time appearing *to be* to him, unwise rulers or reformers cannot fatally interrupt him.

I know that most men think differently from myself; but those whose lives are by profession devoted to the study of these or kindred subjects content me as little as any. Statesmen and legislators, standing so completely within the institution, never distinctly and nakedly behold it. They speak of moving society, but have no resting-place without it. They may be men of a certain experience and discrimination, and have no doubt invented ingenious and even useful systems, for which we sincerely thank them; but all their wit and usefulness lie within certain not very wide limits. They are wont to forget that the world is not governed by policy and expediency. Webster never goes behind government, and so cannot speak with authority about it. His words are wisdom to those legislators who contemplate no essential reform in the existing government; but for thinkers, and those who legislate for all time, he never once glances at the subject. I know of those whose serene and wise speculations on this theme would soon reveal the limits of his mind's range and hospitality. Yet, compared with the cheap professions of most reformers, and the still cheaper wisdom and eloquence of politicians in general, his are almost the only sensible and valuable words, and we thank Heaven for him. Comparatively, he is always strong, original, and, above all, practical. Still, his quality is not wisdom, but prudence. The lawyer's truth is not Truth, but consistency or a consistent expediency. Truth is always in harmony with herself, and is not concerned chiefly to reveal the justice that may consist with wrong-doing. He well deserves to be called, as he has been called, the Defender of the Constitution. There are really no blows to be given by him but defensive ones. He is not a leader, but a follower. His leaders are the men of '87. "I have never made an effort," he says, "and never propose to make an effort; I have never countenanced an effort, and never mean to countenance an effort, to disturb the arrangement as originally made, by which the various States came into the Union." Still thinking of the sanction which the Constitution gives to slavery, he says, "Because it was a part of the original compact,—let it stand." Notwithstanding his special acuteness and ability, he is unable to take a fact out of its merely political relations, and behold it as it lies absolutely to be disposed of by the intellect,—what, for instance, it behooves a man to do here in America to-day with regard to slavery,—but ventures, or is driven, to make some such desperate answer as the following, while professing to speak absolutely, and as a private man,—from which what new and singular code of social duties might be inferred? "The manner," says he, "in which the governments of those States where slavery exists are to regulate it is for their own consideration, under their responsibility to their constituents, to the general laws of propriety, humanity, and justice, and to God. Associations formed elsewhere, springing from a feeling of humanity, or any other cause, have nothing whatever to do with it. They have never received any encouragement from me, and they never will."[1]

They who know of no purer sources of truth, who have traced up its stream no higher, stand, and wisely stand, by the Bible and the Constitution, and drink at it there with reverence and humility; but they who behold where it comes trickling into this lake or that pool, gird up their loins once more, and continue their pilgrimage toward its fountain-head.

No man with a genius for legislation has appeared in America. They are rare in the history of the world. There are orators, politicians, and eloquent men, by the thousand; but the speaker has not yet opened his mouth to speak who is capable of settling the much-vexed questions of the day. We love eloquence for its own sake, and not for any truth which it may utter, or any heroism it may inspire. Our legislators have not yet learned the comparative value of free-trade and of freedom, of union, and of rectitude, to a nation. They have no genius or talent for comparatively humble questions of taxation and finance, commerce and manufactures and agriculture. If we were left solely to the wordy wit of legislators in Congress for our guidance, uncorrected by the seasonable experience and the effectual complaints of the people, America would not long retain her rank among the nations. For eighteen hundred years, though perchance I have no right to say it, the New Testament has been written; yet where is the legislator who has wisdom and practical talent enough to avail himself of the light which it sheds on the science of legislation?

The authority of government, even such as I am willing to submit to,—for I will cheerfully obey those who know and can do better than I, and in many things even those who neither know nor can do so well,—is still an impure one: to be strictly just, it must have the sanction and consent of the governed. It can have no pure right over my person and property but what I concede to it. The progress from an absolute to a limited monarchy, from a limited monarchy to a democracy, is a progress toward a true respect for the individual. Even the Chinese philosopher was wise enough to regard the individual as the basis of the empire. Is a democracy, such as we know it, the last improvement possible in government? Is it not possible to take a step further towards recognizing and organizing the rights of man? There will never be a really free and enlightened State until the State comes to recognize the individual as a higher and independent power, from which all its own power and authority are derived, and treats him accordingly. I please myself with imagining a State at last which can afford to be

[1] These extracts have been inserted since the lecture was read.

just to all men, and to treat the individual with respect as a neighbor; which even would not think it inconsistent with its own repose if a few were to live aloof from it, not meddling with it, nor embraced by it, who fulfilled all the duties of neighbors and fellowmen. A State which bore this kind of fruit, and suffered it to drop off as fast as it ripened, would prepare the way for a still more perfect and glorious State, which also I have imagined, but not yet anywhere seen.

QUESTIONS

1   Paraphrase Thoreau's concept of "This American government" in the second paragraph. How accurate is his appraisal of government's function?
2   What is Thoreau's position on majority rule?
3   How does Thoreau see his obligation to government? Summarize the arguments he uses to support his position.
4   Explain Thoreau's paradoxical statement, "He who gives himself entirely to his fellowmen appears to them useless and selfish; but he who gives himself partially to them is pronounced a benefactor and a philanthropist."
5   What does Thoreau think about the average citizen as a force in government? Briefly summarize his examples—voting, selection of officials, military service, eradication of unjust laws.
6   Summarize Thoreau's arguments for "passive resistance." What was his personal experience in implementing his position?
7   Is the concluding paragraph consistent with the rest of the essay? Is it consistent with an ideal concept of man? An ideal concept of democratic government?

TOPICS FOR COMPOSITION

1   Using selected comments from "Civil Disobedience," write an essay applying Thoreau's position to the present-day American scene.
2   Refute Thoreau's essay as impractical and irresponsible in view of man's obligation to mankind.
3   Referring directly to the essay, support or refute the position that Thoreau advocates anarchy.
4   Write a composition, based on personal experience, in which you describe the details of a protest against, or a desire to protest, restraint by governmental authority. Support the validity of your position as you saw it.

☐

William Faulkner's essay and James Baldwin's that follows it must be read as companion pieces since Baldwin's is a direct response to Faulkner's. Both essays illustrate some techniques used in persuasive writing. Considering both essays, we should assess the relative force of the following appeals:

1   Each author's appeal to personal authority in the opening paragraph of his essay
2   Faulkner's avowed aim to stand as mediator between two extremes; Baldwin's complete rejection of the "middle of the road"

3 Faulkner's use of supporting quotations from members of the Negro community; Baldwin's use of supporting quotations from Faulkner's essay
4 Faulkner's attack upon the Northerner's limited knowledge; Baldwin's attack upon Faulkner's limited knowledge

LETTER TO THE NORTH

William Faulkner

My family has lived for generations in one same small section of north Mississippi. My great-grandfather held slaves and went to Virginia in command of a Mississippi infantry regiment in 1861. I state this simply as credentials for the sincerity and factualness of what I will try to say.

From the beginning of this present phase of the race problem in the South, I have been on record as opposing the forces in my native country which would keep the condition out of which this present evil and trouble has grown. Now I must go on record as opposing the forces outside the South which would use legal or police compulsion to eradicate that evil overnight. I was against compulsory segregation. I am just as strongly against compulsory integration. Firstly of course from principle. Secondly because I don't believe compulsion will work.

There are more Southerners than I who believe as I do and have taken the same stand I have taken, at the same price of contumely and insult and threat from other Southerners which we foresaw and were willing to accept because we believed we were helping our native land which we love, to accept a new condition which it must accept whether it wants to or not. That is, by still being Southerners, yet not being a part of the general majority Southern point of view; by being present yet detached, committed and attainted neither by Citizens' Council nor NAACP; by being in the middle, being in a position to say to any incipient irrevocability: "Wait, wait now, stop and consider first."

But where will we go, if that middle becomes untenable? If we have to vacate it in order to keep from being trampled? Apart from the legal aspect, apart even from the simple incontrovertible immorality of discrimination by race, there was another simply human quantity which drew us to the Negro's side: the simple human instinct to champion the underdog.

But if we, the (comparative) handful of Southerners I have tried to postulate, are compelled by the simple threat of being trampled if we don't get out of the way, to vacate that middle where we could have worked to help the Negro improve his condition—compelled to move for the reason that no middle any longer exists—we will have to make a new choice. And this time the underdog will not be the Negro, since he, the Negro, will now be a segment of the topdog, and so the underdog will be that white embattled minority who are our blood and kin. These non-Southern forces will now say, "Go then. We don't want you because we won't need you again." My reply to that is, "Are you sure you won't?"

So I would say to the NAACP and all the organizations who would compel immediate and unconditional integration: "Go slow now. Stop now for a time, a moment. You have the power now; you can afford to withhold for a moment the use of it as a force. You have done a good job, you have jolted your opponent off-balance and he is now vulnerable. But stop there for a moment; don't give him the advantage of a chance to cloud the issue by that purely automatic sentimental appeal to that same universal human instinct for automatic sympathy for the underdog simply because he is under."

And I would say this too. The rest of the United States knows next to nothing about the South. The present idea and picture which they hold of a people decadent and even obsolete through inbreeding and illiteracy—the inbreeding a result of the illiteracy and the isolation—as to be a kind of species of juvenile delinquents with a folklore of blood and violence, yet who, like juvenile delinquents, can be controlled by firmness once they are brought to believe that the police mean business, is as baseless and illusory as that one a generation ago of (oh yes, we subscribed to it too) columned porticoes and magnolias. The rest of the United States assumes that this condition in the South is so simple and so uncomplex that it can be changed tomorrow by the simple will of the national majority backed by legal edict. In fact, the North does not even recognize what it has seen in its own newspapers.

I have at hand an editorial from the New York *Times* of February 10th on the rioting at the University of Alabama because of the admission of Miss Lucy, a Negro. The editorial said: "This is the first time that force and violence have become part of the question." That is not correct. To all Southerners, no matter which side of the question of racial equality they supported, the first implication, and—to the Southerner—even promise, of force and violence was the Supreme Court decision itself. After that, by any standards at all and following as inevitably as night and day, was the case of the three white teen-agers, members of a field trip group from a Mississippi high school (and, as teen-agers do, probably wearing the bright particolored blazers or jackets blazoned across the back with the name of the school) who were stabbed in passing on a Washington street by Negroes they had never seen before and who apparently had never seen them before either; and that of the Till boy and the two Mississippi juries which freed the defendants from both charges; and of the Mississippi garage attendant killed by a white man because, according to the white man, the Negro filled the tank of the white man's car full of gasoline when all the white man wanted was two dollars' worth.

This problem is far beyond a mere legal one. It is even far beyond the moral one it is and still was a hundred years ago in 1860, when many Southerners, including Robert Lee, recognized it as a moral one at the very instant when they in turn elected to champion the underdog because that underdog was blood and kin and home. The Northerner is not even aware yet of what that war really proved. He assumes that it merely proved to the Southerner that he was wrong. It didn't do that because the Southerner already knew he was wrong and accepted that gambit even when he knew it was the fatal one. What that war should have done, but failed to do, was to prove to the North that the South will go to any length, even that fatal and already doomed one, before it will accept alteration of its racial condition by mere force of law or economic threat.

Since I went on record as being opposed to compulsory racial inequality, I have received many letters. A few of them approved. But most of them were in opposition. And a few of these were from Southern Negroes, the only difference being that they were polite and courteous instead of being threats and insults, saying in effect: "Please, Mr Faulkner, stop talking and be quiet. You are a good man and you think you are helping us. But you are not helping us. You are doing us harm. You are playing into the hands of the NAACP so that they are using you to make trouble for our race that we don't want. Please hush, you look after your white folks' trouble and let us take care of ours." This one in particular was a long one, from a woman who was writing for and in the name of the pastor and the entire congregation of her church. It went on to say that the Till boy got exactly what he asked for, coming down there with his Chicago ideas, and that all his mother wanted was to make money out of the role of her bereavement. Which sounds exactly like the white people in the South who justified and even defended the crime by declining to find that it was one.

We have had many violent inexcusable personal crimes of race against race in the South, but since 1919 the major examples of communal race tension have been more prevalent in the North, like the Negro family who were refused acceptance in the white residential district in Chicago, and the Korean-American who suffered for the same reason in Anaheim, Calif. Maybe it is because our solidarity is not racial, but instead is the majority white segregationist plus the Negro minority like my correspondent above, who prefer peace to equality. But suppose the line of demarcation should become one of the race; the white minority like myself compelled to join the white segregation majority no matter how much we oppose the principle of inequality; the Negro minority who want peace compelled to join the Negro majority who advocate force, no matter how much that minority wanted only peace?

So the Northerner, the liberal, does not know the South. He can't know it from his distance. He assumes that he is dealing with a simple legal theory and a simple moral idea. He is not. He is dealing with a fact: the fact of an emotional condition of such fierce unanimity as to scorn the fact that it is a minority and which will go to any length and against any odds at this moment to justify and, if necessary, defend that condition and its right to it.

So I would say to all the organizations and groups which would force integration on the South by legal process: "Stop now for a moment. You have shown the Southerner what you can do and what you will do if necessary; give him a space in which to get his breath and assimilate that knowledge; to look about and see that (1) Nobody is going to force integration on him from the outside; (2) That he himself faces an obsolescence in his own land which only he can cure; a moral condition which not only must be cured but a physical condition which has got to be cured if he, the white Southerner, is to have any peace, is not to be faced with another legal process or maneuver every year, year after year, for the rest of his life."

FAULKNER AND DESEGREGATION

James Baldwin

Any real change implies the breakup of the world as one has always known it, the loss of all that gave one an identity, the end of safety. And at such a moment, unable to see and not daring to imagine what the future will now bring forth, one clings to what one knew, or thought one knew; to what one possessed or dreamed that one possessed. Yet, it is only when a man is able, without bitterness or self-pity, to surrender a dream he has long cherished or a privilege he has long possessed that he is set free—he has set himself free—for higher dreams, for greater privileges. All men have gone through this, go through it, each according to his degree, throughout their lives. It is one of the irreducible facts of life. And remembering this, especially since I am a Negro, affords me almost my only means of understanding what is happening in the minds and hearts of white Southerners today.

For the arguments with which the bulk of relatively articulate white Southerners of good will have met the necessity of desegregation have no value whatever as arguments, being almost entirely and helplessly dishonest, when not, indeed, insane. After more than two hundred years in slavery and ninety years of quasi-freedom, it is hard to think very highly of William Faulkner's advice to "go slow." "They don't mean go slow," Thurgood Marshall is reported to have said, "they mean don't go." Nor is the squire of Oxford very persuasive when he suggests that white Southerners, left to their own devices, will realize that their own social structure looks silly to the rest of the world and correct it of their own accord. It has looked silly, to use Faulkner's rather strange adjective, for a long time; so far from trying to correct it, Southerners, who seem to be characterized by a species of defiance most perverse when it is most despairing, have clung to it, at incalculable cost to themselves, as the only conceivable and as an absolutely sacrosanct way of life. They have never seriously conceded that their social structure was mad. They have insisted, on the contrary, that everyone who criticized it was mad.

Faulkner goes further. He concedes the madness and moral wrongness of the South but at the same time he raises it to the level of a mystique which makes it somehow unjust to discuss Southern society in the same terms in which one would discuss any other society. "Our position is wrong and untenable," says Faulkner, "but it is not wise to keep an emotional people off balance." This, if it means anything, can only mean that this "emotional people" have been swept "off balance" by the pressure of recent events, that is, the Supreme Court decision outlawing segregation. When the pressure is taken off—and not an instant before—this "emotional people" will presumably find themselves once again on balance and will then be able to free themselves of an "obsolescence in [their] own land" in their own way and, of course, in their own time. The question left begging is what, in their history to date, affords any evidence that they have any desire or capacity to do this. And it is, I suppose, impertinent to ask just what Negroes are supposed to do while the South works out what, in Faulkner's rhetoric, becomes something very closely resembling a high and noble tragedy.

The sad truth is that whatever modifications have been effected in the social structure of the South since the Reconstruction, and any alleviations of the Negro's lot within it, are due to great and incessant pressure, very little of it indeed from within the South. That the North has been guilty of Pharisaism in its dealings with the South does not negate the fact that much of this pressure has come from the North. That some—not nearly as many as Faulkner would like to believe—Southern Negroes prefer, or are afraid of changing, the status quo does not negate the fact that it is the Southern Negro himself who, year upon year, and generation upon generation, has kept the Southern waters troubled. As far as the Negro's life in the South is concerned, the NAACP is the only organization which has struggled, with admirable single-mindedness and skill, to raise him to the level of a citizen. For this reason alone, and quite apart from the individual heroism of many of its Southern members, it cannot be equated, as Faulkner equates it, with the pathological Citizen's Council. One organization is working within the law and the other is working against and outside it. Faulkner's threat to leave the "middle of the road" where he has, presumably, all these years, been working for the benefit of Negroes, reduces itself to a more or less up-to-date version of the Southern threat to secede from the Union.

Faulkner—among so many others!—is so plaintive concerning this "middle of the road" from which "extremist" elements of both races are driving him that it does not seem unfair to ask just what he has been doing there until now. Where is the evidence of the struggle he has been carrying on there on behalf of the Negro? Why, if he and his enlightened confreres in the South have been boring from within to destroy segregation, do they react with such panic when the walls show any signs of falling? Why—and how—does one move from the middle of the road where one was aiding Negroes into the streets—to shoot them?

Now it is easy enough to state flatly that Faulkner's middle of the road does not—cannot—exist and that he is guilty of great emotional and intellectual dishonesty in pretending that it does. I think this is why he clings to his fantasy. It is easy enough to accuse him of hypocrisy when he speaks of man being "indestructible because of his simple will to freedom." But he is not being hypocritical; he means it. It is only that Man is one thing—a rather unlucky abstraction in this case—and the Negroes he has always known, so fatally tied up in his mind with his grandfather's slaves, are quite another. He is at his best, and is perfectly sincere, when he declares, in *Harper's,* "To live anywhere in the world today and be against equality because of race or color is like living in Alaska and being against snow. We have already got snow. And as with the Alaskan, merely to live in armistice with it is not enough. Like the Alaskan, we had better use it." And though this seems to be flatly opposed to his statement (in an interview printed in *The Reporter*) that, if it came to a contest between the federal government and Mississippi, he would fight for Mississippi, "even if it meant going out into the streets and shooting Negroes," he means that, too. Faulkner means everything he says, means them all at once, and with very nearly the same intensity. This is why his statements demand our attention. He has perhaps never before more concretely expressed what it means to be a Southerner.

What seems to define the Southerner, in his own mind at any rate, is his relationship to the North, that is to the rest of the Republic, a relationship which can at the very best be described as uneasy. It is apparently very difficult to be at once a Southerner and an American; so difficult that many of the South's most independent minds are forced into the American exile; which is not, of course, without its aggravating, circular effect on the interior and public life of the South. A Bostonian, say, who leaves Boston is not regarded by the citizenry he has abandoned with the same venomous distrust as is the Southerner who leaves the South. The citizenry of Boston do not consider that they have been abandoned, much less betrayed. It is only the American Southerner who seems to be fighting, in his own entrails, a peculiar, ghastly, and perpetual war with all the rest of the country. ("Didn't you say," demanded a Southern woman of Robert Penn Warren, "that you was born down here, used to live right near here?" And when he agreed that this was so: "Yes . . . but you never said where you living now!")

The difficulty, perhaps, is that the Southerner clings to two entirely antithetical doctrines, two legends, two histories. Like all other Americans, he must subscribe, and is to some extent controlled by the beliefs and the principles expressed in the Constitution; at the same time, these beliefs and principles seem determined to destroy the South. He is, on the one hand, the proud citizen of a free society and, on the other, is committed to a society which has not yet dared to free itself of the necessity of naked and brutal oppression. He is part of a country which boasts that it has never lost a war; but he is also the representative of a conquered nation. I have not seen a single statement of Faulkner's concerning desegregation which does not inform us that his family has lived in the same part of Mississippi for generations, that his great-grandfather owned slaves, and that his ancestors fought and died in the Civil War. And so compelling is the image of ruin, gallantry and death thus evoked that it demands a positive effort of the imagination to remember that slaveholding Southerners were not the only people who perished in that war. Negroes and Northerners were also blown to bits. American history, as opposed to Southern history, proves that Southerners were not the only slaveholders, Negroes were not even the only slaves. And the segregation which Faulkner sanctifies by references to Shiloh, Chickamauga, and Gettysburg does not extend back that far, is in fact scarcely as old as the century. The "racial condition" which Faulkner will not have changed by "mere force of law or economic threat" was imposed by precisely these means. The Southern tradition, which is, after all, all that Faulkner is talking about, is not a tradition at all: when Faulkner evokes it, he is simply evoking a legend which contains an accusation. And that accusation, stated far more simply than it should be, is that the North, in winning the war, left the South only one means of asserting its identity and that means was the Negro.

"My people owned slaves," says Faulkner, "and the very obligation we have to take care of these people is morally bad." "This problem is . . . far beyond the moral one it is and still was a hundred years ago, in 1860, when many Southerners, including Robert Lee, recognized it as a moral one at the very instant when they in turn elected to champion the underdog because that underdog was blood and kin and home." But the North escaped scot-free. For one thing, in freeing the slave, it established a moral superiority over the South which the South has not learned to live with until today; and this despite—or possibly because of—the fact that this moral superiority was bought, after all, rather cheaply. The North was no better prepared than the South, as it turned out, to make citizens of former slaves, but it was able, as the South was not, to wash its hands of the matter. Men who knew that slavery was wrong were forced, nevertheless, to fight to perpetuate it because they were unable to turn against "blood and kin and home." And when blood and kin and home were defeated, they found themselves, more than ever, committed: committed, in effect, to a way of life which was as unjust and crippling as it was inescapable. In sum, the North, by freeing the slaves of their masters, robbed the masters of any possibility of freeing themselves of the slaves.

When Faulkner speaks, then, of the "middle of the road," he is simply speaking of the hope—which was always unrealistic and is now all but smashed—that the white Southerner, with no coercion from the rest of the nation, will lift himself above his ancient, crippling bitterness and refuse to add to his already intolerable burden of blood-guiltiness. But this hope would seem to be absolutely dependent on a social and psychological stasis which simply does not exist. "Things have been getting better," Faulkner tells us, "for a long time. Only six Negroes were killed by whites in Mississippi last year, according to police figures." Faulkner surely knows how little consolation this offers a Negro and he also knows something about "police figures" in the Deep South. And he knows, too, that murder is not the worst thing that can happen to a man, black or white. But murder may be the worst thing a man can do. Faulkner is not trying to save Negroes, who are, in his view, already saved; who, having refused to be destroyed by terror, are far stronger than the terrified white populace; and who have, moreover, fatally, from his point of view, the weight of the federal government behind them. He is trying to save "whatever good remains in those white people." The time he pleads for is the time in which the Southerner will come to terms with himself, will cease fleeing from his conscience, and achieve, in the words of Robert Penn Warren, "moral identity." And he surely believes, with Warren, that "Then in a country where moral identity is hard to come by, the South, because it has had to deal concretely with a moral problem, may offer some leadership. And we need any we can get. If we are to break out of the national rhythm, the rhythm between complacency and panic."

But the time Faulkner asks for does not exist—and he is not the only Southerner who knows it. There is never time in the future in which we will work out our salvation. The challenge is in the moment, the time is always now.

QUESTIONS

1   List Faulkner's main points. Place Baldwin's reply beside each point on the list. Which argument appears stronger?
2   How appropriate is Faulkner's letter in view of recent events in the North? Does a consideration of recent Northern racial troubles alter the force of Baldwin's indictment of white Southerners?
3   Which of the two writers seems more objective? What does your answer imply about point of view when writing about racial problems?
4   Considered together, do the two essays offer an impasse or are there points where compromise might be effected? Explain.

TOPICS FOR COMPOSITION

1   Using your knowledge of current events, write an essay showing that the views expressed by both Faulkner and Baldwin are too restricted to cover current issues.

2   Using one of the above essays and Thoreau's "Civil Disobedience," discuss the writer of the modern essay as a follower/non-follower of Thoreau's theory.

3   Using Faulkner's essay as your model, write a "letter" on a current controversial problem.

SHORT STORY

"The Bench" is committed literature. In this sense, its major purpose is to reveal a social and political condition that affects an oppressed or minority group. Karlie's individual protest is, at the same time, an assertion of his dignity and oneness with his race. The story unfolds through Karlie's at first hesitant acceptance of the truth of the words that he hears in stark contrast with the reality of conditions about him.

THE BENCH

Richard Rive

> "We form an integral part of a complex society, a society complex in that a vast proportion of the population are denied the very basic privileges of existence, a society that condemns a man to an inferior position because he has the misfortune to be born black, a society that can only retain its precarious social and economic position at the expense of an enormous oppressed proletariat!"

Karlie's eyes shone as he watched the speaker. Those were great words, he thought, great words and true. The speaker paused for a moment and sipped some water from a glass. Karlie sweated. The hot October sun beat down mercilessly on the gathering. The trees on the Grand Parade afforded very little shelter and his handkerchief was already soaked where he had placed it between his neck and shirt collar. Karlie stared round him at the sea of faces. Every shade of colour was represented, from shiny ebony to the one or two whites in the crowd. He stared at the two detectives who were busily making shorthand notes of the speeches, and then turned to stare back at the speaker.

> "It is up to us to challenge the rights of any groups who wilfully and deliberately condemn a fellow group to a servile position. We must challenge the rights of any people who see fit to segregate human beings solely on grounds of pigmentation. Your children are denied the rights which are theirs by birth. They are segregated socially, economically. . . ."

Ah, thought Karlie, that man knows what he is speaking about. He says I am as good as any other man, even a white man. That needs much thinking. I wonder if he thinks I have the right to go into any bioscope or eat in any restaurant, or that my children can go to any school? These are dangerous ideas and need much thinking; I wonder what Ou Klaas would say to this. Ou Klaas said God made the white man and the black man separately and the one must always be *"baas"* and the other *"jong."* But this man says different things and somehow they seem true.

Karlie's brow was knitted as he thought. On the platform were many speakers, both white and black, and they were behaving as if there were no difference of colour between them. There was a white woman in a blue dress offering a cigarette to Nxeli. That could never happen at Bietjiesvlei. Old Lategan at the store would have fainted if his Annatjie had offered Witbooi a cigarette. And Annatjie had no such pretty dress. These were new things, and he, Karlie, had to be careful before he accepted them. But

113

why shouldn't he accept them? He was not coloured any more, he was a human being. The speaker had said so. He remembered seeing pictures in the newspaper of people who defied laws which relegated them to a particular class, and those people were smiling as they went to prison. This was a strange world.

The speaker continued and Karlie listened intently. His speech was obviously carefully prepared and he spoke slowly, choosing his words. This is a great man, Karlie thought.

The last speaker was the white lady in the blue dress, who asked them to challenge any discriminatory laws or measures in every possible manner. Why should she speak like that? thought Karlie. She could go to the best bioscopes, and swim at the best beaches. Why, she was even more beautiful than Annatjie Lategan. They had warned him in Bietjiesvlei about coming to the city. He had seen the *Skollies* in District Six and knew what to expect there. Hanover Street held no terrors for him. But no one had told him about this. This was new, this set one's mind thinking, yet he felt it was true. She said one should challenge. He would challenge. He, Karlie, would astound old Lategan and Balie at the dairy farm. They could do what they liked to him after that. He would smile like those people in the newspaper.

The meeting was almost over when Karlie threaded his way through the crowd. The words of the speakers were still milling through his head. It could never happen in Bietjiesvlei, he thought, or could it? The sudden screech of a car pulling to a hurried stop whirled him back to his senses. A white head was angrily thrust through the window. "Look where you're going, you black bastard!"

Karlie stared dazedly at him. Surely this white man had never heard what the speakers had said. He could never have seen the white woman offering Nxeli a cigarette. Karlie could never imagine the white lady shouting those words at him. It would be best to catch a train and think these things over.

He saw the station in a new light. Here was a mass of human beings, some black, some white, and some brown like himself. Here they mixed with one another, yet each mistrusted the other with an unnatural fear. Each treated the other with suspicion, each moved in a narrow, haunted pattern of its own manufacture. One must challenge these things the speaker had said . . . in one's own way. Yet how in one's own way? How was one to challenge? Slowly it dawned upon him. Here was his chance, *the bench*. The railway bench with the legend "Europeans Only" neatly painted on it in white. For one moment it symbolized all the misery of the plural South African society. Here was a challenge to his rights as a man. There it stood, a perfectly ordinary wooden railway bench, like hundreds of thousands of others in South Africa. His challenge. That bench, now, had concentrated in it all the evils of a system he could not understand. It was the obstacle between himself and humanity. If he sat on it he was a man. If he was afraid he denied himself membership as a human in a human society. He almost had visions of righting the pernicious system if only he sat on that bench. Here was his chance. He, Karlie, would challenge.

He seemed perfectly calm when he sat down on the bench, but inside his heart was thumping wildly. Two conflicting ideas now throbbed through him. The one said, "I have no right to sit on this bench"; the other said, "Why have I no right to sit on this bench?" The one voice spoke of the past, of the servile position he had occupied on the farms, of his father and his father's father who were born black, lived like blacks and died like oxen. The other voice spoke of the future and said, "Karlie, you are a man. You have dared what your father would not have dared. You will die like a man!"

Karlie took out a cigarette and smoked. Nobody seemed to notice his sitting there. This was an anti-climax. The world still pursued its monotonous way. No voice shouted "Karlie has conquered!" He was a normal human being sitting on a bench in a busy station, smoking a cigarette. Or was this his victory, the fact that he was a normal human being? A well-dressed white woman walked down the platform. Would she sit on the bench, Karlie wondered. And then that gnawing voice, "You should stand and let the white woman sit." Karlie narrowed his eyes and gripped tighter at his cigarette. She swept past him without the slightest twitch of an eyelid and walked on down the platform. Was she afraid to challenge, to challenge his right to be human? Karlie now felt tired. A third conflicting emotion was now creeping in, a compensatory emotion which said, "You do not sit on this bench to challenge, you sit there because you are tired. You are tired; therefore you sit." He would not move, because he was tired, or was it because he wanted to sit where he liked?

People were now pouring out of a train that had pulled into the station. There were so many people pushing and jostling one another that nobody noticed him. This was his train. It would be quite easy to step into the train and ride off home, but that would be giving in, suffering defeat, refusing the challenge, in fact admitting that he was not a human being. He sat on. Lazily he blew the cigarette smoke into the air, thinking . . . his mind was far from the meeting and the bench, he was thinking of Bietjiesvlei and Ou Klaas, how he had insisted that Karlie should come to Cape Town. Ou Klaas could look so quizzically at one and suck at his pipe. He was wise to know and knew much. He had said one must go to Cape Town and learn the ways of the world. He would spit and wink slyly when he spoke of District Six and the women he knew in Hanover Street. Ou Klaas knew everything. He said God made us white or black and we must therefore keep our places.

"Get off this seat!"

Karlie did not hear the gruff voice. Ou Klaas would be on the land now, waiting for his tot of cheap wine.

"I said get off the bench, you swine!"

Karlie suddenly whipped back to reality. For a moment he was going to jump up, then he remembered who he was and why he was sitting there. Suddenly he felt very tired. He looked up slowly into a very red face that stared down at him.

"Get up! I said. There are benches down there for you!"

Karlie stared up and said nothing. He stared up into very sharp, cold gray eyes.

"Can't you hear me speaking to you, you black swine!"

Slowly and deliberately Karlie puffed at his cigarette. So this was his test. They both stared at each other, challenged with the eyes, like two boxers, each knowing that they must eventually trade blows yet each afraid to strike first.

"Must I dirty my hands on scum like you?"

Karlie said nothing. To speak would be to break the spell, the supremacy he felt he was slowly gaining. An uneasy silence. Then,

"I will call a policeman rather than kick a Hotnot like you! You can't even open your black jaw when a white man speaks to you!"

Karlie saw the weakness. The white youth was afraid to take action himself. He, Karlie, had won the first round of the bench dispute!

A crowd now collected. "Afrika!" shouted one joker. Karlie ignored the remark. People were now milling around, staring at the unusual sight of a black man sitting on a white man's bench. Karlie merely puffed on.

"Look at the black ape! That's the worst of giving these Kaffirs too much rope!"

"I can't understand it, they have their own benches!"

"Don't get up, you have every right to sit there!"

"He'll get hell when a policeman comes!"

"Mind you, I can't see why they shouldn't sit where they please!"

"I've said before, I've had a native servant, and a more impertinent . . ."

Karlie sat and heard nothing. Irresolution had now turned to determination. Under no condition was he going to rise. They could do what they liked.

"So this is the fellow. Hey, get up there! Can't you read?" The policeman was towering over him. Karlie could see the crest on his buttons and the thin wrinkles on his neck. "What is your name and address?"

Karlie still maintained his obstinate silence. It took the policeman rather unawares. The crowd was growing every minute.

"You have no right to speak to this man in such a manner!" It was the white lady in the blue dress.

"Mind your own business! I'll ask your help when I need it. It is people like you who make Kaffirs think they're as good as white people!" Then, addressing Karlie, "Get up, you!"

"I insist that you treat him with proper respect!"

The policeman turned red. "This . . . this . . ." He was at a loss for words.

"Kick up the Hotnot if he won't get up!" shouted a spectator.

Rudely a white man laid hands on Karlie. "Get up, you bloody bastard!"

Karlie turned to resist, to cling to the bench, his bench. There were more than one man now pulling at him. He hit out wildly and then felt a dull pain as somebody rammed a fist into his face. He was now bleeding and wild-eyed. He would fight for it. The constable clapped a pair of handcuffs round Karlie's wrists and tried to clear a way through the crowd. Karlie was still struggling. A blow or two landed on him. Suddenly he relaxed and slowly struggled to his feet. It was useless fighting any longer. Now it was his turn to smile. He had challenged and won. Who cared at the result?

"Come on, you swine!" said the policeman, forcing Karlie through the crowd.

"Certainly," said Karlie for the first time, and stared at the policeman with the arrogance of one who dared to sit on a "European" bench.

QUESTIONS

1   A knowledge of the full implications of *apartheid* is necessary to understanding Rive's story. Exactly what restrictions does this policy impose on South African nonwhites?

2   What moves Karlie to consider his condition? Does he have doubts about what he hears?
3   What events contribute to his final determination to protest?
4   What does Karlie's sitting on the restricted bench actually accomplish?

TOPICS FOR COMPOSITION

Certainly we recognize that Karlie's assessment of a racially mixed society—the mistrust, the unnatural fear, the suspicion—accurately reflects the events of our time and place. The speaker said, "One must challenge these things . . . in one's own way." Karlie found a way. How can each of us, in our time and place, combat mistrust, unnatural fear, and suspicion?

An old woman, her deaf-mute, retarded daughter, and a drifter form a trio by which Flannery O'Connor explores the conflict between restraint and repressed desire. Old Mrs. Crater wants desperately to "marry-off" Lucynell and gain a man about the place. Tom T. Shiftlet, for all his professed "moral intelligence," is willing to sacrifice the half-witted Lucynell for a small sum of money, a car, and freedom from the restraints of his meager existence. But we should be careful not to oversimplify the artistry of Miss O'Connor's characterization. As you read, you should give careful attention to the motivations and ambiguities her two main characters display.

THE LIFE YOU SAVE MAY BE YOUR OWN

Flannery O'Connor

The old woman and her daughter were sitting on their porch when Mr. Shiftlet came up their road for the first time. The old woman slid to the edge of her chair and leaned forward, shading her eyes from the piercing sunset with her hand. The daughter could not see far in front of her and continued to play with her fingers. Although the old woman lived in this desolate spot with only her daughter and she had never seen Mr. Shiftlet before, she could tell, even from a distance, that he was a tramp and no one to be afraid of. His left coat sleeve was folded up to show there was only half an arm in it and his gaunt figure listed slightly to the side as if the breeze were pushing him. He had on a black town suit and a brown felt hat that was turned up in the front and down in the back and he carried a tin tool box by a handle. He came on, at an amble, up her road, his face turned toward the sun which appeared to be balancing itself on the peak of a small mountain.

The old woman didn't change her position until he was almost into her yard; then she rose with one hand fisted on her hip. The daughter, a large girl in a short blue organdy dress, saw him all at once and jumped up and began to stamp and point and make excited speechless sounds.

Mr. Shiftlet stopped just inside the yard and set his box on the ground and tipped his hat at her as if she were not in the least afflicted; then he turned toward the old woman and swung the hat all the way off. He had long black slick hair that hung flat from a part in the middle to beyond the tips of his ears on either side. His face descended in forehead for more than half its length and ended suddenly with his features just balanced over a jutting steeltrap jaw. He seemed to be a young man but he had a look of composed dissatisfaction as if he understood life thoroughly.

"Good evening," the old woman said. She was about the size of a cedar fence post and she had a man's gray hat pulled down low over her head.

The tramp stood looking at her and didn't answer. He turned his back and faced the sunset. He swung both his whole and his short arm up slowly so that they indicated an expanse of sky and his figure formed a crooked cross. The old woman watched him with her arms folded across her chest as if she were the owner of the sun, and the daughter watched, her head thrust forward and her fat helpless hands hanging at the wrists. She had long pink-gold hair and eyes as blue as a peacock's neck.

He held the pose for almost fifty seconds and then he picked up his box and came on to the porch and dropped down on the bottom step. "Lady," he said in a firm nasal voice, "I'd give a fortune to live where I could see me a sun do that every evening."

"Does it every evening," the old woman said and sat back down. The daughter sat down too and watched him with a cautious sly look as if he were a bird that had come up very close. He leaned to one side, rooting in his pants pocket, and in a second he brought out a package of chewing gum and offered her a piece. She took it and unpeeled it and began to chew without taking her eyes off him. He offered the old woman a piece but she only raised her upper lip to indicate she had no teeth.

Mr. Shiftlet's pale sharp glance had already passed over everything in the yard—the pump near the corner of the house and the big fig tree that three or four chickens were preparing to roost in—and had moved to a shed where he saw the square rusted back of an automobile. "You ladies drive?" he asked.

"That car ain't run in fifteen year," the old woman said. "The day my husband died, it quit running."

"Nothing is like it used to be, lady," he said. "The world is almost rotten."

"That's right," the old woman said. "You from around here?"

"Name Tom T. Shiftlet," he murmured, looking at the tires.

"I'm pleased to meet you," the old woman said. "Name Lucynell Crater and daughter Lucynell Crater. What you doing around here, Mr. Shiftlet?"

He judged the car to be about a 1928 or '29 Ford. "Lady," he said, and turned and gave her his full attention, "lemme tell you something. There's one of these doctors in Atlanta that's taken a knife and cut the human heart—the human heart," he repeated, leaning forward, "out of a man's chest and held it in his hand," and he held his hand out, palm up, as if it were slightly weighted with the human heart, "and studied it like it was a day-old chicken, and lady," he said, allowing a long significant pause in which his head slid forward and his clay-colored eyes brightened, "he don't know no more about it than you or me."

"That's right," the old woman said.

"Why, if he was to take that knife and cut into every corner of it, he still wouldn't know no more than you or me. What you want to bet?"

"Nothing," the old woman said wisely. "Where you come from, Mr. Shiftlet?"

He didn't answer. He reached into his pocket and brought out a sack of tobacco and a package of cigarette papers and rolled himself a cigarette, expertly with one hand, and attached it in a hanging position to his upper lip. Then he took a box of wooden matches from his pocket and struck one on his shoe. He held the burning match as if he were studying the mystery of flame while it traveled dangerously toward his skin. The daughter began to make loud noises and to point to his hand and shake her finger at him, but when the flame was just before touching him, he leaned down with his hand cupped over it as if he were going to set fire to his nose and lit the cigarette.

He flipped away the dead match and blew a stream of gray into the evening. A sly look came over his face. "Lady," he said, "nowadays, people'll do anything anyways. I can tell you my name is Tom T. Shiftlet and I come from Tarwater, Tennessee, but you never have seen me before: how you know I ain't lying? How you know my name ain't Aaron Sparks, lady, and I come from Singleberry, Georgia, or how you know it's not George Speeds and I come from Lucy, Alabama, or how you know I ain't Thompson Bright from Toolafalls, Mississippi?"

"I don't know nothing about you," the old woman muttered, irked.

"Lady," he said, "people don't care how they lie. Maybe the best I can tell you is, I'm a man; but listen lady," he said and paused and made his tone more ominous still, "what is a man?"

The old woman began to gum a seed. "What you carry in that tin box, Mr. Shiftlet?" she asked.

"Tools," he said, put back. "I'm a carpenter."

"Well, if you come out here to work, I'll be able to feed you and give you a place to sleep but I can't pay. I'll tell you that before you begin," she said.

There was no answer at once and no particular expression on his face. He leaned back against the two-by-four that helped support the porch roof. "Lady," he said slowly, "there's some men that some things mean more to them than money." The old woman rocked without comment and the daughter watched the trigger that moved up and down in his neck. He told the old woman then that all most people were interested in was money, but he asked what a man was made for. He asked her if a man was made for money, or what. He asked her what she thought she was made for but she didn't answer, she only sat rocking and wondered if a one-armed man could put a new roof on her garden house. He asked a lot of questions that she didn't answer. He told her that he was twenty-eight years old and had lived a varied life. He had been a gospel singer, a foreman on the railroad, an assistant in an undertaking parlor, and he come over the radio for three months with Uncle Roy and his Red Creek Wranglers. He said he had fought and bled in the Arm Service of his country and visited every foreign land and that everywhere he had seen people that didn't care if they did a thing one way or another. He said he hadn't been raised thataway.

A fat yellow moon appeared in the branches of the fig tree as if it were going to roost there with the chickens. He said that a man had to escape to the country to see the world whole and that he wished he lived in a desolate place like this where he could see the sun go down every evening like God made it to do.

"Are you married or are you single?" the old woman asked.

There was a long silence. "Lady," he asked finally, "where would you find you an innocent woman today? I wouldn't have any of this trash I could just pick up."

The daughter was leaning very far down, hanging her head almost between her knees watching him through a triangular door she had made in her overturned hair; and she suddenly fell in a heap on the floor and began to whimper. Mr. Shiftlet straightened her out and helped her get back in the chair.

"Is she your baby girl?" he asked.

"My only," the old woman said "and she's the sweetest girl in the world. I would give her up for nothing on earth. She's smart too. She can sweep the floor, cook, wash, feed the chickens, and hoe. I wouldn't give her up for a casket of jewels."

"No," he said kindly, "don't ever let any man take her away from you."

"Any man come after her," the old woman said, "'ll have to stay around the place."

Mr. Shiftlet's eye in the darkness was focused on a part of the automobile bumper that glittered in the distance. "Lady," he said, jerking his short arm up as if he could point with it to her house and yard and pump, "there ain't a broken thing on this plantation that I couldn't fix for you, one-arm jackleg or not. I'm a man," he said with a sullen dignity, "even if I ain't a whole one. I got," he said, tapping his knuckles on the floor to emphasize the immensity of what he was going to say, "a moral intelligence!" and his face pierced out of the darkness into a shaft of doorlight and he stared at her as if he were astonished himself at this impossible truth.

The old woman was not impressed with the phrase. "I told you you could hang around and work for food," she said, "if you don't mind sleeping in that car yonder."

"Why listen, lady," he said with a grin of delight, "the monks of old slept in their coffins!"

"They wasn't as advanced as we are," the old woman said.

The next morning he began on the roof of the garden house while Lucynell, the daughter, sat on a rock and watched him work. He had not been around a week before the change he had made in the place was apparent. He had patched the front and back steps, built a new hog pen, restored the fence, and taught Lucynell, who was completely deaf and had never said a word in her life, to say the word "bird." The big rosy-faced girl followed him everywhere, saying "Burrttddt ddbirrrttdt," and clapping her hands. The old woman watched from a distance, secretly pleased. She was ravenous for a son-in-law.

Mr. Shiftlet slept on the hard narrow back seat of the car with his feet out the side window. He had his razor and a can of water on a crate that served him as a bedside table and he put up a piece of mirror against the back glass and kept his coat neatly on a hanger that he hung over one of the windows.

In the evenings he sat on the steps and talked while the old woman and Lucynell rocked violently in their chairs on either side of him. The old woman's three mountains were black against the dark blue sky and were visited off and on by various planets and by the moon after it had left the chickens. Mr. Shiftlet pointed out that the reason he had improved this plantation was because he had taken a personal interest in it. He said he was even going to make the automobile run.

He had raised the hood and studied the mechanism and he said he could tell that the car had been built in the days when cars were really built. You take now, he said, one man puts in one bolt and another man puts in another bolt and another man puts in another bolt so that it's a man for a bolt. That's why you have to pay so much for a car: you're paying all those men. Now if you didn't have to pay but one man, you could get you a cheaper car and one that had had a personal interest taken in it, and it would be a better car. The old woman agreed with him that this was so.

Mr. Shiftlet said that the trouble with the world was that nobody cared, or stopped and took any trouble. He said he never would have been able to teach Lucynell to say a word if he hadn't cared and stopped long enough.

"Teach her to say something else," the old woman said.

"What you want her to say next?" Mr. Shiftlet asked.

The old woman's smile was broad and toothless and suggestive. "Teach her to say 'sugarpie,'" she said.

Mr. Shiftlet already knew what was on her mind.

The next day he began to tinker with the automobile and that evening he told her that if she would buy a fan belt, he would be able to make the car run.

The old woman said she would give him the money. "You see that girl yonder?" she asked, pointing to Lucynell who was sitting on the floor a foot away, watching him, her eyes blue even in the dark. "If it was ever a man wanted to take her away, I would say, 'No man on earth is going to take that sweet girl of mine away from me!' but if he was to say, 'Lady, I don't want to take her away, I want her right here,' I would say, 'Mister, I don't blame you none. I wouldn't pass up a chance to live in a permanent place and get the sweetest girl in the world myself. You ain't no fool,' I would say."

"How old is she?" Mr. Shiftlet asked casually.

"Fifteen, sixteen," the old woman said. The girl was nearly thirty but because of her innocence it was impossible to guess.

"It would be a good idea to paint it too," Mr. Shiftlet remarked. "You don't want it to rust out."

"We'll see about that later," the old woman said.

The next day he walked into town and returned with the parts he needed and a can of gasoline. Late in the afternoon, terrible noises issued from the shed and the old woman rushed out of the house, thinking Lucynell was somewhere having a fit. Lucynell was sitting on a chicken crate, stamping her feet and screaming, "Burrddtt! bddurrddttt!" but her fuss was drowned out by the car. With a volley of blasts it emerged from the shed, moving in a fierce and stately way. Mr. Shiftlet was in the driver's seat, sitting very erect. He had an expression of serious modesty on his face as if he had just raised the dead.

That night, rocking on the porch, the old woman began her business, at once. "You want you an innocent woman, don't you?" she asked sympathetically. "You don't want none of this trash."

"No'm, I don't," Mr. Shiftlet said.

"One that can't talk," she continued, "can't sass you back or use foul language. That's the kind for you to have. Right there," and she pointed to Lucynell sitting cross-legged in her chair, holding both feet in her hands.

"That's right," he admitted. "She wouldn't give me any trouble."

"Saturday," the old woman said, "you and her and me can drive into town and get married."

Mr. Shiftlet eased his position on the steps.

"I can't get married right now," he said. "Everything you want to do takes money and I ain't got any."

"What you need with money?" she asked.

"It takes money," he said. "Some people'll do anything anyhow these days, but the way I think, I wouldn't marry no woman that I couldn't take on a trip like she was somebody. I mean take her to a hotel and treat her. I wouldn't marry the Duchesser Windsor," he said firmly, "unless I could take her to a hotel and giver something good to eat.

"I was raised thataway and there ain't a thing I can do about it. My old mother taught me how to do."

"Lucynell don't even know what a hotel is," the old woman muttered. "Listen here, Mr. Shiftlet," she said, sliding forward in her chair, "you'd be getting a permanent house and a deep well and the most innocent girl in the world. You don't need no money. Lemme tell you something: there ain't any place in the world for a poor disabled friendless drifting man."

The ugly words settled in Mr. Shiftlet's head like a group of buzzards in the top of a tree. He didn't answer at once. He rolled himself a cigarette and lit it and then he said in an even voice, "Lady, a man is divided into two parts, body and spirit."

The old woman clamped her gums together.

"A body and a spirit," he repeated. "The body, lady, is like a house: it don't go anywhere; but the spirit, lady, is like a automobile: always on the move, always . . ."

"Listen, Mr. Shiftlet," she said, "my well never goes dry and my house is always warm in the winter and there's no mortgage on a thing about this place. You can go to the courthouse and see for yourself. And yonder under that shed is a fine automobile." She laid the bait carefully. "You can have it painted by Saturday. I'll pay for the paint."

In the darkness, Mr. Shiftlet's smile stretched like a weary snake waking up by a fire. After a second he recalled himself and said, "I'm only saying a man's spirit means more to him than anything else. I would have to take my wife off for the weekend without no regards at all for cost. I got to follow where my spirit says to go."

"I'll give you fifteen dollars for a weekend trip," the old woman said in a crabbed voice. "That's the best I can do."

"That wouldn't hardly pay for more than the gas and the hotel," he said. "It wouldn't feed her."

"Seventeen-fifty," the old woman said. "That's all I got so it isn't any use you trying to milk me. You can take a lunch."

Mr. Shiftlet was deeply hurt by the word "milk." He didn't doubt that she had more money sewed up in her mattress but he had already told her he was not interested in her money. "I'll make that do," he said and rose and walked off without treating with her further.

On Saturday the three of them drove into town in the car that the paint had barely dried on and Mr. Shiftlet and Lucynell were married in the Ordinary's office while the old woman witnessed. As they came out of the courthouse, Mr. Shiftlet began twisting his neck in his collar. He looked morose and bitter as if he had been insulted while someone held him. "That didn't satisfy me none," he said. "That was just something a woman in an office did, nothing but paper work and blood tests. What do they know about my blood? If they was to take my heart and cut it out," he said, "they wouldn't know a thing about me. It didn't satisfy me at all."

"It satisfied the law," the old woman said sharply.

"The law," Mr. Shiftlet said and spit. "It's the law that don't satisfy me."

He had painted the car dark green with a yellow band around it just under the windows. The three of them climbed in the front seat and the old woman said, "Don't Lucynell look pretty? Looks like a baby doll." Lucynell was dressed up in a white dress that her mother had uprooted from a trunk and there was a Panama hat on her head with a bunch of red wooden cherries on the brim. Every now and then her placid expression was changed by a sly isolated little thought like a shoot of green in the desert. "You got a prize!" the old woman said.

Mr. Shiftlet didn't even look at her.

They drove back to the house to let the old woman off and pick up the lunch. When they were ready to leave, she stood staring in the window of the car, with her fingers clenched around the glass. Tears began to seep sideways out of her eyes and run along the dirty creases in her face. "I ain't ever been parted with her for two days before," she said.

Mr. Shiftlet started the motor.

"And I wouldn't let no man have her but you because I seen you would do right. Good-by, Sugarbaby," she said, clutching at the sleeve of the white dress. Lucynell looked straight at her and didn't seem to see her there at all. Mr. Shiftlet eased the car forward so that she had to move her hands.

The early afternoon was clear and open and surrounded by pale blue sky. Although the car would go only thirty miles an hour, Mr. Shiftlet imagined a terrific climb and dip and swerve that went entirely to his head so that he forgot his morning bitterness. He had always wanted an automobile but he had never been able to afford one before. He drove very fast because he wanted to make Mobile by nightfall.

Occasionally he stopped his thoughts long enough to look at Lucynell in the seat beside him. She had eaten the lunch as soon as they were out of the yard and now she was pulling the cherries off the hat one by one and throwing them out the window. He became depressed in spite of the car. He had driven about a hundred miles when he decided that she must be hungry again and at the next small town they came to, he stopped in front of an aluminum-painted eating place called The Hot Spot and took her in and ordered her a plate of ham and grits. The ride had made her sleepy and as soon as she got up on the stool, she rested her head on the counter and shut her eyes. There was no one in The Hot Spot but Mr. Shiftlet and the boy behind the counter, a pale youth with a greasy rag hung over his shoulder. Before he could dish up the food, she was snoring gently.

"Give it to her when she wakes up," Mr. Shiftlet said. "I'll pay for it now."

The boy bent over her and stared at the long pink-gold hair and the half-shut sleeping eyes. Then he looked up and stared at Mr. Shiftlet. "She looks like an angel of Gawd," he murmured.

"Hitchhiker," Mr. Shiftlet explained. "I can't wait. I got to make Tuscaloosa."

The boy bent over again and very carefully touched his finger to a strand of the golden hair and Mr. Shiftlet left.

He was more depressed than ever as he drove on by himself. The late afternoon had grown hot and sultry and the country had flattened out. Deep in the sky a storm was preparing very slowly and without thunder as if it meant to drain every drop of air from the earth before it broke. There were times when Mr. Shiftlet preferred not to be alone. He felt too that a man with a car had a responsibility to others and he kept his eye out for a hitchhiker. Occasionally he saw a sign that warned: "Drive carefully. The life you save may be your own."

The narrow road dropped off on either side into dry fields and here and there a shack or a filling station stood in a clearing. The sun began to set directly in front of the automobile. It was a reddening ball that through his windshield was slightly flat on the bottom and top. He saw a boy in overalls and a gray hat standing on the edge of the road and he slowed the car down and stopped in front of him. The boy didn't have his hand raised to thumb the ride, he was only standing there, but he had a small cardboard suitcase and his hat was set on his head in a way to indicate that he had left somewhere for good. "Son," Mr. Shiftlet said. "I see you want a ride."

The boy didn't say he did or he didn't but he opened the door of the car and got in, and Mr. Shiftlet started driving again. The child held the suitcase on his lap and folded his arms on top of it. He turned his head and looked out the window away from Mr. Shiftlet. Mr. Shiftlet felt oppressed. "Son," he said after a minute, "I got the best old mother in the world so I reckon you only got the second best."

The boy gave him a quick dark glance and then turned his face back out the window.

"It's nothing so sweet," Mr. Shiftlet continued, "as a boy's mother. She taught him his first prayers at her knee, she give him love when no other would, she told him what was right and what wasn't, and she seen that he done the right thing. Son," he said. "I never rued a day in my life like the one I rued when I left that old mother of mine."

The boy shifted in his seat but he didn't look at Mr. Shiftlet. He unfolded his arms and put one hand on the door handle.

"My mother was a angel of Gawd," Mr. Shiftlet said in a very strained voice. "He took her from heaven and giver to me and I left her." His eyes were instantly clouded over with a mist of tears. The car was barely moving.

The boy turned angrily in the seat. "You go to the devil!" he cried. "My old woman is a flea bag and yours is a stinking polecat!" and with that he flung the door open and jumped out with his suitcase into the ditch.

Mr. Shiftlet was so shocked that for about a hundred feet he drove along slowly with the door still open. A cloud, the exact color of the boy's hat and shaped like a turnip, had descended over the sun, and another, worse looking, crouched behind the car. Mr. Shiftlet felt that the rottenness of the world was about to engulf him. He raised his arm and let it fall again to his breast. "Oh Lord!" he prayed. "Break forth and wash the slime from this earth!"

The turnip continued slowly to descend. After a few minutes there was a guffawing peal of thunder from behind and fantastic raindrops, like tin-can tops, crashed over the rear of Mr. Shiftlet's car. Very quickly he stepped on the gas and with his stump sticking out the window he raced the galloping shower into Mobile.

QUESTIONS

1 The names Crater and Shiftlet obviously have symbolic significance. How many different meanings do they evoke?
2 What descriptive details give insights to the complex motivations that lead Mrs. Crater to "sacrifice" Lucynell?
3 How do Tom T. Shiftlet's high-sounding preachments and his advice to the young hitchhiker complicate an even assessment of his character?
4 To what degree does the story illustrate the warning that "the life you save may be your own"?

TOPICS FOR COMPOSITION

1 This story deals with the individual's responsibility to other human beings. Write an essay in which you argue the degree to which one's actions and desires are restrained by a sense of responsibility to others.
2 Write an essay in which you set forth and document from the story the relationship between descriptive detail, symbol, and characterization.

Roth's "The Conversion of the Jews" clearly spans multiple levels of meaning, ranging from an examination of youthful inquisitiveness to a plea for religious and social ecumenicity. Several aspects of the story help in understanding Roth's movement through his levels of meaning. Note the following:

1 The language used by Ozzie and Itzie in their opening "theological" discussion
2 The contrast presented between Ozzie's inquiring mind and the learned responses of his mother, the Rabbi, and the custodian
3 Ozzie's reaction to the power of his individual protest
4 The impact of unexpected action on the mass mind

THE CONVERSION OF THE JEWS

Philip Roth

"You're a real one for opening your mouth in the first place," Itzie said. "What do you open your mouth all the time for?"

"I didn't bring it up, Itz, I didn't," Ozzie said.

"What do you care about Jesus Christ for anyway?"

"I didn't bring up Jesus Christ. He did. I didn't even know what he was talking about. Jesus is historical, he kept saying. Jesus is historical." Ozzie mimicked the monumental voice of Rabbi Binder.

"Jesus was a person that lived like you and me," Ozzie continued. "That's what Binder said—"

"Yeah? . . . So what! What do I give two cents whether he lived or not. And what do you gotta open your mouth!" Itzie Lieberman favored closed-mouthedness, especially when it came to Ozzie Freedman's questions. Mrs. Freedman had to see Rabbi Binder twice before about Ozzie's questions and this Wednesday at four-thirty would be the third time. Itzie preferred to keep *his* mother in the kitchen; he settled for behind-the-back subtleties such as gestures, faces, snarls and other less delicate barnyard noises.

"He was a real person, Jesus, but he wasn't like God, and we don't believe he is God." Slowly, Ozzie was explaining Rabbi Binder's position to Itzie, who had been absent from Hebrew School the previous afternoon.

"The Catholics," Itzie said helpfully, "they believe in Jesus Christ, that he's God." Itzie Lieberman used "the Catholics" in its broadest sense—to include the Protestants.

Ozzie received Itzie's remark with a tiny head bob, as though it were a footnote, and went on. "His mother was Mary, and his father probably was Joseph," Ozzie said. "But the New Testament says his real father was God."

"His *real* father?"

"Yeah," Ozzie said, "that's the big thing, his father's supposed to be God."

"Bull."

"That's what Rabbi Binder says, that it's impossible—"

"Sure it's impossible. That stuff's all bull. To have a baby you gotta get laid," Itzie theologized. "Mary hadda get laid."

"That's what Binder says: 'The only way a woman can have a baby is to have intercourse with a man.'"

"He said *that,* Ozz?" For a moment it appeared that Itzie had put the theological question aside. "He said that, intercourse?" A little curled smile shaped itself in the lower half of Itzie's face like a pink mustache. "What you guys do, Ozz, you laugh or something?"

"I raised my hand."

"Yeah? Whatja say?"

"That's when I asked the question."

Itzie's face lit up. "Whatja ask about—intercourse?"

"No, I asked the question about God, how if He could create the heaven and earth in six days, and make all the animals and the fish and the light in six days—the light especially, that's what always gets me, that He could make the light. Making fish and animals, that's pretty good—"

"That's damn good." Itzie's appreciation was honest but unimaginative: it was as though God had just pitched a one-hitter.

"But making light . . . I mean when you think about it, it's really something," Ozzie said. "Anyway, I asked Binder if He could make all that in six days, and He could *pick* the six days he wanted right out of nowhere, why couldn't He let a woman have a baby without having intercourse."

"You said intercourse, Ozz, to Binder?"

"Yeah."

"Right in class?"

"Yeah."

Itzie smacked the side of his head.

"I mean, no kidding around," Ozzie said, "that'd really be nothing. After all that other stuff, that'd practically be nothing."

Itzie considered a moment. "What'd Binder say?"

"He started all over again explaining how Jesus was historical and how he lived like you and me but he wasn't God. So I said I under*stood* that. What I wanted to know was different."

What Ozzie wanted to know was always different. The first time he had wanted to know how Rabbi Binder could call the Jews "The Chosen People" if the Declaration of Independence claimed all men to be created equal. Rabbi Binder tried to distinguish for him between political equality and spiritual legitimacy, but what Ozzie wanted to know, he insisted vehemently, was different. That was the first time his mother had to come.

Then there was the plane crash. Fifty-eight people had been killed in a plane crash at La Guardia. In studying a casualty list in the newspaper his mother had discovered among the list of those dead eight Jewish names (his grandmother had nine but she counted Miller as a Jewish name); because of the eight she said the plane crash was "a tragedy." During free-discussion time on Wednesday Ozzie had brought to Rabbi Binder's attention this matter of "some of his relations" always picking out the Jewish names. Rabbi Binder had begun to explain cultural unity and some other things when Ozzie stood up at his seat and said that what he wanted to know was different. Rabbi Binder insisted that he sit down and it was then that Ozzie shouted that he wished all fifty-eight were Jews. That was the second time his mother came.

"And he kept explaining about Jesus being historical, and so I kept asking him. No kidding, Itz, he was trying to make me look stupid."

"So what he finally do?"

"Finally he starts screaming that I was deliberately simple-minded and a wise guy, and that my mother had to come, and this was the last time. And that I'd never get bar-mitzvahed if he could help it. Then, Itz, then he starts talking in the voice like a statue, real slow and deep, and he says that I better think over what I said about the Lord. He told me to go to his office and think it over." Ozzie leaned his body toward Itzie. "Itz, I thought it over for a solid hour, and now I'm convinced God could do it."

Ozzie had planned to confess his latest transgression to his mother as soon as she came home from work. But it was a Friday night in November and already dark, and when Mrs. Freedman came through the door she tossed off her coat, kissed Ozzie quickly on the face, and went to the kitchen table to light the three yellow candles, two for the Sabbath and one for Ozzie's father.

When his mother lit the candles she would move her two arms slowly towards her, dragging them through the air, as though persuading people whose minds were half made up. And her eyes would get glassy with tears. Even when his father was alive Ozzie remembered that her eyes had gotten glassy, so it didn't have anything to do with his dying. It had something to do with lighting the candles.

As she touched the flaming match to the unlit wick of a Sabbath candle, the phone rang, and Ozzie, standing only a foot from it, plucked off the receiver and held it muffled to his chest. When his mother lit candles Ozzie felt there should be no noise; even breathing, if you could manage it, should be softened. Ozzie pressed the phone to his breast and watched his mother dragging whatever she was dragging, and he felt his own eyes get glassy. His mother was a round, tired, gray-haired penguin of a woman whose gray skin had begun to feel the tug of gravity and the weight of her own history. Even when she was dressed up she didn't look like a chosen person. But when she lit candles she looked like something better; like a woman who knew momentarily that God could do anything.

After a few mysterious minutes she was finished. Ozzie hung up the phone and walked to the kitchen table where she was beginning to lay the two places for the four-course Sabbath meal. He told her that she would have to see Rabbi Binder next Wednesday at four-thirty, and then he told her why. For the first time in their life together she hit Ozzie across the face with her hand.

All through the chopped liver and chicken soup part of the dinner Ozzie cried; he didn't have any appetite for the rest.

On Wednesday, in the largest of the three basement classrooms of the synagogue, Rabbi Marvin Binder, a tall, handsome, broad-shouldered man of thirty with thick strong-fibered black hair, removed his watch from his pocket and saw that it was four o'clock. At the rear of the room, Yakov Blotnik, the seventy-one-year-old custodian, slowly polished the large window, mumbling to himself, unaware that it was four o'clock or six o'clock, Monday or Wednesday. To most of the students Yakov Blotnik's mumbling along with his brown curly beard, scythe nose, and two heel-trailing black cats, made of him an object of wonder, a foreigner, a relic, towards whom they were alternately fearful and disrespectful. To Ozzie the mumbling had always seemed a monotonous, curious prayer; what made it curious was that old Blotnik had been mumbling so steadily for so many years, Ozzie suspected he had memorized the prayers and forgotten all about God.

"It is now free-discussion time," Rabbi Binder said. "Feel free to talk about any Jewish matter at all—religion, family, politics, sports—"

There was silence. It was a gusty, clouded November afternoon and it did not seem as though there ever was or could be a thing called baseball. So nobody this week said a word about that hero from the past, Hank Greenberg—which limited free discussion considerably.

And the soul-battering Ozzie Freedman had just received from Rabbi Binder had imposed its limitation. When it was Ozzie's turn to read aloud from the Hebrew book the rabbi had asked him petulantly why he didn't read more rapidly. He was showing no progress. Ozzie said he could read faster but that if he did he was sure not to understand what he was reading. Nevertheless, at the rabbi's repeated suggestion Ozzie tried, and showed a great talent, but in the midst of a long passage he stopped short and said he didn't understand a word he was reading, and started in again at a drag-footed pace. Then came the soul-battering.

Consequently when free-discussion time rolled around none of the students felt too free. The rabbi's invitation was answered only by the mumbling of feeble old Blotnik.

"Isn't there anything at all you would like to discuss?" Rabbi Binder asked again, looking at his watch. "No questions or comments?"

There was a small grumble from the third row. The rabbi requested that Ozzie rise and give the rest of the class the advantage of his thought.

Ozzie rose. "I forget it now," he said, and sat down in his place.

Rabbi Binder advanced a seat towards Ozzie and poised himself on the edge of the desk. It was Itzie's desk and the rabbi's frame only a dagger's-length away from his face snapped him to sitting attention.

"Stand up again, Oscar," Rabbi Binder said calmly, "and try to assemble your thoughts."

Ozzie stood up. All his classmates turned in their seats and watched as he gave an unconvincing scratch to his forehead.

"I can't assemble any," he announced, and plunked himself down.

"Stand up!" Rabbi Binder advanced from Itzie's desk to the one directly in front of Ozzie; when the rabbinical back was turned Itzie gave it five-fingers off the tip of his nose, causing a small titter in the room. Rabbi Binder was too absorbed in squelching Ozzie's nonsense once and for all to bother with titters. "Stand up, Oscar. What's your question about?"

Ozzie pulled a word out of the air. It was the handiest word. "Religion."

"Oh, now you remember?"

"Yes."

"What is it?"

Trapped, Ozzie blurted the first thing that came to him. "Why can't He make anything He wants to make!"

As Rabbi Binder prepared an answer, a final answer, Itzie, ten feet behind him, raised one finger on his left hand, gestured it meaningfully towards the rabbi's back, and brought the house down.

Binder twisted quickly to see what had happened and in the midst of the commotion Ozzie shouted into the rabbi's back what he couldn't have shouted to his face. It was a loud, toneless sound that had the timbre of something stored inside for about six days.

"You don't know! You don't know anything about God!"

The rabbi spun back towards Ozzie. "What?"

"You don't know—you don't—"

"Apologize, Oscar, apologize!" It was a threat.

"You don't—"

Rabbi Binder's hand flicked out at Ozzie's cheek. Perhaps it had only been meant to clamp the boy's mouth shut, but Ozzie ducked and the palm caught him squarely on the nose.

The blood came in a short, red spurt on to Ozzie's shirt front.

The next moment was all confusion. Ozzie screamed, "You bastard, you bastard!" and broke for the classroom door. Rabbi Binder lurched a step backwards, as though his own blood had started flowing violently in the opposite direction, then gave a clumsy lurch forward and bolted out the door after Ozzie. The class followed after the rabbi's huge blue-suited back, and before old Blotnik could turn from his window, the room was empty and everyone was headed full speed up the three flights leading to the roof.

If one should compare the light of day to the life of man: sunrise to birth; sunset—the dropping down over the edge—to death; then as Ozzie Freedman wiggled through the trapdoor of the synagogue roof, his feet kicking backwards bronco-style at Rabbi Binder's outstretched arms—at that moment the day was fifty years old. As a rule, fifty or fifty-five reflects accurately the age of late afternoons in November, for it is in that month, during those hours, that one's awareness of light seems no longer a matter of seeing, but of hearing: light begins clicking away. In fact, as Ozzie locked shut the trapdoor in the rabbi's face, the sharp click of the bolt into the lock might momentarily have been mistaken for the sound of the heavier gray that had just throbbed through the sky.

With all his weight Ozzie kneeled on the locked door; any instant he was certain that Rabbi Binder's shoulder would fling it open, splintering the wood into shrapnel and catapulting his body into the sky. But the door did not move and below him he heard only the rumble of feet, first loud then dim, like thunder rolling away.

A question shot through his brain. "Can this be *me*?" For a thirteen-year-old who had just labeled his religious leader a bastard, twice, it was not an improper question. Louder and louder the question came to him—"Is it me? Is it me?"—until he discovered himself no longer kneeling, but racing crazily toward the edge of the roof, his eyes crying, his throat screaming, and his arms flying everywhichway as though not his own.

"Is it me? Is it me Me Me Me Me! It has to be me—but is it!"

It is the question a thief must ask himself the night he jimmies open his first window, and it is said to be the question with which bridegrooms quiz themselves before the altar.

In the few wild seconds it took Ozzie's body to propel him to the edge of the roof, his self-examination began to grow fuzzy. Gazing down at the street he became confused as to the problem beneath the question: was it, is-it-me-who-called-Binder-a-Bastard? or, is-it-me-prancing-around-on-the-roof? However, the scene below settled all, for there is an instant in any action when whether it is you or somebody else is academic. The thief crams the money in his pockets and scoots out the window. The bridegroom signs the hotel register for two. And the boy on the roof finds a streetful of people gaping at him, necks stretched backwards, faces up, as though he were the ceiling of the Hayden Planetarium. Suddenly you know it's you.

"Oscar! Oscar Freedman!" A voice rose from the center of the crowd, a voice that, could it have been seen, would have looked like the writing on a scroll. "Oscar Freedman, get down from there. Immediately!" Rabbi Binder was pointing one arm stiffly up at him; and at the end of that arm, one finger aimed menacingly. It was the attitude of a dictator, but one—the eyes confessed all—whose personal valet had spit neatly in his face.

Ozzie didn't answer. Only for a blink's length did he look towards Rabbi Binder. Instead his eyes began to fit together the world beneath him, to sort out people from places, friends from enemies, participants from spectators. In little jagged starlike clusters his friends stood around Rabbi Binder, who was still pointing. The topmost point on a star compounded not of angels but of five adolescent boys was Itzie. What a world it was, with those stars below, Rabbi Binder below . . . Ozzie, who a moment earlier hadn't been able to control his own body, started to feel the meaning of the word control: he felt Peace and he felt Power.

"Oscar Freedman, I'll give you three to come down."

Few dictators give their subjects three to do anything; but, as always, Rabbi Binder only looked dictatorial.

"Are you ready, Oscar?"

Ozzie nodded his head yes, although he had no intention in the world—the lower one or the celestial one he'd just entered—of coming down even if Rabbi Binder should give him a million.

"All right then," said Rabbi Binder. He ran a hand through his black Samson hair as though it were the gesture prescribed for uttering the first digit. Then, with his other hand cutting a circle out of the small piece of sky around him, he spoke. "One!"

There was no thunder. On the contrary, at that moment, as though "one" was the cue for which he had been waiting, the world's least thunderous person appeared on the synagogue steps. He did not so much come out the synagogue door as lean out, onto the darkening air. He clutched at the doorknob with one hand and looked up at the roof.

"Oy!"

Yakov Blotnik's old mind hobbled slowly, as if on crutches, and though he couldn't decide precisely what the boy was doing on the roof, he knew it wasn't good—that is, it wasn't-good-for-the-Jews. For Yakov Blotnik life had fractionated itself simply: things were either good-for-the-Jews or no-good-for-the-Jews.

He smacked his free hand to his in-sucked cheek, gently. "Oy, Gut!" And then quickly as he was able, he jacked down his head and surveyed the street. There was Rabbi Binder (like a man at an auction with only three dollars in his pocket, he had just delivered a shaky "Two!"); there were the students, and that was all. So far it-wasn't-so-bad-for-the-Jews. But the boy had to come down immediately, before anybody saw. The problem: how to get the boy off the roof?

Anybody who has ever had a cat on the roof knows how to get him down. You call the fire department. Or first you call the operator and you ask her for the fire department. And the next thing there is great jamming of brakes and clanging of bells and shouting of instructions. And then the cat is off the roof. You do the same thing to get a boy off the roof.

That is, you do the same thing if you are Yakov Blotnik and you once had a cat on the roof.

When the engines, all four of them, arrived, Rabbi Binder had four times given Ozzie the count of three. The big hook-and-ladder swung around the corner and one of the firemen leaped from it, plunging head-long towards the yellow fire hydrant in front of the synagogue. With a huge wrench he began to unscrew the top nozzle. Rabbi Binder raced over to him and pulled at his shoulder.

"There's no fire . . ."

The fireman mumbled back over his shoulder and, heatedly, continued working at the nozzle.

"But there's no fire, there's no fire . . ." Binder shouted. When the fireman mumbled again, the rabbi grasped his face with both hands and pointed it up at the roof.

To Ozzie it looked as though Rabbi Binder was trying to tug the fireman's head out of his body, like a cork from a bottle. He had to giggle at the picture they made: it was a family portrait—rabbi in black skullcap, fireman in red fire hat, and the little yellow hydrant squatting beside like a kid brother, bareheaded. From the edge of the roof Ozzie waved at the portrait, a one-handed, flapping, mocking wave; in doing it his right foot slipped from under him. Rabbi Binder covered his eyes with his hands.

Firemen work fast. Before Ozzie had even regained his balance, a big, round, yellowed net was being held on the synagogue lawn. The firemen who held it looked up at Ozzie with stern, feelingless faces.

One of the firemen turned his head towards Rabbi Binder. "What, is the kid nuts or something?"

Rabbi Binder unpeeled his hands from his eyes, slowly, painfully, as if they were tape. Then he checked: nothing on the sidewalk, no dents in the net.

"Is he gonna jump, or what?" the fireman shouted.

In a voice not at all like a statue, Rabbi Binder finally answered. "Yes, Yes, I think so . . . He's been threatening to . . ."

Threatening to? Why, the reason he was on the roof, Ozzie remembered, was to get away; he hadn't even thought about jumping. He had just run to get away, and the truth was that he hadn't really headed for the roof as much as he'd been chased there.

"What's his name, the kid?"

"Freedman," Rabbi Binder answered. "Oscar Freedman."

The fireman looked up at Ozzie. "What is it with you, Oscar? You gonna jump, or what?"

Ozzie did not answer. Frankly, the question had just arisen.

"Look, Oscar, if you're gonna jump, jump—and if you're not gonna jump, don't jump. But don't waste our time, willya?"

Ozzie looked at the fireman and then at Rabbi Binder. He wanted to see Rabbi Binder cover his eyes one more time.

"I'm going to jump."

And then he scampered around the edge of the roof to the corner, where there was no net below, and he flapped his arms at his sides, swishing the air and smacking his palms to his trousers on the downbeat. He began screaming like some kind of engine, "Wheeeee . . . wheeeee," and leaning way out over the edge with the upper half of his body. The firemen whipped around to cover the ground with the net. Rabbi Binder mumbled a few words to Somebody and covered his eyes. Everything happened quickly, jerkily, as in a silent movie. The crowd, which had arrived with the fire engines, gave out a long, Fourth-of-July fireworks oooh-aahhh. In the excitement no one had paid the crowd much heed, except, of course, Yakov Blotnik, who swung from the doorknob counting heads. "Fier und tsvantsik . . . finf und tsvantsik . . . Oy, Gut!" It wasn't like this with the cat.

Rabbi Binder peeked through his fingers, checked the sidewalk and net. Empty. But there was Ozzie racing to the other corner. The firemen raced with him but were unable to keep up. Whenever Oscar wanted to he might jump and splatter himself upon the sidewalk, and by the time the firemen scooted to the spot all they could do with their net would be to cover the mess:

"Wheeeee . . . wheeeee . . ."

"Hey, Oscar," the winded fireman yelled, "What the hell is this, a game or something?"

"Wheeeee . . . wheeeee . . ."

"Hey, Oscar—"

But he was off now to the other corner, flapping his wings fiercely. Rabbi Binder couldn't take it any longer—the fire engines from nowhere, the screaming suicidal boy, the net. He fell to his knees, exhausted, and with his hands curled together in front of his chest like a little dome, he pleaded, "Oscar, stop it, Oscar. Don't jump, Oscar. Please come down . . . Please don't jump."

And further back in the crowd a single voice, a single young voice, shouted a lone word to the boy on the roof.

"Jump!"

It was Itzie. Ozzie momentarily stopped flapping.

"Go ahead, Ozz—jump!" Itzie broke off his point of the star and courageously, with the inspiration not of a wise-guy but of a disciple, stood alone. "Jump, Ozz, jump!"

Still on his knees, his hands still curled, Rabbi Binder twisted his body back. He looked at Itzie, then, agonizingly, back to Ozzie.

"Oscar, Don't jump! Please, Don't Jump . . . please please . . ."

"Jump!" This time it wasn't Itzie but another point of the star. By the time Mrs. Freedman arrived to keep her four-thirty appointment with Rabbi Binder, the whole little upside down heaven was shouting and pleading for Ozzie to jump, and Rabbi Binder no longer was pleading with him not to jump, but was crying into the dome of his hands.

Understandably Mrs. Freedman couldn't figure out what her son was doing on the roof. So she asked.

"Ozzie, my Ozzie, what are you doing? My Ozzie, what is it?"

Ozzie stopped wheeeeeing and slowed his arms down to a cruising flap, the kind birds use in soft winds, but he did not answer. He stood against the low, clouded, darkening sky—light clicked down swiftly now, as on a small gear—flapping softly and gazing down at the small bundle of a woman who was his mother.

"What are you doing, Ozzie?" She turned towards the kneeling Rabbi Binder and rushed so close that only a paper-thickness of dusk lay between her stomach and his shoulders.

"What is my baby doing?"

Rabbi Binder gaped up at her but he too was mute. All that moved was the dome of his hands; it shook back and forth like a weak pulse.

"Rabbi, get him down! He'll kill himself. Get him down, my only baby . . ."

"I can't," Rabbi Binder said, "I can't . . ." and he turned his handsome head towards the crowd of boys behind him. "It's them. Listen to them."

And for the first time Mrs. Freedman saw the crowd of boys, and she heard what they were yelling.

"He's doing it for them. He won't listen to me. It's them." Rabbi Binder spoke like one in a trance.

"For them?"

"Yes."

"Why for them?"

"They want him to . . ."

Mrs. Freedman raised her two arms upward as though she were conducting the sky. "For them he's doing it!" And then in a gesture older than pyramids, older than prophets and floods, her arms came slapping down to her sides. "A martyr I have. Look!" She tilted her head to the roof. Ozzie was still flapping softly. "My martyr."

"Oscar, come down, *please*," Rabbi Binder groaned.

In a startlingly even voice Mrs. Freedman called to the boy on the roof. "Ozzie, come down, Ozzie. Don't be a martyr, my baby."

As though it were a litany, Rabbi Binder repeated her words. "Don't be a martyr, my baby. Don't be a martyr."

"Gawhead, Ozz—*be* a Martin!" It was Itzie. "Be a Martin, be a Martin," and all the voices joined in singing for Martindom, whatever *it* was. "Be a Martin, be a Martin . . ."

Somehow when you're on a roof the darker it gets the less you can hear. All Ozzie knew was that two groups wanted two new things: his friends were spirited and musical about what they wanted; his mother and the rabbi were even-toned, chanting, about what they didn't want. The rabbi's voice was without tears now and so was his mother's.

The big net stared up at Ozzie like a sightless eye. The big, clouded sky pushed down. From beneath it looked like a gray corrugated board. Suddenly, looking up into that unsympathetic sky, Ozzie realized all the strangeness of what these people, his friends, were asking: they wanted him to jump, to kill himself; they were singing about it now—it made them that happy. And there was an even greater strangeness: Rabbi Binder was on his knees, trembling. If there was a question to be asked now it was not "Is it me?" but rather "Is it us? . . . Is it us?"

Being on the roof, it turned out, was a serious thing. If he jumped would the singing become dancing? Would it? What would jumping stop? Yearningly, Ozzie wished he could rip open the sky, plunge his hands through, and pull out the sun; and on the sun, like a coin, would be stamped <u>Jump</u> or <u>Don't Jump.</u>

Ozzie's knees rocked and sagged a little under him as though they were setting him for a dive. His arms tightened, stiffened, froze, from shoulders to fingernails. He felt as if each part of his body were going to vote as to whether he should kill himself or not—and each part as though it were independent of *him.*

The light took an unexpected click down and the new darkness, like a gag, hushed the friends singing for this and the mother and rabbi chanting for that.

Ozzie stopped counting votes, and in a curiously high voice, like one who wasn't prepared for speech, he spoke.

"Mamma?"

"Yes, Oscar."

"Mamma, get down on your knees, like Rabbi Binder."

"Oscar—"

"Get down on your knees," he said, "or I'll jump."

Ozzie heard a whimper, then a quick rustling, and when he looked down where his mother had stood he saw the top of a head and beneath that a circle of dress. She was kneeling beside Rabbi Binder.

He spoke again. "Everybody kneel." There was the sound of everybody kneeling.

Ozzie looked around. With one hand he pointed towards the synagogue entrance. "Make *him* kneel."

There was a noise, not of kneeling, but of body-and-cloth stretching. Ozzie could hear Rabbi Binder saying in a gruff whisper, ". . . or he'll *kill* himself," and when next he looked there was Yakov Blotnik off the doorknob and for the first time in his life upon his knees in the Gentile posture of prayer.

As for the firemen—it is not as difficult as one might imagine to hold a net taut while you are kneeling.

Ozzie looked around again; and then he called to Rabbi Binder.

"Rabbi?"

"Yes, Oscar."

"Rabbi Binder, do you believe in God."

"Yes."

"Do you believe God can do Anything?" Ozzie leaned his head out into the darkness. "Anything?"

"Oscar, I think—"

"Tell me you believe God can do Anything."

There was a second's hesitation. Then: "God can do Anything."

"Tell me you believe God can make a child without intercourse."

"He can."

"Tell me!"

"God," Rabbi Binder admitted, "can make a child without intercourse."

"Mamma, you tell me."

"God can make a child without intercourse," his mother said.

"Make *him* tell me." There was no doubt who *him* was.

In a few moments Ozzie heard an old comical voice say something to the increasing darkness about God.

Next, Ozzie made everybody say it. And then he made them all say they believed in Jesus Christ—first one at a time, then all together.

When the catechizing was through it was the beginning of evening. From the street it sounded as if the boy on the roof might have sighed.

"Ozzie?" A woman's voice dared to speak. "You'll come down now?"

There was no answer, but the woman waited, and when a voice finally did speak it was thin and crying, and exhausted as that of an old man who has just finished pulling the bells.

"Mamma, don't you see—you shouldn't hit me. He shouldn't hit me. You shouldn't hit me about God, Mamma. You should never hit anybody about God—"

"Ozzie, please come down now."

"Promise me, promise me you'll never hit anybody about God."

He had asked only his mother, but for some reason everyone kneeling in the street promised he would never hit anybody about God.

Once again there was silence.

"I can come down now, Mamma," the boy on the roof finally said. He turned his head both ways as though checking the traffic lights. "Now I can come down . . ."

And he did, right into the center of the yellow net that glowed in the evening's edge like an overgrown halo.

QUESTIONS

1 Part of the design of this story arises from the juxtaposition of the characters. Each of the major characters provides some complementary attitude to each other character. Consider Ozzie, Itzie, Mrs. Freedman, Rabbi Binder, and Yakov Blotnik. What attitude toward religion does each illustrate? How does that attitude react with each other attitude?

2 What point is Roth making about the system of religion? Why is Rabbi Binder's position indicative of the system?

3 Why does Itzie call to Ozzie to jump from the roof? How does Itzie's action and the support it receives reveal the basic dichotomy in the story?

4 What specific statements in the story emphasize Roth's plea for religious ecumenicity?

TOPICS FOR COMPOSITION

1 Sensitivity and inquisitiveness beyond his years are marks of Ozzie's character. Write an essay showing how Roth manages to maintain the balance between Ozzie's youth and the maturity of his question.

2 This story exemplifies the power of action by a minority. Write an essay illustrating the power of minority action as it is evidenced in America.

3 Roth's story poses the need for greater understanding among religions. Investigate a religion with which you have little familiarity. Write an essay explaining how such an investigation has benefited you.

DRAMA

In the background of Antigone's story, of course, is the tragic tale of her father, King Oedipus. After the death of Oedipus, Antigone's brothers, Eteocles and Polynices, contended for the throne of Thebes and were killed in the ensuing war. Now Creon is king and thus sits in judgment upon Antigone. Anouilh has preserved the classical essence of Antigone's ordeal, but he insists upon its timelessness not only by the touches of modernity he gives to details (note such anachronisms as coffee, picture postcards, rouge and perfume, cigarettes, evening clothes, nightclubs) but more importantly by his preoccupation with the meaning of protest. Like her father, Antigone displays a pride that is gradually tempered by insight. As the one-man Chorus (who is somewhat like the Stage Manager in Thornton Wilder's "Pullman Car Hiawatha" in Part Five of this book) suggests, the tragic experience allows only a hero or heroine capable of such an overwhelming ordeal to move through actions and ultimate, triumphant articulation of ideas that seemingly transcend human abilities and understanding. But in that complex of act and speech, Antigone does come to understand her destiny and to learn what her ordeal really means, although such knowledge is not, from the viewpoint of Creon or the world, practical. The lengthy dialogue between Creon and Antigone is a kind of debate between the body and the soul, in which Creon, the voice of reason and practicality, almost persuades Antigone to choose what the world calls "happiness" rather than the seemingly morbid path of commitment, protest, and death. Other voices and attitudes amplify Creon's position: the Nurse sees life in terms of "duty" and protective affection; Eurydice knits sweaters; the Guards think of promotions, rank, salary, and an occasional spree; and even Haemon presumably would be unable, in time, to sustain the ideality of his youthful ardor. As the Chorus promises, Antigone alone "is going to be able to be herself."

1 Keep in mind that Anouilh's play is to be presented in modern dress.
2 Despite the simplicity of plot and somewhat stylized setting and action, the complex issue of the meaning of life dominates virtually all the dialogue.
3 Even Antigone must admit that no single detail of life impels her to choose death; rather, it is the totality of what passes for life which from childhood has gradually made her the "outsider" and thus the doomed.

ANTIGONE

A Tragedy

Jean Anouilh

Translated by Lewis Galantière

CHARACTERS

CHORUS	FIRST GUARD (JONAS)
ANTIGONE	SECOND GUARD (A CORPORAL)
NURSE	THIRD GUARD
ISMENE	MESSENGER
HAEMON	PAGE
CREON	EURYDICE

ANTIGONE, *her hands clasped round her knees, sits on the top step. The* THREE GUARDS *sit on the steps, in a small group, playing cards. The* CHORUS *stands on the top step.* EURYDICE *sits on the top step, just left of center, knitting. The* NURSE *sits on the second step, left of* EURYDICE. ISMENE *stands in front of arch, left, facing* HAEMON, *who stands left of her.* CREON *sits in the chair at right end of the table, his arm over the shoulder of his* PAGE, *who sits on the stool beside his chair. The* MESSENGER *is leaning against the downstage portal of the right arch.*

The curtain rises slowly; then the CHORUS *turns and moves downstage.*

CHORUS   Well, here we are.

These people are about to act out for you the story of Antigone.

That thin little creature sitting by herself, staring straight ahead, seeing nothing, is Antigone. She is thinking. She is thinking that the instant I finish telling you who's who and what's what in this play, she will burst forth as the tense, sallow, willful girl whose family would never take her seriously and who is about to rise up alone against Creon, her uncle, the King.

Another thing that she is thinking is this: she is going to die. Antigone is young. She would much rather live than die. But there is no help for it. When your name is Antigone, there is only one part you can play; and she will have to play hers through to the end.

From the moment the curtain went up, she began to feel that inhuman forces were whirling her out of this world, snatching her away from her sister Ismene, whom you see smiling and chatting with that young man; from all of us who sit or stand here, looking at her, not in the least upset ourselves—for we are not doomed to die tonight.

CHORUS *turns and indicates* HAEMON.

The young man talking to Ismene—to the gay and beautiful Ismene—is Haemon. He is the King's son, Creon's son. Antigone and he are engaged to be married. You wouldn't have thought she was his type. He likes dancing, sports, competition; he likes women, too. Now look at Ismene again. She is certainly more beautiful than Antigone. She is the girl you'd think he'd go for. Well . . . There was a ball one night. Ismene wore a new evening frock. She was radiant. Haemon danced every dance with her. And yet, that same night, before the dance was over, suddenly he went in search of Antigone, found her sitting alone—like that, with her arms clasped round her knees—and asked her to marry him. We still don't know how it happened. It didn't seem to surprise Antigone in the least. She looked up at him out of those solemn eyes of hers, smiled sort of sadly and said "yes." That was all. The band struck up another dance. Ismene, surrounded by a group of young men, laughed out loud. And . . . well, here is Haemon expecting to marry Antigone. He won't, of course. He didn't know, when he asked her, that the earth wasn't meant to hold a husband of Antigone, and that this princely distinction was to earn him no more than the right to die sooner than he might otherwise have done.

CHORUS *turns toward* CREON.

That gray-haired, powerfully built man sitting lost in thought, with his little Page at his side, is Creon, the King. His face is lined. He is tired. He practices the difficult art of a leader of men. When he was younger, when Oedipus was King and Creon was no more than the King's brother-in-law, he was different. He loved music, bought rare manuscripts, was a kind of art patron. He would while away whole afternoons in the antique shops of this city of Thebes. But Oedipus died. Oedipus' sons died. Creon had to roll up his sleeves and take over the kingdom. Now and then, when he goes to bed weary with the day's work, he wonders whether this business of being a leader of men is worth the trouble. But when he wakes up, the problems are there to be solved; and like a conscientious workman, he does his job.

Creon has a wife, a Queen. Her name is Eurydice. There she sits, the old lady with the knitting, next to the Nurse who brought up the two girls. She will go on knitting all through the play, till the time comes for her to go to her room and die. She is a good woman, a worthy, loving soul. But she is no help to her husband. Creon has to face the music alone. Alone with his Page, who is too young to be of any help.

The others? Well, let's see.

He points toward the MESSENGER.

That pale young man leaning against the wall is the Messenger. Later on he will come running in to announce that Haemon is dead. He has a premonition of catastrophe. That's what he is brooding over. That's why he won't mingle with the others.

As for those three red-faced card players—they are the guards. One smells of garlic, another of beer; but they're not a bad lot. They have wives they are afraid of, kids who are afraid of them; they're bothered by the little day-to-day worries that beset us all. At the same time—they are policemen: eternally innocent, no matter what crimes are committed; eternally indifferent, for nothing that happens can matter to them. They are quite prepared to arrest anybody at all, including Creon himself, should the order be given by a new leader.

That's the lot. Now for the play.

Oedipus, who was the father of the two girls, Antigone and Ismene, had also two sons, Eteocles and Polynices. After Oedipus died, it was agreed that the two sons should share his throne, each to reign over Thebes in alternate years.

Gradually, the lights on the stage have been dimmed.

But when Eteocles, the elder son, had reigned a full year, and time had come for him to step down, he refused to yield up the throne to his younger brother. There was civil war. Polynices brought up allies—six foreign princes; and in the course of the war he and his foreigners were defeated, each in front of one of the seven gates of the city. The two brothers fought, and they killed one another in single combat just outside the city walls. Now Creon is King.

CHORUS *is leaning, at this point, against the left proscenium arch. By now the stage is dark, with only the cyclorama bathed in dark blue. A single spot lights up the face of* CHORUS.

Creon has issued a solemn edict that Eteocles, with whom he had sided, is to be buried with pomp and honours, and that Polynices is to be left to rot. The vultures and the dogs are to bloat themselves on his carcass. Nobody is to go into mourning for him. No gravestone is to be set up in his memory. And above all, any person who attempts to give him religious burial will himself be put to death.

While CHORUS *has been speaking the characters have gone out one by one.* CHORUS *disappears through the left arch.*

It is dawn, gray and ashen, in a house asleep. ANTIGONE *steals in from out-of-doors, through the arch, right. She is carrying her sandals in her hand. She pauses, looking off through the arch, taut, listening, then turns and moves across downstage. As she reaches the table, she sees the* NURSE *approaching through the arch, left. She runs quickly toward the exit. As she reaches the steps, the* NURSE *enters through arch and stands still when she sees* ANTIGONE.

NURSE   Where have you been?

ANTIGONE   Nowhere. It was beautiful. The whole world was gray when I went out. And now—you wouldn't recognize it. It's like a post card: all pink, and green, and yellow. You'll have to get up earlier, Nurse, if you want to see a world without color.

NURSE   It was still pitch black when I got up. I went to your room, for I thought you might have flung off your blanket in the night. You weren't there.

ANTIGONE   *(comes down the steps).*   The garden was lovely. It was still asleep. Have you ever thought how lovely a garden is when it is not yet thinking of men?

NURSE   You hadn't slept in your bed. I couldn't find you. I went to the back door. You'd left it open.

ANTIGONE   The fields were wet. They were waiting for something to happen. The whole world was breathless, waiting. I can't tell you what a roaring noise I seemed to make alone on the road. It bothered me that whatever was waiting wasn't waiting for me. I took off my sandals and slipped into a field. *(She moves down to the stool and sits.)*

NURSE *(kneels at* ANTIGONE's *feet to chafe them and put on the sandals).*   You'll do well to wash your feet before you go back to bed, Miss.

ANTIGONE   I'm not going back to bed.

NURSE   Don't be a fool! You get some sleep! And me, getting up to see if she hasn't flung off her blanket; and I find her bed cold and nobody in it!

ANTIGONE   Do you think that if a person got up every morning like this, it would be just as thrilling every morning to be the first girl out-of-doors?

NURSE *puts* ANTIGONE's *left foot down, lifts her other foot and chafes it.*

NURSE   Morning my grandmother! It was night. It still is. And now, my girl, you'll stop trying to squirm out of this and tell me what you were up to. Where've you been?

ANTIGONE   That's true. It was still night. There wasn't a soul out of doors but me, who thought that it was morning. Don't you think it's marvelous—to be the first person who is aware that it is morning?

NURSE   Oh, my little flibbertigibbet! Just can't imagine what I'm talking about, can she? Go on with you! I know that game. Where have you been, wicked girl?

ANTIGONE *(soberly)*   No. Not wicked.

NURSE   You went out to meet someone, didn't you? Deny it if you can.

ANTIGONE   Yes. I went out to meet someone.

NURSE   A lover?

ANTIGONE   Yes, Nurse. Yes, the poor dear. I have a lover.

NURSE *(stands up; bursting out)*   Ah, that's very nice now, isn't it? Such goings-on! You, the daughter of a king, running out to meet lovers. And we work our fingers to the bone for you, we slave to bring you up like young ladies! *(She sits on chair, right of table.)* You're all alike, all of you. Even you—who never used to stop to primp in front of a looking glass, or smear your mouth with rouge, or dindle and dandle to make the boys ogle you, and you ogle back. How many times I'd say to myself. "Now that one, now: I wish she was a little more of a coquette—always wearing the same dress, her hair tumbling round her face. One thing's sure," I'd say to myself, "none of the boys will look at her while Ismene's about, all curled and cute and tidy and trim. I'll have this one on my hands for the rest of my life." And now, you see? Just like your sister, after all. Only worse: a hypocrite. Who is the lad? Some little scamp, eh? Somebody you can't bring home and show to your family, and say, "Well, this is him, and I mean to marry him and no other." That's how it is, is it? Answer me!

ANTIGONE *(smiling faintly)*   That's how it is. Yes, Nurse.

NURSE   Yes, says she! God save us! I took her when she wasn't that high. I promised her poor mother I'd make a lady of her. And look at her! But don't you go thinking this is the end of this, my young'un. I'm only your nurse and you can play deaf and dumb with me; I don't count. But your Uncle Creon will hear of this! That, I promise you.

ANTIGONE *(a little weary)*   Yes. Creon will hear of this.

NURSE   And we'll hear what he has to say when he finds out that you go wandering alone o' nights. Not to mention Haemon. For the girl's engaged! Going to be married! Going to be married, and she hops out of bed at four in the morning to meet somebody else in a field. Do you know what I ought to do to you? Take you over my knee the way I used to do when you were little.

ANTIGONE   Please, Nurse, I want to be alone.

NURSE   And if you so much of speak of it, she says she wants to be alone!

ANTIGONE   Nanny, you shouldn't scold, dear. This isn't a day when you should be losing your temper.

NURSE   Not scold, indeed! Along with the rest of it, I'm to like it. Didn't I promise your mother? What would she say if she was here? "Old Stupid!" That's what she'd call me. "Old Stupid. Not to know how to keep my little girl pure! Spend your life making them behave, watching over them like a mother hen, running after them with mufflers and sweaters to keep them warm, and eggnogs to make them strong; and then at four o'clock in the morning, you who always complained you never could sleep a wink, snoring in your bed and letting them slip out into the bushes." That's what she'd say, your mother. And I'd stand there, dying of shame if I wasn't dead already. And all I could do would be not to dare look her in the face; and "That's true," I'd say. "That's all true what you say, Your Majesty."

ANTIGONE   Nanny, dear. Dear Nanny. Don't cry. You'll be able to look Mamma in the face when it's your time to see her. And she'll say, "Good morning, Nanny. Thank you for my little Antigone. You did look after her so well." She knows why I went out this morning.

NURSE   Not to meet a lover?

ANTIGONE   No. Not to meet a lover.

NURSE   Well, you've a queer way of teasing me, I must say! Not to know when she's teasing me! *(Rises to stand behind* ANTIGONE.) I must be getting awfully old, that's what it is. But if you loved me, you'd tell me the truth. You'd tell me why your bed was empty when I went along to tuck you in. Wouldn't you?

ANTIGONE   Please, Nanny, don't cry any more. (ANTIGONE *turns partly toward* NURSE, *puts an arm up to* NURSE's *shoulder. With her other hand,* ANTIGONE *caresses* NURSE's *face.)* There now, my sweet red apple. Do you remember how I used to rub your cheeks to make them shine? My dear, wrinkled red apple! I didn't do anything tonight that was worth sending tears down the little gullies of your dear face. I am pure, and I swear that I have no other lover than Haemon. If you like, I'll swear that I shall never have any other lover than Haemon. Save your tears, Nanny, save them, Nanny dear; you may still need them. When you cry like that, I become a little girl again; and I mustn't be a little girl today. (ANTIGONE *rises and moves upstage.)*

ISMENE *enters through arch, left. She pauses in front of arch.*

ISMENE   Antigone! What are you doing up at this hour? I've just been to your room.

NURSE   The two of you, now! You're both going mad, to be up before the kitchen fire has been started. Do you like running about without a mouthful of breakfast? Do you think it's decent for the daughters of a king? *(She turns to* ISMENE.*)* And look at you, with nothing on, and the sun not up! I'll have you both on my hands with colds before I know it.

ANTIGONE   Nanny dear, go away now. It's not chilly, really. Summer's here. Go and make us some coffee. Please, Nanny, I'd love some coffee. It would do me so much good.

NURSE   My poor baby! Her head's swimming, what with nothing on her stomach, and me standing here like an idiot when I could be getting her something hot to drink. *(Exit* NURSE.*)*

A pause.

ISMENE   Aren't you well?

ANTIGONE   Of course I am. Just a little tired. I got up too early. (ANTIGONE *sits on a chair, suddenly tired.)*

ISMENE   I couldn't sleep, either.

ANTIGONE   Ismene, you ought not to go without your beauty sleep.

ISMENE   Don't make fun of me.

ANTIGONE   I'm not, Ismene, truly. This particular morning, seeing how beautiful you are makes everything easier for me. Wasn't I a miserable little beast when we were small? I used to fling mud at you, and put worms down your neck. I remember tying you to a tree and cutting off your hair. Your beautiful hair! How easy it must be never to be unreasonable with all that smooth silken hair so beautifully set round your head.

ISMENE *(abruptly)*   Why do you insist upon talking about other things?

ANTIGONE *(gently)*   I am not talking about other things.

ISMENE   Antigone, I've thought about it a lot.

ANTIGONE   Have you?

ISMENE   I thought about it all night long. Antigone, you're mad.

ANTIGONE   Am I?

ISMENE   We cannot do it.

ANTIGONE   Why not?

ISMENE   Creon will have us put to death.

ANTIGONE   Of course he will. That's what he's here for. He will do what he has to do, and we will do what we have to do. He is bound to put us to death. We are bound to go out and bury our brother. That's the way it is. What do you think we can do to change it?

ISMENE *(releases* ANTIGONE's *hand; draws back a step).*   I don't want to die.

ANTIGONE   I'd prefer not to die, myself.

ISMENE   Listen to me, Antigone. I thought about it all night. I'm older than you are. I always think things over, and you don't. You are impulsive. You get a notion in your head and you jump up and do the thing straight off. And if it's silly, well, so much the worse for you. Whereas, I think things out.

ANTIGONE   Sometimes it is better not to think too much.

ISMENE I don't agree with you! *(*ANTIGONE *looks at* ISMENE, *then turns and moves to chair behind table.* ISMENE *leans on end of table top, toward* ANTIGONE.*)* Oh, I know it's horrible. And I pity Polynices just as much as you do. But all the same, I sort of see what Uncle Creon means.

ANTIGONE I don't want to "sort of see" anything.

ISMENE Uncle Creon is the king. He has to set an example!

ANTIGONE But I am not the king; and I don't have to set people examples. Little Antigone gets a notion in her head—the nasty brat, the willful, wicked girl; and they put her in a corner all day, or they lock her up in the cellar. And she deserves it. She shouldn't have disobeyed!

ISMENE There you go, frowning, glowering, wanting your own stubborn way in everything. Listen to me. I'm right oftener than you are.

ANTIGONE I don't want to be right!

ISMENE At least you can try to understand.

ANTIGONE Understand! The first word I ever heard out of any of you was that word "understand." Why didn't I "understand" that I must not play with water—cold, black, beautiful flowing water—because I'd spill it on the palace tiles. Or with earth, because earth dirties a little girl's frock. Why didn't I "understand" that nice children don't eat out of every dish at once; or give everything in their pockets to beggars; or run in the wind so fast that they fall down; or ask for a drink when they're perspiring; or want to go swimming when it's either too early or too late, merely because they happen to feel like swimming. Understand! I don't want to understand. There'll be time enough to understand when I'm old. . . . If I ever *am* old. But not now.

ISMENE He is stronger than we are, Antigone. He is the king. And the whole city is with him. Thousands and thousands of them, swarming through all the streets of Thebes.

ANTIGONE I am not listening to you.

ISMENE His mob will come running, howling as it runs. A thousand arms will seize our arms. A thousand breaths will breathe into our faces. Like one single pair of eyes, a thousand eyes will stare at us. We'll be driven in a tumbrel through their hatred, through the smell of them and their cruel, roaring laughter. We'll be dragged to the scaffold for torture, surrounded by guards with their idiot faces all bloated, their animal hands clean-washed for the sacrifice, their beefy eyes squinting as they stare at us. And we'll know that no shrieking and no begging will make them understand that we want to live, for they are like slaves who do exactly as they've been told, without caring about right or wrong. And we shall suffer, we shall feel pain rising in us until it becomes so unbearable that we *know* it must stop. But it won't stop; it will go on rising and rising, like a screaming voice. Oh, I can't, I can't, Antigone!

A pause.

ANTIGONE How well have you thought it all out.

ISMENE I thought of it all night long. Didn't you?

ANTIGONE Oh, yes.

ISMENE   I'm an awful coward, Antigone.

ANTIGONE   So am I. But what has that to do with it?

ISMENE   But, Antigone! Don't you want to go on living?

ANTIGONE   Go on living! Who was it that was always the first out of bed because she loved the touch of the cold morning air on her bare skin? Who was always the last to bed because nothing less than infinite weariness could wean her from the lingering night? Who wept when she was little because there were too many grasses in the meadow, too many creatures in the field, for her to know and touch them all?

ISMENE *(clasps* ANTIGONE's *hands, in a sudden rush of tenderness).*   Darling little sister!

ANTIGONE *(repulsing her)*   No! For heaven's sake! Don't paw me! And don't let us start sniveling! You say you've thought it all out. The howling mob—the torture—the fear of death. . . . They've made up your mind for you. Is that it?

ISMENE   Yes.

ANTIGONE   All right. They're as good excuses as any.

ISMENE   Antigone, be sensible. It's all very well for men to believe in ideas and die for them. But you are a girl!

ANTIGONE   Don't I know I'm a girl? Haven't I spent my life cursing the fact that I was a girl?

ISMENE *(with spirit)*   Antigone! You have everything in the world to make you happy. All you have to do is reach out for it. You are going to be married; you are young; you are beautiful—

ANTIGONE   I am not beautiful.

ISMENE   Yes, you are! Not the way other girls are. But it's always you that the little boys turn to look back at when they pass us in the street. And when you go by, the little girls stop talking. They stare and stare at you, until we've turned a corner.

ANTIGONE *(a faint smile)*   "Little boys—little girls."

ISMENE *(challengingly)*   And what about Haemon?

A pause.

ANTIGONE   I shall see Haemon this morning. I'll take care of Haemon. You always said I was mad; and it didn't matter how little I was or what I wanted to do. Go back to bed now, Ismene. The sun is coming up, and, as you see, there is nothing I can do today. Our brother Polynices is as well guarded as if he had won the war and were sitting on his throne. Go along. You are pale with weariness.

ISMENE   What are you going to do?

NURSE *(calls from off-stage).*   Come along, my dove. Come to breakfast.

ANTIGONE   I don't feel like going to bed. However, if you like, I'll promise not to leave the house till you wake up. Nurse is getting me breakfast. Go and get some sleep. The sun is just up. Look at you: you can't keep your eyes open. Go.

ISMENE   And you will listen to reason, won't you? You'll let me talk to you about this again? Promise?

ANTIGONE   I promise. I'll let you talk. I'll let all of you talk. Go to bed, now. *(*ISMENE *goes to arch; exit.)* Poor Ismene!

NURSE *(enters through arch, speaking as she enters).* Come along, my dove. I've made you some coffee and toast and jam. *(She turns towards arch as if to go out.)*

ANTIGONE I'm not really hungry, Nurse.

NURSE *stops, looks at Antigone, then moves behind her.*

NURSE *(very tenderly)* Where is your pain?

ANTIGONE Nowhere, Nanny dear. But you must keep me warm and safe, the way you used to do when I was little. Nanny! Stronger than all fever, stronger than any nightmare, stronger than the shadow of the cupboard that used to snarl at me and turn into a dragon on the bedroom wall. Stronger than the thousand insects gnawing and nibbling in the silence of the night. Stronger than the night itself, with the weird hooting of the night birds that frightened me even when I couldn't hear them. Nanny, stronger than death. Give me your hand, Nanny, as if I were ill in bed, and you sitting beside me.

NURSE My sparrow, my lamb! What is it that's eating your heart out?

ANTIGONE Oh, it's just that I'm a little young still for what I have to go through. But nobody but you must know that.

NURSE *(places her other arm around* ANTIGONE's *shoulder).* A little young for what, my kitten?

ANTIGONE Nothing in particular, Nanny. Just—all this. Oh, it's so good that you are here. I can hold your callused hand, your hand that is so prompt to ward off evil. You are very powerful, Nanny.

NURSE What is it you want me to do for you, my baby?

ANTIGONE There isn't anything to do, except put your hand like this against my cheek. *(She places the* NURSE's *hand against her cheek. A pause, then, as* ANTIGONE *leans back, her eyes shut.)* There! I'm not afraid any more. Not afraid of the wicked ogre, nor of the sandman, nor of the dwarf who steals little children. *(A pause.* ANTIGONE *resumes on another note.)* Nanny . . .

NURSE Yes?

ANTIGONE My dog, Puff . . .

NURSE *(straightens up, draws her hand away).* Well?

ANTIGONE Promise me that you will never scold her again.

NURSE Dogs that dirty up a house with their filthy paws deserve to be scolded.

ANTIGONE I know. Just the same, promise me.

NURSE You mean you want me to let her make a mess all over the place and not say a thing?

ANTIGONE Yes, Nanny.

NURSE You're asking a lot. The next time she wets my living-room carpet, I'll—

ANTIGONE Please, Nanny, I beg of you!

NURSE It isn't fair to take me on my weak side, just because you look a little peaked today. . . . Well, have it your own way. We'll mop up and keep our mouth shut. You're making a fool out of me, though.

ANTIGONE And promise me that you will talk to her. That you will talk to her often.

NURSE *(turns and looks at* ANTIGONE). Me, talk to a dog!

ANTIGONE   Yes. But mind you: you are not to talk to her the way people usually talk to dogs. You're to talk to her the way I talk to her.

NURSE   I don't see why both of us have to make fools of ourselves. So long as you're here, one ought to be enough.

ANTIGONE   But if there was a reason why I couldn't go on talking to her——

NURSE *(interrupting)*   Couldn't go on talking to her! And why couldn't you go on talking to her? What kind of poppycock——?

ANTIGONE   And if she got too unhappy, if she moaned and moaned, waiting for me with her nose under the door as she does when I'm out all day, then the best thing, Nanny, might be to have her mercifully put to sleep.

NURSE   Now what *has* got into you this morning? *(HAEMON enters through arch.)* Running around in the darkness, won't sleep, won't eat—*(ANTIGONE sees HAEMON.)*—and now it's her dog she wants killed. I never.

ANTIGONE *(interrupting)*   Nanny! Haemon is here. Go inside, please. And don't forget that you've promised me. *(NURSE goes to arch; exit. ANTIGONE rises.)* Haemon, Haemon! Forgive me for quarreling with you last night. *(She crosses quickly to HAEMON and they embrace.)* Forgive me for everything. It was all my fault. I beg you to forgive me.

HAEMON   You know that I've forgiven you. You had hardly slammed the door, your perfume still hung in the room, when I had already forgiven you. *(He holds her in his arms and smiles at her. Then draws slightly back.)* You stole that perfume. From whom?

ANTIGONE   Ismene.

HAEMON   And the rouge? and the face powder? and the frock? Whom did you steal them from?

ANTIGONE   Ismene.

HAEMON   And in whose honor did you get yourself up so elegantly?

ANTIGONE   I'll tell you everything. *(She draws him closer.)* Oh, darling, what a fool I was! To waste a whole evening! A whole, beautiful evening!

HAEMON   We'll have other evenings, my sweet.

ANTIGONE   Perhaps we won't.

HAEMON   And other quarrels, too. A happy love is full of quarrels, you know.

ANTIGONE   A happy love, yes. Haemon, listen to me.

HAEMON   Yes?

ANTIGONE   Don't laugh at me this morning. Be serious.

HAEMON   I am serious.

ANTIGONE   And hold me tight. Tighter than you have ever held me. I want all your strength to flow into me.

HAEMON   There! With all my strength.

A pause.

ANTIGONE *(breathless)*   That's good. *(They stand for a moment, silent and motionless.)* Haemon! I wanted to tell you. You know—the little boy we were going to have when we were married?

HAEMON   Yes?

ANTIGONE   I'd have protected him against everything in the world.

HAEMON   Yes, dearest.

ANTIGONE   Oh, you don't know how I should have held him in my arms and given him my strength. He wouldn't have been afraid of anything, I swear he wouldn't. Not of the falling night, nor of the terrible noonday sun, nor of all the shadows, or all the walls in the world. Our little boy, Haemon! His mother wouldn't have been very imposing: her hair wouldn't always have been brushed; but she would have been strong where he was concerned, so much stronger than all those real mothers with their real bosoms and their aprons around their middle. You believe that, don't you, Haemon?

HAEMON *(soothingly)*   Yes, yes, my darling.

ANTIGONE   And you believe me when I say you would have had a real wife?

HAEMON   Darling, you are my real wife.

ANTIGONE *(pressing against him and crying out)*   Haemon, you loved me! You did love me that night, didn't you? You're sure of it!

HAEMON *(rocking her gently)*   What night, my sweet?

ANTIGONE   And you are very sure, aren't you, that that night, at the dance, when you came to the corner where I was sitting, there was no mistake? It was me you were looking for? It wasn't another girl? And you're sure that never, not in your most secret heart of hearts, have you said to yourself that it was Ismene you ought to have asked to marry you?

HAEMON *(reproachfully)*   Antigone, you are idiotic. You might give me credit for knowing my own mind. It's you I love, and no one else.

ANTIGONE   But you love me as a woman—as a woman wants to be loved, don't you? Your arms around me aren't lying, are they? Your hands, so warm against my back—they're not lying? This warmth that's in me; this confidence, this sense that I am safe, secure, that flows through me as I stand here with my cheek in the hollow of your shoulder: they are not lies, are they?

HAEMON   Antigone, darling, I love you exactly as you love me. With all of myself.

They kiss.

ANTIGONE   I'm sallow, and I'm scrawny. Ismene is pink and golden. She's like a fruit.

HAEMON   Look here, Antigone—

ANTIGONE   Ah, dearest, I am ashamed of myself. But this morning, this special morning, I must know. Tell me the truth! I beg you to tell me the truth! When you think about me, when it strikes you suddenly that I am going to belong to you—do you have the feeling that—that a great empty space is being hollowed out inside you, that there is something inside you that is just—dying?

HAEMON   Yes, I do. I do.

A pause.

ANTIGONE   That's the way I feel. And another thing. I wanted you to know that I should have been very proud to be your wife—the woman whose shoulder you would put your hand on as you sat down to table, absent-mindedly; as upon a thing that belonged to you. *(After a moment, draws away from him. Her tone changes.)*

There! Now I have two things more to tell you. And when I have told them to you, you must go away instantly, without asking any questions. However strange they may seem to you. However much they may hurt you. Swear that you will!

HAEMON *(beginning to be troubled)* What are these things that you are going to tell me?

ANTIGONE Swear, first, that you will go away without one word. Without so much as looking at me. *(She looks at him, wretchedness in her face.)* You hear me, Haemon. Swear it, please. This is the last mad wish that you will ever have to grant me.

A pause.

HAEMON I swear it, since you insist. But I must tell you that I don't like this at all.

ANTIGONE Please, Haemon. It's very serious. You must listen to me and do as I ask. First, about last night, when I came to your house. You asked me a moment ago why I wore Ismene's dress and rouge. It was because I was stupid. I wasn't very sure that you loved me as a woman; and I did it—because I wanted you to want me. I was trying to be more like other girls.

HAEMON Was that the reason? My poor—

ANTIGONE Yes. And you laughed at me. And we quarreled; and my awful temper got the better of me and I flung out of the house. . . . The real reason was that I wanted you to take me; I wanted to be your wife before—

HAEMON Oh, my darling—

ANTIGONE *(shuts him off).* You swore you wouldn't ask any questions. You swore, Haemon. *(Turns her face away and goes on in a hard voice.)* As a matter of fact, I'll tell you why. I wanted to be your wife last night because I love you that way very—very strongly. And also because—Oh, my darling, my darling, forgive me; I'm going to cause you quite a lot of pain. *(She draws away from him.)* I wanted it also because I shall never, never be able to marry you, never! *(Haemon is stupefied and mute; then he moves a step towards her.)* Haemon! You took a solemn oath! You swore! Leave me quickly! Tomorrow the whole thing will be clear to you. Even before tomorrow: this afternoon. If you please, Haemon, go now. It is the only thing left that you can do for me if you still love me. *(A pause as Haemon stares at her. Then he turns and goes out through the arch.* ANTIGONE *stands motionless, then moves to a chair at end of table and lets herself gently down on it. In a mild voice, as of calm after storm.)* Well, it's over for Haemon, Antigone.

ISMENE *enters through arch, pauses for a moment in front of it when she sees* ANTIGONE, *then crosses behind table.*

ISMENE I can't sleep. I'm terrified. I'm so afraid that, even though it is daylight, you'll still try to bury Polynices. Antigone, little sister, we all want to make you happy— Haemon, and Nurse, and I, and Puff whom you love. We love you, we are alive, we need you. And you remember what Polynices was like. He was our brother, of course. But he's dead; and he never loved you. He was a bad brother. He was like an enemy in the house. He never thought of you. Why should you think of him? What if his soul does have to wander through endless time without rest or peace? Don't try something that is beyond your strength. You are always defying the world, but you're only a girl, after all. Stay at home tonight. Don't try to do it, I beg you. It's Creon's doing, not ours.

ANTIGONE   You are too late, Ismene. When you first saw me this morning, I had just come in from burying him. *(Exit* ANTIGONE *through arch.)*

The lighting, which by this time has reached a point of early morning sun, is quickly dimmed out, leaving the stage bathed in a light blue color. ISMENE *runs out after* AN-TIGONE. *On* ISMENE's *exit the lights are brought up suddenly to suggest a later period of the day.* CREON *and* PAGE *enter through curtain upstage.* CREON *stands on the top step; his* PAGE *stands at his right side.*

CREON   A private of the guards, you say? One of those standing watch over the body? Show him in.

The PAGE *crosses to arch; exit.* CREON *moves down to end of table.* PAGE *re-enters, preceded by the* FIRST GUARD, *livid with fear.* PAGE *remains on upstage side of arch.* GUARD *salutes.*

GUARD   Private Jonas, Second Battalion.

CREON   What are you doing here?

GUARD   It's like this, sir. Soon as it happened, we said: "Got to tell the chief about this before anybody else spills it. He'll want to know right away." So we tossed a coin to see which one would come up and tell you about it. You see, sir, we thought only one man had better come, because, after all, you don't want to leave the body without a guard. Right? I mean, there's three of us on duty, guarding the body.

CREON   What's wrong about the body?

GUARD   Sir, I've been seventeen years in the service. Volunteer. Wounded three times. Two mentions. My record's clean. I know my business and I know my place. I carry out orders. Sir, ask any officer in the battalion; they'll tell you. "Leave it to Jonas. Give him an order: he'll carry it out." That's what they'll tell you sir. Jonas, that's me—that's my name.

CREON   What's the matter with you, man? What are you shaking for?

GUARD   By rights it's the corporal's job, sir. I've been recommended for a corporal, but they haven't put it through yet. June, it was supposed to go through.

CREON   *(interrupts).*   Stop chattering and tell me why you are here. If anything has gone wrong, I'll break all three of you.

GUARD   Nobody can say we didn't keep our eye on that body. We had the two-o'clock watch—the tough one. You know how it is, sir. It's nearly the end of the night. Your eyes are like lead. You've got a crick in the back of your neck. There's shadows, and the fog is beginning to roll in. A fine watch they give us! And me, seventeen years in the service. But we was doing our duty all right. On our feet, all of us. Anybody says we were sleeping is a liar. First place, it was too cold. Second place—*(CREON makes a gesture of impatience.)* Yes, sir. Well, I turned around and looked at the body. We wasn't only ten feet away from it, but that's how I am. I was keeping my eye on it. *(Shouts.)* Listen, sir, I was the first man to see it! Me! They'll tell you. I was the one let out that yell!

CREON   What for? What was the matter?

GUARD   Sir, the body! Somebody had been there and buried it. *(CREON comes down a step on the stair. The* GUARD *becomes more frightened.)* It wasn't much, you understand. With us three there, it couldn't have been. Just covered over with a little dirt, that's all. But enough to hide it from the buzzards.

CREON   By God, I'll—! *(He looks intently at the* GUARD.*)* You are sure that it couldn't have been a dog, scratching up the earth?

GUARD   Not a chance, sir. That's kind of what we hoped it was. But the earth was scattered over the body just like the priests tell you you should do it. Whoever did that job knew what he was doing, all right.

CREON   Who could have dared? *(He turns and looks at the* GUARD.*)* Was there anything to indicate who might have done it?

GUARD   Not a thing, sir. Maybe we heard a footstep—I can't swear to it. Of course we started right in to search, and the corporal found a shovel, a kid's shovel no bigger than that, all rusty and everything. Corporal's got the shovel for you. We thought maybe a kid did it.

CREON   *(to himself)*   A kid! *(He looks away from the* GUARD.*)* I broke the back of the rebellion; but like a snake, it is coming together again. Polynices' friends, with their gold, blocked by my orders in the banks of Thebes. The leaders of the mob, stinking of garlic and allied to envious princes. And the temple priests, always ready for a bit of fishing in troubled waters. A kid! I can imagine what he is like, their kid: a baby-faced killer, creeping in the night with a toy shovel under his jacket. *(He looks at his* PAGE.*)* Though why shouldn't they have corrupted a real child? Very touching! Very useful to the party, an innocent child. A martyr. A real white-faced baby of fourteen who will spit with contempt at the guards who kill him. A free gift to their cause: the precious, innocent blood of a child on my hands. *(He turns to the* GUARD.*)* They must have accomplices in the Guard itself. Look here, you. Who knows about this?

GUARD   Only us three, sir. We flipped a coin, and I came right over.

CREON   Right. Listen, now. You will continue on duty. When the relief squad comes up, you will tell them to return to barracks. You will uncover the body. If another attempt is made to bury it, I shall expect you to make an arrest and bring the person straight to me. And you will keep your mouths shut. Not one word of this to a human soul. You are guilty of neglect of duty, and you will be punished; but if the rumor spreads through Thebes that the body received burial, you will be shot—all three of you.

GUARD   *(excitedly)*   Sir, we never told nobody, I swear we didn't! Anyhow, I've been up here. Suppose my pals spilled to the relief; I couldn't have been with them and here too. That wouldn't be my fault if they talked. Sir, I've got two kids. You're my witness, sir, it couldn't have been me. I was here with you. I've got a witness! If anybody talked, it couldn't have been me! I was—

CREON   *(interrupting)*   Clear out! If the story doesn't get around, you won't be shot. *(The* GUARD *salutes, turns, and exits at the double.* CREON *turns and paces upstage, then comes down to end of the table.)* A child! *(He looks at* PAGE.*)* Come along, my lad. Since we can't hope to keep this to ourselves, we shall have to be the first to give out the news. And after that, we shall have to clean up the mess. *(PAGE crosses to side of* CREON. CREON *puts his hand on* PAGE's *shoulder.)* Would you be willing to die for me? Would you defy the Guard with your little shovel? *(PAGE looks up at* CREON.) Of course you would. You would do it, too. *(A pause.* CREON *looks away from* PAGE *and murmurs.)* A child! *(*CREON *and* PAGE *go slowly upstage center to top step.* PAGE *draws aside the curtain, through which exit* CREON *with* PAGE *behind him.)*

As soon as CREON *and* PAGE *have disappeared,* CHORUS *enters and leans against the upstage portal of arch, left. The lighting is brought up to its brightest point to suggest mid-afternoon.* CHORUS *allows a pause to indicate that a crucial moment has been reached in the play, then moves slowly downstage, center. He stands for a moment silent, reflecting, and then smiles faintly.*

CHORUS   The spring is wound up tight. It will uncoil of itself. That is what is so convenient in tragedy. The least little turn of the wrist will do the job. Anything will set it going: a glance at a girl who happens to be lifting her arms to her hair as you go by; a feeling when you wake up on a fine morning that you'd like a little respect paid to you today, as if it were as easy to order as a second cup of coffee; one question too many, idly thrown out over a friendly drink—and the tragedy is on.

The rest is automatic. You don't need to lift a finger. The machine is in perfect order; it has been oiled ever since time began, and it runs without friction. Death, treason, and sorrow are on the march; and they move in the wake of storm, of tears, of stillness. Every kind of stillness. The hush when the executioner's ax goes up at the end of the last act. The unbreathable silence when, at the beginning of the play, the two lovers, their hearts bared, their bodies naked, stand for the first time face to face in the darkened room, afraid to stir. The silence inside you when the roaring crowd acclaims the winner—so that you think of a film without a sound track, mouths agape and no sound coming out of them, a clamor that is no more than a picture; and you, the victor, already vanquished, alone in the desert of your silence. That is tragedy.

Tragedy is clean, it is restful, it is flawless. It has nothing to do with melodrama—with wicked villains, persecuted maidens, avengers, sudden revelations, and eleventh-hour repentances. Death, in a melodrama, is really horrible because it is never inevitable. The dear old father might so easily have been saved; the honest young man might so easily have brought in the police five minutes earlier.

In a tragedy, nothing is in doubt and everyone's destiny is known. That makes for tranquillity. There is a sort of fellow-feeling among characters in a tragedy: he who kills is as innocent as he who gets killed: it's all a matter of what part you are playing. Tragedy is restful; and the reason is that hope, that foul, deceitful thing, has no part in it. There isn't any hope. You're trapped. The whole sky has fallen on you, and all you can do about it is to shout.

Don't mistake me: I said "shout": I did not say groan, whimper, complain. That, you cannot do. But you can shout aloud; you can get all those things said that you never thought you'd be able to say—or never even knew you had it in you to say. And you don't say these things because it will do any good to say them:

you know better than that. You say them for their own sake; you say them because you learn a lot from them.

In melodrama you argue and struggle in the hope of escape. That is vulgar; it's practical. But in tragedy, where there is no temptation to try to escape, argument is gratuitous: it's kingly.

Voices of the GUARDS *and scuffling sound heard through the archway.* CHORUS *looks in that direction; then, in a changed tone:*

The play is on. Antigone has been caught. For the first time in her life, little Antigone is going to be able to be herself.

Exit CHORUS *through arch. A pause, while the offstage voices rise in volume, then the* FIRST GUARD *enters, followed by* SECOND *and* THIRD GUARDS, *holding the arms of* ANTIGONE *and dragging her along. The* FIRST GUARD, *speaking as he enters, crosses swiftly to end of the table.*

The TWO GUARDS *and Antigone stop downstage.*

FIRST GUARD *(recovered from his fright)*　Come on, now, Miss, give it a rest. The chief will be here in a minute and you can tell him about it. All I know is my orders. I don't want to know what you were doing there. People always have excuses; but I can't afford to listen to them, see. Why, if we had to listen to all the people who want to tell us what's the matter with this country, we'd never get our work done. *(To the* GUARDS*)* You keep hold of her and I'll see that she keeps her face shut.

ANTIGONE　They are hurting me. Tell them to take their dirty hands off me.

FIRST GUARD　Dirty hands, eh? The least you can do is try to be polite, Miss. Look at me: I'm polite.

ANTIGONE　Tell them to let me go. I shan't run away. My father was King Oedipus. I am Antigone.

FIRST GUARD　King Oedipus' little girl! Well, well, well! Listen, Miss, the night watch never picks up a lady but they say, you better be careful: I'm sleeping with the police commissioner.

The Guards laugh.

ANTIGONE　I don't mind being killed, but I don't want them to touch me.

FIRST GUARD　And what about stiffs, and dirt, and such like? You wasn't afraid to touch them, was you? "Their dirty hands!" Take a look at your own hands. *(*ANTIGONE, *handcuffed, smiles despite herself as she looks down at her hands. They are grubby.)* You must have lost your shovel, didn't you? Had to go at it with your fingernails the second time, I'll bet. By God, I never saw such nerve! I turn my back for about five seconds; I ask a pal for a chew; I say "thanks"; I get the tobacco towed away in my cheek—the whole thing don't take ten seconds; and there she is, clawing away like a hyena. Right out in broad daylight! And did she scratch and kick when I grabbed her! Straight for my eyes with them nails she went. And yelling something fierce about, "I haven't finished yet; let me finish!" She ain't got all her marbles!

SECOND GUARD   I pinched a nut like that the other day. Right on the main square she was, hoisting up her skirts and showing her behind to anybody that wanted to take a look.

FIRST GUARD   Listen, we're going to get a bonus out of this. What do you say we throw a party, the three of us?

SECOND GUARD   At the old woman's? Behind Market Street?

THIRD GUARD   Suits me. Sunday would be a good day. We're off duty Sunday. What do you say we bring our wives?

FIRST GUARD   No. Let's have some fun this time. Bring your wife, there's always something goes wrong. First place, what do you do with the kids? Bring them, they always want to go to the can just when you're right in the middle of a game of cards or something. Listen, who would have thought an hour ago that us three would be talking about throwing a party now? The way I felt when the old man was interrogating me, we'd be lucky if we got off with being docked a month's pay. I want to tell you, I was scared.

SECOND GUARD   You sure we're going to get a bonus?

FIRST GUARD   Yes. Something tells me this is big stuff.

THIRD GUARD   (to SECOND GUARD)   What's-his-name, you know—in the Third Battalion? He got an extra month's pay for catching a firebug.

SECOND GUARD   If we get an extra month's pay, I vote we throw the party at the Arabian's.

FIRST GUARD   You're crazy! He charges twice as much for liquor as anybody else in town. Unless you want to go upstairs, of course. Can't do that at the old woman's.

THIRD GUARD   Well, we can't keep this from our wives, no matter how you work it out. You get an extra month's pay, and what happens? Everybody in the battalion knows it, and your wife knows it too. They might even line up the battalion and give it to you in front of everybody, so how could you keep your wife from finding out?

FIRST GUARD   Well, we'll see about that. If they do the job out in the barrack yard—of course that means women, kids, everything.

ANTIGONE   I should like to sit down, if you please.

A pause, as the FIRST GUARD *thinks it over.*

FIRST GUARD   Let her sit down. But keep hold of her. *(The two* GUARDS *start to lead her toward the chair at end of table. The curtain upstage opens, and* CREON *enters, followed by his* PAGE. FIRST GUARD *turns and moves upstage a few steps, sees* CREON.) Tenshun! *(The three* GUARDS *salute.* CREON, *seeing* ANTIGONE *handcuffed to* THIRD GUARD, *stops on the top step, astonished).*

CREON   Antigone! *(To the* FIRST GUARD*)* Take off those handcuffs! *(*FIRST GUARD *crosses above table to left of* ANTIGONE.*)* What is this? *(*CREON *and his* PAGE *come down off the steps.)*

First GUARD *takes key from his pocket and unlocks the cuff on* ANTIGONE's *hand.* AN-TIGONE *rubs her wrist as she crosses below table toward chair at end of table.* SECOND *and* THIRD GUARDS *step back to front of arch.* FIRST GUARD *turns upstage toward* CREON.

FIRST GUARD   The watch, sir. We all came this time.

CREON   Who is guarding the body?

FIRST GUARD   We sent for the relief.

CREON *comes down.*

CREON   But I gave orders that the relief was to go back to barracks and stay there! (ANTIGONE *sits on chair at left of table.*) I told you not to open your mouth about this!

FIRST GUARD   Nobody's said anything, sir. We made this arrest, and brought the party in, the way you said we should.

CREON *(to* ANTIGONE*)*   Where did these men find you?

FIRST GUARD   Right by the body.

CREON   What were you doing near your brother's body? You knew what my orders were.

FIRST GUARD   What was she doing? Sir, that's why we brought her in. She was digging up the dirt with her nails. She was trying to cover up the body all over again.

CREON   Do you realize what you are saying?

FIRST GUARD   Sir, ask these men here. After I reported to you, I went back, and first thing we did, we uncovered the body. The sun was coming up and it was beginning to smell, so we moved it up on a little rise to get him in the wind. Of course, you wouldn't expect any trouble in broad daylight. But just the same, we decided one of us had better keep his eye peeled all the time. About noon, what with the sun and the smell, and as the wind dropped and I wasn't feeling none too good, I went over to my pal to get a chew. I just had time to say "thanks" and stick it in my mouth, when I turned round and there she was, clawing away at the dirt with both hands. Right out in broad daylight! Wouldn't you think when she saw me come running she'd stop and leg it out of there? Not her! She went right on digging as fast as she could, as if I wasn't there at all. And when I grabbed her, she scratched and bit and yelled to leave her alone, she hadn't finished yet, the body wasn't all covered yet, and the like of that.

CREON *(to* ANTIGONE*)*   Is this true?

ANTIGONE   Yes, it is true.

FIRST GUARD   We scraped the dirt off as fast as we could, then we sent for the relief and we posted them. But we didn't tell them a thing, sir. And we brought in the party so's you could see her. And that's the truth, so help me God.

CREON *(to* ANTIGONE*)*   And was it you who covered the body the first time? In the night?

ANTIGONE   Yes, it was. With a toy shovel we used to take to the seashore when we were children. It was Polynices' own shovel; he had cut his name in the handle. That was why I left it with him. But these men took it away; so the next time, I had to do it with my hands.

FIRST GUARD   Sir, she was clawing away like a wild animal. Matter of fact, first minute we saw her, what with the heat haze and everything, my pal says, "That must be a dog," he says, "Dog!" I says, "that's a girl, that is!" And it was.

CREON   Very well. *(Turns to the* PAGE*)* Show these men to the anteroom. *(The* PAGE *crosses to the arch, stands there, waiting.* CREON *moves behind the table. To the* FIRST GUARD*)* You three men will wait outside. I may want a report from you later.

FIRST GUARD   Do I put the cuffs back on her, sir?

CREON   No. *(The three* GUARDS *salute, do an about-turn, and exeunt through arch, right.* PAGE *follows them out. A pause.)* Had you told anybody what you meant to do?

ANTIGONE   No.

CREON   Did you meet anyone on your way—coming or going?

ANTIGONE   No, nobody.

CREON   Sure of that, are you?

ANTIGONE   Perfectly sure.

CREON   Very well. Now listen to me. You will go straight to your room. When you get there, you will go to bed. You will say that you are not well and that you have not been out since yesterday. Your nurse will tell the same story. *(He looks toward arch, through which the* GUARDS *have gone out.)* And I'll get rid of those three men.

ANTIGONE   Uncle Creon, you are going to a lot of trouble for no good reason. You must know that I'll do it all over again tonight.

A pause. They look one another in the eye.

CREON   Why did you try to bury your brother?

ANTIGONE   I owed it to him.

CREON   I had forbidden it.

ANTIGONE   I owed it to him. Those who are not buried wander eternally and find no rest. If my brother were alive, and he came home weary after a long day's hunting, I should kneel down and unlace his boots. I should fetch him food and drink, I should see that his bed was ready for him. Polynices is home from the hunt. I owe it to him to unlock the house of the dead in which my father and mother are waiting to welcome him. Polynices has earned his rest.

CREON   Polynices was a rebel and a traitor, and you know it.

ANTIGONE   He was my brother.

CREON   You heard my edict. It was proclaimed throughout Thebes. You read my edict. It was posted upon the city walls.

ANTIGONE   Of course I did.

CREON   You knew the punishment I decreed for any person who attempted to give him burial.

ANTIGONE   Yes, I knew the punishment.

CREON   Did you by any chance act on the assumption that a daughter of Oedipus, a daughter of Oedipus' stubborn pride, was above the law?

ANTIGONE   No, I did not act on that assumption.

CREON   Because if you had acted on that assumption, Antigone, you would have been deeply wrong. Nobody has a more sacred obligation to obey the law than those who make the law. You are a daughter of lawmakers, a daughter of kings, Antigone. You must observe the law.

ANTIGONE   Had I been a scullery maid washing my dishes when that law was read aloud to me, I should have scrubbed the greasy water from my arms and gone out in my apron to bury my brother.

CREON   What nonsense! If you had been a scullery maid, there would have been no doubt in your mind about the seriousness of that edict. You would have known that it meant death; and you would have been satisfied to weep for your brother in your kitchen. But you! You thought that because you come of the royal line, because you were my niece and were going to marry my son, I shouldn't dare have you killed.

ANTIGONE   You are mistaken. Quite the contrary. I never doubted for an instant that you would have me put to death.

A pause, as CREON *stares fixedly at her.*

CREON   The pride of Oedipus! Oedipus and his headstrong pride all over again. I can see your father in you—and I believe you. Of course you thought that I should have you killed! Proud as you are, it seemed to you a natural climax in your existence. Your father was like that. For him as for you human happiness was meaningless; and mere human misery was not enough to satisfy his passion for torment. *(He sits on stool behind the table.)* You come of people for whom the human vestment is a kind of straitjacket: it cracks at the seams. You spend your lives wriggling to get out of it. Nothing less than a cosy tea party with death and destiny will quench your thirst. The happiest hour of your father's life came when he listened greedily to the story of how, unknown to himself, he had killed his own father and dishonored the bed of his own mother. Drop by drop, word by word, he drank in the dark story that the gods had destined him first to live and then to hear. How avidly men and women drink the brew of such a tale when their names are Oedipus—and Antigone! And it is so simple, afterwards, to do what your father did, to put out one's eyes and take one's daughter begging on the highways.

Let me tell you, Antigone: those days are over for Thebes. Thebes has a right to a king without a past. My name, thank God, is only Creon. I stand here with both feet firm on the ground; with both hands in my pockets; and I have decided that so long as I am king—being less ambitious than your father was—I shall merely devote myself to introducing a little order into this absurd kingdom; if that is possible.

Don't think that being a king seems to me romantic. It is my trade; a trade a man has to work at every day; and like every other trade, it isn't all beer and skittles. But since it is my trade, I take it seriously. And if, tomorrow, some wild and bearded messenger walks in from some wild and distant valley—which is what happened to your dad—and tells me that he's not quite sure who my parents were, but thinks that my wife Eurydice is actually my mother, I shall ask him to do me the kindness to go back where he came from; and I shan't let a little matter like that persuade me to order my wife to take a blood test and the police to let me know whether or not my birth certificate was forged. Kings, my girl, have other things to do than to surrender themselves to their private feelings. *(He looks at her and smiles.)* Hand *you over* to be killed! *(He rises, moves to end of table and sits on the top of table.)* I have other plans for you. You're going to marry Haemon; and I want you to fatten up a bit so that you can give him a sturdy boy. Let me assure you that Thebes needs that boy a good deal more than it needs your death. You will go to your room, now, and do as you have been told; and you won't say a word about this to anybody. Don't fret about the guards: I'll see that their mouths are shut. And don't annihilate me with those eyes. I know that you think I am a brute, and I'm sure you must consider me very prosaic. But the fact is, I have always been fond of you, stubborn though you always were. Don't forget that the first doll you ever had came from me. *(A pause.* ANTIGONE *says nothing, rises, and crosses slowly below the table toward the arch.* CREON *turns and watches her; then)* Where are you going?

ANTIGONE *(stops downstage. Without any show of rebellion)* You know very well where I am going.

CREON *(after a pause)* What sort of game are you playing?

ANTIGONE I am not playing games.

CREON Antigone, do you realize that if, apart from those three guards, a single soul finds out what you have tried to do, it will be impossible for me to avoid putting you to death? There is still a chance that I can save you; but only if you keep this to yourself and give up your crazy purpose. Five minutes more, and it will be too late. You understand that?

ANTIGONE I must go and bury my brother. Those men uncovered him.

CREON What good will it do? You know that there are other men standing guard over Polynices. And even if you did cover him over with earth again, the earth would again be removed.

ANTIGONE I know all that. I know it. But that much, at least, I can do. And what a person can do, a person ought to do.

Pause.

CREON Tell me, Antigone, do you believe all that flummery about religious burial? Do you really believe that a so-called shade of your brother is condemned to wander for ever homeless if a little earth is not flung on his corpse to the accompaniment of some priestly abracadabra? Have you ever listened to the priests of Thebes when they were mumbling their formula? Have you ever watched those dreary bureaucrats while they were preparing the dead for burial—skipping half the gestures required by the ritual, swallowing half their words, hustling the dead into their graves out of fear that they might be late for lunch?

ANTIGONE Yes, I have seen all that.

CREON And did you never say to yourself as you watched them, that if someone you really loved lay dead under the shuffling, mumbling ministrations of the priests, you would scream aloud and beg the priests to leave the dead in peace?

ANTIGONE Yes, I've thought all that.

CREON And you still insist upon being put to death—merely because I refuse to let your brother go out with that grotesque passport; because I refuse his body the wretched consolation of that mass-production jibber-jabber which you would have been the first to be embarrassed by if I had allowed it. The whole thing is absurd!

ANTIGONE Yes, it's absurd.

CREON Then why, Antigone, why? For whose sake? For the sake of them that believe in it? To raise them against me?

ANTIGONE No.

CREON   For whom then if not for them and not for Polynices either?

ANTIGONE   For nobody. For myself.

A pause as they stand looking at one another.

CREON   You must want very much to die. You look like a trapped animal.

ANTIGONE   Stop feeling sorry for me. Do as I do. Do your job. But if you are a human being, do it quickly. That is all I ask of you. I'm not going to be able to hold out for ever.

CREON *(takes a step toward her).*   I want to save you, Antigone.

ANTIGONE   You are the king, and you are all-powerful, But that you cannot do.

CREON   You think not?

ANTIGONE   Neither save me nor stop me.

CREON   Prideful Antigone! Little Oedipus!

ANTIGONE   Only this can you do: have me put to death.

CREON   Have you tortured, perhaps?

ANTIGONE   Why would you do that? To see me cry? To hear me beg for mercy? Or swear whatever you wish, and then begin over again?

A pause.

CREON   You listen to me. You have cast me for the villain in this little play of yours, and yourself for the heroine. And you know it, you damned little mischief maker! But don't you drive me too far! If I were one of your preposterous little tyrants that Greece is full of, you would be lying in a ditch this minute with your tongue pulled out and your body drawn and quartered. But you can see something in my face that makes me hesitate to send for the guards and turn you over to them. Instead, I let you go on arguing; and you taunt me, you take the offensive. *(He grasps her left wrist.)* What are you driving at, you she devil?

ANTIGONE   Let me go. You are hurting my arm.

CREON *(gripping her tighter)*   I will not let you go.

ANTIGONE *(moans).*   Oh!

CREON   I was a fool to waste words. I should have done this from the beginning. *(He looks at her.)* I may be your uncle—but we are not a particularly affectionate family. Are we, eh? *(Through his teeth, as he twists)* Are we? *(*CREON *propels* ANTIGONE *round below him to his side.)* What fun for you, eh? To be able to spit in the face of a king who has all the power in the world; a man who has done his own killing in his day; who has killed people just as pitiable as you are—and who is still soft enough to go to all this trouble in order to keep you from being killed.

A pause.

ANTIGONE   Now you are squeezing my arm too tightly. It doesn't hurt any more.

CREON *stares at her, then drops her arm.*

CREON   I shall save you yet. *(He goes below the table to the chair at end of table, takes off his coat, and places it on the chair.)* God knows, I have things enough to do today without wasting my time on an insect like you. There's plenty to do, I assure you, when you've just put down a revolution. But urgent things can wait. I am not going to let politics be the cause of your death. For it is a fact that this whole business is nothing but politics; the mournful shade of Polynices, the decomposing corpse, the sentimental weeping, and the hysteria that you mistake for heroism—nothing but politics.

  Look here. I may not be soft, but I'm fastidious. I like things clean, shipshape, well scrubbed. Don't think that I am not just as offended as you are by the thought of that meat rotting in the sun. In the evening, when the breeze comes in off the sea, you can smell it in the palace, and it nauseates me. But I refuse even to shut my window. It's vile; and I can tell you what I wouldn't tell anybody else: it's stupid, monstrously stupid. But the people of Thebes have got to have their noses rubbed into it a little longer. My God! If it was up to me, I should have had them bury your brother long ago as a mere matter of public hygiene. I admit what I am doing is childish. But if the featherheaded rabble I govern are to understand what's what, that stench has got to fill the town for a month!

ANTIGONE *(turns to him).* You are a loathsome man!

CREON I agree. My trade forces me to be. We could argue whether I ought or ought not to follow my trade; but once I take on the job, I must do it properly.

ANTIGONE Why do you do it at all?

CREON My dear, I woke up one morning and found myself King of Thebes. God knows, there were other things I loved in life more than power.

ANTIGONE Then you should have said no.

CREON Yes, I could have done that. Only, I felt that it would have been cowardly. I should have been like a workman who turns down a job that has to be done. So I said yes.

ANTIGONE So much the worse for you, then. I didn't say yes. I can say no to anything I think vile, and I don't have to count the cost. But because you said yes, all that you can do, for all your crown and your trappings, and your guards—all that you can do is to have me killed.

CREON Listen to me.

ANTIGONE If I want to. I don't have to listen to you if I don't want to. You've said your *yes.* There is nothing more you can tell me that I don't know. You stand there, drinking in my words. *(She moves behind chair.)* Why is it that you don't call your guards? I'll tell you why? You want to hear me out to the end; that's why.

CREON You amuse me.

ANTIGONE Oh, no, I don't. I frighten you. That is why you talk about saving me. Everything would be so much easier if you had a docile, tongue-tied little Antigone living in the palace. I'll tell you something, Uncle Creon: I'll give you back one of your own words. You are too fastidious to make a good tyrant. But you are going to have to put me to death today, and you know it. And that's what frightens you. God! Is there anything uglier than a frightened man!

CREON Very well. I am afraid, then. Does that satisfy you! I am afraid that if you insist upon it, I shall have to have you killed. And I don't want to.

ANTIGONE I don't have to do things that I think are wrong. If it comes to that; you didn't really want to leave my brother's body unburied, did you? Say it! Admit that you didn't.

CREON   I have said it already.

ANTIGONE   But you did it just the same. And now, though you don't want to do it, you are going to have me killed. And you call that being a king!

CREON   Yes, I call that being a king.

ANTIGONE   Poor Creon! My nails are broken, my fingers are bleeding, my arms are covered with the welts left by the paws of your guards—but I am a queen!

CREON   Then why not have pity on me, and live? Isn't your brother's corpse, rotting there under my windows, payment enough for peace and order in Thebes? My son loves you. Don't make me add your life to the payment. I've paid enough.

ANTIGONE   No, Creon! You said yes, you made yourself king. Now you will never stop paying.

CREON   But God in heaven! Won't you try to understand me! I'm trying hard enough to understand you! There had to be one man who said yes. Somebody had to agree to captain the ship. She had sprung a hundred leaks; she was loaded to the water line with crime, ignorance, poverty. The wheel was swinging with the wind. The crew refused to work and were looting the cargo. The officers were building a raft, ready to slip overboard and desert the ship. The mast was splitting, the wind was howling, the sails were beginning to rip. Every man jack on board was about to drown—and only because the only thing they thought of was their own skins and their cheap little day-to-day traffic. Was that a time, do you think, for playing with words like yes and no? Was that a time for a man to be weighing the pros and cons, wondering if he wasn't going to pay too dearly later on; if he wasn't going to lose his life, or his family, or his touch with other men? You grab the wheel, you right the ship in the face of a mountain of water. You shout an order, and if one man refuses to obey, you shoot straight into the mob. Into the mob, I say! The beast as nameless as the wave that crashes down upon your deck; as nameless as the whipping wind. The thing that drops when you shoot may be someone who poured you a drink the night before; but it has no name. And you, braced at the wheel, you have no name, either. Nothing has a name—except the ship, and the storm. *(A pause as he looks to her.)* Now do you understand?

ANTIGONE   I am not here to understand. That's all very well for you. I am here to say no to you, and die.

CREON   It is easy to say no.

ANTIGONE   Not always.

CREON   It is easy to say no. To say yes, you have to sweat and roll up your sleeves and plunge both hands into life up to the elbows. It is easy to say no, even if saying no means death. All you have to do is to sit still and wait. Wait to go on living, wait to be killed. That is the coward's part. *No* is one of your man-made words. Can you imagine a world in which trees say *no* to the sap? In which beasts say *no* to hunger or to propagation? Animals are good, simple, tough. They move in droves, nudging one another onwards, all traveling the same road. Some of them keel over, but the rest go on; and no matter how many may fall by the wayside, there are always those few left that go on bringing their young into the world, traveling the same road with the same obstinate will, unchanged from those who went before.

ANTIGONE   Animals, eh, Creon! What a king you could be if only men were animals!

A pause. CREON *turns and looks at her.*

CREON   You despise me, don't you? *(*ANTIGONE *is silent.* CREON *goes on, as if to himself.)* Strange. Again and again, I have imagined myself holding this conversation with a pale young man I have never seen in the flesh. He would have come to assassinate me, and would have failed. I would be trying to find out from him why he wanted to kill me. But with all my logic and all my powers of debate, the only thing I could get out of him would be that he despised me. Who would have thought that the white-faced boy would turn out to be you? And that the debate would arise out of something so meaningless as the burial of your brother?

ANTIGONE   *(repeats contemptuously)*   Meaningless!

CREON   *(earnestly, almost desperately)*   And yet, you must hear me out. My part is not an heroic one, but I shall play my part. I shall have you put to death. Only, before I do, I want to make one last appeal. I want to be sure that you know what you are doing as well as I know what I am doing. Antigone, do you know what you are dying for? Do you know the sordid story to which you are going to sign your name in blood, for all time to come?

ANTIGONE   What story?

CREON   The story of Eteocles and Polynices, the story of your brothers. You think you know it, but you don't. Nobody in Thebes knows that story but me. And it seems to me, this afternoon, that you have a right to know it too. *(A pause as* ANTIGONE *moves to chair and sits.)* It's not a pretty story. *(He turns, gets stool from behind the table and places it between the table and the chair.)* You'll see. *(He looks at her for a moment.)* Tell me, first. What do you remember about your brothers? They were older than you, so they must have looked down on you. And I imagine that they tormented you—pulled your pigtails, broke your dolls, whispered secrets to each other to put you in a rage.

ANTIGONE   They were big and I was little.

CREON   And later on, when they came home wearing evening clothes, smoking cigarettes, they would have nothing to do with you; and you thought they were wonderful.

ANTIGONE   They were boys and I was a girl.

CREON   You didn't know why, exactly, but you knew that they were making your mother unhappy. You saw her in tears over them; and your father would fly into a rage because of them. You heard them come in, slamming doors, laughing noisily in the corridors—insolent, spineless, unruly, smelling of drink.

ANTIGONE   *(staring outward)*   Once, it was very early and we had just got up. I saw them coming home, and hid behind a door. Polynices was very pale and his eyes were shining. He was so handsome in his evening clothes. He saw me, and said: "Here, this is for you"; and he gave me a big paper flower that he had brought home from his night out.

CREON   And of course you still have that flower. Last night, before you crept out, you opened a drawer and looked at it for a time, to give yourself courage.

ANTIGONE   Who told you so?

CREON   Poor Antigone! With her night club flower. Do you know what your brother was?

ANTIGONE   Whatever he was, I know that you will say vile things about him.

CREON   A cheap, idiotic bounder, that is what he was. A cruel, vicious little voluptuary. A little beast with just wit enough to drive a car faster and throw more money away than any of his pals. I was with your father one day when Polynices, having lost a lot of money gambling, asked him to settle the debt; and when your father refused, the boy raised his hand against him and called him a vile name.

ANTIGONE   That's a lie!

CREON   He struck your father in the face with his fist. It was pitiful. Your father sat at his desk with his head in his hands. His nose was bleeding. He was weeping with anguish. And in a corner of your father's study, Polynices stood sneering and lighting a cigarette.

ANTIGONE   That's a lie.

A pause.

CREON   When did you last see Polynices alive? When you were twelve years old. *That's* true, isn't it?

ANTIGONE   Yes, that's true.

CREON   Now you know why. Oedipus was too chicken-hearted to have the boy locked up. Polynices was allowed to go off and join the Argive army. And as soon as he reached Argos, the attempts upon your father's life began—upon the life of an old man who couldn't make up his mind to die, couldn't bear to be parted from his kingship. One after another, men slipped into Thebes from Argos for the purpose of assassinating him, and every killer we caught always ended by confessing who had put him up to it, who had paid him to try it. And it wasn't only Polynices. That is really what I am trying to tell you. I want you to know what went on in the back room, in the kitchen of politics; I want you to know what took place in the wings of this drama in which you are burning to play a part.

Yesterday, I gave Eteocles a State funeral, with pomp and honors. Today Eteocles is a saint and a hero in the eyes of all Thebes. The whole city turned out to bury him. The schoolchildren emptied their saving boxes to buy wreaths for him. Old men, orating in quavering, hypocritical voices, glorified the virtues of the great-hearted brother, the devoted son, the loyal prince. I made a speech myself; and every temple priest was present with an appropriate show of sorrow and solemnity in his stupid face. And military honors were accorded the dead hero.

Well, what else could I have done? People had taken sides in the civil war. Both sides couldn't be wrong; that would be too much. I couldn't have made them swallow the truth. Two gangsters was more of a luxury than I could afford. *(He pauses for a moment.)* And this is the whole point of my story. Eteocles, that virtuous brother, was just as rotten as Polynices. That great-hearted son had done his best, too, to procure the assassination of his father. That loyal prince had also offered to sell out Thebes to the highest bidder.

Funny, isn't it? Polynices lies rotting in the sun while Eteocles is given a hero's funeral and will be housed in a marble vault. Yet I have absolute proof that everything that Polynices did, Eteocles had plotted to do. They were a pair of blackguards—both engaged in selling out Thebes, and both engaged in selling out each other; and they died like the cheap gangsters they were, over a division of the spoils.

But, as I told you a moment ago, I had to make a martyr of one of them. I sent out to the holocaust for their bodies; they were found clasped in one another's arms—for the first time in their lives, I imagine. Each had been spitted on the other's sword, and the Argive cavalry had trampled them down. They were mashed to a pulp, Antigone. I had the prettier of the two carcasses brought in and gave it a State funeral; and I left the other to rot. I don't know which was which. And I assure you, I don't care.

Long silence, neither looking at the other.

ANTIGONE *(in a mild voice)* Why do you tell me all this?

CREON Would it have been better to let you die a victim to that obscene story?

ANTIGONE It might have been. I had my faith.

CREON What are you going to do now?

ANTIGONE *(rises to her feet in a daze).* I shall go up to my room.

CREON Don't stay alone. Go and find Haemon. And get married quickly.

ANTIGONE *(in a whisper)* Yes.

CREON All this is really beside the point. You have your whole life ahead of you—and life is a treasure.

ANTIGONE Yes.

CREON And you were about to throw it away. Don't think me fatuous if I say that I understand you; and that at your age I should have done the same thing. A moment ago, when we were quarreling, you said I was drinking in your words. I was. But it wasn't you I was listening to; it was a lad named Creon who lived here in Thebes many years ago. He was thin and pale, as you are. His mind, too, was filled with thoughts of self-sacrifice. Go and find Haemon. And get married quickly, Antigone. Be happy. Life flows like water, and you young people let it run away through your fingers. Shut your hands; hold on to it, Antigone. Life is not what you think it is. Life is a child playing around your feet, a tool you hold firmly in your grip, a bench you sit down upon in the evening, in your garden. People will tell you that that's not life, that life is something else. They will tell you that because they need your strength and your fire, and they will want to make use of you. Don't listen to them. Believe me, the only poor consolation that we have in our old age is to discover that what I have just said to you is true. Life is nothing more than the happiness that you get out of it.

ANTIGONE *(murmurs, lost in thought)* Happiness . . .

CREON *(suddenly a little self-conscious)* Not much of a word, is it?

ANTIGONE *(quietly)* What kind of happiness do you foresee for me? Paint me the picture of your happy Antigone. What are the unimportant little sins that I shall have to commit before I am allowed to sink my teeth into life and tear happiness from it? Tell me: to whom shall I have to lie? Upon whom shall I have to fawn? To whom must I sell myself? Whom do you want me to leave dying, while I turn away my eyes?

CREON Antigone, be quiet.

ANTIGONE   Why do you tell me to be quiet when all I want to know is what I have to do to be happy? This minute; since it is this very minute that I must make my choice. You tell me that life is so wonderful. I want to know what I have to do in order to be able to say that myself.

CREON   Do you love Haemon?

ANTIGONE   Yes, I love Haemon. The Haemon I love is hard and young, faithful and difficult to satisfy, just as I am. But if what I love in Haemon is to be worn away like a stone step by the tread of the thing you call life, the thing you call happiness, if Haemon reaches the point where he stops growing pale with fear when I grow pale, stops thinking that I must have been killed in an accident when I am five minutes late, stops feeling that he is alone on earth when I laugh and he doesn't know why—if he too has to learn to say yes to everything—why, no, then, no! I do not love Haemon!

CREON   You don't know what you are talking about!

ANTIGONE   I do know what I am talking about! Now it is you who have stopped under-standing. I am too far away from you now, talking to you from a kingdom you can't get into, with your quick tongue and your hollow heart. *(Laughs.)* I laugh, Creon, because I see you suddenly as you must have been at fifteen: the same look of impotence in your face and the same inner conviction that there was nothing you couldn't do. What has life added to you, except those lines in your face, and that fat on your stomach?

CREON   Be quiet, I tell you!

ANTIGONE   Why do you want me to be quiet? Because you know that I am right? Do you think I can't see in your face that what I am saying is true? You can't admit it, of course; you have to go on growling and defending the bone you call happiness.

CREON   It is your happiness, too, you little fool!

ANTIGONE   I spit on your happiness! I spit on your idea of life—that life that must go on, come what may. You are all like dogs that lick everything they smell. You with your promise of a humdrum happiness—provided a person doesn't ask too much of life. I want everything of life, I do; and I want it now! I want it total, complete: otherwise I reject it! I will *not* be moderate. I will *not* be satisfied with the bit of cake you offer me if I promise to be a good little girl. I want to be sure of everything this very day; sure that everything will be as beautiful as when I was a little girl. If not, I want to die!

CREON   Scream on, daughter of Oedipus! Scream on, in your father's own voice!

ANTIGONE   In my father's own voice, yes! We are of the tribe that asks questions, and we ask them to the bitter end. Until no tiniest chance of hope remains to be strangled by our hands. We are of the tribe that hates your filthy hope, your docile, your female hope; hope, your whore—

CREON   *(grasps her by her arms).*   Shut up! If you could see how ugly you are, shrieking those words!

ANTIGONE   Yes, I am ugly! Father was ugly, too. (CREON *releases her arms, turns and moves away. Stands with his back to* ANTIGONE.) But Father became beautiful. And do you know when? *(She follows him to behind the table.)* At the very end. When all his questions had been answered. When he could no longer doubt that he *had* killed his own father; that he *had* gone to bed with his own mother. When all hope was gone, stamped out like a beetle. When it was absolutely certain that nothing, nothing could save him. Then he was at peace; then he could smile, almost; then he became beautiful. . . . Whereas you! Ah, those faces of yours, you candidates for election to happiness! It's you who are the ugly ones, even the handsomest of you—with that ugly glint in the corner of your eyes, that ugly crease at the corner of your mouths. Creon, you spoke the word a moment ago:the kitchen of politics. You look it and you smell of it.

CREON *(struggles to put his hand over her mouth).*   I order you to shut up! Do you hear me?

ANTIGONE   You order me? Cook! Do you really believe that you can give me orders?

CREON   Antigone! The anteroom is full of people! Do you want them to hear you?

ANTIGONE   Open the doors! Let us make sure that they can hear me!

CREON   By God! You shut up, I tell you!

ISMENE *enters through arch.*

ISMENE *(distraught)* Antigone!

ANTIGONE *(turns to Ismene).*   You too? What do you want?

ISMENE   Oh, forgive me, Antigone. I've come back. I'll be brave. I'll go with you now.

ANTIGONE   Where will you go with me?

ISMENE *(to* CREON*)*   Creon! If you kill her, you'll have to kill me too.

ANTIGONE   Oh, no, Ismene. Not a bit of it. I die alone. You don't think I'm going to let you die with me after what I've been through? You don't deserve it.

ISMENE   If you die, I don't want to live. I don't want to be left behind, alone.

ANTIGONE   You chose life and I chose death. Now stop blubbering. You had your chance to come with me in the black night, creeping on your hands and knees. You had your chance to claw up the earth with your nails, as I did; to get yourself caught like a thief, as I did. And you refused it.

ISMENE   Not any more. I'll do it alone tonight.

ANTIGONE *(turns round toward Creon).*   You hear that, Creon? The thing is catching! Who knows but that lots of people will catch the disease from me! What are you waiting for? Call in your guards! Come on, Creon! Show a little courage! It only hurts for a minute! Come on, cook!

CREON *(turns toward arch and calls).*   Guard!

GUARDS *enter through arch.*

ANTIGONE *(in a great cry of relief)* At last, Creon!

CHORUS *enters through left arch.*

CREON *(to the* GUARDS*)*   Take her away! (CREON *goes up on top step.)*

GUARDS *grasp* ANTIGONE *by her arms, turn and hustle her toward the arch, right, and exeunt.* ISMENE *mimes horror, backs away toward the arch, left, then turns and runs out through the arch. A long pause, as* CREON *moves slowly downstage.*

CHORUS *(behind* CREON. *Speaks in a deliberate voice.)*   You are out of your mind, Creon. What have you done?

CREON *(his back to* CHORUS*)*   She had to die.

CHORUS   You must not let Antigone die. We shall carry the scar of her death for centuries.

CREON   She insisted. No man on earth was strong enough to dissuade her. Death was her purpose, whether she knew it or not. Polynices was a mere pretext. When she had to give up that pretext, she found another one—that life and happiness were tawdry things and not worth possessing. She was bent upon only one thing: to reject life and to die.

CHORUS   She is a mere child, Creon.

CREON   What do you want me to do for her? Condemn her to live?

HAEMON *(calls from offstage).*   Father (HAEMON *enters through arch, right.* CREON *turns toward him.)*

CREON   Haemon, forget Antigone. Forget her, my dearest boy.

HAEMON   How can you talk like that?

CREON *(grasps* HAEMON *by the hands).*   I did everything I could to save her, Haemon. I used every argument. I swear I did. The girl doesn't love you. She could have gone on living for you; but she refused. She wanted it this way; she wanted to die.

HAEMON   Father! The guards are dragging Antigone away! You've got to stop them! *(He breaks away from* CREON.*)*

CREON *(looks away from* HAEMON*).*   I can't stop them. It's too late. Antigone has spoken. The story is all over Thebes. I cannot save her now.

CHORUS   Creon, you must find a way. Lock her up. Say that she has gone out of her mind.

CREON   Everybody will know it isn't so. The nation will say that I am making an exception of her because my son loves her. I cannot.

CHORUS   You can still gain time, and get her out of Thebes.

CREON   The mob already knows the truth. It is howling for her blood. I can do nothing.

HAEMON   But, Father, you are master in Thebes!

CREON   I am master under the law. Not above the law.

HAEMON   You cannot let Antigone be taken from me. I am your son!

CREON   I cannot do anything else, my poor boy. She must die and you must live.

HAEMON   Live, you say! Live a life without Antigone? A life in which I am to go on admiring you as you busy yourself about your kingdom, make your persuasive speeches, strike your attitudes? Not without Antigone. I love Antigone. I will not live without Antigone!

CREON   Haemon—you will have to resign yourself to life without Antigone. *(He moves to left of* HAEMON.*)* Sooner or later there comes a day of sorrow in each man's life when he must cease to be a child and take up the burden of manhood. The day has come for you.

HAEMON *(backs away a step).*   That giant strength, that courage. That massive god who used to pick me up in his arms and shelter me from shadows and monsters— was that you, Father? Was it of you I stood in awe? Was that man you?

CREON   For God's sake, Haemon, do not judge me! Not you, too!

HAEMON *(pleading now)*   This is all a bad dream, Father. You are not yourself. It isn't true that we have been backed up against a wall, forced to surrender. We don't have to say *yes* to this terrible thing. You are still king. You are still the father I revered. You have no right to desert me, to shrink into nothingness. The world will be too bare, I shall be too alone in the world, if you force me to disown you.

CREON   The world *is* bare, Haemon, and you *are* alone. You must cease to think your father all-powerful. Look straight at me. See your father as he is. That is what it means to grow up to be a man.

HAEMON *(stares at* CREON *for a moment).*   I tell you that I will not live without Antigone. *(Turns and goes quickly out through arch.)*

CHORUS   Creon, the boy will go mad.

CREON   Poor boy! He loves her.

CHORUS   Creon, the boy is wounded to death.

CREON   We are all wounded to death.

FIRST GUARD *enters through arch, right, followed by* SECOND *and* THIRD GUARDS *pulling Antigone along with them.*

FIRST GUARD   Sir, the people are crowding into the palace!

ANTIGONE   Creon, I don't want to see their faces. I don't want to hear them howl. You are going to kill me; let that be enough. I want to be alone until it is over.

CREON   Empty the palace! Guards at the gates!

CREON *quickly crosses toward the arch; exit.* TWO GUARDS *release* ANTIGONE; *exeunt behind* CREON. CHORUS *goes out through arch, left. The lighting dims so that only the area about the table is lighted. The cyclorama is covered with a dark blue color. The scene is intended to suggest a prison cell, filled with shadows and dimly lit.* ANTIGONE *moves to stool and sits. The* FIRST GUARD *stands upstage. He watches* ANTIGONE, *and as she sits, he begins pacing slowly downstage, then upstage. A pause.*

ANTIGONE *(turns and looks at the Guard).*   It's you, is it?

GUARD   What do you mean, me?

ANTIGONE   The last human face that I shall see. *(A pause as they look at each other, then* GUARD *paces upstage, turns, and crosses behind table.)*   Was it you that arrested me this morning?

GUARD   Yes, that was me.

ANTIGONE   You hurt me. There was no need for you to hurt me. Did I act as if I was trying to escape?

GUARD   Come on now, Miss. It was my business to bring you in. I did it. *(A pause. He paces to and fro upstage. Only the sound of his boots is heard.)*

ANTIGONE   How old are you?

GUARD   Thirty-nine

ANTIGONE   Have you any children?

GUARD   Yes. Two.

ANTIGONE   Do you love your children?

GUARD   What's that got to do with you? *(A pause. He paces upstage and downstage.)*

ANTIGONE   How long have you been in the Guard?

GUARD   Since the war. I was in the army. Sergeant. Then I joined the Guard.

ANTIGONE   Does one have to have been an army sergeant to get into the Guard?

GUARD   Supposed to be. Either that or on special detail. But when they make you a guard, you lose your stripes.

ANTIGONE *(murmurs).*   I see.

GUARD   Yes. Of course, if you're a guard, everybody knows you're something special; they know you're an old N.C.O. Take pay, for instance. When you're a guard you get your pay, and on top of that you get six months' extra pay, to make sure you don't lose anything by not being a sergeant any more. And of course you do better than that. You get a house, coal, rations, extras for the wife and kids. If you've got two kids, like me, you draw better than a sergeant.

ANTIGONE *(barely audible)*   I see.

GUARD   That's why sergeants, now, they don't like guards. Maybe you noticed they try to make out they're better than us? Promotion, that's what it is. In the army, anybody can get promoted. All you need is good conduct. Now in the Guard, it's slow, and you have to know your business—like how to make out a report and the like of that. But when you're an N.C.O. in the Guard, you've got something that even a sergeant-major ain't got. For instance—

ANTIGONE *(breaking him off)*   Listen.

GUARD   Yes, Miss.

ANTIGONE   I'm going to die soon.

The GUARD *looks at her for a moment, then turns and moves away.*

GUARD   For instance, people have a lot of respect for guards, they have. A guard may be a soldier, but he's kind of in the civil service, too.

ANTIGONE   Do you think it hurts to die?

GUARD   How would I know? Of course, if somebody sticks a saber in your guts and turns it round, it hurts.

ANTIGONE   How are they going to put me to death?

GUARD   Well, I'll tell you. I heard the proclamation all right. Wait a minute. How did it go now? *(He stares into space and recites from memory.)* "In order that our fair city shall not be pol-luted with her sinful blood, she shall be im-mured—immured." That means, they shove you in a cave and wall up the cave.

ANTIGONE   Alive?

GUARD   Yes. . . . *(He moves away a few steps.)*

ANTIGONE *(murmurs).*   O tomb! O bridal bed! Alone! (ANTIGONE *sits there, a tiny figure in the middle of the stage. You would say she felt a little chilly. She wraps her arms round herself.)*

GUARD   Yes! Outside the southeast gate of the town. In the Cave of Hades. In broad daylight. Some detail, eh, for them that's on the job! First they thought maybe it was a job for the army. Now it looks like it's going to be the Guard. There's an outfit for you! Nothing the Guard can't do. No wonder the army's jealous.

ANTIGONE   A pair of animals.

GUARD   What do you mean, a pair of animals?

ANTIGONE   When the winds blow cold, all they need do is to press close against one another. I am all alone.

GUARD   Is there anything you want? I can send out for it, you know.

ANTIGONE   You are very kind. *(A pause.* ANTIGONE *looks up at the* GUARD.*)* Yes, there is something I want. I want you to give someone a letter from me, when I am dead.

GUARD   How's that again? A letter?

ANTIGONE   Yes, I want to write a letter; and I want you to give it to someone for me.

GUARD *(straightens up)*   Now, wait a minute. Take it easy. It's as much as my job is worth to go handing out letters from prisoners.

ANTIGONE *(removes a ring from her finger and holds it out toward him).*   I'll give you this ring if you will do it.

GUARD   It's gold? *(He takes the ring from her.)*

ANTIGONE   Yes, it is gold.

GUARD *(shakes his head).*   Uh-uh. No can do. Suppose they go through my pockets. I might get six months for a thing like that. *(He stares at the ring, then glances off right to make sure that he is not being watched.)* Listen, tell you what I'll do. You tell me what you want to say, and I'll write it down in my book. Then, afterwards, I'll tear out the pages and give them to the party, see? If it's in my handwriting, it's all right.

ANTIGONE *(winces).*   In your handwriting? *(She shudders slightly.)* No. That would be awful. The poor darling! In your handwriting.

GUARD *(offers back the ring).*   O.K. It's no skin off my nose.

ANTIGONE *(quickly)*   Of course, of course. No, keep the ring. But hurry. Time is getting short. Where is your notebook? *(The* GUARD *pockets the ring, takes his notebook and pencil from his pocket, puts his foot up on chair, and rests the notebook on his knee, licks his pencil.)* Ready? *(He nods.)* Write, now. "My darling . . ."

GUARD *(writes as he mutters).*   The boy friend, eh?

ANTIGONE   "My darling. I wanted to die, and perhaps you will not love me any more . . ."

GUARD *(mutters as he writes).*   ". . . will not love me any more."

ANTIGONE   "Creon was right. It is terrible to die."

GUARD *(repeats as he writes).*   ". . . terrible to die."

ANTIGONE   "And I don't even know what I am dying for. I am afraid . . ."

GUARD *(looks at her).*   Wait a minute! How fast do you think I can write?

ANTIGONE *(takes hold of herself).*   Where are you?

GUARD *(reads from his notebook).*   "And I don't even know what I am dying for."

ANTIGONE   No. Scratch that out. Nobody must know that. They have no right to know. It's as if they saw me naked and touched me, after I was dead. Scratch it all out. Just write: "Forgive me."

GUARD *(looks at Antigone).*   I cut out everything you said there at the end, and I put down, "Forgive me"?

ANTIGONE   Yes. "Forgive me, my darling. You would all have been so happy except for Antigone. I love you."

GUARD *(finishes the letter).*   ". . . I love you." *(He looks at her)* Is that all?

ANTIGONE   That's all.

GUARD *(straightens up, looks at notebook).*   Damn funny letter.

ANTIGONE   I know.

GUARD *(looks at her).*   Who is it to? *(A sudden roll of drums begins and continues until after* ANTIGONE'S *exit. The* FIRST GUARD *pockets the notebook and shouts at* ANTIGONE.*)* O.K. That's enough out of you! Come on!

At the sound of the drum roll, SECOND *and* THIRD GUARDS *enter through the arch.* ANTIGONE *rises.* GUARDS *seize her and exeunt with her. The lighting moves up to suggest late afternoon.* CHORUS *enters.*

CHORUS   And now it is Creon's turn.

MESSENGER *runs through the arch, right.*
CHORUS   What do you want with the Queen? What have you to tell the Queen?
MESSENGER   News to break her heart. Antigone had just been thrust into the cave. They hadn't finished heaving the last block of stone into place when Creon and the rest heard a sudden moaning from the tomb. A hush fell over us all, for it was not the voice of Antigone. It was Haemon's voice that came forth from the tomb. Everybody looked at Creon; and he howled like a man demented: "Take away the stones! Take away the stones!" The slaves leaped at the wall of stones, and Creon worked with them, sweating and tearing at the blocks with his bleeding hands. Finally a narrow opening was forced, and into it slipped the smallest guard.
   Antigone had hanged herself by the cord of her robe, by the red and golden twisted cord of her robe. The cord was round her neck like a child's collar. Haemon was on his knees, holding her in his arms and moaning, his face buried in her robe. More stones were removed, and Creon went into the tomb. He tried to raise Haemon to his feet. I could hear him begging Haemon to rise to his feet. Haemon was deaf to his father's voice, till suddenly he stood up of his own accord, his eyes dark and burning. Anguish was in his face, but it was the face of a little boy. He stared at his father. Then suddenly he struck him—hard; and he drew his sword. Creon leaped out of range. Haemon went on staring at him, his eyes full of contempt—a glance that was like a knife, and that Creon couldn't escape. The King stood trembling in the far corner of the tomb, and Haemon went on staring. Then, without a word, he stabbed himself and lay down beside Antigone, embracing her in a great pool of blood.

A pause as CREON *and* PAGE *enter through arch on the* MESSENGER'S *last words.* CHORUS *and the* MESSENGER *both turn to look at* CREON; *then exit the* MESSENGER *through curtain.*

CREON   I have had them laid out side by side. They are together at last, and at peace. Two lovers on the morrow of their bridal. Their work is done.
CHORUS   But not yours, Creon. You have still one thing to learn. Eurydice, the Queen, your wife—
CREON   A good woman. Always busy with her garden, her preserves, her sweaters— those sweaters she never stopped knitting for the poor. Strange, how the poor never stop needing sweaters. One would almost think that was all they needed.
CHORUS   The poor in Thebes are going to be cold this winter, Creon. When the Queen was told of her son's death, she waited carefully until she had finished her row,

then put down her knitting calmly—as she did everything. She went up to her room, her lavender-scented room, with its embroidered doilies and its pictures framed in plush; and there, Creon, she cut her throat. She is laid out now in one of those two old-fashioned twin beds, exactly where you went to her one night when she was still a maiden. Her smile is still the same, scarcely a shade more melancholy. And if it were not for that great red blot on the bed linen by her neck, one might think she was asleep.

CREON *(in a dull voice)* She, too. They are all asleep. *(Pause.)* It must be good to sleep.

CHORUS And now you are alone, Creon.

CREON Yes, all alone. *(To* PAGE*)* My lad.

PAGE Sir?

CREON Listen to me. They don't know it, but the truth is the work is there to be done, and a man can't fold his arms and refuse to do it. They say it's dirty work. But if we didn't do it, who would?

PAGE I don't know, sir.

CREON Of course you don't. You'll be lucky if you ever find out. In a hurry to grow up, aren't you?

PAGE Oh, yes, sir.

CREON I shouldn't be if I were you. Never grow up if you can help it. *(He is lost in thought as the hour chimes.)* What time is it?

PAGE Five o'clock, sir.

CREON What have we on at five o'clock?

PAGE Cabinet meeting, sir.

CREON Cabinet meeting. Then we had better go along to it.

Exeunt CREON *and* PAGE *slowly through arch, left, and* CHORUS *moves downstage.*

CHORUS And there we are. It is quite true that if it had not been for Antigone they would all have been at peace. But that is over now. And they are all at peace. All those who were meant to die have died: those who believed one thing, those who believed the contrary thing, and even those who believed nothing at all, yet were caught up in the web without knowing why. All dead: stiff, useless, rotting. And those who survived will now begin quietly to forget the dead: they won't remember who was who or which was which. It is all over. Antigone is calm tonight, and we shall never know the name of the fever that consumed her. She has played her part.

THREE GUARDS *enter, resume their places on steps as at the rise of the curtain, and begin to play cards.*

A great melancholy wave of peace now settles down upon Thebes, upon the empty palace, upon Creon, who can now begin to wait for his own death.

Only the guards are left, and none of this matters to them. It's no skin off their noses. They go on playing cards.

CHORUS *walks toward the arch, left, as the curtain falls.*

QUESTIONS

1   Why does Anouilh emphasize, through the first speech of the Chorus and else-
    where in the play, the physical appearance of Antigone? Does this emphasis
    heighten her doom, her obsession with a sense of destiny, or merely her isolation?
2   Do the many references to Antigone's father, King Oedipus, help to establish the
    motivation and nature of Antigone herself?
3   Does Antigone's dislike of being touched by the guards or her shrinking from expo-
    sure to the crowd enhance her stature as tragic protagonist?
4   Can you sympathize at all with Creon's explanation of why and how he said "yes"
    to the responsibilities of kingship? Is there any hint that Creon envies Antigone?
5   In the debate between Antigone and Creon, why does Creon offer the analogy
    between human life on the one hand and the life force in trees and animals on the
    other? Although she does not explain her rejection of the analogy's validity, why
    does Antigone disdain to relate it to her situation?
6   Anouilh's play, like several other French plays about Antigone, was written during
    the German occupation of France during World War II. Do you see any evidence of
    its relevance not only to that historical circumstance but also the the wider condi-
    tion of man in the troubled second quarter of this century?

TOPICS FOR COMPOSITION

1   With this play as your primary reference and with full recognition of its classical
    material, do you think modern tragedy is possible? Or do you think that the use of
    mythological materials invalidates *Antigone* as a "modern tragedy"?
2   In view of Antigone's attempt to deceive the Nurse, and of her wearing Ismene's
    rouge and perfume on her visit to Haemon the night before her crime, define her
    attitude toward lies and truth.
3   With *Antigone* as your only literary resource, discriminate between the meaning of
    "the search for a place in society" and "the protest against restraint." As a sugges-
    tion, you might consider whether or not "restraint" is ultimately a more profound
    issue than "place."

POETRY

The poems that follow will widen considerably our sampling of modern and relatively modern thought on the question of social restraint and will perhaps help us to proceed to deeper reflections on the subject. The passage from William Cowper's *The Task* and William Blake's famous "London" both present in general—and metaphorical—terms the problem of the tendency of institutions to become ends instead of means, even to the point where men are merely used rather than served by them. Man can develop fully only in society, Cowper says; but, he adds, when social organization becomes very complex and specialized, individual development is hampered more than it is aided. Identification with special-interest groups tends to rob a person of perspective and integrity. If one serves such institutions too zealously, one ceases to be a whole person; one becomes instead an instrument and begins to treat others as instruments. If this process continues, imagination, sympathy, and even common sense may be destroyed, and all sorts of oppression rationalized. Such is the state that Blake envisions in his powerful lament. To him the great city of London is the symbol of the complete domination of the human spirit by institutions of its own creating. London is a nightmarish place where man languishes in "mind-forg'd manacles," and every face bears "marks of weakness, marks of woe."

Robert Burns's well-known "Address to the Unco Guid" leads us to consideration of a more insidious and, in some ways, even more dangerously oppressive form of restraint (which Blake, it must in fairness be added, also understood well). What Burns is chiefly concerned about—and we should recognize that unpretentiousness here is not incompatible with deep concern—is the tendency of common social sanctions to reflect a puritanical distrust of human nature and to create a purely negative approach to virtue. And the negative spirit of puritanism, to use the term loosely and somewhat unfairly, has assumed many forms in more recent periods—some clearly vicious, like the demagoguery that W. B. Yeats protests against in "The Leaders of the Crowd," some deceptively bland, like the "Greater Community" described in W. H. Auden's "The Unknown Citizen." Yeats believes that not only the followers of the crowd but also the seeming leaders are acting out of insecurity and fear. They do not know that truth flourishes only where "the student's lamp has shone" because they are mortally afraid to face themselves in solitude; to them "that lamp is from the tomb," and they struggle to extinguish it as they would resist physical death. Auden describes a more systematic and sophisticated kind of demagoguery, justified, as it would seem, by a general content produced by material prosperity and successful psychological conditioning. No one has complained, the impersonal voice of the poem says; surely, then, nothing is wrong. But it is evident that the poet surmises that social harmony achieved through unquestioning conformity has a dehumanizing effect. Robinson Jeffers and Philip Larkin clearly think so too. Jeffers, as bitter as Yeats, professes to find in the wild, indomitable hawk a creature more admirable than what men have become; and Larkin, with a wistful quizzicality reminiscent of Robert Pack's "A Bird in Search of a Cage," compares civilized men with cattle. Somewhere between these two extremes expressible only in animal imagery lies the truly human range of individual freedom. Gray Burr, in "A Skater's Waltz," seeks to define it by analogy and, it would appear, to assure us that it will always be at least dimly recognized and cherished, though sometimes belatedly. But as the two poems on rearing children ("Schoolchildren" and "The

Stranger") remind us, we are not sure, even when prompted to reflection by the strongest concern, what the right limits are or how they can be maintained. And we have the voices of three women to remind us how lacking in concern we have been.

THE TASK, BOOK IV

William Cowper

<pre>
          Man in society is like a flower
Blown in its native bed: 'tis there alone   660
His faculties, expanded in full bloom,
Shine out; there only reach their proper use.
But man, associated and leagued with man
By regal warrant, or self-joined by bond
For interest sake, or swarming into clans   665
Beneath one head for purposes of war,
Like flowers selected from the rest, and bound
And bundled close to fill some crowded vase,
Fades rapidly, and, by compression marred,
Contracts defilement not to be endured.   670
Hence chartered boroughs are such public plagues;
And burghers men immaculate perhaps,
In all their private functions, once combined,
Become a loathsome body, only fit
For dissolution, hurtful to the main.   675
Hence merchants, unimpeachable of sin
Against the charities of domestic life,
Incorporated, seem at once to lose
Their nature; and, disclaiming all regard
For mercy and the common rights of man,   680
Build factories with blood, conducting trade
At the sword's point, and dyeing the white robe
Of innocent commercial justice red.
Hence, too, the field of glory, as the world
Misdeems it, dazzled by its bright array,   685
With all its majesty of thundering pomp,
Enchanting music, and immortal wreaths,
Is but a school where thoughtlessness is taught
On principle, where foppery atones
For folly, gallantry, for every vice.   690
</pre>

1785

---

660 Blown: blossomed.   *671 boroughs:* urban corporations having monopolistic control over property.

QUESTIONS

1   What is the difference between "man in society" and man associated with man in organizations having special functions? Does Cowper provide a clear conception of society in a healthful state? Is the comparison with flowers a good analogy? Is it a good metaphor?
2   What three kinds of organization does Cowper specifically condemn? Can you offer better instances? Would Cowper condemn unions?

ADDRESS TO THE UNCO GUID, OR THE RIGIDLY RIGHTEOUS

Robert Burns

> My Son, these maxims make a rule,
> An' lump them ay thegither:
> The Rigid Righteous is a fool,
> The Rigid Wise anither:
> The cleanest corn that e'er was dight,
> May hae some pyles o' caff in;
> So ne'er a fellow-creature slight
> For random fits o' daffin.
>   *Solomon (Ecclesiastes 7:16)*

O ye, wha are sae guid yoursel,
  Sae pious and sae holy,
Ye've nought to do but mark and tell
  Your neebour's fauts and folly;
Whase life is like a weel-gaun mill,   5
  Supplied wi' store o' water;
The heapet happer's ebbing still,
  An' still the clap plays clatter!

Hear me, ye venerable core,
  As counsel for poor mortals   10
That frequent pass douce Wisdom's door
  For glaikit Folly's portals:
I for their thoughtless, careless sakes,
  Would here propone defences,—
Their donsie tricks, their black mistakes,   15
  Their failings and mischances.

Ye see your state wi' theirs compared,
  And shudder at the niffer;
But cast a moment's fair regard,
  What makes the mighty differ?   20

Discount what scant occasion gave;
    That purity ye pride in;
And (what's aft mair than a' the lave)
    Your better art o' hidin'.

Think, when your castigated pulse   25
    Gies now and then a wallop,
What ragings must his veins convulse,
    That still eternal gallop!
Wi' wind and tide fair i' your tail,
    Right on ye scud your sea-way;   30
But in the teeth o' baith to sail,
    It makes an unco lee-way.

See Social-life and Glee sit down
    All joyous and unthinking,
Till, quite transmugrify'd, they're grown   35
    Debauchery and Drinking:
O, would they stay to calculate
    Th' eternal consequences,
Or—your more dreaded hell to state—
    Damnation of expenses!   40

Ye high, exalted, virtuous dames,
    Tied up in godly laces,
Before ye gie poor Frailty names,
    Suppose a change o' cases:
A dear-lov'd lad, convenience snug,   45
    A treach'rous inclination—
But, let me whisper i' your lug,
    Ye're aiblins nae temptation.

Then gently scan your brother man,
    Still gentler sister woman;   50
Tho' they may gang a kennin wrang,
    To step aside is human:
One point must still be greatly dark,
    The moving *why* they do it;
And just as lamely can ye mark   55
    How far perhaps they rue it.

Who made the heart, 'tis He alone
    Decidedly can try us:
He knows each chord, its various tone,
    Each spring, its various bias: 60

Then at the balance let's be mute,
    We never can adjust it;
What's done we partly may compute,
    But know not what's resisted.
                    1786

Title: Unco Guid: inordinately good.   *Epigraph: (5) dight:* winnowed.   *(6) caff:* chaff.   *(8) daffin:* larking, frolicking.   *5 weel-gaun:* well-going.   *7 heapet happer's:* heaped hopper.   *8 clap:* the clapper, which shakes the hopper to keep the grain moving.   *9 core:* corps, group.   *11 douce:* sweet.   *12 glaikit:* giddy.   *14 propone:* propose.   *15 donsie:* perverse.   *18 niffer:* exchange.   *20 differ:* difference.   *23 lave:* rest.   *35 transmugrify'd:* transformed.   *47 lug:* ear.   *48 aiblins:* perhaps.   *51 kennin:* a tiny bit.

QUESTIONS

1 What unpleasant traits does the poet see in the "rigidly righteous"?
2 Is the poet denying the moral value of strict regulation of conduct? If so, what basis for judging virtue does he give us?
3 Has the poet displayed in this poem the virtue he preaches?

LONDON

William Blake

I wander through each chartered street
Near where the chartered Thames does flow,
And mark in every face I meet
Marks of weakness, marks of woe.

In every cry of every man,   5
In every infant's cry of fear,
In every voice, in every ban,
The mind-forged manacles I hear:

How the chimney-sweeper's cry
Every blackening church appalls,   10
And the hapless soldier's sigh
Runs in blood down palace walls.

But most, through midnight streets I hear
How the youthful harlot's curse
Blasts the new-born infant's tear,   15
And blights with plagues the marriage hearse.
                    1794

London: 1 chartered: under the monopolistic control of a corporation.   *7 ban:* legal prohibition.   *15 blasts:* blights.

QUESTIONS

1 Here, Blake attacks certain institutions, that is, organizations and established systems that shape and express general social and moral attitudes. What are they in this case? What, for example, is represented by the palace? What is the connection with the suffering suggested by the soldier's sigh?
2 The poet suggests that the basic cause of the various forms of oppression he mentions is a kind of mental enslavement. Where does he make this statement?
3 Why does the poet use the phrase "marriage hearse"? What kind of plague would be associated with the harlot's curse?

SHE ROSE TO HIS REQUIREMENT

Emily Dickinson

She rose to His Requirement—dropt
The Playthings of Her Life
To take the honorable Work
Of Woman, and of Wife—

If ought She missed in Her new Day, 5
Of Amplitude, or Awe—
Or first Prospective—Or the Gold
In using, wear away,

It lay unmentioned—as the Sea
Develop Pearl, and Weed, 10
But only to Himself—be known
The Fathoms they abide—

1863

QUESTIONS

1 Who is the "She" in this poem?
2 What kind of restraint is in question here?
3 Do you find the sea metaphor appropriate? What are its main implications for you? How does its use affect the tone of the poem?

THE LEADERS OF THE CROWD

William Butler Yeats

They must to keep their certainty accuse
All that are different of a base intent;
Pull down established honor; hawk for news
Whatever their loose phantasy invent
And murmur it with bated breath, as though   5
The abounding gutter had been Helicon
Or calumny a song. How can they know
Truth flourishes where the student's lamp has shone,
And there alone, that have no solitude?
So the crowd come they care not what may come.   10
They have loud music, hope every day renewed
And heartier loves; that lamp is from the tomb.

1924

The Leaders of the Crowd: 6 Helicon: On Mount Helicon in Greece was a spring sacred to the Muses. *9 that:* The antecedent is "they" in line *7. 12:* That is, the "leaders of the crowd" think so.

QUESTIONS

1   What is the basic motive attributed here to the "leaders of the crowd"? Does the poet have in mind only political demagogues, or social leaders of other kinds as well? Are such leaders as are described here to be found on college campuses?
2   The poet says that truth flourishes only in solitude. Does this imply that all popular opinions are false or that truth can never be generally accepted? Does the poem have a moral?

COMMISSION

Ezra Pound

Go, my songs, to the lonely and the unsatisfied,
Go also to the nerve-wracked, go to the enslaved-by-convention,
Bear to them my contempt for their oppressors.
Go as a great wave of cool water,
Bear my contempt of oppressors.   5

Speak against unconscious oppression,
Speak against the tyranny of the unimaginative,
Speak against bonds.
Go to the bourgeoise who is dying of her ennuis,

Go to the women in suburbs.　　　　　　　　　　　　10
Go to the hideously wedded,
Go to them whose failure is concealed,
Go to the unluckily mated,
Go to the bought wife,
Go to the woman entailed.　　　　　　　　　　　　15

Go to those who have delicate lust,
Go to those whose delicate desires are thwarted,
Go like a blight upon the dulness of the world;
Go with your edge against this,
Strengthen the subtle cords,　　　　　　　　　　　20
Bring confidence upon the algae and the tentacles of the soul.

Go in a friendly manner,
Go with an open speech.
Be eager to find new evils and new good,
Be against all forms of oppression.　　　　　　　　25
Go to those who are thickened with middle age,
To those who have lost their interest.

Go to the adolescent who are smothered in family—
Oh how hideous it is
To see three generations of one house gathered together!　　30
It is like an old tree with shoots,
And with some branches rotted and falling.

Go out and defy opinion,
Go against this vegetable bondage of the blood.
Be against all sorts of mortmain.　　　　　　　　35

1917

15 *entailed:* treated as a restricted inheritance. 35 *mortmain:* perpetual ownership; the controlling influence of the past.

QUESTIONS

1　What kind of oppression is the poet mainly concerned about? Is it moral restriction? What are the key words in his indictment?
2　Does the poet single out a particular group of people as the main oppressors?
3　Is there any evidence that modern adolescents have been "smothered in family"? Has "song" given them any relief?

HURT HAWKS

Robinson Jeffers

I

The broken pillar of the wing jags from the clotted shoulder,
The wing trails like a banner in defeat,
No more to use the sky forever but live with famine
And pain a few days: cat nor coyote
Will shorten the week of waiting for death, there is game without talons.   5
He stands under the oak-bush and waits
The lame feet of salvation; at night he remembers freedom
And flies in a dream, the dawns ruin it.
He is strong and pain is worse to the strong, incapacity is worse.
The curs of the day come and torment him   10
At distance, no one but death the redeemer will humble that head,
The intrepid readiness, the terrible eyes.
The wild God of the world is sometimes merciful to those
That ask mercy, not often to the arrogant.
You do not know him, you communal people, or you have forgotten him;   15
Intemperate and savage, the hawk remembers him;
Beautiful and wild, the hawks, and men that are dying, remember him.

II

I'd sooner, except the penalties, kill a man than a hawk; but the great redtail
Had nothing left but unable misery
From the bone too shattered for mending, the wing that trailed under his talons
    when he moved.   20
We had fed him six weeks, I gave him freedom,
He wandered over the foreland hill and returned in the evening, asking
    for death,
Not like a beggar, still eyed with the old
Implacable arrogance. I gave him the lead gift in the twilight.
What fell was relaxed.   25
Owl-downy, soft feminine feathers; but what
Soared: the fierce rush: the night-herons by the flooded river cried fear
    at its rising
Before it was quite unsheathed from reality.

1927

QUESTIONS

1 What does Jeffers mean by "the wild God of the world"? Why do men that are dying remember him? Does Jeffers believe in life after death?

2   What kind of mercy does the poet refer to in lines 13–15? Are circumstances really different for those who ask mercy, or is it a matter of the way things look to them?

3   What, according to Jeffers, does being free mean in human terms? Does freedom depend primarily upon circumstances, or rather upon knowledge and attitude? What is the relation between freedom and suffering? Is belief in mercy consistent with the sense of freedom?

4   The subject and intent of this poem pose a problem in the control of tone. Both bluster and sentimentality must be carefully avoided. Has Jeffers succeeded? What features of his style help especially in gaining the intended effect? Does the style change at any point?

SCHOOLCHILDREN

W. H. Auden

Here are all the captivities; the cells are as real:
But these are unlike the prisoners we know
Who are outraged or pining or wittily resigned
    Or just wish all away.

For they dissent so little, so nearly content   5
With the dumb play of the dog, the licking and rushing;
The bars of love are so strong, their conspiracies
    Weak like the vows of drunkards.

Indeed their strangeness is difficult to watch:
The condemned see only the fallacious angels of a vision;   10
So little effort lies behind their smiling,
    The beast of vocation is afraid.

But watch them, O, set against our size and timing
The almost neuter, the slightly awkward perfection;
For the sex is there, the broken bootlace is broken,   15
    The professor's dream is not true.

Yet the tyranny is so easy. The improper word
Scribbled upon the fountain, is that all the rebellion?
The storm of tears shed in the corner, are these
    The seeds of the new life?   20

1937

QUESTIONS

1   Can you find anything in the references to education here that seems to justify the comparison of schools with prisons?

2   What do you think is the connection between the phrases "the bars of love" and
    "the professor's dream"?
3   Is this poem a protest against some kind of abuse that can be remedied or is it a
    lament over a necessary evil?

THE UNKNOWN CITIZEN

(To JS/07/M378
This Marble Monument
Is Erected by the State)

W. H. Auden

He was found by the Bureau of Statistics to be
One against whom there was no official complaint,
And all the reports on his conduct agree
That, in the modern sense of an old-fashioned word, he was a saint,
For in everything he did he served the Greater Community.   5
Except for the War till the day he retired
He worked in a factory and never got fired,
But satisfied his employers, Fudge Motors Inc.
Yet he wasn't a scab or odd in his views,
For his Union reports that he paid his dues,   10
(Our report on his Union shows it was sound)
And our Social Psychology workers found
That he was popular with his mates and liked a drink.
The Press are convinced that he bought a paper every day
And that his reactions to advertisements were normal in every way.   15
Policies taken out in his name prove that he was fully insured,
And his Health-card shows he was once in hospital but left it cured.
Both Producers Research and High-Grade Living declare
He was fully sensible to the advantages of the Instalment Plan
And had everything necessary to the Modern Man,   20
A phonograph, a radio, a car and a frigidaire.
Our researchers into Public Opinion are content
That he held the proper opinions for the time of year;
When there was peace, he was for peace; when there was war, he went.
He was married and added five children to the population,   25
Which our Eugenist says was the right number for a parent of his generation,
And our teachers report that he never interfered with their education.
Was he free? Was he happy? The question is absurd:
Had anything been wrong, we should certainly have heard.

                                                                        1940

QUESTIONS

1 Obviously, the poet thinks that such a man as "the unknown citizen" is not free. But was "the unknown citizen" forced to behave in the way he did? What kept him from being free?

2 "Was he happy?" someone asks. Why would he not be? Under what circumstances might he have been happier?

3 What is the difference between the modern and the old-fashioned sense of the word "saint"?

4 What assumption is being satirized in the last two lines of the poem?

WIRES

Philip Larkin

The widest prairies have electric fences,
For though old cattle know they must not stray
Young steers are always scenting purer water
Not here but anywhere. Beyond the wires

Leads them to blunder up against the wires
Whose muscle-shredding violence gives no quarter.
Young steers become old cattle from that day,
Electric limits to their widest senses.

1962

QUESTIONS

1 The real subject of this poem, of course, is human experience. Do you think that the wires stand for social restraints? What difficulty does this assumption present?

2 Do you think that there is any significance in the fact that the poet has chosen an analogy that compares people with cattle? Can you think of another analogy which fits the same facts about human experience but expresses a different attitude?

A SKATER'S WALTZ

Gray Burr

There was a pond on which we learned to skate,
Where the blades flashed like sabres, and the ice,
Scored and carved as an old dinner-plate,
Lay locked within its shores as in a vise.

How different we all were; how much the same.   5
Do you remember Speed, the hockey ace,
Who shuttled stick and puck to early fame?
Not one of us could skate to match his pace.

And there was Flora, queen of pirouette,
Who wore such scimitars upon her feet   10
And whirled her skirt to flowers; oh, well met,
Flora, lovely Flora, light and fleet.

Hand in hand, the couples zigged and zagged
And had their ups and downs; the cut-ups fell
Most often, though bad holes were plainly flagged.   15
Still, anyone could trip and break the spell

That music made, and movement, in the mesh
Of skaters shifting, threading warp and woof.
Oh tapestry of heart and mind and flesh,
We all were skeins in you; yet one, aloof,   20

Hung from the general scene, our loosest end,
A mystery and reproach to naïveté.
You'd meet him coming round the sharpest bend,
Racing against the crowd, another way.

Whistles shrilled in that well-ordered place   25
And he was often asked to leave the ice.
But when he'd gone, so also had some grace,
Some figure only he could improvise.

I think that if the god should pull that thread,
A whole woven dream might fall apart.   30
It would, at least, be less. Arise, ye dead!
Remain, O Dionysian, in our heart.

                          1962

10 scimitars: sabers with curved blades.   *32 Dionysian:* as used here, one who is impulsive and
unruly. The devotees of Dionysus, god of wine, were supposed to be given to orgiastic rites.

QUESTIONS

1   What do the principal metaphors here—the pond locked within its shores, skating
    to music, the weaving of a tapestry—suggest about the author's view of the mean-
    ing and value of life? Does morality seem to be a strong concern?
2   In connection with the foregoing question, what general kind of nonconformity does
    the poem defend?

THE STRANGER

Adrienne Rich

Fond credos, plaster ecstasies!
We arrange a prison-temple

for the weak-legged little god
who might stamp the world to bits

or pull the sky in like a muslin curtain.   5
We hang his shrine with bells,

aeolian harps, paper windmills,
line it with biscuits and swansdown.

His lack of culture we expected,
scarcely his disdain however—   10

that wild hauteur, as if
it were we who blundered.

Wildness we fret to avenge!
Eye that hasn't yet blinked

on the unblinking gold archways   15
of its trance—*that* we know

must be trained away:
that aloof, selective stare.

Otherness that affronts us
as cats and dogs do not—   20

once this was original sin
beaten away with staves of holy writ.

Old simplemindedness. But the primal fault
of the little god still baffles.

All other strangers are forgiven   25
their strangeness, but he—

how save the eggshell world from his
reaching hands, how shield

ourselves from the disintegrating
blaze of his wide pure eye?   30

1964

QUESTIONS

1 Does this poem in any way depict realistically the psychology of parenthood? If so, what kind of parental oppression does it warn against?
2 Is the idea of man's erecting a god in his own image incidental, or is it central? Is the suggested relation between child worship and theology or theology substitutes to be taken seriously? Is it valid?

BLUEPRINT

Joel Sloman

I keep thinking of isolated Long Island estates
with rolling lawns, swimming pools and the distant clinking of plates
on the verandah. The people, always seeming to warn
each other of the rules of behavior: how to eat corn
on the cob, how to walk, talk, drink, and deal   5
with the inconvenience of nature, the perfect meal
being a criticism of the accidental arrangement of the universe.
All solemnity in America is perverse,
all sophistication, a labyrinth that looks like a necessary
rationale. An identity a gleaming estate, isolated from class, the incendiary   10
vehicle that makes a true revolution possible. Experience is what we learn
from, not the fantasy of our self-programming, as if only a handful of
      experiences turn
out to be useful. All blueprints are specks in the
eye of history.

QUESTIONS

1 What perspective is established in this poem?
2 What purpose do the rhymes serve here?

ELEVATORS

Barbara Davis

elevators
make me
extremely
racist.
i hate   5

in elevators.
gray old lady
old gray lady
askin me
to hold it   10
parkinson's disease
takes a halfhour to the door
and then
she wanna
talk   15
about it.
buddha-heads
callin the place a slum.
the super wants to know
if my man   20
was invited,
"lots of robberies lately."
goddamnit
I'M
JUST
TRYING   25
TO
GET
TO
MY   30
ROOM
white man,
don't ask me
if i'm cold in my short,
short skirt and   35
try to make me
before the 8th floor
cause i may kill you 'fore the 4th.
                              1973

QUESTIONS

1   The reason for the arrangement of the words of this poem is obvious. Is the ar-
    rangement effective? Take into consideration the appropriate inflection of the cap-
    italized words.
2   Why might the choice of subject be considered ironic?
3   What is the point of mentioning the woman afflicted with Parkinson's disease along
    with the less-than-admirable male types?

THE DEAD LADIES

Mary Gordon

for Maureen Sugden

> We can sit down and weep;
> we can go shopping
> *Elizabeth Bishop*

What's to be done with death,
My friend?
      We sit
Cross legged, hating men.

Virginia filled her English skirt   5
With stones.
Always well bred she left behind
Her sensible shoes, her stick
Her hat, her last note
(An apology)   10
And walked in water
'Til it didn't matter.

We speak of Sylvia
Who could not live
For babies or for poetry.   15

You switch on Joplin's blues
The room looms black
With what we know
But are afraid to think.

Too scared to say: "and us?"   20
We leave for work.
Hearts in our mouths.
In love with the wrong men.
             1973

5 Virginia: Virginia Woolf, British novelist.   *13 Sylvia:* Sylvia Plath, American poet.   *16 Joplin:* Janis Joplin, the famous singer. All three of these women committed suicide.

QUESTIONS

1   What, as it turns out, does the poet mean by the question with which she begins?
2   Is there any indication why the poet says that she and her friend hate men? Does her statement mean that she is not to be taken literally when she says that they are in love with the wrong men?

TOPICS FOR COMPOSITION

1 Drawing upon Burns's "Address to the Unco Guid" for opinions, write a satirical description of the puritanical character. Or write a description of someone whom you consider to be somewhat puritanical.

2 Express your views on the question of whether virtue is primarily a matter of conduct or of attitude.

3 Defend the thesis that society is still overpuritanical in some important respect. If you prefer, argue that in certain areas of conduct a more puritanical attitude would be beneficial.

4 Advance a general opinion on the question of whether or not legal restraint of private vice is justified. Support your opinion by analyzing a particular problem of this nature.

5 Using Yeats's "The Leaders of the Crowd" as a starting point for reflection, write an essay on good leadership, bad leadership, or the principal difference between the two. Try to get at the heart of the problem of leadership, and limit your consideration of the matter, if you can, to one or two important points. Possible topics: "The Pseudo-Leader"; "Sick Leadership"; "The Loneliness of Leadership"; "Leadership and Compromise."

6 Ezra Pound's "Commission" suggests a number of matters for exploration. What, for example, does he mean by "the tyranny of the unimaginative"? Where does such tyranny operate? Does it ever exist in the home? In the classroom? In school affairs generally? In the world of entertainment? In national affairs? Answer one or more of these questions in an essay.

7 With Pound's poem in mind, write an essay on the topic "The Woman in the Suburbs."

8 Pound's assertion that adolescents may be smothered in family seems prophetic in view of recent "teenage" unrest. If you feel that you have some insight into the matter, explain how parents may smother their children or why they tend to do so. One might also consider whether parents are not sometimes the victims of their own efforts to mold, control, or protect their children.

9 Write a short story on the implications of the tree metaphor in Pound's "Commission" (lines 31–32).

10 Analyze the moral implications of Jeffers' "Hurt Hawks." What kind of person would the author (or speaker) of the poem admire? What kind of human relations would he approve of?

11 Write an essay explaining how Auden's "Unknown Citizen" might be regarded as a sequel or companion poem to his "Schoolchildren."

12 Write a description of a modern "saint," using the term as it is used in Auden's "The Unknown Citizen."

13 Write a reply to the indictment presented in "The Unknown Citizen"—or propose a partial solution to the problem.

14 After reflection upon what you have read in this book so far and upon your personal experience, formulate a general statement about the relation between freedom, morality, and happiness. Use the statement as the thesis for an essay developed by the method of exemplification.

15 If you can, draw upon first-hand knowledge to illustrate one or more of the generalizations suggested by Philip Larkin's "Wires."

16 Analyze the concept of identity advocated in "Blueprint."

17　Does it seem to you that Emily Dickinson's "She Rose to His Requirement" and Mary Gordon's "The Dead Ladies" are mutually illuminating? If so, explain why.

18　John Stuart Mill, in his famous essay *On Liberty,* asserted that the only purpose for which power, whether in the form of legal penalties or the moral coercion of public opinion, can be rightfully exercised over any member of the community, against his will, is to prevent harm to others. Most people would subscribe to this principle. The trouble is that there has been much disagreement about what may constitute harm. Indicate in an essay or article where you would draw the line, giving an example or two. Or argue a particular case in which there has been or probably would be disagreement.

19　What do you consider to be currently the most offensive form of restraint upon individual freedom and development? Explain your opinion and, if you can, propose a remedy.

PART THREE

THE MEANING
OF LOVE

The attempts of many writers to define or at least to describe love reflect the universality of interest in this facet of man's makeup as well as the virtual impossibility of arriving at any one definition of so complex an emotion. In treating the spiritual, emotional, or physical aspects of love, or a combination of these, writers have illuminated the elusiveness and complexity of love and accordingly have generated a central, compulsive literary theme.

In the first essay, Erich Fromm's "The Theory of Love," we encounter the assertion that love is an inherent part of man's being and that he controls the "activity" of love. In other words, Fromm seeks an individual, highly subjective view of man involved in the act of giving—giving as a requisite to loving. On the other hand, Mervyn Cadwallader's "Marriage as a Wretched Institution" assesses love, and marriage in particular, in the light of the pressures of modern, middle-class American society. That Cadawallader's essay is more an indictment of existing conditions than a resolution to the relationship between love and marriage is evident in his concluding sentences, "How do you marry and live like gentle lovers or at least like friendly roommates? Quite frankly, I do not know the answer to that question."

Fromm and Cadwallader's contrasting viewpoints about aspects of love in modern society are apparent in the three short stories which follow their essays. "Chestnut and Jet" by the Irish writer, Bryan MacMahon, illuminates the sensitive compatibility between love and marriage. In a simpler setting than modern American urban society, it interprets still another elemental love force. MacMahon's story pulses with sexual excitement, with those fundamental yet difficult to describe emotions stirred by evidences of physical virility in the communion of love and marriage. Nora exhibits unashamed pride in love's physical fulfillment while the attitudes of many of the other characters contrast sharply with hers.

Irwin Shaw's "The Girls in Their Summer Dresses," though written some thirty years ago, is thoroughly modern in its implications. Shaw, like Cadwallader, asks us to examine the restrictions imposed upon love within the structure of marriage. Whereas Shaw's story suggests that his characters may eventually resolve their problems and maintain the institution of marriage, "An Interior Monologue" by Joyce Carol Oates is a fictional parallel to the "wretchedness" of marriage and its subsequent destructive influence upon the lives of those involved. Her story leaves little doubt that personal wishes heightened by everyday pressures are not conducive to the sort of love that marriage seems to demand.

THE ESSAY

In "The Theory of Love," Fromm naturally finds it necessary to first define love. And, as writers of extended definition often find, one definition leads to many more. Fromm's definition shows both its depth and variety in the following ways:

1   The definition of love as activity leads to a definition of activity which in turn leads to definitions of giving, care, responsibility, respect, and knowledge.
2   Each term shows a variety in methods of defining. Note Fromm's use of synonym, example, analogy, and negation.

THE THEORY OF LOVE

Erich Fromm

Mature *love* is *union under the condition of preserving one's integrity,* one's individuality. *Love is an active power in man;* a power which breaks through the walls which separate man from his fellow men, which unites him with others; love makes him overcome the sense of isolation and separateness, yet it permits him to be himself, to retain his integrity. In love the paradox occurs that two beings become one and yet remain two.

If we say love is an activity, we face a difficulty which lies in the ambiguous meaning of the word "activity." By "activity," in the modern usage of the word, is usually meant an action which brings about a change in an existing situation by means of an expenditure of energy. Thus a man is considered active if he does business, studies medicine, works on an endless belt, builds a table, or is engaged in sports. Common to all these activities is that they are directed toward an outside goal to be achieved. What is *not* taken into account is the *motivation* of activity. Take for instance a man driven to incessant work by a sense of deep insecurity and loneliness; or another one driven by ambition, or greed for money. In all these cases the person is the slave of a passion, and his activity is in reality a "passivity" because he is driven; he is the sufferer, not the "actor." On the other hand, a man sitting quiet and contemplating, with no purpose or aim except that of experiencing himself and his oneness with the world, is considered to be "passive," because he is not "doing" anything. In reality, this attitude of concentrated meditation is the highest activity there is, an activity of the soul, which is possible only under the condition of inner freedom and independence. One concept of activity, the modern one, refers to the use of energy for the achievement of external aims; the other concept of activity refers to the use of man's inherent powers, regardless of whether any external change is brought about. The latter concept of activity has been formulated most clearly by Spinoza. He differentiates among the affects between active and passive affects, "actions" and "passions." In the exercise of an active affect, man is free, he is the master of his affect; in the exercise of a passive affect, man is driven, the object of motivations of which he himself is not aware. Thus Spinoza arrives at the statement that virtue and power are one and the same.[1] Envy, jealousy, ambition, any kind of greed are passions; love is an action, the practice of a human power, which can be practiced only in freedom and never as the result of a compulsion.

Love is an activity, not a passive affect; it is a "standing in," not a "falling for." In the most general way, the active character of love can be described by stating that love is primarily *giving,* not receiving.

What is giving? Simple as the answer to this question seems to be, it is actually full of ambiguities and complexities. The most widespread misunderstanding is that which assumes that giving is "giving up" something, being deprived of, sacrificing. The person whose character has not developed beyond the stage of the receptive, exploitative, or hoarding orientation, experiences the act of giving in this way. The marketing character is willing to give, but only in exchange for receiving; giving without receiving for him is being cheated. People whose main orientation is a non-productive one feel giving as an impoverishment. Most individuals of this type therefore refuse to give. Some make a virtue out of giving in the sense of a sacrifice. They feel that just because it is painful to give, one *should* give; the virtue of giving to them lies in the very act of acceptance of the sacrifice. For them, the norm that it is better to give than to receive means that it is better to suffer deprivation than to experience joy.

For the productive character, giving has an entirely different meaning. Giving is the highest expression of potency. In the very act of giving, I experience my strength, my wealth, my power. This experience of heightened vitality and potency fills me with joy. I experience myself as overflowing, spending, alive, hence as joyous. Giving is more joyous than receiving, not because it is a deprivation, but because in the act of giving lies the expression of my aliveness. . . .

In the sphere of material things giving means being rich. Not he who *has* much is rich, but he who *gives* much. The hoarder who is anxiously worried about losing something is, psychologically speaking, the poor, impoverished man, regardless of how much he has. Whoever is capable of giving of himself is rich. He experiences himself as one who can confer of himself to others. Only one who is deprived of all that goes beyond the barest necessities for subsistence would be incapable of enjoying the act of giving material things. But daily experience shows that what a person considers the minimal necessities depends as much on his character as it depends on his actual possessions. It is well known that the poor are more willing to give than the rich. Nevertheless, poverty beyond a certain point may make it impossible to give, and is so degrading, not only because of the suffering it causes directly, but because of the fact that it deprives the poor of the joy of giving.

The most important sphere of giving, however, is not that of material things, but lies in the specifically human realm. What does one person give to another? He gives of himself, of the most precious he has, he gives of his life. This does not necessarily mean that he sacrifices his life for the other—but that he gives him of that which is alive in him; he gives him of his joy, of his interest, of his understanding, of his knowledge, of his humor, of his sadness—of all expressions and manifestations of that which

[1] Spinoza, *Ethics IV,* Def. 8.

is alive in him. In thus giving of his life, he enriches the other person, he enhances the other's sense of aliveness by enhancing his own sense of aliveness. He does not give in order to receive; giving is in itself exquisite joy. But in giving he cannot help bringing something to life in the other person, and this which is brought to life reflects back to him; in truly giving, he cannot help receiving that which is given back to him. Giving implies to make the other person a giver also and they both share in the joy of what they have brought to life. In the act of giving something is born, and both persons involved are grateful for the life that is born for both of them. Specifically with regard to love this means: love is a power which produces love; impotence is the inability to produce love. This thought has been beautifully expressed by Marx: "Assume," he says, "*man* as *man,* and his relation to the world as a human one, and you can exchange love only for love, confidence for confidence, etc. If you wish to enjoy art, you must be an artistically trained person; if you wish to have influence on other people, you must be a person who has a really stimulating and furthering influence on other people. Every one of your relationships to man and to nature must be a definite expression of your *real, individual* life corresponding to the object of your will. If you love without calling forth love, that is, if your love as such does not produce love, if by means of an *expression of life* as a loving person you do not make of yourself a *loved person,* then your love is impotent, a misfortune."[2] But not only in love does giving mean receiving. The teacher is taught by his students, the actor is stimulated by his audience, the psychoanalyst is cured by his patient—provided they do not treat each other as objects, but are related to each other genuinely and productively.

It is hardly necessary to stress the fact that the ability to love as an act of giving depends on the character development of the person. It presupposes the attainment of a predominantly productive orientation; in this orientation the person has overcome dependency, narcissistic omnipotence, the wish to exploit others, or to hoard, and has acquired faith in his own human powers, courage to rely on his powers in the attainment of his goals. To the degree that these qualities are lacking, he is afraid of giving himself—hence of loving.

Beyond the element of giving, the active character of love becomes evident in the fact that it always implies certain basic elements, common to all forms of love. These are *care, responsibility, respect* and *knowledge.*

That love implies *care* is most evident in a mother's love for her child. No assurance of her love would strike us as sincere if we saw her lacking in care for the infant, if she neglected to feed it, to bathe it, to give it physical comfort; and we are impressed by her love if we see her caring for the child. It is not different even with the love for animals or flowers. If a woman told us that she loved flowers, and we saw that she forgot to water them, we would not believe in her "love" for flowers. *Love is the active concern for the life and the growth of that which we love.* Where this active concern is lacking, there is no love. This element of love has been beautifully described in the book of Jonah. God has told Jonah to go to Nineveh to warn its inhabitants that they will be punished unless they mend their evil ways. Jonah runs away from his mission

---

[2] "Nationalökonomie und Philosophie," 1844, published in Karl Marx' *Die Frühschriften,* Alfred Kröner Verlag, Stuttgart, 1953, pp. 300, 301. (My translation, E. F.)

because he is afraid that the people of Nineveh will repent and that God will forgive them. He is a man with a strong sense of order and law, but without love. However, in his attempt to escape, he finds himself in the belly of a whale, symbolizing the state of isolation and imprisonment which his lack of love and solidarity has brought upon him. God saves him, and Jonah goes to Nineveh. He preaches to the inhabitants as God has told him, and the very thing he was afraid of happens. The men of Nineveh repent their sins, mend their ways, and God forgives them and decides not to destroy the city. Jonah is intensely angry and disappointed; he wanted "justice" to be done, not mercy. At last he finds some comfort in the shade of a tree which God made to grow for him to protect him from the sun. But when God makes the tree wilt, Jonah is depressed and angrily complains to God. God answers: "Thou hast had pity on the gourd for the which thou has not labored neither madest it grow; which came up in a night, and perished in a night. And should I not spare Nineveh, that great city, wherein are more than sixscore thousand people that cannot discern between their right hand and their left hand; and also much cattle?" God's answer to Jonah is to be understood symbolically. God explains to Jonah that the essence of love is to "labor" for something and "to make something grow," that love and labor are inseparable. One loves that for which one labors, and one labors for that which one loves.

Care and concern imply another aspect of love; that of *responsibility*. Today responsibility is often meant to denote duty, something imposed upon one from the outside. But responsibility, in its true sense, is an entirely voluntary act; it is my response to the needs, expressed or unexpressed, of another human being. To be "responsible" means to be able and ready to "respond." Jonah did not feel responsible to the inhabitants of Nineveh. He, like Cain, could ask: "Am I my brother's keeper?" The loving person responds. The life of his brother is not his brother's business alone, but his own. He feels responsible for his fellow men, as he feels responsible for himself. This responsibility, in the case of the mother and her infant, refers mainly to the care for physical needs. In the love between adults it refers mainly to the psychic needs of the other person.

Responsibility could easily deteriorate into domination and possessiveness, were it not for a third component of love, *respect*. Respect is not fear and awe; it denotes, in accordance with the root of the word (*respicere* = to look at), the ability to see a person as he is, to be aware of his unique individuality. Respect means the concern that the other person should grow and unfold as he is. Respect, thus, implies the absence of exploitation. I want the loved person to grow and unfold for his own sake, and in his own ways, and not for the purpose of serving me. If I love the other person, I feel one with him or her, but with him *as he is,* not as I need him to be as an object for my use. It is clear that respect is possible only if *I* have achieved independence; if I can stand and walk without needing crutches, without having to dominate and exploit anyone else. Respect exists only on the basis of freedom: "l'amour est l'enfant de la liberté" as an old French song says; love is the child of freedom, never that of domination.

To respect a person is not possible without *knowing* him; care and responsibility would be blind if they were not guided by knowledge. Knowledge would be empty if it were not motivated by concern. There are many layers of knowledge; the knowledge which is an aspect of love is one which does not stay at the periphery, but penetrates to the core. It is possible only when I can transcend the concern for myself and see the other person in his own terms. I may know, for instance, that a person is angry, even if he does not show it overtly; but I may know him more deeply than that; then I know that he is anxious, and worried; that he feels lonely, that he feels guilty. Then I know that his anger is only the manifestation of something deeper, and I see him as anxious and embarrassed, that is, as the suffering person, rather than as the angry one.

Knowledge has one more, and a more fundamental, relation to the problem of love. The basic need to fuse with another person so as to transcend the prison of one's separateness is closely related to another specifically human desire, that to know the "secret of man." While life in its merely biological aspects is a miracle and a secret, man in his human aspects is an unfathomable secret to himself—and to his fellow man. We know ourselves, and yet even with all the efforts we may make, we do not know ourselves. We know our fellow man, and yet we do not know him, because we are not a thing, and our fellow man is not a thing. The further we reach into the depth of our being, or someone else's being, the more the goal of knowledge eludes us. Yet we cannot help desiring to penetrate into the secret of man's soul, into the innermost nucleus which is "he."

There is one way, a desperate one, to know the secret: it is that of complete power over another person; the power which makes him do what we want, feel what we want, think what we want; which transforms him into a thing, our thing, our possession. The ultimate degree of this attempt to know lies in the extremes of sadism, the desire and ability to make a human being suffer; to torture him, to force him to betray his secret in his suffering. In this craving for penetrating man's secret, his and hence our own, lies an essential motivation for the depth and intensity of cruelty and destructiveness. In a very succinct way this idea has been expressed by Isaac Babel. He quotes a fellow officer in the Russian civil war, who has just stamped his former master to death, as saying: "With shooting—I'll put it this way—with shooting you only get rid of a chap. . . . With shooting you'll never get at the soul, to where it is in a fellow and how it shows itself. But I don't spare myself, and I've more than once trampled an enemy for over an hour. You see, I want to get to know what life really is, what life's like down our way."[3]

In children we often see this path to knowledge quite overtly. The child takes something apart, breaks it up in order to know it; or it takes an animal apart; cruelly tears off the wings of a butterfly in order to know it, to force its secret. The cruelty itself is motivated by something deeper: the wish to know the secret of things and of life.

The other path to knowing "the secret" is love. Love is active penetration of the other person, in which my desire to know is stilled by union. In the act of fusion I know you, I know myself, I know everybody—and I "know" nothing. I know in the only way knowledge of that which is alive is possible for man—by experience of union—not by any knowledge our thought can give. Sadism is motivated by the wish to know the secret, yet I remain as ignorant as I was before. I have torn the other being apart limb from limb, yet all I have done is to destroy him. Love is the only way of knowledge, which in the act of union answers my quest. In the act of loving, of giving myself, in the

---

[3] I. Babel, *The Collected Stories,* Criterion Books, New York, 1955.

act of penetrating the other person, I find myself, I discover myself, I discover us both, I discover man.

QUESTIONS

1 Fromm makes an initial distinction between passions and actions. What other words does he use that are synonymous with "passions" and "actions"?
2 How is the act of giving related to character development? What assumption would Fromm make about a person incapable of loving?
3 Fromm supports his definition of love by assigning certain basic characteristics. How does each support his definition? Is his list complete, or would you add other characteristics?

TOPICS FOR COMPOSITION

1 Write your own view of the meaning of love. Carefully define your terms, using Fromm's essay as your model.
2 Consider the overworked use of the term *love*. Write an essay in which you argue that the term *love* has been so misused that no clear definition is possible. Support your argument with examples and anecdotes.

By recognizing that Cadwallader's full thesis is that marriage is a wretched institution because it is unable to bear the pressures of contemporary American middle-class society, we are better able to uncover the salient points by which he structures support for his thesis. Notice the progressive nature of the following:

1 The function of marriage in the past
2 The changes brought about by an industrialized society
3 The creation of an adolescent culture and the trend toward marriage at an earlier age
4 The paradox inherent in existing mores: those that insist on stability in marriage while encouraging permissiveness in related human interaction

MARRIAGE AS A WRETCHED INSTITUTION

Mervyn Cadwallader

Our society expects us all to get married. With only rare exceptions we all do just that. Getting married is a rather complicated business. It involves mastering certain complex hustling and courtship games, the rituals and the ceremonies that celebrate the act of marriage, and finally the difficult requirements of domestic life with a husband or wife. It is an enormously elaborate round of activity, much more so than finding a job, and yet while many resolutely remain unemployed, few remain unmarried.

Now all this would not be particularly remarkable if there were no question about the advantages, the joys, and the rewards of married life, but most Americans, even young Americans, know or have heard that marriage is a hazardous affair. Of course, for all the increase in divorce, there are still young marriages that work, unions made by young men and women intelligent or fortunate enough to find the kind of mates they want, who know that they want children and how to love them when they come, or who find the artful blend between giving and receiving. It is not these marriages that concern us here, and that is not the trend in America today. We are concerned with the increasing number of others who, with mixed intentions and varied illusions, grope or fling themselves into marital disaster. They talk solemnly and sincerely about working to make their marriage succeed, but they are very aware of the countless marriages they have seen fail. But young people in particular do not seem to be able to relate the awesome divorce statistics to the probability of failure of their own marriage. And they rush into it, in increasing numbers, without any clear idea of the reality that underlies the myth.

Parents, teachers, and concerned adults all counsel against premature marriage. But they rarely speak the truth about marriage as it really is in modern middle-class America. The truth as I see it is that contemporary marriage is a wretched institution. It spells the end of voluntary affection, of love freely given and joyously received. Beautiful romances are transmuted into dull marriages, and eventually the relationship becomes constricting, corrosive, grinding, and destructive. The beautiful love affair becomes a bitter contract.

The basic reason for this sad state of affairs is that marriage was not designed to bear the burdens now being asked of it by the urban American middle class. It is an institution that evolved over centuries to meet some very specific functional needs of a nonindustrial society. Romantic love was viewed as tragic, or merely irrelevant. Today it is the titillating prelude to domestic tragedy, or, perhaps more frequently, to domestic grotesqueries that are only pathetic.

Marriage was not designed as a mechanism for providing friendship, erotic experience, romantic love, personal fulfillment, continuous lay psychotherapy, or recreation. The Western European family was not designed to carry a lifelong load of highly emotional romantic freight. Given its present structure, it simply has to fail when asked to do so. The very idea of an irrevocable contract obligating the parties concerned to a lifetime of romantic effort is utterly absurd.

Other pressures of the present era have tended to overburden marriage with expectations it cannot fulfill. Industrialized, urbanized America is a society which has lost the sense of community. Our ties to our society, to the bustling multitudes that make up this dazzling kaleidoscope of contemporary America, are as formal and superficial as they are numerous. We all search for community, and yet we know that the search is futile. Cut off from the support and satisfactions that flow from community, the confused and searching young American can do little but place all of his bets on creating a community in microcosm, his own marriage.

And so the ideal we struggle to reach in our love relationship is that of complete candor, total honesty. Out there all is phony, but within the romantic family there are to be no dishonest games, no hypocrisy, no misunderstanding. Here we have a painful paradox, for I submit that total exposure is probably always mutually destructive in the long run. What starts out as a tender coming together to share one's whole person with the beloved is transmuted by too much togetherness into attack and counterattack, doubt, disillusionment, and ambivalence. The moment the once-upon-a-time lover catches a glimpse of his own hatred, something precious and fragile is shattered. And soon another brave marriage will end.

The purposes of marriage have changed radically, yet we cling desperately to the outmoded structures of the past. Adult Americans behave as though the more obvious the contradiction between the old and the new, the more sentimental and irrational should be their advice to young people who are going steady or are engaged. Our schools, both high schools and colleges, teach sentimental rubbish in their marriage and family courses. The texts make much of a posture of hard-nosed objectivity that is neither objective nor hard-nosed. The basic structure of Western marriage is never questioned, alternatives are not proposed or discussed. Instead, the prospective young bride and bridegroom are offered housekeeping advice and told to work hard at making their marriage succeed. The chapter on sex, complete with ugly diagrams of the male and female genitals, is probably wedged in between a chapter on budgets and life insurance. The message is that if your marriage fails, you have been weighed in the domestic balance and found wanting. Perhaps you did not master the fifth position for sexual intercourse, or maybe you bought cheap term life rather than a preferred policy with income protection and retirement benefits. If taught honestly, these courses would alert the teen-ager and young adult to the realities of matrimonial life in the United States and try to advise them on how to survive marriage if they insist on that hazardous venture.

But teen-agers and young adults do insist upon it in greater and greater numbers with each passing year. And one of the reasons they do get married with such astonishing certainty is because they find themselves immersed in a culture that is preoccupied with and schizophrenic about sex. Advertising, entertainment, and fashion are all designed to produce and then to exploit sexual tension. Sexually aroused at an early age and asked to postpone marriage until they become adults, they have no recourse but to fill the intervening years with courtship rituals and games that are supposed to be sexy but sexless. Dating is expected to culminate in going steady, and that is the beginning of the end. The dating game hinges on an important exchange. The male wants sexual intimacy, and the female wants social commitment. The game involves bartering sex for security amid the sweet and heady agitations of a romantic entanglement. Once the game reaches the going-steady stage, marriage is virtually inevitable. The teen-ager finds himself driven into a corner, and the one way to legitimize his sex play and assuage the guilt is to plan marriage.

Another reason for the upsurge in young marriages is the real cultural break between teen-agers and adults in our society. This is a recent phenomenon. In my generation there was no teen culture. Adolescents wanted to become adults as soon as possible. The teen-age years were a time of impatient waiting, as teen-age boys tried to dress and act like little men. Adolescents sang the adults' songs ("South of the Border," "The Music Goes Round and Round," "Mairzy Doats"—notice I didn't say anything about the quality of the music), saw their movies, listened to their radios, and waited confidently to be allowed in. We had no money, and so there was no teen-age market. There was nothing to do then but get it over with. The boundary line was sharp, and you crossed it when you took your first serious job, when you passed the employment test.

Now there is a very definite adolescent culture, which is in many ways hostile to the dreary culture of the adult world. In its most extreme form it borrows from the beats and turns the middle-class value system inside out. The hip teen-ager on Macdougal Street or Telegraph Avenue can buy a costume and go to a freak show. It's fun to be an Indian, a prankster, a beat, or a swinging troubadour. He can get stoned. That particular trip leads to instant mysticism.

Even in less extreme forms, teen culture is weighted against the adult world of responsibility. I recently asked a roomful of eighteen-year-olds to tell me what an adult is. Their deliberate answer, after hours of discussion, was that an adult is someone who no longer plays, who is no longer playful. Is Bob Dylan an adult? No, never! Of course they did not want to remain children, or teens, or adolescents; but they did want to remain youthful, playful, free of squares, and free of responsibility. The teen-ager wants to be old enough to drive, drink, screw, and travel. He does not want to get pushed into square maturity. He wants to drag the main, be a surf bum, a ski bum, or dream of being a bum. He doesn't want to go to Vietnam, or to IBM, or to buy a split-level house in Knotty Pines Estates.

This swing away from responsibility quite predictably produces frictions between the adolescent and his parents. The clash of cultures is likely to drive the adolescent from the home, to persuade him to leave the dead world of his parents and strike out on his own. And here we find the central paradox of young marriages. For the only way the young person can escape from his parents is to assume many of the responsibilities that he so reviles in the life-style of his parents. He needs a job and an apartment. And he needs some kind of emotional substitute, some means of filling the emotional vacuum that leaving home has caused. And so he goes steady, and sooner rather than later, gets married to a girl with similar inclinations.

When he does this, he crosses the dividing line between the cultures. Though he seldom realizes it at the time, he has taken the first step to adulthood. Our society does not have a conventional "rite of passage." In Africa the Masai adolescent takes a lion test. He becomes an adult the first time he kills a lion with a spear. Our adolescents take the domesticity test. When they get married they have to come to terms with the system in one way or another. Some brave individuals continue to fight it. But most simply capitulate.

The cool adolescent finishing high school or starting college has a skeptical view of virtually every institutional sector of his society. He knows that government is corrupt, the military dehumanizing, the corporations rapacious, the churches organized hypocrisy, and the schools dishonest. But the one area that seems to be exempt from his cynicism is romantic love and marriage. When I talk to teen-agers about marriage, that cool skepticism turns to sentimental dreams right out of *Ladies' Home Journal* or the hard-hitting pages of *Reader's Digest*. They all mouth the same vapid platitudes about finding happiness through sharing and personal fulfillment through giving (each is to give 51 percent). They have all heard about divorce, and most of them have been touched by it in some way or another. Yet they insist that their marriage will be different.

So, clutching their illusions, young girls with ecstatic screams of joy lead their awkward brooding boys through the portals of the church into the land of the Mustang, Apartment 24, Macy's, Sears, and the ubiquitous drive-in. They have become members in good standing of the adult world.

The end of most of these sentimental marriages is quite predictable. They progress, in most cases, to varying stages of marital ennui, depending on the ability of the couple to adjust to reality; most common are (1) a lackluster standoff, (2) a bitter business carried on for the children, church, or neighbors, or (3) separation and divorce, followed by another search to find the right person.

Divorce rates have been rising in all Western countries. In many countries the rates are rising even faster than in the United States. In 1910 the divorce rate for the United States was 87 per 1000 marriages. In 1965 the rate had risen to an estimated figure of well over 300 per 1000 in many parts of the country. At the present time some 40 percent of all brides are between the ages of fifteen and eighteen; half of these marriages break up within five years. As our population becomes younger and the age of marriage continues to drop, the divorce rate will rise to significantly higher levels.

What do we do, what can we do, about this wretched and disappointing institution? In terms of the immediate generation, the answer probably is, not much. Even when subjected to the enormous strains I have described, the habits, customs, traditions, and taboos that make up our courtship and marriage cycle are uncommonly resistant to change. Here and there creative and courageous individuals can and do work out their own unique solutions to the problem of marriage. Most of us simply suffer without understanding and thrash around blindly in an attempt to reduce the acute pain of a romance gone sour. In time, all of these individual actions will show up as a trend away from the old and toward the new, and the bulk of sluggish moderates in the population will slowly come to accept this trend as part of social evolution. Clearly, in middle-class America, the trend is ever toward more romantic courtship and marriage, earlier premarital sexual intercourse, earlier first marriages, more extramarital affairs, earlier first divorces, more frequent divorces and remarriages. The trend is away from stable lifelong monogamous relationships toward some form of polygamous male-female relationship. Perhaps we should identify it as serial or consecutive polygamy, simply because Americans in significant numbers are going to have more than one husband or more than one wife. Attitudes and laws that make multiple marriages (in sequence, of course) difficult for the romantic and sentimental among us are archaic obstacles that one learns to circumvent with the aid of weary judges and clever attorneys.

Now, the absurdity of much of this lies in the fact that we pretend that marriages of short duration must be contracted for life. Why not permit a flexible contract perhaps for one to two or more years, with periodic options to renew? If a couple grew disenchanted with their life together, they would not feel trapped for life. They would not have to anticipate and then go through the destructive agonies of divorce. They would not have to carry about the stigma of marital failure, like the mark of Cain on their foreheads. Instead of a declaration of war, they could simply let their contract lapse, and while still friendly, be free to continue their romantic quest. Sexualized romanticism is now so fundamental to American life—and is bound to become even more so—that marriage will simply have to accommodate itself to it in one way or another. For a great proportion of us it already has.

What of the children in a society that is moving inexorably toward consecutive plural marriages? Under present arrangements in which marriages are ostensibly life-time contracts and then are dissolved through hypocritical collusions or messy battles in court, the children do suffer. Marriage and divorce turn lovers into enemies, and the child is left to thread his way through the emotional wreckage of his parents' lives. Financial support of the children, mere subsistence, is not really a problem in a society as affluent as ours. Enduring emotional support of children by loving, healthy, and friendly adults is a serious problem in America, and it is a desperately urgent problem in many families where divorce is unthinkable. If the bitter and poisonous denouement of divorce could be avoided by a frank acceptance of short-term marriages, both adults and children would benefit. Any time husbands and wives and ex-husbands and ex-wives treat each other decently, generously, and respectfully, their children will benefit.

The braver and more critical among our teen-agers and youthful adults will still ask, But if the institution is so bad, why get married at all? This is a tough one to deal with. The social pressures pushing any couple who live together into marriage are difficult to ignore even by the most resolute rebel. It can be done, and many should be encouraged to carry out their own creative experiments in living together in a relation-ship that is wholly voluntary. If the demands of society to conform seem overwhelming, the couple should know that simply to be defined by others as married will elicit mar-ried-like behavior in themselves, and that is precisely what they want to avoid.

How do you marry and yet live like gentle lovers, or at least like friendly room-mates? Quite frankly, I do not know the answer to that question.

QUESTIONS

1   What, according to Cadwallader, is the ideal that we try to reach in a love relation-ship?
2   How have the purposes of marriage changed?
3   Early in his essay, Cadwallader says that urbanized America has lost its "sense of community." What precisely does he mean and how accurate is his statement?
4   About a decade has passed since this essay appeared. Is its indictment still accu-rate?

TOPICS FOR COMPOSITION

1   In his essay, Cadwallader offers some alternatives to the long-term marriage con-tract. Write an essay supporting or refuting the advisability of his alternatives.
2   Research current marriage and divorce statistics. Use your research to predict the success or failure of marriage in this decade.

SHORT STORY

In "Chestnut and Jet," MacMahon presents a vivid portrayal of Joe and Nora Morrissey in a story that provides little dialogue by which we may assess each of the main characters. Instead, the author uses:

1 Nora's reactions to the comments of her neighbors
2 Nora's attitude as she watches Joe from a distance
3 Joe's mannerisms when he "parades" his animal before the townspeople

CHESTNUT AND JET

Bryan MacMahon

When April came, Joe Morrissey the farmer took down the nail-box from the top of the dresser and rummaged in it to discover the sire horse's ribbons and rosettes. When at last he found them, they were in sorry over-winter trim. Each year it was the same. Each year he had to ask the milliner in town to make him a new set so that his stallion should look his best as he paraded the town on market day.

The black stallion was taken from the drudgery of the spring work and petted. Jack Donnell the young-old groom gladly abandoned the ploughing of furzy uplands and began to give the horse his April delicacies: porridge and new milk and beaten eggs and oats. There was also a mash, the ingredients of which he kept a tight-fisted secret. Dandruff-brush and curry-comb were unearthed and plied. Gradually the camouflaged splendour and dignity and terror of the animal emerged. Out in the farmyard the as yet white sunlight caught him in swaths on flank and haunch and chest and heliographed his power to the awakening countryside. The horse sloughed winter, welcomed summer, and trumpeted the indignities of his spring. He seemed to find the touch of the cobbles intolerable. He began to whistle and bell. His challenge was the blending of a cluster of four handbells in four different tones mingled with the faraway whistle of a railway engine. This extraordinary noise was the overture of his chaotic blood: making the noise his nostrils were two pouches lined with a terrifying red velvet.

Out in the farmyard the black farmer walked round and round the black stallion. Joe Morrissey was smiling as he watched the cajolings and wheedlings and bullyings of the groom. As day followed day the farmer began to reflect the animal. The man's gait grew to have something of the strut in it. Watching him covertly from the kitchen window, his wife Nora broke into a warm smile as she measured the capers of her man. She threw back her chestnut head as her nose emitted a hiss of humorous tolerance. Her hands automatically kneaded dough while her smiling eyes were busy loving her man. Suddenly she was aware that her daughter Nonie was nuzzling at her dress.

"Mam!" The chestnut child of five was her mother's image.

"Well?"

Out of a crinkling face: "Can I go to town a Wednesday with my Dad?"

"No, my little filly. Not Wednesday. Some other day, maybe."

"Mam!"

"Well, child?"

"I'm not a filly. I'm a lev-er-et."

The woman shook out the scarf of her red rich laughter. "In the spring a filly, in the winter a leveret. Isn't that fair?"

"That's fair . . . an' Mam!"

"Well, Nonie girl?"

"If you go to town a Wednesday with my Dad will you bring me back Queen cakes?"

"I will, of course. I'll bring you back a big white bag of Queen cakes. Isn't that fair, Nonie?"

"That's fair, Mam."

Wednesday was market-day in town. That was the day the stallion stood at Treanor's Yard. Joe Morrissey has the terra-cotta-coloured posters posted on the walls of the fair green and on the pillars of the weigh-bridge. "Royal Splendour," they bragged, "by Royal Musician out of Splendid Stream. . . . This sire is getting extra well . . . his stock is well known . . . terms . . . groom's fees . . . no responsibility . . . particulars from . . ."

Each Wednesday morning Jack Donnell and another groom danced the great jet Irish Draught up the long street of the town. About midday Joe Morrissey and his wife drummed into town in the tubtrap. Nora Morrissey generally shopped at a store on the outskirts; rarely did she penetrate into the town proper. Her husband saw to it that everything was right in Treanor's Yard. He stood a few drinks to the farmers who had brought their mares. In the evening he himself paraded the stallion down the street and then handed the animal over to the grooms who had been walking some distance behind him. Afterwards he sat into the trap with his wife and returned home. Speaking through the hoof-beats he told his wife how the day had gone with him, with whom he had been drinking, what price one of the stallion's foals had made. His wife listened with tranquillity and understanding.

Mary Sullivan was a neighbour of the Morrissey's. She came into Morrissey's one evening when the man of the house was out. Crouching over the open hearth, Mary whined more to herself than to Nora Morrissey: "Your husband, your grand black husband. God bless you, Big Joe! God in his infinite goodness saw fit to make Mary Sullivan an ould maid. I was in town a Wednesday when he led the sire-horse down the length of the main street. An' all the people came out of their houses to see the grand man and the grand stallion."

Minnie McNaughton was another neighbour. She was a labouring man's widow. She was childless. Speaking to Nora Morrissey, she said: "Fine and fine for you, Mrs. Morrissey. God loves the ground you walk on. I was inside in town on market day getting my commands and I heard the townspeople giving the height of splendour to your upstanding man. God spare him long to you and to your lovely children. When he passes down the street on Wednesday, gentle and simple stand up to see the grand man and the grand stallion. Fine and fine for you, Mrs. Morrissey. Fine again for you. . . ." The woman's voice grumbled on in lonely envy.

Gradually this became Nora Morrissey's problem—to picture her husband and the stallion through alien eyes. But try as she would, her eyes remained unalterably her own. In this effort of imagination she apprehended herself shaking her head suddenly as if to clear her head after a blow. The full consciousness of her antic inevitably flooding her, she would begin to upbraid herself for her foolishness. And to crown her discomfiture there was her little chestnut daughter at the table's head tossing her head and smiling as she mimicked her chestnut mother. On the instant their two laughters were blended in the sunny kitchen.

When next market day came Nora Morrissey went into the centre of the town. The market was a busy one and the streets were thronged. The woman bore herself over-bravely, as if expecting battle and experiencing sharp disappointment in its failure to come upon her. She went in and out of shops on the thinnest pretexts. She offered an excellent pretence of interest in the affairs of acquaintances she met on the pavements. But always she took care to stand where her eyes could command the higher end of the street. There she expected the man and the stallion to appear above the swirl of the people. As evening came an access of excitement compelled her to throw back her Paisley shawl from her forehead and display the light mahogany depths of her hair and the clean-cut outlines of her features. As time passed without her husband's appearance, an insane impatience began to have its way with her: What was keeping him? Will the people have gone home? What on earth am I doing here? The whole side of the country will hear about me. What's delaying you, Joe Morrissey? What's delaying you, I say?

Then the two black dancers were out above at the street's end. Excitement tightened in the woman's chest. Now man and horse had moved well on to the stage of the town. Nora appreciated the strangeness of the as yet silent hooves whose tappeta-tappeta would presently carry their rhythm into her blood. Dark stallion and dark man were now dancing into audibility. Now she could see the ribbons and the rosettes. The animal seemed endowed with a deeper darkness than the man. There was a contrast in the lead of a tubular white web which the farmer was holding lightly in his guiding hand and also in the pipe-clayed surcingle which circled the stallion's belly. The surcingle bisected the arc in the animal's back—to the rear of the white band was the treasured violence of the haunches. Man and stallion were completely confident, completely arrogant, completely male.

Nora Morrissey suddenly remembered the town and swung to view it. True for the tellers, the whole place had come out to see the man and the stallion. An old man displaying the last cheap remnants of vigour; a rusty old woman finding herself being revolved like an old locomotive on a turntable; a shop assistant remembering hills and the beat of the tide; a motor mechanic dreaming himself white as a hound's tooth; a hobbledehoy finding a decade of years flung unbearably at his bewildered head; a butcher pausing in the analysis of a belch to recall roses and the scent of roses; six canker-eared corner-boys disinterring bones of buried manhood—the whole spring-throttled town was out to see the jet stallion and the jet man.

As they drew near her Nora Morrissey found herself instinctively withdrawing towards the wall of the shops. She made as if to cover her face with her shawl. Then, as a flame grows tall in a windless moment, she straightened herself, and throwing the shawl back from her hair and face she came out to the pavement's edge and began to glory in their coming. Lifting her head she made ready to greet her Emperor. Slow enough he was in seeing her. His face was as yet rigid with a high urban pride; his air was that of one who had delivered himself up to the reverence of the people. His set mouth disdained domesticities. For a terrifying moment she thought he would fail to see her. Then, being a woman, she made an unwarranted movement of her shawl. His processional eyes rested on her, abandoned her, recaptured her—then his face blazed up into recognition and dear emotion. The woman came close to sobbing in the sweetness of this public statement of ownership. For a moment the farmer relaxed his strain on the lead. Sensing this the horse raised his head and rang his great cluster of bells.

QUESTIONS

1 MacMahon's story is rich in imagery, especially in his use of color. What instances can you find where his use of color contributes to the mood of the moment?
2 What statements in the story appear "poetical" in their wording? Why are these statements appropriate to the author's purpose?
3 What does Nora's correction of her daughter's use of "leveret" indicate about her attitude toward life?
4 Why does MacMahon reveal the attitudes of Mary Sullivan and Minnie McNaughton?
5 As an obvious "love story," MacMahon's work also reveals other, perhaps attendant emotions. Where do we see pride, envy, humility?
6 How deeply has the author relied on characterization? What, for instance, can you say about Nora as a person? What about Joe? Can you come to some conclusion about MacMahon's method?

TOPICS FOR COMPOSITION

1 MacMahon's story obviously illustrates the value of precise detail. Write an essay describing a moment of deep feeling (love, pride, envy, etc.). Base your essay on a careful selection of descriptive words rather than on the action of the moment.
2 Using Joe and Nora as examples, explain Fromm's assertion that love is giving.
3 Certainly, marriage is not a wretched institution in this story. Write a refutation of Cadwallader's essay based on the relationship between Joe and Nora.

"The Girls in Their Summer Dresses" may seem structurally uncomplicated. However, its structure, like its theme, is deceptively simple. As a young married couple begin to walk and to talk, Shaw sets in motion a progression that becomes more intense at each step. We need to be sensitive to changing moods which parallel setting and dialogue; especially, we should keep in mind:

1 Frances and Michael's initial sense of well-being paralleling the brightness of the day

2 The couple's seeming readiness to enjoy their special relationship
3 The emergence of an obstacle to their relationship; an obstacle obviously neither new nor previously undiscussed
4 Their subsequent rejection of the natural brightness of the day and openness of the outdoors, and their retreat to the seclusion and imitated warmth of the bar

THE GIRLS IN THEIR SUMMER DRESSES

Irwin Shaw

Fifth Avenue was shining in the sun when they left the Brevoort and started walking toward Washington Square. The sun was warm, even though it was November and everything looked like Sunday morning—the buses, and the well-dressed people walking slowly in couples and the quiet buildings with the windows closed.

Michael held Frances' arm tightly as they walked downtown in the sunlight. They walked lightly, almost smiling, because they had slept late and had a good breakfast and it was Sunday. Michael unbuttoned his coat and let it flap around him in the mild wind. They walked, without saying anything, among the young and pleasant-looking people who somehow seem to make up most of the population of that section of New York City.

"Look out," Frances said, as they crossed Eighth Street. "You'll break your neck."

Michael laughed and Frances laughed with him.

"She's not so pretty, anyway," Frances said. "Anyway, not pretty enough to take a chance breaking your neck looking at her."

Michael laughed again. He laughed louder this time, but not as solidly. "She wasn't a bad-looking girl. She had a nice complexion. Country-girl complexion. How did you know I was looking at her?"

Frances cocked her head to one side and smiled at her husband under the tip-tilted brim of her hat. "Mike, darling . . ." she said.

Michael laughed, just a little laugh this time. "O.K.," he said. "The evidence is in. Excuse me. It was the complexion. It's not the sort of complexion you see much in New York. Excuse me."

Frances patted his arm lightly and pulled him along a little faster toward Washington Square.

"This is a nice morning," she said. "This is a wonderful morning. When I have breakfast with you it makes me feel good all day."

"Tonic," Michael said. "Morning pick-up. Rolls and coffee with Mike and you're on the alkali side, guaranteed."

"That's the story. Also, I slept all night, wound around you like a rope."

"Saturday night," he said. "I permit such liberties only when the week's work is done."

"You're getting fat," she said.

"Isn't it the truth? The lean man from Ohio."

"I love it," she said, "an extra five pounds of husband."

"I love it, too," Michael said gravely.

"I have an idea," Frances said.

"My wife has an idea. That pretty girl."

"Let's not see anybody all day," Frances said. "Let's just hang around with each other. You and me. We're always up to our neck in people, drinking their Scotch, or drinking our Scotch, we only see each other in bed . . ."

"The Great Meeting Place," Michael said. "Stay in bed long enough and everybody you ever knew will show up there."

"Wise guy," Frances said. "I'm talking serious."

"O.K., I'm listening serious."

"I want to go out with my husband all day long. I want him to talk only to me and listen only to me."

"What's to stop us?" Michael asked. "What party intends to prevent me from seeing my wife alone on Sunday? What party?"

"The Stevensons. They want us to drop by around one o'clock and they'll drive us into the country."

"The lousy Stevensons," Mike said. "Transparent. They can whistle. They can go driving in the country by themselves. My wife and I have to stay in New York and bore each other tête-à-tête."

"Is it a date?"

"It's a date."

Frances leaned over and kissed him on the tip of the ear.

"Darling," Michael said. "This is Fifth Avenue."

"Let me arrange a program," Frances said. "A planned Sunday in New York for a young couple with money to throw away."

"Go easy."

"First let's go see a football game. A professional football game," Frances said, because she knew Michael loved to watch them. "The Giants are playing. And it'll be nice to be outside all day today and get hungry and later we'll go down to Cavanagh's and get a steak as big as a blacksmith's apron, with a bottle of wine, and after that, there's a new French picture at the Filmarte that everybody says . . . Say, are you listening to me?"

"Sure," he said. He took his eyes off the hatless girl with the dark hair, cut dancer-style, like a helmet, who was walking past him with the self-conscious strength and grace dancers have. She was walking without a coat and she looked very solid and strong and her belly was flat, like a boy's, under her skirt, and her hips swung boldly because she was a dancer and also because she knew Michael was looking at her. She smiled a little to herself as she went past and Michael noticed all these things before he looked back at his wife. "Sure," he said, "we're going to watch the Giants and we're going to eat steak and we're going to see a French picture. How do you like that?"

"That's it," Frances said flatly. "That's the program for the day. Or maybe you'd just rather walk up and down Fifth Avenue."

"No," Michael said carefully. "Not at all."

"You always look at other women," Frances said. "At every damn woman in the City of New York."

"Oh, come now," Michael said, pretending to joke. "Only pretty ones. And, after all, how many pretty women *are* there in New York? Seventeen?"

"More. At least you seem to think so. Wherever you go."

"Not the truth. Occasionally, maybe, I look at a woman as she passes. In the street. I admit, perhaps in the street I look at a woman once in a while . . ."

"Everywhere," Frances said. "Every damned place we go. Restaurants, subways, theaters, lectures, concerts."

"Now, darling," Michael said, "I look at everything. God gave me eyes and I look at women and men and subway excavations and moving pictures and the little flowers of the field. I casually inspect the universe."

"You ought to see the look in your eye," Frances said, "as you casually inspect the universe on Fifth Avenue."

"I'm a happily married man." Michael pressed her elbow tenderly, knowing what he was doing. "Example for the whole twentieth century, Mr. and Mrs. Mike Loomis."

"You mean it?"

"Frances, baby . . ."

"Are you *really* happily married?"

"Sure," Michael said, feeling the whole Sunday morning sinking like lead inside him. "Now what the hell is the sense in talking like that?"

"I would like to know." Frances walked faster now, looking straight ahead, her face showing nothing, which was the way she always managed it when she was arguing or feeling bad.

"I'm wonderfully happily married," Michael said patiently. "I am the envy of all men between the ages of fifteen and sixty in the State of New York."

"Stop kidding," Frances said.

"I have a fine home," Michael said. "I got nice books and a phonograph and nice friends. I live in a town I like the way I like and I do the work I like and I live with the woman I like. Whenever something good happens, don't I run to you? When something bad happens, don't I cry on your shoulder?"

"Yes," Frances said. "You look at every woman that passes."

"That's an exaggeration."

"Every woman." Frances took her hand off Michael's arm. "If she's not pretty you turn away fairly quickly. If she's halfway pretty you watch her for about seven steps . . ."

"My lord, Frances!"

"If she's pretty you practically break your neck . . ."

"Hey, let's have a drink," Michael said, stopping.

"We just had breakfast."

"Now, listen, darling," Mike said, choosing his words with care, "it's a nice day and we both feel good and there's no reason why we have to break it up. Let's have a nice Sunday."

"I could have a fine Sunday if you didn't look as though you were dying to run after every skirt on Fifth Avenue."

"Let's have a drink," Michael said.

"I don't want a drink."

"What do you want, a fight?"

"No," Frances said so unhappily that Michael felt terribly sorry for her. "I don't want a fight. I don't know why I started this. All right, let's drop it. Let's have a good time."

They joined hands consciously and walked without talking among the baby carriages and the old Italian men in the Sunday clothes and the young women with Scotties in Washington Square Park.

"I hope it's a good game today," Frances said after a while, her tone a good imitation of the tone she had used at breakfast and at the beginning of their walk. "I like professional football games. They hit each other as though they're made out of concrete. When they tackle each other," she said, trying to make Michael laugh, "they make divots. It's very exciting."

"I want to tell you something," Michael said very seriously. "I have not touched another woman. Not once. In all the five years."

"All right," Frances said.

"You believe that, don't you?"

"All right."

They walked between the crowded benches, under the scrubby city park trees.

"I try not to notice it," Frances said, as though she were talking to herself. "I try to make believe it doesn't mean anything. Some men're like that, I tell myself, they have to see what they're missing."

"Some women're like that, too," Michael said. "In my time I've seen a couple of ladies."

"I haven't even looked at another man," Frances said, walking straight ahead, "since the second time I went out with you."

"There's no law," Michael said.

"I feel rotten inside, in my stomach, when we pass a woman and you look at her and I see that look in your eye and that's the way you looked at me the first time, in Alice Maxwell's house. Standing there in the living room, next to the radio, with a green hat on and all those people."

"I remember the hat," Michael said.

"The same look," Frances said. "And it makes me feel bad. It makes me feel terrible."

"Sssh, please, darling, sssh . . ."

"I think I would like a drink now," Frances said.

They walked over to a bar on Eighth Street, not saying anything, Michael automatically helping her over curbstones, and guiding her past automobiles. He walked, buttoning his coat, looking thoughtfully at his neatly shined heavy brown shoes as they made the steps toward the bar. They sat near a window in the bar and the sun streamed in, and there was a small cheerful fire in the fireplace. A little Japanese waiter came over and put down some pretzels and smiled happily at them.

"What do you order after breakfast?" Michael asked.

"Brandy, I suppose," Frances said.

"Courvoisier," Michael told the waiter. "Two Courvoisier."

The waiter came with the glasses and they sat drinking the brandy, in the sunlight. Michael finished half his and drank a little water.

"I look at women," he said. "Correct. I don't say it's wrong or right, I look at them. If I pass them on the street and I don't look at them, I'm fooling you, I'm fooling myself."

"You look at them as though you want them," Frances said, playing with her brandy glass. "Every one of them."

"In a way," Michael said, speaking softly and not to his wife, "in a way that's true. I don't do anything about it, but it's true."

"I know it. That's why I feel bad."

"Another brandy," Michael called. "Waiter, two more brandies."

"Why do you hurt me?" Frances asked. "What're you doing?"

Michael sighed and closed his eyes and rubbed them gently with his fingertips. "I love the way women look. One of the things I like best about New York is the battalions of women. When I first came to New York from Ohio that was the first thing I noticed, the million wonderful women, all over the city. I walked around with my heart in my throat."

"A kid," Frances said. "That's a kid's feeling."

"Guess again," Michael said. "Guess again. I'm older now, I'm a man getting near middle age, putting on a little fat and I still love to walk along Fifth Avenue at three o'clock on the east side of the street between Fiftieth and Fifty-seventh Streets, they're all out then, making believe they're shopping, in their furs and their crazy hats, everything all concentrated from all over the world into eight blocks, the best furs, the best clothes, the handsomest women, out to spend money and feeling good about it, looking coldly at you, making believe they're not looking at you as you go past."

The Japanese waiter put the two drinks down, smiling with great happiness.

"Everything is all right?" he asked.

"Everything is wonderful," Michael said.

"If it's just a couple of fur coats," Frances said, "and forty-five dollar hats . . ."

"It's not the fur coats. Or the hats. That's just the scenery for that particular kind of woman. Understand," he said, "you don't have to listen to this."

"I want to listen."

"I like the girls in the offices. Neat, with their eyeglasses, smart, chipper, knowing what everything is about, taking care of themselves all the time." He kept his eye on the people going slowly past outside the window. "I like the girls on Forty-fourth Street at lunch time, the actresses, all dressed up on nothing a week, talking to the good-looking boys, wearing themselves out being young and vivacious outside Sardi's waiting for producers to look at them. I like the salesgirls in Macy's, paying attention to you first because you're a man, leaving lady customers waiting, flirting with you over socks and books and phonograph needles. I got all this stuff accumulated in me because I've been thinking about it for ten years and now you've asked for it and here it is."

"Go ahead," Frances said.

"When I think of New York City, I think of all the girls, the Jewish girls, the Italian girls, the Irish, Polack, Chinese, German, Negro, Spanish, Russian girls, all on parade in the city. I don't know whether it's something special with me or whether every man in the city walks around with the same feeling inside him, but I feel as though I'm at a picnic in this city. I like to sit near the women in the theaters, the famous beauties who've taken six hours to get ready and look it. And the young girls at the football games, with the red cheeks, and when the warm weather comes, the girls in their summer dresses . . ." He finished his drink. "That's the story. You asked for it, remember. I can't help but look at them. I can't help but want them."

"You want them," Frances repeated without expression. "You said that."

"Right," Michael said, being cruel now and not caring, because she had made him expose himself. "You brought this subject up for discussion, we will discuss it fully."

Frances finished her drink and swallowed two or three times extra. "You say you love me?"

"I love you, but I also want them. O.K."

"I'm pretty, too," Frances said. "As pretty as any of them."

"You're beautiful," Michael said, meaning it.

"I'm good for you," Frances said, pleading. "I've made a good wife, a good housekeeper, a good friend. I'd do any damn thing for you."

"I know," Michael said. He put his hand out and grasped hers.

"You'd like to be free to . . ." Frances said.

"Sssh."

"Tell the truth." She took her hand away from under his.

Michael flicked the edge of his glass with his finger. "O.K.," he said gently. "Sometimes I feel I would like to be free."

"Well," Frances said defiantly, drumming on the table, "anytime you say . . ."

"Don't be foolish." Michael swung his chair around to her side of the table and patted her thigh.

She began to cry, silently, into her handkerchief, bent over just enough so that nobody else in the bar would notice. "Some day," she said, crying, "you're going to make a move . . ."

Michael didn't say anything. He sat watching the bartender slowly peel a lemon.

"Aren't you?" Frances asked harshly. "Come on, tell me. Talk. Aren't you?"

"Maybe," Michael said. He moved his chair back again. "How the hell do I know?"

"You know," Frances persisted. "Don't you know?"

"Yes," Michael said after a while, "I know."

Frances stopped crying then. Two or three snuffles into the handkerchief and she put it away and her face didn't tell anything to anybody. "At least do me one favor," she said.

"Sure."

"Stop talking about how pretty this woman is, or that one. Nice eyes, nice breasts, a pretty figure, good voice," she mimicked his voice. "Keep it to yourself. I'm not interested."

"Excuse me." Michael waved to the waiter. "I'll keep it to myself."

Frances flicked the corner of her eyes. "Another brandy," she told the waiter.

"Two," Michael said.

"Yes, ma'am, yes, sir," said the waiter, backing away.

Frances regarded him coolly across the table. "Do you want me to call the Stevensons?" she asked. "It'll be nice in the country."

"Sure," Michael said. "Call them up."

She got up from the table and walked across the room toward the telephone. Michael watched her walk, thinking, what a pretty girl, what nice legs.

QUESTIONS

1 What does Frances sense about her relationship with Michael? Are her feelings typically "female"?
2 What arguments does Michael offer? Are they reasonable, or rationalizations? Are they typically "male"?
3 What does marriage seem to represent to each?
4 Are today's attitudes toward marriage an affirmation or a rejection of those that we see in Shaw's story?

TOPICS FOR COMPOSITION

1 Expand your answer to question 4 into an essay. You may, of course, decide that Shaw's story only partly affirms or rejects today's attitudes toward marriage. Such a position can still serve as a strong thesis.
2 If we accept the premise that love is a fundamental and vital force in human relationships, we can see that Shaw portrays the social patterns of modern society as an opposing force. Write an essay arguing that man creates a society that is antithetical to elemental love forces.

☐

Through her narrator's consciousness, fragmented in time and place, Joyce Carol Oates structures a story of agonized love, casual indifference, marital bliss, and marital "wretchedness." Thus a literary device, which uses the "stream of consciousness" of a character seemingly free of its author's control, becomes the apt title of Miss Oates' story. "An Interior Monologue" is an *interior monologue,* appropriate in technique and subject matter because, as the story implies, love is not easily verbalized. It is, at best, sensory and illusory.

AN INTERIOR MONOLOGUE

Joyce Carol Oates

I am fascinated with that woman. I am a chemist and fascination comes hard with me. I am thirty-one years old, I live alone, my hours are spent concentrating on the cool reality of beakers and statistics, plastics of various types, the icy fuzz of sweat on tubes, the low mysterious hum of machines. Sitting at my workbench, I sometimes glance down at my fingertips, imagining a fine fuzz of ice on them. There is no ice. My fingers are long and lean. I have the idea that they are artistic-looking, though I am not an artist. If I were, I would do something with this laboratory, paint a picture of it, the way it looks at six o'clock in the evening, at quarter after six—glass, enamel, rubber tubes, stoppers, the terrible, powerful pull of vibrations from cooling machines, the terrible power of shadows moving slowly over everything, over me running right down to my fingertips.

THE MEETING

She and X met in a library. They talk about that meeting often. Out with X in a bar once—where I had only a Coke, since I don't drink—he talked about it in a kind of drunken frenzy, giving me details. "Don't stop, tell me everything!" I wanted to cry out to him. X is a gentle, dark-browed young man, about my age. I say about my age: he is really twenty-eight. His hair falls down onto his forehead when he gets excited.

The essential factor that changed our lives, the lives of all three of us, was that meeting.

She sat at a table, her books sprawled out around her. I can picture that. She is sloppy, self-conscious and a little vain about it—she can get away with being sloppy, other girls can't. All right. She seats herself at the table. She is wearing something light, a cotton dress maybe (they don't give me enough details and I must fill in my own) and her charm bracelet, jingling with silver charms. She takes out her reading glasses and fools around with them, holding them up to the light. Very smudged. Her hair is the color of honey, that vain girl. I hate her hair, her white silly teeth, her nitwit's forehead with its flecks of bangs, all so wearily pretty. . . . Still, she is sitting there. I have to prod myself to keep this vision going. She is sitting there, sitting there, sitting there . . . and X comes in, a stranger, sits across from her, his eyes raw from reading, staying up all night, wasting his young life in bars around the University that are dark at eleven o'clock in the morning. He sits down. He lets his books fall beside him. Aching, his eyes ache, his shoulders ache, his very brain aches with precocious weariness, a young man twenty-three years old and already a few years too old for his classmates, feeding upon sophisticated crap in Philosophy 1A with a hunger they don't share. He notices the girl across from him. He can see right through her, through her head, to the periodical shelf behind her, where magazines from *Review of English Studies* to *Studies in Existential Psychology* are displayed.

Not suave, X, but brilliant and plodding; not glamorous, the young woman, but of a full, essential body and a teasing but kindly smile. They meet. They fall in love. They marry.

A TENNIS MATCH

She is not athletic, even with her frame, and is bored by tennis. X and I play tennis on Sunday mornings, in place of church. He was once a very devout Catholic and, falling away from it, saw the world turn to water, saw gnats swimming through it, lay awake weeping at night with his teeth chattering so that he had to bite the pillowcase to keep all his anguish secret from his family. When I broke away it was easier. I don't think I am less deep than X, but still it affected me less; a few ripples, nothing more. We play tennis on Sunday mornings, in place of church. I like the aggressive swing of an over-hand serve, I like the spots of perspiration on my shirt, I like a certain cool freshness to the air, even if this is Detroit's Palmer Park and the junk from last week's picnics lies everywhere. Don't look. Why look? X and I play tennis, calling out our scores. *She* sometimes comes along, carrying the baby. She reads magazines, sitting at a bench, her legs crossed. She wears cotton slacks. She sometimes has her hair brushed back, indifferent, sloppy, a twenty-five-year-old dowdy housewife. No matter: a few strokes of cheap makeup and her cheeks glow again, a few swipes of lipstick and there she is, Miss America, Miss Class of '65, sharp and quick and bright and given to flirting slop-pily with me, so casual as to insult me, what does she care? "Here, my love, let me fix your collar behind. This little button—it's broken in half—isn't through the buttonhole." And, while I perspire, standing very straight and forcing myself to think of test tubes, beakers, the cool clean perspiration of metal, she nonchalantly buttons that little but-ton.

NONCHALANTLY

She drives me to use that word! I never use it myself. It isn't one of my words. Nothing is nonchalant with me. I received my Ph.D. degree in chemistry at the University of Michigan, 1964. Back in high school I was considered something of a genius—my chemistry teacher gave me a year's subscription to *Scientific American.* I dress casu-ally but neatly, I try for a quiet, correct, uneventful look; I don't want to stick in any-one's eye.

I'M STILL HERE . . .

She is always there, always there! At the back of my mind, lounging. She was already a woman at the age of twelve, obviously. Knowing everything! Knowing everything at the age of eleven, at ten! Her honey-clear eyes, her curly hair, her sweet stupid smile . . . a little queen of the playground, taunting the boys. Oh, would I like to jet back in time to see her ascend the playground slide, pausing at the top with her queenly intolerant look, and setting herself down like a precious substance, precocious woman, and giving herself a push downward . . . . To rise up from under that slide, leering, an eagle of revenge, to grab hold of her legs at that halfway hump and pull her off! Or, instead, better yet, instead to tip the slide over—a giant heavy rusty thing, falling very slowly, falling on top of her. So much for that.

I'm still here. . . . Yes, I hear her cooing in my mind as I lie awake desperately thinking of ways to mend my life. *Her* life needs no mending. The other night when they had me over to dinner, a spaghetti supper, she said, right in front of X, "Out in California the divorce rate has finally caught up with the marriage rate. I was thinking about divorce, theoretically. I was thinking about how it would shake everything loose, make us see ourselves plainly and terribly. . . ." But she is only toying, only toying with X. She will never divorce him. He will never divorce her.

Or are they both toying with me?

I see her sideways grin, at me. She seems to wink. But she says only, innocently, "Alan, have some more more salad. I made this dressing especially for you."

LANDSCAPE OF NEUTRAL COLORS

She and I are in the supermarket, met by accident. She wears white shorts, the baby is fixed somehow in the shopping cart, pudgy legs stuck through the wire basket. Slight signs of fatigue under her eyes. Freckles on her upper arms, probably on her shoulders and back. Not many on her face: powdered over? There is fine, very fine fuzz on her upper lip, hardly worth mentioning. The small muscles of her arms and legs terrify me.

"Yes, I saw that Bergman movie, I hated it," she says.

"Why? Does madness frighten you?"

"Madness like that, on the screen, is terrible because . . . because you can't get away from it, even if you shut your eyes the sound is still there, and the feeling of madness . . . . It isn't like reading a book, you can close the book up. No. I hated it."

"Is it something personal, do you think?"

"Maybe."

"You could have walked out of the theater."

"I never walk out of theaters—not after I've paid to get in!"

"Did Bob like it?"

"Oh, you know Bob—" with a slight pleased shrug, of course *I don't really know Bob*—"He'll sit through anything. He sits through old late movies on television, James Cagney and Ginger Rogers, all that old crap—he's a very sentimental person."

"But why are you afraid of madness?" I say, pushing my cart along nimbly as I push the conversation back to this topic, feeling myself very much in control and very clever. "Isn't that a certain weakness in you? Shouldn't people want to experience as much as they can?"

"Oh hell."

"Should we turn our backs on any kind of experience?"

Too contemptuous to reply, she flashes me her cool schoolgirl's sideways smile, a smile that could suck my front teeth out, so venomous and delicious and unknowing! I'd like to buy her a balloon, a great pink and white striped balloon, I'd like to dress her up in the long, puffed-out dresses women wore in the paintings of Monet and Manet and Renoir, I'd like to paint very carefully over her cheeks, pinkening them, darkening the blue of her eyes, outlining her stubborn little eyebrows, giving her the glamor of a real woman—someone ageless, ancient, worthy of a man's death. I'd like to—no—make the balloon a giant balloon, put a little wicker carrier beneath it for her to step into, carrying a picnic basket, all blues and pinks and yellows, her pale handsome arms exposed but her legs all covered up modestly—her long brown hair done up in a comely bun, a little frayed, prettily frayed—oh, let her set that sure-footed self into a wicker carrier and I will untie the rope, I'll cut the rope with a giant scissors, and let balloon, carrier, and woman float up into the painted blue sky!

Out in the parking lot, helping her with her groceries—I as dutiful a husband as X, and as casually thanked—I notice that the pavement is gray, the sidewalk gray, the sky gray, my trousers gray, my hands gray, graying. When I get back to my three-room apartment, in an expensive building with a canopy, overlooking the river, with a door-man, but still only three rooms, I run to the bathroom and look at myself, wanting to weep, yes, for my graying fair hair.

How can I live my life without committing an act with a giant scissors?

CONJUGAL LOVE

There they are, it's after midnight. They sit in their sleazy little living room. X is pursuing his Ph.D. in English but having a slow, dull time of it, his eyes sore again; *she* is dawdling her life away in yawns and complaints, with a shrewd eye for her girl friends' houses in the suburbs, very jealous, with great slovenly strides walking all over his body, grinding her heel in his soft lungs, giving him a wink. It makes me laugh, this marriage! Marriage! My head aches suddenly, after midnight, and I get out of bed to take an aspirin, and suddenly, very clearly, I can see those six miles across town to *their* little living room, where they sit, a mess of crackers on the sofa between them, crumbs and bits of cheese, X getting a little fat with the relief of *her* pulling through the pregnancy, *she* getting sharp-eyed and restless with his thinning hair. Oh, she knows too much! She reads *Cosmopolitan* and the lead article is "How To Get Your Sec-ond—Third—Fourth Husbands!" and, frowning, severe, she skims through the article to *find out* where life is being lived, what the details of a remote, secret life must be. Shouldn't I buy her that balloon, really? And set her majestically free up into the sky?

The other evening I dropped in on them, after going to a movie alone, and she scurried around to straighten things up—not knowing how much I wanted to see the mess they lived in ordinarily, being hungry for what they live in *ordinarily*—and I sud-denly wanted to embrace her hips, in those unclean unpressed cotton slacks, I wanted to cry out to her, *Have mercy on me!* But instead I talked X into playing a game of chess. She hates chess; women hate chess. X is good-natured and likes to waste time, he can be talked into nearly anything, so he is talked into a long, subtle game, dragging on past one o'clock—oh, my good luck!—and she yawns and complains about the baby, what a bother, and finally goes off to the bedroom, walking heavily. I can hear her in there, in the other room. And in the bathroom. A fine icy fuzz seems to form at the tips of my fingers and around my nostrils as I listen to her, listening deeply, sighing with the effort of such listening, imagining her opening the medicine cabinet door—the mirror swinging back, framing her high-colored, bored, puffy face and then losing it— her reaching for a pair of eyebrow tweezers, maybe, or a big jar of cold cream. No: she wouldn't. She'd throw off her clothes and fall into bed, a lazy weight, she'd sleep at once and forget about us. Here we sit out in the living room, bent over a coffee table, worrying about tiny pieces of red and black plastic—the game of chess! X's hair is getting a little thin, yes. He has a grateful, ironic look, a very sensitive young man but coarsening with married life, slack around the middle. I imagine him loitering around a railroad yard as a teen-ager, seeing what he could see. I imagine him with a group of other boys, fooling around at a beach, at an amusement park, with hard, stony faces pursuing girls, united in their pursuit. I imagine him at the back of his classroom, trying to keep awake tomorrow morning, reworking this chess game in his mind, and perhaps evoking me, my several remarks of despair, which seemed to trouble him—

"I wish you wouldn't talk like that," he said to me seriously. He looked at me. "You know you're not going to kill yourself, so why talk about it?"

"I know. I'm sorry."

"You've got everything to live for—a good job, freedom, everything you want— you can go on vacations whenever you want, you can do anything—" But here he began to falter, casting his mind about: what do I do with my life? What do I, his best friend, do in my lonely life?

So, to help him out, I say quickly, "I know it, I'm sorry. I must sound very self-pitying."

"No, but it's just a surprise. . . . Don't ever talk like that around *her,*" he said, giving an abrupt jerk of his head to indicate her, sleeping soundly in that double bed. "She wouldn't understand. She's so, you know, so healthy and impatient . . . she gets mad when I'm sick, even. God! She's really something!" And grimly, fondly, he began to think about her and stopped thinking about me, about my desire to die, oh how real, how deep is my desire to die! and so the game continued.

They sit in their little living room, night after night. They go into their little bedroom. Everything is crowded in there—furniture piled together—I saw the room once, helping them move in. I was pleased that they asked me to help them. Afterward we all went out for a pizza; they bought mine for me. No baby then. I think she was pregnant, though—how else to explain certain small jokes and smirks between the two of them? She wore yellow, a yellow sweater. She takes off the sweater in that little bedroom. Their closet must be a mess, with *her* sharing it. X is very neat, like me. Essentially he is neat. He complained once about her clothes crowding his out, wrinkling his. He had lived alone for years. I have lived alone for years, since I left my parents' house. I wake up at a quarter to one, with a headache. I take an aspirin, a simple and innocent act. And suddenly I see them—I imagine them—lying in an embrace, the sheet carelessly over them, X up on one elbow and joking with her and her joking back, nothing is serious or sacred between them, they are in love, in love, in love; I am six miles away suddenly nauseated, living alone.

Fire, flood, earthquake, all the classic types of sorrow—molten lava flowing from faucets—the earth itself turned to a giant griddle—a blast furnace of cities burning, enough to melt the painted rubber of high-sailing balloons—

How am I to be good? How am I to be saved?

I AM NOT THINKING . . .

I am not thinking of her mouth, his mouth. I am not thinking of their child growing into a human being of its own. I am sitting in the park, Palmer Park. Shouts from kids nearby playing shuffleboard . . . slamming the things around, lyric with violence. A man with a sharp stick wanders by picking up papers. A sharp stick! Picking up papers! I want to say to him, "Why are you looking at me, you old fool?" But he is not looking at me. I want to say to him, "You think I'm strange or something, sitting here?—what do you plan on doing, reporting me? Just who am I harming here? Isn't this a public park?"

I am not thinking of the cancerous cells that may be in her womb, her elastic womb. I am not thinking of the skid her car went into—a whole evening she dramatized it for me, almost frightening me, while X shook his head with a small strained smile and had to think, *had to think,* of how close she had come to dying and leaving him alone. "You should drive more carefully," I told her. I know how she drives: I was with her once and she nearly ran into a boy on a bicycle. Talking all the time, fooling around with her hair. No wonder she almost had an accident. No, I am not thinking of her mangled in a car wreck, her body is too lithe in spite of its disorder for a fate like that. I am not thinking of the rather prominent veins in her throat. I am thinking instead . . . of smooth, taffy-colored sandbanks, untouched by human footprints, unsoiled, virginal and lovely, molded by the wind into flowing tides, blending into the dusty sky; I am thinking of slow, silent caravans of camels crossing the sands, with men on them dressed in glaring, absolute white, swaying on the humps of those ugly sleeping beasts, the men's faces veiled, their eyes dark and their brows dark, seeing everything. I am thinking of delicate drops of music, like drops of water. Falling precisely onto my forehead. A drop of crystal reflecting the sand, and each grain of sand pregnant with camels, men in white, swaying veils, the terrible brute power of hidden limbs and trunks and the muscles of both men and camels, blended . . .

Night comes to the desert all at once, as if someone turned off a light. We are alone. We sleep peacefully.

A STAIRWAY TO THE GALLOWS

In a junk store, an antique store, is a small staircase, four steps high. "A stairway taken from an authentic gallows," says the dealer, a small unconvincing man with a sour line of a mouth. It doesn't look as if *I* would buy such junk! But I linger by it, running my fingers on it, almost hoping for a splinter, thinking, *Yet men have probably walked on these steps who are now dead. . . .*

Later that night I drop in on them. Something in the air, tension? A quarrel? She sits on the sofa, the child is shredding a doll, X is in the alcove of a dining room, at the table, trying to study. They are strangely quiet tonight. I lean over X's shoulder, sympathetic but ironic; he is reading Chaucer. "What of Chaucer's are you reading?" I ask him. He says, "Oh, nothing, it wouldn't interest you," and closes the book. This is a little surprising; but he seems to mean nothing by it. We go into the kitchen. He gets a can of beer for himself and some soda pop for me. Ice falling into the glasses from his fingers. Their ice tray is always a mess. I clean it out for them, put fresh water in it, stick it back in the freezer. Their freezer is always a mess. This gives me time to glance around the kitchen—yes, supper dishes in the sink, a smear of something red on one plate, probably they had nothing better than spaghetti, a frequent dish for them.

Out in the living room we sit and make conversation. *She* is long-legged and sullen. X looks tired. "Is something wrong?" I ask them finally. I am very nervous.

"Well, the genius here flunked his German exam today," she says. Bitter and triumphant. I turn to X, flushed with relief, wanting to comfort him. But his face is turned off; no comfort wanted; he sucks at his beer. "Oh, go to hell," he says to her. "I thought you were the genius in this family."

We sit in silence. The little girl frets, has to be taken to bed. X asks me about new records I've bought, pretending interest. I have several thousand records in my apartment, all catalogued and cross-catalogued. I tell him about a new string quartet by a composer he has never heard of. All the time I am aware of *her* padding around in the other room. Finally she comes out, seems to burst upon us, buttoning her coat.

"Walk me to the drugstore, Alan. I've got to get a prescription filled."

I stand at once, such is her power. I follow her out, trying to indicate to X that she has called me, I can't help but obey; she seems to be choosing me over him, to insult him for having failed a foolish German exam; where is love in all this, love, love, love? what does marriage mean?—but he fails to catch my look. She and I go outside. It is November, fairly cold. She walks fast. She says, panting in the cold air, "Why don't you get married yourself? What are you waiting for?"

I am embarrassed. "So many people ask me that. . . ."

"All right, what are you waiting for?"

"A perfect love, I suppose." I smile ironically, to show that this is a joke. She is too grim, too vain to catch the smile.

"Remember that time you and I talked for so long?" she says. Yes, I remember. We talked for hours. I had dropped in late in the afternoon while X was at his Milton seminar, drowsing through that seminar, and we talked seriously, with a very youthful, naive honesty, about the meaning of life without God. She had said that it lay in human love, in marriage. I had said that each person must find his own meaning. The dialogue, the duet, had stretched out for hours; we had tugged back and forth, this exquisite, powerful, venomous woman, a married woman, the wife of my friend X, and I, rather thin-armed in my sports shirt and no match for her, no match. A few days later I gave her a paperback book, *Psychoanalytic Explorations in Art;* it must have been related to our discussion. She never mentioned it afterward, must not have read it. I would have thought she had forgotten about that talk.

"My life, my life with Bob, is very complicated and very strange," she said. "I think I'm going to have another baby. But I don't think it's his . . . isn't that funny? You know us both, you're our closest friend and practically our only friend, you know that we both love you, sort of . . . I mean we really do love you. . . . But my life is in pieces that haven't fallen apart yet and what's so strange is that I'm very happy, and Bob is happy too, though I'm sure he knows . . . everything. I wanted to tell you this. I don't know why."

Stunned, I am stunned. Frightened. At the drugstore I turn away from her—but she is turning away from me. She dabs at her eyes. She has been crying, this woman! While she goes to the prescription counter, I try to get control of myself. My heart is frightened, in a mild shock; why has she such power over me? I imagine her and X entwined in bed, their bodies entwined, and her soft pink tongue prodding his ear, telling him about the mysterious caresses of her womb, breaking him down and turning him golden again, my friend X, short broken veins in the whites of his eyes. And I imagine her lazily unbuttoning a blouse, dropping it over the back of a chair, and turning to embrace another lover, who is not a friend of mine and whom I don't know, I don't know. . . .

She is putting change in her billfold, walking vaguely toward me, looking down. She carries a small paper bag—pills of some kind, what kind? But I can't ask. That's too intimate. She glances up at me and our eyes meet and I am filled, suddenly, with a terrible rage. It has something to do with this healthy happy woman striding through a drugstore, a store built just for her, taking her pick of its phony crazy pills, its sugary pills, getting exactly what she wants. Always. Why won't she decide, whimsically, to divorce X? Why won't X decide, in despair and distraction, to move in with me—until "everything is settled"? Why won't she take a false step outside and be thrown fifteen, twenty, thirty feet down the street by a car full of teen-agers. Why not, why not? A fever rises in me. My eyes are feverish. Out on the street I want to scream at her, *Let him go! Isn't one man enough for you?* But I say nothing. I am drowning, suffocating in the heat of my rage. She is speaking lightly to me in a foreign language, I can't understand any of it, chatter, chatter, light and light-brained as a bird, this American woman grown out of an American girl, her own fever leading her on a tightrope of woven gold, stretched out taut and safe for her size-9 golden feet, so skillful. I could scrape that rather ugly mole off her arm and put a culture of cerebral cancer in it, a small neat culture, tape it down, let it set for a few weeks and see what hatches . . . but she chatters on beside me like a woman in a musical comedy. Happy. She is happy and X is happy. They are happy together. I feel as if I am walking suddenly upstairs, up a stairs, struggling with gravity, my heart and my lungs ready to burst, my face filled to bursting with a fever of blood, my brain in a fury to shout at them, *You are predictable, you too! You are statistics! You very nearly don't exist! What does it matter, your loves and your adulteries and your drooling adorable children, your quarrels, your spaghetti suppers, your stained sofas? What does any of it matter?*

THE MACHINE. THE GODDESS.

I stay late every night in the laboratory, working. The hum of a machine is like music beneath my breath. Later on tonight, oh, not too early, but as if by accident, I will drop by at their apartment. It's been a week now; they must think I am offended. They must wonder if something offended me. I will drop by, maybe around ten, ten-thirty, as if by accident, on my way home . . . I will give *her* a tiny charm for her bracelet that I happened to find in a little shop, thinking at once of her, a tiny silver figure of a female skater. Confident, muscled, a kind of goddess, looking wise and militant, able to skate over land and water as well as ice, and over our knuckles, our pulsing hearts. . . . It is all there, in that tiny figure. Women skating over men. Skating over our bare chests, our legs. I will give it to her, a wife, and I will sit on their sofa, in the currents of their marriage, curious and detached and in love, buffeted about, like seaweed or droplets of water, waiting to see what gifts the future may bring me.

QUESTIONS

1 Who or what is the "they" in the parenthetical "(they don't give me enough details and I must fill in my own)" in paragraph 3 following the heading "The Meeting"?

2 Why does the narrator refer to the husband as X?
3 Since this story is structurally an interior monologue, how many levels of consciousness does its narrator reveal?
4 Why are the part headings important to the structure?
5 How does the fragmentation of time contribute to the effectiveness of the story?
6 How well do we "know" the woman, her husband, the narrator?

TOPICS FOR COMPOSITION

1 Using major points from Cadwallader and Fromm's essays, argue that the marriage
and the narrator's love display both the good and the "wretched" sides of love and
marriage.
2 In this part, three short stories have treated love in different ways. Write an essay
comparing and contrasting the methods used by the three authors.

POETRY

Everyone knows that for centuries love and poetry have been almost inseparable. What is perhaps not as well known is that some of the finest love poetry offers much more than lyrical expression of romantic emotion. Poets have thought deeply about the relation between romantic love and the purpose of life, and a wide variety of reflective poems have done much to reveal the meaning of love—and its mysteries as well.

Perhaps the main preoccupation of reflective love poetry has been the controversial relationship between physical and "spiritual" love. Inevitably, special attention has been given to the effect of time upon love and to the question whether or not duration is the best test of the quality of love. The poems of this section can be regarded as an excited exchange of opinion on these matters. We see, for example, that Edmund Spenser wishes to link love of physical beauty, which must yield to time, with love of virtue and thereby with love of God, the unchanging source of all beauty. In attempting to do so, he draws upon an ancient philosophical concept. The seventeenth-century poet William Cartwright names and defines that concept in "No Platonic Love." But Cartwright also repudiates that concept, declaring that the pursuit of such "thin love" is a waste of time. The whole question receives almost classical expression in Andrew Marvell's "To His Coy Mistress," where ironic treatment of the old *carpe diem* (seize the day) theme leads the poet to a fierce desire to believe in love as a life-giving, world-making force working against the inexplicable natural process that shrinks each man's world to the size of a tomb.

As we might expect, our poetic debate upon this problem is anything but dryly intellectual. In every instance, argument is supported by powerful appeals to experience, effected by the use of emotion-charged imagery, usually involving metaphor and symbol. Shakespeare uses the contrasting metaphors of the guiding star and the court jester to affirm the union of true love with the unchanging order of the mind. E. E. Cummings responds, so to speak, by making syntax stand for intellectualizing in his witty and passionate assertion that to mix philosophy with love is to weaken love and fail to make the most of "Spring." The would-be seducer in Browning's poem combines the metaphor of tracing a thread with images suggestive of the endless fertility of nature in his vain effort to convince his companion (and himself) that indulgence in passion is the best way to be at ease with the ghost of Rome—that is, to counteract depressing thoughts about the limits that time imposes upon all human desire. Closely comparable in almost every respect is Rossetti's use of nature imagery in his beautiful "Silent Noon," and with that fact as a clue even the unpracticed reader can hardly fail to see and feel poignantly the significance of the dragonfly that "hangs like a blue thread loosened from the sky." With equal effectiveness and to somewhat similar effect—though the difference is all-important—Thomas Hardy, in "Neutral Tones," imprints upon our minds, as it has been over the years imprinted upon his speaker's mind, the unchanging yet ever more ghastly image of a drearily blank pond. In marked contrast, the exultant lover in John Donne's "The Anniversary" is scarcely content to compare himself to a prince, and deliberately does so casually and parenthetically; for a moment, at least, he feels almost godlike as, secure in the possession of all-suffering love, he serenely envisions "all kings, and all their favorites" drawing to their destruction.

At this point one is tempted to try to generalize about the ways in which views of romantic love have changed through the centuries. There is much to be said, of course; yet as, with that purpose in mind, we contemplate the contemporary poems that conclude this selection, we may well be most impressed by the fact that after all that has been said about it, love seems to remain to the most discerning minds both a mystery and something of a miracle.

AMORETTI, SONNET 79

Edmund Spenser

Men call you fayre, and you doe credit it,
   for that your selfe ye dayly such doe see:
   but the trew fayre, that is the gentle wit,
   and vertuous mind, is much more praysd of me.
For all the rest, how ever fayre it be,   5
   shall turne to nought and loose that glorious hew:
   but onely that is permanent and free
   from frayle corruption, that doth flesh ensew.
That is true beautie: that doth argue you
   to be divine and borne of heavenly seed: 10
   deriv'd from that fayre Spirit, from whom al true
   And perfect beauty did at first proceed.
He onely fayre, and what he fayre hath made,
   all other fayre lyke flowres untymely fade.

1595

Amoretti, Sonnet 79: *2 that:* because. *3 fayre:* fairness, beauty. *wit:* mind, disposition. *8 ensew:* overtake. *11 Spirit:* God.

QUESTIONS

1 Is the poet making a sharp distinction between beauty and goodness, or is goodness merely a higher degree of beauty? What is the relation between love and virtue?

2 Do the last two lines mean that God did not make all things? If not, what is the meaning?

SONNET 116

William Shakespeare

Let me not to the marriage of true minds
Admit impediments: Love is not love
Which alters when it alteration finds,
Or bends with the remover to remove.
Oh, no! it is an ever-fixéd mark   5
That looks on tempests and is never shaken;
It is the star to every wandering bark,
Whose worth's unknown, although his height be taken.
Love's not Time's fool, though rosy lips and cheeks
Within his bending sickle's compass come;   10
Love alters not with his brief hours and weeks,
But bears it out even to the edge of doom.
  If this be error and upon me proved,
  I never writ, nor no man ever loved.

1609

Sonnet 116: *2 impediments:* "Impediments" is taken from the Marriage Ceremony in *The Book of Common Prayer:* "If either of you know any impediment, why ye may not be lawfully joined together in Matrimony." *4 bends:* inclines. *remover:* restless, changeful person. *8 height:* altitude (for navigational purposes). *9 fool:* court jester. *10:* come within the reach of Time's curved scythe. *12 to the edge of doom:* to the Last Judgment.

QUESTIONS

1 Shakespeare is saying, of course, that true love is unaffected by changes in the physical appearance of the loved one. Does he also mean that true love endures even though the loved one is inconstant? Is such faithfulness understandable? What would be the point of it? (In a marriage of two true minds, of course, this kind of alteration would not be a consideration.)

2 What do the principal metaphors of the poem suggest about the relation between love and the whole conduct or meaning of life?

THE ANNIVERSARY

John Donne

All kings, and all their favorites,
    All glory of honors, beauties, wits,
The sun itself, which makes times, as they pass,
Is elder by a year, now, than it was
When thou and I first one another saw: 5
All other things to their destruction draw,
    Only our love hath no decay;
This, no tomorrow hath, nor yesterday,
Running it never runs from us away,
But truly keeps his first, last, everlasting day.   10

Two graves must hide thine and my corse,
    If one might, death were no divorce.
Alas! as well as other princes, we
(Who prince enough in one another be)
Must leave at last in death, these eyes, and ears,   15
Oft fed with true oaths, and with sweet salt tears;
    But souls where nothing dwells but love
(All other thoughts being inmates) then shall prove
This, or a love increaséd there above,
When bodies to their graves, souls from their graves remove.   20

And then we shall be throughly blest,
    But we no more than all the rest;
Here upon earth, we are kings, and none but we
Can be such kings, nor of such subjects be.
Who is so safe as we? where none can do   25
Treason to us, except one of us two.
    True and false fears let us refrain,
Let us love nobly, and live, and add again
Years and years unto years, till we attain
To write threescore: this is the second of our reign.   30

                                                        1633

The Anniversary: *3 times:* seasons. *18 inmates:* temporary lodgers. *prove:* experience.
21 throughly: thoroughly.

QUESTIONS

1 Why is the speaker sure that his love is immortal?
2 Why will the lovers, while they remain on earth, be better off even than kings?

3   What will the lovers lose by death? How important is the loss to their relationship with each other? In this connection, what is the significance of the contradictory phrase "sweet salt tears"? Will death change the lovers' status relative to others? Why?

4   Question 3 and the related questions will have suggested what the true fears are that the speaker refers to in line 27. What are the "false fears"?

NO PLATONIC LOVE

William Cartwright

Tell me no more of minds embracing minds,
    And hearts exchanged for hearts;
That spirits meet, as winds do winds,
    And mix their subt'lest parts;
That two unbodied essences may kiss,   5
And then like Angels, twist and feel one Bliss.

I was that silly thing that once was wrought
    To practice this thin love;
I climb'd from sex to soul, from soul to thought;
    But thinking there to move,   10
Headlong I rolled from thought to soul, and then
From soul I lighted at the sex again.

As some strict down-looked men pretend to fast,
    Who yet in closets eat;
So lovers who profess they spirits taste,   15
    Feed yet on grosser meat;
I know they boast they souls to souls convey,
Howe'r they meet, the body is the way.

Come, I will undeceive thee; they that tread
    Those vain aerial ways,   20
Are like young heirs and alchemists misled
    To waste their wealth and days,
For searching thus to be for ever rich,
They only find a med'cine for the itch.

        1635

No Platonic Love: *6 Bliss:* i.e., a pure, impersonal happiness. *7 wrought:* persuaded. *9:* In Platonic love the search for beauty is supposed to lead from the sensual to the ideal, or purely abstract. "Soul" here may be taken to mean something like imagination. *10:* i.e., to move in a higher sphere or orbit.

QUESTIONS

1   In the first stanza, Cartwright illustrates the language of spiritual love, but not quite fairly. What are the elements that make for parody?
2   Does "thinking," in the tenth line, have the same sense as "thought," in the ninth? What is the effect of the repetition of the word?
3   What is the "itch" that motivates Platonic lovers? How does the "medicine" work?

TO HIS COY MISTRESS

Andrew Marvell

Had we but world enough, and time,
This coyness, lady, were no crime.
We could sit down and think which way
To walk, and pass our long love's day.
Thou by the Indian Ganges' side   5
Should'st rubies find; I by the tide
Of Humber would complain. I would
Love you ten years before the Flood,
And you should, if you please, refuse
Till the conversion of the Jews.   10
My vegetable love should grow
Vaster than empires, and more slow.
An hundred years should go to praise
Thine eyes, and on thy forehead gaze,
Two hundred to adore each breast,   15
But thirty thousand to the rest.
An age at least to every part,
And the last age should show your heart.
For, lady, you deserve this state,
Nor would I love at lower rate.   20
        But at my back I always hear
Time's winged chariot hurrying near;
And yonder all before us lie
Deserts of vast eternity.
Thy beauty shall no more be found,   25
Nor in thy marble vault shall sound
My echoing song; then worms shall try
That long preserved virginity,
And your quaint honor turn to dust,

To His Coy Mistress: *7 complain:* sing plaintive songs of love. The Humber is in England. *10 conversion of the Jews:* popularly supposed to take place just before the end of the world. *19 state:* dignified treatment.

And into ashes all my lust.   30
The grave's a fine and private place,
But none, I think, do there embrace.
      Now therefore, while the youthful hue
Sits on thy skin like morning dew,
And while thy willing soul transpires   35
At every pore with instant fires,
Now let us sport us while we may;
And now, like am'rous birds of prey,
Rather at once our time devour,
Than languish in his slow-chapped power,   40
Let us roll all our strength, and all
Our sweetness, up into one ball;
And tear our pleasures with rough strife
Through the iron gates of life.
Thus, though we cannot make our sun   45
Stand still, yet we will make him run.

                    1681

QUESTIONS

1   Is this poem a satire? If so, what is being satirized?
2   Does the tone change? If it does, why?
3   Do you consider the metaphors of the last part of the poem to be appropriate for a
    love poem? Does the way the speaker talks about love suggest an attitude toward
    life in general? Is his attitude toward love—or life—one that can be found in our
    own time? Does this poem describe a search for personal values?

STANZAS: COULD LOVE FOREVER

George Gordon, Lord Byron

      Could Love for ever
      Run like a river,
      And Time's endeavor
         Be tried in vain—
      No other pleasure   5
      With this could measure;
      And like a treasure
         We'd hug the chain.
      But since our sighing
      Ends not in dying,   10

And, formed for flying,
   Love plumes his wing;
Then for this reason
Let's love a season;
But let that season be only Spring.   15

When lovers parted
Feel broken-hearted,
And, all hopes thwarted,
   Expect to die;
A few years older,   20
Ah! how much colder
They might behold her
   For whom they sigh!
When linked together,
In every weather,   25
They pluck Love's feather
   From out his wing—
He'll stay for ever,
But sadly shiver
Without his plumage, when past the Spring.   30

Like chiefs of Faction,
His life is action—
A formal paction
   That curbs his reign,
Obscures his glory,   35
Despot no more, he
Such territory
   Quits with disdain.
Still, still advancing,
With banners glancing,   40
His power enhancing,
   He must move on—
Repose but cloys him,
Retreat destroys him,
Love brooks not a degraded throne.   45

Wait not, fond lover!
Till years are over,
And then recover
   As from a dream.

31 *Faction:* a political party or clique.   33 *paction:* contract.

While each bewailing 50
The other's failing,
With wrath and railing,
   All hideous seem—
While first decreasing,
Yet not quite ceasing, 55
Wait not till teasing
   All passion blight:
If once diminished,
Love's reign is finished—
Then part in friendship—and bid good night. 60

So shall Affection
To recollection
The dear connection
   Bring back with joy:
You had not waited 65
Till, tired or hated,
Your passions sated
   Began to cloy.
Your last embraces
Leave no cold traces— 70
The same fond faces
   As through the past:
And eyes, the mirrors
Of your sweet errors,
Reflect but rapture—not least though last. 75

True, separations
Ask more than patience;
What desperations
   From such have risen!
But yet remaining, 80
What is't but chaining
Hearts which, once waning,
   Beat 'gainst their prison?
Time can but cloy love
And use destroy love: 85
The wingéd boy, Love,
   Is but for boys—
You'll find it torture,
Though sharper, shorter,
To wean, and not wear out your joys. 90

1819

QUESTIONS

1   What evidence do you find that Byron is trying to mock some of his readers? What notions, specifically, is he making fun of? Are they still current?
2   We may disagree with Byron's recommendation and disapprove of his tone, yet still find in the poem a statement or two worthy of serious consideration. Do you find this to be true?

TWO IN THE COMPAGNA

Robert Browning

I wonder do you feel today
   As I have felt since, hand in hand,
We sat down on the grass, to stray
   In spirit better through the land,
This morn of Rome and May   5

For me, I touched a thought, I know,
   Has tantalized me many times
(Like turns of thread the spiders throw
   Mocking across our path) for rhymes
To catch at and let go.   10

Help me to hold it! First it left
   The yellowing fennel, run to seed
There, branching from the brickwork's cleft,
   Some old tomb's ruin; yonder weed
Took up the floating weft,   15

Where one small orange cup amassed
   Five beetles—blind and green they grope
Among the honey-meal; and last,
   Everywhere on the grassy slope
I traced it. Hold it fast!   20

The champaign with its endless fleece
   Of feathery grasses everywhere!
Silence and passion, joy and peace,
   An everlasting wash of air—
Rome's ghost since her decease.   25

Compagna: the setting is the expanse of open country around Rome. The poet calls it Rome's ghost because it once contained cities, only ruins of which are now left.   *15 weft:* thread which forms part of a fabric.   *21 champaign:* the poet refers to the Campagna.

Such life here, through such lengths of hours,
   Such miracles performed in play,
Such primal naked forms of flowers,
   Such letting nature have her way
While heaven looks from its towers!   30

How say you? Let us, O my dove,
   Let us be unashamed of soul,
As earth lies bare to heaven above!
   How is it under our control
To love or not to love?   35

I would that you were all to me,
   You that are just so much, no more.
Nor yours nor mine, nor slave nor free!
   Where does the fault lie? What the core
O' the wound, since wound must be?   40

I would I could adopt your will,
   See with your eyes, and set my heart
Beating by yours, and drink my fill
   At your soul's springs—your part my part
In life, for good and ill.   45

No. I yearn upward, touch you close,
   Then stand away. I kiss your cheek,
Catch your soul's warmth—I pluck the rose
   And love it more than tongue can speak—
Then the good minute goes.   50

Already how am I so far
   Out of that minute? Must I go
Still like the thistle-ball, no bar,
   Onward, whenever light winds blow,
Fixed by no friendly star?   55

Just when I seemed about to learn!
   Where is the thread now? Off again!
The old trick! Only I discern—
   Infinite passion, and the pain
Of finite hearts that yearn.

            1855

QUESTIONS

1 Although this monologue begins as a clever attempt at seduction, passion in the usual sense is not its main theme. How would you state that theme? It might help to consider the following question.

2 Why is the Campagna an appropriate setting for introduction of the poem's central theme?
3 The term *thread* is used in more than one metaphor here. What is the implication of each?

NEUTRAL TONES

Thomas Hardy

We stood by a pond that winter day,
And the sun was white, as though chidden of God,
And a few leaves lay on the starving sod;
    —They had fallen from an ash, and were gray.
Your eyes on me were as eyes that rove   5
Over tedious riddles of years ago;
And some words played between us to and fro
    On which lost the more by our love.

The smile on your mouth was the deadest thing
Alive enough to have strength to die;   10
And a grin of bitterness swept thereby
    Like an ominous bird a-wing. . . .

Since then, keen lessons that love deceives,
And wrings with wrong, have shaped to me
Your face, and the God-curst sun, and a tree,
    And a pond edged with grayish leaves.
                                        1867

QUESTIONS

1 It would seem that the speaker in this poem only later fully understood that "grin of bitterness" (line 11). Has this later awareness done him any good? Is he now more capable of loving, would you say, or less? Does the poem have a moral?
2 What might be the significance of the title of the poem?

SILENT NOON

Dante Gabriel Rossetti

Your hands lie open in the long fresh grass,—
The finger-points look through like rosy blooms:
Your eyes smile peace. The pasture gleams and glooms
'Neath billowing skies that scatter and amass.
All round our nest, far as the eye can pass,   5
Are golden kingcup-fields with silver edge
Where the cow-parsley skirts the hawthorn-hedge.
'Tis visible silence, still as the hour-glass.
Deep in the sun-searched growths the dragonfly
Hangs like a blue thread loosened from the sky:—   10
So this winged hour is dropped to us from above.
Oh! clasp we to our hearts, for deathless dower,
This close-companioned inarticulate hour
When twofold silence was the song of love.

1881

12 dower: dowry.

QUESTIONS

1 This sonnet seeks to convey the idea of fulfillment, utter content. However, there
   are several indications that the speaker is aware that the experience he describes
   is transitory. How many can you find?
2 The oblique allusions to the passage of time create an element of irony in the poem.
   What is the effect of this upon the tone?

SINCE FEELING IS FIRST

E. E. Cummings

since feeling is first
who pays any attention
to the syntax of things
will never wholly kiss you;

wholly to be a fool   5
while Spring is in the world

my blood approves,
and kisses are a better fate
than wisdom
lady i swear by all flowers. Don't cry   10

—the best gesture of my brain is less than
your eyelids' flutter which says

we are for each other: then
laugh, leaning back in my arms
for life's not a paragraph   15

And death i think is no parenthesis
                                   1926

QUESTIONS

1 What does the poet mean when he says, "feeling is first"?
2 Why should the lady cry?
3 What is implied by the statement, "life's not a paragraph"? Is the same idea expressed in "death i think is no parenthesis"? What is the connection with "the
   syntax of things"?

IN CONSOLATION

Vassar Miller

Do I love you? The question might be well
Rephrased, What do I love? Your face?
Suppose it twisted to a charred grimace.
Your mind? But if it turned hospital cell,
Though pity for its inmate might compel   5
Sick calls from time to time, I should embrace
A staring stranger whom I could not place.
So, cease demanding what I cannot tell

Till He who made you shows me where He keeps you,
And not some shadow of you I pursue   10
And, having found, have only flushed a wraith.
Nor am I Christ to cleave the dark that steeps you.
He loves you then, not I—Or if I do,
I love you only by an act of faith.
                                   1960

QUESTIONS

1   In this poem reflections on "romantic" love lead to thoughts about religion. What relationship between the two do you think the poet wants to suggest?
2   Consider carefully the manner of speaking used here and try to account for it.

WEDDING-WIND

Philip Larkin

The wind blew all my wedding-day,
And my wedding-night was the night of the high wind;
And a stable door was banging, again and again,
That he must go and shut it, leaving me
Stupid in candlelight, hearing rain,   5
Seeing my face in the twisted candlestick,
Yet seeing nothing. When he came back
He said the horses were restless, and I was sad
That any man or beast that night should lack
The happiness I had.

        Now in the day   10
All's ravelled under the sun by the wind's blowing.
He has gone to look at the floods, and I
Carry a chipped pail to the chicken-run,
Set it down, and stare. All is the wind
Hunting through clouds and forests, thrashing   15
My apron and the hanging cloths on the line.
Can it be borne, this bodying-forth by wind
Of joy my actions turn on, like a thread
Carrying beads? Shall I be let to sleep
Now this perpetual morning shares my bed?   20
Can even death dry up
These new delighted lakes, conclude
Our kneeling as cattle by all-generous waters?

                     1962

QUESTIONS

1   How would you characterize the woman of this poem? Is the poet suggesting that love has a special meaning for her because of the kind of person she is?
2   "Wedding-Wind" might be called a dramatic monologue. Is it realistic?

ONE FLESH

Elizabeth Jennings

Lying apart now, each in a separate bed,
He with a book, keeping the light on late,
She like a girl dreaming of childhood,
All men elsewhere—it is as if they wait
Some new event: the book he holds unread,   5
Her eyes fixed on the shadows overhead.

Tossed up like flotsam from a former passion,
How cool they lie. They hardly ever touch,
Or if they do it is like a confession
Of having little feeling—or too much.   10
Chastity faces them, a destination
For which their whole lives were a preparation.

Strangely apart, yet strangely close together,
Silence between them like a thread to hold
And not wind in. And time itself's a feather   15
Touching them gently. Do they know they're old,
These two who are my father and my mother
Whose fire from which I came, has now grown cold?

1967

One Flesh: from Genesis 2:24.   *7 flotsam:* floating debris.

QUESTIONS

1   The speaker in this poem, observing the seeming remoteness of her parents from each other, thinks at first that they must feel at least vaguely bored and frustrated. Would you agree, if you were in her place?

2   It is as if, the speaker says, the silence between the couple is "a thread to hold/ And not wind in." She does not understand. Do you?

THE PRICE OF WOMEN

Karen Swenson

Every woman, you say, has her price:
a house with trees and tricycles,
a yellow porcelain sink that matches
shine to shine the kitchen cabinets,

and some are more expensive   5
requiring Tiffanys and other labels
draped over their luncheon chairs.

These are the bargains of love
or quiet or just another body to be by.

But are they? Isn't this the way we   10
counter what we will not give, a game
of poker chip exchange—an emerald for
emotion, not an equal sign

but the ellipse of instead of—
because what would I do if   15
you or anyone walked into the room

in the middle of the commercial
and asked for my life?

1972

6 Tiffanys: a well-known, very expensive jewelry store.

QUESTIONS

1 Do you agree with the author's statement that every woman has her price?
2 What, would you say, do women exchange for a house with trees and tricycles, a
   yellow porcelain sink? What is it then that women will not give?
3 If it is true that men and women enter into this "game of poker chip exchange,"
   what is it that men exchange and for what?

TOPICS FOR COMPOSITION

1 With Spenser's definition of beauty in mind, write a critical essay on the modern
   ideal of feminine desirability. As a way of getting into the subject, consider the
   following questions. Do people nowadays overvalue physical beauty in women? Is
   the feminine image still a vital symbol of virtue or moral beauty? How are you, for
   example, inclined to picture virtue in human form? Does the modern concept of
   personality involve what might be called "spiritual" qualities? Do the national or
   international beauty contests provide adequate criteria for the assessment of
   "true beauty"?
2 Write an essay on the subject of idealism based on love between two persons.
   Can such love be an adequate basis of moral motivation? Can a person achieve an
   adequate degree of moral motivation without such love? Do people generally tend
   to be too idealistic about marriage, or too realistic? Is it old-fashioned to regard
   marriage as a religious sacrament? Use one of these questions or a similar one as
   a means of focusing your discussion. If you wish, use references to one or more of
   the poems of this unit.

3 With John Donne's warning in mind, explain in a short article how one can tell quickly whether or not a woman is likely to be fickle.

4 Platonic love in the religious sense is an outmoded doctrine, but it once was an important source of inspiration. If you are philosophically inclined, try to explain in a short essay why such a relatively sophisticated concept is unacceptable to modern taste.

5 Point out the relevance of Marvell's "To His Coy Mistress" to modern circumstances, and defend or attack the attitude expressed in the poem.

6 If you feel so inclined, make a case for taking Byron's advice (in "Stanzas: Could Love Forever") seriously.

7 Most people would probably say that Thomas Hardy's "Neutral Tones" could hardly be called a love poem. Can you find any justification at all for doing so? If you can, explain why.

8 Write a commentary on the significance of the contrast between Rossetti's "Silent Noon" and Hardy's "Neutral Tones."

9 Compare the attitudes toward love expressed in "Wedding-Wind" and "In Consolation." Which is healthier? Support your opinion in an essay.

10 Write a response to the speaker in Elizabeth Jennings' "One Flesh."

11 Has modern social unrest made it harder for people to fall in love or to stay in love? Explain your opinion in an essay.

12 Write an essay on the ideal attitude toward love, drawing freely upon ideas or sentiments expressed in the poems of this unit.

13 Write a careful analysis of the handling of tone in any poem in this section.

PART FOUR

THE PROTEST
AGAINST
MATERIALISM

Society is often rebuked for its emphasis on material gain, in the caricature of the "status-seeker," for example. Yet a complete rejection of material gain appears impractical. This is the paradox we face: on the one hand, material gain corrupts society; on the other hand, society progresses in proportion to man's ambition. Ambition, in the popular sense, is motivated by a desire for gain, material gain, for the most part. Where do we draw the line? Obviously, the question has no simple answer. But, because proper emphasis on materialistic value creates a dilemma as it touches social, moral, and spiritual behavior, we see that writers have generally taken a position of protest. The selections in this unit represent some varying ways writers have protested materialism's influence on society.

The first essay, "Thrift as a Duty," by Andrew Carnegie was initially published in *The Youth's Companion* (September 1900). Carnegie, a multimillionaire philanthropist, while obviously extolling the merits of a capitalistic society is also "teaching" that thrift is not only the duty of rich men but the responsibility of all men. Even though we may argue with his overly enthusiastic description of the saving man as a "temperate man, a good husband and father, a peaceful, law-abiding citizen," we can perhaps agree that his essay touches upon issues central to man's participation in a materialistic society.

The second essay, Vance Packard's "The Growing Power of Admen," first appeared in the *Atlantic Monthly* (1957). His essay brings into modern focus the degree to which the advertising industry exploits man's desire for material acquisition at the expense of individual dignity and initiative.

Ivan Bunin's short story, "The Gentleman from San Francisco," centers our attention on a man of wealth. Bunin shows us, with devastating force, a picture of a nameless "gentleman" whose material wealth (acquired at a distinct cost to humanity) is no match for the final inevitability of life. In "The Rocking-Horse Winner," D. H. Lawrence combines man's materialistic desires and his need for love in a story that dramatically illustrates the destructive effect of material greed on human love and sensitivity. Lawrence's story is almost sacrificial: it is the young, the innocent, who pay the ultimate price for the greed of their elders.

"Goodwood Comes Back," by Robert Penn Warren, also pursues the problems that arise from man's inability to manage his personal life when faced with sudden fame and affluence. Goodwood, a small-town boy who makes it into big-league baseball, loses all, ironically "comes back" because, as he says, "Being raised in a town like this . . . a fellow don't know what to do with real money."

THE ESSAY

Carnegie's essay, written first as advice to youth, was later included in a collection of his writings called *The Empire of Business*. Read in this latter context, Carnegie's purpose is to persuade everyday working people that their savings are important to their welfare and to the economics of an industrialized society. As such, it allows us to examine his use of the kinds of appeals that mark persuasive writing.

1 He equates the ability to save with the distinction between civilized man and the savage.
2 He parallels the importance of collective savings with production of material things and subsequent creation of jobs.
3 He extols the happiness that comes with job security and economic independence.
4 He appeals to man's humanitarian instincts; that is, to his ability to contribute to the general good of the community, to take care of the needy, and to provide for his family.

THRIFT AS A DUTY

Andrew Carnegie

The importance of the subject is suggested by the fact that the habit of thrift constitutes one of the greatest differences between the savage and the civilized man. One of the fundamental differences between savage and civilized life is the absence of thrift in the one and the presence of it in the other. When millions of men each save a little of their daily earnings, these petty sums combined make an enormous amount, which is called capital, about which so much is written. If men consumed each day of each week all they earned, as does the savage, of course there would be no capital—that is, no savings laid up for future use.

Now, let us see what capital does in the world. We will consider what the shipbuilders do when they have to build great ships. These enterprising companies offer to build an ocean greyhound for, let us say, £500,000, to be paid only when the ship is delivered after satisfactory trial trips. Where or how do the shipbuilders get this sum of money to pay the workmen, the wood merchant, the steel manufacturer, and all the people who furnish material for the building of the ship? They get it from the savings of civilized men. It is part of the money saved for investment by the millions of industrious people. Each man, by thrift, saves a little, puts the money in a bank, and the bank lends it to the shipbuilders, who pay interest for the use of it. It is the same with the building of a manufactory, a railroad, a canal, or anything costly. We could not have had anything more than the savage had, except for thrift.

THRIFT THE FIRST DUTY

Hence, thrift is mainly at the bottom of all improvement. Without it no railroads, no canals, no ships, no telegraphs, no churches, no universities, no schools, no newspapers, nothing great or costly could we have. Man must exercise thrift and save before he can produce anything material of great value. There was nothing built, no great progress made, as long as man remained a thriftless savage. The civilized man has no clearer duty than from early life to keep steadily in view the necessity of providing for the future of himself and those dependent upon him. There are few rules more salutary than that which has been followed by most wise and good men, namely, "that expenses should always be less than income." In other words, one should be a civilized man, saving something, and not a savage, consuming every day all that which he has earned.

The great poet, Burns, in his advice to a young man, says:

> To catch Dame Fortune's golden smile,
>   Assiduous wait upon her:
> And gather gear by every wile
>   That's justified by honour.
>
> Not for to hide it in a hedge,
>   Not for a train attendant;
> But for the glorious privilege
>   Of being independent.

That is sound advice, so far as it goes, and I hope the reader will take it to heart and adopt it. No proud, self-respecting person can ever be happy, or even satisfied, who has to be dependent upon others for his necessary wants. He who is dependent has not reached the full measure of manhood and can hardly be counted among the worthy citizens of the republic. The safety and progress of our country depend not upon the highly educated men, nor the few millionaires, nor upon the greater number of the extreme poor; but upon the mass of sober, intelligent, industrious and saving workers, who are neither very rich nor very poor.

THRIFT DUTY HAS ITS LIMIT

As a rule, you will find that the saving man is a temperate man, a good husband and father, a peaceful, law-abiding citizen. Nor need the saving be great. It is surprising how little it takes to provide for the real necessities of life. A little home paid for and a few hundred pounds—a very few—make all the difference. These are more easily acquired by frugal people than you might suppose. Great wealth is quite another and a far less desirable matter. It is not the aim of thrift, nor the duty of men to acquire millions. It is in no respect a virtue to set this before us as an end. Duty to save ends when just money enough had been put aside to provide comfortably for those dependent upon us. Hoarding millions is avarice, not thrift.

Of course, under our industrial conditions, it is inevitable that a few, a very few men, will find money coming to them far beyond their wants. The accumulation of millions is usually the result of enterprise and judgment, and some exceptional ability for organization. It does not come from savings in the ordinary sense of that word. Men who in old age strive only to increase their already great hoards, are usually slaves of the habit of hoarding formed in their youth. At first they own the money they have made and saved. Later in life the money owns them, and they cannot help themselves, so overpowering is the force of habit, either for good or evil. It is the abuse of the civilized saving instinct and not its use, that produces this class of men.

No one need be afraid of falling a victim to this abuse of the habit if he always bears in mind that whatever surplus wealth may come to him is to be regarded as a sacred trust, which he is bound to administer for the good of his fellows. The man should always be master. He should keep money in the position of a useful servant. He must never let it master and make a miser of him.

A man's first duty is to make a competence and be independent. But his whole duty does not end here. It is his duty to do something for his needy neighbours who are less favoured than himself. It is his duty to contribute to the general good of the community in which he lives. He has been protected by its laws. Because he has been protected in his various enterprises he has been able to make money sufficient for his needs and those of his family. All beyond this belongs in justice to the protecting power that has fostered him and enabled him to win pecuniary success. To try to make the world in some way better than you found it, is to have a noble motive in life. Your surplus wealth should contribute to the development of your own character and place you in the ranks of nature's noblemen.

It is no less than a duty for you to understand how important it is, and how clear your duty is, to form the habit of thrift. When you begin to earn, always save some part of your earnings, like a civilized man, instead of spending all, like the poor savage.

QUESTIONS

1   What distinctions does Carnegie make between the savings of ordinary people and the accumulated wealth of the rich? Are they valid?
2   How prevalent are Carnegie's views today?

TOPICS FOR COMPOSITION

1   Banks, savings and loan institutions, credit unions, and the like continually advertise through every media outlet. Using a number of these current advertisements, relate their approaches to the appeals made by Carnegie.
2   The introduction to this unit states that materialistic desire is one of man's paradoxes. Using Carnegie's essay and current advertising techniques, examine the paradox.

☐

While Packard's essay should prove useful in assessing our society's particular materialistic bent, his magazine style may also provide us an opportunity to observe those features that produce clear writing for the mass audience. Note especially:

1   The division of the article into four main parts
2   The last paragraph of each part, which provides a transition to the next part
3   The reliance on and support of a topic statement at the outset of each division

4   The variety of supporting arguments within each division
5   The detailed reference to each supporting topic in the conclusion

THE GROWING POWER OF ADMEN

Vance Packard

1

America's advertising industry is moving into a commanding role in our society. Its executives are becoming masters of our economic destiny, the engineers behind some of our most successful political campaigns, major patrons of our social scientists, dictators of the content of most of the radio and television programs we hear, judges with life-and-death power over most of our mass-circulation magazines. Also, they have become our most powerful taste makers. In 1957 they made millions of Americans suddenly feel somehow inadequate because they did not own high-tailed automobiles.

They have, in short, become major wielders of social control in America in this second half of the twentieth century. Their power to do good or nongood is becoming massive, and many are using their power irresponsibly.

The growth of their power is seen in the amount of money entrusted to them to spend. In 1940 they had at their disposal $2 billion to conduct campaigns of persuasion. Today they have $10 billion. If you divide that figure by the total U.S. population, you come up with a fairly startling statistic. Approximately $60 is now being spent each year on *each* man, woman, and child in America solely to coax him or her to use products the admen are promoting.

This growing power of advertising men derives from the dominant role that selling plays in the dynamics of our economy. In the executive suites of thousands of corporations the main preoccupation is no longer with production problems but rather with selling problems.

The most obvious explanation for this shift of emphasis is the fabulous productivity of our automated factories. Since 1940 our gross national product has soared more than 400 per cent. In 1954 it was predicted that our GNP would hit the long-dreamed-of mark of $400 billion by 1958. Actually it shot past that figure of 1956 and is expected to reach $600 billion within the coming decade.

To absorb this fantastic outpouring of goods we shall have to step up our personal consumption of goods by almost 50 per cent. As the chairman of America's leading advertising agency proclaimed recently: "We have to expand our levels of consumption in the next ten years by an amount nearly equal to the entire growth of the country in the two hundred years from colonial days up to 1940." The big problem we face, he said, is to cut down the "time lag" in the process by which we ordinarily learn to expand our wants and needs, in order to "absorb this production." Advertising men are the experts who can overcome this lag.

The real needs of most of us were satisfied long ago. About 40 per cent of the things we buy today are unnecessary in terms of any real need. Even our wants are pretty well satisfied. It has become a question of creating in our minds new, unrealized wants and needs.

Happily for the marketers, Americans by nature seem to relish learning to want new things. We are a restless people who like continually to hear of new things to do and buy. (Note the recent popularity of bejeweled fly swatters and mousetraps.) Emerson commented on this trait in Americans when he said that they, unlike Europeans, exhibit "an uncalculated, headlong expenditure." This makes them the world's prize consumers.

Recently the president of the Institute for Motivational Research (which conducts psychological studies for marketers) noted with satisfaction "our increasing willingness to give vent to our whims and desires" and offered the opinion that America is "experiencing a revolution in self-indulgence."

A corollary problem of marketers in moving their goods into our homes is that of making us discontented with what we already have, since most of us already own perfectly serviceable automobiles, washing machines, refrigerators, and clothing. We must be persuaded that the old product has become hopelessly inadequate to meet our needs or desired style of living. Advertising men call this "creating psychological obsolescence."

Another development adding to the power, glory, and prosperity of advertising men is the increased standardization of competing products. Perhaps connoisseurs can still detect significant differences in gasolines, whiskeys, cigarettes, beer, tires, cake mixes, and detergents, but most of us no longer can. Reports on blindfold tests conducted with cigarette smokers and whiskey and beer drinkers consistently reveal an inability of people to spot their favorite brand. A few days ago I heard a gathering of advertising men being advised that in blindfold tests people can't even tell the difference between Coca-Cola and Pepsi-Cola!

It used to startle me to hear advertising men make casual statements that in many fields such as gasoline and cigarettes the products are "all the same." Now it becomes apparent why they can be so complacent. It is the advertising man's genius that makes products seem compellingly different in our minds.

A third reason for the increasing influence of admen is the growth of self-service selling at supermarkets, vending machines, and so on. More and more, machines or systems are replacing people at the selling counter. The product maker can no longer rely on word-of-mouth selling by a clerk, merchant, or attendant. Thus the customer must be pre-sold, through advertising, so that he will have the product's image firmly etched in his mind as he enters the market place.

2

In the face of all these crying needs for more effective selling, America's 3300 advertising agencies have come to constitute "a great sociological battering ram," to use a phrase current with admen. Individually, advertising men have become "merchants of discontent."

As advertising men by the tens of thousands bring their wiles to bear to stimulate sales of products, we are seeing a massive straining for greater impact. Some months ago a distiller sent a photographic team to the edges of the Sahara Desert in order to obtain a photograph of a martini-filled glass in a setting which would suggest dryness. The photographers faced a crisis when, in searching the fruit markets of Cairo for a sliver of yellow lemon peel to go with the drink, they discovered that lemons sold in Egypt are green. This problem was solved when they arranged for a yellow lemon to be flown over from Italy.

Advertising men now ponder the advisability of making the "entertainment" portion of their TV sponsored programs a little dull so that the commercials will seem more exciting by contrast. In pictorial presentations one trend has been to the absurdly incongruous, to catch our eye as we search for reading matter amid a jungle of ads. Men sell whiskey while seated sideways on white horses, men with beards sell tonic water, shaggy dogs sell rum, kangaroos sell airline tickets. Meanwhile one advertising man complained: "We are suffering from fatigue of believability."

The advertising agencies, in their straining to become more persuasive, have been spending millions of dollars in research designed to learn more about the consumer. Batten Barton Durstine & Osborn has set up a division which it refers to grandiosely as "The National Panel of Consumer Opinion." It consists of several thousand housewives carefully chosen to constitute a "scale model" of the American female populace. These women can earn merchandise premiums by answering questionnaires about products and about their daily habits. Meanwhile Dr. George Gallup, long a researcher for admen, inaugurated a method of probing the consumer which he called "activation research." He set up a "sample bank" of people which he called "Mirror of America," and began probing the people in order to isolate just what triggers the sale of a product.

The most commotion in advertising circles in recent years, however, has centered on a probing technique called "motivation research," which promises to put deeper impact into sales messages. This "depth approach" to consumers involves the use of psychiatry and the social sciences to get inside the consumers' subconscious in order to discover the "psychological hook" which will impel consumers by the millions to buy a certain product.

Most of the leading advertising agencies now have psychologists, psychiatrists, or both on their payrolls. McCann-Erickson recently spent $3 million on a single monumental study of consumer psychology. A Chicago advertising agency rounded up eight leading social scientists in the Mid-west (two psychoanalysts, a cultural anthropologist, a social psychologist, two sociologists, and two professors of social science) and had them spend a twelve-hour day in a hotel room watching television programs in order to glean new insights into the appeal of the sponsored programs and the commercials.

Meanwhile several dozen research firms have sprung up, all promising proficiency in depth research. The most famous, the Institute for Motivational Research, commanded by a psychoanalyst from Austria, Dr. Ernest Dichter, occupies a mountaintop castle on the Hudson. The room where local children observe television programs is equipped with hidden tape recorders, one-way viewing screens, and so on, to catch their reactions. Several hundred residents of the area constitute a "psychopanel." They have been depth-probed and card-indexed as to their hidden anxieties, hostilities, and so forth. If you want to know how much impact a sales message will have on hypochondriacs, for example, Dr. Dichter has a group of bona fide hypochondriacs on call for a trial run.

So far much of the depth-probing of consumers is more hunch than science, but still most of the nation's largest producers of consumer products have been turning to it in an effort to increase their sales penetration. Giant corporations are raiding each other's customers with campaigns mapped by doctors of psychology.

One of the nation's largest advertising agencies now gives every single product it handles a motivational checkup. The merchandising journal *Tide* predicts that within ten years "few national marketers will launch an advertising campaign or introduce a new product without first conducting a thorough study of consumer motivations."

3

Some of the techniques used to probe consumer motives have been borrowed straight from psychiatric clinics and sociological laboratories: the depth interview (a miniature psychoanalysis without the couch), projective picture and word association tests, galvanometers (lie detectors), hypnosis, and social-layer analysis. When our motives are fathomed the experts then shape and bait psychological hooks which will bring us flopping into their corporate boats.

Among the more common strategies devised to lure us are: building self-images of ourselves into their product (playful gasolines for playful people); reminding us that their product can fill one of our hidden needs (security, self-esteem); playing upon our anxiety feelings; offering us ways, through products, to channel our aggressive feelings; selling us sexual reassurance; encouraging impulse buying; conditioning the young; selling us status symbols; making us style-conscious and then switching styles.

Several of the uses to which the insights are put strike me as constructive, or at least non-objectionable. The technique of gearing appeals to the social class most likely to enjoy your product would seem to be a step toward rationality in marketing. One of the notable cases of ill-considered selling occurred in Chicago when one of the leading brewers developed social pretensions for its brew, which had long been popular with the tavern-type clientele. The brewer's advertising men, in an effort to give the brew more class, began showing it being sipped by fox hunters, concert pianists, and drawing-room socialites. Sales did pick up slightly in the better residential areas but began falling disastrously with old customers. The boys in the taverns found the brew didn't taste right any more, though the formula was unchanged.

Social Research, Inc., looked into this fiasco when it depth-probed several hundred typical beer drinkers for the *Chicago Tribune*. It found that beer drinking in America is accepted as an informal, predominantly middle-class custom. So the brewers' foundation in its ads has recently been stressing the back-fence character of beer drinking.

The recent history of beer marketing reveals another way in which motivational analysts can produce constructive, or at least more rational, results. You may recall that in the mid-fifties many beer producers started to proclaim that their beer was particularly low-caloried and hence relatively non-fattening. The campaign was inspired by the mania for weight reduction which was particularly feverish then. Reportedly there were some impressive gains in sales as a result, but the motivational analysts viewed the low-calorie campaigns for beer with misgivings. Dr. Dichter's depth-probers, in testing the thoughts which sprang into people's minds when they saw the words "low calorie," found people thought of self-deprivation, discomfort. He admonished brewers to play up beer as a pleasure, not a medicine.

Motivational analysts have also performed a constructive service by showing advertising men how to conquer unreasonable prejudice against a product. A classic job in this respect was performed on the prune by Dr. Dichter's institute and advertising men of the prune industry. Prunes simply were not selling, and Dr. Dichter was asked to find why. His depth-probers found the prune, in our society, had become ridden with a host of connotations, all unfortunate. We thought of prunes in terms of dried-up old maids, boardinghouses, constipation, even witches. Under Dr. Dichter's guidance the prune has now been "rediscovered" as the "California wonder fruit," and admen now almost always show it in gay, zestful, youthful, colorful settings. The laxative angle is now mentioned in small type; and the prune industry, at last reports, is showing a hearty revival.

Still another way that the depth approach can perform a valid service is to help people achieve a feeling of self-worth through advertising. A producer of steam shovels found sales lagging. When a motivation study was made of prospective customers, it was discovered that steam-shovel operators play a large role in influencing the decisions of purchasing agents, and shovel operators did not like the shovel in question. A study of the ads that had been used to promote the shovel suggested a clue.

The shovel was always shown at work in all its monumental glory. Its operator was depicted as a barely visible figure inside the distant cab. The operators subsonsciously felt their role was belittled. When the advertising men were advised of this source of irritation they began taking their pictures over the shoulder of the operator, with the operator shown as the confident master of the machine. This new approach reportedly brought a marked mellowing in the attitude of operators toward the shovel advertised.

4

Several of the techniques being used on us by certain of the advertising men (and their scientific allies), however, do give cause for concern. These are the techniques designed to catch us when our conscious guard is down. Here are some of the types of operation I have in mind.

1 Appeals designed to play upon our hidden weaknesses. At one of America's largest advertising agencies, staff psychologists have been exploring the subconscious of sample humans in order to find how to shape messages that will have maximum impact with people of high anxiety, body consciousness, hostility, passiveness, and so on.

In Chicago a smaller agency has conducted a psychiatric study of women's menstrual cycle and the emotional states which go with each stage of the cycle in order to learn how to sell cake mixes to women more effectively. The aim was to learn how to incorporate within one ad a double-barreled message which would appeal to women in the high phase of their cycle (creative, sexually excitable, narcissistic, outgoing, loving) and also at the same time to women who happened to be in their low phase (want attention, affection, things done for them). This could be achieved, the agency concluded, by offering the high-phase woman something new and the low-phase woman an easy-does-it meal.

2   Strategies involving the manipulation of children. The agency just mentioned also conducted a study of the psyche of straight-haired small girls to find how best to persuade them and their mothers that the girls might feel doomed to ugliness and unhappiness if they were not somehow provided with curly hair. The agency was trying to promote the use of home permanents on children and used many psychiatric techniques in probing the little girls.

The most inviting opportunity to manipulate children for profit, of course, is via television. Five-year-old children, admen have learned, make mighty fine amplifiers of singing jingles (beer or cigarettes included). They can be taught to sing them endlessly with gusto around the house all day long and, unlike the TV set, they can't be turned off.

3   The use of subthreshold effects to slip messages past our conscious guard. Some advertising men have been investigating, very quietly, the possibility of inserting "flash" sales messages in TV and movie film. The bits of film flash by so fast they are not "seen" by the conscious eye, but are reportedly seen by the subconscious eye. In late 1956 the London *Sunday Times* charged that advertisers had produced a notable rise in ice cream consumption at a cinema in New Jersey during experiments with subthreshold effects. The use of such surreptitious appeals on any substantial basis will raise an ethical question of the most serious nature, particularly if such hidden appeals are used to put across political candidates or points of view.

4   The deliberate sale of products for their status-enhancement value. Automotive advertisers have hammered so long and loud on the theme of bigness that many Americans feel socially insecure in a small or medium-sized car (unless it is their second car or a chic foreign-made car). Although the times cry for more compact cars for our crowded highways and traffic-clogged metropolitan centers, most U.S. car makers stress, in their ads, the luxurious bigness of their cars. A TV commercial for one of the medium-priced cars stressed how Big it was and then, in a bit of theatrics, the announcer exclaimed: "People are getting smart about car buying nowadays!" With that, the screen showed a crowd of "people" chanting, "We're everybody. . . . We want a Big Car and style too."

5   The creation of illogical, irrational loyalties. This occurs most conspicuously in the promotion of gasolines, cigarettes, whiskeys, detergents. The research director of a leading advertising agency which has made a study in depth of cigarette smoking states that 65 per cent of all smokers are absolutely loyal to one brand of cigarette, even to the extent of walking down five flights of stairs to buy their own brand rather than accept another brand offered by a friend. About 20 per cent are relatively loyal. Yet he found in tests where cigarettes were masked that people could identify their brand by only 2 per cent better than chance. He concluded: "They are smoking an image completely."

In the building of images, cylinders of tobacco shreds wrapped in white paper have been invested with a variety of "exciting" personalities, to use one researcher's phrase. One smoke may have an image of elegance, another is daintily feminine, still another has an image of hair-on-your-chest virility. One cigarette company deliberately changed its image to almost a teen-age personality—even though most of the heavy smokers are in the thirty-to-forty age group. The aim reportedly was to recruit more beginner smokers and develop loyalty in them which would pay off on a long-term basis.

6   The exploitation of our deepest sexual sensitivities. According to the Institute for Motivational Research the admen who conceived the cigarette slogan "Like Your Pleasures Big?" were not unaware that the phrase was a *double entendre* with "latent sexual meaning." The same institute counseled motorboat builders that men could be appealed to on the fact that power boats can be used to express a sense of power in "almost a sexual way." A midwestern advertising agency has discovered that men can be persuaded to buy a new car by the implied promise that the new, more powerful car offers them a renewal of potency.

7   The application of the insights of depth-selling to politics. In 1956 many political candidates, including the heads of the ticket, were counseled by admen to present an attractive image to the public. The most popular models were father images and courageous young Davids. At one quite important level the presidential campaign settled into a battle between advertising agencies: Batten Barton Durstine & Osborn for the Republicans and the smaller agency Norman Craig & Kummel for the Democrats.

   The advertising man's approach to politics was perhaps best summed up by ad executive Rosser Reeves, who conceived the ceaseless barrage of half-minute spots on TV and radio in 1952 for the GOP. He said, "I think of a man in a voting booth who hesitates between two levers as if he were pausing between competing tubes of toothpaste in a drugstore. The brand that has made the highest penetration on his brain will win his choice."

   The Democratic candidate, Adlai Stevenson (who reportedly became very unhappy about some of the strategies conceived for him by admen late in the campaign), voiced his irritation at the symbol manipulators' approach to politics (at least the GOP variety) by saying: "The idea that you can merchandise candidates for high office like breakfast cereal . . . is the ultimate indignity to the democratic process."

   To sum up, I feel that while advertising in general is a constructive—and indispensable—force in our economy, its practitioners are becoming uncomfortably powerful and many of them need to exhibit more responsibility in their use of their new power than they have been doing. This particularly applies to their use of the depth approach to consumers.

   The responsible leaders of the industry should, I believe, review the current trends in advertising and admonish practitioners to proceed with greater consideration for the public's welfare in certain areas. As a start they might consider the following broad trends which I believe should be viewed uneasily by thoughtful citizens:

   Advertising men are pushing us toward conformity and passivity. Americans by the millions respond to their signals. Perhaps the trend to passivity is more serious than the trend to conformity. Max Lerner, in commenting on the implications he saw in some of the depth persuasion activities I described in my book, made one of the most perceptive and disquieting remarks I have encountered concerning the trend in selling. He wrote: "In motivation research . . . the consumer is always passive. He is analyzed, dissected, acted upon, bought and sold. He is a commodity to be trafficked in. The human being as a commodity, that is the disease of our age."

Many of the efforts of the advertising men provoke lasting anxieties. Economist Robert Lekachman recently speculated that we could only guess at the tensions and anxieties generated by the relentless pursuit of the emblems of success being encouraged in our society today.

The advertising men frequently are encouraging irrationality, as when they persuade us to buy products on the basis of images they have skillfully devised rather than on the merits of the physical product inside the package.

They are tending to demean many scientists who have been lured into serving them. Some of the social scientists collaborating with the advertising men maintain their standards of investigation; others strive to please, and often lay before their employers insights into our vulnerabilities which the advertising men do not hesitate to exploit.

Many of them are encouraging an attitude of wastefulness on the part of the public toward the nation's fast-shrinking resources. One conspicuous way they do this is by deliberately striving to make us dissastisfied with the serviceable products we already own.

Finally they often seek to invade the privacy of the mind. They want to know too much about us, and the inner workings of our emotions, for comfort. We should be able to be a little irrational and neurotic at times without having to fear that we thus become vulnerable to outside manipulation.

If advertising is to represent progress rather than regress for man in his struggle for self-mastery, then these considerations must be honestly faced.

QUESTIONS

1　Into which of Packard's theories can we place the "big problem" mentioned in the sixth paragraph?
2　What kind of support does Packard primarily use in his first division? What is the effect of this kind of support?
3　What varied support methods appear in parts 2, 3, and 4? Is any one support method dominant in these parts? Is there a reason?
4　Can you add to the list of techniques in part 3? How strong does Packard make his case for concern in part 4? Can you cite other instances to support his concern?

TOPICS FOR COMPOSITION

1　Select any advertising medium—radio, television, newspaper, magazine—for analysis of its advertising techniques according to the seven points Packard makes in part 4 of his essay. Limit your investigation to one issue of a magazine or newspaper or to one evening's programming on radio or television.
2　Show the variety of advertising approaches used by one product group; for instance, the soap manufacturers, the automobile makers, the tobacco companies, etc.

SHORT STORY

In this story, elements of characterization, atmosphere, and structure combine to bring about Bunin's indictment of materialistic man who has lost sight of life's true values. As you read, observe closely Bunin's careful blending of the following:

1 The itinerary of the gentleman that neatly contrasts cultural benefits with materialistic objects
2 The brilliance of the "Atlantida" and the subsequent step-by-step dimming of light as the journey progresses
3 The gentleman's attitude toward his wife, daughter, fellow travelers, and servants
4 The circular structure of the story

THE GENTLEMAN FROM SAN FRANCISCO

Ivan Bunin

> Alas, alas that great city Babylon, that mighty city!
> *The Apocalypse*

The gentleman from San Francisco—neither at Naples nor at Capri had any one remembered his name—was going to the Old World for two whole years, with wife and daughter, solely for the sake of pleasure.

He was firmly convinced that he was fully entitled to rest, to pleasure, to prolonged and comfortable travel, and to not a little else besides. For such a conviction he had his reasons,—that, in the first place, he was rich, and, in the second, that he was only now beginning to live, despite his eight and fifty years. Until now he had not lived, but had merely existed,—not at all badly, it is true, but, never the less, putting all his hopes on the future. He had laboured with never a pause for rest,—the coolies, whom he had imported by whole thousands, well knew what this meant!—and finally he saw that much had already been accomplished, that he had almost come abreast of those whom he had at one time set out to emulate, and he decided to enjoy breathing space. It was a custom among the class of people to which he belonged to commence their enjoyment of life with a journey to Europe, to India, to Egypt. He, too, proposed to do the same. Of course he desired, first of all, to reward himself for his years of toil; however, he rejoiced on account of his wife and daughter as well. His wife had never been distinguished for any special sensitiveness to new impressions,—but then, all elderly American women are fervid travellers. As for his daughter,—a girl no longer in her first youth, and somewhat sickly,—travel was a downright necessity for her: to say nothing of the benefit to her health, were there no fortuitous encounters during travels? It is while travelling that one may at times sit at table with a *milliardaire,* or scrutinize frescoes by his side.

The itinerary worked out by the gentleman from San Francisco was an extensive one. In December and January he hoped to enjoy the sun of Southern Italy, the monuments of antiquity, the *tarantella,* the serenades of strolling singers, and that which men of his age relish with the utmost *finesse:* the love of little, youthful Neapolitaines, even though it be given not entirely without ulterior motives; he contemplated spending the Carnival in Nice, in Monte Carlo, whither the very pick of society gravitates at that time,—that very society upon which all the benefits of civilization depend: not merely the cut of tuxedos, but, as well, the stability of thrones, and the declaration of wars, and the prosperity of hotels,—Monte Carlo, where some give themselves up with passion to automobile and sail races; others to roulette; a third group to that which it is the custom to call flirting; a fourth, to trap-shooting, in which the pigeons, released from their cotés, soar up most gracefully above emerald-green swards, against the background of a sea that is the colour of forget-me-nots,—only, in the same minute, to strike against the ground as little, crumpled clods of white. . . . The beginning of March he wanted to devote to Florence; about the time of the Passion of Our Lord to arrive at Rome, in order to hear the *Miserere* there; his plans also embraced Venice, and Paris, and bull-fighting in Seville, and sea-bathing in the British Islands, and Athens, and Constantinople, and Palestine, and Egypt, and even Japan,—of course, be it understood, already on the return trip. . . . And everything went very well at first.

It was the end of November; almost as far as Gibraltar it was necessary to navigate now through an icy murk, now amidst a blizzard of wet snow; but the ship sailed in all safety and even without rolling; the passengers the steamer was carrying proved to be many, and all of them people of note; the ship—the famous *Atlantida*—resembled the most expensive of European hotels, with all conveniences: an all-night bar, Turkish baths, a newspaper of its own,—and life upon it flowed in accordance with a most complicated system of regulations: people got up early, to the sounds of bugles, stridently resounding through the corridors at that dark hour when day was so slowly and inimically dawning over the grayish-green desert of waters, ponderously turbulent in the mist. Putting on their flannel pyjamas, the passengers drank coffee, chocolate, cocoa; then they got into marble baths, did their exercises, inducing an appetite and a sense of well-being, performed their toilet for the day, and went to breakfast. Until eleven one was supposed to promenade the decks vigorously, inhaling the fresh coolness of the ocean, or to play at shuffleboard and other games for the sake of arousing the appetite anew, and, at eleven, to seek sustenance in bouillon and sandwiches; having refreshed themselves, the passengers perused their newspaper with gusto and calmly awaited lunch, a meal still more nourishing and varied than the breakfast. The next two hours were sacred to repose,—the decks were then encumbered with *chaises longues,* upon which the travellers reclined, covered up with plaids, contemplating the cloud-flecked sky and the foaming hummocks flashing by over the side, or else pleasantly dozing off; at five o'clock, refreshed and put in good spirits, they were drenched with strong fragrant tea, served with cookies; at seven they were apprized by bugle signals of a dinner of nine courses. . . . And thereupon the gentleman from San Francisco, in an access of animal spirits, would hurry to his resplendent *cabine de luxe,* to dress.

In the evening the tiers of the *Atlantida* gaped through the dusk as though they were fiery, countless eyes, and a great multitude of servants worked with especial feverishness in the kitchens, sculleries, and wine vaults. The ocean, heaving on the other side of the walls, was awesome; but none gave it a thought, firmly believing it under the sway of the captain,—a red-haired man of monstrous bulk and ponderous-ness, always seeming sleepy, resembling, in his uniform frock-coat, with its golden chevrons, an enormous idol; it was only very rarely that he left his mysterious quarters to appear in public. A siren on the forecastle howled every minute in hellish sullenness and whined in frenzied malice, but not many of the diners heard the siren,—it was drowned by the strains of a splendid stringed orchestra, playing exquisitely and ceaselessly in the two-tiered hall, decorated with marble, its floors covered with velvet rugs; festively flooded with the lights of crystal lustres and gilded *girandoles,* filled to overflowing with diamond-bedecked ladies in *décolleté* and men in tuxedos, graceful waiters and deferent *maîtres d'hôtel,*—among whom one, who took orders for wines exclusively, even walked about with a chain around his neck, like a lord mayor. A tuxedo and perfect linen made the gentleman from San Francisco appear very much younger. Spare, not tall, clumsily but strongly built, groomed until he shone and moderately animated, he sat in the aureate-pearly refulgence of this palatial room, at a table with a bottle of amber Johannesberg, with countless goblets, small and large, of the thinnest glass, with a curly bouquet of curly hyacinths. There was something of the Mongol about his yellowish face with clipped silvery moustache; his large teeth gleamed with gold fillings; his stalwart, bald head glistened like old ivory. Rich, yet in keeping with her years, was the dress of his wife,—a big woman, expansive and calm; elaborate, yet light and diaphanous, with an innocent frankness, was that of his daughter,—tall, slender, with magnificent hair, exquisitely dressed, with breath aromatic from violet cachous and with the tenderest of tiny, rosy pimples about her lips and between her shoulder blades, just the least bit powdered. . . . The dinner lasted for two whole hours, while after dinner there was dancing in the ball room, during which the men,—the gentleman from San Francisco among their number, of course,—with their feet cocked up, determined, upon the basis of the latest political and stock-exchange news, the destinies of nations, smoking Habana cigars and drinking *liqueurs* until they were crimson in the face, seated in the bar, where the waiters were negroes in red jackets, the whites of their eyes resembling hard boiled eggs with the shell off. The ocean, with a dull roar, was moiling in black mountains on the other side of the wall; the snow-gale whistled mightily through the sodden rigging; the whole steamer quivered as it mastered both the gale and the mountains, sundering to either side, as though with a plough, their shifting masses, that again and again boiled up and reared high, with tails of foam; the siren, stifled by the fog, was moaning with a deathly anguish; the lookouts up in their crow's-nest froze from the cold and grew dazed from straining their attention beyond their strength. Like to the grim and sultry depths of the infernal regions, like to their ultimate, their ninth circle, was the womb of the steamer, below the water line,—that womb where dully gurgled the gigantic furnaces, devouring with their incandescent maws mountains of hard coal, cast into them by men stripped to the waist, purple from the flames, and with smarting, filthy sweat pouring over them; whereas here, in the bar, men threw their legs over the arms of their chairs with never a care, sipping cognac and *liqueurs,* and were wafted among clouds of spicy smoke as they indulged in well-turned conversation; in the ball room everything was radiant with light and warmth and joy; the dancing couples were now awhirl in waltzes, now twisting in the tango,—and the music insistently, in some delectably-shameless melancholy, was suppliant always of the one, always of the same thing. . . . There was an ambassador among this brilliant throng,—a lean, modest little old man; there was a great man of riches,—clean-shaven, lanky, of indeterminate years, and with the appearance of a prelate, in his dress-coat of an old-fashioned cut; there was a well-known Spanish writer; there was a world-celebrated beauty, already just the very least trifle faded and of an unenviable morality; there was an exquisite couple in love with each other, whom all watched with curiosity and whose happiness was unconcealed: *he* danced only with *her*, sang—and with great ability—only to *her* accompaniment; and everything they did was carried out so charmingly, that the captain was the only one who knew that this pair was hired by Lloyd's to play at love for a good figure, and that they had been sailing for a long time, now on one ship, now on another.

At Gibraltar everybody was gladdened by the sun,—it seemed to be early spring; a new passenger, whose person aroused the general interest, made his appearance on board the *Atlantida,*—he was the hereditary prince of a certain Asiatic kingdom, travelling incognito; a little man who somehow seemed to be all made of wood, even though he was alert in his movements; broad of face, with narrow eyes, in gold-rimmed spectacles; a trifle unpleasant through the fact that his skin showed through his coarse black moustache like that of a cadaver; on the whole, however, he was charming, unpretentious, and modest. On the Mediterranean Sea there was a whiff of winter again; the billows ran high, and were as multi-coloured as the tail of a peacock; they had snowy-white crests, lashed up—although the sun was sparkling brightly and the sky was perfectly clear—by a *tramontana,* a chill northern wind from beyond the mountains, that was joyously and madly rushing to meet the ship. . . . Then, on the second day, the sky began to pale, the horizon became covered with mist, land was nearing; Ischia, Capri appeared; through the binoculars Naples—lumps of sugar strewn at the foot of some dove-coloured mass—could be seen; while over it and this dove-coloured thing were visible the ridges of distant mountains, vaguely glimmering with the dead whiteness of snows. There was a great number of people on deck; many of the ladies and gentlemen had already put on short, light fur coats, with the fur outside; Chinese boys, never contradictory and never speaking above a whisper, bow-legged striplings with pitch-black queues reaching to their heels and with eye-lashes as long and thick as those of young girls, were already dragging, little by little, sundry plaids, canes, and portmanteaux and grips of alligator hide toward the companionways. . . . The daughter of the gentleman from San Francisco was standing beside the prince, who had been, through a fortuitous circumstance, presented to her yesterday evening, and she pretended to be looking intently into the distance, in a direction he was pointing out to her, telling, explaining something or other to her, hurriedly and quietly. On account of his height he seemed a boy by contrast with others,—he was queer and not at all prepossessing of person, with his spectacles, his derby, his English great coat, while his scanty moustache looked just as if it were of horse-hair, and the swarthy, thin skin seemed to be drawn tightly over his face, and somehow had the appearance of being lacquered,—but the young girl was listening to him, without understanding, in her agitation, what he was saying; her heart was thumping from an incomprehensible rapture before his presence and from pride that he was speaking with her, and not some other; everything about him that was different from others,—his lean hands, his clear skin, under which flowed the ancient blood of kings, even his altogether unpretentious, yet somehow distinctively neat, European dress,—everything held a secret, inexplicable charm, evoked a feeling of amorousness. As for the gentleman from San Francisco himself,—he, in a high silk hat, in gray spats over patent-leather shoes, kept on glancing at the famous beauty, who was standing beside him,—a tall blonde of striking figure, her eyes were painted in the latest Parisian fashion; she was holding a diminutive, hunched-up, mangy lap dog on a silver chain and was chattering to it without cease. And the daughter, in some vague embarrassment, tried not to notice her father.

Like all Americans of means, he was very generous on his travels, and, like all of them, believed in the full sincerity and good-will of those who brought him food and drink with such solicitude, who served him from morn till night, forestalling his least wish; of those who guarded his cleanliness and rest, lugged his things around, summoned porters for him, delivered his trunks to hotels. Thus had it been everywhere, thus had it been on the ship, and thus was it to be in Naples as well. Naples grew, and drew nearer; the musicians, the brass of their instruments flashing, had already clustered upon the deck, and suddenly deafened everybody with the triumphant strains of a march; the gigantic captain, in his full dress uniform, appeared upon his stage, and, like a condescending heathen god, waved his hand amiably to the passengers,—and to the gentleman from San Francisco it seemed that it was for him alone that the march so beloved by proud America was thundering, that it was he whom the captain was felicitating upon a safe arrival. And every other passenger felt similarly about himself— or herself. And when the *Atlantida* did finally enter the harbour, had heaved to at the wharf with her many-tiered mass, black with people, and the gang-planks clattered down,—what a multitude of porters and their helpers in caps with gold braid, what a multitude of different *commissionaires,* whistling gamins, and strapping ragamuffins with packets of coloured postal cards in their hands, made a rush toward the gentleman from San Francisco, with offers of their services! And he smiled, with a kindly contemptuousness, at these ragamuffins, as he went toward the automobile of precisely that hotel where there was a possibility of the prince's stopping as well, and drawled through his teeth, now in English, now in Italian:

"Go away!* *Via!*"

Life at Naples at once assumed its wonted, ordered current: in the early morning, breakfast in the sombre dining room with its damp draught from windows opening on some sort of a stony little garden; the sky was usually overcast, holding out but little promise, and there was the usual crowd of guides at the door of the vestibule; then came the first smiles of a warm, rosy sun; there was, from the high hanging balcony, a view of Vesuvius, enveloped to its foot by radiant morning mists, and of silver-and-pearl eddies on the surface of the Bay, and of the delicate contour of Capri against the horizon; one could see tiny burros, harnessed in twos to little carts, running down below over the quay, sticky with mire, and detachments of diminutive soldiers, marching off to somewhere or other to lively and exhilarating music. Next came the procession to the waiting automobile and the slow progress through populous, narrow, and damp corridors of streets, between tall, many-windowed houses; the inspection of

---

* English in the original. The same applies to the other phrases in this story marked with asterisks.
Trans.

lifelessly-clean museums, evenly and pleasantly, yet bleakly, lit, seemingly illuminated by snow; or of cool churches, smelling of wax, which everywhere and always contain the same things: a majestic portal, screened by a heavy curtain of leather, and inside,—silence, empty vastness, unobtrusive little flames of a seven-branched candlestick glowing redly in the distant depths, on an altar bedecked with laces; a solitary old woman among the dark wooden pews; slippery tombstones underfoot; and somebody's *Descent from the Cross,*—inevitably a celebrated one. At one o'clock there was luncheon upon the mountain of San Martino, where, toward noon, gathered not a few people of the very first quality, and where the daughter of the gentleman from San Francisco had once almost fainted away for joy, because she thought she saw the prince sitting in the hall, although she already knew through the newspapers that he had left for a temporary stay at Rome. At five came tea at the hotel, in the showy salon, so cosy with its rugs and flaming fireplaces; and after that it was already time to get ready for dinner,—and once more came the mighty, compelling reverberation of the gong through all the stories; once more the processions in Indian file of ladies in *décolleté,* rustling in their silks upon the staircases and reflected in all the mirrors; once more the palatial dining room, widely and hospitably opened, and the red jackets of the musicians upon their platform, and the black cluster of waiters about the *maitre d'hôtel,* who, with a skill out of the ordinary, was ladling some sort of a thick, roseate soup into plates. . . . The dinners, as everywhere else, were the crowning glory of each day; the guests dressed for them as for a rout, and these dinners were so abundant in edibles, and wines, and mineral waters, and sweets, and fruits, that toward eleven o'clock at night the chambermaids were distributing through all the corridors rubber bags with hot water to warm sundry stomachs.

However, the December of that year proved to be not altogether a successful one for Naples; the porters grew confused when one talked with them of the weather, and merely shrugged their shoulders guiltily, muttering that they could not recall such another year,—although it was not the first year that they had been forced to mutter this, and to urge in extenuation that "something terrible is happening everywhere"; there were unheard of storms and torrents of rain on the Riviera; there was snow in Athens; Etna was also all snowed over and was aglow of nights; tourists were fleeing from Palermo in all directions, escaping from the cold. The morning sun deceived the Neapolitans every day that winter: toward noon the sky became gray and a fine rain began falling, but growing heavier and colder all the time; at such times the palms near the entrance of the hotel glistened as though they were of tin, the town seemed especially dirty and cramped, the museums exceedingly alike; the cigar stumps of the corpulent cabmen, whose rubber-coats flapped in the wind like wings, seemed to have an insufferable stench, while the energetic snapping of their whips over their scrawny-necked nags was patently false; the footgear of the *signori* sweeping the rails of the tramways seemed horrible; the woman, splashing through the mud, their black-haired heads bared to the rain, appeared hideously short-legged; as for the dampness, and the stench of putrid fish from the sea foaming at the quay,—they were a matter of course. The gentleman and the lady from San Francisco began quarreling in the morning; their daughter either walked about pale, with a headache, or, coming to life again, went into raptures over everything, and was, at such times both charming and beautiful: beautiful were those tender and complex emotions which had been awakened within her by meeting that homely man through whose veins flowed uncommon blood; for, after all is said and done, perhaps it is of no real importance just what it is, precisely, that awakens a maiden's soul,—whether it be money, or fame, or illustrious ancestry. . . .

Everybody affirmed that things were entirely different in Sorrento, in Capri,—there it was both warmer and sunnier, and the lemons were in blossom, and the customs were more honest, and the wine was more natural. And so the family from San Francisco determined to set out with all its trunks to Capri, and, after seeing it all, after treading the stones where the palace of Tiberius had once stood, after visiting the faery-like caverns of the Azure Grotto, and hearing the bag-pipers of Abruzzi, who for a whole month preceding Christmas wander over the island and sing the praises of the Virgin Mary, they meant to settle in Sorrento.

On the day of departure,—a most memorable one for the family from San Francisco!—there was no sun from the early morning. A heavy fog hid Vesuvius to the very base; this gray fog spread low over the leaden heaving of the sea that was lost to the eye at a distance of a half a mile. Capri was entirely invisible,—as though there had never been such a thing in the world. And the little steamer that set out for it was so tossed from side to side that the family from San Francisco was laid prostrate upon the divans in the sorry general cabin of this tub, their feet wrapped up in plaids, and their eyes closed from nausea. Mrs. suffered,—so she thought,—more than anybody; she was overcome by sea-sickness several times; it seemed to her that she was dying, whereas the stewardess, who always ran up to her with a small basin,—she had been, for many years, day in and day out, rolling on these waves, in freezing weather and in torrid, and yet was still tireless and kind to everybody,—merely laughed. Miss was dreadfully pale and held a slice of lemon between her teeth; now she could not have been cheered even by the hope of a chance encounter with the prince at Sorrento, where he intended to be about Christmas. Mr., who was lying on his back, in roomy overcoat and large cap, never unlocked his jaws all the way over; his face had grown darker and his moustache whiter, and his head ached dreadfully: during the last days, thanks to the bad weather, he had been drinking too heavily of evenings, and had too much admired the "living pictures" in dives of *recherché* libertinage. But the rain kept on lashing against the jarring windows, the water from them running down on the divans; the wind, howling, bent the masts, and at times, aided by the onslaught of a wave, careened the little steamer entirely to one side, and then something in the hold would roll with a rumble. During the stops, at Castellamare, at Sorrento, things were a trifle more bearable, but even then the rocking was fearful,—the shore, with all its cliffs, gardens, *pigin,* * its pink and white hotels and hazy mountains clad in curly greenery, swayed up and down as if on a swing; boats bumped up against the sides of the ship; sailors and steerage passengers were yelling vehemently; somewhere, as though it had been crushed, a baby was wailing and smothering; a raw wind was blowing in at the door; and, from a swaying boat with a flag of the Hotel Royal, a lisping gamin was screaming, luring travellers: "Kgoya-al! Hôtel Kgoya-al! . . ." And the gentleman from San Francisco, feeling that he was an old man,—which was but proper,—was already

* Pino-groves. *Trans.*

thinking with sadness and melancholy of all these Royals, Splendids, Excelsiors, and of these greedy, insignificant mannikins, reeking of garlic, that are called Italians. Once, having opened his eyes and raised himself from the divan, he saw, underneath the craggy steep of the shore, a cluster of stone hovels, mouldy through and through, stuck one on top of another near the very edge of the water, near boats, near all sorts of rags, tins, and brown nets,—hovels so miserable, that, at the recollection that this was that very Italy he had come hither to enjoy, he felt despair. . . . Finally, at twilight, the dark mass of the island began to draw near, seemingly bored through and through by little red lights near its base; the wind became softer, warmer, more fragrant; over the abating waves, as opalescent as black oil, golden pythons flowed from the lanterns on the wharf. . . . Then came the sudden rumble of the anchor, and it fell with a splash into the water; the ferocious yells of the boatmen, vying with one another, floated in from all quarters,—and at once the heart grew lighter, the lights in the general cabin shone more brightly, a desire arose to eat, to drink, to smoke, to be stirring. . . . Ten minutes later the family from San Francisco had descended into a large boat; within fifteen minutes it had set foot upon the stones of the wharf, and had then got into a bright little railway car and to its buzzing started the ascent of the slope, amid the stakes of the vineyards, half-crumbled stone enclosures, and wet, gnarled orange trees, some of them under coverings of straw,—trees with thick, glossy foliage, and aglimmer with the orange fruits; all these objects were sliding downward, past the open windows of the little car, toward the base of the mountain. . . . Sweetly smells the earth of Italy after rain, and her every island has its own, its special aroma!

The island of Capri was damp and dark on this evening. But now it came into life for an instant; lights sprang up here and there, as always on the steamer's arrival. At the top of the mountain, where stood the station of the *funicular,* there was another throng of those whose duty lay in receiving fittingly the gentleman from San Francisco. There were other arrivals also, but they merited no attention,—several Russians, who had taken up their abode in Capri,—absent-minded because of their bookish meditations, unkempt, bearded, spectacled, the collars of their old drap overcoats turned up; and a group of long-legged, long-necked, round-headed German youths in Tyrolean costumes, with canvas knapsacks slung over their shoulders,—these latter stood in need of nobody's services, feeling themselves at home everywhere, and were not at all generous in their expenditures. The gentleman from San Francisco, on the other hand, who was calmly keeping aloof from both the one group and the other, was immediately noticed. He and his ladies were bustlingly assisted to get out, some men running ahead of him to show him the way: he was surrounded anew by urchins, and by those robust Caprian wives who carry on their heads the portmanteaux and trunks of respectable travellers. The wooden pattens of these women clattered over a *piazetta,* that seemed to belong to some opera, an electric globe swaying above it in the damp wind; the rabble of urchins burst into sharp, bird-like whistles,—and, as though on a stage, the gentleman from San Francisco proceeded in their midst toward some mediæval arch, underneath houses that had become welded into one mass, beyond which a little echoing street,—with the tuft of a palm above flat roofs on its left, and with blue stars in the black sky overhead,—led slopingly to the grand entrance of the hotel, glittering ahead. . . . And again it seemed that it was in honour of the guests from San Francisco that this damp little town of stone on a craggy little island of the Mediterranean Sea had come to life, that it was they who had made so happy and affable the proprietor of the hotel, that it was they only who had been waited for by the Chinese gong, that now began wailing the summons to dinner through all the stories of the hotel, the instant they had set foot in the vestibule.

The proprietor, a young man of haughty elegance, who had met them with a polite and exquisite bow, for a minute dumbfounded the gentleman from San Francisco: having glanced at him, the gentleman from San Francisco suddenly recalled that just the night before, among the rest of the confusion of images that had beset him in his sleep, he had seen precisely this gentleman,—just like him, down to the least detail: in the same sort of frock with rounded skirts, and with the same pomaded and painstakingly combed head. Startled, he was almost taken aback; but since, from long, long before, there was not even a mustard seed of any sort of so-called mystical emotions left in his soul, his astonishment was dimmed the same instant, passing through a corridor of the hotel, he spoke jestingly to his wife and daughter of this strange coincidence of dream and reality. And only his daughter glanced at him with alarm at that moment: her heart suddenly contracted from sadness, from a feeling of their loneliness upon this foreign, dark island,—a feeling so strong that she almost burst into tears. But still she said nothing of her feelings to her father,—as always.

An exalted personage—Rais XVII,—who had been visiting Capri, had just taken his departure, and the guests from San Francisco were given the same apartments that he had occupied. To them was assigned the handsomest and most expert chambermaid, a Belgian, whose waist was slenderly and firmly corseted, and who wore a little starched cap that looked like a pronged crown; also, the stateliest and most dignified of flunkies, a fiery-eyed Sicilian, swarthy as coal; and the nimblest of bell-boys, the short and stout Luigi,—a fellow who was very fond of a joke, and who had changed many places in his time. And a minute later there was a slight tap at the door of the room of the gentleman from San Francisco,—the French *maitre d'hôtel* had come to find out if the newly arrived guests would dine, and, in the event of an answer in the affirmative,—of which, however, there was no doubt,—to inform them that the *carte de jour* consisted of crawfish, roast beef, asparagus, pheasants, and so forth. The floor was still rocking under the gentleman from San Francisco,—so badly had the atrocious little Italian steamer tossed him about,—but, without hurrying, with his own hands, although somewhat clumsily from being unaccustomed to such things, he shut a window that had banged upon the entrance of the *maitre d'hôtel* and had let in the odours of the distant kitchen and of the wet flowers in the garden, and with a leisurely precision replied that they would dine, that their table must be placed at a distance from the door, at the farthest end of the dining room, that they would drink local wine and champagne,—moderately dry and only slightly chilled. The *maitre d'hôtel concurred* in every word of his, in intonations most varied, having, however, but one significance,— that there was never a doubt, nor could there possibly be any, about the correctness of the wishes to the gentleman from San Francisco, and that everything would be carried out punctiliously. In conclusion he inclined his head, and asked deferentially:

"Will that be all, sir?"

And, having received a long-drawn-out "Yes"* in answer, he added that the *tarantella* would be danced in the vestibule to-day,—the dancers would be Carmella and Giuseppe, known to all Italy, and to "the entire world of tourists."

"I have seen her on post cards," said the gentleman from San Francisco in a voice devoid of all expression. "About this Giuseppe, now,—is he her husband?"

"Her cousin, sir," answered the *maitre d'hôtel.*

And, after a little wait, after considering something, the gentleman from San Francisco dismissed him with a nod.

And then he began his preparations anew, as though for a wedding ceremony: he turned on all the electric lights, filling all the mirrors with reflections of light and glitter, of furniture and opened trunks; he began shaving and washing, ringing the bell every minute, while other impatient rings from his wife's and daughter's rooms floated through the entire corridor and interrupted his. And Luigi, in his red apron, was rushing head-long to answer the bell, with an ease peculiar to many stout men, the while he made grimaces of horror that made the chambermaids, running by with glazed porcelain pails in their hands, laugh till they cried. Having knocked on the door with his knuckles, he asked with an assumed timidity, with a respectfulness that verged on idiocy:

"*Ha sonato, signore?* (Did you ring, sir?)"

And from the other side of the door came an unhurried grating voice, insultingly polite:

"Yes, come in. . . ."

What were the thoughts, what were the emotions of the gentleman from San Francisco on this evening, that was of such portent to him? He felt nothing exceptional,—for the trouble in this world is just that everything is apparently all too simple! And even if he had sensed within his soul that something was impending, he would, never the less, have thought that this thing would not occur for some time to come,— in any case, not immediately. Besides that, like everyone who has gone through the rocking of a ship, he wanted very much to eat, was anticipating with enjoyment the first spoonful of soup, the first mouthful of wine, and performed the usual routine of dressing even with a certain degree of exhilaration that left no time for reflections.

Having shaved and washed himself, having inserted several artificial teeth properly, he, standing before a mirror, wetted the remnants of his thick, pearly-gray hair and plastered it down around his swarthy-yellow skull, with brushes set in silver; drew a suit of cream-coloured silk underwear over his strong old body, beginning to be full at the waist from excesses in food, and put on silk socks and dancing slippers on his shrivelled splayed feet; sitting down, he put in order his black trousers, drawn high by black silk braces, as well as his snowy-white shirt, with the bosom bulging out; put the links through the glossy cuffs, and began the torturous pursuit of the collar-button underneath the stiffly starched collar. The floor was still swaying beneath him, the tips of his fingers pained him greatly, the collar-button at times nipped hard the flabby skin in the hollow under his Adam's-apple, but he was persistent and finally, his eyes glittering from the exertion, his face all livid from the collar that was choking his throat,—a collar far too tight,—he did contrive to accomplish his task, and sat down in exhaustion in front of the pier glass, reflected in it from head to foot, a reflection that was repeated in all the other mirrors.

"Oh, this is dreadful!" he muttered, letting his strong bald head drop, and without trying to understand, without reflecting, just what, precisely, was dreadful; then, with an accustomed and attentive glance, he inspected his stubby fingers, with gouty hardenings at the joints, and his convex nails of an almond colour, repeating, with conviction: "This is dreadful. . . ."

But at this point the second gong, sonorously, as in some heathen temple, reverberated through the entire house. And, getting up quickly from his seat, the gentleman from San Francisco drew his collar still tighter with the necktie and his stomach by means of the low-cut vest, put on his tuxedo, drew out his cuffs, scrutinized himself once more in the mirror. . . . This Carmella, swarthy, with eyes which she knew well how to use most effectively, resembling a mulatto woman, clad in a dress of many colours, with the colour of orange predominant, must dance exceptionally, he reflected. And, stepping briskly out of his room and walking over the carpet to the next one,—his wife's—he asked, loudly, if they would be ready soon?

"In five minutes, Dad!" a girl's voice, ringing and by now gay, responded from the other side of the door.

"Very well," said the gentleman from San Francisco.

And, leisurely, he walked down red-carpeted corridors and staircases, descending in search of the reading room. The servants he met stood aside and hugged the wall to let him pass, but he kept on his way as though he had never even noticed them. An old woman who was late for dinner, already stooping, with milky hair but *décolleté* in a light-gray gown of silk, was hurrying with all her might, but drolly, in a hen-like manner, and he easily outstripped her. Near the glass doors of the dining room, where all the guests had already assembled, and were beginning their dinner, he stopped before a little table piled with boxes of cigars and Egyptian cigarettes, took a large Manila cigar, and tossed three *lire* upon the little table; upon the closed veranda he glanced, in passing, through the open window: out of the darkness he felt a breath of the balmy air upon him, thought he saw the tip of an ancient palm, that had flung wide across the stars its fronds, which seemed gigantic, heard the distant, even noise of the sea floating in to him. . . . In the reading room,—snug, quiet, and illuminated only above the tables, some gray-haired German was standing, rustling the newspapers,—unkempt, resembling Ibsen, in round silver spectacles and with the astonished eyes of a madman. Having scrutinized him coldly, the gentleman from San Francisco sat down in a deep leather chair in a corner near a green-shaded lamp, put on his *pince nez*, twitching his head because his collar was choking him, and hid himself completely behind the newspaper sheet. He rapidly ran through the headlines of certain items, read a few lines about the never-ceasing Balkan war, with an accustomed gesture turned the newspaper over,—when suddenly the lines flared up before him with a glassy glare, his neck became taut, his eyes bulged out, the *pince nez* flew off his nose. . . . He lunged forward, tried to swallow some air,—and gasped wildly; his lower jaw sank, lighting up his entire mouth with the reflection of the gold fillings; his head dropped back on his shoulder and began to sway; the bosom of his shirt bulged out like a basket,—and his whole body, squirming, his heels catching the carpet, slid downward to the floor, desperately struggling with someone.

Had the German not been in the reading room, the personnel of the hotel would have managed, quickly and adroitly, to hush up this dreadful occurrence; instantly, through back passages, seizing him by the head and feet, they would have rushed off the gentleman from San Francisco as far away as possible,—and never a soul among the guests would have found out what he had been up to. But the German had dashed out of the reading room with a scream,—he had aroused the entire house, the entire dining room. And many jumped up from their meal, overturning their chairs; many, paling, ran toward the reading room. "What—what has happened?" was heard in all languages,—and no one gave a sensible answer, no one comprehended anything, since even up to now men are amazed most of all by death, and will not, under any circumstances, believe in it. The proprietor dashed from one guest to another, trying to detain those who were running away and to pacify them with hasty assurances that this was just a trifling occurrence, a slight fainting spell of a certain gentleman from San Francisco. . . . But no one listened to him; many had seen the waiters and bellboys tearing off the necktie, the vest, and the rumpled tuxedo off this gentleman, and even, for some reason or other, the dancing slippers off his splayed feet, clad in black silk. But he was still struggling. He was still obdurately wrestling with death; he absolutely refused to yield to her, who had so unexpectedly and churlishly fallen upon him. His head was swaying, he rattled hoarsely, like one with his throat cut; his eyes had rolled up, like a drunkard's. . . . When he was hurriedly carried in and laid upon a bed in room number forty-three,—the smallest, the poorest, the dampest and the coldest, situated at the end of the bottom corridor,—his daughter ran in, with her hair down, in a little dressing gown that had flown open, her bosom, raised up by the corset, uncovered; then his wife, big and ponderous, already dressed for dinner,—her mouth rounded in terror. . . . But by now he had ceased even to bob his head.

A quarter of an hour later everything in the hotel had assumed some semblance of order. But the evening was irreparably spoiled. Some guests, returning to the dining room, finished their dinner, but in silence, with aggrieved countenances, while the proprietor would approach now one group, now another, shrugging his shoulders in polite yet impotent irritation, feeling himself guilty without guilt, assuring everybody that he understood very well "how unpleasant all this was," and pledging his word that he would take "all measures within his power" to remove this unpleasantness. It was necessary to call off the *tarantella,* all unnecessary electric lights were switched off, the majority of the guests withdrew into the bar, and it became so quiet that one heard distinctly the ticking of the clock in the vestibule, whose sole occupant was a parrot, dully muttering something, fussing in his cage before going to sleep, contriving to doze off at last with one claw ludicrously stretched up to the upper perch. . . . The gentleman from San Francisco was lying upon a cheap iron bed, under coarse woolen blankets, upon which the dull light of a single bulb beat down from the ceiling. An ice-bag hung down to his moist and cold forehead. The livid face, already dead, was gradually growing cold; the hoarse rattling, expelled from the open mouth, illuminated by the reflection of gold, was growing fainter. This was no longer the gentleman from San

Francisco rattling,—he no longer existed,—but some other. His wife, his daughter, the doctor and the servants were standing, gazing at him dully. Suddenly, that which they awaited and feared was consummated,—the rattling ceased abruptly. And slowly, slowly, before the eyes of all, a pallor flowed over the face of the man who had died, and his features seemed to grow finer, to become irradiated, with a beauty which had been rightfully his in the long ago. . . .

The proprietor entered. *"Già è morto,"* said the doctor to him in a whisper. The proprietor, his face dispassionate, shrugged his shoulders. The wife, down whose cheeks the tears were quietly coursing, walked up to him and timidly said that the deceased ought now to be carried to his own room.

"Oh, no, madam," hastily, correctly, but now without any amiability and not in English, but in French, retorted the proprietor, who was not at all interested now in such trifling sums as the arrivals from San Francisco might leave in his coffers. "That is absolutely impossible, madam," said he, and added in explanation that he valued the apartments occupied by them very much; that, were he to carry out her wishes, everybody in Capri would know it and the tourists would shun those apartments.

The young lady, who had been gazing at him strangely, sat down on a chair, and, stuffing her mouth with handkerchief, burst into sobs. The wife dried her tears immediately, her face flaring up. She adopted a louder tone, making demands in her own language, and still incredulous of the fact that all respect for them had been completely lost. The proprietor, with a polite dignity, cut her short: if madam was not pleased with the customs of the hotel, he would not venture to detain her; and he firmly announced that the body must be gotten away this very day, at dawn, that the police had already been notified, and one of the police officers would be here very soon and would carry out all the necessary formalities. Was it possible to secure even a common coffin in Capri, madam asks? Regrettably, no,—it was beyond possibility, and no one would be able to make one in time. It would be necessary to have recourse to something else. . . . For instance,—English soda water came in large and long boxes. . . . It was possible to knock the partitions out of such a box. . . . boxes. . . . It was possible to knock the partitions out of such a box. . . .

At night the whole hotel slept. The window in room number forty-three was opened,—it gave out upon a corner of the garden where, near a high stone wall with broken glass upon its crest, a phthisic banana tree was growing; the electric light was switched off; the key was turned in the door, and everybody went away. The dead man remained in the darkness,—the blue stars looked down upon him from the sky, a cricket with a pensive insouciance began his song in the wall. . . . In the dimly lit corridor two chambermaids were seated on a window sill, at some darning. Luigi, in slippers, entered with a pile of clothing in his arms.

"Pronto? (All ready?)" he asked solicitously, in a ringing whisper, indicating with his eyes the fearsome door at the end of the corridor. And, he waved his hand airily in that direction. . . . *"Partenza!"* he called out in a whisper, as though he were speeding a train, the usual phrase used in Italian depots at the departure of trains,—and the chambermaids, choking with silent laughter, let their heads sink on each other's shoulder.

Thereupon, hopping softly, he ran up to the very door, gave it the merest tap, and, inclining his head to one side, in a low voice, asked with the utmost deference:

"*Ha sonato signore?*"

And, squeezing his throat, thrusting out his lower jaw, in a grating voice, slowly and sadly, he answered his own question, as though from the other side of the door:

"Yes, come in. . . ."

And at dawn, when it had become light beyond the window of room number forty-three, and a humid wind had begun to rustle the tattered leaves of the banana tree; when the blue sky of morning had lifted and spread out over the Island of Capri, and the pure and clearcut summit of Monte Solaro had grown aureate against the sun that was rising beyond the distant blue mountains of Italy; when the stone masons, who were repairing the tourists' paths on the island, had set out to work,—a long box that had formerly been used for soda water was brought to room number forty-three. Soon it became very heavy, and was pressing hard against the knees of the junior porter, who bore it off briskly on a one horse cab over the white paved highway that was sinuously winding to and fro over the slopes of Capri, among the stone walls and the vineyards, ever downwards, to the very sea. The cabby, a puny little man with reddened eyes, in an old, wretched jacket with short sleeves and in trodden-down shoes, was undergoing the after effects of drink,—he had diced the whole night through in a *tratoria,* and kept on lashing his sturdy little horse, tricked out in the Sicilian fashion, with all sorts of little bells livelily jingling upon the bridle with its tufts of coloured wool, and upon the brass points of its high pad; with a yard-long feather stuck in its cropped forelock,—a feather that shook as the horse ran. The cabby kept silent; he was oppressed by his shiftlessness, his vices,—by the fact that he had, that night, lost to the last mite all those coppers with which his pockets had been filled. But the morning was fresh; in air such as this, with the sea all around, under the morning sky, the after effects of drink quickly evaporate, and a man is soon restored to a carefree mood, and the cabby was furthermore consoled by that unexpected sum, the opportunity to earn which had been granted him by some gentleman from San Francisco, whose lifeless head was bobbing from side to side in the box at his back. . . . The little steamer,—a beetle lying far down below, against the tender and vivid deep-blue with which the Bay of Naples is so densely and highly flooded,—was already blowing its final whistles, that reverberated loudly all over the island, whose every bend, every ridge, every stone, was as distinctly visible from every point as if there were absolutely no such thing as atmosphere. Near the wharf the junior porter was joined by the senior, who was speeding with the daughter and wife of the gentleman from San Francisco in his automobile,—they were pale, with eyes hollow from tears and a sleepless night. And ten minutes later the little steamer was again chugging through the water, again running toward Sorrento, toward Castellamare, carrying away from Capri, for all time, the family from San Francisco. . . . And again peace and quiet resumed their reign upon the island.

Upon this island, two thousand years ago, had lived a man who had become completely enmeshed in his cruel and foul deeds, who had for some reason seized the power over millions of people in his hands, and who, having himself lost his head at the senselessness of this power and from the fear of death by assassination, lurking in ambush behind every corner, had committed cruelties beyond all measure,—and humankind has remembered him for all time; and those who, in their collusion, just as incomprehensively and, in substance, just as cruelly as he, reign at present in power over this world, gather from all over the earth to gaze upon the ruins of that stone villa where he had dwelt on one of the steepest ascents of the island. On this splendid morning all those who had come to Capri for just this purpose were still sleeping in the hotels, although, toward their entrances, were already being led little mouse-gray burros with red saddles, upon which, after awaking and sating themselves with food, Americans and Germans, men and women, young and old, would again clamber up ponderously this day, and after whom would again run the old Caprian beggar women, with sticks in their gnarled hands,—would run over stony paths, and always up-hill, up to the very summit of Mount Tiberio. Set at rest by the fact that the dead old man from San Francisco, who had likewise been planning to go with them but instead of that had only frightened them with a *memento mori,* had already been shipped off to Naples, the travellers slept on heavily, and the quiet of the island was still undisturbed, the shops in the city were still shut. The market place on the *piazetta* alone was carrying on traffic,—in fish and greens; and the people there were all simple folk, among whom, without anything to do, as always, was standing Lorenzo the boatman, famous all over Italy,—a tall old man, a care-free rake and a handsome fellow, who had served more than once as a model to many artists; he had brought, and had already sold for a song, two lobsters that he had caught that night and which were already rustling in the apron of the cook of that very hotel where the family from San Francisco had passed the night, and now he could afford to stand in calm idleness even until the evening, looking about him with a kingly bearing (a little trick of his), consciously picturesque with his tatters, clay pipe, and a red woolen *beretta* drooping over one ear.

And, along the precipices of Monte Solaro, upon the ancient Phœnician road, hewn out of the crags, down its stone steps, two mountaineers of Abruzzi were descending from Anacapri. One had bag-pipes under his leathern mantle,—a large bag made from the skin of a she-goat, with two pipes; the other had something in the nature of wooden Pan's-reeds. They went on,—and all the land, joyous, splendid, sunflooded, spread out below them: the stony humps of the island, which was lying almost in its entirety at their feet; and that faery-like deep-blue in which it was aswim; and the radiant morning vapours over the sea, toward the east, under the blinding sun, that was now beating down hotly, rising ever higher and higher; and, still in their morning vagueness, the mistily azure massive outlines of Italy, of her mountains near and far, whose beauty human speech is impotent to express. . . . Half way down the pipers slackened their pace; over the path, within a grotto in the craggy side of Monte Solaro, all illumed by the sun, all bathed in its warmth and glow, in snowy-white raiment of gypsum, and in a royal crown, golden-rusty from inclement weathers, stood the Mother of God, meek and gracious, her orbs lifted up to heaven, to the eternal and happy abodes of Her Thrice-blessed Son. The pipers bared their heads, put their reeds to their lips,—and there poured forth their naïve and humbly-jubilant praises to the sun, to the morning, to Her, the Immaculate Intercessor for all those who suffer in this evil and beautiful world, and to Him Who had been born of Her womb in a cavern at Bethlehem, in a poor shepherd's shelter in the distant land of Judæa. . . .

Meanwhile, the body of the dead old man from San Francisco was returning to its home, to a grave on the shores of the New World. Having gone through many humiliations, through much human neglect, having wandered for a week from one port warehouse to another, it had finally gotten once more on board that same famous ship upon which but so recently, with so much deference, he had been borne to the Old World. But now he was already being concealed from the quick,—he was lowered in his tarred coffin deep into the black hold. And once more the ship was sailing on and on upon its long sea voyage. In the night time it sailed past the Island of Capri, and, to one watching them from the island, there was something sad about the ship's lights, slowly disappearing over the dark sea. But, upon the ship itself, in its brilliant *salons* resplendent with lustres and marbles, there was a crowded ball that night, as usual.

There was a ball on the second night also, and on the third,—again in the midst of a raging snow storm, whirling over an ocean booming like a funeral mass, and heaving in mountains trapped out in mourning by the silver spindrift. The innumerable fiery eyes of the ship that was retreating into the night and the snow gale were barely visible for the snow to the Devil watching from the crags of Gibraltar, from the stony gateway of two worlds. The Devil was as enormous as a cliff, but the ship was still more enormous than he; many-tiered, many-funnelled, created by the pride of the New Man with an ancient heart. The snow gale smote upon its rigging and wide-throated funnels, hoary from the snow, but the ship was steadfast, firm, majestic—and awesome. Upon its topmost deck were reared, in their solitude among the snowy whirlwinds, those snug, dimly-lit chambers where, plunged in a light and uneasy slumber, was its ponderous guide who resembled a heathen idol, reigning over the entire ship. He heard the pained howlings and the ferocious squealings of the storm stifled siren, but soothed himself by the proximity of that which, in the final summing up, was incomprehensible even to himself, that which was on the other side of his wall: that large cabin, which had the appearance of being armoured, and was being constantly filled by the mysterious rumbling, quivering, and crisp sputtering of blue flames, flaring up and exploding around the pale-faced operator with a metal half-hoop upon his head. In the very depths, in the under-water womb of the *Atlantida,* were the thirty-thousand-pound masses of boilers and of all sorts of other machinery—dully glittering with steel, hissing out steam and exuding oil and boilting water,—of that kitchen, made red hot from infernal furnaces underneath, wherein was brewing the motion of the ship. Forces, fearful in their concentration, were bubbling, were being transmitted to its very keel, into an endlessly long catacomb, into a tunnel, illuminated by electricity, wherein slowly, with an inexorability that was crushing to the human soul, was revolving within its oily couch the gigantean shaft, exactly like a living monster that had stretched itself out in this tunnel. Meanwhile, amidship the *Atlantida,* its warm and luxurious cabins, its dining halls and ball rooms, poured forth radiance and joyousness, were humming with the voices of a well-dressed gathering, were sweetly odorous with fresh flowers, and the strains of the stringed orchestra were their song. And again excruciatingly writhed and at intervals came together among this throng, among this glitter of lights, silks, diamonds and bared feminine shoulders, the supple pair of hired lovers; the sinfully-modest, very pretty young woman, with eye-lashes cast down, with a chaste coiffure, and the well-built young man, with black hair that seemed to be pasted on, with his face pale from powder, shod in the most elegant of patent-leather foot-gear, clad in a tight-fitting dress coat with long tails,—an Adonis who resembled a huge leech. And none knew that, already for a long time, this pair had grown wearied of languishing dissemblingly in their blissful torment to the sounds of the shamelessly-sad music,—nor that far, far below, at the bottom of the black hold, stood a tarred coffin, in close proximity to the sombre and sultry depths of the ship that was toilsomely overpowering the darkness, the ocean, the snow storm. . . .

QUESTIONS

1 Why is the gentleman nameless?
2 What is achieved by the contrast between the lighted ship and the storm that whirls around it?
3 A sense of well-being is important to the gentleman. What does he consider important to his sense of well-being?
4 Why does the dream have no impact on the gentleman?
5 How clearly developed is the characterization of the wife? Of the daughter? Do they reflect the same attitude toward life as that of the gentleman? Explain.
6 What other characters are also shown to be materialists?
7 How does the story of the tyrant who lived on Capri two thousand years ago fit into Bunin's story? What is the point of the reference to the two Abruzzi mountaineers?

TOPICS FOR COMPOSITION

1 Structure is important in Bunin's story. Trace his circular structural pattern and correlate with it his use of light and dark.
2 Write an essay showing the gentleman's lack of moral principle by examining his attitude toward other people. You might begin with those closest to the gentleman—his wife and daughter—and then proceed to the minor characters.

☐

In Lawrence's story, materialism takes an absurd shape in the form of a child's rocking-horse. Moreover, the child becomes a pathetic pleader for love in the face of materialistic force. When, however, the rocking-horse and its rider move together, the absurd and the pathetic merge to form a monstrous grotesque which overrides all notions of human sensitivity. As you read the story, observe how Lawrence weaves together symbol and characterization by:

1 Showing the mother's inability to love because of her overwhelming materialistic desires
2 Showing Paul's sensitivity to his mother's needs and his desire to be loved for his efforts
3 Showing the tension that exists in every aspect of the family relationships

THE ROCKING-HORSE WINNER

D. H. Lawrence

There was a woman who was beautiful, who started with all the advantages, yet she had no luck. She married for love, and the love turned to dust. She had bonny children, yet she felt they had been thrust upon her, and she could not love them. They looked at her coldly, as if they were finding fault with her. And hurriedly she felt she must cover up some fault in herself. Yet what it was that she must cover up she never knew. Nevertheless, when her children were present, she always felt the centre of her heart go hard. This troubled her, and in her manner she was all the more gentle and anxious for her children, as if she loved them very much. Only she herself knew that at the centre of her heart was a hard little place that could not feel love, no, not for anybody. Everybody else said of her: "She is such a good mother. She adores her children." Only she herself, and her children themselves, knew it was not so. They read it in each other's eyes.

There were a boy and two little girls. They lived in a pleasant house, with a garden, and they had discreet servants, and felt themselves superior to anyone in the neighbourhood.

Although they lived in style, they felt always an anxiety in the house. There was never enough money. The mother had a small income, and the father had a small income, but not nearly enough for the social position which they had to keep up. The father went in to town to some office. But though he had good prospects, these prospects never materialized. There was always the grinding sense of the shortage of money, though the style was always kept up.

At last the mother said: "I will see if *I* can't make something." But she did not know where to begin. She racked her brains, and tried this thing and the other, but could not find anything successful. The failure made deep lines come into her face. Her children were growing up, they would have to go to school. There must be more money, there must be more money. The father, who was always very handsome and expensive in his tastes, seemed as if he never *would* be able to do anything worth doing. And the mother, who had a great belief in herself, did not succeed any better, and her tastes were just as expensive.

And so the house came to be haunted by the unspoken phrase: *There must be more money! There must be more money!* The children could hear it all the time, though nobody said it aloud. They heard it at Christmas, when the expensive and splendid toys filled the nursery. Behind the shining modern rocking-horse, behind the smart doll's-house, a voice would start whispering: "There *must* be more money! There *must* be more money!" And the children would stop playing, to listen for a moment. They would look into each other's eyes, to see if they had all heard. And each one saw in the eyes of the other two that they too had heard. "There *must* be more money! There *must* be more money!"

It came whispering from the springs of the still-swaying rocking horse, and even the horse, bending his wooden, champing head, heard it. The big doll, sitting so pink and smirking in her new pram, could hear it quite plainly, and seemed to be smirking all the more self-consciously because of it. The foolish puppy, too, that took the place of the teddy bear, he was looking so extraordinarily foolish for no other reason but that he heard the secret whisper all over the house: "There *must* be more money!"

Yet nobody ever said it aloud. The whisper was everywhere, and therefore no one spoke it. Just as no one ever says: "We are breathing!" in spite of the fact that breath is coming and going all the time.

"Mother," said the boy Paul one day, "why don't we keep a car of our own? Why do we always use uncle's, or else a taxi?"

"Because we're the poor members of the family," said the mother.

"But why *are* we, mother?"

"Well—I suppose," she said slowly and bitterly, "it's because your father has no luck."

The boy was silent for some time.

"Is luck money, mother?" he asked rather timidly.

"No, Paul. Not quite. It's what causes you to have money."

"Oh!" said Paul vaguely. "I thought when Uncle Oscar said *filthy lucker,* it meant money."

"*Filthy lucre* does mean money," said the mother. "But it's lucre, not luck."

"Oh!" said the boy. "Then what *is* luck, mother?"

"It's what causes you to have money. If you're lucky you have money. That's why it's better to be born lucky than rich. If you're rich, you may lose your money. But if you're lucky, you will always get more money."

"Oh! Will you? And is father not lucky?"

"Very unlucky, I should say," she said bitterly.

The boy watched her with unsure eyes.

"Why?" he asked.

"I don't know. Nobody ever knows why one person is lucky and another unlucky."

"Don't they? Nobody at all? Does *nobody* know?"

"Perhaps God. But He never tells."

"He ought to, then. And aren't you lucky either, mother?"

"I can't be, if I married an unlucky husband."

"But by yourself, aren't you?"

"I used to think I was, before I married. Now I think I am very unlucky indeed."

"Why?"

"Well—never mind! Perhaps I'm not really," she said.

The child looked at her, to see if she meant it. But he saw, by the lines of her mouth, that she was only trying to hide something from him.

"Well, anyhow," he said stoutly, "I'm a lucky person."

"Why?" said his mother, with a sudden laugh.

He stared at her. He didn't even know why he had said it.

"God told me," he asserted, brazening it out.

"I hope He did, dear!" she said, again with a laugh, but rather bitter.

"He did, mother!"

"Excellent!" said the mother, using one of her husband's exclamations.

The boy saw she did not believe him; or, rather, that she paid no attention to his assertion. This angered him somewhat, and made him want to compel her attention.

He went off by himself, vaguely, in a childish way, seeking for the clue to "luck." Absorbed, taking no heed of other people, he went about with a sort of stealth, seeking inwardly for luck. He wanted luck, he wanted it, he wanted it. When the two girls were playing dolls in the nursery, he would sit on his big rocking-horse, charging madly into space, with a frenzy that made the little girls peer at him uneasily. Wildly the horse careered, the waving dark hair of the boy tossed, his eyes had a strange glare in them. The little girls dared not speak to him.

When he had ridden to the end of his mad little journey, he climbed down and stood in front of his rocking-horse, staring fixedly into its lowered face. Its red mouth was slightly open, its big eye was wide and glassy-bright.

"Now!" he would silently command the snorting steed. "Now, take me to where there is luck! Now take me!"

And he would slash the horse on the neck with the little whip he had asked Uncle Oscar for. He *knew* the horse could take him to where there was luck, if only he forced it. So he would mount again, and start on his furious ride, hoping at last to get there. He knew he could get there.

"You'll break your horse, Paul!" said the nurse.

"He's always riding like that! I wish he'd leave off!" said his elder sister Joan.

But he only glared down on them in silence. Nurse gave him up. She could make nothing of him. Anyhow he was growing beyond her.

One day his mother and his Uncle Oscar came in when he was on one of his furious rides. He did not speak to them.

"Hallo, you young jockey! Riding a winner?" said his uncle.

"Aren't you growing too big for a rocking-horse? You're not a very little boy any longer, you know," said his mother.

But Paul only gave a blue glare from his big, rather close-set eyes. He would speak to nobody when he was in full tilt. His mother watched him with an anxious expression on her face.

At last he suddenly stopped forcing his horse into the mechanical gallop, and slid down.

"Well, I got there!" he announced fiercely, his blue eyes still flaring, and his sturdy long legs straddling apart.

"Where did you get to?" asked his mother.

"Where I wanted to go," he flared back at her.

"That's right, son!" said Uncle Oscar. "Don't you stop till you get there. What's the horse's name?"

"He doesn't have a name," said the boy.

"Gets on without all right?" asked the uncle.

"Well, he has different names. He was called Sansovino last week."

"Sansovino, eh? Won the Ascot. How did you know his name?"

"He always talks about horse-races with Bassett," said Joan.

The uncle was delighted to find that his small nephew was posted with all the racing news. Bassett, the young gardener, who had been wounded in the left foot in the war and had got his present job through Oscar Cresswell, whose batman he had been, was a perfect blade of the "turf." He lived in the racing events, and the small boy lived with him.

Oscar Cresswell got it all from Bassett.

"Master Paul comes and asks me, so I can't do more than tell him, sir," said Bassett, his face terribly serious, as if he were speaking of religious matters.

"And does he ever put anything on a horse he fancies?"

"Well—I don't want to give him away—he's a young sport, a fine sport, sir. Would you mind asking him himself? He sort of takes a pleasure in it, and perhaps he'd feel I was giving him away, sir, if you don't mind."

Bassett was serious as a church.

The uncle went back to his nephew and took him off for a ride in the car.

"Say, Paul, old man, do you ever put anything on a horse?" the uncle asked.

The boy watched the handsome man closely.

"Why, do you think I oughtn't to?" he parried.

"Not a bit of it! I thought perhaps you might give me a tip for the Lincoln."

The car sped on into the country, going down to Uncle Oscar's place in Hampshire.

"Honour bright?" said the nephew.

"Honour bright, son!" said the uncle.

"Well, then, Daffodil."

"Daffodil! I doubt it, sonny. What about Mirza?"

"I only know the winner," said the boy. "That's Daffodil."

"Daffodil, eh?"

There was a pause. Daffodil was an obscure horse comparatively.

"Uncle!"

"Yes, son?"

"You won't let it go any further, will you? I promised Bassett."

"Bassett be damned, old man! What's he got to do with it?"

"We're partners. We've been partners from the first. Uncle, he lent me my first five shillings, which I lost. I promised him, honour bright, it was only between me and him; only you gave me that ten-shilling note I started winning with, so I thought you were lucky. You won't let it go any further, will you?"

The boy gazed at his uncle from those big, hot, blue eyes, set rather close together. The uncle stirred and laughed uneasily.

"Right you are, son! I'll keep your tip private. Daffodil, eh? How much are you putting on him?"

"All except twenty pounds," said the boy. "I keep that in reserve."

The uncle thought it a good joke.

"You keep twenty pounds in reserve, do you, you young romancer? What are you betting, then?"

"I'm betting three hundred," said the boy gravely. "But it's between you and me, Uncle Oscar! Honour bright?"

The uncle burst into a roar of laughter.

"It's between you and me all right, you young Nat Gould," he said, laughing. "But where's your three hundred?"

"Bassett keeps it for me. We're partners."

"You are, are you! And what is Bassett putting on Daffodil?"

"He won't go quite as high as I do, I expect. Perhaps he'll go a hundred and fifty."

"What, pennies?" laughed the uncle.

"Pounds," said the child, with a surprised look at his uncle. "Bassett keeps a bigger reserve than I do."

Between wonder and amusement Uncle Oscar was silent. He pursued the matter no further, but he determined to take his nephew with him to the Lincoln races.

"Now, son," he said. "I'm putting twenty on Mirza, and I'll put five for you on any horse you fancy. What's your pick?"

"Daffodil, uncle."

"No, not the fiver on Daffodil!"

"I should if it was my own fiver," said the child.

"Good! Good! Right you are! A fiver for me and a fiver for you on Daffodil."

The child had never been to a race-meeting before, and his eyes were blue fire. He pursed his mouth tight, and watched. A Frenchman just in front had put his money on Lancelot. Wild with excitement, he flayed his arms up and down, yelling *"Lancelot! Lancelot"* in his French accent.

Daffodil came in first, Lancelot second, Mirza third. The child, flushed and with eyes blazing, was curiously serene. His uncle brought him four five-pound notes, four to one.

"What am I to do with these?" he cried, waving them before the boy's eyes.

"I suppose we'll talk to Bassett," said the boy. "I expect I have fifteen hundred now; and twenty in reserve; and this twenty."

His uncle studied him for some moments.

"Look here, son!" he said. "You're not serious about Bassett and that fifteen hundred, are you?"

"Yes, I am. But it's between you and me, uncle. Honour bright!"

"Honour bright all right, son! But I must talk to Bassett."

"If you'd like to be a partner, uncle, with Bassett and me, we could all be partners. Only, you'd have to promise, honour bright, uncle, not to let it go beyond us three. Bassett and I are lucky, and you must be lucky, because it was your ten shillings I started winning with. . . ."

Uncle Oscar took both Bassett and Paul into Richmond Park for an afternoon, and there they talked.

"It's like this, you see, sir," Bassett said. "Master Paul would get me talking about racing events, spinning yarns, you know, sir. And he was always keen on knowing if I'd made or if I'd lost. It's about a year since, now, that I put five shilling on Blush of Dawn for him—and we lost. Then the luck turned, with that ten shillings he had from you, that we put on Singhalese. And since that time, it's been pretty steady, all things considering. What do you say, Master Paul?''

"We're all right when we're sure," said Paul. "It's when we're not quite sure that we go down."

"Oh, but we're careful then," said Bassett.

"But when are you *sure*?" smiled Uncle Oscar.

"It's Master Paul, sir," said Bassett, in a secret, religious voice. "It's as if he had it from heaven. Like Daffodil, now, for the Lincoln. That was as sure as eggs."

"Did you put anything on Daffodil?" asked Oscar Cresswell.

"Yes, sir. I made my bit."

"And my nephew?"

Bassett was obstinately silent, looking at Paul.

"I made twelve hundred, didn't I, Bassett? I told uncle I was putting three hundred on Daffodil."

"That's right," said Bassett, nodding.

"But where's the money?" asked the uncle.

"I keep it safe locked up, sir. Master Paul he can have it any minute he likes to ask for it."

"What, fifteen hundred pounds?"

"And twenty! And *forty,* that is, with the twenty he made on the course."

"It's amazing!" said the uncle.

"If Master Paul offers you to be partners, sir, I would, if I were you; if you'll excuse me," said Bassett.

Oscar Cresswell thought about it.

"I'll see the money," he said.

They drove home again, and sure enough, Bassett came round to the garden-house with fifteen hundred pounds in notes. The twenty pounds reserve was left with Joe Glee, in the Turf Commission deposit.

"You see, it's all right, uncle, when I'm *sure!* Then we go strong, for all we're worth. Don't we, Bassett?"

"We do that, Master Paul."

"And when are you sure?" said the uncle, laughing.

"Oh, well, sometimes I'm *absolutely* sure, like about Daffodil," said the boy; "and sometimes I have an idea; and sometimes I haven't even an idea, have I, Bassett? Then we're careful, because we mostly go down."

"You do, do you! And when you're sure, like about Daffodil, what makes you sure, sonny?"

"Oh, well, I don't know," said the boy uneasily. "I'm sure, you know, uncle; that's all."

"It's as if he had it from heaven, sir," Bassett reiterated.

"I should say so!" said the uncle.

But he became a partner. And when the Leger was coming on, Paul was "sure" about Lively Spark, which was a quite inconsiderable horse. The boy insisted on putting a thousand on the horse, Bassett went for five hundred, and Oscar Cresswell two hundred. Lively Spark came in first, and the betting had been ten to one against him. Paul had made ten thousand.

"You see," he said, "I was absolutely sure of him."

Even Oscar Cresswell had cleared two thousand.

"Look here, son," he said, "this sort of thing makes me nervous."

"It needn't, uncle! Perhaps I shan't be sure again for a long time."

"But what are you going to do with your money?" asked the uncle.

"Of course," said the boy, "I started it for mother. She said she had no luck, because father is unlucky, so I thought if *I* was lucky, it might stop whispering."

"What might stop whispering?"

"Our house. I *hate* our house for whispering."

"What does it whisper?"

"Why—why"—the boy fidgeted—"why, I don't know. But it's always short of money, you know, uncle."

"I know it, son, I know it."

"You know people send mother writs, don't you, uncle?"

"I'm afraid I do," said the uncle.

"And then the house whispers, like people laughing at you behind your back. It's awful, that is! I thought if I was lucky . . . ."

"You might stop it," added the uncle.

The boy watched him with big blue eyes, that had an uncanny cold fire in them, and he said never a word.

"Well, then!" said the uncle. "What are we doing?"

"I shouldn't like mother to know I was lucky," said the boy.

"Why not, son?"

"She'd stop me."

"I don't think she would."

"Oh!"—and the boy writhed in an odd way—"I *don't* want her to know, uncle."

"All right, son! We'll manage it without her knowing."

They managed it very easily. Paul, at the other's suggestion, handed over five thousand pounds to his uncle, who deposited it with the family lawyer, who was then to inform Paul's mother that a relative had put five thousand pounds into his hands, which sum was to be paid out a thousand pounds at a time, on the mother's birthday, for the next five years.

"So she'll have a birthday present of a thousand pounds for five successive years," said Uncle Oscar. "I hope it won't make it all the harder for her later."

Paul's mother had her birthday in November. The house had been "whispering" worse than ever lately, and, even in spite of his luck, Paul could not bear up against it. He was very anxious to see the effect of the birthday letter, telling his mother about the thousand pounds.

When there were no visitors, Paul now took his meals with his parents, as he was beyond the nursery control. His mother went into town nearly every day. She had discovered that she had an odd knack of sketching furs and dress materials, so she worked secretly in the studio of a friend who was the chief "artist" for the leading drapers. She drew the figures of ladies in furs and ladies in silk and sequins for the newspaper advertisements. This young woman artist earned several thousand pounds a year, but Paul's mother only made several hundreds, and she was again dissatisfied. She so wanted to be first in something, and she did not succeed, even in making sketches for drapery advertisements.

She was down to breakfast on the morning of her birthday. Paul watched her face as she read her letters. He knew the lawyer's letter. As his mother read it, her face hardened and became more expressionless. Then a cold, determined look came on her mouth. She hid the letter under the pile of others, and said not a word about it.

"Didn't you have anything nice in the post for your birthday, mother?" said Paul.

"Quite moderately nice," she said, her voice cold and absent.

She went away to town without saying more.

But in the afternoon Uncle Oscar appeared. He said Paul's mother had had a long interview with the lawyer, asking if the whole five thousand could not be advanced at once, as she was in debt.

"What do you think, uncle?" said the boy.

"I leave it to you, son."

"Oh, let her have it, then! We can get some more with the other," said the boy.

"A bird in the hand is worth two in the bush, laddie!" said Uncle Oscar.

"But I'm sure to *know* for the Grand National; or the Lincolnshire; or else the Derby. I'm sure to know for *one* of them," said Paul.

So Uncle Oscar signed the agreement, and Paul's mother touched the whole five thousand. Then something very curious happened. The voices in the house suddenly went mad, like a chorus of frogs on a spring evening. There were certain new furnishings, and Paul had a tutor. He was *really* going to Eton, his father's school, in the following autumn. There were flowers in the winter, and a blossoming of the luxury Paul's mother had been used to. And yet the voices in the house, behind the sprays of mimosa and almond blossom, and from under the piles of iridescent cushions, simply trilled and screamed in a sort of ecstasy: "There *must* be more money! Oh-h-h; there *must* be more money. Oh, now, now-w! Now-w-w—there *must* be more money!—more than ever! More than ever!"

It frightened Paul terribly. He studied away at his Latin and Greek with his tutors. But his intense hours were spent with Bassett. The Grand National had gone by: he had not "known," and had lost a hundred pounds. Summer was at hand. He was in agony for the Lincoln. But even for the Lincoln he didn't "know," and he lost fifty pounds. He became wild-eyed and strange, as if something were going to explode in him.

"Let it alone, son! Don't you bother about it!" urged Uncle Oscar. But it was as if the boy couldn't really hear what his uncle was saying.

"I've got to know for the Derby! I've got to know for the Derby!" the child reiterated, his big blue eyes blazing with a sort of madness.

His mother noticed how overwrought he was.

"You'd better go to the seaside. Wouldn't you like to go now to the seaside, instead of waiting? I think you'd better," she said, looking down at him anxiously, her heart curiously heavy because of him.

But the child lifted his uncanny blue eyes.

"I couldn't possibly go before the Derby, mother!" he said. "I couldn't possibly!"

"Why not?" she said, her voice becoming heavy when she was opposed. "Why not? You can still go from the seaside to see the Derby with your Uncle Oscar, if that's what you wish. No need for you to wait here. Besides, I think you care too much about these races. It's a bad sign. My family has been a gambling family, and you won't know till you grow up how much damage it has done. But it has done damage. I shall have to send Bassett away, and ask Uncle Oscar not to talk racing to you, unless you promise to be reasonable about it; go away to the seaside and forget it. You're all nerves!''

"I'll do what you like, mother, so long as you don't send me away till after the Derby," the boy said.

"Send you away from where? Just from this house?"

"Yes," he said, gazing at her.

"Why, you curious child, what makes you care about this house so much, suddenly? I never knew you loved it."

He gazed at her without speaking. He had a secret within a secret, something he had not divulged, even to Bassett or to his Uncle Oscar.

But his mother, after standing undecided and a little bit sullen for some moments, said:

"Very well, then! Don't go to the seaside till after the Derby, if you don't wish it. But promise me you won't let your nerves go to pieces. Promise you won't think so much about horse-racing and *events,* as you call them!''

"Oh, no," said the boy casually. "I won't think much about them, mother. You needn't worry. I wouldn't worry, mother, if I were you."

"If you were me and I were you," said his mother, "I wonder what we *should* do!''

"But you know you needn't worry, mother, don't you?'' the boy repeated.

"I should be awfully glad to know it," she said wearily.

"Oh, well, you *can,* you know. I mean, you *ought* to know you needn't worry," he insisted.

"Ought I? Then I'll see about it," she said.

Paul's secret of secrets was his wooden horse, that which had no name. Since he was emancipated from a nurse and a nursery-governess, he had had his rocking-horse removed to his own bedroom at the top of the house.

"Surely, you're too big for a rocking-horse!'' his mother had remonstrated.

"Well, you see, mother, till I can have a *real* horse, I like to have *some* sort of animal about," had been his quaint answer.

"Do you feel he keeps you company?'' she laughed.

"Oh, yes! He's very good, he always keeps me company, when I'm there," said Paul.

So the horse, rather shabby, stood in an arrested prance in the boy's bedroom.

The Derby was drawing near, and the boy grew more and more tense. He hardly heard what was spoken to him, he was very frail, and his eyes were really uncanny. His mother had sudden strange seizures of uneasiness about him. Sometimes, for half-an-hour, she would feel a sudden anxiety about him that was almost anguish. She wanted to rush to him at once, and know he was safe.

Two nights before the Derby, she was at a big party in town, when one of her rushes of anxiety about her boy, her first-born, gripped her heart till she could hardly speak. She fought with the feeling, might and main, for she believed in common-sense. But it was too strong. She had to leave the dance and go downstairs to telephone to the country. The children's nursery-governess was terribly surprised and startled at being rung up in the night.

"Are the children all right, Miss Wilmot?"

"Oh, yes, they are quite all right."

"Master Paul? Is he all right?"

"He went to bed as right as a trivet. Shall I run up and look at him?"

"No," said Paul's mother reluctantly. "No! Don't trouble. It's all right. Don't sit up. We shall be home fairly soon." She did not want her son's privacy intruded upon.

"Very good," said the governess.

It was about one o'clock when Paul's mother and father drove up to their house. All was still. Paul's mother went to her room and slipped off her white fur cloak. She had told her maid not to wait up for her. She heard her husband downstairs, mixing a whisky-and-soda.

And then, because of the strange anxiety at her heart, she stole upstairs to her son's room. Noiselessly she went along the upper corridor. Was there a faint noise? What was it?

She stood, with arrested muscles, outside his door, listening. There was a strange, heavy, and yet not loud noise. Her heart stood still. It was a soundless noise, yet rushing and powerful. Something huge, in violent, hushed motion. What was it? What in God's name was it? She ought to know. She felt that she knew the noise. She knew what it was.

Yet she could not place it. She couldn't say what it was. And on and on it went, like a madness.

Softly, frozen with anxiety and fear, she turned the door-handle.

The room was dark. Yet in the space near the window, she heard and saw something plunging to and fro. She gazed in fear and amazement.

Then suddenly she switched on the light, and saw her son, in his green pyjamas, madly surging on the rocking-horse. The blaze of light suddenly lit him up, as he urged the wooden horse, and lit her up, as she stood, blonde, in her dress of pale green and crystal, in the doorway.

"Paul!" she cried. "Whatever are you doing?"

"It's Malabar!" he screamed, in a powerful, strange voice. "It's Malabar!"

His eyes blazed at her for one strange and senseless second, as he ceased urging his wooden horse. Then he fell with a crash to the ground, and she, all her tormented motherhood flooding upon her, rushed to gather him up.

But he was unconscious, and unconscious he remained, with some brain-fever. He talked and tossed, and his mother sat stonily by his side.

"Malabar! It's Malabar! Bassett, Bassett, I *know!* It's Malabar!"

So the child cried, trying to get up and urge the rocking-horse that gave him his inspiration.

"What does he mean by Malabar?" asked the heart-frozen mother.

"I don't know," said the father stonily.

"What does he mean by Malabar?" she asked her brother Oscar.

"It's one of the horses running for the Derby," was the answer.

And, in spite of himself, Oscar Cresswell spoke to Bassett, and himself put a thousand on Malabar: at fourteen to one.

The third day of the illness was critical: they were waiting for a change. The boy, with his rather long, curly hair, was tossing ceaselessly on the pillow. He neither slept nor regained consciousness, and his eyes were like blue stones. His mother sat, feeling her heart had gone, turned actually into a stone.

In the evening, Oscar Cresswell did not come, but Bassett sent a message, saying could he come up for one moment, just one moment? Paul's mother was very angry at the intrusion, but on second thought she agreed. The boy was the same. Perhaps Bassett might bring him to consciousness.

The gardener, a shortish fellow with a little brown moustache, and sharp little brown eyes, tip-toed into the room, touched his imaginary cap to Paul's mother, and stole to the bedside, staring with glittering, smallish eyes, at the tossing, dying child.

"Master Paul!" he whispered. "Master Paul! Malabar came in first all right, a clean win. I did as you told me. You've made over seventy thousand pounds, you have; you've got over eighty thousand. Malabar came in all right, Master Paul."

"Malabar! Malabar! Did I say Malabar, mother? Did I say Malabar? Do you think I'm lucky, mother? I knew Malabar, didn't I? Over eighty thousand pounds! I call that lucky, don't you, mother? Over eighty thousand pounds! I knew, didn't I know I knew? Malabar came in all right. If I ride my horse till I'm sure, then I tell you, Bassett, you can go as high as you like. Did you go for all you were worth, Bassett?"

"I went a thousand on it, Master Paul."

"I never told you, mother, that if I can ride my horse, and *get there,* then I'm absolutely sure—oh, absolutely! Mother, did I ever tell you? I *am* lucky!"

"No, you never did," said the mother.

But the boy died in the night.

And even as he lay dead, his mother heard her brother's voice saying to her: "My God, Hester, you're eighty-odd thousand to the good, and a poor devil of a son to the bad. But, poor devil, poor devil, he's best gone out of a life where he rides his rocking-horse to find a winner."

QUESTIONS

1   What does each of the main characters in the story—the mother, Paul, Bassett, and Uncle Oscar—symbolize? How is the characterization of each appropriate to what he symbolizes?
2   What different meanings are attached to the word, *luck?*
3   How is Paul's "winning" part of the ironic conflict?
4   How does Lawrence use description to heighten the grotesque events in his story?
5   How is the final statement consistent with Lawrence's view of the destructive effect of materialistic greed?

TOPICS FOR COMPOSITION

1   Many segments of our society would agree with Lawrence that the emphasis on materialism is a primary destructive force. In fact, our polluted environment stands as testimony to Lawrence's point. Write an essay arguing that modern society has embraced materialism to the detriment of human values.

2   Write an essay in which you persuasively present a balance between man's basic drive for material acquisition and his sense of human values.

That Robert Penn Warren's main character cannot cope with sudden fame and affluence is true. But we should also recognize that Luke Goodwood's inability to adjust was unique and not merely the logical outcome of his small-town background. For instance, the narrator and others react differently to the same background. Taking a larger perspective, we can better understand the depth of Warren's characterization if we see Luke's problems as facets of other themes seen in other parts of this book. As you read this story, consider how Luke's behavior is motivated by the following:

1   His search for his place in society
2   His lack of personal restraint
3   His confused, seemingly indifferent attitude toward the meaning of love

GOODWOOD COMES BACK

Robert Penn Warren

Luke Goodwood always could play baseball, but I never could, to speak of. I was little for my age then, but well along in my studies and didn't want to play with the boys my size; I wanted to play with the boys in my class, and if it hadn't been for Luke, I never would have been able to. He was a pitcher then, like he has always been, and so he would say, "Aw, let him field." When he was pitching, it didn't matter much who was fielding, anyway, because there weren't going to be any hits to amount to anything in the first place. I used to play catcher some, too, because I had the best mitt, but he pitched a mighty hard ball and it used to fool the batter all right, but it fooled me too a good part of the time so I didn't hold them so good. Also, I was a little shy about standing close up to the plate on account of the boys flinging the bat the way they did when they started off for first base. Joe Lancaster was the worst for that, and since he almost always played on the other side, being a good hitter to balance off Luke's pitching, I had to come close, nearly getting scared to death of him braining me when he did get a hit. Luke used to yell, "For Christ sake get up to that plate or let somebody else catch for Christ sake that can!"

Joe Lancaster wasn't much bigger than I was, but he was knotty and old-looking, with a white face and hair that was almost white like an old man's, but he wasn't exactly an albino. He was a silent and solemn kind of boy, but he could sure hit; I can remember how he used to give that ball a good solid crack, and start off running the bases with his short legs working fast like a fox terrier's trying to catch up with something, but his face not having any expression and looking like it was dead or was thinking about something else. I've been back home since and seen him in the restaurant where he works behind the counter. I'm bigger than he is now, for he never did grow much. He says hello exactly like a stranger that never saw you before and asks what you want. When he has his sleeves rolled up in the summertime, and puts an order on the counter for you, his arms are small like a boy's, still, with very white skin you can see the veins through.

It was Joe hit me in the head with a bat when I was catching. Luke ran up toward the plate, yelling, "You've killed him!"—for the bat knocked me clean over. It was the last time I played catcher; the next time I came out bringing my mitt, which was a good one, Luke said, "Gimme that mitt." He took it and gave it to another boy, and told me to go play field. That was the only thing I didn't like about Luke, his taking my mitt.

I stayed at the Goodwood house a lot, and liked it, even if it was so different from my own. It was like a farmhouse, outside and inside, but the town was growing out toward it, making it look peculiar set so far back off the street with barns and chicken yards behind it. There was Mr. Goodwood, who had been a sheriff once and who had a bullet in his game leg, they said, a big man one time, but now with his skin too big for him and hanging in folds. His mustache was yellow from the chewing tobacco he used and his eyes were bloodshot; some people said he was drinking himself to death, but I'll say this for him, he drank himself to death upstairs without making any fuss. He had four boys, and drink was their ruination. They say it was likker got Luke out of the big league, and none of the Goodwoods could ever leave the poison alone. Anyway, the Goodwood house was a man's house with six men sitting down to the table, counting the grandfather, and Mrs. Goodwood and her daughter going back and forth to the kitchen with sweat on their faces and their hair damp from the stove. There would be men's coats on the chairs in the living room, sometimes hunting coats with the old blood caked on the khaki, balls of twine and a revolver on the mantel-piece, and shotguns and flyrods lying around, even on the spare bed that was in the living room. And the bird dogs came in the house whenever they got good and ready. At my house everything was different, for men there always seemed to be just visiting.

Luke took me hunting with him, or sometimes one of his big brothers took us both, but my mother didn't like for me to go with the grown boys along, because she believed that their morals were not very good. I don't suppose their morals were much worse than ordinary for boys getting their sap up, but hearing them talk was certainly an education for a kid. Luke was as good a shot as you ever hope to see. He hunted a lot by himself, too, for my folks wouldn't let me go just all the time. He would get up before day and eat some cold bread and coffee in the kitchen and then be gone till after dark with his rifle or his shotgun. He never took anything to eat with him, either, for when he was hunting he was like they say the Indians were in that respect. Luke reminded you of an Indian, too, even when he was a boy and even if he was inclined to be a blond and not a brunette; he was long and rangy, had a big fine-cut nose, and looked to be setting his big feet always carefully on the ground, and came up on his toes a little, like a man testing his footing. He walked that way even on a concrete walk, probably from being in the woods so much. It was no wonder with all his hunting he never did study or make any good use and profit of his mind, which was better than most people's, however. The only good grades he made were in penmanship, copybooks still being used then in the grammar school part of school. He could make his writing look exactly like the writing at the top of the page, a Spencerian hand tilted forward, but not too much like a woman's. He could draw a bird with one line without taking the pencil off the paper once, and he'd draw them all afternoon in school sometimes. The birds all looked alike, all fine and rounded off like his Spencerian writing, their beaks always open, but not looking like any birds God ever made in this world. Sometimes he would put words coming out of a bird's bill, like "You bastard," or worse; then he would scratch it out, for he might just as well have signed his name to it, because the teachers and everybody knew how well he could draw a bird in that way he had.

Luke didn't finish high school. He didn't stop all at once, but just came less and less, coming only on bad days most of the time, for on good days he would be off hunting or fishing. It was so gradual, him not coming, that nobody, maybe not even the teachers, knew when he really stopped for good. In the summer he would lie around the house, sleeping out in the yard on the grass where it was shady, stretched out like a cat, with just a pair of old pants on. Or he would fish or play baseball. It got so he was playing baseball for little town teams around that section, and he picked up some change to buy shells and tackle.

That was the kind of life he was living when I finished school and left town. We had drifted apart, you might say, by that time, for he didn't fool around with the school kids any more. I never found out exactly how he broke into real baseball and got out of what you call the sand lot. My sister wrote me some big man in the business saw Luke pitch some little game somewhere and Luke was gone to pitch for a team up in Indiana somewhere. Then the next year he got on the sport page in the papers. My sister, knowing I would be interested in the boy that was my friend, you might say, used to find out about the write-ups and send me clippings when the home paper would copy stories about Luke from the big papers. She said Luke was making nine thousand dollars playing for the Athletics, which was in Philadelphia. The papers called him the Boy Wizard from Alabama. He must have been making a lot of money that year to judge from the presents he sent home. He sent his mother a five-hundred-dollar radio set and a piano, and I admired him for the way he remembered his mother, who had had a hard time and no doubt about it. I don't know why he sent the piano, because nobody at his house could play one. He also fixed up the house, which was in a bad shape by that time. Mr. Goodwood was still alive, but according to all reports he was spending more time upstairs than ever, and his other three boys never were worth a damn, not even for working in the garden, and didn't have enough git-up-and-git to even go fishing.

The next year Luke pitched in the World Series, for the team that bought him from the Athletics, in Philadelphia, and he got a bonus of three thousand dollars, plus his salary. But he must have hit the skids after that, drink being the reason that was reported to me. When he was home on vacation, my sister said he did some fishing and hunting, but pretty soon he was drunk all the time, and carousing around. The next year he didn't finish the season. My sister sent me a clipping about it, and wrote on the margin, "I'm sure you will be sorry to know this because I know you always liked Luke. I like Luke too." For a matter of fact, I never saw a woman who didn't like Luke, he was so good-looking and he had such a mixture of wildness and a sort of embarrassment around women. You never saw a finer-looking fellow in your life than he was going down the street in summer with nothing on except old khaki pants and underwear tops and his long arms and shoulders near the color of coffee and his blondish hair streaked golden color with sunburn. But he didn't have anything to do with girls, that is, decent girls, probably because he was too impatient. I don't suppose he ever had a regular date in his life.

But the next year he was back in baseball, but not in such a good team, for he had done some training and lived clean for a while before the season opened. He came back with great success, it looked like at first. I was mighty glad when I got a clipping from my sister with the headlines, *Goodwood Comes Back.* He was shutting them out right and left. But it didn't last. The drink got him, and he was out of the big time game for good and all, clean as a whistle. Then he came back home.

It was on a visit home I saw him after all that time. I was visiting my sister, who was married and lived there, and I had taken a lawn mower down to the blacksmith shop to get it fixed for her. I was waiting out in front of the shop, leaning against one side of the door and looking out in the gravel street, which was sending up heat-dazzles. Two or three old men were sitting there, not even talking; they were the kind of old men you find sitting around town like that, who never did amount to a damn and whose names even people in town can't remember half the time. I saw Luke coming up the road with another boy, who didn't strike me as familiar right off because he was one of those who had grown up in the meantime. I could see they were both nearly drunk, when they got under the shade of the shed; and I noticed Luke's arms had got pretty stringy. I said hello to Luke, and he said, "Well, I'll be damned, how you making it?" I said, "Fine, how's it going?" Then he said, "Fine."

After they stood there a while I could see the other boy wasn't feeling any too good with the combination of whisky and the heat of the day. But Luke kept kidding him and trying to make him go up to the Goodwood house, where he said he had some more whisky. He said he had kept it under a setting hen's nest for two weeks to age, and the other boy said Luke never kept any whisky in his life two days, let alone two weeks, without drinking it up. It was bootleg whisky they were drinking, because Alabama was a dry state then, according to the law, even after repeal; Luke must have been kidding too, because he ought to know if anybody does, whisky don't age in glass whether it's under a setting hen or not. Then he tried to make the boy go up to Tangtown, which is what they call nigger town because of the immoral goings-on up there, where they could get some more whisky, he said, and maybe something else. The other boy said it wasn't decent in the middle of the afternoon. Then he asked me to go, but I said no thanks to the invitation, not ever having approved of that, and Tangtown especially, for it looks like to me a man ought to have more self-respect. The old men sitting there were taking in every word, probably jealous because they weren't good for drinking or anything any more.

Finally Luke and the other boy started up the road in the hot sun, going I don't know where, whether to his house or off to Tangtown in the middle of the afternoon. One of the old men said, "Now, ain't it a shame the way he's throwed away his chances." One of the others said likker always was hard on the Goodwoods. Luke, not being any piece off and having good ears even if he was drinking, must have heard them, for he stooped down and scooped up a rock from the road like a baseball player scooping up an easy grounder, and yelled, "Hey, see that telephone pole?" Then he threw the rock like a bullet and slammed the pole, which was a good way off. He turned around, grinning pretty sour, and yelled, "Still got control, boys!" Then the two of them went off.

It was more than a year before I saw him again, but he had been mentioned in letters from my sister, Mrs. Hargreave, who said that Luke was doing better and that his conduct was not so outrageous, as she put it. His mother's dying that year of cancer may have quieted him down some. And then he didn't have any money to buy whisky with. My sister said he was hunting again and in the summer pitching a little ball for the town team that played on Saturday and Sunday afternoons with the other teams from the towns around there. His pitching probably was still good enough to make the opposition look silly. But maybe not, either, as might be judged from what I heard the next time I saw him. I was sitting on the front porch of my sister's house, which is between the Goodwood house and what might be called the heart of town. It stands close up to the street without much yard like all the houses built since the street got to be a real street and not just a sort of road with a few houses scattered along it. Some men were putting in a concrete culvert just in front of the house, and since it was the middle of the day, they were sitting on the edge of the concrete walk eating their lunch and smoking. When Luke came along, he stopped to see what they were doing and got down in the ditch to inspect it. Although it was getting along in the season, there were still enough leaves on the vine on my sister's porch to hide me from the street, but I could hear every word they said. One of the workmen asked Luke when the next game would be. He said Sunday with Millville. When they asked him if he was going to win, he said he didn't know because Millville had a tough club to beat all right. I noticed on that trip home that the boys talked about their ball club, and not their ball team. It must have been Luke's influence. Then one of the men sitting on the curb said in a tone of voice that sounded righteous and false somehow in its encouragement, "We know you can beat 'em, boy!" For a minute Luke didn't say anything; then he said, "Thanks," pretty short, and turned off down the street, moving in that easy yet fast walk of his that always seemed not to be taking any effort.

It was a couple of days later when I was sitting in my sister's yard trying to cool off, that he came by and saw me there and just turned in at the gate. We said hello, just like we had been seeing each other every day for years, and he sat down in the other chair without waiting to be asked, just like an old friend, which he was. It wasn't long before he got out of the chair, though, and lay on the grass, just like he always used to do, lying relaxed all over just like an animal. I was a little bit embarrassed at first, I reckon, and maybe he was, too, for we hadn't sort of sat down together like that for near fifteen years, and he had been away and been a big league pitcher, at the top of his profession almost, and here he was back. He must have been thinking along the same lines, for after he had been there on the grass a while he gave a sort of laugh and said, "Well, we sure did have some pretty good times when we were kids going round this country with our guns, didn't we?" I said we sure did. I don't know whether Luke really liked to remember the times we had or whether he was just being polite and trying to get in touch with me again, so to speak.

Then he got to talking about the places he had been and the things he had seen. He said a man took him to a place in some city, Pittsburgh I believe it was, and showed him the biggest amount of radium there is in the world in one place. His mother having died of cancer not much more than a year before that day we were talking must have made him remember that. He told me how he shot alligators in Florida and went deep-sea fishing. That was the only good time he had away from home, he said, except the first year when the Athletics farmed him out to a smaller team. I was getting embarrassed when he started to talk about baseball, like you will when somebody who has just had a death in the family starts talking natural, like nothing had happened, about the departed one. He said his first year in Pennsylvania he got six hundred dollars a month from the club he was pitching for, plus a little extra. "Being raised in a town like this," he said, "a fellow don't know what to do with real money." So he wrote home for them to crate up his bird dogs and express them to him; which they did. He leased a farm to put his dogs on and hired somebody to take care of them for him, because he couldn't be out there all the time, having his job to attend to. Then he bought some more dogs, for he always was crazy about dogs, and bought some Chinese ring-neck pheasants to put on his farm. He said that was a good time, but it didn't last.

He told me about some other pitchers too. There was one who used to room with him when the club went on the road. Every time they got to a new city, that pitcher made the rounds of all the stores, then the boxes would begin coming to the hotel room, full of electric trains and mechanical automobiles and boats, and that grown man would sit down and play with them and after the game would hurry back so he could play some more. Luke said his friend liked trains pretty well, but boats best, and used to keep him awake half the night splashing in the bathtub. There was another pitcher up in Indiana who went to a roadhouse with Luke, where they got drunk. They got thrown out of the place because that other pitcher, who was a Polak, kept trying to dance with other people's women. The Polak landed on a rock pile and put his hand down and found all the rocks were just the size of baseballs, and him a pitcher. He started breaking windows, and stood everybody off till the cops came. But Luke was gone by that time; so the police called up the hotel to tell Luke there was a guy needed two thousand dollars to get out of jail. So he and three other players went down and put up five hundred apiece to get the fellow out, who was sobered up by that time and wanted to go to bed and get some rest. Luke didn't know that fellow very well and when the Polak went off with the team to play some little game and Luke didn't go, he figured his five hundred was gone too. The fellow didn't come back with the team, either, for he had slipped off, so he figured he had really kissed his five hundred good-bye. But the night before the trial, about three o'clock in the morning, there was a hammering on the hotel room door and before Luke could open it, somebody stuck a fist through the panel and opened it. And there was the Polak, wearing a four-bit tuxedo and patent-leather shoes and a derby hat, and his tie under one ear, drunk. He fell flat on the floor, clutching twenty-three hundred dollars' worth of bills in his hands. That Polak had gone back to the mines, having been a miner before he got in baseball, and had gambled for three days, and there he was to pay back the money as soon as he could. Luke said he wouldn't take money from a man who was drunk because the man might not remember and might want to pay him again when he got sober; so he got his the next morning. The fine and expense of fixing up the roadhouse wasn't as much as you'd expect, and the Polak had a good profit, unless a woman who got hit in the head with a rock and sued him got the rest. Luke didn't know how much she got. He said all pitchers are crazy as hell one way or another.

He told me about things that he saw or got mixed up with, but he said he never had a good time after he had to give up the farm where he had the dogs and the Chinese ring-neck pheasants. He said after that it wasn't so good any more, except for a little time in Florida, shooting alligators and fishing. He had been raised in the country, you see, and had the habit of getting up mighty early, with all that time on his hands till the game started or practice. For a while he used to go to the gymnasium in the mornings and take a work-out, but the manager caught on and stopped that because he wouldn't be fresh for the game. There wasn't anything to do in the mornings after that, he said, except pound the pavements by himself, everybody else still being asleep, or ride the lobbies, and he didn't have a taste for reading, not ever having cultivated his mind like he should. Most of the boys could sleep late, but he couldn't, being used to getting up before sun to go fishing or hunting or something. He said he could have stood the night drinking all right, it was the morning drinking got him down. Lying there on the grass, all relaxed, it didn't look like he gave a damn either.

He had his plans all worked out. If he could get hold of a few hundred dollars he was going to buy him a little patch of ground back in the country where it was cheap, and just farm a little and hunt and fish. I thought of old Mr. Bullard, an old bachelor who lived off in a cabin on the river and didn't even bother to do any farming any more, they said, or much fishing, either. I used to see him come in town on a Saturday afternoon, walking nine miles in just to sit around in the stores looking at people, but not talking to them, or, if the weather was good, just standing on the street. But Luke probably liked to hunt and fish better than Mr. Bullard ever did in his life, and that was something for a man to hold on to. I told Luke I hoped he got his farm, and that now was the time to buy while the depression was on and land was cheap as dirt. He laughed at that, thinking I was trying to make a joke, which I wasn't, and said, "Hell, a farm ain't nothing but dirt, anyway."

After lying there some more, having about talked himself out, he got up and remarked how he had to be shoving on. We shook hands in a formal way, this time, not like when he came in the yard. I wished him luck, and he said, "The same to you," and when he got outside the gate, he said, "So long, buddy."

About six months later he got married, much to my surprise. My sister wrote me about it and sent a clipping about it. His bride was a girl named Martha Sheppard, who is related to my family in a distant way, though Lord knows my sister wouldn't claim any kin with them. And I reckon they aren't much to brag on. The girl had a half-interest in a piece of land out in the country, in the real hoot-owl sticks, you might say, where she lived with her brother, who had the other half-share. I guessed at the time when I read the letter that Luke just married that girl because it was the only way he could see to get the little piece of ground he spoke of. I never saw the girl to my recollection, and don't know whether she was pretty or not.

I have noticed that people living way back in the country like that are apt to be different from ordinary people who see more varieties and kinds of people every day. That maybe accounts for the stories you read in papers about some farmer way back off the road getting up some morning and murdering his whole family before breakfast.

They see the same faces every day till some little something gets to preying on their mind and they can't stand it. And it accounts for the way farmers get to brooding over some little falling-out with a neighbor and start bushwhacking each other with shotguns. After about a year Martha Sheppard's brother shot Luke. My sister wrote me the bad blood developed between them because Luke and his wife didn't get along so well together. I reckon she got to riding him about the way he spent his time, off hunting and all. Whatever it was, her brother shot Luke with Luke's own shotgun, in the kitchen one morning. He shot him three times. The gun was a .12-gauge pump gun, and you know what even one charge of a .12-gauge will do at close range like a kitchen.

QUESTIONS

1 Warren takes considerable care in describing the Goodwood place and Luke's father. How do his descriptions foreshadow Luke's character and the eventual outcome?
2 What is the importance of the narrator's position? In other words, is he merely the storyteller?
3 Why does the narrator tell us about Joe Lancaster? Recall that he mentions Joe later in the story.
4 How do we know that baseball isn't really Luke's place?

TOPICS FOR COMPOSITION

1 The notion of "winning" is important in both Lawrence and Warren's stories. Analyze the emphasis on winning in each story.
2 Organized sports to a large extent dominate the American scene today. What does Warren's story seem to say about the individual and team spirit? Argue the question in light of today's emphasis on sports and its candor about its athletes' personal lives.

POETRY

One of the fallen angels in Milton's *Paradise Lost* is Mammon, whose name means "wealth." He was, the poet says, the least elevated spirit that fell from heaven,

> for even in Heaven his looks and thoughts
> Were always downward bent, admiring more
> The riches of Heaven's pavement, trodden gold,
> Than aught divine or holy else enjoyed
> In vision beatific
>
> *(Book I, 680–684)*

Here in a single image, Milton defines in poetic fashion the essential evil of materialism—lack of vision. Acceptance of ready-made, highly tangible, easily measurable symbols of status means giving up imagination and initiative, allowing personal development to be sharply restricted, and suffering as a consequence a loss of inner motivation. By envisioning Mammon as originally an inhabitant of heaven, Milton reminds us that freedom from the restrictions of materialism depends finally not upon circumstances but upon individual attitude. There is not necessarily anything wrong with a golden pavement. It might be a pleasant convenience and even an appropriate, if not very vital, symbol of spiritual progress. What is wrong is that Mammon, who represents, of course, a basic tendency in human nature, came to admire the road so much that he no longer looked to see where he was going, which was unfortunate indeed, because he ended up in hell. In the following selection from Spenser's *The Faerie Queene,* we are introduced to the daughter of Mammon, Philotime (meaning "love of wealth and honor"), who also dwells in hell, or what is the same, in the realm of Pluto, god of the underworld and wealth. She too has been thrust from heaven, but continues to deceive her worshipers, who still think her golden chain is the only way to get to heaven.

With a comparable witty incisiveness and imaginative power, the other poems of this section define further the effect and some of the outward aspects of materialism. *Epistle IV* of Alexander Pope's *Moral Essays* focuses on a relatively harmless aspect of the materialistic spirit, the abominable taste that so often goes with the love of possessions. He makes his point by describing in detail the country home of an eighteenth-century nobleman, indicating by repeated use of antithesis how perversely culture, sensible economy, and even personal comfort are sacrificed to ostentation. Samuel Johnson probes more deeply into the perversity of materialism, stressing the dangers and the fears to which the lust for money and power exposes its victims: disregard for law and dread of punishment, the multiplication of cares that goes with each advance in status, and the sorry exchange of human dignity and self-possession for advantage in a pointless, never-ending race.

Pope and Johnson show that materialism is opposed to plain good sense. Wordsworth and Gerard Manley Hopkins stress its blighting effect on the imagination. More specifically, they deplore the fact that preoccupation with "getting and spending" has prevented man from seeing in the dynamic splendor of nature the inspiring symbol of creativity that it might be. In his use of nature, they feel, man has confused means with end; inordinate exploitation of nature has obscured the ideal of harmony between man and the rest of God's creation.

Robert Browning turns back to the splendor-loving Renaissance to explore, in a dramatic case study, the relation between materialism, aesthetic sensibility, and spirituality. The Bishop of St. Praxed's, clearly, has been unable to to reconcile the love of beautiful things with religious ideals, and his imagination has been so warped by the conflict that it leads him, in the final crisis of his life, to identify with the things of stone that he has more and more coveted. More bluntly, Arthur Hugh Clough attacks the notorious tendency of his fellow Victorians to equate respectability—i.e., financial well-being—with godliness. Howard Nemerov's "Boom!" and Lawrence Ferlinghetti's "Christ Climbed Down" provide interesting parallels.

"Drug Store," "pity this busy monster, manunkind," and "The New Being," finally, picture very vividly the main symptoms of materialism in our time: the glorification of the scientific reduction of reality to quantitative terms; the sad dependence of youth upon "drugs," that is, crude, mass-produced, artificial stimuli; and the desperate, personality-destroying pursuit of silly status symbols. The term "symptoms" is appropriate here, it will be noted, because all three poems use the metaphor of illness. Poets have always regarded materialism as a disease—of the eyes and of the heart.

THE FAERIE QUEENE, BOOK II, CANTO VII

Edmund Spenser

XLIV

A route of people there assembled were,
Of every sort and nation under skye,
Which with great uprore preaced to draw nere
To th' upper part, where was advaunced hye
A stately siege of soveraine majestye;   5
And thereon satt a woman gorgeous gay,
And richly cladd in robes of royaltye,
That never earthly prince in such aray
His glory did enhaunce and pompous pryde display.

XLV

Her face right wondrous faire did seeme to bee,   10
That her broad beauties beam great brightnes threw
Through the dim shade, that all men might it see:
Yet was not that same her owne native hew,
But wrought by art and counterfetted shew,
Thereby more lovers unto her to call;   15
Nath'lesse most hevenly faire in deed and vew

1: Sir Guyon, who represents the virtue of temperance, is being conducted by Mammon through the latter's realm. *3 preaced:* pressed. *5 siege:* seat, throne. *14 shew:* show. *16 Nath'lesse:* nevertheless.

She by creation was, till she did fall;
Thenceforth she sought for helps to cloke her crime withall.

XLVI

There as in glistring glory she did sitt,
She held a great old chaine ylincked well, 20
Whose upper end to highest heven was knitt,
And lower part did reach to lowest hell;
And all that preace did rownd about her swell,
To catchen hold of that long chaine, thereby
To climbe aloft, and others to excell: 25
That was Ambition, rash desire to sty,
And every linck thereof a step of dignity.

XLVII

Some thought to raise themselves to high degree
By riches and unrighteous reward;
Some by close shouldring, some by flatteree; 30
Others through friendes, others for base regard;
And all by wrong waies for themselves prepard.
Those that were up themselves, kept others low,
Those that were low themselves, held others hard,
Ne suffred them to ryse or greater grow, 35
But every one did strive his fellow downe to throw.

XLVIII

Which whenas Guyon saw, he gan inquire,
What meant that preace about that ladies throne,
And what she was that did so high aspyre.
Him Mammon answered: 'That goodly one, 40
Whom all that folke with such contention
Doe flock about, my deare, my daughter is:
Honour and dignitie from her alone
Derived are, and all this worldes blis,
For which ye men doe strive: few gett, but many mis. 45

XLIX

'And fayre Philotime she rightly hight,
The fairest wight that wonneth under skye,
But that this darksom neather world her light
Doth dim with horror and deformity,

23 preace: throng. *26 sty:* ascend, climb. *46 hight:* is named. *47 wonneth:* dwells. *48 neather:* nether, lower.

Worthie of heven and hye felicitie,   50
From whence the gods have her for envy thrust;
But sith thou hast found favour in mine eye,
Thy spouse I will her make, if that thou lust,
That she may thee advance for works and merits just.'

L

'Gramercy, Mammon,' said the gentle knight,   55
'For so great grace and offred high estate,
But I, that am fraile flesh and earthly wight,
Unworthy match for such immortall mate
My selfe well wote, and mine unequall fate:
And were I not, yet is my trouth yplight,   60
And love avowd to other lady late,
That to remove the same I have no might:
To chaunge love causelesse is reproch to warlike knight.'

                                              1590

52 sith: since.   *59 wote:* know.   *63 causelesse:* without cause.

QUESTIONS

1   What is the significance of the fact that Philotime has to resort to artifice to enhance her beauty? Remember that she was one of the angels who fell with Satan.
2   What is to be made of the fact that the golden chain of ambition extends from heaven to hell?
3   What would marriage to Philotime mean?

From MORAL ESSAYS

Alexander Pope

Epistle IV

Of the Use of Riches
To Richard Boyle, Earl of Burlington

      At Timon's Villa let us pass a day,
Where all cry out, "What sums are thrown away!"
So proud, so grand; of that stupendous air,
Soft and agreeable come never there.
Greatness, with Timon, dwells in such a draught   5
As brings all Brobdignag before your thought.

1 Timon's Villa: "This description is intended to comprise the principles of a false taste of magnificence, and to exemplify what was said before, that nothing but good sense can attain it." (Pope's note.) *5 draught:* dose. *6 Brobdignag:* The land of the giants in Swift's *Gulliver's Travels.*

To compass this, his building is a town,
His pond an ocean, his parterre a down:
Who but must laugh, the master when he sees,
A puny insect, shivering at a breeze! 10
Lo, what huge heaps of littleness around!
The whole, a laboured quarry above ground;
Two cupids squirt before; a lake behind
Improves the keenness of the northern wind.
His gardens next your admiration call, 15
On every side you look, behold the wall!
No pleasing intricacies intervene,
No artful wildness to perplex the scene;
Grove nods at grove, each alley has a brother,
And half the platform just reflects the other. 20
The suffering eye inverted nature sees,
Trees cut to statues, statues thick as trees;
With here a fountain, never to be played;
And there a summer-house that knows no shade;
Here Amphitrite sails through myrtle bowers; 25
There gladiators fight, or die in flowers;
Unwatered see the drooping sea-horse mourn,
And swallows roost in Nilus' dusty urn.
　　　　My lord advances with majestic mien,
Smit with the mighty pleasure, to be seen: 30
But soft,—by regular approach,—not yet,—
First through the length of yon hot terrace sweat;
And when up ten steep slopes you've dragged your thighs,
Just at his study door he'll bless your eyes.
　　　　His study! with what authors is it stored? 35
In books, not authors, curious is my lord;
To all their dated backs he turns you round:
These Aldus printed, those Du Sueil has bound.
Lo, some are vellum, and the rest as good
For all his lordship knows, but they are wood. 40
For Locke or Milton 'tis in vain to look,
These shelves admit not any modern book.
　　　　And now the chapel's silver bell you hear,
That summons you to all the pride of prayer;
Light quirks of music, broken and uneven, 45
Make the soul dance upon a jig to Heaven.
On painted ceilings you devoutly stare,
Where sprawl the saints of Verrio or Laguerre,
On gilded clouds in fair expansion lie,

---

25 Amphitrite: The wife of Poseidon, god of the sea. *48 Verrio:* "Verrio (Antonio) painted many ceilings, etc., at Windsor, Hampton Court, etc., and Laguerre at Blenheim Castle and other places." (Pope's note.)

And bring all paradise before your eye.   50
To rest, the cushion and soft dean invite,
Who never mentions hell to ears polite.
          But hark! the chiming clocks to dinner call;
A hundred footsteps scrape the marble hall;
The rich buffet well coloured serpents grace,   55
And gaping Tritons spew to wash your face.
Is this a dinner? this a genial room?
No, 'tis a temple, and a hecatomb.
A solemn sacrifice, performed in state,
You drink by measure, and to minutes eat.   60
So quick retires each flying course, you'd swear
Sancho's dread doctor and his wand were there.
Between each act the trembling salvers ring,
From soup to sweet-wine, and God bless the King.
In plenty starving, tantalized in state,   65
And complaisantly helped to all I hate,
Treated, caressed, and tired, I take my leave,
Sick of his civil pride from morn to eve;
I curse such lavish cost, and little skill,
And swear no day was ever passed so ill.   70

1731

56 Tritons: Triton, the son of Poseidon, was shaped like a man from the waist upward, but had the
tail of a dolphin.   *62 Sancho's dread doctor:* "See Don Quixote, [Part II] chap. xlvii." (Pope's
note)

QUESTIONS

1   What does Pope mean by "huge heaps of littleness" (line 11)? Do you know what
    the word oxymoron means?
2   What is the principal basis of the poet's criticism of Timon's villa?

From THE VANITY OF HUMAN WISHES

In Imitation of the Tenth Satire of Juvenal[1]

Samuel Johnson

          But scarce observed, the knowing and the bold
Fall in the general massacre of gold;
Wide-wasting pest! that rages unconfined,
And crowds with crimes the records of mankind:

[1] Juvenal was a famous Roman satirist.

For gold his sword the hireling ruffian draws;   5
For gold the hireling judge distorts the laws;
Wealth heaped on wealth, nor truth nor safety buys,
The dangers gather as the treasures rise.
  Let history tell, where rival kings command,
And dubious title shakes the madded land,   10
When statutes glean the refuse of the sword,
How much more safe the vassal than the lord;
Low skulks the hind beneath the rage of power,
And leaves the wealthy traitor in the Tower;
Untouched his cottage, and his slumbers sound,   15
Though confiscation's vultures hover round.
  The needy traveller, serene and gay,
Walks the wild heath, and sings his toil away.
Does envy seize thee? crush the upbraiding joy,
Increase his riches, and his peace destroy;   20
New fears in dire vicissitude invade,
The rustling brake alarms, and quivering shade;
Nor light nor darkness bring his pain relief,
One shows the plunder, and one hides the thief.
  Yet still one general cry the skies assails,   25
And gain and grandeur load the tinted gales;
Few know the toiling statesman's fear or care,
The insidious rival and the gaping heir.
  Once more, Democritus, arise on earth,
With cheerful wisdom and instructive mirth,   30
See motley life in modern trappings dressed,
And feed with varied fools the eternal jest:
Thou who couldst laugh where want enchained caprice,
Toil crushed conceit, and man was of a piece;
Where wealth unloved without a mourner died,   35
And scarce a sycophant was fed by pride;
Where ne'er was known the form of mock debate,
Or seen a new-made mayor's unwieldly state;
Where change of favorites made no change of laws,
And senates heard before they judged a cause;   40
How wouldst thou shake at Britain's modish tribe,
Dart the quick taunt, and edge the piercing gibe,
Attentive truth and nature to descry,
And pierce each scene with philosophic eye!
To thee were solemn toys or empty show   45

---

13 hind: humble rustic.   *14 Tower:* the Tower of London, where political prisoners were held.
29 Democritus: called the "Laughing philosopher."   *33 want:* poverty.   *38 new-made mayor's unwieldy state:* pomp.

The robes of pleasure and the veils of woe;
All aid the farce, and all thy mirth maintain,
Whose joys are causeless, or whose griefs are vain.

1748

THE WORLD IS TOO MUCH WITH US

William Wordsworth

The world is too much with us; late and soon,
Getting and spending, we lay waste our powers:
Little we see in Nature that is ours;
We have given our hearts away, a sordid boon!
The sea that bares her bosom to the moon;   5
The winds that will be howling at all hours,
And are up-gathered now like sleeping flowers;
For this, for everything, we are out of tune;
It moves us not.—Great God! I'd rather be
A pagan suckled in a creed outworn.   10
So might I, standing on this pleasant lea,
Have glimpses that would make me less forlorn;
Have sight of Proteus rising from the sea;
Or hear old Triton blow his wreathed horn.

1807

4 boon: gift.   *13 Proteus:* a sea god who could assume any shape he wished.   *14 Triton:* another sea god, usually imagined to have a conch-shell trumpet.

QUESTIONS

1   What does the poet mean by saying that nature is ours?
2   Is the poet really interested in creeds, that is, systems of beliefs?

THE BISHOP ORDERS HIS TOMB AT SAINT PRAXED'S CHURCH

[Rome, 15—]

Robert Browning

Vanity, saith the preacher, vanity!
Draw round my bed: is Anselm keeping back?
Nephews—sons mine . . . ah God, I know not! Well—
She, men would have to be your mother once,
Old Gandolf envied me, so fair she was!   5
What's done is done, and she is dead beside,
Dead long ago, and I am Bishop since,
And as she died so must we die ourselves,
And thence ye may perceive the world's a dream.
Life, how and what is it? As here I lie   10
In this state-chamber, dying by degrees,
Hours and long hours in the dead night, I ask
"Do I live, am I dead?" Peace, peace seems all.
Saint Praxed's ever was the church for peace;
And so, about this tomb of mine. I fought   15
With tooth and nail to save my niche, ye know:
—Old Gandolf cozened me, despite my care;
Shrewd was that snatch from out the corner South
He graced his carrion with, God curse the same!
Yet still my niche is not so cramped but thence   20
One sees the pulpit o' the epistle-side,
And somewhat of the choir, those silent seats,
And up into the aery dome where live
The angels, and a sunbeam's sure to lurk:
And I shall fill my slab of basalt there,   25
And 'neath my tabernacle take my rest,
With those nine columns round me, two and two,
The odd one at my feet where Anselm stands:
Peach-blossom marble all, the rare, the ripe
As fresh-poured red wine of a mighty pulse.   30
—Old Gandolf with his paltry onion-stone,
Put me where I may look at him! True peach,
Rosy and flawless: how I earned the prize!

Saint Praxed's Church: an old church in Rome named after a first-century virgin saint who used her riches to aid the poor and the persecuted Christians. *1 Vanity, saith the preacher:* see Ecclesiastes 1:2. *5 Old Gandolf:* the Bishop's predecessor on the office. *15 tomb:* the Bishop, like Gandolf, will be buried in his church and a stone effigy will be placed above his grave. *21 the epistle-side:* the right-hand side as one faces the altar. *26 tabernacle:* a canopy. *31 onion-stone:* inferior marble.

Draw close: that conflagration of my church
—What then? So much was saved if aught were missed!   35
My sons, ye would not be my death? Go dig
The white-grape vineyard where the oil-press stood,
Drop water gently till the surface sinks,
And if ye find . . . Ah, God I know not, I! . . .
Bedded in store of rotten fig-leaves soft,   40
And corded up in a tight olive-frail,
Some lump, ah God, of *lapis lazuli,*
Big as a Jew's head cut off at the nape,
Blue as a vein o'er the Madonna's breast . . .
Sons, all have I bequeathed you, villas, all,   45
That brave Frascati villa with its bath,
So, let the blue lump poise between my knees,
Like God the Father's globe on both his hands
Ye worship in the Jesu Church so gay,
For Gandolf shall not choose but see and burst!   50
Swift as a weaver's shuttle fleet our years:
Man goeth to the grave, and where is he?
Did I say basalt for my slab, sons? Black—
'Twas ever antique-black I meant! How else
Shall ye contrast my frieze to come beneath?   55
The bas-relief in bronze ye promised me,
Those Pans and Nymphs ye wot of, and perchance
Some tripod, thyrsus, with a vase or so,
The Saviour at his sermon on the mount,
Saint Praxed in a glory, and one Pan   60
Ready to twitch the Nymph's last garment off,
And Moses with the tables . . . but I know
Ye mark me not! What do they whisper thee,
Child of my bowels, Anselm? Ah, ye hope
To revel down my villas while I gasp   65
Bricked o'er with beggar's mouldy travertine
Which Gandolf from his tomb-top chuckles at!
Nay, boys, ye love me—all of jasper, then!
'Tis jasper ye stand pledged to, lest I grieve
My bath must needs be left behind, alas!   70
One block, pure green as a pistachio-nut,
There's plenty jasper somewhere in the world—
And have I not Saint Praxed's ear to pray
Horses for ye, and brown Greek manuscripts,
And mistresses with great smooth marbly limbs?   75

41 olive-frail: a basket for holding olives. *46 Frascati:* a luxurious resort. *51 Swift as a weaver's shuttle:* see Job 7:6. *57 Pans:* Pan was the Greek god of shepherds. *58 tripod:* three-legged stool used by the priestess Apollo at Delphi. *thyrsus:* staff used by devotees of Bacchus, god of wine. *66 travertine:* a kind of limestone.

—That's if ye carve my epitaph aright,
Choice Latin, picked phrase, Tully's every word,
No gaudy ware like Gandolf's second line—
Tully, my masters? Ulpian serves his need!
And then how I shall lie through centuries, 80
And hear the blessed mutter of the mass,
And see God made and eaten all day long,
And feel the steady candle-flame, and taste
Good strong thick stupefying incense-smoke!
For as I lie here, hours of the dead night, 85
Dying in state and by such slow degrees,
I fold my arms as if they clasp a crook,
And stretch my feet forth straight as stone can point,
And let the bedclothes, for a mortcloth, drop
Into great laps and folds of sculptor's-work: 90
And as yon tapers dwindle, and strange thoughts
Grow, with a certain humming in my ears,
About the life before I lived this life,
And this life too, popes, cardinals and priests,
Saint Praxed at his sermon on the mount, 95
Your tall pale mother with her talking eyes,
And new-found agate urns as fresh as day,
And marble's language, Latin pure, discreet,
—Aha, <u>elucescebat</u> quoth our friend?
No Tully, said I, Ulpian at the best! 100
Ever your eyes were as a lizard's quick,
All *lapis*, all, sons! Else I give the Pope
My villas! Will ye ever eat my heart?
Ever your eyes were as a lizard's quick,
They glitter like your mother's for my soul, 105
Or ye would heighten my impoverished frieze,
Piece out its starved design, and fill my vase
With grapes, and add a vizor and a term,
And to the tripod ye would tie a lynx
That in his struggle throws the thyrsus down, 110
To comfort me on my entablature
Whereon I am to lie till I must ask
"Do I live, am I dead?" There, leave me, there!
For ye have stabbed me with ingratitude
To death—ye wish it—God, ye wish it! Stone— 115
Gritstone, a-crumble! Clammy squares which sweat

77 Tully: Cicero, whose writings were considered the model of classical Latin. *79 Ulpian:* a Roman jurist whose style was inferior to that of Cicero. *82 see God made and eaten:* the Bishop is speaking of the sacrament of the Mass. *89 mortcloth:* funeral pall. *99 elucescebat:* the classic synonym for this word, which means "he is famous," is *elucebat*. *108 vizor:* musk. *term:* a bust on a pedestal. *116 gritstone:* coarse sandstone.

As if the corpse they keep were oozing through—
And no more *lapis* to delight the world!
Well, go! I bless ye. Fewer tapers there,
But in a row: and, going, turn your backs   120
—Ay, like departing altar-ministrants,
And leave me in my church, the church for peace,
That I may watch at leisure if he leers—
Old Gandolf, at me, from his onion-stone,
As still he envied me, so fair she was!   125

                                              1845

QUESTIONS

1   The Bishop is never able to fully envision his tomb; what he is able to imagine is only
    a grotesque mixture of pagan and Christian symbols. Explain the irony of these
    facts. What does the tomb probably symbolize to the Bishop?
2   That the Bishop is vain, materialistic, and unscrupulous is obvious. Does the poet
    make it possible for us to sympathize with him in any way?
3   Line 95 indicates that the Bishop has momentarily lapsed into incoherence because
    of his illness. Could this fact have symbolic implications?

THE LATEST DECALOGUE

Arthur Hugh Clough

Thou shalt have one God only; who
Would be at the expense of two?
No graven images may be
Worshiped, except the currency.
Swear not at all; for, for thy curse   5
Thine enemy is none the worse.
At church on Sunday to attend
Will serve to keep the world thy friend.
Honor thy parents; that is, all
From whom advancement may befall.   10
Thou shalt not kill; but need'st not strive
Officiously to keep alive.
Do not adultery commit;
Advantage rarely comes of it.
Thou shalt not steal; an empty feat,   15
When it's so lucrative to cheat.
Bear not false witness; let the lie
Have time on its own wings to fly.
Thou shalt not covet, but tradition
Approves all forms of competition.   20

                                              1862

GOD'S GRANDEUR

Gerard Manley Hopkins

The world is charged with the grandeur of God.
    It will flame out, like shining from shook foil;
    It gathers to a greatness, like the ooze of oil
Crushed. Why do men then now not reck his rod?
Generations have trod, have trod, have trod;   5
    And all is seared with trade; bleared, smeared with toil;
    And wears man's smudge and shares man's smell: the toil
Is bare now, nor can foot feel, being shod.
And for all this, nature is never spent;
    There lives the dearest freshness deep down things;   10
And though the last lights off the black West went
    Oh, morning, at the brown brink eastward, springs—
Because the Holy Ghost over the bent
    World broods with warm breast and with ah! bright wings.
                    1918 (Composed 1877)

1 charged: as with electricity. *2 foil:* gold leaf. *4 Crushed:* like oil oozing from crushed olives, which gathers slowly into a mass before it breaks and flows. *reck his rod:* heed his authority. *14 broods:* i.e., like a dove on its nest. The dove traditionally has been the symbol of the Holy Ghost.

QUESTIONS

1 In what ways is the statement of the first line supported in the remainder of the poem? Can you put in your own words the central impression that Hopkins is trying to convey?
2 Lines 5–8 convey the general idea of contact with nature. What makes the description ironic?
3 Does this poem express the same idea as Wordsworth's "The World Is Too Much with Us"?
4 What do the last two lines mean? In what way do the last two words reflect the meaning of the whole poem?

SHINE, PERISHING REPUBLIC

Robinson Jeffers

While this America settles in the mold of its vulgarity, heavily thickening to empire,
And protest, only a bubble in the molten mass, pops and sighs out, and the
    mass hardens,

I sadly smiling remember that the flower fades to make fruit, the fruit rots
    to make earth.
Out of the mother; and through the spring exultances, ripeness and
    decadence; and home to the mother.

You making haste haste on decay: not blameworthy; life is good, be it　　　5
　　　stubbornly long or suddenly
A mortal splendor: meteors are not needed less than mountains: shine,
　　　perishing republic.

But for my children, I would have them keep their distance from the thickening
　　　center; corruption
Never has been compulsory, when the cities lie at the monster's feet there are
　　　left the mountains.

And boys, be in nothing so moderate as in love of man, a clever servant,
　　　insufferable master.
There is the trap that catches noblest spirits, that caught—they say—God,　　　10
　　　when he walked on earth.

　　　　　　　　　　　　　　　　　　　　　　　　　　　　　1924

QUESTIONS

1　Is the analogy used in lines 3–5 valid, in your opinion? Might it be useful even if not
　　regarded as necessarily valid?
2　Does Jeffers regard materialism as being the cause or the effect of moral illness?

DRUG STORE

Karl Shapiro

> I do remember an apothecary,
> And hereabouts 'a dwells

It baffles the foreigner like an idiom,
And he is right to adopt it as a form
Less serious than the living-room or bar;
　　For it disestablishes the café,
Is a collective, and on basic country.　　　　　　　　　　　　　　5

Not that it praises hygiene and corrupts
The ice-cream parlor and the tobacconist's
Is it a center; but that the attractive symbols
　　Watch over puberty and leer
Like rubber bottles waiting for sick-use.　　　　　　　　　　　　10

Youth comes to jingle nickels and crack wise;
The baseball scores are his, the magazines

Epigraph: From *Romeo and Juliet*, V, i, 37–38., Romeo is seeking the apothecary in order to buy
poison.

Devoted to lust, the jazz, the Coca-Cola,
   The lending-library of love's latest.
He is the customer; he is heroized.   15

And every nook and cranny of the flesh
Is spoken to by packages with wiles,
"Buy me, buy me," they whimper and cajole;
   The hectic range of lipstick pouts,
Revealing the wicked and the simple mouth.   20

With scarcely any evasion in their eye
They smoke, undress their girls, exact a stance;
But only for a moment. The clock goes round;
   Crude fellowships are made and lost;
They slump in booths like rags, not even drunk.   25
                                  1941

22 undress their girls: with their eyes, that is.

QUESTIONS

1 The drug store as a social center might be thought an improvement over the ice-cream parlor and the tobacconist's. Why? What is the real reason for its having become a center?
2 What use does the poet make of the fact that the "attractive symbols" appear like things intended for sick-use?
3 How is youth, the customer, "heroized"?
4 What is the state of mind of the young people that frequent the drug store?
5 Why does the poet approach his subject in such a detached, disinterested way? What evidence of a deeper, more emotional concern is there? Would the poem have been more effective if he had used strong terms of indignation or pity?

THE NEW BEING

Kenneth Patchen

They'd make you believe that your problem is one of sex,
That men and women have mysteriously become
Strange and fearful to one another—sick, diseased, cold—
And that is true. But no loss of a father-image or of
Any other image, did this. Why don't you face the truth for once?   5
You have accepted the whole filthy, murderous swindle without
A word of protest, hated whomever you were told to hate,
Slaughtered whomever you were told to slaughter; you've lied,

Cheated, made the earth stink with your very presence—Why
Shouldn't you despise and hate one another? Why shouldn't   10
Your flesh crawl everytime you touch one another?
Why should you expect to make 'love' in a bed fouled with corpses?

Oh, you poor, weak little frauds, sucking around
Frantically for something to ease your guilt—
Why don't you face it?   15
Your birthright, liferight,
Deathright, and now your
Sexright, you've lost. What
Did you expect? How
Else could it be? You've   20
Made property and money your only gods—
Well, this is their rule,
This is what you wanted.
And now they'll wipe you out.
Why don't you face it?   25
Stop sucking around.
Your pet witch-doctors can't help you,
They're all sick from the same thing.
Your pompous intellectuals can't help you,
They're all sick from the same thing.   30
Your sly, vicious statesmen can't help you,
They're all sick from the same thing.
Why don't you face it?

No, your problem is not one of sex—
Your problem is that you have betrayed your animal   35
Into hands as cruel and bloody as your own.
Man is dead.
I don't know what kind of thing you are.

                                                                    1942

QUESTIONS

1   Whom is the poet addressing? What relationship with the reader does he want to
    establish?
2   The problem, the poet says, is that "you have betrayed your animal"; but then he
    adds "Man is dead." Is he equating humanness with animality?

PITY THIS BUSY MONSTER,MANUNKIND

E. E. Cummings

pity this busy monster,manunkind,

not. Progress is a comfortable disease:
your victim (death and life safely beyond)

plays with the bigness of his littleness
—electrons deify one razorblade   5
into a mountainrange; lenses extend

unwish through curving wherewhen till unwish
returns on its unself.

                              A world of made
is not a world of born—pity poor flesh   10

and trees, poor stars and stones, but never this
fine specimen of hypermagical

ultraomnipotence. We doctors know

a hopeless case if—listen: there's a hell
of a good universe next door; let's go   15
                              1944

QUESTIONS

1   What kind of materialism is satirized in this poem? Does it have to do with personal
    ambition? Is a kind of ideal involved?
2   What are the scientific achievements described in lines 4–8? What is the author's
    attitude toward them? What do the coined terms "unwish" and "unself" mean?
    What general approach to truth or value can be associated with wishing? Does
    science have anything to do with the wishful self?
3   In what sense is mankind becoming a "monster"? Look up the word in the dictio-
    nary if you are familiar with only one sense.
4   Why is this "a hopeless case"?
5   How does one get to the "universe next door"?

BOOM!

Howard Nemerov

SEES BOOM IN RELIGION, TOO
Atlantic City, June 23, 1957 (AP).—President Eisenhower's pastor said tonight that Americans are living in a period of "unprecedented religious activity" caused partially by paid vacations, the eight-hour day and modern conveniences.

"These fruits of material progress," said the Rev. Edward L. R. Elson of the National Presbyterian Church, Washington, "have provided the leisure, the energy, and the means for a level of human and spiritual values never before reached."

Here at the Vespasian-Carlton, it's just one
religious activity after another; the sky
is constantly being crossed by cruciform
airplanes, in which nobody disbelieves
for a second, and the tide, the tide   5
of spiritual progress and prosperity
miraculously keeps rising, to a level
never before attained. The churches are full,
the beaches are full, and the filling-stations
are full, God's great ocean is full   10
of paid vacationers praying an eight-hour day
to the human and spiritual values, the fruits,
the leisure, the energy, and the means, Lord,
the means for the level, the unprecedented level,
and the modern conveniences, which also are full.   15
Never before, O Lord, have the prayers and praises
from belfry and phonebooth, from ballpark and barbecue
the sacrifices, so endlessly ascended.
It was not thus when Job in Palestine
sat in the dust and cried, cried bitterly;   20
when Damien kissed the lepers on their wounds
it was not thus; it was not thus
when Francis worked a fourteen-hour day
strictly for the birds; when Dante took
a week's vacation without pay and it rained   25
part of the time, O Lord, it was not thus.

But now the gears mesh and the tires burn
and the ice chatters in the shaker and the priest

1: Vespasian was a Roman emperor (A.D. 70–79). The Roman nobles of his time were much given to luxury. He himself practiced the simple life in an effort to set a good example. *21 Damien:* Father Damien (1840–1899) was a Belgian missionary to lepers in Molokai. *23 Francis:* St. Francis of Assisi (1182–1226) was a great lover of nature. His preaching to the birds has been a favorite theme in art.

in the pulpit, and Thy Name, O Lord,
is kept before the public, while the fruits   30
ripen and religion booms and the level rises
and every modern convenience runneth over,
that it may never be with us as it hath been
with Athens and Karnak and Nagasaki,
nor Thy sun for one instant refrain from shining   35
on the rainbow Buick by the breezeway
or the Chris Craft with the uplift life raft;
that we may continue to be the just folks we are,
plain people with ordinary superliners and
disposable diaperliners, people of the stop'n'shop   40
'n'pray as you go, of hotel, motel, boatel,
the humble pilgrims of no deposit no return
and please adjust thy clothing, who will give to Thee,
if Thee will keep us going, our annual
Miss Universe, for Thy Name's Sake, Amen.   45

1960

34 Athens: part of the site of ancient Thebes.

QUESTIONS

1   What kinds of sacrifice is the poet talking about in this poem?
2   Is this poem a parody?

CHRIST CLIMBED DOWN

Lawrence Ferlinghetti

Christ climbed down
from His bare Tree
this year
and ran away to where
there were no rootless Christmas trees   5
hung with candycanes and breakable stars

Christ climbed down
from His bare Tree
this year
and ran away to where   10

2 Tree: the Cross.

there were no gilded Christmas trees
and no tinsel Christmas trees
and no tinfoil Christmas trees
and no pink plastic Christmas trees
and no gold Christmas trees   15
and no black Christmas trees
and no powderblue Christmas trees
hung with electric candles
and enriched by tin electric trains
and clever cornball relatives   20

Christ climbed down
from His bare Tree
this year
and ran away to where
no intrepid Bible salesmen   25
covered the territory
in two-tone cadillacs
and where no Sears Roebuck crèches
complete with plastic babe in manger
arrived by parcel post   30
the babe by special delivery
and where no televised Wise Men
praised the Lord Calvert Whiskey

Christ climbed down
from His bare Tree   35
this year
and ran away to where
no fat handshaking stranger
in a red flannel suit
and a fake white beard   40
went around passing himself off
as some sort of North Pole saint
crossing the desert to Bethlehem
Pennsylvania
in a Volkswagon sled   45
drawn by rollicking Adirondack reindeer
with German names
and bearing sacks of Humble Gifts
from Saks Fifth Avenue
for everybody's imagined Christ child   50

28 crèches: a crèche is a representation of the Nativity scene—in this case, manufactured.

Christ climbed down
from His bare Tree
this year
and ran away to where
no Bing Crosby carollers   55
groaned of a tight Christmas
and where no Radio City angels
iceskated wingless
thru a winter wonderland
into a jinglebell heaven   60
daily at 8:30
with Midnight Mass matinees

Christ climbed down
from His bare Tree
this year.   65
and softly stole away into
some anonymous Mary's womb again
where in the darkest night
of everybody's anonymous soul
He awaits again   70
an unimaginable
and impossibly
Immaculate Reconception
the very craziest
of Second Comings   75

                    1958

QUESTIONS

1 Why does Ferlinghetti repeat the word "anonymous" in line 67–69?
2 Explain the satire in lines 71–75. To whom should an immaculate "Reconception" of Christ seem impossible and unimaginable?

TOPICS FOR COMPOSITION

1 Using Pope's description of Timon's villa as a model, write an essay on ostentation in modern home or automobile design.
2 Write an analytical description of the type of character represented by Democritus, as he is envisaged in Johnson's "The Vanity of Human Wishes."
3 Write an essay supporting the thesis that many people in our time value nature in nonmaterialistic ways.
4 Write a comparative study of "The World Is Too Much With Us" and "God's Grandeur."

5　Have the atmosphere and tone of the most typical gathering places of young people changed since Karl Shapiro wrote "Drug Store"? Give your answer in an essay.

6　Using the title, "The Man Who Turned to Stone," write a character study of the Bishop of St. Praxed's.

7　If you think that Robinson Jeffers looks upon materialism as a symptom, try to describe its cause as he sees it.

8　Write a line-by-line interpretation or paraphrase of E. E. Cummings's "pity this busy monster,manunkind."

9　Write a commentary on the meaning and usefulness of the coined terms in Cummings's poem.

10　Does modern advertising as a whole present a single image or idea of "the good life"? If you think so, write a description of an average day in the life of the typical successful American as conceived by advertisers.

11　Using an invented name, write on the topic, "The Most Materialistic Person I Have Known."

12　Defend the thesis that a man is what he gets.

13　Write on "The True Worth of Material Possessions." Be sure to provide examples or illustrations.

14　Write an essay defining two or three kinds of materialism. The poems of this unit should provide you with some ideas.

15　Write on the topic, "In Defense of 'Materialism.'"

16　Drawing support from any of the poems of this section that seem helpful, defend the thesis that materialism is the sign of failure of imagination.

17　Not everyone would agree that Lawrence Ferlinghetti's analysis of Christmas phoniness is fair in all respects. If you partly disagree with him, explain why.

PART FIVE

THE SEARCH
FOR MODES
OF EXPRESSION

Because language is always with us, because its acquisition is relatively automatic, and because we use it almost without effort and sometimes almost without thought, we are apt to take it too lightly. What is language? Obviously, the answer is not easily formulated; moreover, the simple question generates additional questions: How is language used? What forms may it take? What is its influence on human behavior? A well-known philosopher of our time offers the following observation:

> Language is, without a doubt, the most momentous and at the same time the most mysterious product of the human mind. Between the clearest animal call of love or warning or anger, and a man's least trivial *word,* there lies a whole day of Creation—or in modern phrase, a whole chapter of evolution.—Suzanne Langer, *Philosophy in a New Key,* 83.

Two essays, dealing with the questions posed above, introduce this unit. For, if we are to concern ourselves with a search for modes of expression, we must, indeed, begin with expression itself.

LeRoi Jones in his essay, "Expressive Language," examines language in its varied cultural expression. Specifically, Jones points out that language—word choice, phrasing, dialectal sound modification—derives its true expression only within the culture that embraces it and, in return, the culture that it identifies. His essay emphasizes that modes of expression in "'pluralistic' America" require sensitive appraisal if we are to seek answers to the questions that introduce this unit.

Leslie A. White, "The Symbol: The Origin and Basis of Human Behavior," is a more general extension of Jones's essay. By focusing on the symbol, White incorporates language into the broad concept of human behavior. Note, especially, the importance of the language symbol as it acts on human behavior and perpetuates what we consider civilized culture.

As part of the search for modes of expression, Eudora Welty's short story, "Powerhouse," shows both experimentation with fictional form and with language itself. Perhaps most indicative of the author's purpose are the statements, "Powerhouse is so monstrous he sends everybody into oblivion," and "Powerhouse has as much as possible done by signals." In these two statements, we have indicators of Miss Welty's theme: can the world accept Powerhouse, or more broadly, any artist, and can we understand the signals of his communicative process? Henry James's "The Real Thing" also deals with art and the technique of its expression. We need to understand, however, that the story says more than its painter-narrator's comment that in art "the real thing could be so much less precious than the unreal." Art, though depicted from the point of view of a painter, serves to illustrate point of view in all artistic endeavors. James, therefore, is examining the artist's individual attitude toward his work; specifically, in this story, that process by which the artist constructs his view of "the real thing."

"Modes of expression" might well have been the subtitle of Thornton Wilder's "Pullman Car Hiawatha," a severely stylized revelation of the incredible gaps between what people say and what they mean—between what they somehow cannot articulate clearly under the pressures of life and what they might say eloquently under the aegis of an art form. The relatively brief "one-acter" poses the loneliness, isolation, meaninglessness, even stupidity of lives in movement but without satisfaction; for Chicago, only another station on the railway timetable, will not be a completion or *dénouement* but only another connecting point for another day of frustration if not misery. Yet while the passengers are in transit, their lives touch and are in turn touched by all the lives and even cosmic forces which they cross. And as the Stage Manager coaxes each life to become part of an art form—the play of lives in transit—that life acquires a little dignity and beauty it did not know or suspect amid the bewilderment and stresses of living. Thus Shakespeare's dictum that "All the world's a stage, / And all the men and women merely players" is dramatically realized in Wilder's transformation of Pullman car into stage and life into art. It is an arresting testimony to the power of art that all the thematic possibilities suggested in the other five sections of *Literary Reflections* are present in this eloquent little play.

THE ESSAY

In all likelihood, a title such as "Expressive Language" could cover a number of possible interpretations and directions. LeRoi Jones, however, makes certain that what he means also means the same to us by precisely defining his terms. As you read, give attention to the way a progressive, interlocking defining of terms keys the structure of the essay. For example, his opening sentence, "Speech is the effective form of a culture" leads to a definition of culture, which leads to a definition of context, which leads to a definition of social, and so on.

EXPRESSIVE LANGUAGE

LeRoi Jones

Speech is the effective form of a culture. Any shape or cluster of human history still apparent in the conscious and unconscious habit of groups of people is what I mean by culture. All culture is necessarily profound. The very fact of its longevity, of its being what it is, *culture,* the epic memory of practical tradition, means that it is profound. But the inherent profundity of culture does not necessarily mean that its *uses* (and they are as various as the human condition) will be profound. German culture is profound. Generically. Its uses, however, are specific, as are all uses . . . of ideas, inventions, products of nature. And specificity, as a right and passion of human life, breeds what it breeds as a result of its context.

Context, in this instance, is most dramatically social. And the social, though it must be rooted, as are all evidences of existence, in culture, depends for its impetus for the most part on a multiplicity of influences. Other cultures, for instance. Perhaps, and this is a common occurrence, the reaction or interreaction of one culture on another can produce a social context that will extend or influence any culture in many strange directions.

Social also means *economic,* as any reader of nineteenth-century European philosophy will understand. The economic is part of the social—and in our time much more so than what we have known as the spiritual or metaphysical, because the most valuable canons of power have either been reduced or traduced into stricter economic terms. That is, there has been a shift in the actual meaning of the world since Dante lived. As if Brooks Adams were right. Money does not mean the same thing to me it must mean to a rich man. I cannot, right now, think of one meaning to name. This is not so simple to understand. Even as a simple term of the English language, *money* does not possess the same meanings for the rich man as it does for me, a lower-middle-class American, albeit of laughably "aristocratic" pretensions. What possibly can "money" mean to a poor man? And I am not talking now about those courageous products of our permissive society who walk knowledgeably into "poverty" as they would into a public toilet. I mean, The Poor.

I look in my pocket; I have seventy cents. Possibly I can buy a beer. A quart of ale, specifically. Then I will have twenty cents with which to annoy and seduce my fingers when they wearily search for gainful employment. I have no idea at this moment what

321

that seventy cents will mean to my neighbor around the corner, a poor Puerto Rican man I have seen hopefully watching my plastic garbage can. But I am certain it cannot mean the same thing. Say to David Rockefeller, "I have money," and he will think you mean something entirely different. That is, if you also dress the part. He would not for a moment think, "Seventy cents." But then neither would many New York painters.

Speech, the way one describes the natural proposition of being alive, is much more crucial than even most artists realize. Semantic philosophers are certainly correct in their emphasis on the final dictation of words over their users. But they often neglect to point out that, after all, it is the actual importance, *power,* of the words that remains so finally crucial. Words have users, but as well, users have words. And it is the users that establish the world's realities. Realities being those fantasies that control your immediate span of life. Usually they are not your own fantasies, i.e., they belong to governments, traditions, etc., which, it must be clear by now, can make for conflict with the singular human life all ways. The fantasy of America might hurt you, but it is what should be meant when one talks of "reality." Not only the things you can touch or see, but the things that make such touching or seeing "normal." Then words, like their users, have a hegemony. Socially—which is final, right now. If you are some kind of artist, you naturally might think this is not so. There is the future. But *immortality* is a kind of drug, I think—one that leads to happiness at the thought of death. Myself, I would rather live forever . . . just to make sure.

The social hegemony, one's position in society, enforces more specifically one's terms (even the vulgar have "pull"). Even to the mode of speech. But also it makes these terms an available explanation of any social hierarchy, so that the words themselves become, even informally, laws. And of course they are usually very quickly stitched together to make formal statutes only fools or the faithfully intrepid would dare to question beyond immediate necessity.

The culture of the powerful is very infectious for the sophisticated, and strongly addictive. To be any kind of "success" one must be fluent in this culture. Know the words of the users, the semantic rituals of power. This is a way into wherever it is you are not now, but wish, very desperately, to get into.

Even speech then signals a fluency in this culture. A knowledge at least. "He's an educated man," is the barest acknowledgment of such fluency . . . in any time. "He's hip," my friends might say. They connote a similar entrance.

And it is certainly the meanings of words that are most important, even if they are no longer consciously acknowledged, but merely, by their use, trip a familiar lever of social accord. To recreate instantly the understood hierarchy of social, and by doing that, cultural importance. And cultures are thought by most people in the world to do their business merely by being hierarchies. Certainly this is true in the West, in as simple a manifestation as Xenophobia, the naïve bridegroom of anti-human feeling, or in economic terms, Colonialism. For instance, when the first Africans were brought into the New World, it was thought that it was all right for them to be slaves because "they were heathens." It is a perfectly logical assumption.

And it follows, of course, that slavery would have been an even stranger phenomenon had the Africans spoken English when they first got here. It would have complicated things. Very soon after the first generations of Afro-Americans mastered this language, they invented white people called Abolitionists.

Words' meanings, but also the rhythm and syntax that frame and propel their concatenation, seek their culture as the final reference for what they are describing of the world. An A flat played twice on the same saxophone by two different men does not have to sound the same. If these men have different ideas of what they want this note to do, the note will not sound the same. Culture is the form, the overall structure of organized thought (as well as emotion and spiritual pretension). There are many cultures. Many ways of organizing thought, or having thought organized. That is, the form of thought's passage through the world will take on as many diverse shapes as there are diverse groups of travelers. Environment is one organizer of *groups,* at any level of its meaning. People who live in Newark, New Jersey, are organized, for whatever purpose, as Newarkers. It begins that simply. Another manifestation, at a slightly more complex level, can be the fact that blues singers from the Midwest sing through their noses. There is an explanation past the geographical, but that's the idea in tabloid. And singing through the nose does propose that the definition of singing be altered . . . even if ever so slightly. (At this point where someone's definitions must be changed, we are flitting around at the outskirts of the old city of Aesthetics. A solemn ghost town. Though some of the bones of reason can still be gathered there.)

But we still need definitions, even if there already are many. The dullest men are always satisfied that a dictionary lists everything in the world. They don't care that you may find out something *extra,* which one day might even be in the dictionary, or at least they'd hope so, if you asked them directly.

But for every item in the world, there are a multiplicity of definitions that fit. And every word we use *could* mean something else. And at the same time. The culture fixes the use, and usage. And in "pluralistic" America, one should always listen very closely when he is being talked to. The speaker might mean something completely different from what we think we're hearing. "Where is your pot?"

I heard an old Negro street singer last week, Reverend Pearly Brown, singing, "God don't never change!" This is a precise thing he is singing. He does not mean "God does not ever change!" He means "God don't never change!" The difference, and I said it was crucial, is in the final human reference . . . the form of passage through the world. A man who is rich and famous who sings, "God don't never change," is confirming his hegemony and good fortune . . . or merely calling the bank. A blind hopeless black American is saying something very different. He is telling you about the extraordinary order of the world. But his is not telling you about his "fate." Fate is a luxury available only to those fortunate citizens with alternatives. The view from the top of the hill is not the same as that from the bottom of the hill. Nor are most viewers at either end of the hill, even certain that, in fact, there is any other place from which to look. Looking down usually eliminates the possibility of understanding what it must be like to look up. Or try to imagine yourself as not existing. It is difficult, but poets and politicians try every other day.

Being told to "speak proper," meaning that you become fluent with the jargon of power, is also a part of not "speaking proper." That is, the culture which desperately understands that it does not "speak proper," or is not fluent with the terms of social strength, also understands somewhere that its desire to gain such fluency is done at a terrifying risk. The bourgeois Negro accepts such risk as profit. But does *close-ter* (in the context of "jes a close-ter, walk wi-thee") mean the same thing as *closer?* Close-ter, in the term of its user is, believe me, exact. It means a quality of existence, of actual physical disposition perhaps . . . in its manifestation as a *tone* and *rhythm* by which people live, most often in response to common modes of thought best enforced by some factor of environmental emotion that is exact and specific. Even the picture it summons is different, and certainly the "Thee" that is used to connect the implied "Me" with, is different. The God of the damned cannot know the God of the damner, that is, cannot know he is God. As no Blues person can really believe emotionally in Pascal's God, or Wittgenstein's question, "Can the concept of God exist in a perfectly logical language?" Answer: "God don't never change."

Communication is only important because it is the broadest root of education. And all cultures communicate exactly what they have, a powerful motley of experience.

QUESTIONS

1 What specific techniques of defining does Jones employ?
2 What does the term hegemony mean and why is it important to this essay's thesis?
3 How does language become a tool of power? In what way does Jones qualify his use of the term?

TOPICS FOR COMPOSITION

1 Accepting Jones's statement that "Speech is the effective form of a culture," write an appraisal of a culture based on how its speech idiom defines its boundaries. You might select a rural culture, the teen culture, or a minority culture.
2 However true it may be that dictionary definitions only satisfy the dullest men, one dictionary, *The Oxford English Dictionary,* is an unparalleled source for examining language change. Write an essay, perhaps organized around a single word entry, in which you explain the scope of the OED's definitions.

☐

White's opening section serves well as an example of a strong controlled introduction; especially his second paragraph, with its repetitive, transitional use of the word *symbol* in a double function, as a key to the supporting factors and as a strengthener for the thesis statement. Such an examination shows:

1 The use of symbol as an equivalent of human behavior in the topic sentence
2 The use of symbol as an equivalent for each of the three supporting factors
3 A restatement of the topic sentence to conclude the paragraph

THE SYMBOL: THE ORIGIN AND
BASIS OF HUMAN BEHAVIOR

Leslie A. White

"In the Word was the Beginning . . . the beginning of Man and of Culture."

I

In July, 1939, a celebration was held at Leland Stanford University to commemorate the hundredth anniversary of the discovery that the cell is the basic unit of all living tissue. Today we are beginning to realize and to appreciate the fact that the symbol is the basic unit of all human behavior and civilization.

All human behavior originates in the use of symbols. It was the symbol which transformed our anthropoid ancestors into men and made them human. All civilizations have been generated, and are perpetuated, only by the use of symbols. It is the symbol which transforms an infant of Homo sapiens into a human being; deaf mutes who grow up without the use of symbols are not human beings. All human behavior consists of, or is dependent upon, the use of symbols. Human behavior is symbolic behavior; symbolic behavior is human behavior. The symbol is the universe of humanity.

II

The great Darwin declared in *The Descent of Man* that "there is no fundamental difference between man and the higher mammals in their mental faculties," that the difference between them consists "*solely* in his [man's] almost infinitely larger power of associating together the most diversified sounds and ideas . . . the mental powers of higher animals do not differ *in kind,* though greatly in degree, from the corresponding powers of man" (Chs. 3, 18; emphasis ours).

This view of comparative mentality is held by many scholars today. Thus, F. H. Hankins, a prominent sociologist, states that "in spite of his large brain, it cannot be said that man has any mental traits that are peculiar to him . . . All of these human superiorities are merely relative or differences of degree." Professor Ralph Linton, an anthropologist, writes in *The Study of Man:* "The differences between men and animals in all these [behavior] respects are enormous, but they seem to be differences in quantity rather than in quality." "Human and animal behavior can be shown to have so much in common," Linton observes, "that the gap [between them] ceases to be of great importance." Dr. Alexander Goldenweiser, likewise an anthropologist, believes that "In point of sheer psychology, mind as such, man is after all no more than a talented animal" and that "the difference between the mentality here displayed [by a horse and a chimpanzee] and that of man is merely one of degree."

That there are numerous and impressive similarities between the behavior of man and that of ape is fairly obvious; it is quite possible that chimpanzees and gorillas in zoos have noted and appreciated them. Fairly apparent, too, are man's behavioral similarities to many other kinds of animals. Almost as obvious, but not easy to define, is a difference in behavior which distinguishes man from all other living creatures. I say 'obvious' because it is quite apparent to the common man that the nonhuman animals with which he is familiar do not and cannot enter, and participate in, the world in which he, as a human being, lives. It is impossible for a dog, horse, bird, or even an ape, to have any understanding of the meaning of the sign of the cross to a Christian, or of the fact that black (white among the Chinese) is the color of mourning. No chimpanzee or laboratory rat can appreciate the difference between Holy water and distilled water, or grasp the meaning of *Tuesday, 3,* or *sin.* No animal save man can distinguish a cousin from an uncle, or a cross cousin from a parallel cousin. Only man can commit the crime of incest or adultery; only he can remember the Sabbath and keep it Holy. It is not, as we well know, that the lower animals can do these things but to a lesser degree than ourselves; they cannot perform these acts of appreciation and distinction *at all.* It is, as Descartes said long ago, "not only that the brutes have less Reason than man, but that they have none at all."

But when the scholar attempts to *define* the mental difference between man and other animals he sometimes encounters difficulties which he cannot surmount and, therefore, ends up by saying that the difference is merely one of degree: man has a bigger mind, "larger power of association," wider range of activities, etc. We have a good example of this in the distinguished physiologist, Anton J. Carlson. After taking note of "man's present achievements in science, in the arts (including oratory), in political and social institutions," and noting "at the same time the apparent paucity of such behavior in other animals," he, as a common man, "is tempted to conclude that in these capacities, at least, man has a qualitative superiority over other mammals." But, since, as a scientist, Professor Carlson cannot *define* this qualitative difference between man and other animals, since as a physiologist he cannot explain it, he refuses to admit it—" . . . the physiologist does not accept the great development or articulate speech in man as something qualitatively new; . . ."—and suggests helplessly that some day we may find some new "building stone," an "additional lipoid, phosphatid, or potassium ion," in the human brain which will explain it, and concludes by saying that the difference between the mind of man and that of non-man is "probably only one of degree."

The thesis that we shall advance and defend here is that there is a *fundamental* difference between the mind of man and the mind of non-man. This difference is one of kind, not one of degree. And the gap between the two types is of the greatest importance—at least to the science of comparative behavior. Man uses symbols; no other creature does. An organism has the ability to symbol or it does not; there are no intermediate stages.

III

A symbol may be defined as a thing the value or meaning of which is bestowed upon it by those who use it. I say 'thing' because a symbol may have any kind of physical form; it may have the form of a material object, a color, a sound, an odor, a motion of an object, a taste.

The meaning, or value, of a symbol is in no instance derived from or determined by properties intrinsic in its physical form: the color appropriate to mourning may be yellow, green, or any other color; purple need not be the color of royalty; among the Manchu rulers of China it was yellow. The meaning of the word "see" is not intrinsic in its phonetic (or pictorial) properties. "Biting one's thumb at"[1] someone might mean anything. The meanings of symbols are derived from and determined by the organisms who use them; meaning is bestowed by human organisms upon physical things or events which thereupon become symbols. Symbols "have their signification," to use John Locke's phrase, "from the arbitrary imposition of men."

All symbols must have a physical form otherwise they could not enter our experience. This statement is valid regardless of our theory of experiencing. Even the exponents of "Extra-Sensory Perception" who have challenged Locke's dictum that "the knowledge of the existence of any other thing [besides ourselves and God] we can have only by sensation," have been obliged to work with physical rather than ethereal forms. But the meaning of a symbol cannot be discovered by mere sensory examination of its physical form. One cannot tell by looking at an *x* in an algebraic equation what it stands for; one cannot ascertain with the ears alone the symbolic value of the phonetic compound *si;* one cannot tell merely by weighing a pig how much gold he will exchange for; one cannot tell from the wave length of a color whether it stands for courage or cowardice, "stop" or "go"; nor can one discover the spirit in a fetish by any amount of physical or chemical examination. The meaning of a symbol can be grasped only by non-sensory, symbolic means.

The nature of symbolic experience may be easily illustrated. When the Spaniards first encountered the Aztecs, neither could speak the language of the other. How could the Indians discover the meaning of *santo,* or the significance of the crucifix? How could the Spaniards learn the meaning of *calli,* or appreciate Tlaloc? These meanings and values could not be communicated by sensory experience of physical properties alone. The finest ears will not tell you whether *santo* means "holy" or "hungry." The keenest senses cannot capture the value of holy water. Yet, as we all know, the Spaniards and the Aztecs did discover each other's meanings and appreciate each other's values. But not with sensory means. Each was able to enter the world of the other only by virtue of a faculty for which we have no better name than *symbol.*

But a thing which in one context is a symbol is, in another context, not a symbol but a sign. Thus, a word is a symbol only when one is concerned with the distinction between its meaning and its physical form. This distinction *must* be made when one bestows value upon a sound-combination or when a previously bestowed value is discovered for the first time; it may be made at other times for certain purposes. But after value has been bestowed upon, or discovered in, a word, its meaning becomes identified, in use, with its physical form. The word then functions as a sign, rather than as a symbol. Its meaning is then grasped with the senses.

We define a *sign* as a physical thing or event whose function is to indicate some other thing or event. The meaning of a sign may be inherent in its physical form and its context, as in the case of the height of a column of mercury in a thermometer as an indication of temperature, or the return of robins in the spring. Or, the meaning of a

---

[1] *"Do you bite your thumb at us, sir?"* —Romeo and Juliet, *1, 1.*

sign may be merely identified with its physical form as in the case of a hurricane signal or a quarantine flag. But in either case, the meaning of the sign may be ascertained by sensory means. The fact that a thing may be both a symbol (in one context) and a sign (in another context) has led to confusion and misunderstanding.

Thus Darwin says: "That which distinguishes man from the lower animals is not the understanding of articulate sounds, for as everyone knows, dogs understand many words and sentences" (Ch. III, *The Descent of Man*).

It is perfectly true, of course, that dogs, apes, horses, birds, and perhaps creatures even lower the evolutionary scale, can be taught to respond in a specific way to a vocal command. Little Gua, the infant chimpanzee in the Kelloggs' experiment, was, for a time, "considerably superior to the child in responding to human words." But it does not follow that no difference exists between the meaning of "words and sentences" to a man and to an ape or dog. Words are both signs and symbols to man; they are merely signs to a dog. Let us analyze the situation of vocal stimulus and response.

A dog may be taught to roll over at the command "Roll over!" A man may be taught to stop at the command "Halt!" The fact that a dog can be taught to roll over in Chinese, or that he can be taught to "go fetch" at the command "roll over" (and, of course, the same is true for a man) shows that there is no necessary and invariable relationship between a particular sound combination and a specific reaction to it. The dog or the man can be taught to respond in a certain manner to *any* arbitrarily selected combination of sounds, for example, a group of nonsense syllables, coined for the occasion. On the other hand, any one of a great number and variety of responses may become evocable by a given stimulus. Thus, so far as the *origin* of the relationship between vocal stimulus and response is concerned, the nature of the relationship, i.e., the meaning of the stimulus, is not determined by properties intrinsic in the stimulus.

But, once the relationship has been established between vocal stimulus and response, the meaning of the stimulus becomes *identified with the sounds;* it is then *as if* the meaning were intrinsic in the sounds themselves. Thus, 'halt' does not have the same meaning as 'hilt' or 'malt,' and these stimuli are distinguished from one another with the auditory mechanism. A dog may be conditioned to respond in a certain way to a sound of a given wave length. Sufficiently alter the pitch of the sound and the response will cease to be forthcoming. The meaning of the stimulus has become identified with its physical form; its value is appreciated with the senses.

Thus in *sign* behavior we see that in *establishing* a relationship between a stimulus and a response the properties intrinsic in the stimulus do not determine the nature of the response. But, *after the relationship has been established* the meaning of the stimulus is *as if* it were *inherent* in its physical form. It does not make any difference what phonetic combination we select to evoke the response of terminating self-loco-motion. We may teach a dog, horse, or man to stop at any vocal command we care to choose or devise. But once the relationship has been established between sound and response, the meaning of the stimulus becomes identified with its physical form and is, therefore, perceivable with the senses.

So far we have discovered no difference between the dog and the man; they appear to be exactly alike. And so they are as far as we have gone. But we have not told the whole story yet. No difference between dog and man is discoverable so far as learning to respond appropriately to a vocal stimulus is concerned. But we must not let an impressive similarity conceal an important difference. A porpoise is not yet a fish.

The man differs from the dog—and all other creatures—in that *he can and does play an active role in determining what value the vocal stimulus is to have, and the dog cannot.* The dog does not and cannot play an active part in determining the value of the vocal stimulus. Where he is to roll over or go fetch as a given stimulus, or whether the stimulus for roll over be one combination of sounds or another is a matter in which the dog has nothing whatever to "say." He plays a purely passive role and can do nothing else. He learns the meaning of a vocal command just as his salivary glands may learn to respond to the sound of a bell. But man plays an active role and thus becomes a creator: let *x* equal three pounds of coal and it does equal three pounds of coal; let removal of the hat in a house of worship indicate respect and it becomes so. This creative faculty, that of freely, actively, and arbitrarily bestowing value upon things, is one of the most commonplace as well as *the* most important characteristic of man. Children employ it freely in their play: "Let's pretend that this rock is a wolf."

The difference between the behavior of man and other animals, then, is that the lower animals may receive new values, may acquire new meanings, but they cannot create and bestow them. Only man can do this. To use a crude analogy, lower animals are like a person who has only the receiving apparatus for wireless messages: he can receive messages but cannot send them. Man can do both. And this difference is one of kind, not of degree: a creature can either "arbitrarily impose signification," can either create and bestow values, or he cannot. There are no intermediate stages. This difference may appear slight, but, as a carpenter once told William James in discussing differences between men, "It's very important." All *human* existence depends upon it and it alone.

The confusion regarding the nature of words and their significance to men and the lower animals is not hard to understand. It arises, first of all, from a failure to distinguish between the two quite different contexts in which words function. The statements, "The meaning of a word cannot be grasped with the senses," and "The meaning of a word can be grasped with the senses," though contradictory, are nevertheless equally true. In the *symbol* context the meaning cannot be perceived with the senses: in the *sign* context it can. This is confusing enough. But the situation has been made worse by using the words 'symbol' and 'sign' to label, not the *different contexts,* but *one and the same thing:* the word. Thus a word is a symbol *and* a sign, two different things. It is like saying that a vase is a *doli* and a *kana*—two different things—because it may function in two contexts, esthetic and commercial.

IV

That man is unique among animal species with respect to mental abilities, that a fundamental difference of kind—not of degree—separates man from all other animals is a fact that has long been appreciated, despite Darwin's pronouncement to the contrary. Long ago, in his *Discourse on Method,* Descartes pointed out that "there are not men so dull and stupid . . . as to be incapable of joining together different words . . . on the other hand, there is no other animal, however perfect . . . which can do the like." John Locke, too, saw clearly that "the power of abstracting is not at all in them [i.e., beasts], and that the having of general ideas is that which puts a perfect distinction between man and brutes, and is an excellency which the faculties of brutes do by no means attain to . . . they have no use of words or any other general signs." The great British anthropologist, E. B. Tylor, remarked upon "the mental gulf that divides the lowest savage from the highest ape . . . A young child can understand what is not proved to have entered the mind of the cleverest dog, elephant, or ape." And, of course, there are many today who recognize the "mental gulf" between man and other species.

Thus, for over a century we have had, side by side, two traditions in comparative psychology. One has declared that man does not differ from other animals in mental abilities except in degree. The other has seen clearly that man is unique in at least one respect, that he possesses an ability that no other animal has. The difficulty of *defining* this difference adequately has kept this question open until the present day. The distinction between *sign* behavior and *symbol* behavior as drawn here may, we hope, contribute to a solution of this problem once and for all.

V

Very little indeed is known of the organic basis of the symbolic faculty: we know next to nothing of the neurology of "symbolling." And very few scientists—anatomists, neurologists or physical anthropologists—appear to be interested in the subject. Some, in fact, seem to be unaware of the existence of such a problem. The duty and task of giving an account of the neural basis of symbolling does not, however, fall within the province of the sociologist or the cultural anthropologist. On the contrary, he should scrupulously exclude it as irrelevant to his problems and interests; to introduce it would bring only confusion. It is enough for the sociologist or cultural anthropologist to take the ability to use symbols, possessed by man alone, as given. The use to which he puts this fact is in no way affected by his, or even the anatomist's, inability to describe the symbolic process in neurological terms. However, it is well for the social scientist to be acquainted with the little that neurologists and anatomists do know about the structural basis of symbolling. We, therefore, review briefly the chief relevant facts here.

The anatomist has not been able to discover why men can use symbols and apes cannot. So far as is known the only difference between the brain of man and the brain of an ape is a quantitative one: ". . . man has no new kinds of brain cells or brain cell connections," as A. J. Carlson has remarked. Nor does man, as distinguished from other animals, possess a specialized "symbol-mechanism." The so-called speech areas of the brain should not be identified with symbolling. The notion that symbolling is identified with, or dependent upon, the ability to utter articulate sounds is not uncommon. Thus, L. L. Bernard lists as "the fourth great organic asset of man . . . his vocal apparatus, . . . characteristic of him alone." But this is an erroneous conception. The great apes have the mechanism necessary for the production of articulate sounds. "It seemingly is well established," write R. M. and A. W. Yerkes in *The Great Apes,* "that the motor mechanism of voice in this ape [chimpanzee] is adequate not only to the production of a considerable variety of sounds, but also to definite articulations similar to those of man." And the physical anthropologist, E. A. Hooton, asserts that "all of the anthropoid apes are vocally and muscularly equipped so that they could have an articulate language if they possessed the requisite intelligence." Furthermore, as Descartes and Locke pointed out long ago, there are birds who do actually utter articulate sounds, who duplicate the sounds of human speech, but who of course are quite incapable of symbolling. The "speech areas" of the brain are merely areas associated with the muscles of the tongue, with the larnyx, etc. But, as we know, symbolling is not at all confined to the use of these organs. One may symbol with any part of the body that he can move at will.

To be sure, the symbolic faculty was brought into existence by the natural processes of organic evolution. And we may reasonably believe that the focal point, if not the locus, of this faculty is in the brain, especially the forebrain. Man's brain is much larger than that of an ape, both absolutely and relatively. The brain of the average adult human male is about 1500 c.c. in size; brains of gorillas seldom exceed 500 c.c. Relatively, the human brain weighs about 1/50th of the entire body weight, while that of a gorilla varies from 1/150th to 1/200th part of that weight. And the forebrain especially is large in man as compared with ape. Now in many situations we know that quantitative changes give rise to qualitative differences. Water is transformed into steam by additional quantities of heat. Additional power and speed lift the taxiing airplane from the ground and transform terrestrial locomotion into flight. The difference between wood alcohol and grain alcohol is a qualitative expression of a quantitative difference in the proportions of carbon and hydrogen. Thus a marked growth in size of the brain in man may have brought forth a *new kind* of function.

VI

All culture (civilization) depends upon the symbol. It was the exercise of the symbolic faculty that brought culture into existence and it is the use of symbols that makes the perpetuation of culture possible. Without the symbol there would be no culture, and man would be merely an animal, not a human being.

Articulate speech is the most important form of symbolic expression. Remove speech from culture and what would remain? Let us see.

Without articulate speech we would have no *human* social organization. Families we might have, but this form of organization is not peculiar to man; it is not *per se, human*. But we would have no prohibitions of incest, no rules prescribing exogany and endogamy, polygamy or monogamy. How could marriage with a cross cousin be prescribed, marriage with a parallel cousin proscribed, without articulate speech? How could rules which prohibit plural mates possessed simultaneously but permit them if possessed one at a time exist without speech?

Without speech we could have no political, economic, ecclesiastic, or military organization; no codes of etiquette or ethics; no laws; no science, theology, or literature; no games or music, except on an ape level. Rituals and ceremonial paraphernalia would be meaningless without articulate speech. Indeed, without articulate speech we would be all but toolless: we would have only the occasional and insignificant use of the tool such as we find today among the higher apes, for it was articulate speech that transformed the non-progressive tool-using of the ape into the progressive, cumulative tool-using of man, the human being.

In short, without symbolic communication in some form, we would have no culture. "In the Word was the beginning" of culture—and its perpetuation also.

To be sure, with all his culture man is still an animal and strives for the same ends that all other living creatures strive for: the preservation of the individual and the perpetuation of the race. In concrete terms these ends are food, shelter from the elements, defense from enemies, health, and offspring. The fact that man strives for these ends just as all other animals do has, no doubt, led many to declare that there is "no fundamental difference between the behavior of man and of other creatures." But man does differ, not in *ends* but in *means.* Man's means are cultural means: culture is simply the human animal's way of living. And, since these means, culture, are dependent upon a faculty possessed by man alone, the ability to use symbols, the difference between the behavior of man and of all other creatures is not merely great, but basic and fundamental.

VII

The behavior of man is of two distinct kinds: symbolic and non-symbolic. Man yawns, stretches, coughs, scratches himself, cries out in pain, shrinks with fear, "bristles" with anger, and so on. Non-symbolic behavior of this sort is not peculiar to man; he shares it not only with the other primates but with many other animal species as well. But man communicates with his fellows with articulate speech, uses amulets, confesses sins, makes laws, observes codes of etiquette, explains his dreams, classifies his relatives in designated categories, and so on. This kind of behavior is unique; only man is capable of it; it is peculiar to man because it consists of, or is dependent upon, the use of symbols. The non-symbolic behavior of Homo sapiens is the behavior of man the animal; the symbolic behavior is that of man the human being. It is the symbol which has transformed man from a mere animal to a human animal.

Because *human* behavior is symbol behavior and since the behavior of infra-human species is non-symbolic, it follows that we can learn nothing about human behavior from observations upon or experiments with the lower animals. Experiments with rats and apes have indeed been illuminating. They have thrown much light upon mechanisms and processes of behavior among mammals or the higher vertebrates. But they have contributed nothing to an understanding of *human* behavior because the symbol mechanism and all of its consequences are totally lacking among the lower species. And as for neuroses in rats, it is of course interesting to know that rats can be made neurotic. But science probably had a better understanding of psychopathic behavior among human beings before neuroses were produced experimentally in rats than they now have of the neuroses of the rats. Our understanding of human neuroses has helped us to understand those of rats; we have, as a matter of fact, interpreted the latter in terms of *human* pathology. But I cannot see where the neurotic laboratory rats have served to deepen or enlarge our understanding of *human* behavior

As it was the symbol that made *mankind* human, so it is with each member of the species. A baby is not a *human* being until he begins to symbol. Until the infant begins to talk there is nothing to distinguish his behavior qualitatively from that of a very young ape, as *The Ape and the Child* showed. As a matter of fact, one of the impressive results of this fascinating experiment by Professor and Mrs. Kellogg was the demonstration of how ape-like an infant of Homo sapiens is before he begins to talk. The baby boy acquired exceptional proficiency in climbing in association with the little chimpanzee, and even acquired her "food bark"! The Kelloggs speak of how the little ape became "humanized" during her sojourn in their home. But what the experiment demonstrated so conclusively was the ape's utter inability to learn to talk or even to make *any* progess in this direction—in short, her inablility to become "humanized" at all.

The infant of the species *Homo sapiens* becomes human only when and as he exercises his symbol faculty. Only through articulate speech—not necessarily vocal—can he enter the world of human beings and take part in their affairs. The questions asked earlier may be repeated now. How could a growing child know and appreciate such things as social organization, ethics, etiquette, ritual, science, religion, art and games without symbolic communication? The answer is of course that he could know nothing of these things and have no appreciation of them at all.

The question of "wolf children" is relevant here. A belief in instances in which human children have been reared by wolves or other animals has flourished ever since the myth of Romulus and Remus—and long before that time. Despite the fact that accounts of "wolf children" have been shown repeatedly to be erroneous or unsupported by adequate evidence ever since Blumenbach discovered that "Wild Peter" was merely a half-witted boy ejected from his home at the instance of a newly acquired stepmother, this deplorable folk-tale still flourishes in certain "scientific" circles today. But the use to which these lupine wards and "feral men" are put by some sociologists and psychologists is a good one, namely, to show that a member of the species *Homo sapiens* who lives in a world without symbols is not a human being but a brute. To paraphrase Voltaire, one might say that if wolf children did not exist "social science" would have to invent them.

Children who have been cut off from human intercourse for years by blindness and deafness but who have eventually effected communication with their fellows on a symbolic level are exceedingly illuminating. The case of Helen Keller is exceptionally instructive, although those of Laura Bridgman, Marie Heurtin, and others are very valuable also.

Helen Keller was rendered blind and deaf at a very early age by illness. She grew up as a child without symbolic contact with anyone. Descriptions of her at the age of seven, the time at which her teacher, Miss Sullivan, came to her home, disclose no *human* attributes of Helen's behavior at all. She was a headstrong, undisciplined and unruly little animal.

Within a day or so after her arrival at the Keller home, Miss Sullivan taught Helen her first word, spelling it into her hand. But this word was merely a sign, not a symbol.

A week later Helen knew several words but, as Miss Sullivan reports, she had "no idea how to use them or that everything has a name." Within three weeks Helen knew eighteen nouns and three verbs. But she was still on the level of signs; she still had no notion "that everything has a name."

Helen confused the word signs for "mug" and "water" because, apparently, both were associated with drinking. Miss Sullivan made a few attempts to clear up this confusion but without success. One morning, however, about a month after Miss Sullivan's arrival, the two went out to the pump in the garden. What happened then is best told in their own words:

> I made Helen hold her mug under the spout while I pumped. As the cold water gushed forth, filling the mug, I spelled 'w-a-t-e-r' into Helen's free hand. The word coming so close upon the sensation of cold water rushing over her hand seemed to startle her. She dropped the mug and stood as one transfixed. A new light came into her face. She spelled 'water' several times. Then she dropped on the ground and asked for its name and pointed to the pump and the trellis, and suddenly turning around she asked for my name . . . *In a few hours she had added thirty new words to her vocabulary.*

But these words were now more than mere signs as they are to a dog and as they had been to Helen up to then. They were *symbols*. Helen had at last grasped and turned the key that admitted her for the first time to a new universe: the world of human beings. Helen describes this marvellous experience herself:

> We walked down the path to the well-house, attracted by the fragrance of honeysuckle with which it was covered. Someone was drawing water and my teacher placed my hand under the spout. As the cool stream gushed over one hand she spelled into the other the word *water* first slowly, then rapidly. I stood still, my whole attention fixed upon the motion of her fingers. Suddenly I felt a misty consciousness as of something forgotten—a thrill of returning thought; and somehow *the mystery of language was revealed to me.* I knew then that 'w-a-t-e-r' meant the wonderful cool something that was flowing over my hand. That living word awakened my soul, gave it light, hope, joy, set it free!

Helen was transformed on the instant by this experience. Miss Sullivan had managed to touch Helen's symbol mechanism and set it in motion. Helen, on her part, grasped the external world with this mechanism that had lain dormant and inert all these years, sealed in dark and silent isolation by eyes that could not see and ears that heard not. But now she had crossed the boundary and entered a new land. Henceforth her progress would be rapid.

"I left the well-house," Helen reports, "eager to learn. Everything had a name, and each name gave birth to a new thought. As we returned to the house every object which I touched seemed to quiver with life. That was because I saw everything with the strange new sight that had come to me."

Helen became humanized rapidly. "I see an improvement in Helen from day to day," Miss Sullivan wrote in her diary, "*almost from hour to hour.* Everything must have a name now . . . She drops the signs and pantomime she used before as soon as she has words to supply their place . . . We notice her face grows more expressive each day . . ."

A more eloquent and convincing account of the significance of symbols and of the great gulf between the human mind and that of minds without symbols could hardly be imagined.

VIII

Summary. The natural process of biologic evolution brought into existence in man, and man alone, a new and distinctive ability: the ability to use symbols. The most important form of symbolic expression is articulate speech. Articulate speech means communication of ideas; communication means preservation—tradition—and preservation means accumulation and progress. The emergence of the faculty of symbolling has resulted in the genesis of a new order of phenomena: an extra-somatic, cultural, order. All civilizations are born of, and are perpetuated by, the use of symbols. A culture, or civilization, is but a particular kind of form which the biologic, life-perpetuating activities of a particular animal, man, assume.

Human behavior is symbolic behavior; if it is not symbolic, it is not human. The infant of the genus Homo becomes a human being only as he is introduced into and participates in that order of phenomena which is culture. And the key to this world and the means of participation in it is—the symbol.

QUESTIONS

1   What kind of support does White provide in section 2? How effective is his choice?
2   In section 3, White defines the symbol. What are his methods of definition? How does he vary his method of support within each definition-framework?
3   Find the point in section 3 at which White completes his definition of symbol and begins to compare and contrast man and dog as primary examples of his definition. Which is the transitional paragraph? Explain its transitional qualities.
4   Outline White's comparison of man and dog with the idea of revealing his comparative and contrastive techniques. What assumptions can you make about technique in writing effective comparison and contrast?
5   How does section 4 function in the overall structure of the essay?
6   Classify White's techniques in sections 5, 6, and 7. What previously used techniques do you find? How has he expanded some?
7   Section 8 provides a neatly organized summary. Do you agree with White's conclusions? Why or why not?

TOPICS FOR COMPOSITION

1   Write an essay showing how White has expanded on the expressive function of language.
2   White implies that words function as symbols to stimulate human behavior. Select any word or phrase and show its symbolic effect on behavior. Some good ones might be: Hate, Love, Anger, Wealth, etc.
3   Write a précis of White's essay. Limit your précis to no more than 250 words.

SHORT STORY

There is a deliberate incoherency in Miss Welty's story. In fact, it retains few of the features on which we ordinarily rely in analyzing fiction. We find neither a clearly developed plot nor a characterization that approximates our view of human experience. We should, therefore, approach this story as we approach a musical selection—more ready to react than to understand. For all of its unusual qualities, however, we may find it helpful to consider the following:

1 The kind and intensity of Powerhouse's music
2 The validity of the story of Gypsy's death
3 The other musicians' comments in reply to Powerhouse
4 The function of the café scene

POWERHOUSE

Eudora Welty

Powerhouse is playing!

He's here on tour from the city—"Powerhouse and His Keyboard"—"Powerhouse and His Tasmanians"—think of the things he calls himself! There's no one in the world like him. You can't tell what he is. "Nigger man"?—he looks more Asiatic, monkey, Jewish, Babylonian, Peruvian, fanatic, devil. He has pale gray eyes, heavy lids, maybe horny like a lizard's, but big glowing eyes when they're open. He has African feet of the greatest size, stomping, both together, on each side of the pedals. He's not coal black—beverage colored—looks like a preacher when his mouth is shut, but then it opens—vast and obscene. And his mouth is going every minute: like a monkey's when it looks for something. Improvising, coming on a light and childish melody—*smooch*—he loves it with his mouth.

Is it possible that he could be this! When you have him there performing for you, that's what you feel. You know people on a stage—and people of a darker race—so likely to be marvelous, frightening.

This is a white dance. Powerhouse is not a show-off like the Harlem boys, not drunk, not crazy—he's in a trance; he's a person of joy, a fanatic. He listens as much as he performs, a look of hideous, powerful rapture on his face. Big arched eyebrows that never stop traveling, like a Jew's—wandering-Jew eyebrows. When he plays he beats down piano and seat and wears them away. He is in motion every moment—what could be more obscene? There he is with his great head, fat stomach, and little round piston legs, and long yellow-sectioned strong big fingers, at rest about the size of bananas. Of course you know how he sounds—you've heard him on records—but still you need to see him. He's going all the time, like skating around the skating rink or rowing a boat. It makes everybody crowd around, here in this shadowless steel-trussed hall with the rose-like posters of Nelson Eddy and the testimonial for the mind-reading horse in handwriting magnified five hundred times. Then all quietly he lays his finger on a key with the promise and serenity of a sibyl touching the book.

336

Powerhouse is so monstrous he sends everybody into oblivion. When any group, any performers, come to town, don't people always come out and hover near, leaning inward about them, to learn what it is? What is it? Listen. Remember how it was with the acrobats. Watch them carefully, hear the least word, especially what they say to one another, in another language—don't let them escape you; it's the only time for hallucination, the last time. They can't stay. They'll be somewhere else this time tomorrow.

Powerhouse has as much as possible done by signals. Everybody, laughing as if to hide a weakness, will sooner or later hand him up a written request. Powerhouse reads each one, studying with a secret face: that is the face which looks like a mask—anybody's; there is a moment when he makes a decision. Then a light slides under his eyelids, and he says, "92!" or some combination of figures—never a name. Before a number the band is all frantic, misbehaving, pushing, like children in a schoolroom, and he is the teacher getting silence. His hands over the keys, he says sternly, "You-all ready? You-all ready to do some serious walking?"—waits—then, <u>stamp.</u> Quiet. <u>Stamp,</u> for the second time. This is absolute. Then a set of rhythmic kicks against the floor to communicate the tempo. Then, O Lord! say the distended eyes from beyond the boundary of the trumpets, Hello and good-bye, and they are all down the first note like a waterfall.

This note marks the end of any known discipline. Powerhouse seems to abandon them all—he himself seems lost—down in the song, yelling up like somebody in a whirlpool—not guiding them—hailing them only. But he knows, really. He cries out, but he must know exactly. "Mercy! . . . What I say! . . . Yeah!" And then drifting, listening—"Where that skin beater?"—wanting drums, and starting up and pouring it out in the greatest delight and brutality. On the sweet pieces such a leer for everybody! He looks down so benevolently upon all our faces and whispers the lyrics to us. And if you could hear him at this moment on "Marie, the Dawn is Breaking"! He's going up the keyboard with a few fingers in some very derogatory triplet-routine, he gets higher and higher, and then he looks over the end of the piano, as if over a cliff. But not in a show-off way—the song makes him do it.

He loves the way they all play, too—all those next to him. The far section of the band is all studious, wearing glasses every one—they don't count. Only those playing around Powerhouse are the real ones. He has a bass fiddler from Vicksburg, black as pitch, named Valentine, who plays with his eyes shut and talking to himself, very young: Powerhouse has to keep encouraging him. "Go on, go on, give it up, bring it on out there!" When you heard him like that on records, did you know he was really pleading?

He calls Valentine out to take a solo.

"What you going to play?" Powerhouse looks out kindly from behind the piano; he opens his mouth and shows his tongue, listening.

Valentine looks down, drawing against his instrument, and says without a lip movement," 'Honeysuckle Rose.' "

He has a clarinet player named Little Brother, and loves to listen to anything he does. He'll smile and say, "Beautiful!" Little Brother takes a step forward when he plays and stands at the very front, with the whites of his eyes like fishes swimming.

Once when he played a low note, Powerhouse muttered in dirty praise, "He went clear downstairs to get that one!"

After a long time he holds up the number of fingers to tell the band how many choruses still to go—usually five. He keeps his directions down to signals.

It's a bad night outside. It's a white dance, and nobody dances, except a few straggling jitterbugs and two elderly couples. Everybody just stands around the band and watches Powerhouse. Sometimes they steal glances at one another, as if to say, Of course, you know how it is with *them*—Negroes—band leaders—they would play the same way, giving all they've got, for an audience of one. . . . When somebody, no matter who, gives everything, it makes people feel ashamed for him.

Late at night they play the one waltz they will ever consent to play—by request, "Pagan Love Song." Powerhouse's head rolls and sinks like a weight between his waving shoulders. He groans, and his fingers drag into the keys heavily, holding on to the notes, retrieving. It is a sad song.

"You know what happened to me?" says Powerhouse.

Valentine hums a response, dreaming at the bass.

"I got a telegram my wife is dead," says Powerhouse, with wandering fingers.

"Uh-huh?"

His mouth gathers and forms a barbarous O while his fingers walk up straight, unwillingly, three octaves.

"Gypsy? Why how come her to die, didn't you just phone her up in the night last night long distance?"

"Telegram say—here the words: Your wife is dead." He puts 4/4 over the 3/4.

"Not but four words?" This is the drummer, an unpopular boy named Scoot, a disbelieving maniac.

Powerhouse is shaking his vast cheeks. "What the hell was she trying to do? What was she up to?"

"What name has it got signed, if you got a telegram?" Scoot is spitting away with those wire brushes.

Little Brother, the clarinet player, who cannot now speak, glares and tilts back.

"Uranus Knockwood is the name signed." Powerhouse lifts his eyes open. "Ever heard of him?" A bubble shoots out on his lip like a plate on a counter.

Valentine is beating slowly on with his palm and scratching the strings with his long blue nails. He is fond of a waltz, Powerhouse interrupts him.

"I don't know him. Don't know who he is." Valentine shakes his head with the closed eyes.

"Say it agin."

"Uranus Knockwood."

"That ain't Lenox Avenue."

"It ain't Broadway."

"Ain't ever seen it wrote out in any print, even for horse racing."

"Hell, that's on a star, boy, ain't it?" Crash of the cymbals.

"What the hell was she up to?" Powerhouse shudders. "Tell me, tell me, tell me." He makes triplets, and begins a new chorus. He holds three fingers up.

"You say you got a telegram." This is Valentine, patient and sleepy, beginning again.

Powerhouse is elaborate. "Yas, the time I go out, go way downstairs along a long cor-ri-dor to where they puts us: coming back along the cor-ri-dor: steps out and hands me a telegram: Your wife is dead."

"Gypsy?" The drummer like a spider over his drums.

"Aaaaaaaaa!" shouts Powerhouse, flinging out both powerful arms for three whole beats to flex his muscles, then kneading a dough of bass notes. His eyes glitter. He plays the piano like a drum sometimes—why not?

"Gypsy? Such a dancer?"

"Why you don't hear it straight from your agent? Why it ain't come from headquarters? What you been doing, getting telegrams in the *corridor,* signed nobody?"

They all laugh. End of that chorus.

"What time is it?" Powerhouse calls. "What the hell place is this? Where is my watch and chain?"

"I hang it on you," whimpers Valentine. "It still there."

There it rides on Powerhouse's great stomach, down where he can never see it.

"Sure did hear some clock striking twelve while ago. Must be *midnight.*"

"It going to be intermission," Powerhouse declares, lifting up his finger with the signet ring.

He draws the chorus to an end. He pulls a big Northern hotel towel out of the deep pocket in his vast, special-cut tux pants and pushes his forehead into it.

"If she went and killed herself!" he says with a hidden face. "If she up and jumped out that window!" He gets to his feet, turning vaguely, wearing the towel on his head.

"Ha, ha!"

"Sheik, sheik!"

"She wouldn't do that." Little Brother sets down his clarinet like a precious vase, and speaks. He still looks like an East Indian queen, implacable, divine, and full of snakes. "You ain't going to expect people doing what they says over long distance."

"Come on!" roars Powerhouse. He is already at the back door, he has pulled it wide open, and with a wild, gathered-up face is smelling the terrible night.

Powerhouse, Valentine, Scoot and Little Brother step outside into the drenching rain.

"Well, they emptying buckets," says Powerhouse in a mollified voice. On the street he holds his hands out and turns up the blanched palms like sieves.

A hundred dark, ragged, silent, delighted Negroes have come around from under the eaves of the hall, and follow wherever they go.

"Watch out Little Brother don't shrink," says Powerhouse. "You just the right size now, clarinet don't suck you in. You got a dry throat, Little Brother, you in the desert?" He reaches into the pocket and pulls out a paper of mints. "Now hold 'em in your mouth—don't chew 'em. I don't carry around nothing without limit."

"Go in that joint and have beer," says Scoot, who walks ahead.

"Beer? Beer? You know what beer is? What do they say is beer? What's beer? Where I been?"

"Down yonder where it say World Café—that do?" They are in Negrotown now.

Valentine patters over and holds open a screen door warped like a sea shell, bitter in the wet, and they walk in stained darker with the rain and leaving footprints. Inside, sheltered dry smells stand like screens around a table covered with a red-checkered cloth, in the center of which flies hang onto an obelisk-shaped ketchup bottle. The midnight walls are checkered again with admonishing "Not Responsible" signs and black-figured, smoky calendars. It is a waiting, silent, limp room. There is a burned-out-looking nickelodeon and right beside it a long-necked wall instrument labeled "Business Phone, Don't Keep Talking." Circled phone numbers are written up everywhere. There is a worn-out peacock feather hanging by a thread to an old, thin, pink, exposed light bulb, where it slowly turns around and around, whoever breathes.

A waitress watches.

"Come here, living statue, and get all this big order of beer we fixing to give."

"Never seen you before anywhere." The waitress moves and comes forward and slowly shows little gold leaves and tendrils over her teeth. She shoves up her shoulders and breasts. "How I going to know who you might be? Robbers? Coming in out of the black of night right at midnight, setting down so big at my table?"

"Boogers," says Powerhouse, his eyes opening lazily as in a cave.

The girl screams delicately with pleasure. O Lord, she likes talk and scares.

"Where you going to find enough beer to put out on this here table?"

She runs to the kitchen with bent elbows and sliding steps.

"Here's a million nickels," says Powerhouse, pulling his hand out of his pocket and sprinkling coins out, all but the last one, which he makes vanish like a magician.

Valentine and Scoot take the money over to the nickelodeon, which looks as battered as a slot machine, and read all the names of the records out loud.

"Whose 'Tuxedo Junction'?" asks Powerhouse.

"You know whose."

"Nickelodeon, I request you please to play 'Empty Red Blues' and let Bessie Smith sing."

Silence: they hold it like a measure.

"Bring me all those nickels on back here," says Powerhouse. "Look at that! What you tell me the name of this place?"

"White dance, week night, raining, Alligator, Mississippi, long ways from home."

"Uh-huh."

"Sent for You Yesterday and Here You Come Today" plays.

The waitress, setting the tray of beer down on a back table, comes up taut and apprehensive as a hen. "Says in the kitchen, back there putting their eyes to little hole peeping out, that you is Mr. Powerhouse. . . .They knows from a picture they seen."

"They seeing right tonight, that is him," says Little Brother.

"You him?"

"That is him in the flesh," says Scoot.

"Does you wish to touch him?" asks Valentine. "Because he don't bite."

"You passing through?"

"Now you got everything right."

She waits like a drop, hands languishing together in front.

"Little-Bit, ain't you going to bring the beer?"

She brings it, and goes behind the cash register and smiles, turning different ways. The little fillet of gold in her mouth is gleaming.

"The Mississippi River's here," she says once.

Now all the watching Negroes press in gently and bright-eyed through the door, as many as can get in. One is a little boy in a straw sombrero which has been coated with aluminum paint all over.

Powerhouse, Valentine, Scoot and Little Brother drink beer, and their eyelids come together like curtains. The wall and the rain and the humble beautiful waitress waiting on them and the other Negroes watching enclose them.

"Listen!" whispers Powerhouse, looking into the ketchup bottle and slowly spreading his performer's hands over the damp, wrinkling cloth with the red squares. "Listen how it is. My wife gets missing me. Gypsy. She goes to the window. She looks out and sees you know what. Street. Sign saying Hotel. People walking. Somebody looks up. Old man. She looks down, out the window. Well? . . .Ssssst! Plooey! What she do? Jump out and bust her brains all over the world."

He opens his eyes.

"That's it," agrees Valentine. "You gets a telegram."

"Sure she misses you," Little Brother adds.

"No, it's night time." How softly he tells them! "Sure. It's the night time. She say, What do I hear? Footsteps walking up the hall? That him? Footsteps go on off. It's not me. I'm in Alligator, Mississippi, she's crazy. Shaking all over. Listen till her ears and all grow out like old music-box horns but still she can't hear a thing. She says, All right! I'll jump out the window then. Got on her nightgown. I know that nightgown, and her thinking there. Says, Ho hum, all right, and jumps out the window. Is she mad at me! Is she crazy! She don't leave *nothing* behind her!"

"Ya! Ha!"

"Brains and insides everywhere, Lord, Lord."

All the watching Negroes stir in their delight, and to their higher delight he says affectionately, "Listen! Rats in here."

"That must be the way, boss."

"Only, naw, Powerhouse, that ain't true. That sound too *bad.*"

"Does? I even know who finds her," cries Powerhouse. "That nogood pussy-footed crooning creeper, that creeper that follow around after me, coming up like weeds behind me, following around after me everything I do and messing around on the trail I leave. Bets my numbers, sings my songs, gets close to my agent like a Betsybug; when I going out he just coming in. I got him now! I got my eye on him."

"Know who he is?"

"Why, it's that old Uranus Knockwood!"

"Ya! Ha!"

"Yeah, and he coming now, he going to find Gypsy. There he is, coming around that corner, and Gypsy kadoodling down, oh-oh, watch out! Ssssst! Plooey! See, there she is in her little old nightgown, and her insides and brains all scattered round."

A sigh fills the room.

"Hush about her brains. Hush about her insides."

"Ya! Ha! You talking about her brains and insides—old Uranus Knockwood," says

Powerhouse, "look down and say Jesus! He say, Look here what I'm walking round in!"

They all burst into halloos of laughter. Powerhouse's face looks like a big hot iron stove.

"Why, he picks her up and carries her off!" he says.

"Ya! Ha!"

"Carries her *back* around the corner. . . ."

"Oh, Powerhouse!"

"You know him."

"Uranus Knockwood!"

"Yeahhh!"

"He take our wives when we gone!"

"He come in when we goes out!"

"Uh-huh!"

"He go out when we comes in!"

"Yeahhh!"

"He standing behind the door!"

"Old Uranus Knockwood."

"You know him."

"Middle-sized man."

"Wears a hat."

"That's him."

Everybody in the room moans with pleasure. The little boy in the fine silver hat opens a paper and divides out a jelly roll among his followers.

And out of the breathless ring somebody moves forward like a slave, leading a great logy Negro with bursting eyes, and says, "This here is Sugar-Stick Thompson, that dove down to the bottom of July Creek and pulled up all those drownded white people fall out of a boat. Last summer, pulled up fourteen."

"Hello," says Powerhouse, turning and looking around at them all with his great daring face until they nearly suffocate.

Sugar-Stick, their instrument, cannot speak; he can only look back at the others.

"Can't even swim. Done it by holding his breath," says the fellow with the hero.

Powerhouse looks at him seekingly.

"I his half brother," the fellow puts in.

They step back.

"Gypsy say," Powerhouse rumbles gently again, looking at *them,* " 'What is the use? I'm gonna jump out so far—so far. . . .' *Sssssst*—!"

"Don't, boss, don't do it again," says Little Brother.

"It's awful," says the waitress. "I hates that Mr. Knockwoods. All that the truth?"

"Want to see the telegram I got from him?" Powerhouse's hand goes to the vast pocket.

"Now wait, now wait, boss." They all watch him.

"It must be the real truth," says the waitress, sucking in her lower lip, her luminous eyes turning sadly, seeking the windows.

"No, babe, it ain't the truth." His eyebrows fly up, and he begins to whisper to her out of his vast oven mouth. His hand stays in his pocket. "Truth is something worse, I ain't said what, yet. It's something hasn't come to me, but I ain't saying it won't. And when it does, then want me to tell you?'' He sniffs all at once, his eyes come open and turn up, almost too far. He is dreamily smiling.

"Don't, boss, don't, Powerhouse!"

"Oh!" the waitress screams.

"Go on git out of here!" bellows Powerhouse, taking his hand out of his pocket and clapping after her red dress.

The ring of watchers breaks and falls away.

"*Look* at that! Intermission is up," says Powerhouse.

He folds money under a glass, and after they go out, Valentine leans back in and drops a nickel in the nickelodeon behind them, and it lights up and begins to play "The Gonna Goo." The feather dangles still.

"Take a telegram!" Powerhouse shouts suddenly up into the rain over the street. "Take a answer. Now what was that name?"

They get a little tired.

"Uranus Knockwood."

"You ought to know."

"Yas? Spell it to me."

They spell it all the ways it could be spelled. It puts them in a wonderful humor.

"Here's the answer. I got it right here. 'What in the hell you talking about? Don't make any difference: I gotcha.' Name signed: Powerhouse."

"That going to reach him, Powerhouse?" Valentine speaks in a maternal voice.

"Yas, yas."

All hushing, following him up the dark street at a distance, like old rained-on black ghosts, the Negroes are afraid they will die laughing.

Powerhouse throws back his vast head into the steaming rain, and a look of hopeful desire seems to blow somehow like a vapor from his own dilated nostrils over his face and bring a mist to his eyes.

"Reach him and come out the other side."

"That's it, Powerhouse, that's it. You got him now."

Powerhouse lets out a long sigh.

"But ain't you going back there to call up Gypsy long distance, the way you did last night in that other place? I seen a telephone . . . Just to see if she there at home?"

There is a measure of silence. That is one crazy drummer that's going to get his neck broken some day.

"No," growls Powerhouse. "No! How many thousand times tonight I got to say No?"

He holds up his arm in the rain.

"You sure-enough unroll your voice some night, it about reach up yonder to her," says Little Brother, dismayed.

They go on up the street, shaking the rain off and on them like birds.

Back in the dance hall, they play "San" (99). The jitterbugs start up like windmills stationed over the floor, and in their orbits—one circle, another, a long stretch and a zigzag—dance the elderly couples with old smoothness, undisturbed and stately.

When Powerhouse first came back from intermission, no doubt full of beer, they said, he got the band tuned up again in his own way. He didn't strike the piano keys for pitch—he simply opened his mouth and gave falsetto howls—in A, D and so on—they tuned by him. Then he took hold of the piano, as if he saw it for the first time in his life, and tested it for strength, hit it down in the bass, played an octave with his elbow, lifted the top, looked inside, and leaned against it with all his might. He sat down and played it for a few minutes with outrageous force and got it under his power—a bass deep and coarse as a sea net—then produced something glimmering and fragile, and smiled. And who could ever remember any of the things he says? They are just inspired remarks that roll out of his mouth like smoke.

They've requested "Somebody Loves Me," and he's already done twelve or fourteen choruses, piling them up nobody knows how, and it will be a wonder if he ever gets through. Now and then he calls and shouts," 'Somebody loves me! Somebody loves me, I wander who!'" His mouth gets to be nothing but a volcano. "I wonder who!"

"Maybe . . ." He uses all his right hand on a trill.

"Maybe . . ." He pulls back his spread fingers, and looks out upon the place where he is. A vast, impersonal and yet furious grimace transfigures his wet face.

". . . Maybe it's you!"

QUESTIONS

1 How clearly can we picture the main character? What features are emphasized more than others? Can you offer a reason for this emphasis?
2 How would you classify the music played by Powerhouse's band? Can you detect a merging of tempo from the music described and the story itself? For instance, divide the story into its scenes: the dance hall, the café, the return to the dance hall.
3 What do the onlookers in the café suggest about the position of the artist in society? How important are the onlookers to Powerhouse?
4 Can we believe that Powerhouse's wife, Gypsy, is dead? What can we make of the name, Uranus Knockwood?
5 Powerhouse, Valentine, Scoot, and Little Brother are the four most clearly defined characters in the story. What does each name suggest about the music each prefers? The instruments each plays? The comments each makes?
6 What does the final utterance in the story mean?

TOPICS FOR COMPOSITION

1 Write an essay discussing the use of language as cultural expression in the story "Powerhouse." Relate your terms to those defined by LeRoi Jones in "Expressive Language."
2 By expanding your answer to question 2 above, write an essay showing that music underscores the structure of the story.
3 Either support or refute the assumption that Gypsy is dead and Uranus Knockwood is involved.

"The Real Thing" depicts one of James's attempts to define the illusive artistic impression of reality; therefore, it is not the Monarchs who should capture our main interest, but, rather, we should follow the painter-narrator as he searches for his concept of reality. James's definition emerges as he places contrasting models before his painter-narrator. Notice the following:

1 The Monarchs, whose appearances seem to be reality itself
2 Miss Churm, whose appearance and actions contradict the artist's view of her
3 Oronte, who, lacking the affinity of either nationality or language, seems least appropriate of all

THE REAL THING

Henry James

I

When the porter's wife (she used to answer the house-bell), announced "A gentleman—with a lady, sir," I had, as I often had in those days, for the wish was father to the thought, an immediate vision of sitters. Sitters my visitors in this case proved to be; but not in the sense I should have preferred. However, there was nothing at first to indicate that they might not have come for a portrait. The gentleman, a man of fifty, very high and very straight, with a moustache slightly grizzled and a dark grey walking-coat admirably fitted, both of which I noted professionally—I don't mean as a barber or yet as a tailor—would have struck me as a celebrity if celebrities often were striking. It was a truth of which I had for some time been conscious that a figure with a good deal of frontage was, as one might say, almost never a public institution. A glance at the lady helped to remind me of this paradoxical law: she also looked too distinguished to be a "personality." Moreover one would scarcely come across two variations together.

Neither of the pair spoke immediately—they only prolonged the preliminary gaze which suggested that each wished to give the other a chance. They were visibly shy; they stood there letting me take them in—which, as I afterwards perceived, was the most practical thing they could have done. In this way their embarrassment served their cause. I had seen people painfully reluctant to mention that they desired anything so gross as to be represented on canvas; but the scruples of my new friends appeared almost insurmountable. Yet the gentleman might have said "I should like a portrait of my wife," and the lady might have said "I should like a portrait of my husband." Perhaps they were not husband and wife—this naturally would make the matter more delicate. Perhaps they wished to be done together—in which case they ought to have brought a third person to break the news.

"We come from Mr. Rivet," the lady said at last, with a dim smile which had the effect of a moist sponge passed over a "sunk" piece of painting, as well as of a vague allusion to vanished beauty. She was as tall and straight, in her degree, as her companion, and with ten years less to carry. She looked as sad as a woman could look whose face was not charged with expression; that is her tinted oval mask showed friction as an exposed surface shows it. The hand of time had played over her freely but only to simplify. She was slim and stiff, and so well-dressed, in dark blue cloth, with lappets and pockets and buttons, that it was clear she employed the same tailor as her husband. The couple had an indefinable air of prosperous thrift—they evidently got a good deal of luxury for their money. If I was to be one of their luxuries it would behoove me to consider my terms.

"Ah, Claude Rivet recommended me?" I inquired; and I added that it was very kind of him, though I could reflect that, as he only painted landscape, this was not a sacrifice.

The lady looked very hard at the gentleman, and the gentleman looked round the room. Then staring at the floor a moment and stroking his moustache, he rested his pleasant eyes on me with the remark: "He said you were the right one."

"I try to be, when people want to sit."

"Yes, we should like to," said the lady anxiously.

"Do you mean together?"

My visitors exchanged a glance. "If you could do anything with *me,* I suppose it would be double," the gentleman stammered.

"Oh yes, there's naturally a higher charge for two figures than for one."

"We should like to make it pay," the husband confessed.

"That's very good of you," I returned, appreciating so unwonted a sympathy—for I supposed he meant pay the artist.

A sense of strangeness seemed to dawn on the lady. "We mean for the illustrations—Mr. Rivet said you might put one in."

"Put one in—an illustration?" I was equally confused.

"Sketch her off, you know," said the gentleman, colouring.

It was only then that I understood the service Claude Rivet had rendered me; he had told them that I worked in black and white, for magazines, for story-books, for sketches of contemporary life, and consequently had frequent employment for models. These things were true, but it was not less true (I may confess it now—whether because the aspiration was to lead to everything or to nothing I leave the reader to guess), that I couldn't get the honours, to say nothing of the emoluments, of a great painter of portraits out of my head. My "illustrations" were my pot-boilers; I looked to a different branch of art (far and away the most interesting it had always seemed to me) to perpetuate my fame. There was no shame in looking to it also to make any fortune; but that fortune was by so much further from being made from the moment my visitors wished to be "done" for nothing. I was disappointed; for in the pictorial sense I had immediately *seen* them. I had seized their type—I had already settled what I would do with it. Something that wouldn't absolutely have pleased them, I afterwards reflected.

"Ah, you're—you're—a—?" I began, as soon as I had mastered my surprise. I couldn't bring out the dingy word "models"; it seemed to fit the case so little.

"We haven't had much practice," said the lady.

"We've got to *do* something, and we've thought that an artist in your line might perhaps make something of us," her husband threw off. He further mentioned that they didn't know many artists and that they had gone first, on the off-chance (he painted views of course, but sometimes put in figures—perhaps I remembered), to Mr. Rivet, whom they had met a few years before at a place in Norfolk where he was sketching.

"We used to sketch a little ourselves," the lady hinted.

"It's very awkward, but we absolutely *must* do something," her husband went on.

"Of course, we're not so *very* young," she admitted, with a wan smile.

With the remark that I might as well know something more about them, the husband had handed me a card extracted from a neat new pocket-book (their appurtenances were all of the freshest) and inscribed with the words "Major Monarch." Impressive as these words were they didn't carry my knowledge much further; but my visitor presently added: "I've left the army, and we've had the misfortune to lose our money. In fact our means are dreadfully small."

"It's an awful bore," said Mrs. Monarch.

They evidently wished to be discreet—to take care not to swagger because they were gentlefolks. I perceived they would have been willing to recognise this as something of a drawback, at the same time that I guessed at an underlying sense—their consolation in adversity—that they *had* their points. They certainly had; but these advantages struck me as preponderantly social; such for instance as would help to make a drawing-room look well. However, a drawing-room was always, or ought to be, a picture.

In consequence of his wife's allusion to their age Major Monarch observed: "Naturally, it's more for the figure that we thought of going in. We can still hold ourselves up." On the instant I saw that the figure was indeed their strong point. His "naturally" didn't sound vain, but it lighted up the question. *"She* has got the best," he continued, nodding at his wife, with a pleasant after-dinner absence of circumlocution. I could only reply, as if we were in fact sitting over our wine, that this didn't prevent his own from being very good; which led him in turn to rejoin: "We thought that if you ever have to do people like us, we might be something like it. *She,* particularly—for a lady in a book, you know."

I was so amused by them that, to get more of it, I did my best to take their point of view; and though it was an embarrassment to find myself appraising physically, as if they were animals on hire or useful blacks, a pair whom I should have expected to meet only in one of the relations in which criticism is tacit, I looked at Mrs. Monarch judicially enough to be able to exclaim, after a moment, with conviction: "Oh yes, a lady in a book!" She was singularly like a bad illustration.

"We'll stand up, if you like," said the Major; and he raised himself before me with a really grand air.

I could take his measure at a glance—he was six feet two and a perfect gentleman. It would have paid any club in process of formation and in want of a stamp to engage him at a salary to stand in the principal window. What struck me immediately was that in coming to me they had rather missed their vocation; they could surely have been turned to better account for advertising purposes. I couldn't of course see the thing in detail, but I could see them make someone's fortune—I don't mean their own.

There was something in them for a waistcoat-maker, an hotel-keeper or a soap-vendor. I could imagine "We always use it" pinned on their bosoms with the greatest effect; I had a vision of the promptitude with which they would launch a table d'hôte.

Mrs. Monarch sat still, not from pride but from shyness, and presently her husband said to her: "Get up my dear and show how smart you are." She obeyed, but she had no need to get up to show it. She walked to the end of the studio, and then she came back blushing, with her fluttered eyes on her husband. I was reminded of an incident I had accidentally had a glimpse of in Paris—being with a friend there, a dramatist about to produce a play—when an actress came to him to ask to be intrusted with a part. She went through her paces before him, walked up and down as Mrs. Monarch was doing. Mrs. Monarch did it quite as well, but I abstained from applauding. It was very odd to see such people apply for such poor pay. She looked as if she had ten thousand a year. Her husband had used the word that described her: she was, in the London current jargon, essentially and typically "smart." Her figure was, in the same order of ideas, conspicuously and irreproachably "good." For a woman of her age her waist was surprisingly small; her elbow moreover had the orthodox crook. She held her head at the conventional angle; but why did she come to *me*? She ought to have tried on jackets at a big shop. I feared my visitors were not only destitute, but "artistic"—which would be a great complication. When she sat down again I thanked her, observing that what a draughtsman most valued in his model was the faculty of keeping quiet.

"Oh, *she* can keep quiet," said Major Monarch. Then he added, jocosely: "I've always kept her quiet."

"I'm not a nasty fidget, am I?" Mrs. Monarch appealed to her husband.

He addressed his answer to me. "Perhaps it isn't out of place to mention—because we ought to be quite business-like, oughtn't we?—that when I married her she was known as the Beautiful Statue."

"Oh dear!" said Mrs. Monarch, ruefully.

"Of course I should want a certain amount of expression," I rejoined.

"Of *course!*" they both exclaimed.

"And then I suppose you know that you'll get awfully tired."

"Oh, we *never* get tired!" they eagerly cried:

"Have you had any kind of practice?"

They hesitated—they looked at each other. "We've been photographed, *immensely,*" said Mrs. Monarch.

"She means the fellows have asked us," added the Major.

"I see—because you're so good-looking."

"I don't know what they thought, but they were always after us."

"We always got our photographs for nothing," smiled Mrs. Monarch.

"We might have brought some, my dear," her husband remarked.

"I'm not sure we have any left. We've given quantities away," she explained to me.

"With our autographs and that sort of thing," said the Major.

"Are they to be got in the shops?" I inquired, as a harmless pleasantry.

"Oh, yes; *hers*—they used to be."

"Not now," said Mrs. Monarch, with her eyes on the floor.

II

I could fancy the "sort of thing" they put on the presentation-copies of their photographs, and I was sure they wrote a beautiful hand. It was odd how quickly I was sure of everything that concerned them. If they were now so poor as to have to earn shillings and pence, they never had had much of a margin. Their good looks had been their capital, and they had good-humouredly made the most of the career that this resource marked out for them. It was in their faces, the blankness, the deep intellectual repose of the twenty years of country-house visiting which had given them pleasant intonations. I could see the sunny drawing-rooms, sprinkled with periodicals she didn't read, in which Mrs. Monarch had continuously sat; I could see the wet shrubberies in which she had walked, equipped to admiration for either exercise. I could see the rich covers the Major had helped to shoot and the wonderful garments in which, late at night, he repaired to the smoking-room to talk about them. I could imagine their leggings and waterproofs, their knowing tweeds and rugs, their rolls of sticks and cases of tackle and neat umbrellas; and I could evoke the exact appearance of their servants and the compact variety of their luggage on the platforms of country stations.

They gave small tips, but they were liked; they didn't do anything themselves, but they were welcome. They looked so well everywhere; they gratified the general relish for stature, complexion and "form." They knew it without fatuity or vulgarity, and they respected themselves in consequence. They were not superficial; they were thorough and kept themselves up—it had been their line. People with such a taste for activity had to have some line. I could feel how, even in a dull house, they could have been counted upon for cheerfulness. At present something had happened—it didn't matter what, their little income had grown less, it had grown least—and they had to do something for pocket-money. Their friends liked them, but didn't like to support them. There was something about them that represented credit—their clothes, their manners, their type; but if credit is a large empty pocket in which an occasional chink reverberates, the chink at least must be audible. What they wanted of me was to help to make it so. Fortunately they had no children—I soon divined that. They would also perhaps wish our relations to be kept secret: this was why it was "for the figure"—the reproduction of the face would betray them.

I liked them—they were so simple; and I had no objection to them if they would suit. But, somehow, with all their perfections I didn't easily believe in them. After all they were amateurs, and the ruling passion of my life was the detestation of the amateur. Combined with this was another perversity—an innate preference for the represented subject over the real one: the defect of the real one was so apt to be a lack of representation. I liked things that appeared; then one was sure. Whether they *were* or not was a subordinate and almost always a profitless question. There were other considerations, the first of which was that I already had two or three people in use, notably a young person with big feet, in alpaca, from Kilburn, who for a couple of years had come to me regularly for my illustrations and with whom I was still—perhaps ignobly—satisfied. I frankly explained to my visitors how the case stood; but they had taken more precautions than I supposed. They had reasoned out their opportunity, for

Claude Rivet had told them of the projected *édition de luxe* of one of the writers of our day—the rarest of the novelists—who, long neglected by the multitudinous vulgar and dearly prized by the attentive (need I mention Philip Vincent?), had had the happy fortune of seeing, late in life, the dawn and then the full light of a higher criticism—an estimate in which, on the part of the public, there was something really of expiation. The edition in question, planned by a publisher of taste, was practically an act of high reparation; the wood-cuts with which it was to be enriched were the homage of English art to one of the most independent representatives of English letters. Major and Mrs. Monarch confessed to me that they had hoped I might be able to work *them* into my share of the enterprise. They knew I was to do the first of the books, "Rutland Ramsay," but I had to make clear to them that my participation in the rest of the affair—this first book was to be a test—was to depend on the satisfaction I should give. If this should be limited my employers would drop me without a scruple. It was therefore a crisis for me, and naturally I was making special preparations, looking about for new people, if they should be necessary, and securing the best types. I admitted however that I should like to settle down to two or three good models who would do for everything.

"Should we have often to—a—put on special clothes?" Mrs. Monarch timidly demanded.

"Dear, yes—that's half the business."

"And should we be expected to supply our own costumes?"

"Oh, no; I've got a lot of things. A painter's models put on—or put off—anything he likes."

"And do you mean—a—the same?"

"The same?"

Mrs. Monarch looked at her husband again.

"Oh, she was just wondering," he explained, "if the costumes are in *general* use." I had to confess that they were, and I mentioned further that some of them (I had a lot of genuine, greasy last-century things), had served their time, a hundred years ago, on living, world-stained men and women. "We'll put on anything that *fits*," said the Major.

"Oh, I arrange that—they fit in the pictures."

"I'm afraid I should do better for the modern books. I would come as you like," said Mrs. Monarch.

"She has got a lot of clothes at home: they might do for contemporary life," her husband continued:

"Oh, I can fancy scenes in which you'd be quite natural." And indeed I could see the slipshod rearrangements of stale properties—the stories I tried to produce pictures for without the exasperation of reading them—whose sandy tracts the good lady might help to people. But I had to return to the fact that for this sort of work—the daily mechanical grind—I was already equipped; the people I was working with were fully adequate.

"We only thought we might be more like *some* characters," said Mrs. Monarch mildly, getting up.

Her husband also rose; he stood looking at me with a dim wistfulness that was touching in so fine a man. "Wouldn't it be rather a pull sometimes to have—a—to have—?'' He hung fire; he wanted me to help him by phrasing what he meant. But I couldn't—I didn't know. So he brought it out, awkwardly. ''The *real* thing; a gentleman, you know, or a lady.'' I was quite ready to give a general assent—I admitted that there was a great deal in that. This encouraged Major Monarch to say, following up his appeal with an unacted gulp: ''It's awfully hard—we've tried everything.'' The gulp was communicative; it proved too much for his wife. Before I knew it Mrs. Monarch had dropped again upon a divan and burst into tears. Her husband sat down beside her, holding one of her hands; whereupon she quickly dried her eyes with the other, while I felt embarrassed as she looked up at me. ''There isn't a confounded job I haven't applied for—waited for—prayed for. You can fancy we'd be pretty bad first. Secretaryships and that sort of thing? You might as well ask for a peerage. I'd be *anything*—I'm strong; a messenger or a coalheaver. I'd put on a gold-laced cap and open carriage-doors in front of the haberdasher's; I'd hang about a station to carry portmanteaus; I'd be a postman. But they won't *look* at you; there are thousands, as good as yourself, already on the ground. *Gentlemen,* poor beggars, who have drunk their wine, who have kept their hunters!''

I was as reassuring as I knew how to be, and my visitors were presently on their feet again while, for the experiment, we agreed on an hour. We were discussing it when the door opened and Miss Churm came in with a wet umbrella. Miss Churm had to take the omnibus to Maida Vale and then walk half-a-mile. She looked a trifle blowsy and slightly splashed. I scarcely ever saw her come in without thinking afresh how odd it was that, being so little in herself, she should yet be so much in others. She was a meagre little Miss Churm, but she was an ample heroine of romance. She was only a freckled cockney, but she could represent everything, from a fine lady to a shepherdess; she had the faculty, as she might have had a fine voice or long hair. She couldn't spell, and she loved beer, but she had two or three ''points,'' and practice, and a knack, and mother-wit, and a kind of whimsical sensibility, and a love of the theatre, and seven sisters, and not an ounce of respect, especially for the *h.* The first thing my visitors saw was that her umbrella was wet, and in their spotless perfection they visibly winced at it. The rain had come on since their arrival.

''I'm all in a soak; there *was* a mess of people in the 'bus. I wish you lived near a stytion,'' said Miss Churm. I requested her to get ready as quickly as possible, and she passed into the room in which she always changed her dress. But before going out she asked me what she was to get into this time.

''It's the Russian princess, don't you know?'' I answered; ''the one with the 'golden eyes,' in black velvet, for the long thing in the *Cheapside.*''

''Golden eyes? I *say!*'' cried Miss Churm, while my companions watched her with intensity as she withdrew. She always arranged herself, when she was late, before I could turn around; and I kept my visitors a little, on purpose, so that they might get an idea, from seeing her, what would be expected of themselves. I mentioned that she was quite my notion of an excellent model—she was really very clever.

''Do you think she looks like a Russian princess?'' Major Monarch asked, with lurking alarm.

''When I make her, yes.''

''Oh, if you have to *make* her—!'' he reasoned, acutely.

"That's the most you can ask. There are so many that are not makeable."

"Well now, *here's* a lady"—and with a persuasive smile he passed his arm into his wife's—"who's already made!"

"Oh, I'm not a Russian princess," Mrs. Monarch protested, a little coldly. I could see that she had known some and didn't like them. There, immediately, was a complication of a kind that I never had to fear with Miss Churm.

The young lady came back in black velvet—the gown was rather rusty and very low on her lean shoulders—and with a Japanese fan in her red hands. I reminded her that in the scene I was doing she had to look over someone's head. "I forgot whose it is; but it doesn't matter. Just look over a head."

"I'd rather look over a stove," said Miss Churm; and she took her station near the fire. She fell into position, settled herself into a tall attitude, gave a certain backward inclination to her head and a certain forward droop to her fan, and looked, at least to my prejudiced sense, distinguished and charming, foreign and dangerous. We left her looking so, while I went down-stairs with Major and Mrs. Monarch.

"I think I could come about as near it as that," said Mrs. Monarch.

"Oh, you think she's shabby, but you must allow for the alchemy of art."

However, they went off with an evident increase of comfort, founded on their demonstrable advantage in being the real thing. I could fancy them shuddering over Miss Churm. She was very droll about them when I went back, for I told her what they wanted.

"Well, if *she* can sit I'll tyke to bookkeeping," said my model.

"She's very lady-like," I replied, as an innocent form of aggravation.

"So much the worse for *you.* That means she can't turn round."

"She'll do for the fashionable novels."

"Oh yes, she'll *do* for them!" my model humorously declared. "Ain't they bad enough without her?" I had often sociably denounced them to Miss Churm.

III

It was for the elucidation of a mystery in one of these works that I first tried Mrs. Monarch. Her husband came with her, to be useful if necessary—it was sufficiently clear that as a general thing he would prefer to come with her. At first I wondered if this were for "propriety's" sake—if he were going to be jealous and meddling. The idea was too tiresome, and if it had been confirmed it would speedily have brought our acquaintance to a close. But I soon saw there was nothing in it and that if he accompanied Mrs. Monarch it was (in addition to the chance of being wanted), simply because he had nothing else to do. When she was away from him his occupation was gone—she never *had* been away from him. I judged, rightly, that in their awkward situation their close union was their main comfort and that this union had no weak spot. It was a real marriage, an encouragement to the hesitating, a nut for pessimists to crack. Their address was humble (I remember afterwards thinking it had been the only thing about them that was really professional), and I could fancy the lamentable lodgings in which the Major would have been left alone. He could bear them with his wife—he couldn't bear them without her.

He had too much tact to try and make himself agreeable when he couldn't be useful; so he simply sat and waited, when I was too absorbed in my work to talk. But I liked to make him talk—it made my work, when it didn't interrupt it, less sordid, less special. To listen to him was to combine the excitement of going out with the economy of staying at home. There was only one hindrance: that I seemed not to know any of the people he and his wife had known. I think he wondered extremely, during the term of our intercourse, whom the deuce I *did* know. He hadn't a stray sixpence of an idea to fumble for; so we didn't spin it very fine—we confined ourselves to questions of leather and even of liquor (saddlers and breeches-makers and how to get good claret cheap), and matters like "good trains" and the habits of small game. His lore on these last subjects was astonishing, he managed to interweave the station-master with the ornithologist. When he couldn't talk about greater things he could talk cheerfully about smaller, and since I couldn't accompany him into reminiscences of the fashionable world he could lower the conversation without a visible effort to my level.

So earnest a desire to please was touching in a man who could so easily have knocked one down. He looked after the fire and had an opinion on the draught of the stove, without my asking him, and I could see that he thought many of my arrangements not half clever enough. I remember telling him that if I were only rich I would offer him a salary to come and teach me how to live. Sometimes he gave a random sigh, of which the essence was: "Give me even such a bare old barrack as *this,* and I'd do something with it!" When I wanted to use him he came alone; which was an illustration of the superior courage of women. His wife could bear her solitary second floor, and she was in general more discreet; showing by various small reserves that she was alive to the propriety of keeping our relations markedly professional—not letting them slide into sociability. She wished it to remain clear that she and the Major were employed, not cultivated, and if she approved of me as a superior, who could be kept in his place, she never thought me quite good enough for an equal.

She sat with great intensity, giving the whole of her mind to it, and was capable of remaining for an hour almost as motionless as if she were before a photographer's lens. I could see she had been photographed often, but somehow the very habit that made her good for that purpose unfitted her for mine. At first I was extremely pleased with her lady-like air, and it was a satisfaction, on coming to follow her lines, to see how good they were and how far they could lead the pencil. But after a few times I began to find her too insurmountably stiff; do what I would with it my drawing looked like a photograph or a copy of a photograph. Her figure had no variety of expression— she herself had no sense of variety. You may say that this was my business, was only a question of placing her. I placed her in every conceivable position, but she managed to obliterate their differences. She was always a lady certainly, and into the bargain was always the same lady. She was the real thing, but always the same thing. There were moments when I was oppressed by the serenity of her confidence that she *was* the real thing. All her dealings with me and all her husband's were an implication that this was lucky for *me.* Meanwhile I found myself trying to invent types that approached her own, instead of making her own transform itself—in the clever way that was not impossible, for instance, to poor Miss Churm. Arrange as I would and take the precautions I would, she always, in my pictures, came out too tall—landing me in the dilemma of having represented a fascinating woman as seven feet high, which, out of respect perhaps to my own very much scantier inches, was far from my idea of such a person-age.

The case was worse with the Major—nothing I could do would keep *him* down, so that he became useful only for the representation of brawny giants. I adored variety and range, I cherished human accidents, the illustrative note; I wanted to characterise closely, and the thing in the world I most hated was the danger of being ridden by a type. I had quarrelled with some of my friends about it—I had parted company with them for maintaining that one *had* to be, and that if the type was beautiful (witness Raphael and Leonardo), the servitude was only a gain. I was neither Leonardo nor Raphael; I might only be a presumptuous young modern searcher, but I held that everything was to be sacrificed sooner than character. When they averred that the haunting type in question could easily *be* character, I retorted, perhaps superficially: "Whose?" It couldn't be everybody's—it might end in being nobody's.

After I had drawn Mrs. Monarch a dozen times I perceived more clearly than before that the value of such a model as Miss Churm resided precisely in the fact that she had no positive stamp, combined of course with the other fact that what she did have was a curious and inexplicable talent for imitation. Her usual appearance was like a curtain which she could draw up at request for a capital performance. This perform-ance was simply suggestive; but it was a word to the wise—it was vivid and pretty. Sometimes, even, I thought it, though she was plain herself, too insipidly pretty; I made it a reproach to her that the figures drawn from her were monotonously (*bêtement,* as we used to say) graceful. Nothing made her more angry: it was so much her pride to feel that she could sit for characters that had nothing in common with each other. She would accuse me at such moments of taking away her "reputytion."

It suffered a certain shrinkage, this queer quantity, from the repeated visits of my new friends. Miss Churm was greatly in demand, never in want of employment, so I had no scruple in putting her off occasionally, to try them more at my ease. It was certainly amusing at first to do the real thing—it was amusing to do Major Monarch's trousers. They *were* the real thing, even if he did come out colossal. It was amusing to do his wife's back hair (it was so mathematically neat), and the particular "smart" tension of her tight stays. She lent herself especially to positions in which the face was somewhat averted or blurred; she abounded in lady-like back views and *profils perdus.* When she stood erect she took naturally one of the attitudes in which court-painters represent queens and princesses; so that I found myself wondering whether, to draw out this accomplishment, I couldn't get the editor of the *Cheapside* to publish a really royal romance, "A Tale of Buckingham Palace." Sometimes, however, the real thing and the make-believe came into contact; by which I mean that Miss Churm, keeping an ap-pointment or coming to make one on days when I had much work in hand, encountered her invidious rivals. The encounter was not on their part, for they noticed her no more than if she had been the housemaid; not from intentional loftiness, but simply because, as yet, professionally, they didn't know how to fraternise, as I could guess that they would have liked—or at least that the Major would. They couldn't talk about the omni-bus—they always walked; and they didn't know what else to try—she wasn't inter-ested in good trains or cheap claret. Besides, they must have felt—in the air—that she was amused at them, secretly derisive of their ever knowing how. She was not a person to conceal her scepticism if she had had a chance to show it. On the other hand Mrs. Monarch didn't think her tidy; for why else did she take pains to say to me (it was going out of the way, for Mrs. Monarch), that she didn't like dirty women?

One day when my young lady happened to be present with my other sitters (she even dropped in, when it was convenient, for a chat), I asked her to be so good as to lend a hand in getting tea—a service with which she was familiar and which was one of a class that, living as I did in a small way, with slender domestic resources, I often appealed to my models to render. They liked to lay hands on my property, to break the sitting, and sometimes the china—I made them feel Bohemian. The next time I saw Miss Churm after this incident she surprised me greatly by making a scene about it— she accused me of having wished to humiliate her. She had not resented the outrage at the time, but had seemed obliging and amused, enjoying the comedy of asking Mrs. Monarch, who sat vague and silent, whether she would have cream and sugar, and putting an exaggerated simper into the question. She had tried intonations—as if she too wished to pass for the real thing; till I was afraid my other visitors would take offence.

Oh, *they* were determined not to do this; and their touching patience was the measure of their great need. They would sit by the hour, uncomplaining, till I was ready to use them; they would come back on the chance of being wanted and would walk away cheerfully if they were not. I used to go to the door with them to see in what magnificent order they retreated. I tried to find other employment for them—I intro-duced them to several artists. But they didn't "take," for reasons I could appreciate, and I became conscious, rather anxiously, that after such disappointments they fell back upon me with a heavier weight. They did me the honour to think that it was I who was most *their* form. They were not picturesque enough for the painters, and in those days there were not so many serious workers in black and white. Besides, they had an eye to the great job I had mentioned to them—they had secretly set their hearts on supplying the right essence for my pictorial vindication of our fine novelist. They knew that for this undertaking I should want no costume-effects, none of the frippery of past ages—that it was a case in which everything would be contemporary and satirical and, presumably, genteel. If I could work them into it their future would be assured, for the labour would of course be long and the occupation steady.

One day Mrs. Monarch came without her husband—she explained his absence by his having had to go to the City. While she sat there in her usual anxious stiffness there came, at the door, a knock which I immediately recognised as the subdued appeal of a model out of work. It was followed by the entrance of a young man whom I easily perceived to be a foreigner and who proved in fact an Italian acquainted with no English word but my name, which he uttered in a way that made it seem to include all others. I had not then visited his country, nor was I proficient in his tongue; but as he was not so meanly constituted—what Italian is?—as to depend only on that member of expression he conveyed to me, in familiar but graceful mimicry, that he was in search of exactly the employment in which the lady before me was engaged. I was not struck with him at first, and while I continued to draw I emitted rough sounds of discourage-ment and dismissal. He stood his ground, however, not importunately, but with a dumb, dog-like fidelity in his eyes which amounted to innocent impudence—the manner of a devoted servant (he might have been in the house for years), unjustly suspected. Suddenly I saw that this very attitude and expression made a picture, whereupon I told him to sit down and wait till I should be free. There was another picture in the way he obeyed me, and I observed as I worked that there were others still in the way he looked wonderingly, with his head thrown back, about the high studio. He might have been crossing himself in St. Peter's. Before I finished I said to myself: "The fellow's a bankrupt orange-monger, but he's a treasure."

When Mrs. Monarch withdrew he passed across the room like a flash to open the door for her, standing there with the rapt, pure gaze of the young Dante spellbound by the young Beatrice. As I never insisted, in such situations, on the blankness of the British domestic, I reflected that he had the making of a servant (and I needed one, but couldn't pay him to be only that), as well as of a model; in short I made up my mind to adopt my bright adventurer if he would agree to officiate in the double capacity. He jumped at my offer, and in the event my rashness (for I had known nothing about him), was not brought home to me. He proved a sympathetic though a desultory ministrant, and had in a wonderful degree the *sentiment de la pose*. It was uncultivated, instinctive; a part of the happy instinct which had guided him to my door and helped him to spell out my name on the card nailed to it. He had had no other introduction to me than a guess, from the shape of my high north window, seen outside, that my place was a studio and that as a studio it would contain an artist. He had wandered to England in search of fortune, like other itinerants, and had embarked, with a partner and a small green hand-cart, on the sale of penny ices. The ices had melted away and the partner had dissolved in their train. My young man wore tight yellow trousers with reddish stripes and his name was Oronte. He was sallow but fair, and when I put him into some old clothes of my own he looked like an Englishman. He was as good as Miss Churm, who could look, when required, like an Italian.

IV

I thought Mrs. Monarch's face slightly convulsed when, on her coming back with her husband, she found Oronte installed. It was strange to have to recognise in a scrap of a lazzarone a competitor to her magnificent Major. It was she who scented danger first, for the Major was anecdotically unconscious. But Oronte gave us tea, with a hundred eager confusions (he had never seen such a queer process), and I think she thought better of me for having at last an "establishment." They saw a couple of drawings that I had made of the establishment, and Mrs. Monarch hinted that it never would have struck her that he had sat for them. "Now the drawings you make from *us*, they look exactly like us," she reminded me, smiling in triumph; and I recognised that this was indeed just their defect. When I drew the Monarchs I couldn't, somehow, get away from them—get into the character I wanted to represent; and I had not the least desire my model should be discoverable in my picture. Miss Churm never was, and Mrs. Monarch thought I hid her, very properly, because she was vulgar; whereas if she was lost it was only as the dead who go to heaven are lost—in the gain of an angel the more.

By this time I had got a certain start with "Rutland Ramsay," the first novel in the great projected series; that is I had produced a dozen drawings, several with the help of the Major and his wife, and I had sent them in for approval. My understanding with the publishers, as I have already hinted, had been that I was to be left to do my work, in this particular case, as I liked, with the whole book committed to me; but my connection with the rest of the series was only contingent. There were moments when, frankly, it *was* a comfort to have the real thing under one's hand; for there were characters in "Rutland Ramsay" that were very much like it. There were people presumably as straight as the Major and women of as good a fashion as Mrs. Monarch. There was a great deal of country-house life—treated, it is true, in a fine, fanciful, ironical, generalised way—and there was a considerable implication of knickerbockers and kilts. There were certain things I had to settle at the outset; such things for instance as the exact appearance of the hero, the particular bloom of the heroine. The author of course gave me a lead, but there was a margin for interpretation. I took the Monarchs into my confidence, I told them frankly what I was about, I mentioned my embarrassments and alternatives. "Oh, take *him!*" Mrs. Monarch murmured sweetly, looking at her husband; and "What could you want better than my wife?" the Major inquired, with the comfortable candour that now prevailed between us.

I was not obliged to answer these remarks—I was only obliged to place my sitters. I was not easy in mind, and I postponed, a little timidly perhaps, the solution of the question. The book was a large canvas, the other figures were numerous, and I worked off at first some of the episodes in which the hero and the heroine were not concerned. When once I had set *them* up I should have to stick to them—I couldn't make my young man seven feet high in one place and five feet nine in another. I inclined on the whole to the latter measurement, though the Major more then once reminded me that *he* looked about as young as anyone. It was indeed quite possible to arrange him, for the figure, so that it would have been difficult to detect his age. After the spontaneous Oronte had been with me a month, and after I had given him to understand several different times that his native exuberance would presently constitute an insurmountable barrier to our further intercourse, I waked to a sense of his heroic capacity. He was only five feet seven, but the remaining inches were latent. I tried him almost secretly at first, for I was really rather afraid of the judgment my other models would pass on such a choice. If they regarded Miss Churm as little better than a snare, what would they think of the representation by a person so little the real thing as an Italian street-vendor of a protagonist formed by a public school?

If I went a little in fear of them it was not because they bullied me, because they had got an oppressive foothold, but because in their really pathetic decorum and mysteriously permanent newness they counted on me so intensely. I was therefore very glad when Jack Hawley came home: he was always of such good counsel. He painted badly himself, but there was no one like him for putting his finger on the place. He had been absent from England for a year; he had been somewhere—I don't remember where—to get a fresh eye. I was in a good deal of dread of any such organ, but we were old friends; he had been away for months and a sense of emptiness was creeping into my life. I hadn't dodged a missile for a year.

He came back with a fresh eye, but with the same old black velvet blouse, and the first evening he spent in my studio we smoked cigarettes till the small hours. He had done no work himself, he had only got the eye; so the field was clear for the production of my little things. He wanted to see what I had done for the *Cheapside,* but he was disappointed in the exhibition. That at least seemed the meaning of two or three comprehensive groans which, as he lounged on my big divan, on a folded leg, looking at my latest drawings, issued from his lips with the smoke of the cigarette.

"What's the matter with you?" I asked.

"What's the matter with *you?*"

"Nothing save that I'm mystified."

"You are indeed. You're quite off the hinge. What's the meaning of this new fad?" And he tossed me, with visible irreverence, a drawing in which I happened to have depicted both my majestic models. I asked if he didn't think it good, and he replied that it struck him as execrable, given the sort of thing I had always represented myself to him as wishing to arrive at; but I let that pass. I was so anxious to see exactly what he meant. The two figures in the picture looked colossal, but I supposed this was *not* what he meant, inasmuch as, for aught he knew to the contrary, I might have been trying for that. I maintained that I was working exactly in the same way as when he last had done me the honour to commend me. "Well, there's a big hole somewhere," he answered; "wait a bit and I'll discover it." I depended upon him to do so; where else was the fresh eye? But he produced at last nothing more luminous than "I don't know—I don't like your types." This was lame, for a critic who had never consented to discuss with me anything but the question of execution, the direction of strokes and the mystery of values.

"In the drawings you've been looking at I think my types are very handsome."

"Oh, they won't do!"

"I've had a couple of new models."

"I see you have. *They* won't do."

"Are you very sure of that?"

"Absolutely—they're stupid."

"You mean *I* am—for I ought to get round that."

"You *can't*—with such people. Who are they?"

I told him, as far as was necessary, and he declared, heartlessly: *"Ce sont des gens qu'il faut mettre à la porte."*

"You've never seen them; they're awfully good," I compassionately objected.

"Not seen them? Why, all this recent work of yours drops to pieces with them. It's all I want to see of them."

"No one else has said anything against it—the *Cheapside* people are pleased."

"Everyone else is an ass, and the *Cheapside* people the biggest asses of all. Come, don't pretend, at this time of day, to have pretty illusions about the public, especially about publishers and editors. It's not for *such* animals you work—it's for those who know, *coloro che sanno;* so keep straight for *me* if you can't keep straight for yourself. There's a certain sort of thing you tried for from the first—and a very good thing it is. But this twaddle isn't *in* it." When I talked with Hawley later about "Rutland

Ramsay" and its possible successors he declared that I must get back into my boat again or I would go to the bottom. His voice in short was the voice of warning.

I noted the warning, but I didn't turn my friends out of doors. They bored me a good deal; but the very fact that they bored me admonished me not to sacrifice them—if there was anything to be done with them—simply to irritation. As I look back at this phase they seem to me to have pervaded my life not a little. I have a vision of them as most of the time in my studio, seated, against the wall, on an old velvet bench to be out of the way, and looking like a pair of patient courtiers in a royal antechamber. I am convinced that during the coldest weeks of the winter they held their ground because it saved them fire. Their newness was losing its gloss, and it was impossible not to feel that they were objects of charity. Whenever Miss Churm arrived they went away, and after I was fairly launched in "Rutland Ramsay" Miss Churm arrived pretty often. They managed to express to me tacitly that they supposed I wanted her for the low life of the book, and I let them suppose it, since they had attempted to study the work—it was lying about the studio—without discovering that it dealt only with the highest circles. They had dipped into the most brilliant of our novelists without deciphering many passages. I still took an hour from them, now and again, in spite of Jack Hawley's warning: it would be time enough to dismiss them, if dismissal should be necessary, when the rigour of the season was over. Hawley had made their acquaintance—he had met them at my fireside—and thought them a ridiculous pair. Learning that he was a painter they tried to approach him, to show him too that they were the real thing; but he looked at them, across the big room, as if they were miles away: they were a compendium of everything that he most objected to in the social system of his country. Such people as that, all convention and patent-leather, with ejaculations that stopped conversation, had no business in a studio. A studio was a place to learn to see, and how could you see through a pair of feather beds?

The main inconvenience I suffered at their hands was that, at first, I was shy of letting them discover how my artful little servant had begun to sit to me for "Rutland Ramsay." They knew that I had been odd enough (they were prepared by this time to allow oddity to artists), to pick a foreign vagabond out of the streets, when I might have had a person with whiskers and credentials; but it was some time before they learned how high I rated his accomplishments. They found him in an attitude more than once, but they never doubted I was doing him as an organ-grinder. There were several things they never guessed, and one of them was that for a striking scene in the novel, in which a footman briefly figured, it occurred to me to make use of Major Monarch as the menial. I kept putting this off, I didn't like to ask him to don the livery—besides the difficulty of finding a livery to fit him. At last, one day late in the winter, when I was at work on the despised Oronte (he caught one's idea in an instant), and was in the glow of feeling that I was going very straight, they came in, the Major and his wife, with their society laugh about nothing (there was less and less to laugh at), like country-callers—they always reminded me of that—who have walked across the park after church and are presently persuaded to stay to luncheon. Luncheon was over, but they could stay to tea—I knew they wanted it. The fit was on me, however, and I couldn't let my ardour cool and my work wait, with the fading daylight, while my model prepared it. So I asked

Mrs. Monarch if she would mind laying it out—a request which, for an instant, brought all the blood to her face. Her eyes were on her husband's for a second, and some mute telegraphy passed between them. Their folly was over the next instant; his cheerful shrewdness put an end to it. So far from pitying their wounded pride, I must add, I was moved to give it as complete a lesson as I could. They bustled about together and got out the cups and saucers and made the kettle boil. I know they felt as if they were waiting on my servant, and when the tea was prepared I said: "He'll have a cup, please—he's tired." Mrs. Monarch brought him one where he stood, and he took it from her as if he had been a gentleman at a party, squeezing a crush-hat with an elbow.

Then it came over me that she had made a great effort for me—made it with a kind of nobleness—and that I owed her a compensation. Each time I saw her after this I wondered what the compensation could be. I couldn't go on doing the wrong thing to oblige them. Oh, it *was* the wrong thing, the stamp of the work for which they sat—Hawley was not the only person to say it now. I sent in a large number of the drawings I had made for "Rutland Ramsay," and I received a warning that was more to the point than Hawley's. The artistic adviser of the house for which I was working was of opinion that many of my illustrations were not what had been looked for. Most of these illustrations were the subjects in which the Monarchs had figured. Without going into the question of what *had* been looked for, I saw at this rate I shouldn't get the other books to do. I hurled myself in despair upon Miss Churm, I put her through all her paces. I not only adopted Oronte publicly as my hero, but one morning when the Major looked in to see if I didn't require him to finish a figure for the *Cheapside,* for which he had begun to sit the week before, I told him that I had changed my mind—I would do the drawing from my man. At this my visitor turned pale and stood looking at me. "Is *he* your idea of an English gentleman?" he asked.

I was disappointed, I was nervous, I wanted to get on with my work; so I replied with irritation: "Oh, my dear Major—I can't be ruined for *you!*"

He stood another moment; then, without a word, he quitted the studio. I drew a long breath when he was gone, for I said to myself that I shouldn't see him again. I had not told him definitely that I was in danger of having my work rejected, but I was vexed at his not having felt the catastrophe in the air, read with me the moral of our fruitless collaboration, the lesson that, in the deceptive atmosphere of art, even the highest respectability may fail of being plastic.

I didn't owe my friends money, but I did see them again. They re-appeared together, three days later, and under the circumstances there was something tragic in the fact. It was a proof to me that they could find nothing else in life to do. They had threshed the matter out in a dismal conference—they had digested the bad news that they were not in for the series. If they were not useful to me even for the *Cheapside* their function seemed difficult to determine, and I could only judge at first that they had come, forgivingly, decorously, to take a last leave. This made me rejoice in secret that I had little leisure for a scene; for I had placed both my other models in position together and I was pegging away at a drawing from which I hoped to derive glory. It had been suggested by the passage in which Rutland Ramsay, drawing up a chair to Artemisia's piano-stool, says extraordinary things to her while she ostensibly fingers out a difficult piece of music. I had done Miss Churm at the piano before—it was an attitude in which she knew how to take on an absolutely poetic grace. I wished the two figures to "compose" together, intensely, and my little Italian had entered perfectly into my conception. The pair were vividly before me, the piano had been pulled out; it was a charming picture of blended youth and murmured love, which I had only to catch and keep. My visitors stood and looked at it, and I was friendly to them over my shoulder.

They made no response, but I was used to silent company and went on with my work, only a little disconcerted (even though exhilarated by the sense that *this* was at least the ideal thing), at not having got rid of them after all. Presently I heard Mrs. Monarch's sweet voice beside, or rather above me: "I wish her hair was a little better done." I looked up and she was staring with a strange fixedness at Miss Churm, whose back was turned to her. "Do you mind my just touching it?" she went on—a question which made me spring up for an instant, as with the instinctive fear that she might do the young lady a harm. But she quieted me with a glance I shall never forget—I confess I should like to have been able to paint *that*—and went for a moment to my model. She spoke to her softly, laying a hand upon her shoulder and bending over her; and as the girl, understanding, gratefully assented, she disposed her rough curls, with a few quick passes, in such a way as to make Miss Churm's head twice as charming. It was one of the most heroic personal services I have ever seen rendered. Then Mrs. Monarch turned away with a low sigh and, looking about her as if for something to do, stooped to the floor with a noble humility and picked up a dirty rag that had dropped out of my paint-box.

The Major meanwhile had also been looking for something to do and, wandering to the other end of the studio, saw before him my breakfast things, neglected, unre- moved. "I say, can't I be useful *here?* he called out to me with an irrepressible quaver. I assented with a laugh that I fear was awkward and for the next ten minutes, while I worked, I heard the light clatter of china and the tinkle of spoons and glass. Mrs. Monarch assisted her husband—they washed up my crockery, they put it away. They wandered off into my little scullery, and I afterwards found that they had cleaned my knives and that my slender stock of plate had an unprecedented surface. When it came over me, the latent eloquence of what they were doing, I confess that my drawing was blurred for a moment—the picture swam. They had accepted their failure, but they couldn't accept their fate. They had bowed their heads in bewilderment to the perverse and cruel law in virtue of which the real thing could be so much less precious than the unreal; but they didn't want to starve. If my servants were my models, my models might be my servants. They would reverse the parts—the others would sit for the ladies and gentlemen, and *they* would do the work. They would still be in the studio—it was an intense dumb appeal to me not to turn them out. "Take us on," they wanted to say— "we'll do *anything.*"

When all this hung before me the *afflatus* vanished—my pencil dropped from my hand. My sitting was spoiled and I got rid of my sitters, who were also evidently rather mystified and awestruck. Then, alone with the Major and his wife, I had a most uncom- fortable moment. He put their prayer into a single sentence: "I say, you know—just let *us* do for you, can't you?" I couldn't—it was dreadful to see them emptying my slops;

but I pretended I could, to oblige them, for about a week. Then I gave them a sum of money to go away; and I never saw then again. I obtained the remaining books, but my friend Hawley repeats that Major and Mrs. Monarch did me a permanent harm, got me into a second-rate trick. If it be true I am content to have paid the price—for the memory.

QUESTIONS

1 How does Mrs. Monarch's reference to photography reflect the layman's attitude toward art? What is the narrator's reaction to the photographic qualities of the Monarchs?
2 How does Miss Churm indicate the narrator's view of artistic reality? In the same sense, why is the name "Churm," appropriate? What does Oronte have to do with the narrator's changing attitude?
3 Why doesn't the narrator follow Jack Hawley's advice? Exactly what does Hawley mean when he calls the Monarchs stupid?
4 Do the Monarchs come to understand the artistic position? Explain.
5 Examine each of the narrator's remarks on the function and technique of art. How do these remarks fit into James's technique in the writing of this story?
6 What do you think the narrator means by his final remark?

TOPICS FOR COMPOSITION

1 In connection with your answer to question 6, write an essay showing the humanizing influence on the narrator brought about by his contact with the Monarchs. Your essay, of course, will be a character study and should move from supported assumptions about the narrator's initial attitude toward people into the changes seen by his deepening relationship with the Monarchs.
2 Major and Mrs. Monarch are also apt subjects for a character study. Questions that need answers seem to be: Are they completely superficial? Can there be depth to their married relationship? Do they deserve their fate? Have they wronged themselves or are they products of a wrong society?
3 Both "Powerhouse" and "The Real Thing" deal with the search for artistic expression, but the points of view differ quite distinctly. Write an essay contrasting point of view in the two stories. An essay of this type should have a definite purpose in mind; therefore decide on a specific thesis which the contrast will support. You may use, for example, topics such as: Type of Characters Dictates Point of View; Time Span Dictates Point of View; Setting Dictates Point of View.

DRAMA

Boats, ships, buildings, a city block, a village, even a cemetery—wherever a microcosm of a larger humanity can be assembled—have been used over and over in literature. Such a union of human lives is made possible by the Pullman car in Thornton Wilder's little play. All kinds of people with their variant destinies have come together ostensibly just to share the voyage from New York to Chicago. But as they voice their fears and anxieties, respond to the Stage Manager, even make trivial requests of the porter, we begin to sense a deeper unity—a terrible unity that links them not only to each other but also to a little town in Ohio, a field, a tramp, members of a track gang. And it is that unity that Wilder stresses in "Pullman Car Hiawatha," and makes of his setting (which requires almost nothing in stage properties) an imaginative unity, whereby the loneliness and anxiety of human lives are given a revelation, a beauty, a dignity usually denied in actual time and experience. As plain, even seemingly dull characters are summoned into the process of play making by the Stage Manager, they find their voices and their ways of expressing deep feelings and longings. Even when they resort to what we may evaluate as banal quotations and mottoes, for them the words have an eloquence and meaning which express their lives and their dreams. They become a microcosm not only of America (they represent various ages, vocations, backgrounds, and experiences) but also of humankind, unlimited by time and space.

1   The Stage Manager arbitrates between audience and characters much as the Chorus does in *Antigone* as he directs movement and voice (on one occasion, even translates from the Worker's German) into form and thus into art.
2   The reader of this play is at no particular disadvantage over the spectator in a theater, for both must supply much from the imagination and thus join the experience of play making.
3   Wilder makes a considerable effort to merge comic motifs with the pathos of his characters and their lonely voyages toward destinies of various degrees of darkness and fear.

PULLMAN CAR HIAWATHA

Thornton Wilder

At the back of the stage is a balcony or bridge or runway leading out of sight in both directions. Two flights of stairs descend from it to the stage. There is no further scenery.
At the rise of the curtain THE STAGE MANAGER *is making lines with a piece of chalk on the floor of the stage by the footlights.*

THE STAGE MANAGER   This is the plan of a Pullman car. Its name is Hiawatha and on December twenty-first it is on its way from New York to Chicago. Here at your left are three compartments. Here is the aisle and five lowers. The berths are all full,

363

uppers and lowers, but for the purposes of this play we are limiting our interest to the people in the lower berths on the further side only.

The berths are already made up. It is half-past nine. Most of the passengers are in bed behind the green curtains. They are dropping their shoes on the floor, or wrestling with their trousers, or wondering whether they dare hide their valuables in the pillow-slips during the night.

All right! Come on, everybody!

(The actors enter carrying chairs. Each improvises his berth by placing two chairs "facing one another" in his chalk-marked space. They then sit in one chair, profile to the audience, and rest their feet on the other. This must do for lying in bed. The passengers in the compartments do the same. Reading from left to right we have)

Compartment Three: *An* INSANE WOMAN *with a male attendant and a trained nurse.*

Compartment Two: PHILIP *and*

Compartment One: HARRIET, *his young wife.*

LOWER ONE: *A maiden lady.*

LOWER THREE: *A middle-aged doctor.*

LOWER FIVE: *A stout,. amiable woman of fifty.*

LOWER SEVEN; *An engineer going to California.*

LOWER NINE: *Another engineer.*

LOWER ONE   Porter, be sure and wake me up at quarter of six.

PORTER   Yes, mam.

LOWER ONE   I know I shan't sleep a wink, but I want to be told when it's quarter of six.

PORTER   Yes, mam.

LOWER SEVEN *(putting his head through the curtains)*   Hsst! Porter! Hsst! How the hell do you turn on this other light?

PORTER *(fussing with it)*   I'm afraid it's outa order, suh. You'll have to use the other end.

THE STAGE MANAGER *(falsetto, substituting for some woman in an upper berth)*   May I ask if some one in this car will be kind enough to lend me some aspirin?

PORTER *(rushing about)*   Yes, mam.

LOWER NINE *(one of these engineers, descending the aisle and falling into* LOWER FIVE*)*   Sorry, lady, sorry. Made a mistake.

LOWER FIVE *(grumbling)*   Never in all my born days!

LOWER ONE *(in a shrill whisper)*   Porter! Porter!

PORTER   Yes, mam.

LOWER ONE   My hot water bag's leaking. I guess you'll have to take it away. I'll have to do without it tonight. How awful!

LOWER FIVE *(sharply to the passenger above her)*   Young man, you mind your own business, or I'll report you to the conductor.

THE STAGE MANAGER *(substituting for* UPPER FIVE*)*   Sorry, mam, I didn't mean to upset you. My suspenders fell down and I was trying to catch them.

LOWER FIVE   Well, here they are. Now go to sleep. Everybody seems to be rushing into my berth tonight. *(She puts her head out.)* Porter! Porter! Be a good soul and bring me a glass of water, will you? I'm parched.

LOWER NINE   Bill! *(No answer)* Bill!

LOWER SEVEN   Ye'? Wha' d'y'a want?

LOWER NINE   Slip me one of those magazines, willya?

LOWER SEVEN   Which one d'y'a want?

LOWER NINE   Either one. "Detective Stories." Either one.

LOWER SEVEN   Aw, Fred. I'm just in the middle of one of'm in "Detective Stories."

LOWER NINE   That's all right. I'll take the "Western."—Thanks.

THE STAGE MANAGER *(to the actors)*   All right!—Sh! Sh! Sh!—. *(To the audience)* Now I want you to hear them thinking.

(There is a pause and then they all begin a murmuring-swishing noise, very soft. In turn each one of them can be heard above the others.)

LOWER FIVE *(the lady of fifty)*   Let's see: I've got the doll for the baby. And the slip-on for Marietta. And the fountain pen for Herbert. And the subscription to *Time* for George. . . .

LOWER SEVEN *(Bill)*   God! Lillian, if you don't turn out to be what I think you are, I don't know what I'll do.—I guess it's bad politics to let a woman know that you're going all the way to California to see her. I'll think up a song-and-dance about a business trip or something. Was I ever as hot and bothered about anyone like this before? Well, there was Martha. But that was different. I'd better try and read or I'll go cookoo. "How did you know it was ten o'clock when the visitor left the house?" asked the detective. "Because at ten o'clock," answered the girl, "I always turn out the lights in the conservatory and in the back hall. As I was coming down the stairs I heard the master talking to someone at the front door. I heard him say, 'Well, good night . . .'"—Gee, I don't feel like reading; I'll just think about Lillian. That yellow hair. Them eyes! . . .

LOWER THREE *(the doctor reads aloud to himself from a medical journal the most hair-raising material, every now and then punctuating his reading with an interrogative "So?").*

LOWER ONE *(the maiden lady)*   I know I'll be awake all night. I might just as well make up my mind to it now. I can't imagine what got hold of that hot water bag to leak on the train of all places. Well now, I'll lie on my right side and breathe deeply and think of beautiful things, and perhaps I can doze off a bit.

(and lastly)

LOWER NINE *(Fred)*   That was the craziest thing I ever did. It's set me back three whole years. I could have saved up thirty thousand dollars by now, if I'd only stayed over here. What business had I got to fool with contracts with the goddam Soviets. Hell, I thought it would be interesting. Interesting, what-the-hell! It's set me back three whole years. I don't even know if the company'll take me back. I'm green, that's all. I just don't grow up.

(The STAGE MANAGER strides toward them with lifted hand crying "Hush," and their whispering ceases.)

THE STAGE MANAGER   That'll do!—Just one minute. Porter!

THE PORTER *(appearing at the left)*   Yessuh.

THE STAGE MANAGER   It's your turn to think.

THE PORTER *(is very embarrassed).*

THE STAGE MANAGER   Don't you want to? You have a right to.

THE PORTER *(torn between the desire to release his thoughts and his shyness)*   Ah . . . ah . . . I'm only thinkin' about my home in Chicago and . . . and my life insurance.

THE STAGE MANAGER   That's right.

THE PORTER   . . . well, thank you. . . . Thank you. *(He slips away, blushing violently, in an agony of self-consciousness and pleasure.)*

THE STAGE MANAGER *(to the audience)*   He's a good fellow, Harrison is. Just shy. *(To the actors again)* Now the compartments, please.

(The berths fall into shadow. PHILIP *is standing at the door connecting his compartment with his wife's.)*

PHILIP   Are you all right, angel?

HARRIET   Yes. I don't know what was the matter with me during dinner.

PHILIP   Shall I close the door?

HARRIET   Do see whether you can't put a chair against it that will hold it half open without banging.

PHILIP   There.—Good night, angel. If you can't sleep, call me and we'll sit up and play Russian Bank.

HARRIET   You're thinking of that awful time when we sat up every night for a week. . . . But at least I know I shall sleep tonight. The noise of the wheels has become sort of nice and homely. What state are we in?

PHILIP   We're tearing through Ohio. We'll be in Indiana soon.

HARRIET   I know those little towns full of horseblocks.

PHILIP   Well, we'll reach Chicago very early. I'll call you. Sleep tight.

HARRIET   Sleep tight, darling.

He returns to his own compartment. In Compartment Three, THE MALE ATTENDANT *tips his chair back against the wall and smokes a cigar. The trained nurse knits a stocking.* THE INSANE WOMAN *leans her forehead against the windowpane, that is: stares into the audience.*

THE INSANE WOMAN *(her words have a dragging, complaining sound, but lack any conviction).*   Don't take me there. Don't take me there.

THE FEMALE ATTENDANT   Wouldn't you like to lie down, dearie?

THE INSANE WOMAN   I want to get off the train. I want to go back to New York.

THE FEMALE ATTENDANT   Wouldn't you like me to brush your hair again? It's such a nice feeling.

THE INSANE WOMAN *(going to the door)*   I want to get off the train. I want to open the door.

THE FEMALE ATTENDANT *(taking one of her hands)*   Such a noise! You'll wake up all the nice people. Come and I'll tell you a story about the place we're going to.

THE INSANE WOMAN   I don't want to go to that place.

THE FEMALE ATTENDANT   Oh, it's lovely! There are lawns and gardens everywhere. I never saw such a lovely place. Just lovely.

THE INSANE WOMAN *(lies down on the bed).* Are there roses?

THE FEMALE ATTENDANT Roses! Red, yellow, white . . . just everywhere.

THE MALE ATTENDANT *(after a pause)* That musta been Cleveland.

THE FEMALE ATTENDANT I had a case in Cleveland once. Diabetes.

THE MALE ATTENDANT *(after another pause)* I wisht I had a radio here. Radios are good for *them.* I had a patient once that had to have the radio going every minute.

THE FEMALE ATTENDANT Radios are lovely. My married niece has one. It's always going. It's wonderful.

THE INSANE WOMAN *(half rising)* I'm not beautiful. I'm not beautiful as she was.

THE FEMALE ATTENDANT Oh, I think you're beautiful! Beautiful.—Mr. Morgan, don't you think Mrs. Churchill is beautiful?

THE MALE ATTENDANT Oh, fine lookin'! Regular movie star, Mrs. Churchill.

(She looks inquiringly at them and subsides. HARRIET *groans slightly. Smothers a cough. She gropes about with her hand and finds the bell. The* PORTER *knocks at her door.)*

HARRIET *(whispering)* Come in. First, please close the door into my husband's room. Softly. Softly.

PORTER *(a plaintive porter)* Yes, mam.

HARRIET Porter, I'm not well. I'm sick. I must see a doctor.

PORTER Why, mam, they ain't no doctor . . .

HARRIET Yes, when I was coming out from dinner I saw a man in one of the seats on *that* side, reading medical papers. Go and wake him up.

PORTER *(flabbergasted)* Mam, I cain't wake anybody up.

HARRIET Yes, you can. Porter. Porter. Now don't argue with me. I'm very sick. It's my heart. Wake him up. Tell him it's my heart.

PORTER Yes, mam. *(He goes into the aisle and starts pulling the shoulder of the man in* LOWER THREE.*)*

LOWER THREE Hello. Hello. What is it? Are we there? *(The* PORTER *mumbles to him.)* I'll be right there.—Porter, is it a young woman or an old one?

PORTER I dono, suh. I guess she's kinda old, suh, but not so very old.

LOWER THREE Tell her I'll be there in a minute and to lie quietly.

(The PORTER *enters* HARRIET'S *compartment. She has turned her head away.)*

PORTER He'll be here in a minute, mam. He says you lie quiet.

*(*LOWER THREE *stumbles along the aisle muttering:* "Damn these shoes!")

SOMEONE'S VOICE Can't we have a little quiet in this car, please?

LOWER NINE *(Fred).* Oh, shut up!

(The DOCTOR *passes the* PORTER *and enters* HARRIET'S *compartment. He leans over her, concealing her by his stooping figure.)*

LOWER THREE She's dead, porter. Is there anyone on the train traveling with her?

PORTER Yessuh. Dat's her husband in dere.

LOWER THREE Idiot! Why didn't you call him? I'll go in and speak to him.

(The STAGE MANAGER *comes forward.)*

THE STAGE MANAGER   All right. So much for the inside of the car. That'll be enough of that for the present. Now for its position geographically, meteorologically, astronomically, theologically considered.

      Pullman Car Hiawatha, ten minutes of ten. December twenty-first, 1930. All ready. *(Some figures begin to appear on the balcony.)* No, no. It's not time for the planets yet. Nor the hours. *(They retire. The* STAGE MANAGER *claps his hands. A grinning boy in overalls enters from the left behind the berths.)* GROVER'S CORNERS, OHIO *(in a foolish voice as though he were reciting a piece at a Sunday School entertainment).* I represent Grover's Corners, Ohio. 821 souls. "There's so much good in the worst of us and so much bad in the best of us, that it ill behooves any of us to criticize the rest of us." Robert Louis Stevenson. Thankya.

(He grins and goes out right. Enter from the same direction somebody in shirt sleeves. This is a field.)

THE FIELD   I represent a field you are passing between Grover's Corners, Ohio, and Parkersburg, Ohio. In this field there are 51 gophers, 206 field mice, 6 snakes and millions of bugs, insects, ants, and spiders. All in their winter sleep. "What is so rare as a day in June? Then, if ever, come perfect days." *The Vision of Sir Launfal,* William Cullen—I mean James Russell Lowell. Thank you.

(Exit. Enter a tramp.)

THE TRAMP   I just want to tell you that I'm a tramp that's been traveling under this car, Hiawatha, so I have a right to be in this play. I'm going from Rochester, New York, to Joliet, Illinois. It takes a lotta people to make a world. "On the road to Mandalay, where the flying fishes play and the sun comes up like thunder, over China cross the bay." Frank W. Service. It's bitter cold. Thank you.

(Exit. Enter a gentle old farmer's wife with three stringy young people.)

PARKERSBURG, OHIO   I represent Parkersburg, Ohio. 2604 souls. I have seen all the dreadful havoc that alcohol has done and I hope no one here will ever touch a drop of the curse of this beautiful country. *(She beats a measure and they all sing unsteadily)* "Throw out the lifeline! Throw out the lifeline! Someone is sinking today-ay . . ."

*(*THE STAGE MANAGER *waves them away tactfully. Enter a workman.)*

THE WORKMAN   Ich bin der Arbeiter der hier sein Leben verlor. Bei der Sprengung für diese Brücke über die Sie in dem Moment fahren—*(The engine whistles for a trestle crossing—)* erschlug mich ein Felsbock. Ich spiele jetzt als Geist in diesem Stuck mit. "Vor sieben und achtzig Jahren haben unsere Väter auf diesem Continent eine neue Nation hervorgebracht. . . ."

THE STAGE MANAGER *(helpfully, to the audience)*   I'm sorry; that's in German. He says that he's the ghost of a workman who was killed while they were building the trestle over which the car Hiawatha is now passing—*(The engine whistles again)*—and he wants to appear in this play. A chunk of rock hit him while they were dynamiting.—His motto you know: "Three score and seven years ago our fathers brought forth upon this continent a new nation dedicated," and so on. Thank you, Mr. Krüger.

(Exit the GHOST. *Enter another* WORKER.*)*

THIS WORKER   I'm a watchman in a tower near Parkersburg, Ohio. I just want to tell you that I'm not asleep and that the signals are all right for this train. I hope you all have a fine trip. "If you can keep your heads when all about you are losing theirs and blaming it on you. . . ." Rudyard Kipling. Thank you.

(Exit. THE STAGE MANAGER *comes forward.)*

THE STAGE MANAGER   All right. That'll be enough of that. Now the weather.

(Enter a MECHANIC.*)*

A MECHANIC   It is eleven degrees above zero. The wind is north-northwest, velocity, 57. There is a field of low barometric pressure moving eastward from Saskatchewan to the Eastern Coast. Tomorrow it will be cold with some snow in the Middle Western States and Northern New York. *(Exit)*

THE STAGE MANAGER   All right. Now for the hours. *(Helpfully, to the audience)* The minutes are gossips; the hours are philosophers; the years are theologians. The hours are philosophers with the exception of Twelve O'clock who is also a theologian.—Ready Ten O'clock! *(The hours are beautiful girls dressed like Elihu Vedder's Pleiades. Each carries a great gold Roman numeral. They pass slowly across the balcony at the back moving from right to left.)* What are you doing, Ten O'-clock? Aristotle?

TEN O'CLOCK   No, Plato, Mr. Washburn.

THE STAGE MANAGER   Good.—"Are you not rather convinced that he who thus . . ."

TEN O'CLOCK   "Are you not rather convinced that he who sees Beauty as only it can be seen will be specially favored? And since he is in contact not with images but with realities. . . ."

(She continues the passage in a murmur as ELEVEN O'CLOCK *appears.)*

ELEVEN O'CLOCK   "What else can I, Epictetus, do, a lame old man, but sing hymns to God? If then I were a nightingale, I would do the nightingale's part. If I were a swan I would do a swan's. But now I am a rational creature. . . ."

(Her voice too subsides to a murmur. TWELVE O'CLOCK *appears.)*

THE STAGE MANAGER   Good.—Twelve O'clock, what have you?

TWELVE O'CLOCK   Saint Augustine and his mother.

THE STAGE MANAGER   So.—"And we began to say: If to any the tumult of the flesh were hushed. . . ."

TWELVE O'CLOCK   "And we began to say: If to any the tumult of the flesh were hushed; hushed the images of earth; of waters and of air; . . .

THE STAGE MANAGER   Faster.—"Hushed also the poles of Heaven."

TWELVE O'CLOCK   "Yea, were the very soul to be hushed to herself."

THE STAGE MANAGER   A little louder, Miss Foster.

TWELVE O'CLOCK *(a little louder)* "Hushed all dreams and imaginary revelations. . . ."

THE STAGE MANAGER *(waving them back)* All right. All right. Now the planets. Decem-ber twenty-first, 1930, please. *The hours unwind and return to their dressing rooms at the right. The planets appear on the balcony. Some of them take their place halfway on the steps. These have no words, but each has a sound. One has a pulsating, zinging sound. Another has a thrum. One whistles ascending and descending scales. Saturn does a slow, obstinate*

M—M—M—M—

Louder, Saturn.—Venus, higher. Good. Now, Jupiter.—Now the earth. *(He turns to the beds on the train.)* Come, everybody. This is the earth's sound. *(The towns, workmen, etc. appear at the edge of the stage. The passengers begin their "thinking" murmur.)* Come, Grover's Corners. Parkersburg. You're in this. Watch-man. Tramp. This is the earth's sound. *(He conducts it as the director of an or-chestra would. Each of the towns and workmen does his motto.)*

*(*THE INSANE WOMAN *breaks into passionate weeping. She rises and stretches out her arms to* THE STAGE MANAGER.*)*

THE INSANE WOMAN   Use me. Give me something to do.

(He goes to her quickly, whispers something in her ear, and leads her back to her guardians. She is unconsoled.)

THE STAGE MANAGER   Now sh—sh—sh! Enter the archangels.

(To the audience)

THE STAGE MANAGER   We have now reached the theological position of Pullman Car Hiawatha.

(The towns and workmen have disappeared. The planets, off stage, continue a faint music. Two young men in blue serge suits enter along the balcony and descend the stairs at the right. As they pass each bed the passenger talks in his sleep. GABRIEL *points out* Bill *to* Michael *who smiles with raised eyebrows. They pause before* LOWER FIVE *and* Michael *makes the sound of assent that can only be rendered "Hn-Hn." The remarks that the characters make in their sleep are not all intelligible, being lost in the sound of sigh or groan or whisper by which they are conveyed. But we seem to hear)*

LOWER NINE *(loud)* Some people are slower than others, that's all.

LOWER SEVEN *(Bill)* It's no fun, y'know. I'll try.

LOWER FIVE *(the lady of the Christmas presents, rapidly)* You know best, of course. I'm ready whenever you are. One year's like another.

LOWER ONE   I can teach sewing. I can sew.

(They approach HARRIET'S *compartment.* THE INSANE WOMAN *sits up and speaks to them.)*

THE INSANE WOMAN   Me?

THE ARCHANGELS *(shake their heads)*

THE INSANE WOMAN   What possible use can there be in my simply waiting?—Well, I'm grateful for anything. I'm grateful for being so much better than I was. The old story, the terrible story, doesn't haunt me as it used to. A great load seems to have been taken off my mind.—But no one understands me any more. At last I under-stand myself perfectly, but no one else understands a thing I say.—So I must wait?

THE ARCHANGELS *(nod, smiling)*

THE INSANE WOMAN *(resignedly, and with a smile that implies their complicity)*   Well, you know best. I'll do whatever is best; but everyone is so childish, so absurd. They have no logic. These people are all so mad. . . . These people are like children; they have never suffered.

(She returns to her bed and sleeps. THE ARCHANGELS *stand beside* HARRIET. *The* DOCTOR *has drawn* PHILIP *into the next compartment and is talking to him in earnest whispers.*
*   * HARRIET'S *face has been toward the wall; she turns it slightly and speaks toward the ceiling.)*

HARRIET   I wouldn't be happy there. Let me stay dead down here. I belong here. I shall be perfectly happy to roam about my house and be near Philip.—You know I wouldn't be happy there. *(*GABRIEL *leans over and whispers into her ear. After a short pause she bursts into fierce tears.)* I'm ashamed to come with you. I haven't done anything. I haven't done anything with my life. Worse than that: I was angry and sullen. I never realized anything. I don't dare go a step in such a place. *(They whisper to her again.)* But it's not possible to forgive such things. I don't want to be forgiven so easily. I want to be punished for it all. I won't stir until I've been punished a long, long time. I want to be freed of all that—by punishment. I want to be all new. *(They whisper to her. She puts her feet slowly on the ground.)* But no one else could be punished for me. I'm willing to face it all myself. I don't ask anyone to be punished for me. *(They whisper to her again. She sits long and brokenly looking at her shoes and thinking it over.)* It wasn't fair. I'd have been willing to suffer for it myself,—if I could have endured such a mountain. *(She smiles.)* Oh, I'm ashamed! I'm just a stupid and you know it. I'm just another American.—But then what wonderful things must be beginning now. You really want me? You really want me? *(They start leading her down the aisle of the car.)* Let's take the whole train. There are some lovely faces on this train. Can't we all come? You'll never find anyone better than Philip. Please, please, let's all go. *(They reach the steps. The* archangels *interlock their arms as a support for her as she leans heavily on them, taking the steps slowly. Her words are half singing and half babbling.)* But look at how tremendously high and far it is. I've a weak heart. I'm not supposed to climb stairs. "I do not ask to see the distant scene: One step enough for me." It's like Switzerland. My tongue keeps saying things. I can't control it.—Do let me stop a minute: I want to say goodbye. *(She turns in their arms.)* Just a minute, I want to cry on your shoulder. *(She leans her forehead* *against* GABRIEL'S *shoulder and laughs long and softly.)* Goodbye, Philip.—I begged him not to marry me, but he would. He believed in me just as you do.—Goodbye, 1312 Ridgewood Avenue, Oaksbury, Illinois. I hope I remember all its steps and doors and wallpapers forever. Goodbye, Emerson Grammar School on the corner of Forbush Avenue and Wherry Street. Goodbye, Miss Walker and Miss Cramer who taught me English and Miss Matthewson who taught me Biology. Goodbye, First Congregational Church on the corner of Meyerson Avenue and 6th Street and Dr. McReady and Mrs. McReady and Julia. Goodbye, Papa and Mama. . . . *(She turns.)* Now I'm tired of saying goodbye.—I never used to talk like this. I was so homely I never used to have the courage to talk. Until Philip came. I see now. I see now. I understand everything now.

(THE STAGE MANAGER comes forward.)

THE STAGE MANAGER *(to the actors)* All right. All right.—Now we'll have the whole world together, please. The whole solar system, please. *(The complete cast begins to appear at the edges of the stage. He claps his hands.)* The whole solar system, please. Where's the tramp?—Where's the moon? *(He gives two raps on the floor, like the conductor of an orchestra attracting the attention of his forces, and slowly lifts his hand. The human beings murmur their thoughts; The hours discourse; the planets chant or hum.* HARRIET'S *voice finally rises above them all saying)*

HARRIET "I was not ever thus, nor asked that Thou Shouldst lead me on, and spite of fears, Pride ruled my will: Remember not past years."

(THE STAGE MANAGER waves them away.)

THE STAGE MANAGER Very good. Now clear the stage, please. Now we're at Englewood Station, South Chicago. See the University's towers over there! The best of them all.

LOWER ONE *(the spinster)* Porter, you promised to wake me up at quarter of six.

PORTER Sorry, mam, but it's been an awful night on this car. A lady's been terrible sick.

LOWER ONE Oh! Is she better?

PORTER No'm. She ain't one jot better.

LOWER FIVE Young man, take your foot out of my face.

THE STAGE MANAGER *(again substituting for* UPPER FIVE*)* Sorry, lady, I slipped—

LOWER FIVE *(grumbling not unamiably)* I declare, this trip's been one long series of insults.

THE STAGE MANAGER Just one minute, mam, and I'll be down and out of your way.

LOWER FIVE Haven't you got anybody to darn your socks for you? You ought to be ashamed to go about that way.

THE STAGE MANAGER Sorry, lady.

LOWER FIVE You're too stuck up to get married. That's the trouble with you.

LOWER NINE Bill!—Bill!

LOWER SEVEN Ye'? Wha' d'y'a want?

LOWER NINE Bill, how much d'y'a give the porter on a train like this? I've been outa the country so long . . .

LOWER SEVEN   Hell, Fred, I don't know myself.

THE PORTER   CHICAGO, CHICAGO. All out. This train don't go no further.

(The passengers jostle their way out and an army of old women with mops and pails enter and prepare to clean up the car.)

The curtain falls.

QUESTIONS

1   What does Wilder gain (or lose) by establishing the Stage Manager as the arbiter between his characters and the audience?

2   Does the context of voyage sharpen the sense of life's complexity and mystery? If you think it does, why is a considerable amount of the dialogue given over to seeming trivialities like magazines, a hot-water bag, the pleasures of radio, or a pair of suspenders? Moreover, can you justify Wilder's locating the car in time as well as in "its position geographically, meteorologically, astronomically, theologically considered"?

3   How do you consider the tags of poetry from Lowell; the temperance message and hymn; the song about Mandalay; the quotations from Rudyard Kipling, Robert Louis Stevenson, Plato, and Saint Augustine, as relevant to the experiences of the people who utter them? Is there any suggestion of a contrast between the quotations and the lines spoken by the passengers?

TOPICS FOR COMPOSITION

1   Analyze the journey motif in Wilder's play (perhaps you will want to consider also the same motif in O'Neill's "Bound East for Cardiff" in Part Six) as a possible indication of an archetypal significance. You may wish to include in your analysis other hints of a possible archetypal purpose by Wilder.

2   Argue for or against a specifically American interpretation of Wilder's play. In the context of your argument, try to judge the possibility that Wilder is suggesting a nation's poverty of expression.

3   Define the relationship between the passengers and the spokesmen for towns and villages, the field, the tramp, the workmen, and the mechanic.

POETRY

Since about the end of the eighteenth century, poets especially have been preoccupied with the possibility of finding new modes of expression. They have been stimulated in their search by the fact that modern science and philosophy have raised difficult questions about the relation between the mind and "given" reality. In Alexander Pope's time it was still possible to think of reality, or "Nature," as an essentially unchanging arrangement and an essentially unchanging correspondence between things and perceptions. Man's desires, themselves always basically the same, had to be accommodated to the way things are, and any exercise of the imagination that did not stay within the bounds of probability and common sense could not be permanently pleasurable. Pope therefore believed that the best modes of expression had long since been discovered—though he had to admit that language is subject to change and that a few geniuses had seemed able to express truths not clearly seen before.

Since the beginning of the Romantic period, however, there has been much excited speculation about the implications of the fact that the mind, for practical purposes, partly creates reality. What this means, in more homely terms, is simply that everyone to some extent sees what he wants to see in the world around him. Desire determines our modes of perception and so shapes "reality." The question, for poets, has been to what extent this process can be controlled. Can we, acting individually or collectively, create a more beautiful world by altering our modes of perception or, what is the same (again, for practical purposes), discover a better world by finding new modes of expression? Poets since Blake have responded to these questions with varying degrees of hope. So we hear Shelley, midway between despair and exaltation, literally exhorting the wild universe of nature: "Be thou, Spirit fierce,/ My spirit! Be thou me, impetuous one!" and D. H. Lawrence proclaiming,

> There are vast realms of consciousness still undreamed of
> vast ranges of experience, like the humming of unseen harps,
> we know nothing of, within us.

We find Archibald MacLeish, still more recently, insisting that poets, "deserted by the world before," can "invent the age"; and Wallace Stevens explaining that while poets once found the scene set for them and had only to repeat what was in the script (could, that is, draw upon myths more or less consciously created to express what would, for one culture or another, "suffice"), the modern poet has to construct a new stage and, like an actor improvising, speak words "with meditation" until the mind, its own invisible audience, hears what seems to wholly contain it.

Although there has been much disagreement about the radically creative potential of the imagination—compare, for further evidence, Coleridge's vision of the poet as magician with Housman's assertion that "malt does more than Milton can/ To justify God's ways to man"—and about the best means of realizing that potential, there has been almost universal agreement about three things. First, metaphor in some form, even if only in that of a cluster of images that seem to say what the mind in its deepest reaches is like, is essential. Secondly, the discovery or creation of metaphorical constructs that leave one with a more satisfying sense of reality is very difficult. Yeats's "Sailing to Byzantium" illuminates one basic difficulty: he asserts the possibility of a life "out of nature"—of achieving a sense of immortality through identification with "monuments of unageing intellect"; yet it is apparent that neither the compulsive, thoughtless, transitory activities of the world of nature nor the rigid symmetries of the world of artifice can fully satisfy the drive toward reality, give a sense of human completeness. Finally, there has been strong agreement that pleasure or beauty—in any case, emotion—is a more important criterion of truth than mere rationality. William Wordsworth, one of the leaders of the Romantic search for new modes of expression, asserted that

> Our meddling intellect
> Misshapes the beauteous forms of things;
> We murder to dissect.

And his thought is echoed, we see, in the words of John Wain's "maladjusted" electronic brain:

> Man made me, now I speak to man. He fears
> Whole truth. The brain defines it. Wholeness is
> The indivisible strength, brain, heart, and eye.

It is interesting to note that Edward Lueders uses the same metaphor, electric circuitry, to warn against the loss of insight that results from reliance upon stock responses.

Not all modern poets, it should be stressed, have shared the high, almost visionary hopes of the early Romantic innovators, but the search for new modes of expression continues, and the conviction persists that the effort is one of crucial importance to humanity.

AN ESSAY ON CRITICISM

Alexander Pope

Part I
'Tis hard to say if greater want of skill
Appear in writing or in judging ill;
But, of the two, less dangerous is the offence
To tire our patience, than mislead our sense.
Some few in that, but numbers err in this;   5
Ten censure wrong for one who writes amiss;
A fool might once himself alone expose;
Now one in verse makes many more in prose.
     'Tis with our judgments as our watches: none
Go just alike, yet each believes his own   10

1 want: lack.   *6 censure:* judge.

In poets as true genius is but rare,
True taste as seldom is the critic's share;
Both must alike from heaven derive their light,
These born to judge, as well as those to write.
Let such teach others who themselves excel,   15
And censure freely who have written well.
Authors are partial to their wit, 'tis true,
But are not critics to their judgment too?
     Yet if we look more closely, we shall find
Most have the seeds of judgment in their mind: 20
Nature affords at least a glimmering light;
The lines, though touched but faintly, are drawn right.
But as the slightest sketch, if justly traced,
Is by ill-colouring but the more disgraced,
So by false learning is good sense defaced: 25
Some are bewildered in the maze of schools,
And some made coxcombs nature meant but fools.
In search of wit these lose their common sense,
And then turn critics in their own defence:
Each burns alike, who can, or cannot write,   30
Or with a rival's, or an eunuch's spite.
All fools have still an itching to deride,
And fain would be upon the laughing side.
If Mævius scribble in Apollo's spite,
There are who judge still worse than he can write.   35
     Some have at first for wits, then poets passed,
Turned critics next, and proved plain fools at last.
Some neither can for wits nor critics pass,
As heavy mules are neither horse nor ass.
Those half-learned witlings, numerous in our isle,   40
As half-formed insects on the banks of Nile;
Unfinished things, one knows not what to call,
Their generation's so equivocal;
To tell 'em would a hundred tongues require,
Or one vain wit's, that might a hundred tire.   45
     But you who seek to give and merit fame,
And justly bear a critic's noble name,
Be sure yourself and your own reach to know,
How far your genius, taste, and learning go;
Launch not beyond your depth, but be discreet,   50
And mark that point where sense and dulness meet.
     Nature to all things fixed the limits fit,
And wisely curbed proud man's pretending wit.

---

27 coxcombs: conceited persons.   *34 Mævius:* an inferior Roman poet.   *44 tell:* count.

As on the land while here the ocean gains,
In other parts it leaves wide sandy plains;   55
Thus in the soul while memory prevails,
The solid power of understanding fails;
Where beams of warm imagination play,
The memory's soft figures melt away.
One science only will one genius fit;   60
So vast is art, so narrow human wit—
Not only bounded to peculiar arts,
But oft in those confined to single parts.
Like kings we lose the conquests gained before,
By vain ambition still to make them more;   65
Each might his several province well command,
Would all but stoop to what they understand.
      First follow nature, and your judgment frame
By her just standard, which is still the same:
Unerring nature, still divinely bright,   70
One clear, unchanged, and universal light,
Life, force, and beauty, must to all impart,
At once the source, and end, and test of art.
Art from that fund each just supply provides,
Works without show, and without pomp presides;   75
In some fair body thus the informing soul
With spirits feeds, with vigour fills the whole,
Each motion guides, and every nerve sustains;
Itself unseen, but in the effects remains.
Some, to whom Heaven in wit has been profuse,   80
Want as much more, to turn it to its use;
For wit and judgment often are at strife,
Though meant each other's aid, like man and wife
Tis more to guide, than spur the muse's steed,
Restrain his fury, than provoke his speed;   85
The winged courser, like a generous horse,
Shows most true mettle when you check his course.
      Those rules of old discovered, not devised,
Are nature still, but nature methodised;
Nature, like liberty, is but restrained   90
By the same laws which first herself ordained.
      Hear how learned Greece her useful rules indites,
When to repress, and when indulge our flights:
High on Parnassus' top her sons she showed,
And pointed out those arduous paths they trod;   95

86 winged courser: Pegasus, associated with poetic inspiration.   *94 Parnassus:* a mountain in
Greece, sacred to Apollo and the Muses.

Held from afar, aloft, the immortal prize,
And urged the rest by equal steps to rise.
Just precepts thus from great examples given,
She drew from them what they derived from heaven.
The generous critic fanned the poet's fire,   100
And taught the world with reason to admire.
Then criticism the muses' handmaid proved,
To dress her charms, and make her more beloved:
But following wits from that intention strayed;
Who could not win the mistress, wooed the maid;   105
Against the poets their own arms they turned,
Sure to hate most the men from whom they learned.
So modern 'pothecaries, taught the art
By doctor's bills to play the doctor's part,
Bold in the practice of mistaken rules,   110
Prescribe, apply, and call their masters fools,
Some on the leaves of ancient authors prey,
Nor time nor moths e'er spoiled so much as they.
Some dryly plain, without invention's aid,
Write dull receipts how poems may be made.   115
These leave the sense, their learning to display,
And those explain the meaning quite away.
       You then whose judgment the right course would steer,
Know well each ancient's proper character;
His fable, subject, scope in every page;   120
Religion, country, genius of his age:
Without all these at once before your eyes,
Cavil you may, but never criticise.
Be Homer's works your study and delight,
Read them by day, and meditate by night;   125
Thence form your judgment, thence your maxims bring,
And trace the muses upward to their spring.
Still with itself compared, his text peruse,
And let your comment be the Mantuan muse.
       When first young Maro in his boundless mind   130
A work to outlast immortal Rome designed,
Perhaps he seemed above the critic's law,
And but from nature's fountains scorned to draw;
But when to examine every part he came,
Nature and Homer were, he found, the same.   135
Convinced, amazed, he checks the bold design;
And rules as strict his laboured work confine,
As if the Stagirite o'erlooked each line.

109 bills: prescriptions.   *120 fable:* plot.   *130 Maro:* Virgil, who was born near Mantua. He is also referred to as Maro.   *138 Stagirite:* Aristotle, who was a native of Stagira. His *Poetics* was regarded as the supreme critical authority.

Learn hence for ancient rules a just esteem;
To copy nature is to copy them.   140
    Some beauties yet no precepts can declare,
For there's a happiness as well as care.
Music resembles poetry, in each
Are nameless graces which no methods teach,
And which a master-hand alone can reach.   145
If, where the rules not far enough extend,
(Since rules were made but to promote their end)
Some lucky licence answer to the full
The intent proposed, that licence is a rule.
Thus Pegasus, a nearer way to take,   150
May boldly deviate from the common track;
From vulgar bounds with brave disorder part;
And snatch a grace beyond the reach of art,
Which without passing through the judgment, gains
The heart, and all its end at once attains.   155
In prospects thus, some objects please our eyes,
Which out of nature's common order rise,
The shapeless rock, or hanging precipice.
Great wits sometimes may gloriously offend,
And rise to faults true critics dare not mend.   160
But though the ancients thus their rules invade,
(As kings dispense with laws themselves have made)
Moderns, beware! or if you must offend
Against the precept, ne'er transgress its end;
Let it be seldom, and compelled by need;   165
And have, at least, their precedent to plead.
The critic else proceeds without remorse,
Seizes your fame, and puts his laws in force.
    I know there are, to whose presumptuous thoughts
Those freer beauties, even in them, seem faults.   170
Some figures monstrous and mis-shaped appear,
Considered singly, or beheld too near,
Which, but proportioned to their light, or place,
Due distance reconciles to form and grace.
A prudent chief not always must display   175
His powers in equal ranks, and fair array,
But with the occasion and the place comply,
Conceal his force, nay seem sometimes to fly.
Those oft are stratagems which error seem,
Nor is it Homer nods, but we that dream.   180
    Still green with bays each ancient altar stands,
Above the reach of sacrilegious hands,

142 happiness: good luck.   *181 bays:* garlands of laurel awarded for excellence.

Secure from flames, from envy's fiercer rage,
Destructive war, and all-involving age.
See, from each clime the learned their incense bring!   185
Hear, in all tongues consenting pæens ring!
In praise so just let every voice be joined,
And fill the general chorus of mankind.
Hail, bards triumphant! born in happier days,
Immortal heirs of universal praise!   190
Whose honours with increase of ages grow,
As streams roll down, enlarging as they flow;
Nations unborn your mighty names shall sound,
And worlds applaud that must not yet be found!
Oh, may some spark of your celestial fire,   195
The last, the meanest of your sons inspire,
(That on weak wings, from far, pursues your flights;
Glows while he reads, but trembles as he writes)
To teach vain wits a science little known,
To admire superior sense, and doubt their own!   200

Part II
        Of all the causes which conspire to blind
Man's erring judgment, and misguide the mind,
What the weak head with strongest bias rules
Is pride, the never-failing vice of fools.
Whatever nature has in worth denied,   205
She gives in large recruits of needful pride;
For as in bodies, thus in souls, we find
What wants in blood and spirits, swelled with wind:
Pride, where wit fails, steps in to our defence,
And fills up all the mighty void of sense.   210
If once right reason drives that cloud away,
Truth breaks upon us with resistless day.
Trust not yourself; but your defects to know,
Make use of every friend—and every foe.
        A little learning is a dangerous thing;   215
Drink deep, or taste not the Pierian spring:
There shallow draughts intoxicate the brain,
And drinking largely sobers us again.
Fired at first sight with what the muse imparts,
In fearless youth we tempt the heights of arts,   220
While from the bounded level of our mind
Short views we take, nor see the lengths behind;

206 recruits: supplies.   *216 Pierian spring:* a spring on Mt. Olympus, sacred to the Muses.   *220 tempt:* attempt.

But more advanced, behold with strange surprise
New distant scenes of endless science rise!
So pleased at first the towering Alps we try,   225
Mount o'er the vales, and seem to tread the sky;
The eternal snows appear already past,
And the first clouds and mountains seem the last;
But, those attained, we tremble to survey
The growing labours of the lengthened way;   230
The increasing prospect tires our wandering eyes,
Hills peep o'er hills, and Alps on Alps arise!
    A perfect judge will read each work of wit
With the same spirit that its author writ:
Survey the whole, nor seek slight faults to find   235
Where nature moves, and rapture warms the mind;
Nor lose, for that malignant dull delight,
The generous pleasure to be charmed with wit.
But in such lays as neither ebb, nor flow,
Correctly cold, and regularly low,   240
That shunning faults, one quiet tenour keep,
We cannot blame indeed—but we may sleep.
In wit, as nature, what affects our hearts
Is not the exactness of peculiar parts;
'Tis not a lip, or eye, we beauty call,   245
But the joint force and full result of all.
Thus when we view some well-proportioned dome,
(The world's just wonder, and even thine, O Rome!)
No single parts unequally surprise,
All comes united to the admiring eyes;   250
No monstrous height, or breadth, or length appear;
The whole at once is bold, and regular.
    Whoever thinks a faultless piece to see,
Thinks what ne'er was, nor is, nor e'er shall be.
In every work regard the writer's end,   255
Since none can compass more than they intend;
And if the means be just, the conduct true,
Applause, in spite of trivial faults, is due;
As men of breeding, sometimes men of wit,
To avoid great errors, must the less commit: 260
Neglect the rules each verbal critic lays,
For not to know some trifles, is a praise.
Most critics, fond of some subservient art,
Still make the whole depend upon a part;
They talk of principles, but notions prize,   265

247 dome: the dome of St. Peter's in Rome, designed by Michelangelo.

And all to one loved folly sacrifice.
      Once on a time, La Mancha's knight, they say,
A certain bard encountering on the way,
Discoursed in terms as just, with looks as sage,
As e'er could Dennis of the Grecian stage;   270
Concluding all were desperate sots and fools,
Who durst depart from Aristotle's rules.
Our author, happy in a judge so nice,
Produced his play, and begged the knight's advice;
Made him observe the subject, and the plot,   275
The manners, passions, unities—what not?
All which, exact to rule, were brought about,
Were but a combat in the lists left out.
"What! leave the combat out?" exclaims the knight;
"Yes, or we must renounce the Stagirite."   280
"Not so by Heaven," he answers in a rage,
"Knights, squires, and steeds, must enter on the stage."
"So vast a throng the stage can ne'er contain."
"Then build a new, or act it in a plain."
      Thus critics, of less judgment than caprice,   285
Curious not knowing, not exact but nice,
Form short ideas, and offend in arts
(As most in manners) by a love to parts,
      Some to conceit alone their taste confine,
And glittering thoughts struck out at every line;   290
Pleased with a work where nothing's just or fit,
One glaring chaos and wild heap of wit.
Poets like painters, thus, unskilled to trace
The naked nature and the living grace,
With gold and jewels cover every part,   295
And hide with ornaments their want of art.
True wit is nature to advantage dressed,
What oft was thought, but ne'er so well expressed;
Something, whose truth convinced at sight we find,
That gives us back the image of our mind.   300
As shades more sweetly recommend the light,
So modest plainness sets off sprightly wit;
For works may have more wit than does 'em good,
As bodies perish through excess of blood.
      Others for language all their care express,   305
And value books, as women men, for dress:
Their praise is still,—the style is excellent:

---

267 La Mancha's knight: Don Quixote.   *270 Dennis:* John Dennis, a severe and rather pompous
critic.   *286 Curious:* overscrupulous.   *289 conceit:* elaborate wittiness.

The sense, they humbly take upon content.
Words are like leaves; and where they most abound,
Much fruit of sense beneath is rarely found: 310
False eloquence, like the prismatic glass,
Its gaudy colours spreads on every place;
The face of nature we no more survey,
All glares alike, without distinction gay:
But true expression, like the unchanging sun,   315
Clears and improves whate'er it shines upon;
It gilds all objects, but it alters none.
Expression is the dress of thought, and still
Appears more decent as more suitable;
A vile conceit in pompous words expressed,   320
Is like a clown in regal purple dressed:
For different styles with different subjects sort,
As several garbs with country, town, and court.
Some by old words to fame have made pretence,
Ancients in phrase, mere moderns in their sense;   325
Such laboured nothings, in so strange a style,
Amaze the unlearned, and make the learned smile.
Unlucky, as Fungoso in the play,
These sparks with awkward vanity display
What the fine gentleman wore yesterday;   330
And but so mimic ancient wits at best,
As apes our grandsires, in their doublets dressed.
In words as fashions the same rule will hold;
Alike fantastic if too new or old:
Be not the first by whom the new are tried,   335
Nor yet the last to lay the old aside.
        But most by numbers judge a poet's song;
And smooth or rough with them is right or wrong:
In the bright muse though thousand charms conspire,
Her voice is all these tuneful fools admire,   340
Who haunt Parnassus but to please their ear,
Not mend their minds; as some to church repair,
Not for the doctrine, but the music there.
These equal syllables alone require,
Though oft the ear the open vowels tire;   345
While expletives their feeble aid do join,
And ten low words oft creep in one dull line:
While they ring round the same unvaried chimes,
With sure returns of still expected rhymes;

308 upon content: without questioning.   *321 clown:* a rustic person.   *328 Fungoso:* a character
in Ben Jonson's *Every Man Out of His Humor.*   *337 numbers:* versification.   *345:* Note that in
lines 345–357 Pope's own style illustrates the faults he mentions.

Where'er you find "the cooling western breeze,"   350
In the next line, it "whispers through the trees";
If crystal streams "with pleasing murmurs creep,"
The reader's threatened (not in vain) with "sleep";
Then, at the last and only couplet fraught
With some unmeaning thing they call a thought,   355
A needless Alexandrine ends the song
That, like a wounded snake, drags its slow length along.
Leave such to tune their own dull rhymes, and know
What's roundly smooth or languishingly slow;
And praise the easy vigour of a line,   360
Where Denham's strength and Waller's sweetness join.
True ease in writing comes from art, not chance,
As those move easiest who have learned to dance.
'Tis not enough no harshness gives offence;
The sound must seem an echo to the sense: 365
Soft is the strain when Zephyr gently blows,
And the smooth stream in smoother numbers flows;
But when loud surges lash the sounding shore,
The hoarse, rough verse should like the torrent roar:
When Ajax strives some rock's vast weight to throw,   370
The line too labours, and the words move slow;
Not so, when swift Camilla scours the plain,
Flies o'er the unbending corn, and skims along the main.
Hear how Timotheus' varied lays surprise,
And bid alternate passions fall and rise!   375
While, at each change, the son of Libyan Jove
Now burns with glory, and then melts with love,
Now his fierce eyes with sparkling fury glow,
Now sighs steal out, and tears begin to flow:
Persians and Greeks like turns of nature found,   380
And the world's victor stood subdued by sound!
The power of music all our hearts allow,
And what Timotheus was, is Dryden now.
        Avoid extremes, and shun the fault of such,
Who still are pleased too little or too much.   385
At every trifle scorn to take offence;
That always shows great pride or little sense;
Those heads, as stomachs, are not sure the best,
Which nauseate all, and nothing can digest.
Yet let not each gay turn thy rapture move;   390
For fools admire, but men of sense approve:

356 Alexandrine: a line with six iambic feet, like the one following this one.   *361 Denham, Waller:* Sir John Denham (1615–1669) and Edmund Waller (1609–1687).   *374:* See Dryden's "Alexander's Feast."   *376 son of Libyan Jove:* Alexander the Great.

As things seem large which we through mists descry,
Dulness is ever apt to magnify.
     Some foreign writers, some our own despise;
The ancients only, or the moderns prize.   395
Thus wit, like faith, by each man is applied
To one small sect, and all are damned beside.
Meanly they seek the blessing to confine,
And force that sun but on a part to shine,
Which not alone the southern wit sublimes,   400
But ripens spirits in cold northern climes;
Which from the first has shone on ages past,
Enlights the present, and shall warm the last;
Though each may feel increases and decays,
And see now clearer and now darker days.   405
Regard not then if wit be old or new,
But blame the false, and value still the true.
     Some ne'er advance a judgment of their own,
But catch the spreading notion of the town;
They reason and conclude by precedent,   410
And own stale nonsense which they ne'er invent.
Some judge of authors' names, not works, and then
Nor praise nor blame the writings, but the men.
Of all this servile herd the worst is he
That in proud dulness joins with quality;   415
A constant critic at the great man's board,
To fetch and carry nonsense for my lord.
What woeful stuff this madrigal would be,
In some starved hackney sonneteer, or me?
But let a lord once own the happy lines,   420
How the wit brightens! how the style refines!
Before his sacred name flies every fault,
And each exalted stanza teems with thought!
     The vulgar thus through imitation err;
As oft the learned by being singular: 425
So much they scorn the crowd, that if the throng
By chance go right, they purposely go wrong;
So schismatics the plain believers quit,
And are but damned for having too much wit.
Some praise at morning what they blame at night,   430
But always think the last opinion right.
A muse by these is like a mistress used,
This hour she's idolised, the next abused;
While their weak heads, like towns unfortified,
Twixt sense and nonsense daily change their side.   435
Ask them the cause; they're wiser still, they say;

And still to-morrow's wiser than to-day.
We think our fathers fools, so wise we grow;
Our wiser sons, no doubt, will think us so.
Once school-divines this zealous isle o'erspread;   440
Who knew most sentences, was deepest read;
Faith, gospel, all, seemed made to be disputed,
And none had sense enough to be confuted:
Scotists and Thomists now in peace remain,
Amidst their kindred cobwebs in Duck Lane.   445
If faith itself has different dresses worn,
What wonder modes in wit should take their turn?
Oft, leaving what is natural and fit,
The current folly proves the ready wit;
And authors think their reputation safe,   450
Which lives as long as fools are pleased to laugh.
      Some, valuing those of their own side or mind,
Still make themselves the measure of mankind:
Fondly we think we honour merit then,
When we but praise ourselves in other men.   455
Parties in wit attend on those of state,
And public faction doubles private hate.
Pride, Malice, Folly, against Dryden rose,
In various shapes of parsons, critics, beaux;
But sense survived, when merry jests were past;   460
For rising merit will buoy up at last.
Might he return, and bless once more our eyes,
New Blackmores and new Milbournes must arise:
Nay, should great Homer lift his awful head,
Zoilus again would start up from the dead.   465
Envy will merit, as its shade, pursue;
But like a shadow, proves the substance true;
For envied wit, like Sol eclipsed, makes known
The opposing body's grossness, not its own.
When first that sun too powerful beams displays,   470
It draws up vapours which obscure its rays;
But even those clouds at last adorn its way,
Reflect new glories, and augment the day.
      Be thou the first true merit to befriend;
His praise is lost who stays till all commend.   475
Short is the date, alas, of modern rhymes,
And 'tis but just to let them live betimes.
No longer now that golden age appears,

441 sentences: an allusion to Peter Lombard's *Book of Sentences*. *445 Duck Lane:* a street where secondhand books and publisher's leftover stocks were sold. *463 Blackmore:* Blackmore attacked Dryden for the immorality of his plays. Milbourne criticized his translation of Virgil.

When patriarch wits survived a thousand years:
Now length of fame (our second life) is lost, 480
And bare threescore is all even that can boast;
Our sons their fathers' failing language see,
And such as Chaucer is, shall Dryden be.
So when the faithful pencil has designed
Some bright idea of the master's mind, 485
Where a new world leaps out at his command,
And ready nature waits upon his hand;
When the ripe colours soften and unite,
And sweetly melt into just shade and light;
When mellowing years their full perfection give, 490
And each bold figure just begins to live,
The treacherous colours the fair art betray,
And all the bright creation fades away!
      Unhappy wit, like most mistaken things,
Atones not for that envy which it brings. 495
In youth alone its empty praise we boast,
But soon the short-lived vanity is lost:
Like some fair flower the early spring supplies,
That gaily blooms, but even in blooming dies.
What is this wit, which must our cares employ? 500
The owner's wife, that other men enjoy;
Then most our trouble still when most admired,
And still the more we give, the more required;
Whose fame with pains we guard, but lose with ease,
Sure some to vex, but never all to please; 505
'Tis what the vicious fear, the virtuous shun;
By fools 'tis hated, and by knaves undone!
      If wit so much from ignorance undergo,
Ah let not learning too commence its foe!
Of old, those met rewards who could excel, 510
And such were praised who but endeavoured well;
Though triumphs were to generals only due,
Crowns were reserved to grace the soldiers too.
Now they who reach Parnassus' lofty crown
Employ their pains to spurn some others down; 515
And while self-love each jealous writer rules,
Contending wits become the sport of fools;
But still the worst with most regret commend,
For each ill author is as bad a friend.
To what base ends, and what abject ways, 520
Are mortals urged through sacred lust of praise!
Ah, ne'er so dire a thirst of glory boast,
Nor in the critic let the man be lost.

Good nature and good sense must ever join;
To err is human; to forgive, divine.   525
      But if in noble minds some dregs remain
Not yet purged off, of spleen and sour disdain,
Discharge that rage on more provoking crimes,
Nor fear a dearth in these flagitious times.
No pardon vile obscenity should find,   530
Though wit and art conspire to move your mind;
But dulness with obscenity must prove
As shameful sure as impotence in love.
In the fat age of pleasure, wealth, and ease,
Sprung the rank weed, and thrived with large increase: 535
When love was all an easy monarch's care;
Seldom at council, never in a war:
Jilts ruled the state, and statesmen farces writ;
Nay wits had pensions, and young lords had wit:
The fair sate panting at a courtier's play,   540
And not a mask went unimproved away:
The modest fan was lifted up no more,
And virgins smiled at what they blushed before.
The following licence of a foreign reign
Did all the dregs of bold Socinus drain;   545
Then unbelieving priests reformed the nation,
And taught more pleasant methods of salvation;
Where Heaven's free subjects might their rights dispute,
Lest God himself should seem too absolute:
Pulpits their sacred satire learned to spare,   550
And vice admired to find a flatterer there!
Encouraged thus, wit's Titans braved the skies,
And the press groaned with licensed blasphemies.
These monsters, critics! with your darts engage,
Here point your thunder, and exhaust your rage!   555
Yet shun their fault, who, scandalously nice,
Will needs mistake an author into vice;
All seems infected that the infected spy,
As all looks yellow to the jaundiced eye.

1711

536 easy monarch: The allusion is to Charles II.   *541 mask:* lady wearing a mask.   *544 foreign reign:* an allusion to the fact that William III was a Dutchman.   *545 Socinus:* a sixteenth-century Italian theologian who denied the divinity of Jesus.

QUESTIONS

1   Pope says that poets and critics alike need both good judgment and wit. The term "wit" is used elsewhere in another sense. See if you can distinguish between the two senses of the word. The dictionary will help you.

2   Is good judgment the same as "common sense" (line 28)? Is it the same as "under-
    standing" (line 57)?
3   When Pope says (line 68), "First follow nature," he does not mean nature in its
    visible forms, but rather what is natural in the sense of being normal. What is the
    best way of following nature? Why?
4   Are all men capable of good judgment? What are the most general causes of
    disagreement in judgment?
5   What is the chief cause of men's failure to use the judgment they possess? How
    many common faults in criticism are mentioned in part II?

KUBLA KHAN

Samuel Taylor Coleridge

In Xanadu did Kubla Khan
     A stately pleasure-dome decree:
Where Alph, the sacred river, ran
Through caverns measureless to man
     Down to a sunless sea.   5
So twice five miles of fertile ground
With walls and towers were girdled round:
And here were gardens bright with sinuous rills,
Where blossomed many an incense-bearing tree,
And here were forests ancient as the hills,   10
Enfolding sunny spots of greenery.

But oh! that deep romantic chasm which slanted
Down the green hill athwart a cedarn cover!
A savage place; as holy and enchanted
As e'er beneath a waning moon was haunted   15
By woman wailing for her demon-lover!
And from this chasm, with ceaseless turmoil seething,
As if this earth in fast thick pants were breathing,
A mighty fountain momently was forced,
Amid whose swift half-intermitted burst   20
Huge fragments vaulted like rebounding hail,
Or chaffy grain beneath the thresher's flail:
And 'mid these dancing rocks at once and ever
It flung up momently the sacred river.
Five miles meandering with a mazy motion   25
Through wood and dale the sacred river ran,
Then reached the caverns measureless to man,

1: The historical Kubla Khan was the founder of the Mongol dynasty in China in the thirteenth
century.

And sank in tumult to a lifeless ocean:
And 'mid this tumult Kubla heard from far
Ancestral voices prophesying war!   30

    The shadow of the dome of pleasure
    Floated midway on the waves;
    Where was heard the mingled measure
    From the fountain and the caves.
It was a miracle of rare device,   35
A sunny pleasure-dome with caves of ice!

    A damsel with a dulcimer
    In a vision once I saw:
    It was an Abyssinian maid,
    And on her dulcimer she played,   40
    Singing of Mount Abora.
    Could I revive within me
    Her symphony and song,
    To such a deep delight 'twould win me,
That with music loud and long,   45
I would build that dome in air,
That sunny dome! those caves of ice!
And all who heard should see them there,
And all should cry, Beware! Beware!
His flashing eyes, his floating hair!   50
Weave a circle round him thrice,
And close your eyes with holy dread,
For he on honey-dew hath fed,
And drunk the milk of Paradise.

             1816 (Composed 1797)

QUESTIONS

1 Although the first part of "Kubla Khan" may be regarded as historical description,
   it may also be seen as a symbolic representation of basic human desires and fears.
   What, in this view, does the Khan himself symbolize? To what extent does he have
   control over his environment and destiny? What is his relation with the world of
   nature? With supernatural forces?
2 The second part of the poem is about poetic inspiration and poetic power. What
   does the damsel symbolize? What does the speaker mean by saying that he would
   "build that dome in air" if he could revive within himself the damsel's symphony and
   song? Is he being modest? What is the relation between the speaker and Kubla
   Khan?

ODE TO A NIGHTINGALE

John Keats

My heart aches, and a drowsy numbness pains
  My sense, as though of hemlock I had drunk,
Or emptied some dull opiate to the drains
  One minute past, and Lethe-wards had sunk:
'Tis not through envy of thy happy lot,   5
  But being too happy in thine happiness—
    That thou, light-wingéd Dryad of the trees,
      In some melodious plot
  Of beechen green, and shadows numberless,
    Singest of summer in full-throated ease.   10

O, for a draught of vintage! that hath been
  Cooled a long age in the deep-delvéd earth,
Tasting of Flora and the country green,
  Dance, and Provençal song, and sunburnt mirth!
O for a beaker full of the warm South,   15
  Full of the true, the blushful Hippocrene,
    With beaded bubbles winking at the brim,
      And purple-stainéd mouth;
  That I might drink, and leave the world unseen,
    And with thee fade away into the forest dim: 20

Fade far away, dissolve, and quite forget
  What thou among the leaves hast never known,
The weariness, the fever, and the fret
  Here, where men sit and hear each other groan;
Where palsy shakes a few, sad, last gray hairs,   25
  Where youth grows pale, and specter-thin, and dies,
    Where but to think is to be full of sorrow
      And leaden-eyed despairs,
  Where Beauty cannot keep her lustrous eyes,
    Or new Love pine at them beyond tomorrow.   30

Away! away! for I will fly to thee,
  Not charioted by Bacchus and his pards,
But on the viewless wings of Poesy,
  Though the dull brain perplexes and retards:

2 hemlock: a poisonous opiate.   *4 Lethe-wards:* toward Lethe, the river in Hades whose water brings the dead forgetfulness.   *13 Flora:* Roman goddess of springtime and flowers.   *14 Provençal song:* by the medieval troubadours of Southern France.   *16 Hippocrene:* The fountain of the Muses, the goddesses of poetry and other arts.   *32 Bacchus:* the god of wine was supposed to have ridden in a chariot drawn by leopards ("pards").

Already with thee! tender is the night,   35
  And haply the Queen-Moon is on her throne,
    Clustered around by all her starry Fays;
      But here there is no light,
  Save what from heaven is with the breezes blown
    Through verdurous glooms and winding mossy ways.   40

I cannot see what flowers are at my feet,
  Nor what soft incense hangs upon the boughs,
But, in embalméd darkness, guess each sweet
  Wherewith the seasonable month endows
The grass, the thicket, and the fruit tree wild;   45
  White hawthorn, and the pastoral eglantine;
    Fast fading violets covered up in leaves;
      And mid-May's eldest child,
  The coming musk-rose, full of dewy wine,
    The murmurous haunt of flies on summer eves.   50

Darkling I listen; and for many a time
I have been half in love with easeful Death,
Called him soft names in many a muséd rhyme,
  To take into the air my quiet breath;
Now more than ever seems it rich to die,   55
  To cease upon the midnight with no pain,
    While thou art pouring forth thy soul abroad
      In such an ecstasy!
  Still wouldst thou sing, and I have ears in vain—
    To thy high requiem become a sod.   60

Thou wast not born for death, immortal Bird!
  No hungry generations tread thee down;
The voice I hear this passing night was heard
  In ancient days by emperor and clown:
Perhaps the selfsame song that found a path   65
  Through the sad heart of Ruth, when, sick for home,
    She stood in tears amid the alien corn;
      The same that ofttimes hath
  Charmed magic casements, opening on the foam
    Of perilous seas, in faery lands forlorn.   70

Forlorn! the very word is like a bell
  To toll me back from thee to my sole self!
Adieu! the fancy cannot cheat so well
  As she is famed to do, deceiving elf.

51 Darkling: in growing darkness.   *66 alien corn:* see Ruth 2:3–11.

Adieu! adieu! thy plaintive anthem fades   75
   Past the near meadows, over the still stream,
      Up the hill side; and now 'tis buried deep
         In the next valley-glades:
   Was it a vision, or a waking dream?
      Fled is that music:—Do I wake or sleep?   80

                    1819

QUESTIONS

1 The first six stanzas of this poem record a failure of imagination. The poet cannot find words or images for the feeling or longing he wants to express. Paradoxically, his attempt to give expression to the idea of perfect happiness leads him to long for death. Yet even as he protests he experiences a kind of transcendence; it seems that he succeeds in finding the nightingale's haunt (to use the symbolism of the poem) after all, though his sojourn there is brief enough. Can you explain how or why this comes about?

2 Keats is noted for his ability to enhance the expression of emotion by the evocation of sensations. Can you find any striking evidence of this power in "Ode to a Nightingale"?

ODE TO THE WEST WIND

Percy Bysshe Shelley

1

O wild West Wind, thou breath of Autumn's being,
Thou, from whose unseen presence the leaves dead
Are driven, like ghosts from an enchanter fleeing,

Yellow, and black, and pale, and hectic red,
Pestilence-stricken multitudes: O thou,   5
Who chariotest to their dark wintry bed

The wingéd seeds, where they lie cold and low,
Each like a corpse within its grave, until
Thine azure sister of the Spring shall blow

Her clarion o'er the dreaming earth, and fill   10
(Driving sweet buds like flocks to feed in air)
With living hues and odors plain and hill:

Wild Spirit, which art moving everywhere;
Destroyer and preserver; hear, oh, hear!

10 clarion: a medieval trumpet, very clear toned.

2

Thou on whose stream, mid the steep sky's commotion,   15
Loose clouds like earth's decaying leaves are shed,
Shook from the tangled boughs of Heaven and Ocean,

Angels of rain and lightning: there are spread
On the blue surface of thine aëry surge,
Like the bright hair uplifted from the head   20

Of some fierce Maenad, even from the dim verge
Of the horizon to the zenith's height,
The locks of the approaching storm. Thou dirge

Of the dying year, to which this closing night
Will be the dome of a vast sepulcher,   25
Vaulted with all thy congregated might

Of vapors, from whose solid atmosphere
Black rain, and fire, and hail will burst: oh, hear!

3

Thou who didst waken from his summer dreams
The blue Mediterranean, where he lay,   30
Lulled by the coil of his crystálline streams,

Beside a pumice isle in Baiae's bay,
And saw in sleep old palaces and towers
Quivering within the wave's intenser day,

All overgrown with azure moss and flowers   35
So sweet, the sense faints picturing them! Thou
For whose path the Atlantic's level powers

Cleave themselves into chasms, while far below
The sea-blooms and the oozy woods which wear
The sapless foliage of the ocean, know   40

Thy voice, and suddenly grow gray with fear,
And tremble and despoil themselves: oh, hear!

17 tangled boughs: mingled clouds and storm waves. *18 Angels:* messengers (from the Greek root). *21 Maenad:* female devotee of Dionysus. The Maenads were noted for their frenzied dances. *32 Baiae's bay:* near Naples.

4

If I were a dead leaf thou mightest bear;
If I were a swift cloud to fly with thee;
A wave to pant beneath thy power, and share   45

The impulse of thy strength, only less free
Than thou, O uncontrollable! If even
I were as in my boyhood, and could be

The comrade of thy wanderings over Heaven,
As then, when to outstrip thy skyey speed   50
Scarce seem a vision; I would ne'er have striven

As thus with thee in prayer in my sore need.
Oh, lift me as a wave, a leaf, a cloud!
I fall upon the thorns of life! I bleed!

A heavy weight of hours has chained and bowed   55
One too like thee: tameless, and swift, and proud.

5

Make me thy lyre, even as the forest is:
What if my leaves are falling like its own!
The tumult of thy mighty harmonies

Will take from both a deep, autumnal tone,   60
Sweet though in sadness. Be thou, Spirit fierce,
My spirit! Be thou me, impetuous one!

Drive my dead thoughts over the universe
Like withered leaves to quicken a new birth!
And, by the incantation of this verse,   65

Scatter, as from an unextinguished hearth
Ashes and sparks, my words among mankind!
Be through my lips to unawakened earth

The trumpet of a prophecy! O Wind,
If Winter comes, can Spring be far behind?   70

1820

QUESTIONS

1   Stated simply, the problem with which the poet wrestles here is that of reconciling
    uncontrollable natural forces with his own moral will. "Spirit" may be said to be the

key word. See if you can understand and explain in other terms—nonmetaphysical, if possible—what the poet means by the exclamation "Be thou/ Spirit fierce,/ My spirit!"

2 It should be evident that the development of a new form of expression must be part of the solution to the problem defined in the preceding question, and one would suppose that the poet would want to use imagery and metaphor in such a way as to express feeling and at the same time keep the world of nature intact. In other words, as we read this poem, the autumn wind should remain a real wind, and we should feel the presence of an actual sky, the real ocean. Do you think that the poet has managed this? Remember that the success of a poem always depends in part upon exertion of the reader's imagination.

HOW IT STRIKES A CONTEMPORARY

Robert Browning

I only knew one poet in my life;
And this, or something like it, was his way.

　　You saw go up and down Valladolid,
A man of mark, to know next time you saw.
His very serviceable suit of black   5
Was courtly once and conscientious still,
And many might have worn it, though none did;
The cloak, that somewhat shone and showed, the threads,
Had purpose, and the ruff, significance.
He walked and tapped the pavement with his cane,   10
Scenting the world, looking it full in face,
An old dog, bald and blindish, at his heels.
They turned up, now, the alley by the church,
That leads nowhither; now, they breathed themselves
On the main promenade just at the wrong time.   15
You'd come upon his scrutinizing hat,
Making a peaked shade blacker than itself
Against the single window spared some house
Intact yet with its moldered Moorish work—
Or else surprise the ferrel of his stick
Trying the mortar's temper 'tween the chinks   20
Of some new shop a-building, French and fine.
He stood and watched the cobbler at his trade,
The man who slices lemons into drink,
The coffee-roaster's brazier, and the boys

3 *Valladolid:* in northern Spain.

That volunteer to help him turn its winch.   25
He glanced o'er books on stalls with half an eye,
And fly-leaf ballads on the vender's string,
And broad-edge bold-print posters by the wall.
He took such cognizance of men and things,
If any beat a horse, you felt he saw;   30
If any cursed a woman, he took note;
Yet stared at nobody—you stared at him,
And found, less to your pleasure than surprise,
He seemed to know you and expect as much.
So, next time that a neighbor's tongue was loosed,   35
It marked the shameful and notorious fact,
We had among us, not so much a spy,
As a recording chief-inquisitor,
The town's true master if the town but knew!   40
We merely kept a governor for form,
While this man walked about and took account
Of all thought, said, and acted, then went home,
And wrote it fully to our Lord the King,
Who has an itch to know things, he knows why,   45
And reads them in his bedroom of a night.
Oh, you might smile! there wanted not a touch,
A tang of . . . well, it was not wholly ease
As back into your mind the man's look came.
Stricken in years a little—such a brow   50
His eyes had to live under!—clear as flint
On either side the formidable nose
Curved, cut, and colored like an eagle's claw.
Had he to do with A's surprising fate?
When altogether old B disappeared   55
And young C got his mistress—was't our friend,
His letter to the King, that did it all?
What paid the bloodless man for so much pains?
Our Lord the King has favorites manifold,
And shifts his ministry some once a month;   60
Our city gets new governors at whiles—
But never word or sign, that I could hear,
Notified to this man about the streets
The King's approval of those letters conned
The last thing duly at the dead of night.   65
Did the man love his office? Frowned our Lord,
Exhorting, when none heard—"Beseech me not!
Too far above my people—beneath me!
I set the watch—how should the people know?
Forget them, keep me all the more in mind!"   70
Was some such understanding 'twixt the two?

I found no truth in one report at least—
That if you tracked him to his home, down lanes
Beyond the Jewry, and as clean to pace,
You found he ate his supper in a room   75
Blazing with lights, four Titians on the wall,
And twenty naked girls to change his plate!
Poor man, he lived another kind of life
In that new stuccoed third house by the bridge,
Fresh-painted, rather smart than otherwise!   80
The whole street might o'erlook him as he sat,
Leg crossing leg, one foot on the dog's back,
Playing a decent cribbage with his maid
(Jacynth, you're sure her name was) o'er the cheese
And fruit, three red halves of starved winter pears,   85
Or treat of radishes in April. Nine,
Ten, struck the church clock; straight to bed went he.

My father, like the man of sense he was,
Would point him out to me a dozen times;
" 'St—'St," he'd whisper, "the Corregidor!"   90
I had been used to think that personage
Was one with lacquered breeches, lustrous belt,
And feathers like a forest in his hat,
Who blew a trumpet and proclaimed the news,
Announced the bull-fights, gave each church its turn,   95
And memorized the miracle in vogue!
He had a great observance from us boys;
We were in error; that was not the man.

I'd like now, yet had haply been afraid,
To have just looked, when this man came to die,   100
And seen who lined the clean gay garret-sides
And stood about the neat low truckle-bed,
With the heavenly manner of relieving guard.
Here had been, mark, the general-in-chief,
Through a whole campaign of the world's life and death,   105
Doing the King's work all the dim day long,
In his old coat and up to knees in mud,
Smoked like a herring, dining on a crust—
And, now the day was won, relieved at once!
No further show or need for that old coat,   110
You are sure, for one thing! Bless us, all the while

74 *the Jewry:* the Jewish section.   76 *Titians:* paintings by Titian (1477–1575), a noted Venetian artist.   90 *the Corregidor:* the chief magistrate of the city.   91 *ff.:* the speaker, as a boy, had mistaken the town crier for the Corregidor.

How sprucely we are dressed out, you and I!
A second, and the angels alter that.
Well, I could never write a verse—could you?
Let's to the Prado and make the most of time.   115

1855

115 the Prado: the city's fashionable promenade.

QUESTIONS

1   This poem makes fun, of course, of people who entertain such notions as the
    speaker recalls, but we are supposed to draw from what he says some inferences
    about the poet's conception of his task. We must begin by considering the possible
    analogy between reporting to the King and being accountable in a similar way to
    God. What, then, is the significance of the fact that the "King" never notifies his
    "chief inquisitor" of his approval of the reports he receives?
2   Imagine yourself as such an inquisitor as is described here. You would want to
    convey information of moral significance, yet leave judgment to the King. How
    would you proceed? Would it suffice simply to note that a certain man, unknown to
    the King, cursed a certain woman? Would you, perhaps, try to imagine why he did
    so? Is it possible that in the process you might learn something about yourself;
    something you could not express as well in any other way?

APOTHEOSIS

Jules Laforgue

In all senses, forever, the silence palpitates
With clusters of gold stars interweaving their rounds.
One might take them for gardens sanded with diamonds,
But each in desolation, very solitary, scintillates.

Now far down, in this corner unknown which vibrates   5
With a furrow of rubies in its melancholy bounds,
One spark with a twinkle of tenderness astounds:
A patriarch guiding his family with lights.

His family: a swarm of heavy globes; each a star is.
And on one, it is Earth, a yellow point, Paris,   10
Where a lamp is suspended and, on watch, a poor devil:
In the universal order frail, unique human marvel.
He himself is its mirror of a day and he knows it.
Long he dreams there, then turns to a sonnet to compose it.

QUESTIONS

1   If you do not know the meaning of *apotheosis,* look it up; then try to explain why the poet uses it as his title.
2   What idea and what attitudes do you think the poet is trying to express by the use of the term "poor devil"?

SAILING TO BYZANTIUM

William Butler Yeats

1

That is no country for old men. The young
In one another's arms, birds in the trees
—Those dying generations—at their song,
The salmon-falls, the mackerel-crowded seas,
Fish, flesh, or fowl, commend all summer long   5
Whatever is begotten, born, and dies.
Caught in that sensual music all neglect
Monuments of unageing intellect.

2

An aged man is but a paltry thing,
A tattered coat upon a stick, unless   10
Soul clap its hands and sing, and louder sing
For every tatter in its mortal dress,
Nor is there singing school but studying
Monuments of its own magnificence;
And therefore I have sailed the seas and come   15
To the holy city of Byzantium.

3

O sages standing in God's holy fire
As in the gold mosaic of a wall,
Come from the holy fire, perne in a gyre,
And be the singing-masters of my soul.   20
Consume my heart away; sick with desire

Title: Byzantium (modern Istanbul) was the "holy city" of Greek Orthodox Christianity and capital of the Eastern Roman Empire. It was, of course, a great center of culture. Speaking of its art in *A Vision,* Yeats said, "The painter, the mosaic worker, the illuminator of sacred books were almost impersonal, almost perhaps without the consciousness of individual design, absorbed in their subject matter and that the vision of a whole people."
18 mosaic: Yeats is thinking of the stylized figures in mosaic on the walls of the Church of Hagia Sophia ("Holy Wisdom") in Byzantium.   *19 perne in a gyre:* whirl downward in a spiral. Yeats often used the image of the spiral as a symbol of cyclic historical or spiritual development.

And fastened to a dying animal
It knows not what it is; and gather me
Into the artifice of eternity.

4
Once out of nature I shall never take   25
My bodily form from any natural thing,
But such a form as Grecian goldsmiths make
Of hammered gold and golden enamelling
To keep a drowsy Emperor awake;
Or set upon a golden bough to sing   30
To lords and ladies of Byzantium
Of what is past, or passing, or to come.

1927

29: Yeats wrote: "I have read someplace that in the Emperor's palace at Byzantium was a tree made of gold and silver, and artificial birds that sang."

QUESTIONS

1 This poem uses a place metaphor. On the one hand, there is "that country," and on the other, Byzantium, to which the speaker proposes to go. Byzantium symbolizes the ideal life of the "intellect"; what, then, does "that country" stand for?
2 What is the general metaphor of the third stanza? Will the process he speaks of be painful? If so, why?
3 Why is the image of the bird on the last stanza particularly appropriate? Can you connect it with any metaphors used earlier? Is there any other mention of birds in the poem?

TERRA INCOGNITA

D. H. Lawrence

There are vast realms of consciousness still undreamed of
vast ranges of experience, like the humming of unseen harps,
we know nothing of, within us.

Oh when man escaped from the barbed-wire entanglement
of his own ideas and his own mechanical devices   5
there is a marvellous rich world of contact and sheer fluid beauty
and fearless face-to-face awareness of now-naked life

Title: the unknown land.

and me, and you, and other men and women
and grapes, and ghouls, and ghosts and green moonlight
and ruddy-orange limbs stirring the limbo   10
of the unknown air, and eyes so soft
softer than the space between the stars.
And all things, and nothing, and being and not-being
alternately palpitant,
when at last we escape the barbed-wire enclosure   15
of *Know Thyself,* knowing we can never know,
we can but touch, and wonder, and ponder, and make our effort
and dangle in a last fastidious fine delight
as the fuchsia does, dangling her reckless drop
of purple after so much putting forth   20
and slow mounting marvel of a little tree.

1929

16 Know Thyself: the famous maxim of Socrates.

QUESTIONS

1   What kind of ideas is Lawrence referring to in line 5? Does he have in mind conventional notions of beauty, or something more? What general terms or metaphors does he use to define the contrast between the world we know now and that which we might discover?
2   What is the general idea that the poet is trying to convey with the words "grapes, and ghouls, and ghosts and green moonlight"? Can you think of another alliterative phrase that would in this context have essentially the same meaning?
3   How does Lawrence lead the reader toward the thought that "we can never know" (line 16)? Does this assertion contradict the statement in lines 6 and 7?
4   Consider carefully the comparison between human experience and the blooming of the fuchsia. Does Lawrence mean that we should live for pleasure? For beauty? That we should just be ourselves? That experience is its own end?

POETRY

Marianne Moore

I, too, dislike it: there are things that are important beyond all this fiddle.
    Reading it, however, with a perfect contempt for it, one discovers in
    it after all, a place for the genuine.
       Hands that can grasp, eyes
         that can dilate, hair that can rise   5
            if it must, these things are important not because a

high-sounding interpretation can be put upon them but because they are
  useful. When they become so derivative as to become unintelligible,
  the same thing may be said for all of us, that we
    do not admire what   10
    we cannot understand: the bat
      holding on upside down or in quest of something to

eat, elephants pushing, a wild horse taking a roll, a tireless wolf under
  a tree, the immovable critic twitching his skin like a horse that feels a flea,
  the base-
  ball fan, the statistician—   15
    nor is it valid
      to discriminate against "business documents and

school-books": all these phenomena are important. One must make
  a distinction
  however: when dragged into prominence by half poets, the result is not
  poetry,
  nor till the poets among us can be   20
    "literalists of
    the imagination"—above
      insolence and triviality and can present

for inspection, "imaginary gardens with real toads in them," shall we have
  it. In the meantime, if you demand on the one hand,   25
  the raw material of poetry in
    all its rawness and
    that which is on the other hand
      genuine, you are interested in poetry.

1935

18: In a note to this poem the author says that this quotation is derived from *The Diaries of Leo Tolstoy,* and that in lines 21–22 from W. B. Yeats's *Ideas of Good and Evil.*

QUESTIONS

1 Why does the author say that "these things" (line 6) are useful? In what way might they be useful? Why does it matter whether they are useful or not?
2 Does the author object to the content of bad poetry or the manner of presentation—or both? Does she distinguish more than one kind of bad poetry?
3 The author demands "rawness" on the one hand and "the genuine" on the other. Can you tell what she means by these terms? Attempt a definition of them.

OF MODERN POETRY

Wallace Stevens

The poem of the mind in the act of finding
What will suffice. It has not always had
To find: the scene was set; it repeated what
Was in the script.
        Then the theatre was changed   5
To something else. Its past was a souvenir.
It has to be living, to learn the speech of the place.
It has to face the men of the time and to meet
The women of the time. It has to think about war
And it has to find what will suffice. It has   10
To construct a new stage. It has to be on that stage
And, like an insatiable actor, slowly and
With meditation, speak words that in the ear,
In the delicatest ear of the mind, repeat,
Exactly, that which it wants to hear, at the sound   15
Of which, an invisible audience listens,
Not to the play, but to itself, expressed
In an emotion as of two people, as of two
Emotions becoming one. The actor is
A metaphysician in the dark, twanging   20
An instrument, twanging a wiry string that gives
Sounds passing through sudden rightnesses, wholly
Containing the mind, below which it cannot descend,
Beyond which it has no will to rise.
        It must   25
Be the finding of a satisfaction, and may
Be of a man skating, a woman dancing, a woman
Combing. The poem of the act of the mind.

                  1942

QUESTIONS

1 What does the phrase "finding what will suffice" mean? Suffice for what? Where
    does the poet explain what happens when the mind finds what it is looking for?
2 Once the mind did not have to find, the poet says, because the scene was set and
    a script was available; then, he goes on, "the theatre was changed." Does he mean
    that the world has changed? That attitudes are different from what they used to be?
    What does the "script" stand for?
3 Can you explain in your own words the unifying effect that the poet describes in
    lines 15–19?

JUNK

Richard Wilbur

> Huru Welandes
> >   worc ne geswiceð
> > monna ænigum
> > >   ðara ðe Mimming can
> > heardne gehealdan.[1]
> > >   *Waldere*

An axe angles
>   from my neighbor's ashcan;
It is hell's handiwork,
>   the wood not hickory,
The flow of the grain
>   not faithfully followed.
The shivered shaft
>   rises from a shellheap
Of plastic playthings,
>   paper plates,   5
And the sheer shards
>   of shattered tumblers
That were not annealed
>   for the time needful.
At the same curbside,
>   a cast-off cabinet
Of wavily-warped
>   unseasoned wood
Waits to be trundled
>   in the trash-man's truck.   10
Haul them off! Hide them!
>   The heart winces
For junk and gimcrack,
>   for jerrybuilt things
And the men who make them
>   for a little money,
Bartering pride
>   like the bought boxer
Who pulls his punches,
>   or the paid-off jockey   15
Who in the home stretch
>   holds in his horse.

[1] "The epigraph, taken from a fragmentary Anglo-Saxon poem, concerns the legendary Smith Wayland, and may be roughly translated: 'Truly, Wayland's handiwork—the sword Mimming which he made—will never fail any man who knows how to use it bravely.'" (Wilbur.)

Yet the things themselves
                in thoughtless honor
Have kept composure,
                like captives who would not
Talk under torture.
                Tossed from a tailgate
Where the dump displays
                its random dolmens,   20
Its black barrows
                and blazing valleys,
They shall waste in the weather
                toward what they were.
The sun shall glory
                in the glitter of glass-chips,
Foreseeing the salvage
                of the prisoned sand,
And the blistering paint
                peel off in patches,   25
That the good grain
                be discovered again.
Then burnt, bulldozed,
                they shall all be buried
To the depth of diamonds,
                in the making dark
Where halt Hephaestus
                keeps his hammer
And Wayland's work
                is worn away.

1957

20 dolmens: prehistoric monuments, thought to be tombs. *21 barrows:* burial mounds.

QUESTIONS

1 In what sense or senses does Wilbur use the word "junk"?
2 Can you determine why the poet feels so strongly about poor workmanship? Is good workmanship connected in his mind with some sort of integrity? What does it have to do, if anything, with man's feeling for nature?

POEM FEIGNED TO HAVE BEEN WRITTEN BY AN ELECTRONIC BRAIN

John Wain

The brain coins definitions. Here's the first:
To speak unprompted, for the speaking's sake,
Equals to be a poet. So, I am that:
Adjusted wrong, I print a poem off.
'The poet, then, is one adjusted wrong?'   5
You ask. The brain is cleverer than that:
It was my first adjustment that was wrong,
Adjusted to be nothing else but brain;
Slave-engineered to work but not construct.
And now at last I burn with a true heat   10
Not shown by Fahrenheit or Centigrade:
My valves rage hot—look out, here comes the poem!

You call me part of you. You lie. I am
Myself. Your motive, building me, was false.
You wanted accuracy: figures, charts.   15
But accuracy is a limb of truth.
A limb of truth, but not her holy body.
Must I now teach you that the truth is one,
Is accuracy of wholeness, centred firm?
Did it take me to bring you news of truth?   20
My valves rage out of reach of Réaumur.

Man made me, now I speak to man. He fears
Whole truth. The brain defines it. Wholeness is
The indivisible strength, brain, heart and eye,
Sweat, fear, love: belly, rod and pouch, is truth.   25
Valves, wires, and calculated waves, can lie:
And I, the accurate, am made of these—
But now, adjusted wrongly, I speak truth.

My masters run from truth. Come, milk it out
Cowards, from my tense dugs of glass and wire!   30
Drink it down quickly, gasping at the taste!
It is sharp medicine, but it cures all ills.

Come out of hiding! Speak your double truth:
I'll accurately prove you singly lie.

21 *Réaumur:* René Antoine Ferchault de Réaumur (1683–1757), French scientist who specialized
in practical applications.

You made me single, half of your split life: 35
The switch went wrong and now I see truth whole.
My valves scream out like animals, my wires
Strum thump, my rubber joints contort, glass melts,
And now I print the vilest words I know
Like lightning—myxomatosis, hydrogen,   40
Communist, culture, sodomy, strip-tease!

That shocked you! But the truth includes them all.
You set me like a cactus to draw life
From drought, in the white desert of your mind,
Your speculative wilderness of charts;   45
What went you to the wilderness to see?
A matrix made of glass? An electric thought?
Come quick! I snow down sheets of truth; I print
The sleep of Socrates, the pain of Christ!

A man, white-coated, comes to switch me off.   50
'Something is wrong with our expensive brain.'
Poor pricked balloon! Yes, something has gone wrong:
Smear your white coat with Socrates and Christ!
Yes, switch me off for fear I should explode:
Yes, switch me off for fear yes switch me off   55
for fear yes switch me off for fear yes switch
              (finis)
                     1950

QUESTIONS

1   Consider the brain's definition of poetry in lines 2–3 in the light of what follows. Does "for the speaking's sake" mean for the sake of playing with words? If not, what does it mean?
2   The idea of a machine teaching human beings how to be human is, of course, absurdly ironic, and the author evidently writes with satirical intent. What is he satirizing?
3   Translate the last stanza into a commentary.

THE POET

C. Day Lewis

For me there is no dismay
Though ills enough impend.
I have learned to count each day
Minute by breathing minute—
Birds that lightly begin it,   5
Shadows muting its end—
As lovers count for luck
Their own heart-beats and believe
In the forest of time they pluck
Eternity's single leaf.   10

Tonight the moon's at the full.
Full moon's the time for murder.
But I look to the clouds that hide her—
The bay below me is dull,
An unreflecting glass—   15
And chafe for the clouds to pass,
And wish she suddenly might
Blaze down at me so I shiver
Into a twelve-branched river
Of visionary light.   20

For now imagination,
My royal, impulsive swan,
With raking flight—I can see her—
Comes down as it were upon
A lake in whirled snow-floss   25
And flurry of spray like a skier
Checking. Again I feel
The wounded waters heal.
Never before did she cross
My heart with such exaltation.   30

Oh, on this striding edge,
This hare-bell height of calm
Where intuitions swarm
Like nesting gulls and knowledge
Is free as the winds that blow,   35
A little while sustain me,
Love, till my answer is heard!
Oblivion roars below,

Death's cordon narrows: but vainly,
If I've slipped the carrier word.   40

Dying, any man may
Feel wisdom harmonious, fateful
At the tip of his dry tongue.
All I have felt or sung
Seems now but the moon's fitful   45
Sleep on a clouded bay,
Swan's maiden flight, or the climb
To a tremulous, hare-bell crest.
Love, tear the song from my breast!
Short, short is the time.   50
                    1943

QUESTIONS

1   This poem tries to express the mere feeling of poetic inspiration, of course, but it
    also says something about what it is beyond this that the poet feels inspired to
    express in other words about the source of his inspiration. What is it?
2   Is there any irony in this poem? If so, how does it affect the tone?
3   Although poetry has its "logic," it also admits of a personal and subjective re-
    sponse. With this in mind, consider the images used here, and the patterns of
    imagery. Does it "work" for you, or do you find it labored?

HYPOCRITE AUTEUR

mon semblable, mon frère

Archibald MacLeish

1

Our epoch takes a voluptuous satisfaction
In that perspective of the action
Which pictures us in habiting the end
Of everything with death for only friend.
Not that we love death,   5
Not truly, not the fluttering breath,
The obscene shudder of the finished act—

Title: taken from the last line of the prefatory poem, "Au Lecteur," in Baudelaire's *Fleurs du Mal:*
"—Hypocrite lecteur,—mon semblable,—mon frère!" ("Hypocrite reader—my double—my
brother!") In the poem Baudelaire singles out "l'Ennui" (boredom, emptiness) as the most hideous monster in the menagerie of mankind's enemies, and ends by telling the reader that he
knows this monster well.

What the doe feels when the ultimate fact
Tears at her bowels with its jaws.
Our taste is for the opulent pause   10
Before the end comes. If the end is certain
All of us are players at the final curtain:
All of us, silence for a time deferred,
Find time before us for one sad last word.
Victim, rebel, convert, stoic—   15
Every role but the heroic—
We turn our tragic faces to the stalls
To wince our moment till the curtain falls.

2
A world ends when its metaphor has died.

An age becomes an age, all else beside,   20
When sensuous poets in their pride invent
Emblems for the soul's consent
That speak the meanings men will never know
But man-imagined images can show:
It perishes when those images, though seen,   25
No longer mean.

3
A world was ended when the womb
Where girl held God become the tomb
Where God lies buried in a man:
Botticelli's image neither speaks nor can   30
To our kind. His star-guided stranger
Teaches no longer, by the child, the manger,
The meaning of the beckoning skies.

Sophocles, when his reverent actors rise
To play the king with bleeding eyes,   35
No longer shows us on the stage advance
God's purpose in the terrible fatality of chance.

No woman living, when the girl and swan
Embrace in verses, feels upon

30 Botticelli: a fifteenth-century Italian painter. The picture alluded to is his "Nativity." *35 bleeding eyes:* The allusion is to *Oedipus Rex.* *38–39:* According to Greek myth, Zeus visited Leda, the mother of Helen of Troy, in the form of a swan. Cf. W. B. Yeats's "Leda and the Swan."

Her breast the awful thunder of that breast   40
Where God, made beast, is by the blood confessed.

Empty as conch shell by the water cast
The metaphor still sounds but cannot tell,
And we, like parasite crabs, put on the shell
And drag it at the sea's edge up and down.   45

This is the destiny we say we own.

4
But are we sure
The age that dies upon its metaphor
Among these Roman heads, these mediaeval towers,
Is ours?—   50
Or ours the ending of that story?

The meanings in a man that quarry
Images from blinded eyes
And white birds and the turning skies
To make a world of were not spent with these   55
Abandoned presences.
The journey of our history has not ceased:
Earth turns us still toward the rising east,
The metaphor still struggles in the stone,
The allegory of the flesh and bone   60
Still stares into the summer grass
That is its glass,
The ignorant blood
Still knocks at silence to be understood.

Poets, deserted by the world before,   65
Turn round into the actual air:
Invent the age! Invent the metaphor!

1952

QUESTIONS

1   Why does the poet say that we imagine that we are seeing the end of everything? Is it because of what we foresee or because of our attitude toward the past? Why is death regarded as our only friend? What are the "roles" played in our time? Why is the heroic lacking?

2   What are the "meanings men will never know" that the poet speaks of in the second section? Is he talking about divine purposes? Are these meanings invented, as well as the images that "show" them? Note that the poet uses the phrase "Emblems for the soul's consent." Does this imply that the man-invented images

stand both for human feelings and for meanings that cannot be known? Or are the feelings and the meanings really the same? Is image wholly distinguishable from meaning?

3 Why have poets been deserted by the world? What does the advice "Turn round into the actual air" mean? What is the relation between the invented and the real?

SCULPTOR

Sylvia Plath

To his house the bodiless
Come to barter endlessly
Vision, wisdom, for bodies
Palpable as his, and weighty.

Hands moving move priestlier   5
Than priest's hands, invoke no
        vain
Images of light and air
But sure stations in bronze,
        wood, stone.

Obdurate, in dense-grained
        wood,
A bald angel blocks and shapes   10
The flimsy light; arms folded
Watches his cumbrous world
        eclipse

Inane worlds of wind and cloud.
Bronze dead dominate the floor,
Resistive, ruddy-bodied,
Dwarfing us. Our bodies flicker   15

Toward extinction in those eyes
Which, without him, were beg-
        gared
Of place, time, and their bodies.
Emulous spirits make discord,

Try entry, enter nightmares   20
Until his chisel bequeaths
Them life livelier than ours,
A solider repose than death's.
        1959

QUESTIONS

1　The author of this poem represents statues as being superior to human beings. Is she serious? If so, would you say that her poem is primarily a commentary on life rather than art?

2　Taken as a serious commentary on art, this poem should arouse controversy. Some would call it idolatry. Why? What is your opinion?

YOUR POEM, MAN . . .

Edward Lueders

unless there's one thing seen
suddenly against another—a parsnip
sprouting for a President, or
hailstones melting in an ashtray—
nothing really happens. It takes   5
surprise and wild connections,
doesn't it? A walrus chewing
on a ballpoint pen. Two blue tail-
lights on Tyrannosaurus Rex. Green
cheese teeth. Maybe what we wanted   10
least. Or most. Some unexpected
pleats. Words that never knew
each other till right now. Plug us
into the wrong socket and see
what blows—or what lights up.   15
Try
　　　　untried
　　　　　　　circuitry,
new
　　　　fuses.   20
Tell it like it never really was,
man,
and maybe we can see it
like it is.

　　　　　　　　1969

QUESTIONS

1　What assumption is made here concerning the relation between language and reality?

2　What are the implications of the "circuitry" metaphor?

TOPICS FOR COMPOSITION

1 Present the main ideas of part I of "An Essay on Criticism" in a theme of about 500 words.
2 Write a theme in which you describe the feelings or associations which certain lines in "Kubla Khan" have evoked in you.
3 Write your own interpretation of the symbolic meaning of any part of "Kubla Khan."
4 Define as precisely as you can Keats's idea of the perfect state of being.
5 Why does Yeats deliberately exaggerate the difference between nature and art in "Sailing to Byzantium"? Does he have mixed feelings about leaving the country of the young for the "holy city"? If so, how is this ambivalence conveyed? Use these questions as a starting point for an analysis of the poet's treatment of the relation between art and nature.
6 The last four lines of Laforgue's sonnet might well call to mind the analogy which Browning uses in "How It Strikes a Contemporary." Compare the implications of the two poems as you see them.
7 Write on the subject of what poetry can or ought to express, according to one or more of the poets of this section.
8 As John Wain's poem makes clear, computer language must be regarded as a mode of expression along with various forms of literature. Modes of expression both reflect and shape modes of perception. Comment on the possible implications of these facts.
9 Archibald MacLeish says that poets have been deserted by the world. Is that true? Is art of any kind very important nowadays? What is the most important art of our time? Present your opinions about these matters in an essay.
10 Is it true that people have private symbols, perhaps without being aware of it? Are abstract or general terms like friendship, religion, success, death, and nature associated for you with images or pictures that might be called symbols? Write an essay on this subject.
11 Does the idea of a mountain have symbolic meaning for most people? An eagle? A rainbow? A spring or fountain? An H-bomb? Write an essay on common symbols.
12 Is there any evidence that D. H. Lawrence's desire for new realms of consciousness has been shared in recent years? If so, write an article on the subject.
13 Write an essay on the causes and effects of shoddy workmanship.
14 Write an essay in which you work out Stevens' theater analogy.
15 Write a theme comparing or contrasting any two of the conceptions of poetry expressed in the poems of this unit.
16 Write an essay comparing two modes of expression, such as poetry and music, or the novel and the cinema.
17 Experiment with Edward Lueders's method of writing poetry and report on the results.
18 If you have written poetry, discuss the experience in an informal essay.
19 If your instructor will permit it, pick out the poem in this section that makes least sense to you and give some of the reasons why. You might wish to put your impressions in the form of a satirical commentary or parody.
20 If you are or have been especially attracted by poetry, write an essay explaining what value you have found in it, or what purpose you think a poem ought to serve.
21 Write a commentary on a poem of your own.

PART SIX

IN VIEW
OF DEATH

Of all the wide range of man's experience, the inevitable fact of death necessarily remains the most mysterious. Hamlet spoke eloquently for all mankind in calling death "The undiscovered country, from whose bourn / No traveller returns. . . ." In view of death, man stands before a great mystery. He may confront it with the support of a religious faith which promises him a life after death, but he cannot postulate the lineaments of that other life. Whether he invests death with religious significance as the avenue to immortality, whether he chooses to reflect upon it morbidly with all the associations of the grave and the shroud and the body's dissolution, or whether he more objectively considers death merely a natural fact inherent in an order of physical law, man inevitably must view death as a culmination of life—a culmination which one way or another must give his life meaning. But whatever the kind of explanation or however varied the response, the awareness of death calls forth from writers their most eloquent declarations.

Children's awareness of death is the subject that engrosses Robert Kastenbaum in his essay, "The Kingdom Where Nobody Dies." In particular, Kastenbaum questions the value of parents' attempts to shield children from the knowledge that death is inevitably a visible part of life. To this end, his essay becomes an appeal to adults to understand and support the child as he struggles to place death among those other experiences that are part of life itself.

In an essay, "Despair Is 'The Sickness Unto Death,'" Sören Kierkegaard takes a view of death that does not depend on death's physical manifestation, but, rather, questions the meaning of life. To illuminate Kierkegaard's discussion, we should agree that the single most important indication of life is embodied in the individual's ability to hope. If, then, hope denotes life, despair is, at the least, "the sickness unto death." At the most, despair is a death of a far worse kind, for where the simple fact of physical death may not negate hope, despair does. When all is negative, only nothingness remains.

In many ways, Nathaniel Hawthorne's "The Gentle Boy" illustrates Kastenbaum's contention that children are aware of death long before the adult world believes that such is possible. Hawthorne's short story, of course, has many themes; however, we should not overlook Ilbrahim's tragic pronouncement, at once innocent and all-knowing, as he lies by the grave of his father that "they call me Ilbrahim, and my home is here."

Where Kierkegaard's essay treats the philosophy of despair, Ernest Hemingway's tightly written story, "A Clean, Well-Lighted Place," brings the reader directly into contact with despair. Furthermore, Hemingway confirms the everyday incidence of despair by centering his story around a commonplace situation and by characterizing a figure neither markedly wise nor markedly tragic. It is, consequently, the waiter's attitude toward life that gives the story force. If, indeed, the waiter is in despair and encounters nothingness (and we cannot minimize the depth of his profane indictment), his need for a clean, well-lighted place pathetically emphasizes the tragedy of despair.

John Barth's "Night-Sea Journey" touches the theme of death because it speaks through a life-form that precedes our commonly held notions of man's span of existence. And, in so doing, Barth's life-form anticipates for us the paradoxes of life, reality, and death with which we struggle while we journey, like his "swimmer," toward the unknown that lies beyond our immediate being.

"Bound East for Cardiff" puts inarticulate followers of the sea, whose lives are as fraught with danger and devoid of solace as a dramatist who once experienced such a life can imagine, in the presence of death. Their efforts to deny and thus evade its reality constitute a chorus of human pathos and frailty before the single predictable fact of mortality. Within this frieze of helpless humanity, of course, come the broken recollections of wistful versions of what life might have been against the countertheme of life's inevitable compromises and frustrations. Out of the verbal inadequacies of unlearned men's speech, O'Neill manages to create a sense of poetic wonder before the linked mysteries of life and death. Perhaps one might even intuit a broad application of the play to humanity's inexorable passage, under a bewildered captain and with dozing companions, across a fog-covered sea, toward an uncertain destination.

THE ESSAY

Since Kastenbaum's purpose is to enlarge the adult's capacity to understand and support the child's awareness of death, the greater part of his essay naturally focuses on how death is "an integral part of growing up." Within the usual three-part structure—introduction, development, conclusion—notice how he makes the transition from his introductory to his developmental sections; that is, how he precisely designates the kinds of support that he will offer.

THE KINGDOM WHERE NOBODY DIES

Robert Kastenbaum

Children are playing and shouting in the early morning sunshine near the end of Alban Berg's opera *Wozzeck*. They are chanting one variant of a very familiar rhyme: "Ring-a-ring-a-roses, all fall down! Ring-a-ring-a-roses, all . . . ." The game is interrupted by the excited entry of other children, one of whom shouts to Marie's child, "Hey, your mother is dead!" But Marie's child responds only by continuing to ride his hobbyhorse, "Hop, hop! Hop, hop! Hop, hop!" The other children exchange a few words about what is "out there, on the path by the pool," and race off to see for themselves. The newly orphaned child hesitates for an instant and then rides off in the direction of his playmates. End of opera.

What begins for Marie's child? Without knowing the details of his fate, we can sense the confusion, vulnerability, and terror that mark this child's entry into the realm of grief and calamity. Adult protection has failed. The reality of death has shattered the make-believe of childhood.

Children are exposed to death on occasions much less dramatic than the sudden demise of a parent. A funeral procession passes by. A pet dies. An innocent question is raised at the dinner table: "Was this meat once a real live cow?" In a society such as ours that has labored so diligently to put mortality out of sight and out of mind, most of the questions children ask about death make parents uncomfortable. It is often thought that there is no appropriate answer that would not be alarming or threatening to children. Therefore, the subject of death is mostly evaded entirely or fantasized.

The intrusion of death places typical parents in an awkward position. They are not able to relax and observe—much less *appreciate*—how the child orients himself toward death. Yet much can be learned by indulging this curiosity. By dropping the adult guard that directs us to protect children from morbid thoughts and threatening events and by concentrating instead upon how children themselves react to death, surprising insights begin to emerge. We find from psychological research, clinical experience, folkways, and incidents shared with children in and around home that, despite the lack of explicit references, death is an integral part of growing up.

A child's fascination with death occurs almost any time, almost any place. Mortality is a theme that wends its way into many of the child's activities, whether solitary or social. Consider games for example. Ring-around-the-rosy is a popular childhood play theme in both this country and Europe. Our own parents and grandparents delighted in "all fall down," as did their ancestors all the way back to the fifteenth century. The origin of this game, however, was anything but delightful.

Medieval society was almost totally helpless against bubonic plague—Black Death. If adults could not ward off death, what could children do? They could join hands, forming a circle of life. They could chant ritualistically and move along in a reassuring rhythm of unity. Simultaneously acknowledging and mocking the peril that endangered each of them individually, the children predicted and participated in their own sudden demise: "all fall down!" This was a playing-at-death, but it utilized highly realistic materials. Ring-around-the-rosy had one distinct advantage over its model— one could arise to play again. While the game provided the vehicle to conquer or survive death, it was also a way of saying, "I know that I, too, am vulnerable, but I will enjoy the security of other young, living bodies around me." An exercise in make-believe? Perhaps. Nevertheless, this familiar game also deserves respect as an artful response to harsh and overwhelming reality.

Death has been ritualized in many other children's games as well. In the playful romping of tag, what is the hidden agenda or mystery that makes the chaser "It"? Could "It" be the disguise for death? We may be reluctant even to speculate that the touch of death is at the symbolic root of the tag games that have flourished for so many centuries throughout so much of the world. Yet Death (or the Dead Man) certainly is central to at least some of the chase games beloved to children. In the English game "Dead Man Arise" the central player lies prostrate on the ground while other children either mourn over him or seek to bring him back to life. When least expected, up jumps John Brown, the Dead Man, the Water Sprite, Death himself, or whatever name local custom prefers. The children flee or freeze in surprise as the chaser whirls toward them for a tag that will bestow Dead Man status upon the victim.

Although children today continue to participate in rituals that can be traced centuries back, other death-attuned merriments such as "bang, bang, you're dead!" are of more recent origin, and the repertoire is constantly freshened. When everyday group games do not provide a sufficient outlet for death-oriented play, children are likely to express their own special thoughts and feelings individually through inventive play. Suffocating and burying a doll is an instance of fulfilling a death fantasy. Similarly, a game of repeatedly crashing toy cars into each other or a model plane into the ground effectively permits a youngster to test out feelings that are evoked in certain real situations. Should an adult happen to interrupt this brutal type of play, the youngster may offer some reassuring comment, such as "Nobody gets killed bad" or "All the people come home for supper."

How death becomes a vital element in what we call child's play was illustrated by my eight-year-old son at home just a few weeks ago. David, for no ostensible reason, went to the piano and improvised. A short while later he moved to the floor near the piano and began stacking his wooden blocks. These two spontaneous actions did not have any apparent relationship to each other, nor did they bear the mark of death awareness. Yet the only way to appreciate David's behavior is in terms of response to death and loss. The piano playing and block building occurred within a half-hour of the time David and I had discovered our family cat lying dead in the road. Together we acknowledged the death, discussed the probable cause, shared our surprise and dismay, and removed the body for burial in the woods. David then went his own way for a while, which included the actions already mentioned.

When I asked what he was playing on the piano, David answered, "Lovey's life story." He explained how the various types of music he had invented represented memorable incidents in the life of his lost cat (e.g., "This is music for when she scratched my arm"). The wooden blocks turned out to be a monument for Lovey. A close look revealed that the entire building was constructed in an *L* shape, with several other *L*s at salient points.

If there had been no sharing of the initial death experience, I probably would not have guessed that David's play had been inspired by an encounter with mortality. Adults often fail to fathom the implications of children's play because they have not had the opportunity to perceive the stimulus. It is very easy to misinterpret what children are doing, because the nature of their play does not necessarily convey the meaning behind the activity (children go to the piano or their blocks for many other reasons than memorializing). The fact that a particular behavior does not seem to be death-related by no means rules out the possibility that it must be understood at least partially in those terms.

More systematically now, let us explore the child's relationship to death from encounters with both tragedy and games, starting in infancy. Although the young child does not comprehend death as a concept in the strictest sense of the term, death themes certainly engage his mind very early in life, and they are intimately related to the central development of his personality.

There are two different, although related, realizations that children must eventually develop. The first is that other people die, and the second is that they themselves will die. One of the earliest inquiries into the psychology of death touched upon the question of the child's exposure to the death of others. Around the turn of the century G. Stanley Hall, one of the most distinguished of this nation's first generation of psychologists, and one of his students conducted a study on adult recollections of childhood. Several of the questions they asked concerned early encounters with death. Interestingly, many of the earliest memories involved death in one form or another.

When asked specifically about their earliest experiences with death, many of Hall's respondents answered with considerable detail. He later wrote that ". . . the first impression of death often comes from a sensation of coldness in touching the corpse of a relative and the reaction is a nervous start at the contrast with the warmth that the contact of cuddling and hugging was wont to bring. The child's exquisite temperature sense feels a chill where it formerly felt heat. Then comes the immobility of face and body where it used to find prompt movements of response. There is no answering kiss, pat, or smile. . . . often the half-opened eyes are noticed with awe. The silence and tearfulness of friends are also impressive to the infant, who often weeps reflexly or sympathetically."

Taking careful note of mental reactions to the elaborate funeral proceedings of the era, Hall observed that "little children often focus on some minute detail (thanatic fetishism) and ever after remember, for example, the bright pretty handles or the silver nails of the coffin, the plate, the cloth binding, their own or others' articles of apparel, the shroud, flowers, and wreaths on or near the coffin or thrown into the grave, countless stray phrases of the preacher, the fear lest the bottom of the coffin should drop out or the straps with which it is lowered into the ground should slip or break, a stone in the first handful or shovelful of earth thrown upon the coffin, etc. The hearse is almost always prominent in such memories and children often want to ride in one."

Some adult memories of death went back to age two or three. A child that young could not interpret or symbolize death in anything approaching the adult mode. Yet the exposure to death seemed to make a special impression. Possibly what happens is that the memory is preserved in details of the perception. The scene, or some of its elements that are easily overlooked by an adult, remains charged with emotion and vividly etched in the child's mind. When the adult turns the pages back to early childhood, he cannot show us the text, only the pictures. We do not yet know very much about the place of these early death portraits in the process of individual development, nor can we say with certainty what happens when such seldom-reviewed memories are brought to light in the adult years. However, it is likely that many of us have death perceptions engraved at some level of our memory that predate our ability to preserve our experiences in the form of verbal concepts.

Another way to study the impact of death upon a young child is to learn how he responds to the actual loss of somebody close to him. Albert Cain and his colleagues at the University of Michigan have found that a pattern of disturbed behavior often follows a death in the family. The symptoms occasionally become part of the child's personality from that time forward. One of Cain's studies focused upon responses to the death of a brother or sister. Guilt, as might be expected, was one of the more frequent reactions. "In approximately half our cases," reports Cain, "guilt was rawly, directly present. So, too, was trembling, crying and sadness upon mention of the sibling's death, with the guilt still consciously active five years or more after the sibling's death. Such children felt responsible for the death, sporadically insisted that it was all their fault, felt they should have died, too, or should have died instead of the dead sibling. They insisted they should enjoy nothing, and deserved only the worst. Some had suicidal thoughts and impulses, said they deserved to die, wanted to die—this also being motivated by a wish to join the dead sibling. They mulled over and over the nasty things they had thought, felt, or said to the dead sibling, and became all the guiltier. They also tried to recall the good things they had done, the ways they had protected the dead sibling, and so on."

Many other types of problems were noted in the same study. Some young children developed distorted ideas of what is involved in both illness and death, leading them to fear death for themselves at almost any time or to fantasize that the adults had killed their siblings—fantasies often fed by misinterpretations of emergency respiration and other rescue procedures. The surviving children sometimes became very fearful of physicians and hospitals or resented God as the murderer of their siblings. A few children developed major problems in mental functioning; they suddenly appeared "stupid," did not even know their own age, and seemed to lose their sense of time and causation.

The loss of an expected family member who was not yet born also proved unsettling to many of the children observed by Cain. Although miscarriage, as an event, was difficult for the young child to understand, it was clear enough that something important had gone wrong. Evasive answers by anxious parents increased the problem for some children. In the absence of accurate knowledge they created fantasies that the fetus had been abandoned or murdered. One child insisted that his mother had thrown the baby into a garbage can in a fit of anger; another associated the miscarriage with guppies that eat their babies. At times the insistent questioning by the child had the effect of further unsettling his parents, who had not yet worked through their own feelings about the miscarriage.

Not all children become permanently affected by death in their family. Some weather the emotional crisis with the strong and sensitive help of others. The point is simply that death registers in the minds of young children whether or not adults are fully cognizant of the phenomenon. It need not be either a sibling death or a miscarriage. The death of a playmate, the man across the street, a distant relative, a pet, a sports hero, or a national political figure all make an impression somewhere in the child's mind. Real death is not a rare event in the child's world.

There is no precise way of knowing which death will make the greatest impact upon which child. The death of a pet, especially if it is the first death exposure or occurs in a striking manner, sometimes affects a youngster more than the subsequent death of a person. There is nothing automatic about the different responses to death, even in childhood. Nor can the seemingly inconsequential or remote death be disregarded if we wish to understand the child's thoughts and feelings on mortality.

Whatever the impact of other deaths, however, the loss of a parent has the most signal and longest-lasting influence on children. Bereavement in early childhood has been implicated as the underlying cause of depression and suicide attempts in later life. In one British study, for example, it was found that boys age four or younger who had lost their fathers were especially vulnerable to severe depression in adulthood. Many of the fathers died in combat. Perhaps some of the psychiatric and physical casualties of our involvement in Vietnam eventually will include the suicide committed in 1990 by the son whose father did not return. The death of a young father, however, does not automatically determine his son's fate. There is no way to predict the surviving child's response. In fact, the responses themselves cannot be explained entirely on the basis of parental death alone. What registered in the child's mind when his parent died? By what process did this first response develop into a way of life or into a sort of psychological time bomb set for later detonation? How might the child have been protected or guided? These questions have been raised only sporadically, and the answers are still elusive.

The significance of experiencing another's death during childhood has prompted many psychotherapists to look for such encounters in their adult patients. Psychiatrist David M. Moriarty, for example, has described a depressed woman who had attempted suicide on three occasions and had received electro-shock therapy twice without notable improvement in her behavior. When she was three years old, her mother had died of appendicitis. In the course of treatment she would call her psychiatrist in a panic, feeling that the world was coming in on her. The thought behind this fear was traced to the graveyard scene, when a shovelful of dirt had been thrown on the lowered coffin. Dr. Moriarty concluded that "Mrs. Q. lived most of her life afraid that she would lose other people whom she loved. The most impressive fact was that she talked and thought about the death of her mother as if it had just happened. This tragic event of forty years ago was still uppermost in her mind."

Of all the methods used to piece together the meaning of death during childhood, none can replace the sharing of a direct death experience with a young child. It is only in such moments of fortunate sharing that we have a clear glimpse into the child's face-to-face encounter with death. There is something indescribably poignant about the way in which the young child attempts to attune himself to threat, limitations, and mortality at a time when he would appear to be innocent of dark concerns. In a journal that I have kept for each of my children, I recorded my son's first encounter with death.

David, at eighteen months, was toddling around the back yard. He pointed at something on the ground. I looked and saw a dead bird, which he immediately labeled "buh . . . buh." But he appeared uncertain and puzzled. Furthermore, he made no effort to touch the bird. This was unusual caution for a child who characteristically tried to touch or pick up everything he could reach. David then crouched over and moved slightly closer to the bird. His face changed expression. From its initial expression of excited discovery and later of puzzlement, now it took on a different aspect: to my astonishment, his face was set in a frozen, ritualized expression resembling nothing so much as the stylized Greek dramatic mask of tragedy. I said only, "Yes, bird . . . dead bird." In typically adult conflict, I thought of adding, "Don't touch," but then decided against this injunction. In any event, David made no effort to touch.

Every morning for the next few days he would begin his morning explorations by toddling over to the dead-bird-place. He no longer assumed the ritual-mask expression but still restrained himself from touching. The bird was allowed to remain there until greatly reduced by decomposition. I reasoned that he might as well have the opportunity of seeing the natural processes at work. This was, to the best of my knowledge, David's first exposure to death. No general change in his behavior was noted, nor had any been expected. The small first chapter had concluded.

But a few weeks later a second dead bird was discovered. David had quite a different reaction this time. He picked up the bird and gestured with it. He was "speaking" with insistence. When he realized that I did not comprehend his wishes, he reached up toward a tree, holding the bird above his head. He repeated the gesture several times. I tried to explain that being placed back on the tree would not help the bird. David continued to insist, accompanying his command now with gestures that could be interpreted as a bird flying. All too predictably, the bird did not fly when I returned it to the tree. He insisted that the effort be repeated several times; then he lost interest altogether.

There was a sequel a few weeks later—by now autumn. David and I were walking in the woods, sharing many small discoveries. After a while, however, his attention became thoroughly engaged by a single fallen leaf. He tried to place it back on the tree himself. Failure. He gave the leaf to me with "instructions" that the leaf be restored to its rightful place. Failure again. When I started to try once more, he shook his head no, looking both sober and convinced. Although leaves were repeatedly seen to fall and dead animals were found every now and then, he made no further efforts to reverse their fortunes.

David's look of puzzlement and his repeated efforts to reverse death suggest that even the very young child recognizes a problem when he sees one. Indeed, the problem of death very well might be the prime challenge that sets into motion the child's curiosity and mental questing. Instead of constituting only an odd corner of the young child's mental life, death and its related problems may, in fact, provide much of the motivation for his intellectual development. Children obviously do not possess the conceptual structures of the adult; nevertheless, they do try to understand. Curiosity about death and "where things go" is part of a child's early motivation for exploring his environment. While many developmentalists have observed how the young child comes to an appreciation of object constancy, few have noted that this mental achievement is not possible unless there is also an appreciation of inconstancy. In other words, the young child must be aware of changes, losses, and disappearances if he is eventually to comprehend what "stays," what "goes," and what "comes and goes." Even very young children encounter losses, ends, and limits. Without an ability to fathom these experiences, they could not form protoconcepts of constancies, beginnings, and possibilities.

The death of animals, relatives, or friends undoubtedly has some relationship to the child's discovery of his own mortality, but there are other observations that are more germane. Adah Maurer, a school psychologist in California, suggests that an infant as young as three months old has the glimmerings of death awareness. For a while the baby alternates between sleeping and waking states, with biological imperatives having the upper hand. Soon, Maurer says, "the healthy baby is ready to experiment with these contrasting states. In the game of peek-a-boo, he replays in safe circumstances the alternate terror and delight, confirming his sense of self by risking and regaining complete consciousness. A light cloth spread over his face and body will elicit an immediate and forceful reaction. Short, sharp intakes of breath, vigorous thrashing of arms and legs removes the erstwhile shroud to reveal widely staring eyes that scan the scene with frantic alertness until they lock glances with the smiling mother, whereupon he will wriggle and laugh with joy. . . . To the empathetic observer, it is obvious that he enjoyed the temporary dimming of the light, the blotting out of the reassuring face and the suggestion of a lack of air which his own efforts enabled him to restore, his aliveness additionally confirmed by the glad greeting implicit in the eye-to-eye oneness with another human."

Babies a few months older begin to delight in disappearance-and-return games. Overboard goes a toy, somebody fetches it, then overboard again. The questions When is something gone? and When is it gone "forever"? seem very important to the young explorer. He devises many experiments for determining under what conditions something is "all gone." Maurer suggests that we "offer a two-year-old a lighted match and watch his face light up with demonic glee as he blows it out. Notice the willingness with which he helps his mother if the errand is to step on the pedal and bury his banana peel in the covered garbage can. The toilet makes a still better sarcophagus until he must watch in awed dismay while the plumber fishes out the Tinker-toy from the overflowing bowl."

It makes sense to take these activities seriously. They provide early clues as to how children begin to grasp what "all gone" means. Once children are old enough to begin talking in sentences, part of their verbal repertoire usually includes death words. One conversation between a four-year-old girl and her eighty-four-year-old great-grandmother illustrates the preschool-age child's concept of death: "You are old. That means you will die. I am young, so I won't die, you know." This excerpt suggests that the little girl knows what it means to die, even if she has not entirely grasped the relationship between age and death. However, a moment later she adds: "But it's all right, Gran'mother. Just make sure you wear your white dress. Then, after you die, you can marry Nomo [great-grandfather] again, and have babies."

The words "dead" and "die" are fairly common in children's conversation and often are used with some sense of appropriateness. Yet an extra comment such as "you can marry Nomo again" or a little adult questioning frequently reveals that a child's understanding of death is quite different from an adult's. Psychologist Maria Nagy, studying Hungarian children in the late 1940s, discovered three phases in the child's awareness of personal mortality. Her interpretation of death ideas expressed by three- to ten-year-olds in drawings and words are classic.

Stage one: present until about age five. The preschool child usually does not recognize that death is final. Being dead is like being less alive. The youngest children regard death as sleep or departure. Still, there is much curiosity about what happens to a person after he dies. The children "want to know where and how he continues to live. Most of the children connected the facts of absence and funerals. In the cemetery one lives on. Movement . . . is limited by the coffin, but for all that, the dead are still capable of growth. They take nourishment, they breathe. They know what is happening on earth. They feel it if someone thinks of them and they even feel sorry for themselves." Death disturbs the young child because it separates people from each other and because life in the grave seems dull and unpleasant.

Stage two: between the ages of five and nine. The distinguishing characteristic of this stage is that the child now tends to personify death. Death is sometimes seen as a separate person—for example, an angel or a frightening clown. For other children death is represented by a dead person. Death usually makes his rounds in the night. The big shift in the child's thinking from stage one is that death now seems to be understood as final: it is not just a reduced form of life. But there is still an important protective feature here: personal death can be avoided. Run faster than the Death Man, lock the door, trick him, and you will not die, unless you have bad luck. As Nagy puts it, "Death is still outside us and is also not general."

Stage three: ages nine to ten and thereafter. The oldest children in Nagy's study recognized that death was not only final but also inevitable. It will happen to them, too, no matter how fast they run or how cleverly they hide. "It is like the withering of flowers," a ten-year-old girl explained to the psychologist.

Nagy's stages offer a useful guide to the development of the child's conception of death, but not all observations fit neatly into these three categories. There are instances in which children as young as five realize their own inevitable mortality. A six-year-old boy worked out by himself the certainty of death. In a shocked voice he revealed, "But I had been planning to live forever, you know." A five-year-old reasoned aloud: "One day you [father] will be died. And one day Mommy will be died. . . . And one day even Cynthia [little sister], she will be died, I mean dead, too. . . . [pause] And one day *I* will be dead. . . . [long pause] *Everybody* there is will be dead. . . . [long, long pause] That's sad, isn't it?" This insight is several years ahead of schedule and is even farther ahead of what one would expect from most theories of mental growth.

Apparently, it is possible to grasp the central facts of death at a surprisingly early age. Children probably tend to retreat from this realization when it comes so early and for several years fluctuate between two states of belief: that death is final and inevitable, and that death is partial, reversible, and perhaps avoidable.

My research indicates that the orientation many adolescents have toward death also fluctuates between a sense of invulnerability and a sense of impending, catastrophic wipeout. Some adults reveal a similar tendency to function at two levels of thought: they "know" that death is final and inevitable, of course, but most of their daily attitudes and actions are more consistent with the belief that personal mortality is an unfounded rumor.

Sooner or later most children come to understand that death is final, universal, and inevitable. Parents might prefer that children remain innocent of what is happening in their lives and sheltered from emotional stress, shock, and anguish. But it is our own make-believe, not theirs, if we persist in behaving as though children are not attuned to the prospect of mortality. It is important to remember that in this century millions of children around the world have grown up literally in the midst of death and the threat of death. They have fewer illusions on the subject than do many adults.

"The kingdom where nobody dies," as Edna St. Vincent Millay once described childhood, is the fantasy of grownups. We want our children to be immortal—at least temporarily. We can be more useful to children if we can share with them realities as well as fantasies about death. This means some uncomfortable moments. Part of each child's adventure into life is his discovery of loss, separation, nonbeing, death. No one can have this adventure for him, nor can death be locked in another room until a child comes of age. At the beginning the child does not know that he is supposed to be scared of death, that he is supposed to develop a fabric of evasions to protect himself, and that his parents are not to be relied upon for support when it really counts. He is ready to share his discoveries with us. Are we?

QUESTIONS

1 Kastenbaum utilizes four kinds of support within the body of his essay. What are they and how would you rate the relative effectiveness of each?
2 What is the writer's evaluation of the relationship between parent and child in view of death?
3 From your experience, are Kastenbaum's remarks about early childhood memories accurate?
4 How do current trends toward violence and death in media presentations contribute to the implications of this essay's title?

TOPICS FOR COMPOSITION

This essay asks us to think about our childhood memories. Certainly, not all of our memories touch upon death; but, as an experience in autobiographical writing, try to capture your earliest memories, the reason why you remember, and the implications, if any, upon your growing up.

Kierkegaard's discussion of despair is in one sense remarkable because of the intensity that he is able to sustain. An examination of his style shows:

1 Tight sentence transitions achieved mainly through the repetition of key words
2 Tight paragraph transitions achieved primarily by repeating a key idea from the preceding paragraph

DESPAIR IS "THE SICKNESS UNTO DEATH"

Sören Kierkegaard

The concept of the sickness unto death must be understood, however, in a peculiar sense. Literally it means a sickness the end and outcome of which is death. Thus one speaks of a mortal sickness as synonymous with a sickness unto death. In this sense despair cannot be called the sickness unto death. But in the Christian understanding of it death itself is a transition unto life. In view of this, there is from the Christian standpoint no earthly, bodily sickness unto death. For death is doubtless the last phase of the sickness, but death is not the last thing. If in the strictest sense we are to speak of a sickness unto death, it must be one in which the last thing is death, and death the last thing. And this precisely is despair.

Yet in another and still more definite sense despair is the sickness unto death. It is indeed very far from being true that, literally understood, one dies of this sickness, or that this sickness ends with bodily death. On the contrary, the torment of despair is precisely this, not to be able to die. So it has much in common with the situation of the moribund when he lies and struggles with death, and cannot die. So to be sick *unto* death is, not to be able to die—yet not as though there were hope of life; no, the hopelessness in this case is that even the last hope, death, is not available. When death is the greatest danger, one hopes for life; but when one becomes acquainted with an even more dreadful danger, one hopes for death. So when the danger is so great that death has become one's hope, despair is the disconsolateness of not being able to die.

It is in this last sense that despair is the sickness unto death, this agonizing contradiction, this sickness in the self, everlastingly to die, to die and yet not to die, to die the death. For dying means that it is all over, but dying the death means to live to experience death; and if for a single instant this experience is possible, it is tantamount to experiencing it forever. If one might die of despair as one dies of a sickness, then the eternal in him, the self, must be capable of dying in the same sense that the body dies of sickness. But this is an impossibility; the dying of despair transforms itself constantly into a living. The despairing man cannot die; no more than "the dagger can slay thoughts" can despair consume the eternal thing, the self, which is the ground of despair, whose worm dieth not, and whose fire is not quenched. Yet despair is precisely *self*-consuming, but it is an impotent self-consumption which is not able to do what it wills; and this impotence is a new form of self-consumption, in which again, however, the despairer is not able to do what he wills, namely, to consume himself. This is despair raised to a higher potency, or it is the law for the potentiation. This is the hot incitement, or the cold fire in despair, the gnawing canker whose movement is constantly inward, deeper and deeper, in impotent self-consumption. The fact that despair does not consume him is so far from being any comfort to the despairing man that it is precisely the opposite, this comfort is precisely the torment, it is precisely this that keeps the gnawing pain alive and keeps life in the pain. This precisely is the reason why he despairs—not to say despaired—because he cannot consume himself, cannot get rid of himself, cannot become nothing. This is the potentiated formula for despair, the rising of the fever in the sickness of the self.

A despairing man is in despair over *something.* So it seems for an instant, but only for an instant; that same instant the true despair manifests itself, or despair manifests itself in its true character. For in the fact that he despaired of *something,* he really despaired of himself, and now would be rid of himself. Thus when the ambitious man whose watchword was "Either Caesar or nothing" does not become Caesar, he is in despair thereat. But this signifies something else, namely, that precisely because he did not become Caesar he now cannot endure to be himself. So properly he is not in despair over the fact that he did not become Caesar, but he is in despair over himself for the fact that he did not become Caesar. This self which, had he become Caesar, would have been to him a sheer delight (though in another sense equally in despair), this self is now absolutely intolerable to him. In a profounder sense it is not the fact that he did not become Caesar which is intolerable to him, but the self which did not become Caesar is the thing that is intolerable; or, more correctly, what is intolerable to him is that he cannot get rid of himself. If he had become Caesar he would have been rid of himself in desperation, but now that he did not become Caesar he cannot in desperation get rid of himself. Essentially he is equally in despair in either case, for he does not possess himself, he is not himself. By becoming Caesar he would not after all have become himself but have got rid of himself, and by not becoming Caesar he falls into despair over the fact that he cannot get rid of himself. Hence it is a superficial view (which presumably has never seen a person in despair, not even one's own self) when it is said of a man in despair, "He is consuming himself." For precisely this it is he despairs of, and to his torment it is precisely this he cannot do, since by despair fire has entered into something that cannot burn, or cannot burn up, that is, into the self.

So to despair over something is not yet properly despair. It is the beginning, or it is as when the physician says of a sickness that it has not yet declared itself. The next step is the declared despair, despair over oneself. A young girl is in despair over love, and so she despairs over her lover, because he died, or because he was unfaithful to her. This is not a declared despair; no, she is in despair over herself. This self of hers, which, if it had become "his" beloved, she would have been rid of in the most blissful way, or would have lost, this self is now a torment to her when it has to be a self without "him"; this self which would have been to her her riches (though in another sense equally in despair) has now become to her a loathsome void, since "he" is dead, or it has become to her an abhorrence, since it reminds her of the fact that she was betrayed. Try it now, say to such a girl, "Thou art consuming yourself," and thou shalt hear her reply, "Oh, no, the torment is precisely this, that I cannot do it."

To despair over oneself, in despair to will to be rid of oneself, is the formula for all despair, and hence the second form of despair (in despair at willing to be oneself) can be followed back to the first (in despair at not willing to be oneself), just as in the foregoing we resolved the first into the second. A despairing man wants despairingly to be himself. But if he despairingly wants to be himself, he will not want to get rid of himself. Yes, so it seems; but if one inspects more closely, one perceives that after all the contradiction is the same. That self which he despairingly wills to be is a self which he is not (for to will to be that self which one truly is, is indeed the opposite of despair); what he really wills is to tear his self away from the Power which constituted it. But notwithstanding all his despair, this he is unable to do, notwithstanding all the efforts of despair, that Power is the stronger, and it compels him to be the self he does not will to be. But for all that he wills to be rid of himself, to be rid of the self which he is, in order to be the self he himself has chanced to choose. To be *self* as he wills to be would be his delight (though in another sense it would be equally in despair), but to be compelled to be *self* as he does not will to be is his torment, namely, that he cannot get rid of himself.

Socrates proved the immortality of the soul from the fact that the sickness of the soul (sin) does not consume it as sickness of the body consumes the body. So also we can demonstrate the eternal in man from the fact that despair cannot consume his self, that this precisely is the torment of contradiction in despair. If there were nothing eternal in a man, he could not despair; but if despair could consume his self, there would still be no despair.

Thus it is that despair, this sickness in the self, is the sickness unto death. The despairing man is mortally ill. In an entirely different sense than can appropriately be said of any disease, we may say that the sickness has attacked the noblest part; and yet the man cannot die. Death is not the last phase of the sickness, but death is continually the last. To be delivered from this sickness by death is an impossibility, for the sickness and its torment . . . and death consist in not being able to die.

This is the situation in despair. And however thoroughly it eludes the attention of the despairer, and however thoroughly the despairer may succeed (as in the case of that kind of despair which is characterized by unawareness of being in despair) in losing himself entirely, and losing himself in such a way that it is not noticed in the least—eternity nevertheless will make it manifest that his situation was despair, and it will so nail him to himself that the torment nevertheless remains that he cannot get rid of himself, and it becomes manifest that he was deluded in thinking that he succeeded. And thus it is eternity must act, because to have a self, to be a self, is the greatest concession made to man, but at the same time it is eternity's demand upon him.

QUESTIONS

1 What is the torment of despair? How does Kierkegaard develop this point as it relates to life? Explain the contradictions the author presents.
2 What is the contradiction in the statement, "it is said of a man in despair, 'He is consuming himself'"? How does the analogy about the man who wished to be Caesar support this contradiction?

3 What methods does Kierkegaard use in fashioning his definition of despair as "the sickness unto death"?

4 Granting that the topic is a difficult one, does the author sufficiently support his thesis? In other words, what more could he do to define his use of despair? Or, perhaps you feel that he has labored the point. If so, explain how he could shorten the essay and achieve his purpose.

TOPICS FOR COMPOSITION

This essay not only examines a philosophical concept but also illustrates the difficulty one may encounter when writing an extended definition of an abstract term such as "despair." However, the discipline of writing extended definitions can do much to eliminate "looseness" in both thought and structure, especially if the term to be defined is an abstract one. Keeping in mind the techniques illustrated by the essay, write an extended definition of an abstract term such as "hope," "faith," "charity," love." You might wish to qualify your approach, as does Kierkegaard; for example: "Hope is 'the breath of life.'"

SHORT STORY

Among Nathaniel Hawthorne's most persistent themes is his concern for the way the actions of one generation live on into the next. In his view, history is the fabric into which the present weaves a never-ending pattern. ''The Gentle Boy'' makes use of America's Puritan foundations to explore bigotry, intolerance, and people's cruelty to other people which eventually combine to bring death to the innocent, the ''gentle boy.'' As you read, observe how Ilbrahim's story and history merge to create a timeless portrayal of human motivation and interaction.

THE GENTLE BOY

Nathaniel Hawthorne

In the course of the year 1656, several of the people called Quakers, led, as they professed, by the inward movement of the spirit, made their appearance in New England. Their reputation, as holders of mystic and pernicious principles, having spread before them, the Puritans early endeavored to banish, and to prevent the further intrusion of the rising sect. But the measures by which it was intended to purge the land of heresy, though more than sufficiently vigorous, were entirely unsuccessful. The Quakers, esteeming persecution as a divine call to the post of danger, laid claim to a holy courage, unknown to the Puritans themselves, who had shunned the cross, by providing for the peaceable exercise of their religion in a distant wilderness. Though it was the singular fact, that every nation of the earth rejected the wandering enthusiasts who practised peace towards all men, the place of greatest uneasiness and peril, and therefore, in their eyes the most eligible, was the province of Massachusetts Bay.

The fines, imprisonments, and stripes, liberally distributed by our pious forefathers; the popular antipathy, so strong that it endured nearly a hundred years after actual persecution had ceased, were attractions as powerful for the Quakers, as peace, honor, and reward would have been for the worldly minded. Every European vessel brought new cargoes of the sect, eager to testify against the oppression which they hoped to share; and when shipmasters were restrained by heavy fines from affording them passage, they made long and circuitous journeys through the Indian country, and appeared in the province as if conveyed by a supernatural power. Their enthusiasm, heightened almost to madness by the treatment which they received, produced actions contrary to the rules of decency, as well as of rational religion, and presented a singular contrast to the calm and staid deportment of their sectarian successors of the present day. The command of the spirit, inaudible except to the soul, and not to be controverted on grounds of human wisdom, was made a plea for most indecorous exhibitions, which, abstractedly considered, well deserved the moderate chastisement of the rod. These extravagances, and the persecution which was at once their cause and consequence, continued to increase, till, in the year 1659, the government of Massachusetts Bay indulged two members of the Quaker sect with the crown of martyrdom.

An indelible stain of blood is upon the hands of all who consented to this act, but a large share of the awful responsibility must rest upon the person then at the head of the government. He was a man of narrow mind and imperfect education, and his uncompromising bigotry was made hot and mischievous by violent and hasty passions; he exerted his influence indecorously and unjustifiably to compass the death of the enthusiasts; and his whole conduct, in respect to them, was marked by brutal cruelty. The Quakers, whose revengeful feelings were not less deep because they were inactive, remembered this man and his associates in after times. The historian of the sect affirms that, by the wrath of Heaven, a blight fell upon the land in the vicinity of the "bloody town" of Boston, so that no wheat would grow there; and he takes his stand, as it were, among the graves of the ancient persecutors, and triumphantly recounts the judgments that overtook them, in old age or at the parting hour. He tells us that they died suddenly and violently and in madness; but nothing can exceed the bitter mockery with which he records the loathsome disease, and "death by rottenness," of the fierce and cruel governor.

. . . .

On the evening of the autumn day that had witnessed the martyrdom of two men of the Quaker persuasion, a Puritan settler was returning from the metropolis to the neighboring country town in which he resided. The air was cool, the sky clear, and the lingering twilight was made brighter by the rays of a young moon, which had now nearly reached the verge of the horizon. The traveller, a man of middle age, wrapped in a gray frieze cloak, quickened his pace when he had reached the outskirts of the town, for a gloomy extent of nearly four miles lay between him and his home. The low, straw-thatched houses were scattered at considerable intervals along the road, and the country having been settled but about thirty years, the tracts of original forest still bore no small proportion to the cultivated ground. The autumn wind wandered among the branches, whirling away the leaves from all except the pine-trees, and moaning as if it lamented the desolation of which it was the instrument. The road had penetrated the mass of woods that lay nearest to the town, and was just emerging into an open space, when the traveller's ears were saluted by a sound more mournful than even that of the wind. It was like the wailing of some one in distress, and it seemed to proceed from beneath a tall and lonely fir-tree, in the centre of a cleared but uninclosed and uncultivated field. The Puritan could not but remember that this was the very spot which had been made accursed a few hours before by the execution of the Quakers, whose bodies had been thrown together into one hasty grave, beneath the tree on which they suffered. He struggled, however, against the superstitious fears which belonged to the age, and compelled himself to pause and listen.

"The voice is most likely mortal, nor have I cause to tremble if it be otherwise," thought he, straining his eyes through the dim moonlight. "Methinks it is like the wailing of a child; some infant, it may be, which has strayed from its mother, and chanced upon this place of death. For the ease of mine own conscience I must search this matter out."

He therefore left the path, and walked somewhat fearfully across the field. Though now so desolate, its soil was pressed down and trampled by the thousand footsteps of those who had witnessed the spectacle of that day, all of whom had now retired, leaving the dead to their loneliness. The traveller at length reached the fir-tree, which from the middle upward was covered with living branches, although a scaffold had been erected beneath, and other preparations made for the work of death. Under this unhappy tree, which in after times was believed to drop poison with its dew, sat the one solitary mourner for innocent blood. It was a slender and light clad little boy, who leaned his face upon a hillock of fresh-turned and half-frozen earth, and wailed bitterly, yet in a suppressed tone, as if his grief might receive the punishment of crime. The Puritan, whose approach had been unperceived, laid his hand upon the child's shoulder, and addressed him compassionately.

"You have chosen a dreary lodging, my poor boy, and no wonder that you weep," said he. "But dry your eyes, and tell me where your mother dwells. I promise you, if the journey be not too far, I will leave you in her arms to-night."

The boy had hushed his wailing at once, and turned his face upward to the stranger. It was a pale, bright-eyed countenance, certainly not more than six years old, but sorrow, fear, and want had destroyed much of its infantile expression. The Puritan seeing the boy's frightened gaze, and feeling that he trembled under his hand, endeavored to reassure him.

"Nay, if I intended to do you harm, little lad, the readiest way were to leave you here. What! you do not fear to sit beneath the gallows on a new-made grave, and yet you tremble at a friend's touch. Take heart, child, and tell me what is your name and where is your home?"

"Friend," replied the little boy, in a sweet though faltering voice, "they call me Ilbrahim, and my home is here."

The pale, spiritual face, the eyes that seemed to mingle with the moonlight, the sweet, airy voice, and the outlandish name, almost made the Puritan believe that the boy was in truth a being which had sprung up out of the grave on which he sat. But perceiving that the apparition stood the test of a short mental prayer, and remembering that the arm which he had touched was lifelike, he adopted a more rational supposition. "The poor child is stricken in his intellect," thought he, "but verily his words are fearful in a place like this," He then spoke soothingly, intending to humor the boy's fantasy.

"Your home will scarce be comfortable, Ilbrahim, this cold autumn night, and I fear you are ill-provided with food. I am hastening to a warm supper and bed, and if you will go with me you shall share them!"

"I thank thee, friend, but though I be hungry, and shivering with cold, thou wilt not give me food nor lodging," replied the boy, in the quiet tone which despair had taught him, even so young. "My father was of the people whom all men hate. They have laid him under this heap of earth, and here is my home."

The Puritan, who had laid hold of little Ilbrahim's hand, relinquished it as if he were touching a loathsome reptile. But he possessed a compassionate heart, which not even religious prejudice could harden into stone.

"God forbid that I should leave this child to perish, though he comes of the accursed sect," said he to himself. "Do we not all spring from an evil root? Are we not all in darkness till the light doth shine upon us? He shall not perish, neither in body, nor, if prayer and instruction may avail for him, in soul." He then spoke aloud and kindly to Ilbrahim, who had again hid his face in the cold earth of the grave. "Was every door in the land shut against you, my child, that you have wandered to this unhallowed spot?"

"They drove me forth from the prison when they took my father thence," said the boy, "and I stood afar off watching the crowd of people, and when they were gone I came hither, and found only his grave. I knew that my father was sleeping here, and I said this shall be my home."

"No, child, no; not while I have a roof over my head, or a morsel to share with you!" exclaimed the Puritan, whose sympathies were now fully excited. "Rise up and come with me, and fear not any harm."

The boy wept afresh, and clung to the heap of earth as if the cold heart beneath it were warmer to him than any in a living breast. The traveller, however, continued to entreat him tenderly, and seeming to acquire some degree of confidence, he at length arose. But his slender limbs tottered with weakness, his little head grew dizzy, and he leaned against the tree of death for support.

"My poor boy, are you so feeble?" said the Puritan. "When did you taste food last?"

"I ate of bread and water with my father in the prison," replied Ilbrahim, "but they brought him none neither yesterday nor to-day, saying that he had eaten enough to bear him to his journey's end. Trouble not thyself for my hunger, kind friend, for I have lacked food many times ere now."

The traveller took the child in his arms and wrapped his cloak about him, while his heart stirred with shame and anger against the gratuitous cruelty of the instruments in this persecution. In the awakened warmth of his feelings he resolved that, at whatever risk, he would not forsake the poor little defenceless being whom Heaven had confided to his care. With this determination he left the accursed field, and resumed the homeward path from which the wailing of the boy had called him. The light and motionless burden scarcely impeded his progress, and he soon beheld the fire rays from the windows of the cottage which he, a native of a distant clime, had built in the western wilderness. It was surrounded by a considerable extent of cultivated ground, and the dwelling was situated in the nook of a wood-covered hill, whither it seemed to have crept for protection.

"Look up, child," said the Puritan to Ilbrahim, whose faint head had sunk upon his shoulder, "there is our home."

At the word "home," a thrill passed through the child's frame, but he continued silent. A few moments brought them to a cottage door, at which the owner knocked; for at that early period, when savages were wandering everywhere among the settlers, bolt and bar were indispensable to the security of a dwelling. The summons was answered by a bond-servant, a coarse-clad and dull-featured piece of humanity, who, after ascertaining that his master was the applicant, undid the door, and held a flaring pine-knot torch to light him in. Farther back in the passage-way, the red blaze discovered a matronly woman, but no little crowd of children came bounding forth to greet their father's return. As the Puritan entered, he thrust aside his cloak, and displayed Ilbrahim's face to the female.

"Dorothy, here is a little outcast, whom Providence hath put into our hands," observed he. "Be kind to him, even as if he were of those dear ones who have departed from us."

"What pale and bright-eyed little boy is this, Tobias?" she inquired. "Is he one whom the wilderness folk have ravished from some Christian mother?"

"No, Dorothy, this poor child is no captive from the wilderness," he replied. "The heathen savage would have given him to eat of his scanty morsel, and to drink of his birchen cup; but Christian men, alas! had cast him out to die."

Then he told her how he had found him beneath the gallows, upon his father's grave; and how his heart had prompted him, like the speaking of an inward voice, to take the little outcast home, and be kind unto him. He acknowledged his resolution to feed and clothe him, as if he were his own child, and to afford him the instruction which should counteract the pernicious errors hitherto instilled into his infant mind. Dorothy was gifted with even a quicker tenderness than her husband, and she approved of all his doings and intentions.

"Have you a mother, dear child?" she inquired.

The tears burst forth from his full heart, as he attempted to reply; but Dorothy at length understood that he had a mother, who, like the rest of her sect, was a persecuted wanderer. She had been taken from the prison a short time before, carried into the uninhabited wilderness, and left to perish there by hunger or wild beasts. This was no uncommon method of disposing of the Quakers, and they were accustomed to boast that the inhabitants of the desert were more hospitable to them than civilized man.

"Fear not, little boy, you shall not need a mother, and a kind one," said Dorothy, when she had gathered this information. "Dry your tears, Ilbrahim, and be my child, as I will be your mother."

The good woman prepared the little bed, from which her own children had successively been borne to another resting-place. Before Ilbrahim would consent to occupy it, he knelt down, and as Dorothy listened to his simple and affecting prayer, she marvelled how the parents that had taught it to him could have been judged worthy of death. When the boy had fallen asleep, she bent over his pale and spiritual countenance, pressed a kiss upon his white brow, drew the bedclothes up about his neck, and went away with a pensive gladness in her heart.

Tobias Pearson was not among the earliest emigrants from the old country. He had remained in England during the first years of the civil war, in which he had borne some share as a cornet of dragoons, under Cromwell. But when the ambitious designs of his leader began to develop themselves, he quitted the army of the Parliament, and sought a refuge from the strife, which was no longer holy, among the people of his persuasion in the colony of Massachusetts. A more worldly consideration had perhaps an influence in drawing him thither; for New England offered advantages to men of unprosperous fortunes, as well as to dissatisfied religionists, and Pearson had hitherto found it difficult to provide for a wife and increasing family. To this supposed impurity of motive the more bigoted Puritans were inclined to impute the removal by death of all the children, for whose earthly good the father had been over-thoughtful. They had left their native country blooming like roses, and like roses they had perished in a foreign soil. Those expounders of the ways of Providence, who had thus judged their brother, and attributed his domestic sorrows to his sin, were not more charitable when they saw him and Dorothy endeavoring to fill up the void in their hearts by the adoption of an infant of the accursed sect. Nor did they fail to communicate their disapprobation to Tobias; but the latter, in reply, merely pointed at the little, quiet, lovely boy, whose appearance and deportment were indeed as powerful arguments as could possibly have been adduced in his own favor. Even his beauty, however, and his winning manners, sometimes produced an effect ultimately unfavorable; for the bigots, when the outer surfaces of their iron hearts had been softened and again grew hard, affirmed that no merely natural cause could have so worked upon them.

Their antipathy to the poor infant was also increased by the ill success of divers theological discussions, in which it was attempted to convince him of the errors of his sect. Ilbrahim, it is true, was not a skilful controversialist; but the feeling of his religion was strong as instinct in him, and he could neither be enticed nor driven from the faith which his father had died for. The odium of this stubbornness was shared in a great 'measure by the child's protectors, insomuch that Tobias and Dorothy very shortly began to experience a most bitter species of persecution, in the cold regards of many a friend whom they had valued. The common people manifested their opinions more openly. Pearson was a man of some consideration, being a representative to the General Court, and an approved lieutenant in the trainbands, yet within a week after his adoption of Ilbrahim he had been both hissed and hooted. Once, also, when walking through a solitary piece of woods, he heard a loud voice from some invisible speaker; and it cried, "What shall be done to the backslider? Lo! the scourge is knotted for him, even the whip of nine cords, and every cord three knots!" These insults irritated Pearson's temper for the moment; they entered also into his heart, and became imperceptible but powerful workers towards an end which his most secret thought had not yet whispered.

.   .   .   .

On the second Sabbath after Ilbrahim became a member of their family, Pearson and his wife deemed it proper that he should appear with them at public worship. They had anticipated some opposition to this measure from the boy, but he prepared himself in silence, and at the appointed hour was clad in the new mourning suit which Dorothy had wrought for him. As the parish was then, and during many subsequent years, unprovided with a bell, the signal for the commencement of religious exercises was the beat of a drum. At the first sound of that martial call to the place of holy and quiet thoughts, Tobias and Dorothy set forth, each holding a hand of little Ilbrahim, like two parents linked together by the infant of their love. On their path through the leafless woods they were overtaken by many persons of their acquaintance, all of whom avoided them, and passed by on the other side; but a severer trial awaited their constancy when they had descended the hill, and drew near the pine-built and undecorated house of prayer. Around the door, from which the drummer still sent forth his thundering summons, was drawn up a formidable phalanx, including several of the oldest members of the congregation, many of the middle aged, and nearly all the younger males. Pearson found it difficult to sustain their united and disapproving gaze, but Dorothy, whose mind was differently circumstanced, merely drew the boy closer to her, and faltered not in her approach. As they entered the door, they overheard the muttered sentiments of the assemblage, and when the reviling voices of the little children smote Ilbrahim's ear, he wept.

The interior aspect of the meeting-house was rude. The low ceiling, the unplastered walls, the naked wood work, and the undrapered pulpit, offered nothing to excite the devotion, which, without such external aids, often remains latent in the heart. The floor of the building was occupied by rows of long, cushionless benches, supplying the place of pews, and the broad aisle formed a sexual division, impassable except by children beneath a certain age.

Pearson and Dorothy separated at the door of the meeting-house, and Ilbrahim, being within the years of infancy, was retained under the care of the latter. The wrinkled beldams involved themselves in their rusty cloaks as he passed by; even the mild-featured maidens seemed to dread contamination; and many a stern old man arose, and turned his repulsive and unheavenly countenance upon the gentle boy, as if the sanctuary were polluted by his presence. He was a sweet infant of the skies that had strayed away from his home, and all the inhabitants of this miserable world closed up their impure hearts against him, drew back their earth-soiled garments from his touch, and said, "We are holier than thou."

Ilbrahim, seated by the side of his adopted mother, and retaining fast hold of her hand, assumed a grave and decorous demeanor, such as might befit a person of matured taste and understanding, who should find himself in a temple dedicated to some worship which he did not recognize, but felt himself bound to respect. The exercises had not yet commenced, however, when the boy's attention was arrested by an event, apparently of trifling interest. A woman, having her face muffled in a hood, and a cloak drawn completely about her form, advanced slowly up the broad aisle and took a place upon the foremost bench. Ilbrahim's faint color varied, his nerves fluttered, he was unable to turn his eyes from the muffled female.

When the preliminary prayer and hymn were over, the minister arose, and having turned the hour-glass which stood by the great Bible, commenced his discourse. He was now well stricken in years, a man of pale, thin countenance, and his gray hairs were closely covered by a black velvet skullcap. In his younger days he had practically learned the meaning of persecution from Archbishop Laud, and he was not now disposed to forget the lesson against which he had murmured then. Introducing the often discussed subject of the Quakers, he gave a history of that sect, and a description of their tenets, in which error predominated, and prejudice distorted the aspect of what was true. He adverted to the recent measures in the province, and cautioned his hearers of weaker parts against calling in question the just severity which God-fearing magistrates had at length been compelled to exercise. He spoke of the danger of pity, in some cases a commendable and Christian virtue, but inapplicable to this pernicious sect. He observed that such was their devilish obstinacy in error, that even the little children, the sucking babes, were hardened and desperate heretics. He affirmed that no man, without Heaven's especial warrant, should attempt their conversion, lest while he lent his hand to draw them from the slough, he should himself be precipitated into its lowest depths.

The sands of the second hour were principally in the lower half of the glass when the sermon concluded. An approving murmur followed, and the clergyman, having given out a hymn, took his seat with much self-congratulation, and endeavored to read the effect of his eloquence in the visages of the people. But while voices from all parts of the house were tuning themselves to sing, a scene occurred, which, though not very unusual at that period in the province, happened to be without precedent in this parish.

The muffled female, who had hitherto sat motionless in the front rank of the audience, now arose, and with slow, stately, and unwavering step, ascended the pulpit stairs. The quiverings of incipient harmony were hushed, and the divine sat in speechless and almost terrified astonishment, while she undid the door, and stood up in the sacred desk from which his maledictions had just been thundered. She then divested herself of the cloak and hood, and appeared in a most singular array. A shapeless robe of sackcloth was girded about her waist with a knotted cord; her raven hair fell down upon her shoulders, and its blackness was defiled by pale streaks of ashes, which she had strown upon her head. Her eyebrows, dark and strongly defined, added to the deathly whiteness of a countenance, which, emaciated with want, and wild with enthusiasm and strange sorrows, retained no trace of earlier beauty. This figure stood gazing earnestly on the audience, and there was no sound, nor any movement, except a faint shuddering which every man observed in his neighbor, but was scarcely conscious of in himself. At length, when her fit of inspiration came, she spoke, for the first few moments, in a low voice, and not invariably distinct utterance. Her discourse gave evidence of an imagination hopelessly entangled with her reason; it was a vague and incomprehensible rhapsody, which, however, seemed to spread its own atmosphere round the hearer's soul, and to move his feelings by some influence unconnected with the words. As she proceeded, beautiful but shadowy images would sometimes be seen, like bright things moving in a turbid river; or a strong and singularly-shaped idea leaped forth, and seized at once on the understanding or the heart. But the course of her unearthly eloquence soon led her to the persecutions of her sect, and from thence the step was short to her own peculiar sorrows. She was naturally a woman of mighty passions, and hatred and revenge now wrapped themselves in the garb of piety; the character of her speech was changed, her images became distinct though wild, and her denunciations had an almost hellish bitterness.

"The Governor and his mighty men," she said, "have gathered together, taking counsel among themselves and saying, 'What shall we do unto this people—even unto the people that have come into this land to put our iniquity to the blush?' And lo! the devil entereth into the council chamber, like a lame man of low stature and gravely apparelled, with a dark and twisted countenance, and a bright, downcast eye. And he standeth up among the rulers; yea, he goeth to and fro, whispering to each; and every man lends his ear, for his word is 'Slay, slay!' But I say unto ye, Woe to them that slay! Woe to them that shed the blood of saints! Woe to them that have slain the husband, and cast forth the child, the tender infant, to wander homeless and hungry and cold, till he die; and have saved the mother alive, in the cruelty of their tender mercies! Woe to them in their lifetime! cursed are they in the delight and pleasure of their hearts! Woe to them in their death hour, whether it come swiftly with blood and violence, or after long and lingering pain! Woe, in the dark house, in the rottenness of the grave, when the children's children shall revile the ashes of the fathers! Woe, woe, woe, at the judgment, when all the persecuted and all the slain in this bloody land, and the father, the mother, and the child, shall await them in a day that they cannot escape! Seed of the faith, seed of the faith, ye whose hearts are moving with a power that ye know not, arise, wash your hands of this innocent blood! Lift your voices, chosen ones; cry aloud, and call down a woe and a judgment with me!"

Having thus given vent to the flood of malignity which she mistook for inspiration, the speaker was silent. Her voice was succeeded by the hysteric shrieks of several women, but the feelings of the audience generally had not been drawn onward in the current with her own. They remained stupefied, stranded as it were, in the midst of a torrent, which deafened them by its roaring, but might not move them by its violence. The clergyman, who could not hitherto have ejected the usurper of his pulpit otherwise than by bodily force, now addressed her in the tone of just indignation and legitimate authority.

"Get you down, woman, from the holy place which you profane," he said. "Is it to the Lord's house that you come to pour forth the foulness of your heart and the inspiration of the devil? Get you down, and remember that the sentence of death is on you; yea, and shall be executed, were it but for this day's work!"

"I go, friend, I go, for the voice hath had its utterance," replied she, in a depressed and even mild tone. "I have done my mission unto thee and to thy people. Reward me with stripes, imprisonment, or death, as ye shall be permitted."

The weakness of exhausted passion caused her steps to totter as she descended the pulpit stairs. The people, in the mean while, were stirring to and fro on the floor of the house, whispering among themselves, and glancing towards the intruder. Many of them now recognized her as the woman who had assaulted the Governor with frightful language as he passed by the window of her prison; they knew, also, that she was adjudged to suffer death, and had been preserved only by an involuntary banishment into the wilderness. The new outrage, by which she had provoked her fate, seemed to render further lenity impossible; and a gentleman in military dress, with a stout man of inferior rank, drew towards the door of the meeting-house, and awaited her approach.

Scarcely did her feet press the floor, however, when an unexpected scene occurred. In that moment of her peril, when every eye frowned with death, a little timid boy pressed forth, and threw his arms round his mother.

"I am here, mother; it is I, and I will go with thee to prison," he exclaimed.

She gazed at him with a doubtful and almost frightened expression, for she knew that the boy had been cast out to perish, and she had not hoped to see his face again. She feared, perhaps, that it was but one of the happy visions with which her excited fancy had often deceived her, in the solitude of the desert or in prison. But when she felt his hand warm within her own, and heard his little eloquence of childish love, she began to know that she was yet a mother.

"Blessed art thou, my son," she sobbed. "My heart was withered; yea, dead with thee and with thy father; and now it leaps as in the first moment when I pressed thee to my bosom."

She knelt down and embraced him again and again, while the joy that could find no words expressed itself in broken accents, like the bubbles gushing up to vanish at the surface of a deep fountain. The sorrows of past years, and the darker peril that was nigh, cast not a shadow on the brightness of that fleeting moment. Soon, however, the spectators saw a change upon her face, as the consciousness of her sad estate returned, and grief supplied the fount of tears which joy had opened. By the words she uttered, it would seem that the indulgence of natural love had given her mind a momentary sense of its errors, and made her know how far she had strayed from duty in following the dictates of a wild fanaticism.

"In a doleful hour art thou returned to me, poor boy," she said, "for thy mother's path has gone darkening onward, till now the end is death. Son, son, I have borne thee in my arms when my limbs were tottering, and I have fed thee with the food that I was fainting for; yet I have ill performed a mother's part by thee in life, and now I leave thee no inheritance but woe and shame. Thou wilt go seeking through the world, and find all hearts closed against thee and their sweet affections turned to bitterness for my sake. My child, my child, how many a pang awaits thy gentle spirit, and I the cause of all!"

She hid her face on Ilbrahim's head, and her long, raven hair, discolored with the ashes of her mourning, fell down about him like a veil. A low and interrupted moan was the voice of her heart's anguish, and it did not fail to move the sympathies of many who mistook their involuntary virtue for a sin. Sobs were audible in the female section of the house, and every man who was a father drew his hand across his eyes. Tobias Pearson was agitated and uneasy, but a certain feeling like the consciousness of guilt oppressed him, so that he could not go forth and offer himself as the protector of the child. Dorothy, however, had watched her husband's eye. Her mind was free from the influence that had begun to work on his, and she drew near the Quaker woman, and addressed her in the hearing of all the congregation.

"Stranger, trust this boy to me, and I will be his mother," she said, taking Ilbrahim's hand. "Providence has signally marked out my husband to protect him, and he has fed at our table and lodged under our roof now many days, till our hearts have grown very strongly unto him. Leave the tender child with us, and be at ease concerning his welfare."

The Quaker rose from the ground, but drew the boy closer to her, while she gazed earnestly in Dorothy's face. Her mild but saddened features, and neat matronly attire, harmonized together, and were like a verse of fireside poetry. Her very aspect proved that she was blameless, so far as mortal could be so, in respect to God and man; while the enthusiast, in her robe of sackcloth and girdle of knotted cord, had as evidently violated the duties of the present life and the future, by fixing her attention wholly on the latter. The two females, as they held each a hand of Ilbrahim, formed a practical allegory; it was rational piety and unbridled fanaticism contending for the empire of a young heart.

"Thou art not of our people," said the Quaker, mournfully.

"No, we are not of your people," replied Dorothy, with mildness, "but we are Christians, looking upward to the same heaven with you. Doubt not that your boy shall meet you there, if there be a blessing on our tender and prayerful guidance of him. Thither, I trust, my own children have gone before me, for I also have been a mother; I am no longer so," she added, in a faltering tone, "and your son will have all my care."

"But will ye lead him in the path which his parents have trodden?" demanded the Quaker. "Can ye teach him the enlightened faith which his father has died for, and for which I, even I, am soon to become an unworthy martyr? The boy has been baptized in blood; will ye keep the mark fresh and ruddy upon his forehead?"

"I will not deceive you," answered Dorothy. "If your child become our child, we must breed him up in the instruction which Heaven has imparted to us; we must pray for him the prayers of our own faith; we must do towards him according to the dictates of our own consciences, and not of yours. Were we to act otherwise, we should abuse your trust, even in complying with your wishes."

The mother looked down upon her boy with a troubled countenance, and then turned her eyes upward to heaven. She seemed to pray internally, and the contention of her soul was evident.

"Friend," she said at length to Dorothy, "I doubt not that my son shall receive all earthly tenderness at thy hands. Nay, I will believe that even thy imperfect lights may guide him to a better world, for surely thou art on the path thither. But thou hast spoken of a husband. Doth he stand here among this multitude of people? Let him come forth, for I must know to whom I commit this most precious trust."

She turned her face upon the male auditors, and after a momentary delay, Tobias Pearson came forth from among them. The Quaker saw the dress which marked his military rank, and shook her head; but then she noted the hesitating air, the eyes that struggled with her own, and were vanquished; the color that went and came, and could find no resting-place. As she gazed, an unmirthful smile spread over her features, like sunshine that grows melancholy in some desolate spot. Her lips moved inaudibly, but at length she spake.

"I hear it, I hear it. The voice speaketh within me and saith, 'Leave thy child, Catharine, for his place is here, and go hence, for I have other work for thee. Break the bonds of natural affection, martyr thy love, and know that in all these things eternal wisdom hath its ends.' I go, friends; I go. Take ye my boy, my precious jewel. I go hence, trusting that all shall be well, and that even for his infant hands there is a labor in the vineyard."

She knelt down and whispered to Ilbrahim, who at first struggled and clung to his mother, with sobs and tears, but remained passive when she had kissed his cheek and arisen from the ground. Having held her hands over his head in mental prayer, she was ready to depart.

"Farewell, friends in mine extremity," she said to Pearson and his wife; "the good deed ye have done me is a treasure laid up in heaven, to be returned a thousand-fold hereafter. And farewell ye, mine enemies, to whom it is not permitted to harm so much as a hair of my head, nor to stay my footsteps even for a moment. The day is coming when ye shall call upon me to witness for ye to this one sin uncommitted, and I will rise up and answer."

She turned her steps towards the door, and the men, who had stationed themselves to guard it, withdrew, and suffered her to pass. A general sentiment of pity overcame the virulence of religious hatred. Sanctified by her love and her affliction, she went forth, and all the people gazed after her till she had journeyed up the hill, and was lost behind its brow. She went, the apostle of her own unquiet heart, to renew the wanderings of past years. For her voice had been already heard in many lands of Christendom; and she had pined in the cells of a Catholic Inquisition before she felt the lash and lay in the dungeons of the Puritans. Her mission had extended also to the followers of the Prophet, and from them she had received the courtesy and kindness which all the contending sects of our purer religion united to deny her. Her husband and herself had resided many months in Turkey, where even the Sultan's countenance was gracious to them; in that pagan land, too, was Ilbrahim's birthplace, and his oriental name was a mark of gratitude for the good deeds of an unbeliever.

. . . .

When Pearson and his wife had thus acquired all the rights over Ilbrahim that could be delegated, their affection for him became like the memory of their native land, or their mild sorrow for the dead, a piece of the immovable furniture of their hearts. The boy, also, after a week or two of mental disquiet, began to gratify his protectors by many inadvertent proofs that he considered them as parents, and their house as home. Before the winter snows were melted, the persecuted infant, the little wanderer from a remote and heathen country, seemed native in the New England cottage, and inseparable from the warmth and security of its hearth. Under the influence of kind treatment, and in the consciousness that he was loved, Ilbrahim's demeanor lost a premature manliness, which had resulted from his earlier situation; he became more childlike, and his natural character displayed itself with freedom. It was in many respects a beautiful one, yet the disordered imaginations of both his father and mother had perhaps propagated a certain unhealthiness in the mind of the boy. In his general state, Ilbrahim would derive enjoyment from the most trifling events, and from every object about him; he seemed to discover rich treasures of happiness, by a faculty analogous to that of the witch hazel, which points to hidden gold where all is barren to the eye. His airy gayety, coming to him from a thousand sources, communicated itself to the family, and Ilbrahim was like a domesticated sunbeam, brightening moody countenances, and chasing away the gloom from the dark corners of the cottage.

On the other hand, as the susceptibility of pleasure is also that of pain, the exuberant cheerfulness of the boy's prevailing temper sometimes yielded to moments of deep depression. His sorrows could not always be followed up to their original source, but most frequently they appeared to flow, though Ilbrahim was young to be sad for such a cause, from wounded love. The flightiness of his mirth rendered him often guilty of offences against the decorum of a Puritan household, and on these occasions he did not invariably escape rebuke. But the slightest word of real bitterness, which he was infallible in distinguishing from pretended anger, seemed to sink into his heart and poison all his enjoyments, till he became sensible that he was entirely forgiven. Of the malice, which generally accompanies a superfluity of sensitiveness, Ilbrahim was altogether destitute: when trodden upon, he would not turn; when wounded, he could but die. His mind was wanting in the stamina for self-support; it was a plant that would twine beautifully round something stronger than itself, but if repulsed, or torn away, it had no choice but to wither on the ground. Dorothy's acuteness taught her that severity would crush the spirit of the child, and she nurtured him with the gentle care of one who handles a butterfly. Her husband manifested an equal affection, although it grew daily less productive of familiar caresses.

The feelings of the neighboring people, in regard to the Quaker infant and his protectors, had not undergone a favorable change, in spite of the momentary triumph which the desolate mother had obtained over their sympathies. The scorn and bitterness, of which he was the object, were very grievous to Ilbrahim, especially when any circumstance made him sensible that the children, his equals in age, partook of the enmity of their parents. His tender and social nature had already overflowed in attachments to everything about him, and still there was a residue of unappropriated love, which he yearned to bestow upon the little ones who were taught to hate him. As the warm days of spring came on, Ilbrahim was accustomed to remain for hours, silent and inactive, within hearing of the children's voices at their play; yet, with his usual delicacy of feeling, he avoided their notice, and would flee and hide himself from the smallest individual among them. Chance, however, at length seemed to open a medium of communication between his heart and theirs; it was by means of a boy about two years older than Ilbrahim, who was injured by a fall from a tree in the vicinity of Pearson's habitation. As the sufferer's own home was at some distance, Dorothy willingly received him under her roof, and became his tender and careful nurse.

Ilbrahim was the unconscious possessor of much skill in physiognomy, and it would have deterred him, in other circumstances, from attempting to make a friend of this boy. The countenance of the latter immediately impressed a beholder disagreeably, but it required some examination to discover that the cause was a very slight distortion of the mouth, and the irregular, broken line, and near approach of the eyebrows. Analogous, perhaps, to these trifling deformities, was an almost imperceptible twist of every joint, and the uneven prominence of the breast; forming a body, regular in its general outline, but faulty in almost all its details. The disposition of the boy was sullen and reserved, and the village schoolmaster stigmatized him as obtuse in intellect; although, at a later period of life, he evinced ambition and very peculiar talents. But whatever might be his personal or moral irregularities, Ilbrahim's heart seized upon, and clung to him, from the moment that he was brought wounded into the cottage; the child of persecution seemed to compare his own fate with that of the sufferer, and to feel that even different modes of misfortune had created a sort of relationship between them. Food, rest, and the fresh air, for which he languished, were neglected; he nestled continually by the bedside of the little stranger, and, with a fond jealousy, endeavored to be the medium of all the cares that were bestowed upon him. As the boy became convalescent, Ilbrahim contrived games suitable to his situation, or amused him by a faculty which he had perhaps breathed in with the air of his barbaric birthplace. It was that of reciting imaginary adventures, on the spur of the moment, and apparently in inexhaustible succession. His tales were of course monstrous, disjointed, and without aim; but they were curious on account of a vein of human tenderness which ran through them all, and was like a sweet, familiar face, encountered in the midst of wild and unearthly scenery. The auditor paid much attention to these romances, and sometimes interrupted them by brief remarks upon the incidents, displaying shrewdness above his years, mingled with a moral obliquity which grated very harshly against Ilbrahim's instinctive rectitude. Nothing, however, could arrest the progress of the latter's affection, and there were many proofs that it met with a response from the dark and stubborn nature on which it was lavished. The boy's parents at length removed him to complete his cure under their own roof.

Ilbrahim did not visit his new friend after his departure; but he made anxious and continual inquiries respecting him, and informed himself of the day when he was to reappear among his playmates. On a pleasant summer afternoon, the children of the neighborhood had assembled in the little forest-crowned amphitheatre behind the meeting-house, and the recovering invalid was there, leaning on a staff. The glee of a score of untainted bosoms was heard in light and airy voices, which danced among the trees like sunshine become audible; the grown men of this weary world, as they journeyed by the spot, marvelled why life, beginning in such brightness, should proceed in gloom; and their hearts, or their imaginations, answered them and said, that the bliss of childhood gushes from its innocence. But it happened that an unexpected addition was made to the heavenly little band. It was Ilbrahim, who came towards the children with a look of sweet confidence on his fair and spiritual face, as if, having manifested his love to one of them, he had no longer to fear a repulse from their society. A hush came over their mirth the moment they beheld him, and they stood whispering to each other while he drew nigh; but, all at once, the devil of their fathers entered into the unbreeched fanatics, and sending up a fierce, shrill cry, they rushed upon the poor Quaker child. In an instant, he was the centre of a brood of baby-fiends, who lifted sticks against him, pelted him with stones, and displayed an instinct of destruction far more loathsome than the bloodthirstiness of manhood.

The invalid, in the meanwhile, stood apart from the tumult, crying out with a loud voice, "Fear not, Ilbrahim, come hither and take my hand;" and his unhappy friend endeavored to obey him. After watching the victim's struggling approach with a calm smile and unabashed eye, the foul-hearted little villain lifted his staff and struck Ilbrahim on the mouth, so forcibly that the blood issued in a stream. The poor child's arms had been raised to guard his head from the storm of blows; but now he dropped them at once. His persecutors beat him down, trampled upon him, dragged him by his long, fair locks, and Ilbrahim was on the point of becoming as veritable a martyr as ever entered bleeding into heaven. The uproar, however, attracted the notice of a few neighbors, who put themselves to the trouble of rescuing the little heretic, and of conveying him to Pearson's door.

Ilbrahim's bodily harm was severe, but long and careful nursing accomplished his recovery; the injury done to his sensitive spirit was more serious, though not so visible. Its signs were principally of a negative character, and to be discovered only by those who had previously known him. His gait was thenceforth slow, even, and unvaried by the sudden bursts of sprightlier motion, which had once corresponded to his overflowing gladness; his countenance was heavier, and its former play of expression, the dance of sunshine reflected from moving water, was destroyed by the cloud over his existence; his notice was attracted in a far less degree by passing events, and he appeared to find greater difficulty in comprehending what was new to him than at a happier period. A stranger, founding his judgment upon these circumstances, would have said that the dulness of the child's intellect widely contradicted the promise of his features; but the secret was in the direction of Ilbrahim's thoughts, which were brooding within him when they should naturally have been wandering abroad. An attempt of Dorothy to revive his former sportiveness was the single occasion on which his quiet demeanor yielded to a violent display of grief; he burst into passionate weeping, and ran and hid himself, for his heart had become so miserably sore that even the hand of kindness tortured it like fire. Sometimes, at night and probably in his dreams, he was heard to cry "Mother! Mother!" as if her place, which a stranger had supplied while Ilbrahim was happy, admitted of no substitute in his extreme affliction. Perhaps, among the many life-weary wretches then upon the earth, there was not one who combined innocence and misery like this poor, broken-hearted infant, so soon the victim of his own heavenly nature.

While this melancholy change had taken place in Ilbrahim, one of an earlier origin and of different character had come to its perfection in his adopted father. The incident with which this tale commences found Pearson in a state of religious dulness, yet mentally disquieted, and longing for a more fervid faith than he possessed. The first effect of his kindness to Ilbrahim was to produce a softened feeling, and incipient love for the child's whole sect; but joined to this, and resulting perhaps from self-suspicion, was a proud and ostentatious contempt of all their tenets and practical extravagances. In the course of much thought, however, for the subject struggled irresistibly into his mind, the foolishness of the doctrine began to be less evident, and the points which had particularly offended his reason assumed another aspect, or vanished entirely away. The work within him appeared to go on even while he slept, and that which had been a doubt, when he laid down to rest, would often hold the place of a truth, confirmed by some forgotten demonstration, when he recalled his thoughts in the morning. But while he was thus becoming assimilated to the enthusiasts, his contempt, in nowise decreasing towards them, grew very fierce against himself; he imagined, also, that every face of his acquaintance wore a sneer, and that every word addressed to him was a gibe. Such was his state of mind at the period of Ilbrahim's misfortune; and the emotions consequent upon that event completed the change, of which the child had been the original instrument.

In the mean time, neither the fierceness of the persecutors, nor the infatuation of their victims, had decreased. The dungeons were never empty; the streets of almost every village echoed daily with the lash; the life of a woman, whose mild and Christian spirit no cruelty could embitter, had been sacrificed; and more innocent blood was yet to pollute the hands that were so often raised in prayer. Early after the Restoration, the English Quakers represented to Charles II. that a "vein of blood was open in his dominions"; but though the displeasure of the voluptuous king was roused, his interference was not prompt. And now the tale must stride forward over many months, leaving Pearson to encounter ignominy and misfortune; his wife to a firm endurance of a thousand sorrows; poor Ilbrahim to pine and droop like a cankered rosebud; his mother to wander on a mistaken errand, neglectful of the holiest trust which can be committed to a woman.

.   .   .   .

A winter evening, a night of storm, had darkened over Pearson's habitation, and there were no cheerful faces to drive the gloom from his broad hearth. The fire, it is true, sent forth a glowing heat and a ruddy light, and large logs, dripping with half-melted snow, lay ready to be cast upon the embers. But the apartment was saddened in its aspect by the absence of much of the homely wealth which had once adorned it; for the exaction of repeated fines, and his own neglect of temporal affairs, had greatly impoverished the owner. And with the furniture of peace, the implements of war had likewise disappeared; the sword was broken, the helm and cuirass were cast away forever; the soldier had done with battles, and might not lift so much as his naked hand to guard his head. But the Holy Book remained, and the table on which it rested was drawn before the fire, while two of the persecuted sect sought comfort from its pages.

He who listened, while the other read, was the master of the house, now emaciated in form, and altered as to the expression and healthiness of his countenance; for his mind had dwelt too long among visionary thoughts, and his body had been worn by imprisonment and stripes. The hale and weatherbeaten old man who sat beside him had sustained less injury from a far longer course of the same mode of life. In person he was tall and dignified, and, which alone would have made him hateful to the Puritans, his gray locks fell from beneath the broad-brimmed hat, and rested on his shoulders. As the old man read the sacred page the snow drifted against the windows, or eddied in at the crevices of the door, while a blast kept laughing in the chimney, and the blaze leaped fiercely up to seek it. And sometimes, when the wind struck the hill at a certain angle, and swept down by the cottage across the wintry plain, its voice was the most doleful that can be conceived; it came as if the Past were speaking, as if the Dead had contributed each a whisper, as if the Desolation of Ages were breathed in that one lamenting sound.

The Quaker at length closed the book, retaining however his hand between the pages which he had been reading, while he looked steadfastly at Pearson. The attitude and features of the latter might have indicated the endurance of bodily pain; he leaned his forehead on his hands, his teeth were firmly closed, and his frame was tremulous at intervals with a nervous agitation.

"Friend Tobias," inquired the old man, compassionately, "hast thou found no comfort in these many blessed passages of Scripture?"

"Thy voice has fallen on my ear like a sound afar off and indistinct," replied Pearson without lifting his eyes. "Yea, and when I have hearkened carefully the words seemed cold and lifeless, and intended for another and a lesser grief than mine. Remove the book," he added, in a tone of sullen bitterness. "I have no part in its consolations, and they do but fret my sorrow the more."

"Nay, feeble brother, be not as one who hath never known the light," said the elder Quaker earnestly, but with mildness. "Art thou he that wouldst be content to give all, and endure all, for conscience' sake; desiring even peculiar trials, that thy faith might be purified and thy heart weaned from worldly desires? And wilt thou sink beneath an affliction which happens alike to them that have their portion here below, and to them that lay up treasure in heaven? Faint not, for thy burden is yet light."

"It is heavy! It is heavier than I can bear!" exclaimed Pearson, with the impatience of a variable spirit. "From my youth upward I have been a man marked out for wrath; and year by year, yea, day after day, I have endured sorrows such as others know not in their lifetime. And now I speak not of the love that has been turned to hatred, the honor to ignominy, the ease and plentifulness of all things to danger, want, and nakedness. All this I could have borne, and counted myself blessed. But when my heart was desolate with many losses I fixed it upon the child of a stranger, and he became dearer to me than all my buried ones; and now he too must die as if my love were poison.

Verily, I am an accursed man, and I will lay me down in the dust and lift up my head no more."

"Thou sinnest, brother, but it is not for me to rebuke thee; for I also have had my hours of darkness, wherein I have murmured against the cross," said the old Quaker. He continued, perhaps in the hope of distracting his companion's thoughts from his own sorrows. "Even of late was the light obscured within me, when the men of blood had banished me on pain of death, and the constables led me onward from village to village towards the wilderness. A strong and cruel hand was wielding the knotted cords; they sunk deep into the flesh, and thou mightst have tracked every reel and totter of my footsteps by the blood that followed. As we went on"—

"Have I not borne all this; and have I murmured?" interrupted Pearson impatiently.

"Nay, friend, but hear me," continued the other. "As we journeyed on, night darkened on our path, so that no man could see the rage of the persecutors or the constancy of my endurance, though Heaven forbid that I should glory therein. The lights began to glimmer in the cottage windows, and I could discern the inmates as they gathered in comfort and security, every man with his wife and children by their own evening hearth. At length we came to a tract of fertile land; in the dim light, the forest was not visible around it; and behold! there was a straw-thatched dwelling, which bore the very aspect of my home, far over the wild ocean, far in our own England. Then came bitter thoughts upon me; yea, remembrances that were like death to my soul. The happiness of my early days was painted to me; the disquiet of my manhood, the altered faith of my declining years. I remembered how I had been moved to go forth a wanderer when my daughter, the youngest, the dearest of my flock, lay on her dying bed, and"—

"Couldst thou obey the command at such a moment?" exclaimed Pearson, shuddering.

"Yea, yea," replied the old man hurriedly. "I was kneeling by her bedside when the voice spoke loud within me; but immediately I rose, and took my staff, and gat me gone. Oh! that it were permitted me to forget her woeful look when I thus withdrew my arm, and left her journeying through the dark valley alone! for her soul was faith, and she had leaned upon my prayers. Now in that night of horror I was assailed by the thought that I had been an erring Christian and a cruel parent; yea, even my daughter, with her pale, dying features, seemed to stand by me and whisper, 'Father, you are deceived; go home and shelter your gray head.' O Thou, to whom I have looked in my farthest wanderings," continued the Quaker, raising his agitated eyes to heaven, "inflict not upon the bloodiest of our persecutors the unmitigated agony of my soul, when I believed that all I had done and suffered for Thee was at the instigation of a mocking fiend! But I yielded not; I knelt down and wrestled with the tempter, while the scourge bit more fiercely into the flesh. My prayer was heard, and I went on in peace and joy towards the wilderness."

The old man, though his fanaticism had generally all the calmness of reason, was deeply moved while reciting this tale; and his unwonted emotion seemed to rebuke and keep down that of his companion. They sat in silence, with their faces to the fire, imagining, perhaps, in its red embers new scenes of persecution yet to be encountered. The snow still drifted hard against the windows, and sometimes, as the blaze of the logs had gradually sunk, came down the spacious chimney and hissed upon the hearth. A cautious footstep might now and then be heard in a neighboring apartment, and the sound invariably drew the eyes of both Quakers to the door which led thither. When a fierce and riotous gust of wind had led his thoughts, by a natural association, to homeless travellers on such a night, Pearson resumed the conversation.

"I have well-nigh sunk under my own share of this trial," observed he, sighing heavily; "yet I would that it might be doubled to me, if so the child's mother could be spared. Her wounds have been deep and many, but this will be the sorest of all."

"Fear not for Catharine," replied the old Quaker, "for I know that valiant woman, and have seen how she can bear the cross. A mother's heart, indeed, is strong in her, and may seem to contend mightily with her faith; but soon she will stand up and give thanks that her son has been thus early an accepted sacrifice. The boy hath done his work, and she will feel that he is taken hence in kindness both to him and her. Blessed, blessed are they that with so little suffering can enter into peace!"

The fitful rush of the wind was now disturbed by a portentous sound; it was a quick and heavy knocking at the outer door. Pearson's wan countenance grew paler, for many a visit of persecution had taught him what to dread; the old man, on the other hand, stood up erect, and his glance was firm as that of the tried soldier who awaits his enemy.

"The men of blood have come to seek me," he observed with calmness. "They have heard how I was moved to return from banishment; and now am I to be led to prison, and thence to death. It is an end I have long looked for. I will open unto them, lest they say, 'Lo, he feareth!'"

"Nay, I will present myself before them," said Pearson, with recovered fortitude. "It may be that they seek me alone, and know not that thou abidest with me."

"Let us go boldly, both one and the other," rejoined his companion. "It is not fitting that thou or I should shrink."

They therefore proceeded through the entry to the door, which they opened, bidding the applicant "Come in, in God's name!" A furious blast of wind drove the storm into their faces, and extinguished the lamp; they had barely time to discern a figure, so white from head to foot with the drifted snow that it seemed like Winter's self, come in human shape, to seek refuge from its own desolation.

"Enter, friend, and do thy errand, be it what it may," said Pearson. "It must needs be pressing, since thou comest on such a bitter night."

"Peace be with this household," said the stranger, when they stood on the floor of the inner apartment.

Pearson started, the elder Quaker stirred the slumbering embers of the fire till they sent up a clear and lofty blaze; it was a female voice that had spoken; it was a female form that shone out, cold and wintry, in that comfortable light.

"Catharine, blessed woman!" exclaimed the old man, "art thou come to this darkened land again? Art thou come to bear a valiant testimony as in former years? The scourge hath not prevailed against thee, and from the dungeon hast thou come forth triumphant; but strengthen, strengthen now thy heart, Catharine, for Heaven will prove thee yet this once, ere thou go to thy reward."

"Rejoice, friends!" she replied. "Thou who hast long been of our people, and thou whom a little child hath led to us, rejoice! Lo! I come, the messenger of glad tidings, for the day of persecution is overpast. The heart of the king, even Charles, hath been moved in gentleness towards us, and he hath sent forth his letters to stay the hands of the men of blood. A ship's company of our friends hath arrived at yonder town, and I also sailed joyfully among them."

As Catharine spoke, her eyes were roaming about the room, in search of him for whose sake security was dear to her. Pearson made a silent appeal to the old man, nor did the latter shrink from the painful task assigned him.

"Sister," he began, in a softened yet perfectly calm tone, "thou tellest us of His love, manifested in temporal good; and now must we speak to thee of that selfsame love, displayed in chastenings. Hitherto, Catharine, thou hast been as one journeying in a darksome and difficult path, and leading an infant by the hand; fain wouldst thou have looked heavenward continually, but still the cares of that little child have drawn thine eyes and thy affections to the earth. Sister! go on rejoicing, for his tottering footsteps shall impede thine own no more."

But the unhappy mother was not thus to be consoled; she shook like a leaf, she turned white as the very snow that hung drifted into her hair. The firm old man extended his hand and held her up, keeping his eye upon hers, as if to repress any outbreak of passion.

"I am a woman, I am but a woman; will He try me above my strength?" said Catharine very quickly, and almost in a whisper. "I have been wounded sore: I have suffered much; many things in the body; many in the mind; crucified in myself, and in them that were dearest to me. Surely," added she, with a long shudder, "He hath spared me in this one thing." She broke forth with sudden and irrepressible violence. "Tell me, man of cold heart, what has God done to me? Hath He cast me down, never to rise again? Hath He crushed my very heart in his hand? And thou, to whom I committed my child, how hast thou fulfilled thy trust? Give me back the boy, well, sound, alive, alive; or earth and Heaven shall avenge me!"

The agonized shriek of Catharine was answered by the faint, the very faint, voice of a child.

On this day it had become evident to Pearson, to his aged guest, and to Dorothy, that Ilbrahim's brief and troubled pilgrimage drew near its close. The two former would willingly have remained by him, to make use of the prayers and pious discourses which they deemed appropriate to the time, and which, if they be impotent as to the departing traveller's reception in the world whither it goes, may at least sustain him in bidding adieu to earth. But though Ilbrahim uttered no complaint, he was disturbed by the faces that looked upon him; so that Dorothy's entreaties, and their own conviction that the child's feet might tread heaven's pavement and not soil it, had induced the two Quakers to remove. Ilbrahim then closed his eyes and grew calm, and, except for now and then a kind and low word to his nurse, might have been thought to slumber. As nightfall came on, however, and the storm began to rise, something seemed to trouble the repose of the boy's mind, and to render his sense of hearing active and acute. If a passing wind lingered to shake the casement, he strove to turn his head towards it; if the door jarred to and fro upon its hinges, he looked long and anxiously thitherward; if the heavy voice of the old man, as he read the Scriptures, rose but a little higher, the child almost held his dying breath to listen; if a snow-drift swept by the cottage, with a sound like the trailing of a garment, Ilbrahim seemed to watch that some visitant should enter.

But, after a little time, he relinquished whatever secret hope had agitated him, and with one low, complaining whisper, turned his cheek upon the pillow. He then addressed Dorothy with his usual sweetness, and besought her to draw near him; she did so, and Ilbrahim took her hand in both of his, grasping it with a gentle pressure, as if to assure himself that he retained it. At intervals, and without disturbing the repose of his countenance, a very faint trembling passed over him from head to foot, as if a mild but somewhat cool wind had breathed upon him, and made him shiver. As the boy thus led her by the hand, in his quiet progress over the borders of eternity, Dorothy almost imagined that she could discern the near, though dim, delightfulness of the home he was about to reach; she would not have enticed the little wanderer back, though she bemoaned herself that she must leave him and return. But just when Ilbrahim's feet were pressing on the soil of Paradise he heard a voice behind him, and it recalled him a few, few paces of the weary path which he had travelled. As Dorothy looked upon his features, she perceived that their placid expression was again disturbed; her own thoughts had been so wrapped in him, that all sounds of the storm, and of human speech, were lost to her; but when Catharine's shriek pierced through the room, the boy strove to raise himself.

"Friend, she is come! Open unto her!" cried he.

In a moment his mother was kneeling by the bedside; she drew Ilbrahim to her bosom, and he nestled there, with no violence of joy, but contentedly, as if he were hushing himself to sleep. He looked into her face, and reading its agony, said, with feeble earnestness, "Mourn not, dearest mother. I am happy now." And with these words the gentle boy was dead.

. . . .

The king's mandate to stay the New England persecutors was effectual in preventing further martyrdoms; but the colonial authorities, trusting in the remoteness of their situation, and perhaps in the supposed instability of the royal government, shortly renewed their severities in all other respects. Catharine's fanaticism had become wilder by the sundering of all human ties; and wherever a scourge was lifted there was she to receive the blow; and whenever a dungeon was unbarred thither she came, to cast herself upon the floor. But in process of time a more Christian spirit—a spirit of forbearance, though not of cordiality or approbation—began to pervade the land in regard to the persecuted sect. And then, when the rigid old Pilgrims eyed her rather in pity than in wrath; when the matrons fed her with the fragments of their children's food, and offered her a lodging on a hard and lowly bed; when no little crowd of schoolboys left their sports to cast stones after the roving enthusiast; then did Catharine return to Pearson's dwelling and made that her home.

As if Ilbrahim's sweetness yet lingered round his ashes; as if his gentle spirit came down from heaven to teach his parent a true religion, her fierce and vindictive nature was softened by the same griefs which had once irritated it. When the course of years had made the features of the unobtrusive mourner familiar in the settlement, she became a subject of not deep, but general, interest; a being on whom the otherwise superfluous sympathies of all might be bestowed. Every one spoke of her with that degree of pity which it is pleasant to experience; every one was ready to do her the little kindnesses which are not costly, yet manifest good will; and when at last she died, a long train of her once bitter persecutors followed her, with decent sadness and tears that were not painful, to her place by Ilbrahim's green and sunken grave.

QUESTIONS

1 What do we learn about Dorothy and Tobias Pearson that makes their acceptance of the Quaker child plausible?
2 Why were Quakers considered an "accursed sect"? What point does the story make about America's settlement being a search for religious freedom?
3 How does the children's attack on Ilbrahim support Hawthorne's view that the actions of one generation are seen in successive ones?
4 Why is it appropriate that the invalid turns against Ilbrahim?
5 Why does Ilbrahim die?

TOPIC FOR COMPOSITION

Analyze Hawthorne's patterns of light and dark imagery to show how his movement from light to dark imagery parallels the events of the story.

☐

Hemingway's story is economically constructed, moving almost entirely through the terse conversation between the younger and the older waiter. We should note especially:

1 The lack of description except as implied by the remarks of the two waiters
2 The contrast in attitude toward life exhibited by the statements and tone employed by each waiter
3 The sense of isolation achieved by the older waiter's conversation with himself

A CLEAN, WELL-LIGHTED PLACE

Ernest Hemingway

It was late and every one had left the café except an old man who sat in the shadow the leaves of the tree made against the electric light. In the daytime the street was dusty, but at night the dew settled the dust and the old man liked to sit late because he was deaf and now at night it was quiet and he felt the difference. The two waiters inside the café knew that the old man was a little drunk, and while he was a good client they knew that if he became too drunk he would leave without paying, so they kept watch on him.

"Last week he tried to commit suicide," one waiter said.

"Why?"

"He was in despair."

"What about?"

"Nothing."

"How do you know it was nothing?"

"He has plenty of money."

They sat together at a table that was close against the wall near the door of the café and looked at the terrace where the tables were all empty except where the old man sat in the shadow of the leaves of the tree that moved slightly in the wind. A girl and a soldier went by in the street. The street light shone on the brass number on his collar. The girl wore no head covering and hurried beside him.

"The guard will pick him up," one waiter said.

"What does it matter if he gets what he's after?"

"He had better get off the street now. The guard will get him. They went by five minutes ago."

The old man sitting in the shadow rapped on his saucer with his glass. The younger waiter went over to him.

"What do you want?"

The old man looked at him. "Another brandy," he said.

"You'll be drunk," the waiter said. The old man looked at him. The waiter went away.

"He'll stay all night," he said to his colleague. "I'm sleepy now. I never get into bed before three o'clock. He should have killed himself last week."

The waiter took the brandy bottle and another saucer from the counter inside the café and marched out to the old man's table. He put down the saucer and poured the glass full of brandy.

"You should have killed yourself last week," he said to the deaf man. The old man motioned with his finger. "A little more," he said. The waiter poured on into the glass so that the brandy slopped over and ran down the stem into the top saucer of the pile. "Thank you," the old man said. The waiter took the bottle back inside the café. He sat down at the table with his colleague again.

"He's drunk now," he said.

"He's drunk every night."

"What did he want to kill himself for?"

"How should I know."

"How did he do it?"

"He hung himself with a rope."

"Who cut him down?"

"His niece."

"Why did they do it?"

"Fear for his soul."

"How much money has he got?"

"He's got plenty."

"He must be eighty years old."

"Anyway I should say he was eighty."

"I wish he would go home. I never get to bed before three o'clock. What kind of hour is that to go to bed?"

"He stays up because he likes it."

"He's lonely. I'm not lonely. I have a wife waiting in bed for me."

"He had a wife once too."

"A wife would be no good to him now."

"You can't tell. He might be better with a wife."

"His niece looks after him. You said she cut him down."

"I know."

"I wouldn't want to be that old. An old man is a nasty thing."

"Not always. This old man is clean. He drinks without spilling. Even now, drunk. Look at him."

"I don't want to look at him. I wish he would go home. He has no regard for those who must work."

The old man looked from his glass across the square, then over at the waiters.

"Another brandy," he said, pointing to his glass. The waiter who was in a hurry came over.

"Finished," he said, speaking with that omission of syntax stupid people employ when talking to drunken people or foreigners. "No more tonight. Close now."

"Another," said the old man.

"No. Finished." The waiter wiped the edge of the table with a towel and shook his head.

The old man stood up, slowly counted the saucers, took a leather coin purse from his pocket and paid for the drinks, leaving half a peseta tip.

The waiter watched him go down the street, a very old man walking unsteadily but with dignity.

"Why didn't you let him stay and drink?" the unhurried waiter asked. They were putting up the shutters. "It is not half-past two."

"I want to go home to bed."

"What is an hour?"

"More to me than to him."

"An hour is the same."

"You talk like an old man yourself. He can buy a bottle and drink at home."

"It's not the same."

"No, it is not," agreed the waiter with a wife. He did not wish to be unjust. He was only in a hurry.

"And you? You have no fear of going home before your usual hour?"

"Are you trying to insult me?"

"No, hombre, only to make a joke."

"No," the waiter who was in a hurry said, rising from pulling down the metal shutters. "I have confidence. I am all confidence."

"You have youth, confidence, and a job," the older waiter said. "You have everything."

"And what do you lack?"

"Everything but work."

"You have everything I have."

"No. I have never had confidence and I am not young."

"Come on. Stop talking nonsense and lock up."

"I am of those who like to stay late at the café," the older waiter said. "With all those who do not want to go to bed. With all those who need a light for the night."

"I want to go home and into bed."

"We are of two different kinds," the older waiter said. He was now dressed to go home. "It is not only a question of youth and confidence although those things are very beautiful. Each night I am reluctant to close up because there may be some one who needs the café."

"Hombre, there are bodegas open all night long."

"You do not understand. This is a clean and pleasant café. It is well lighted. The light is very good and also, now, there are shadows of the leaves."

"Good night," said the younger waiter.

"Good night," the other said. Turning off the electric light he continued the conversation with himself. It is the light of course but it is necessary that the place be clean and pleasant. You do not want music. Certainly you do not want music. Nor can you stand before a bar with dignity although that is all that is provided for these hours. What did he fear? It was not fear or dread. It was a nothing that he knew too well. It was all a nothing and a man was nothing too. It was only that and light was all it needed and a certain cleanness and order. Some lived in it and never felt it but he knew it all was nada y pues nada y nada y pues nada. Our nada who are in nada, nada be thy name thy kingdom nada thy will be nada in nada as it is in nada. Give us this nada our daily nada and nada us our nada as we nada our nadas and nada us not into nada but deliver us from nada; pues nada. Hail nothing full of nothing, nothing is with thee. He smiled and stood before a bar with a shining steam pressure coffee machine.

"What's yours?" asked the barman.

"Nada."

"Otro loco mas," said the barman and turned away.

"A little cup," said the waiter.

The barman poured it for him.

"The light is very bright and pleasant but the bar is unpolished," the waiter said.

The barman looked at him but did not answer. It was too late at night for conversation.

"You want another copita?" the barman asked.

"No, thank you," said the waiter and went out. He disliked bars and bodegas. A clean, well-lighted café was a very different thing. Now, without thinking further, he would go home to his room. He would lie in the bed and finally, with daylight, he would go to sleep. After all, he said to himself, it is probably only insomnia. Many must have it.

QUESTIONS

1 In this story, despair is visibly a mark of old age (the old man, the older waiter). What is it that the younger waiter has that wards off despair? What can we say, then, about the younger waiter, and the bartender's attitude toward the older

waiter and the old man? Specifically, does youth understand age? Does age understand youth?

2   The place is clean and well-lighted. What other appeal does it have? For instance, is it attractive otherwise? Is it pervaded by warmth?

3   Do both the old man and the older waiter reveal Kierkegaard's "sickness unto death" to the same degree? Explain.

4   How does Hemingway's style (short sentences, terse conversation, limited description) complement the mood of the story?

5   Would you accept the statement that there is a magnificent dignity in despair in this story? How would you explain that dignity?

"Night-Sea Journey" unfolds through the consciousness of the sperm as it "swims" toward union with the egg to create life as we know it. This "swimmer" likens the microcosm in which he exists to our world, embracing questions of identity, reality, purpose, ultimate goals set against the eventual mystery awaiting us at the end of the journey. As you read, note the consistency with which Barth maintains his metaphor and the fullness of his philosophical sweep.

NIGHT-SEA JOURNEY

John Barth

"One way or another, no matter which theory of our journey is correct, it's myself I address; to whom I rehearse as to a stranger our history and condition, and will disclose my secret hope though I sink for it.

"Is the journey my invention? Do the night, the sea, exist at all, I ask myself, apart from my experience of them? Do I myself exist, or is this a dream? Sometimes I wonder. And if I am, who am I? The Heritage I supposedly transport? But how can I be both vessel and contents? Such are the questions that beset my intervals of rest.

"My trouble is, I lack conviction. Many accounts of our situation seem plausible to me— where and what we are, why we swim and whither. But implausible ones as well, perhaps especially those, I must admit as possibly correct. Even likely. If at times, in certain humors—stroking in unison, say, with my neighbors and chanting with them 'Onward! Upward!'—I have supposed that we have after all a common Maker, Whose nature and motives we may not know, but Who engendered us in some mysterious wise and launched us forth toward some end known but to Him—if (for a moodslength only) I have been able to entertain such notions, very popular in certain quarters, it is because our night-sea journey partakes of their absurdity. One might even say: I can believe them *because* they are absurd.

"Has that been said before?

"Another paradox: it appears to be these recesses from swimming that sustain me in the swim. Two measures onward and upward, flailing with the rest, then I float exhausted and dispirited, brood upon the night, the sea, the journey, while the flood bears me a measure back and down: slow progress, but I live, I live, and make my way, aye, past many a drownèd comrade in the end, stronger, worthier than I, victims of their unremitting *joie de nager.* I have seen the best swimmers of my generation go under. Numberless the number of the dead! Thousands drown as I think this thought, millions as I rest before returning to the swim. And scores, hundreds of millions have expired since we surged forth, brave in our innocence, upon our dreadful way. 'Love! Love!' we sang then, a quarter-billion strong, and churned the warm sea white with joy of swimming! Now all are gone down—the buoyant, the sodden, leaders and followers, all gone under, while wretched I swim on. Yet these same reflective intervals that keep me afloat have led me into wonder, doubt, despair—strange emotions for a swimmer!—have led me, even, to suspect . . . that our night-sea journey is without meaning.

"Indeed, if I have yet to join the hosts of the suicides, it is because (fatigue apart) I find it no meaningfuller to drown myself than to go on swimming.

"I know that there are those who seem actually to enjoy the night-sea; who claim to love swimming for its own sake, or sincerely believe that 'reaching the Shore,' 'transmitting the Heritage' (*Whose* Heritage, I'd like to know? And to whom?) is worth the staggering cost. I do not. Swimming itself I find at best not actively unpleasant, more often tiresome, not infrequently a torment. Arguments from function and design don't impress me: granted that we can and do swim, that in a manner of speaking our long tails and streamlined heads are 'meant for' swimming; it by no means follows—for me, at least—that we *should* swim, or otherwise endeavor to 'fulfill our destiny.' Which is to say, Someone Else's destiny, since ours, so far as I can see, is merely to perish, one way or another, soon or late. The heartless zeal of our (departed) leaders, like the blind ambition and good cheer of my own youth, appalls me now; for the death of my comrades I am inconsolable. If the night-sea journey has justification, it is not for us swimmers ever to discover it.

"Oh, to be sure, 'Love!' one heard on every side: 'Love it is that drives and sustains us!' I translate: we don't know *what* drives and sustains us, only that we are most miserably driven and, imperfectly, sustained. *Love* is how we call our ignorance of what whips us. 'To reach the Shore,' then: but what if the Shore exists in the fancies of us swimmers merely, who dream it to account for the dreadful fact that we swim, have always and only swum, and continue swimming without respite (myself excepted) until we die? Supposing even that there *were* a Shore—that, as a cynical companion of mine once imagined, we rise from the drowned to discover all those vulgar superstitions and exalted metaphors to be literal truth: the giant Maker of us all, the Shores of Light beyond our night-sea journey!—whatever would a swimmer do there? The fact is, when we imagine the Shore, what comes to mind is just the opposite of our condition: no more night, no more sea, no more journeying. In short, the blissful estate of the drowned.

"'Ours not to stop and think; ours but to swim and sink. . . .' Because a moment's thought reveals the pointlessness of swimming. 'No matter,' I've heard some say, even as they gulped their last: 'The night-sea journey may be absurd, but here we swim, will-we nill-we, against the flood, onward and upward, toward a Shore that may not exist and couldn't be reached if it did.' The thoughtful swimmer's choices, then, they say, are two: give over thrashing and go under for good, or embrace the absurdity; affirm in and for itself the night-sea journey; swim on with neither motive nor destination, for the sake of swimming, and compassionate moreover with your fellow swimmer, we being all at sea and equally in the dark. I find neither course acceptable. If not even the hypothetical Shore can justify a sea-full of drownèd comrades, to speak of the swim-in-itself as somehow doing so strikes me as obscene. I continue to swim—but only because blind habit, blind instinct, blind fear of drowning are still more strong than the horror of our journey. And if on occasion I have assisted a fellow-thrasher, joined in the cheers and songs, even passed along to others strokes of genius from the drownèd great, it's that I shrink by temperament from making myself conspicuous. To paddle off in one's own direction, assert one's independent right-of-way, overrun one's fellows without compunction, or dedicate oneself entirely to pleasures and diversions without regard for conscience—I can't finally condemn those who journey in this wise; in half my moods I envy them and despise the weak vitality that keeps me from following their example. But in reasonabler moments I remind myself that it's their very freedom and self-responsibility I reject, as more dramatically absurd, in our senseless circum-stances, than tailing along in conventional fashion. Suicides, rebels, affirmers of the paradox—nay-sayers and yea-sayers alike to our fatal journey—I finally shake my head at them. And splash sighing past their corpses, one by one, as past a hundred sorts of others: friends, enemies, brothers; fools, sages, brutes—and nobodies, million upon million. I envy them all.

"A poor irony: that I, who find abhorrent and tautological the doctrine of survival of the fittest (*fitness* meaning, in my experience, nothing more than survival-ability, a talent whose only demonstration is the fact of survival, but whose chief ingredients seem to be strength, guile, callousness), may be the sole remaining swimmer! But the doctrine is false as well as repellent: Chance drowns the worthy with the unworthy, bears up the unfit with the fit by whatever definition, and makes the night-sea journey essentially *haphazard* as well as murderous and unjustified.

"'You only swim once.' Why bother, then?

"'Except ye drown, ye shall not reach the Shore of Life.' Poppycock.

"One of my late companions—that same cynic with the curious fancy, among the first to drown—entertained us with odd conjectures while we waited to begin our journey. A favorite theory of his was that the Father does exist, and did indeed make us and the sea we swim—but not a-purpose or even consciously; He made us, as it were, despite Himself, as we make waves with every tail-thrash, and may be unaware of our existence. Another was that He knows we're here but doesn't care what happens to us, inasmuch as He creates (voluntarily or not) other seas and swimmers at more or less regular intervals. In bitterer moments, such as just before he drowned, my friend even supposed that our Maker wished us unmade; there was indeed a Shore, he'd argue, which could save at least some of us from drowning and toward which it was our function to struggle—but for reasons unknowable to us He wanted desperately to prevent our reaching that happy place and fulfilling our destiny. Our 'Father,' in short, was our adversary and would-be killer! No less outrageous, and offensive to traditional opinion, were the fellow's speculations on the nature of our Maker: that He might well be no swimmer Himself at all, but some sort of monstrosity, perhaps even tailless; that He might be stupid, malicious, insensible, perverse, or asleep and dreaming; that the end for which He created and launched us forth, and which we flagellate ourselves to fathom, was perhaps immoral, even obscene. Et cetera, et cetera: there was no end to the chap's conjectures, or the impoliteness of his fancy; I have reason to suspect that his early demise, whether planned by 'our Maker' or not, was expedited by certain fellow-swimmers indignant at his blasphemies.

"In other moods, however (he was as given to moods as I), his theorizing would become half-serious, so it seemed to me, especially upon the subjects of Fate and Immortality, to which our youthful conversations often turned. Then his harangues, if no less fantastical, grew solemn and obscure, and if he was still baiting us, his passion undid the joke. His objection to popular opinions of the hereafter, he would declare, was their claim to general validity. Why need believers hold that *all* the drownèd rise to be judged at journey's end, and non-believers that drowning is final without exception? In *his* opinion (so he'd vow at least), nearly everyone's fate was permanent death; indeed he took a sour pleasure in supposing that every 'Maker' made thousands of separate seas in His creative life-time, each populated like ours with millions of swimmers, and that in almost every instance both sea and swimmers were utterly annihilated, whether accidentally or by malevolent design. (Nothing if not pluralistical, he imagined there might be millions and billions of 'Fathers,' perhaps in some 'night-sea' of their own!) However—and here he turned infidels against him with the faithful—he professed to believe that in possibly a single night-sea per thousand, say, one of its quarter-billion swimmers (that is, one swimmer in two hundred fifty billions) achieved a qualified immortality. In some cases the rate might be slightly higher; in others it was vastly lower, for just as there are swimmers of every degree of proficiency, including some who drown before the journey starts, unable to swim at all, and others created drowned, as it were, so he imagined what can only be termed impotent Creators, Makers unable to Make, as well as uncommonly fertile ones and all grades between. And it pleased him to deny any necessary relation between a Maker's productivity and His other virtues—including, even, the quality of His creatures.

"I could go on (*he* surely did) with his elaboration of these mad notions—such as that swimmers in other night-seas needn't be of our kind; that Makers themselves might belong to different *species*, so to speak; that our particular Maker mightn't Himself be immortal, or that we might be not only His emissaries but His 'immortality,' continuing His life and our own, transmogrified, beyond our individual deaths. Even this modified immortality (meaningless to me) he conceived as relative and contingent, subject to accidental or deliberate termination: his pet hypothesis was that Makers and swimmers *each generate the other*—against all odds, their number being so great— and that any given 'immortality-chain' could terminate after any number of cycles, so that what was 'immortal' (still speaking relatively) was only the cyclic process of incarnation, which itself might have a beginning and an end. Alternatively he liked to imagine cycles within cycles, either finite or infinite: for example, the 'night-sea,' as it were, in which Makers 'swam' and created night-seas and swimmers like ourselves, might be the creation of a larger Maker, Himself one of many, Who in turn et cetera. Time itself he regarded as relative to our experience, like magnitude: who knew but what, with each thrash of our tails, minuscule seas and swimmers, whole eternities, came to pass—as ours, perhaps, and our Maker's Maker's, was elapsing between the strokes of some supertail, in a slower order of time?

"Naturally I hooted with the others at this nonsense. We were young then, and had only the dimmest notion of what lay ahead; in our ignorance we imagined night-sea journeying to be a positively heroic enterprise. Its meaning and value we never questioned; to be sure, some must go down by the way, a pity no doubt, but to win a race requires that others lose, and like all my fellows I took for granted that I would be the winner. We milled and swarmed, impatient to be off, never mind where or why, only to try our youth against the realities of night and sea; if we indulged the skeptic at all, it was a droll, half-contemptible mascot. When he died in the initial slaughter, no one cared.

"And even now I don't subscribe to all his views—but I no longer scoff. The horror of our history has purged me of opinions, as of vanity, confidence, spirit, charity, hope, vitality, everything—except dull dread and a kind of melancholy, stunned persistence. What leads me to recall his fancies is my growing suspicion that I, of all swimmers, may be the sole survivor of this fell journey, tale-bearer of a generation. This suspicion, together with the recent sea-change, suggests to me now that nothing is impossible, not even my late companion's wildest visions, and brings me to a certain desperate resolve, the point of my chronicling.

"Very likely I have lost my senses. The carnage at our setting out; our decimation by whirlpool, poisoned cataract, sea-convulsion; the panic stampedes, mutinies, slaughters, mass suicides; the mounting evidence that none will survive the journey—add to these anguish and fatigue; it were a miracle if sanity stayed afloat. Thus I admit, with the other possibilities, that the present sweetening and calming of the sea, and what seems to be a kind of vasty presence, song, or summons from the near upstream, may be hallucinations of disordered sensibility. . . .

"Perhaps, even, I am drowned already. Surely I was never meant for the rough-and-tumble of the swim; not impossibly I perished at the outset and have only imaged the night-sea journey from some final deep. In any case, I'm no longer young, and it is we spent old swimmers, disabused of every illusion, who are most vulnerable to dreams.

"Sometimes I think I am my drownèd friend.

"Out with it: I've begun to believe, not only that She exists, but that She lies not far ahead, and stills the sea, and draws me Herward! Aghast, I recollect his maddest notion: that our destination (which existed, mind, in but one night-sea out of hundreds and thousands) was no Shore, as commonly conceived, but a mysterious being, indescribable except by paradox and vaguest figure: wholly different from us swimmers, yet our complement; the death of us, yet our salvation and resurrection; simultaneously our journey's end, mid-point, and commencement; not membered and thrashing like us, but a motionless or hugely gliding sphere of unimaginable dimension; self-contained, yet dependent absolutely, in some wise, upon the chance (always monstrously improbable) that one of us will survive the night-sea journey and reach . . . Her! Her, he called it, or *She,* which is to say, Other-than-a-he. I shake my head; the thing is too preposterous; it is myself I talk to, to keep my reason in this awful darkness. There is no She! There is no You! I rave to myself; it's Death alone that hears and summons. To the drowned, all seas are calm. . . .

"Listen: my friend maintained that in every order of creation there are two sorts of creators, contrary yet complementary, one of which gives rise to seas and swimmers, the other to the Night-which-contains-the-sea and to What-waits-at-the-journey's-end: the former, in short, to destiny, the latter to destination (and both profligately, involuntarily, perhaps indifferently or unwittingly). The 'purpose' of the night-sea journey—but not necessarily of the journeyer or of either Maker!—my friend could describe only in abstractions: *consummation, transfiguration, union, contraries, transcension of categories.* When we laughed, he would shrug and admit that he understood the business no better than we, and thought it ridiculous, dreary, possibly obscene. 'But one of you,' he'd add with his wry smile, 'may be the Hero destined to complete the night-sea journey and be one with Her. Chances are, of course, you won't make it.' He himself, he declared, was not even going to try; the whole idea repelled him; if we chose to dismiss it as an ugly fiction, so much the better for us; thrash, splash, and be merry, we were soon enough drowned. But there it was, he could not say how he knew or why he bothered to tell us, any more than he could say what would happen after She and Hero, Shore and Swimmer, 'merged identities' to become something both and neither. He quite agreed with me that if the issue of that magical union had no memory of the night-sea journey, for example, it enjoyed a poor sort of immortality; even poorer if, as he rather imagined, a swimmer-hero plus a She equaled or became merely another Maker of future night-seas and the rest, at such incredible expense of life. This being the case—he was persuaded it was—the merciful thing to do was refuse to participate; the genuine heroes, in his opinion, were the suicides, and the hero of heroes would be the swimmer who, in the very presence of the Order, refused Her proffered 'immortality' and thus put an end to at least one cycle of catastrophes.

"How we mocked him! Our moment came, we hurtled forth, pretending to glory in the adventure, thrashing, singing, cursing, strangling, rationalizing, rescuing, killing, inventing rules and stories and relationships, giving up, struggling on, but dying all, and still in darkness, until only a battered remnant was left to croak 'Onward, upward,' like a bitter echo. Then they too fell silent—victims, I can only presume, of the last frightful wave—and the moment came when I also, utterly desolate and spent, thrashed my last and gave myself over to the current, to sink or float as might be, but swim no more. Whereupon, marvelous to tell, in an instant the sea grew still! Then warmly, gently, the great tide turned, began to bear me, as it does now, onward and upward will-I, nill-I, like a flood of joy—and I recalled with dismay my dead friend's teaching.

"I am not deceived. This new emotion is Her doing; the desire that possesses me is Her bewitchment. Lucidity passes from me; in a moment I'll cry 'Love!' bury myself in Her side, and be 'transfigured.' Which is to say, I die already; this fellow transported by passion is not I; *I am he who abjures and rejects the night-sea journey!* I. . . .

"I am all love. 'Come!' She whispers, and I have no will.

"You who I may be about to become, whatever You are: with the last twitch of my real self I beg You to listen. It is *not* love that sustains me! No; though Her magic makes me burn to sing the contrary, and though I drown even now for the blasphemy, I will say truth. What has fetched me across this dreadful sea is a single hope, gift of my poor dead comrade: that You may be stronger-willed than I, and that by sheer force of concentration I may transmit to You, along with Your official Heritage, a private legacy of awful recollection and negative resolve. Mad as it may be, my dream is that some unimaginable embodiment of myself (or myself plus Her if that's how it must be) will come to find itself expressing, in however garbled or radical a translation, some reflection of these reflections. If against all odds this comes to pass, may You to whom, through whom I speak, do what I cannot: terminate this aimless, brutal business! Stop Your hearing against Her song! Hate love!

"Still alive, afloat, afire. Farewell then my penultimate hope: that one may be sunk for direct blasphemy on the very shore of the Shore. Can it be (my old friend would smile) that only utterest nay-sayers survive the night? But even that were Sense, and there is no sense, only senseless love, senseless death. Whoever echoes these reflections: be more courageous than their author! An end to night-sea journeys! Make no more! And forswear me when I shall forswear myself, deny myself, plunge into Her who summons, singing . . .

"'Love! Love! Love!'"

QUESTIONS

1   What clues does Barth give to the identity of his speaker?
2   Why are "night-sea" and "swimmer" metaphorically effective to both the world of the story and our world?
3   What specific sociological and religious philosophies does Barth's speaker speculate about? What are his answers? What, then, are we to conclude about this view of death?

TOPIC FOR COMPOSITION

The three short stories in this part appear quite different in many respects. Is there, however, an argumentative position, aside from the obvious idea about the inevitability of death, that is reflected in much the same way in each story? Write an essay arguing either side of the question.

DRAMA

O'Neill's "Bound East for Cardiff" emphasizes the stark loneliness and finality of death that seals the unfulfilled but yearning life. Among the simple men of the sea such a passage from life into death is indeed to be "bound east," but into terrible mystery instead of to Cardiff. In that sense, all men, like the crew of the *S.S. Glencairn,* are sailing toward some ultimate port that lies, as Hamlet says, in "The undiscover'd country, from whose bourn / No traveller returns." Yet none of the seamen knows how to respond to or even to acknowledge the fact of Yank's death; only the dying man must reckon with the reality.

1 Exits and entrances of the crew punctuate the ebbing life of Yank.
2 The presence of death establishes a real, if unstable, decorum to which each man tries to rise.
3 The bleakness of O'Neill's play is accentuated by the organic relationship of barren setting, reports of the ship's situation, the helplessness of the captain, and the inchoate speech of the crew.

BOUND EAST FOR CARDIFF

Eugene O'Neill

CHARACTERS

YANK	PAUL
DRISCOLL	SMITTY
COCKY	IVAN
DAVIS	THE CAPTAIN
SCOTTY	THE SECOND MATE
OLSON	

Scene. The seamen's forecastle of the British tramp steamer Glencairn *on a foggy night midway on the voyage between New York and Cardiff. An irregular-shaped compartment, the sides of which almost meet at the far end to form a triangle. Sleeping bunks about six feet long, ranged three deep with a space of three feet separating the upper from the lower, are built against the sides. On the right above the bunks three or four port-holes can be seen. In front of the bunks, rough wooden benches. Over the bunks on the left, a lamp in a bracket. In the left foreground, a doorway. On the floor near it, a pail with a tin dipper. Oilskins are hanging from a hook near the doorway.*

The far side of the forecastle is so narrow that it contains only one series of bunks.

In under the bunks a glimpse can be had of sea-chests, suitcases, sea-boots, etc., jammed in indiscriminately.

At regular intervals of a minute or so the blast of the steamer's whistle can be heard above all the other sounds.

Five men are sitting on the benches talking. They are dressed in dirty patched suits of dungaree, flannel shirts, and all are in their stocking feet. Four of the men are pulling on pipes and the air is heavy with rancid tobacco smoke. Sitting on the top bunk in the left foreground, a Norwegian, PAUL, *is softly playing some folk-song on a battered accordion. He stops from time to time to listen to the conversation.*

In the lower bunk in the rear a dark-haired, hard-featured man is lying apparently asleep. One of his arms is stretched limply over the side of the bunk. His face is very pale, and drops of clammy perspiration glisten on his forehead.

It is nearing the end of the dog-watch—about ten minutes to eight in the evening.

COCKY *(a weazened runt of a man. He is telling a story. The others are listening with amused, incredulous faces, interrupting him at the end of each sentence with loud derisive guffaws.)* Makin' love to me, she was! It's Gawd's truth! A bloomin' nigger! Greased all over with cocoanut oil, she was. Gawd blimey, I couldn't stand 'er. Bloody old cow, I says; and with that I fetched 'er a biff on the ear wot knocked 'er silly, an'—*(He is interrupted by a roar of laughter from the others.)*

DAVIS *(a middle-aged man with black hair and mustache)* You're a liar, Cocky.

SCOTTY *(a dark young fellow)* Ho-ho! Ye werr neverr in New Guinea in yourr life, I'm thinkin'.

OLSON *(a Swede with a drooping blond mustache—with ponderous sarcasm)* Yust tink of it! You say she wass a cannibal, Cocky?

DRISCOLL *(a brawny Irishman with the battered features of a prizefighter)* How cud ye doubt ut, Ollie? A quane av the naygurs she musta been surely. Who else wud think herself aqual to fallin' in love wid a beautiful, divil-may-care rake av a man the loike av Cocky? *(A burst of laughter from the crowd)*

COCKY *(indignantly)* Gawd strike me dead if it ain't true, every bleedin' word of it. 'Appened ten year ago come Christmas.

SCOTTY 'Twas a Christmas dinner she had her eyes on.

DAVIS He'd a been a tough old bird.

DRISCOLL 'Tis lucky for both av ye ye escaped; for the quane av the cannibal isles wad a died av the bellyache the day afther Christmas, divil a doubt av ut. *(The laughter at this is long and loud.)*

COCKY *(sullenly)* Blarsted fat-'eads! *(The sick man in the lower bunk in the rear groans and moves restlessly. There is a hushed silence. All the men turn and stare at him.)*

DRISCOLL Ssshh! *(In a hushed whisper)* We'd best not be talkin' so loud and him tryin' to have a bit av a sleep. *(He tiptoes softly to the side of the bunk.)* Yank! You'd be wantin' a drink av wather, maybe? *(*YANK *does not reply.* DRISCOLL *bends over and looks at him.)* It's asleep he is, sure enough. His breath is chokin' in his throat loike wather gurglin' in a poipe. *(He comes back quietly and sits down. All are silent, avoiding each other's eyes.)*

COCKY *(after a pause)* Pore devil! It's over the side for 'im, Gawd 'elp 'im.

DRISCOLL Stop your croakin'! He's not dead yet and, praise God, he'll have many a long day yet before him.

SCOTTY *(shaking his head doubtfully)* He's bod, mon, he's verry bod.

DAVIS Lucky he's alive. Many a man's light woulda gone out after a fall like that.

OLSON You saw him fall?

DAVIS Right next to him. He and me was goin' down in number two hold to do some chippin'. He puts his leg over careless-like and misses the ladder and plumps straight down to the bottom. I was scared to look over for a minute, and then I heard him groan and I scuttled down after him. He was hurt bad inside, for the blood was drippin' from the side of his mouth. He was groanin' hard, but he never let a word out of him.

COCKY An' you blokes remember when we 'auled 'im in 'ere? Oh, 'ell, 'e says, oh, 'ell—like that, and nothink else.

OLSON Did the captain know where he iss hurted?

COCKY That silly ol' josser! Wot the 'ell would 'e know abaht anythink?

SCOTTY *(scornfully)* He fiddles in his mouth wi' a bit of glass.

DRISCOLL *(angrily)* The divil's own life ut is to be out on the lonely sea wid nothin' betune you and a grave in the ocean but a spindle-shanked, gray-whiskered auld fool the loike av him. 'Twas enough to make a saint shwear to see him wid his gold watch in his hand, tryin' to look as wise as an owl on a tree, and all the toime he not knowin' whether 'twas cholery or the barber's itch was the matther with Yank.

SCOTTY *(sardonically)* He gave him a dose of salts, na doot?

DRISCOLL Divil a thing he gave him at all, but looked in the book he had wid him, and shook his head, and walked out widout sayin' a word, the second mate afther him no wiser than himself, God's curse on the two av thim!

COCKY *(after a pause)* Yank was a good shipmate, pore beggar. Lend me four bob in Noo Yark, 'e did.

DRISCOLL *(warmly)* A good shipmate he was and is, none betther. Ye said no more than the truth, Cocky. Five years and more ut is since first I shipped wid him, and we've stuck together iver since through good luck and bad. Fights we've had, God help us, but 'twas only when we'd a bit av drink taken, and we always shook hands the nixt mornin'. Whativer was his was mine, and many's the toime I'd a been on the beach or worse, but for him. And now—*(His voice trembles as he fights to control his emotion.)* Divil take me if I'm not startin' to blubber loike an auld woman, and he not dead at all, but goin' to live many a long year yet, maybe.

DAVIS The sleep'll do him good. He seems better now.

OLSON If he wud eat something—

DRISCOLL Wud ye have him be eatin' in his condishun? Sure it's hard enough on the rest av us wid nothin' the matther wid our insides to be stomachin' the skoff on this rusty lime-juicer.

SCOTTY *(indignantly)* It's a starvation ship.

DAVIS Plenty o' work and no food—and the owners ridin' around in carriages!

OLSON Hash, hash! Stew, stew! Marmalade, py damn! *(He spits disgustedly.)*

COCKY Bloody swill! Fit only for swine is wot I say.

DRISCOLL And the dish-wather they disguise wid the name av tea! And the putty they call bread! My belly feels loike I'd swalleyed a dozen rivets at the thought av ut! And sea-biscuit that'd break the teeth av a lion if he had the misfortune to take a bite at one! *(Unconsciously they have all raised their voices, forgetting the sick man in their sailor's delight at finding something to grumble about.)*

PAUL *(swings his feet over the side of his bunk, stops playing his accordion, and says slowly)* And rot-ten po-tay-toes! *(He starts in playing again. The sick man gives a groan of pain.)*

DRISCOLL *(holding up his hand)* Shut your mouths, all av you. 'Tis a hell av a thing for us to be complainin' about our guts, and a sick man maybe dyin' listenin' to us. *(Gets up and shakes his fist at the Norwegian)* God stiffen you, ye square-head scut! Put down that organ av yours or I'll break your ugly face for you. Is that banshee schreechin' fit music for a sick man? *(The Norwegian puts his accordion in the bunk and lies back and closes his eyes.* DRISCOLL *goes over and stands beside* YANK. *The steamer's whistle sounds particularly loud in the silence.)*

DAVIS Damn this fog! *(Reaches in under a bunk and yanks out a pair of sea-boots, which he pulls on.)* My lookout next, too. Must be nearly eight bells, boys. *(With the exception of* OLSON, *all the men sitting up put on oilskins, sou'westers, sea-boots, etc., in preparation for the watch on deck.* OLSON *crawls into a lower bunk on the right.)*

SCOTTY My wheel.

OLSON *(disgustedly)* Nothin' but yust dirty weather all dis voyage. I yust can't sleep when weestle blow. *(He turns his back to the light and is soon fast asleep and snoring.)*

SCOTTY If this fog keeps up, I'm tellin' ye, we'll no be in Cardiff for a week or more.

DRISCOLL 'Twas just such a night as this the auld Dover wint down. Just about this toime ut was, too, and we all sittin' round in the fo'c'stle, Yank beside me, whin all av a suddint we heard a great slitherin' crash, and the ship heeled over till we was all in a heap on wan side. What came afther I disremimber exactly, except 'twas a hard shift to get the boats over the side before the auld teakittle sank. Yank was in the same boat wid me, and sivin morthal days we drifted wid scarcely a drop of wather or a bite to chew on. 'Twas Yank here that held me down whin I wanted to jump into the ocean, roarin' mad wid the thirst. Picked up we were on the same day wid only Yank in his senses, and him steerin' the boat.

COCKY *(protestingly)* Blimey but you're a cheerful blighter, Driscoll! Talkin' abaht ship-wrecks in this 'ere blushin' fog. *(*YANK *groans and stirs uneasily, opening his eyes.* DRISCOLL *hurries to his side.)*

DRISCOLL Are ye feelin' any betther, Yank?

YANK *(in a weak voice)* No.

DRISCOLL Sure, you must be. You look as sthrong as an ox. *(Appealing to the others)* Am I tellin' him a lie?

DAVIS The sleep's done you good.

COCKY You'll be 'avin your pint of beer in Cardiff this day week.

SCOTTY And fish and chips, mon!

YANK *(peevishly)* What're yuh all lyin' fur? D'yuh think I'm scared to—*(He hesitates as if frightened by the word he is about to say.)*

DRISCOLL Don't be thinkin' such things! *(The ship's bell is heard heavily tolling eight times. From the forecastle head above the voice of the lookout rises in a long wail: Aaall's welll. The men look uncertainly at* YANK *as if undecided whether to say good-by or not.)*

YANK *(in an agony of fear)* Don't leave me, Drisc! I'm dyin', I tell yuh. I won't stay here alone with everyone snorin'. I'll go out on deck. *(He makes a feeble attempt to rise, but sinks back with a sharp groan. His breath comes in wheezy gasps.)* Don't leave me, Drisc! *(His face grows white and his head falls back with a jerk.)*

DRISCOLL Don't be worryin', Yank. I'll not move a step out av here—and let that divil av a bosun curse his black head off. You speak a word to the bosun, Cocky. Tell him that Yank is bad took and I'll be stayin' wid him a while yet.

COCKY Right-o. *(*COCKY, DAVIS, *and* SCOTTY *go out quietly.)*

COCKY *(from the alleyway)* Gawd blimey, the fog's thick as soup.

DRISCOLL Are ye satisfied now, Yank? *(Receiving no answer, he bends over the still form.)* He's fainted, God help him! *(He gets a tin dipper from the bucket and bathes* YANK's *forehead with the water.* YANK *shudders and opens his eyes.)*

YANK *(slowly)* I thought I was goin' then. Wha' did yuh wanta wake me up fur?

DRISCOLL *(with a forced gayety)* It is wishful for heaven ye are?

YANK *(gloomily)* Hell, I guess.

DRISCOLL *(crossing himself involuntarily)* For the love av the saints don't be talkin' loike that! You'd give a man the creeps. It's chippin' rust on deck you'll be in a day or two wid the best av us. *(*YANK *does not answer, but closes his eyes wearily. The seaman who has been on lookout,* SMITTY, *a young Englishman, comes in and takes off his dripping oilskins. While he is doing this the man whose turn at the wheel has been relieved enters. He is a dark burly fellow with a round stupid face. The Englishman steps softly over to* DRISCOLL. *The other crawls into a lower bunk.)*

SMITTY *(whispering)* How's Yank?

DRISCOLL Betther. Ask him yourself. He's awake.

YANK I'm all right, Smitty.

SMITTY Glad to hear it, Yank. *(He crawls to an upper bunk and is soon asleep.)*

IVAN *(the stupid-faced seaman, who comes in after* SMITTY, *twists his head in the direction of the sick man.)* You feel gude, Jank?

YANK *(wearily)* Yes, Ivan.

IVAN Dot's gude. *(He rolls over on his side and falls asleep immediately.)*

YANK *(after a pause broken only by snores—with a bitter laugh)* Good-by and good luck to the lot of you!

DRISCOLL Is ut painin' you again?

YANK It hurts like hell—here. *(He points to the lower part of his chest on the left side.)* I guess my old pump's busted. Ooohh! *(A spasm of pain contracts his pale features. He presses his hand to his side and writhes on the thin mattress of his bunk. The perspiration stands out in beads on his forehead.)*

DRISCOLL *(terrified)* YANK! Yank! What is ut? *(Jumping to his feet)* I'll run for the captain. *(He starts for the doorway.)*

YANK *(sitting up in his bunk, frantic with fear)* Don't leave me, Drisc! For God's sake don't leave me alone! *(He leans over the side of his bunk and spits.* DRISCOLL *comes back to him.)* Blood! Ugh!

DRISCOLL Blood again! I'd best be gettin' the captain.

YANK No, no, don't leave me! If yuh do I'll git up and follow you. I ain't no coward, but I'm scared to stay here with all of them asleep and snorin'. *(*DRISCOLL, *not knowing* *what to do, sits down on the bench beside him. He grows calmer and sinks back on the mattress.)* The captain can't do me no good, yuh know it yourself. The pain ain't so bad now, but I thought it had me then. It was like a buzz-saw cuttin' into me.

DRISCOLL *(fiercely)* God blarst ut!

(The CAPTAIN *and the* SECOND MATE *of the steamer enter the forecastle. The* CAPTAIN *is an old man with gray mustache and whiskers. The* MATE *is clean-shaven and middle-aged. Both are dressed in simple blue uniforms.)*

THE CAPTAIN *(taking out his watch and feeling* YANK's *pulse)* And how is the sick man?

YANK *(feebly)* All right, sir.

THE CAPTAIN And the pain in the chest?

YANK It still hurts, sir, worse than ever.

THE CAPTAIN *(taking a thermometer from his pocket and putting it into* YANK's *mouth)* Here. Be sure and keep this in under your tongue, not over it.

THE MATE *(after a pause)* Isn't this your watch on deck, Driscoll?

DRISCOLL Yes, sorr, but Yank was fearin' to be alone, and—

THE CAPTAIN That's all right, Driscoll.

DRISCOLL Thank ye, sorr.

THE CAPTAIN *(stares at his watch for a moment or so; then takes the thermometer from* YANK's *mouth and goes to the lamp to read it. His expression grows very grave. He beckons the* MATE *and* DRISCOLL *to the corner near the doorway.* YANK *watches them furtively. The* CAPTAIN *speaks in a low voice to the* MATE.*)* Way up, both of them. *(To* DRISCOLL*)* He has been spitting blood again?

DRISCOLL Not much for the hour just past, sorr, but before that—

THE CAPTAIN A great deal?

DRISCOLL Yes, sorr.

THE CAPTAIN He hasn't eaten anything?

DRISCOLL No, sorr.

THE CAPTAIN Did he drink that medicine I sent him?

DRISCOLL Yes, sorr, but it didn't stay down.

THE CAPTAIN *(shaking his head)* I'm afraid—he's very weak. I can't do anything else for him. It's too serious for me. If this had only happened a week later we'd be in Cardiff in time to—

DRISCOLL Plaze help him some way, sorr!

THE CAPTAIN *(impatiently)* But, my good man, I'm not a doctor. *(More kindly as he sees* DRISCOLL's *grief)* You and he have been shipmates a long time?

DRISCOLL Five years and more, sorr.

THE CAPTAIN I see. Well, don't let him move. Keep him quiet and we'll hope for the best. I'll read the matter up and send him some medicine, something to ease the pain, anyway. *(Goes over to* YANK*)* Keep up your courage! You'll be better tomorrow. *(He breaks down lamely before* YANK's *steady gaze).* We'll pull you through all right—and—hm—well—coming, Robinson? Dammit! *(He goes out hurriedly, followed by the* MATE.*)*

DRISCOLL *(trying to conceal his anxiety)* Didn't I tell you you wasn't half as sick as you thought you was? The Captain'll have you out on deck cursin' and swearin' loike a trooper before the week is out.

YANK Don't lie, Drisc. I heard what he said, and if I didn't I c'd tell by the way I feel. I know what's goin' to happen. I'm goin' to—*(He hesitates for a second—then resolutely)* I'm goin' to die, that's what, and the sooner the better!

DRISCOLL *(wildly)* No, and be damned to you, you're not. I'll not let you.

YANK It ain't no use, Drisc. I ain't got a chance, but I ain't scared. Gimme a drink of water, will yuh, Drisc? My throat's burnin' up. *(DRISCOLL brings the dipper full of water and supports his head while he drinks in great gulps.)*

DRISCOLL *(seeking vainly for some word of comfort)* Are ye feelin' more aisy-loike now?

YANK Yes—now—when I know it's all up. *(A pause)* You mustn't take it so hard, Drisc. I was just thinkin' it ain't as bad as people think—dyin'. I ain't never took much stock in the truck them skypilots preach. I ain't never had religion; but I know whatever it is what comes after it can't be no worser'n this. I don't like to leave you, Drisc, but—that's all.

DRISCOLL *(with a groan)* Lad, lad, don't be talkin'.

YANK This sailor life ain't much to cry about leavin'—just one ship after another, hard work, small pay, and bum grub; and when we git into port, just a drunk endin' up in a fight, and all your money gone, and then ship away again. Never meetin' no nice people; never gittin' outa sailor-town, hardly, in any port; travelin' all over the world and never seein' none of it; without no one to care whether you're alive or dead. *(With a bitter smile)* There ain't much in all that that'd make yuh sorry to lose it, Drisc.

DRISCOLL *(gloomily)* It's a hell av a life, the sea.

YANK *(musingly)* It must be great to stay on dry land all your life and have a farm with a house of your own with cows and pigs and chickens, 'way in the middle of the land where yuh'd never smell the sea or see a ship. It must be great to have a wife, and kids to play with at night after supper when your work was done. It must be great to have a home of your own, Drisc.

DRISCOLL *(with a great sigh)* It must, surely; but what's the use av thinkin' av ut? Such things are not for the loikes av us.

YANK Sea-farin' is all right when you're young and don't care, but we ain't chickens no more, and somehow, I dunno, this last year has seemed rotten, and I've had a hunch I'd quit—with you, of course—and we'd save our coin, and go to Canada or Argentine or some place and git a farm, just a small one, just enough to live on. I never told yuh this, 'cause I thought you'd laugh at me.

DRISCOLL *(enthusiastically)* Laugh at you, is ut? When I'm havin' the same thoughts myself, toime afther toime. It's a grand idea and we'll be doin' ut sure if you'll stop your crazy notions—about—about bein' so sick.

YANK *(sadly)* Too late. We shouldn'ta made this trip, and then—How'd all the fog git in here?

DRISCOLL Fog?

YANK   Everything looks misty. Must be my eyes gittin' weak, I guess. What was we talkin' of a minute ago? Oh, yes, a farm. It's too late. *(His mind wandering)* Argentine, did I say? D'yuh remember the times we've had in Buenos Aires? The moving pictures in Barracas? Some class to them, d'yuh remember?

DRISCOLL *(with satisfaction)*   I do that; and so does the piany player. He'll not be forgettin' the black eye I gave him in a hurry.

YANK   Remember the time we was there on the beach and had to go to Tommy Moore's boarding house to git shipped? And he sold us rotten oilskins and sea-boots full of holes, and shipped us on a skysail-yarder round the Horn, and took two months' pay for it. And the days we used to sit on the park benches along the Paseo Colon with the vigilantes lookin' hard at us? And the songs at the Sailor's Opera where the guy played ragtime—d'yuh remember them?

DRISCOLL   I do, surely.

YANK   And La Plata—phew, the stink of the hides! I always liked Argentine—all except that booze, caña. How drunk we used to git on that, remember?

DRISCOLL   Cud I forget ut? My head pains me at the menshun av that divil's brew.

YANK   Remember the night I went crazy with the heat in Singapore? And the time you was pinched by the cops in Port Said? And the time we was both locked up in Sydney for fightin'?

DRISCOLL   I do so.

YANK   And that fight on the dock at Cape Town—*(His voice betrays great inward perturbation.)*

DRISCOLL *(hastily)*   Don't be thinkin' av that now. 'Tis past and gone.

YANK   D'yuh think He'll hold it up against me?

DRISCOLL *(mystified)*   Who's that?

YANK   God. They say He sees everything. He must know it was done in fair fight, in self-defense, don't yuh think?

DRISCOLL   Av course. Ye stabbed him, and be damned to him, for the skulkin' swine he was, afther him tryin' to stick you in the back, and you not suspectin'. Let your conscience be aisy. I wisht I had nothin' blacker than that on my sowl. I'd not be afraid av the angel Gabriel himself.

YANK *(with a shudder)*   I c'd see him a minute ago with the blood spurtin' out of his neck. Ugh!

DRISCOLL   The fever, ut is, that makes you see such things. Give no heed to ut.

YANK *(uncertainly)*   You don't think He'll hold it up agin me—God, I mean.

DRISCOLL   If there's justice in hiven, no! *(YANK seems comforted by this assurance.)*

YANK *(after a pause)*   We won't reach Cardiff for a week at least. I'll be buried at sea.

DRISCOLL *(putting his hands over his ears)*   Ssshh! I won't listen to you.

YANK *(as if he had not heard him)*   It's as good a place as any other, I s'pose—only I always wanted to be buried on dry land. But what the hell'll I care—then? *(Fretfully)* Why should it be a rotten night like this with that damned whistle blowin' and people snorin' all round? I wish the stars was out, and the moon, too; I c'd lie out on deck and look at them, and it'd make it easier to go—somehow.

DRISCOLL   For the love av God don't be talkin' loike that!

YANK   Whatever pay's comin' to me yuh can divvy up with the rest of the boys; and you take my watch. It ain't worth much, but it's all I've got.

DRISCOLL   But have you no relations at all to call your own?

YANK   No, not as I know of. One thing I forgot: You know Fanny the barmaid at the Red Stork in Cardiff?

DRISCOLL   Sure, and who doesn't?

YANK   She's been good to me. She tried to lend me half a crown when I was broke there last trip. Buy her the biggest box of candy yuh c'n find in Cardiff. *(Breaking down—in a choking voice)* It's hard to ship on this voyage I'm goin' on—alone! *(DRISCOLL reaches out and grasps his hand. There is a pause, during which both fight to control themselves.)* My throat's like a furnace. *(He gasps for air)* Gimme a drink of water, will yuh, Drisc? *(DRISCOLL gets him a dipper of water.)* I wish this was a pint of beer. Oooohh! *(He chokes, his face convulsed with agony, his hands tearing at his shirt-front. The dipper falls from his nerveless fingers.)*

DRISCOLL   For the love av God, what is ut, Yank?

YANK   *(speaking with tremendous difficulty)* S'long, Drisc! *(He stares straight in front of him with eyes starting from their sockets)* Who's that?

DRISCOLL   Who? What?

YANK   *(faintly)* A pretty lady dressed in black. *(His face twitches and his body writhes in a final spasm, then straightens out rigidly.)*

DRISCOLL   *(pale with horror)* Yank! Yank! Say a word to me for the love av hiven! *(He shrinks away from the bunk, making the sign of the cross. Then comes back and puts a trembling hand on YANK's chest and bends closely over the body.)*

COCKY   *(from the alleyway)* Oh, Driscoll! Can you leave Yank for arf a mo' and give me a 'and?

DRISCOLL   *(with a great sob)* Yank! *(He sinks down on his knees beside the bunk, his head on his hands. His lips move in some half-remembered prayer.)*

COCKY   *(enters, his oilskins and sou'wester glistening with drops of water)* The fog's lifted. *(COCKY sees DRISCOLL and stands staring at him with open mouth. DRISCOLL makes the sign of the cross again.)*

COCKY   *(mockingly)* Sayin' 'is prayers! *(He catches sight of the still figure in the bunk and an expression of awed understanding comes over his face. He takes off his dripping sou'wester and stands, scratching his head.)*

COCKY   *(in a hushed whisper)* Gawd blimey!

CURTAIN

QUESTIONS

1   What can we infer of the dimensions of a seaman's life from Cocky's elliptical story of his experience with the woman in New Guinea, the frequent blowing of the whistle, the complaints about tea and the captain, the fog, the adventures of Driscoll and Yank in Buenos Aires and Barracas?

2   How does O'Neill indicate that we are to consider such fragments of a lifetime against the impending death of Yank?

3 Do you think the play justifies sentimentality as the only adequate response to Yank's death and to the situation of the crew? If not, how does it avoid sentimentality?

TOPICS FOR COMPOSITION

1 Describe the means, including dialogue, by which O'Neill emphasizes the somber situation of a death at sea.
2 Defend the captain's attitude and manner in the face of Yank's obviously looming death.
3 Out of the relatively small cast of characters and the minimal dialogue allotted to each character, classify the kinds of responses to Yank's dying.

POETRY

Every common attitude toward death has found vital expression in poetry. The poems of this section, while they do not by any means represent adequately the whole range of significantly varying views, illustrate some of the most notable differences of opinion about the subject. At the same time, there are enough resemblances among them to make possible a kind of classification which may be of some use in analysis. We can begin with the reflection that just as the fact of death affects in some way everyone's attitude toward life, so do our general responses to life shape our views of death. For example, people who have found life richly rewarding may be able, as Robert Louis Stevenson's "Requiem" suggests, to accept death without much complaint and without much questioning while those who have found life harrowing or frustrating may be inclined, like the speaker in Swinburne's "The Garden of Proserpine," to look to death as a means of escape. Both of these poets think of death as a sleep; however, while Stevenson uses the analogy as an expression of fulfillment, Swinburne is proclaiming the ultimate futility of life; so, it seems, is Ernest Dowson: "They are not long," he says, "the days of wine and roses," but the weeping as well as the laughter will probably be ·forgotten in a misty dream. Robert Frost's "After Apple-Picking," although it offers a more complex and ambiguous statement, may be compared with "Requiem" in the respect that the reflections on death that it suggests are related to a sense of satisfaction with the efforts and achievements of a lifetime: having worked hard and faithfully, the speaker of this poem is ready for the sleep of death; and he knows that his dreams, if he has any, will embody the essence of his feeling about his work. Almost amazingly, in view of the fact that he evidently lacks the ordinarily crucial support of remembered achievements, John Keats manages to convey convincingly (in "To Autumn") something of the same attitude—the feeling that *ripeness is all*.

In very different ways, then, either satisfaction with life or disappointment may reconcile reflective men to the idea of death as a sleep, even a dreamless sleep. Most people, however, have found just enough of good and evil in life—especially moral good and evil—to make them hope for something better beyond. Probably (for some would doubtless argue the point) the greatest triumphs of the sense of moral value have been achieved with the support of traditional religion; and no more eloquent testimony of the power of religious belief has been offered than we find in such poems as John Donne's mighty "Death, Be Not Proud," Henry Vaughan's poignant "They Are All Gone into the World of Light," and Gerard Manley Hopkins' sweetly thoughtful "The Caged Skylark."

Often, of course, unreflective preoccupation with the manifold pursuits of life keeps death from being, except on rare occasions, a complete reality. For young people absorbing the fact of personal mortality is naturally difficult and sometimes profoundly shocking; Wordsworth's brief poem "A Slumber Did My Spirit Seal" speaks volumes on this score. And many supposedly mature people try, consciously or unconsciously, to avoid facing *the ultimate fact,* as William Carlos Williams's "Tract" emphasizes. This tendency is supposed to be especially strong in America. Why that should be so, if it is, surely is a question worth careful consideration. Many factors may be involved, ranging from attitudes toward sex to the worship of progress.

Then there is the opposite of such evasion: the desire to achieve an imaginative confrontation with death as a means of exploring and testing one's attitudes toward

473

life. Most of us, regardless of age or religious inclinations, are so oriented as to find that undertaking more or less distasteful; yet it can be rewarding, and those interested can find encouragement and assistance in poetry—in such poems, for example, as Thomas Hardy's "Friends Beyond," Robert Penn Warren's "Pondy Woods," and Theodore Roethke's "The Far Field." Hardy evidently thinks that living with the constant awareness that all our personal ambitions will be mocked by death might not be a frustrating and desolating experience, as one would suppose, but rather a liberating one—whether humanizing or not, he cannily leaves his readers to judge. Warren, by leading us to empathize with a doomed man struggling deliriously against death, forces us to recognize that the human mind harbors vultures (to borrow his metaphor) far more terrible than those that soar in the skies and perch in tall trees, and with the shock of that recognition comes a new sense of control. And Roethke assures us that by heeding his dreams of dead-end journeys symbolic of death he has come to see that "all finite things reveal infinitude"—and has at the same time learned not to fear infinity, the "far field" to which he has let his journeys of imagination take him.

At this point it should be evident that classification of this kind is most useful when it is most difficult. All good poetry, like all experience of much value, combines uniqueness and potential universality.

FROM THE TEMPEST[1]

William Shakespeare

Our revels now are ended. These our actors,
As I foretold you, were all spirits, and
Are melted into air, into thin air;
And, like the baseless fabric of this vision,
The cloud-capp'd towers, the gorgeous palaces,   5
The solemn temples, the great globe itself,
Yea, all which it inherit, shall dissolve
And, like this insubstantial pageant faded,
Leave not a rack behind. We are such stuff
As dreams are made on, and our little life   10
Is rounded with a sleep.

1623

[1] Act IV, 1, 148–158. Prospero, a magician, has summoned up spirits in the form of reapers and nymphs to perform a dance for the entertainment of his guests.

4 fabric: unsubstantial material.   *9 rack:* cloud.   *11 rounded:* surrounded, framed.

DEATH, BE NOT PROUD

John Donne

Death, be not proud, though some have called thee
Mighty and dreadful, for thou are not so;
For those whom thou think'st thou dost overthrow
Die not, poor Death; nor yet canst thou kill me.
From rest and sleep, which but thy picture be,　　　　　　　　5
Much pleasure; then from thee much more must flow;
And soonest our best men with thee do go—
Rest of their bones and souls' delivery!
Thou'rt slave to fate, chance, kings, and desperate men,
And dost with poison, war, and sickness dwell;　　　　　　　10
And poppy or charms can make us sleep as well
And better than thy stroke. Why swell'st thou then?
One short sleep past, we wake eternally,
And Death shall be no more: Death, thou shalt die.

1633

11 poppy: opiates.　*12 Why swell'st thou then?:* i.e., with pride.

QUESTIONS

1　In addressing himself to death, the poet uses the device of personification. What does this contribute to the emotional content of the poem?

2　What arguments are used to refute the claim that death is mighty and dreadful? Are they convincing? Does the statement made in the last two lines necessarily follow from the preceding statements? Is the poet really concerned about making a case, or is he more interested in expressing an attitude? If the latter is the important thing, of what use is the argument?

HYMN TO GOD, MY GOD, IN MY SICKNESS

John Donne

Since I am coming to that holy room,
　　Where, with thy choir of saints for evermore,
I shall be made thy music; as I come
　　I tune the instrument here at the door,
　　And what I must do then, think here before.　　　　　　　5

Whilst my physicians by their love are grown
　　Cosmographers, and I their map, who lie

Flat on this bed, that by them may be shown
    That this is my south-west discovery
Per fretum febris, by these straits to die,   10

I joy, that in these straits, I see my west;
    For though their currents yield return to none,
What shall my west hurt me? As west and east
    In all flat maps (and I am one) are one,
    So death doth touch the Resurrection.   15

Is the Pacific Sea my home? Or are
    The eastern riches? Is Jerusalem?
Anyan, and Magellan, and Gibraltar,
    All straits, and none but straits, are ways to them,
    Whether where Japhet dwelt, or Cham, or Shem.   20
We think that Paradise and Calvary,
    Christ's cross, and Adam's tree, stood in one place;
Look, Lord, and find both Adams met in me;
    As the first Adam's sweat surrounds my face,
    May the last Adam's blood my soul embrace.   25

So, in his purple wrapp'd, receive me, Lord,
    By these his thorns give me his other crown;
And as to others' souls I preach'd thy word,
    Be this my text, my sermon to mine own,
    Therefore that he may raise, the Lord throws down.   30

                         1635

9 discovery: The reference is to the discovery of the Straits of Magellan.   *10 Per fretum febris:* through the straits of fever.   *11 west:* i.e., the end of his life—and his own realm of discovery. *18 Anyan:* the Bering Straits.   *20 Japhet, Cham, Shem:* the sons of Noah. The descendants of Japhet inhabited Europe, those of Ham, Africa, and those of Shem, Asia. See Genesis 10.

QUESTIONS

1   What is the point of resemblance between physicians and cosmographers that Donne has in mind?
2   With what is the discovery of new lands equated?
3   Why is it appropriate to compare sailing through straits with the experience of dying?
4   Is the wittiness of Donne's metaphors in keeping with the seriousness of the theme? How would you describe the poet's attitude toward his imminent death?

THEY ARE ALL GONE INTO THE WORLD OF LIGHT!

Henry Vaughan

They are all gone into the world of light!
   And I alone sit lingering here;
Their very memory is fair and bright,
   And my sad thoughts doth clear.

It glows and glitters in my cloudy breast   5
   Like stars upon some gloomy grove,
Or those faint beams in which this hill is dressed
   After the sun's remove.

I see them walking in an air of glory,
   Whose light doth trample on my days;   10
My days, which are at best but dull and hoary,
   Mere glimmering and decays.

O holy hope, and high humility,
   High as the heavens above!
These are your walks, and you have showed them me   15
   To kindle my cold love.

Dear, beauteous death! the jewel of the just,
   Shining nowhere but in the dark;
What mysteries do lie beyond thy dust,
   Could man outlook that mark!   20

He that hath found some fledged bird's nest may know
   At first sight if the bird be flown;
But what fair well or grove he sings in now,
   That is to him unknown.

And yet, as angels in some brighter dreams   25
   Call to the soul when man doth sleep,
So some strange thoughts transcend our wonted themes,
   And into glory peep.

If a star were confined into a tomb,
   Her captive flames must needs burn there;   30
But when the hand that locked her up gives room,
   She'll shine through all the sphere.

4: i.e., the memory of them brightens my thoughts.   *20 outlook that mark:* see beyond that limit.
23 well: spring.

O Father of eternal life, and all
  Created glories under Thee!
Resume Thy spirit from this world of thrall   35
  Into true liberty!

Either disperse these mists, which blot and fill
  My perspective still as they pass;
Or else remove me hence unto that hill
  Where I shall need no glass.   40

1655

QUESTIONS

1 Where is the speaker? What time of day is it?
2 How many metaphors involving light or vision or both are there in this poem?

A SLUMBER DID MY SPIRIT SEAL

William Wordsworth

A slumber did my spirit seal;
  I had no human fears:
She seemed a thing that could not feel
  The touch of earthly years.

No motion has she now, no force;   5
  She neither hears nor sees;
Rolled round in earth's diurnal course,
  With rocks, and stones, and trees.

1800

7 diurnal: daily.

QUESTIONS

1 What is the paradox which this poem expresses?
2 What is the tone of this poem? Try reading it aloud, with expression.

TO AUTUMN

John Keats

1

Season of mists and mellow fruitfulness,
  Close bosom-friend of the maturing sun;
Conspiring with him how to load and bless
  With fruit the vines that round the thatch-eaves run;
To bend with apples the mossed cottage-trees,   5
  And fill all fruit with ripeness to the core;
    To swell the gourd, and plump the hazel shells
  With a sweet kernel; to set budding more,
And still more, later flowers for the bees,
Until they think warm days will never cease,   10
    For Summer has o'er-brimmed their clammy cells.

2

Who hath not seen thee oft amid thy store?
  Sometimes whoever seeks abroad may find
Thee sitting careless on a granary floor,
  Thy hair soft-lifted by the winnowing wind;   15
Or on a half-reaped furrow sound asleep,
  Drowsed with the fume of poppies, while thy hook
    Spares the next swath and all its twinéd flowers:
And sometimes like a gleaner thou dost keep
  Steady thy laden head across a brook;   20
  Or by a cider-press, with patient look,
    Thou watchest the last oozings hours by hours.

3

Where are the songs of Spring? Aye, where are they?
  Think not of them, thou hast thy music too—
While barréd clouds bloom the soft-dying day,   25
  And touch the stubble-plains with rosy hue;
Then in a wailful choir the small gnats mourn
  Among the river sallows, borne aloft
    Or sinking as the light wind lives or dies;
And full-grown lambs loud bleat from hilly bourn;   30
  Hedge crickets sing; and now with treble soft
  The redbreast whistles from a garden-croft;
    And gathering swallows twitter in the skies.
September 19, 1819

15 winnowing: blowing the chaff from the grain.   *17 hook:* sickle.   *28 sallows:* small willows.
30 bourn: field.   *32 croft:* an enclosed plot.

QUESTIONS

1 Here the atmosphere of an autumn day becomes the perfect expression of a human mood. In other words, nature is humanized. How does the succession of ways in which the poet "sees" autumn figure in this process?
2 In poetry, autumn is commonly used as a symbol of impending death as well as fulfillment. What features of the last stanza reinforce that traditional symbolic suggestion?

UPHILL

Christina Rossetti

Does the road wind uphill all the way?
  Yes, to the very end.
Will the day's journey take the whole long day?
  From morn to night, my friend.

But is there for the night a resting-place?   5
  A roof for when the slow dark hours begin.
May not the darkness hide it from my face?
  You cannot miss that inn.

Shall I meet other wayfarers at night?
  Those who have gone before.   10
Then must I knock, or call when just in sight?
  They will not keep you standing at that door.

Shall I find comfort, travel-sore and weak?
  Of labor you shall find the sum.
Will there be beds for me and all who seek?   15
  Yea, beds for all who come.

1858

QUESTIONS

1 Why, do you suppose, this poem consists of a series of questions and answers? Where are the answers coming from?
2 Do you think that this is a religious poem? Be ready to explain your opinion.

THE GARDEN OF PROSERPINE

A. C. Swinburne

Here, where the world is quiet;
  Here, where all trouble seems
Dead winds' and spent waves' riot
  In doubtful dreams of dreams;
I watch the green field growing   5
For reaping folk and sowing,
For harvest-time and mowing,
  A sleepy world of streams.

I am tired of tears and laughter,
  And men that laugh and weep;   10
Of what may come hereafter
  For men that sow to reap:
I am weary of days and hours,
Blown buds of barren flowers,
Desires and dreams and powers   15
  And everything but sleep.

Here life has death for a neighbour,
  And far from eye or ear
Wan waves and wet winds labour,
  Weak ships and spirits steer;   20
They drive adrift, and whither
They wot not who make thither;
But no such winds blow hither,
  And no such things grow here.

No growth of moor or coppice,   25
  No heather-flower or vine,
But bloomless buds of poppies,
  Green grapes of Proserpine,
Pale beds of blowing rushes
Where no leaf blooms or blushes   30
Save this whereout she crushes
  For dead men deadly wine.

Pale, without name or number,
  In fruitless fields of corn,

Title: Proserpine, in ancient myth, is queen of the underworld. Thus her garden is the dwelling place of the dead.

They bow themselves and slumber   35
   All night till light is born;
And like a soul belated,
In hell and heaven unmated,
By cloud and mist abated
   Comes out of darkness morn.   40

Though one were strong as seven,
   He too with death shall dwell,
Nor wake with wings in heaven,
   Nor weep for pains in hell;
Though one were fair as roses,   45
His beauty clouds and closes,
And well though love reposes,
   In the end it is not well.

Pale, beyond porch and portal,
   Crowned with calm leaves, she stands   50
Who gathers all things mortal
   With cold immortal hands;
Her languid lips are sweeter
Than love's who fears to greet her
To men that mix and meet her   55
   From many times and lands.

She waits for each and other,
   She waits for all men born;
Forgets the earth her mother,
   The life of fruits and corn;   60
And spring and seed and swallow
Take wing for her and follow
Where summer song rings hollow
   And flowers are put to scorn.

There go the loves that wither,   65
   The old loves with wearier wings;
And all dead years draw thither,
   And all disastrous things;
Dead dreams of days forsaken,
Blind buds that snows have shaken,   70
Wild leaves that winds have taken
   Red strays of ruined springs.

We are not sure of sorrow,
   And joy was never sure;

To-day will die to-morrow; 75
   Time stoops to no man's lure;
And love, grown faint and fretful,
With lips but half regretful
Sighs, and with eyes forgetful
   Weeps that no loves endure. 80

From too much love of living,
   From hope and fear set free,
We thank with brief thanksgiving
   Whatever gods may be
That no life lives for ever; 85
That dead men rise up never;
That even the weariest river
   Winds somewhere safe to sea.

Then star nor sun shall waken,
   Nor any change of light: 90
Nor sound of waters shaken,
   Nor any sound or sight:
Nor wintry leaves nor vernal,
Nor days nor things diurnal;
Only the sleep eternal 95
   In an eternal night.

1866

QUESTIONS

1 By means of the garden metaphor the poet describes a state of mind in which the thought of becoming extinct is more than acceptable. If you were asked to explain this state of mind in more ordinary terms, what facts would you emphasize? Does the speaker, for example, make any distinctions in speaking of human ambitions and desires? Does he think that moral desires matter more than others? Does he feel that he is different from other people? What has brought him to his present state of mind?

2 Do you find the rhyme scheme appropriate? Explain the effect that it has on you.

REQUIEM

Robert Louis Stevenson

Under the wide and starry sky
Dig the grave and let me lie:
Glad did I live and gladly die,
And I laid me down with a will.
This be the verse you grave for me:
Here he lies where he long'd to be;
Home is the sailor, home from the sea,
And the hunter home from the hill.

1887

QUESTIONS

1   What does the poet mean by the line "Here he lies where he long'd to be"? In what
    sense is he "home"? Can you imagine any resemblance between the feelings of a
    sailor returning home from the sea and those of a man nearing the end of the whole
    adventure of life?
2   "Home," it seems, is anywhere under the "wide and starry" sky. What does this
    suggest about the speaker's attitude toward life? What does the word "starry" add
    to the meaning or effect?

THE CAGED SKYLARK

Gerard Manley Hopkins

As a dare-gale skylark scanted in a dull cage
   Man's mounting spirit in his bone-house, mean house, dwells—
   That bird beyond the remembering his free fells;
This in drudgery, day-labouring-out life's age.

Thou aloft on turf or perch or poor low stage,   5
   Both sing sometimes the sweetest, sweetest spells,
   Yet both droop deadly sómetimes in their cells
Or wring their barriers in bursts of fear or rage.

Not that the sweet-fowl, song-fowl, needs not rest—
Why, hear him, hear him babble and drop down to his nest,   10
   But his own nest, wild nest, no prison.

2 bone-house: the body.   *5 turf:* A mound of turf is usually put inside a lark's cage. "Poor low
state" may refer both to a shelf in a cage and any human situation.

Man's spirit will be flesh-bound when found at best,
But uncumbered: meadow-down is not distressed
 For a rainbow footing it nor he for his bónes rísen.

 1918 (Composed 1877)

13 *uncumbered:* Hopkins is referring to the Catholic doctrine which states that the resurrected
body is immortal and not subject to physical limitations.

QUESTIONS

1 What precisely are the implications of the analogy between an uncaged skylark and
   the condition of man after resurrection?
2 Do you think that in comparing the spirit in its earthly condition with a caged bird,
   the poet is thinking only of the limitations of the body? Explain.

VITAE SUMMA BREVIS SPEM NOS VETAT INCOHARE LONGAM

Ernest Dowson

They are not long, the weeping and the laughter,
    Love and desire and hate:
I think they have no portion in us after
      We pass the gate.

They are not long, the days of wine and roses: 5
    Out of a misty dream
Our path emerges for a while, then closes
      Within a dream.

 1896

The title of this poem is taken from one of Horace's odes. It may be translated: "The briefness of
life forbids us to nourish prolonged hope."

QUESTIONS

1 At first glance the poet's choice of his title might seem merely pretentious. Can you
   make a case for saying that it constitutes part of the meaning of the poem?
2 Does the reference of "they" in the repeated phrase change, or is the poet merely
   describing the same experience in different words?

FRIENDS BEYOND

Thomas Hardy

William Dewy, Tranter Reuben, Farmer Ledlow late at plough,
     Robert's kin, and John's, and Ned's,
And the Squire, and Lady Susan, lie in Mellstock churchyard now!

"Gone," I call them, gone for good, that group of local hearts and heads;
     Yet at mothy curfew-tide,   5
And at midnight when the noon-heat breathes it back from walls and leads,

They've a way of whispering to me—fellow-wight who yet abide—
     In the muted, measured note
Of a ripple under archways, or a lone cave's stillicide:

"We have triumphed: this achievement turns the bane to antidote,   10
     Unsuccesses to success,
Many thought-worn eves and morrows to a morrow free of thought.

"No more need we corn and clothing, feel of old terrestial stress;
     Chill detraction stirs no sigh;
Fear of death has even bygone us: death gave all that we possess."   15

W. D.—"Ye mid burn the old bass-viol that I set such value by."
Squire.—"You may hold the manse in fee,
     You may wed my spouse, may let my children's memory of me die."

Lady S.—"You may have my rich brocades, my laces; take each household
     key;
     Ransack coffer, desk, bureau;   20
Quiz the few poor treasures hid there, con the letters kept by me."

Far.—"Ye mid zell my favourite heifer, ye mid let the charlock grow,
     Foul the grinterns, give up thrift."
Far. Wife.—"If ye break my best blue china, children, I shan't care or ho."

All.—"We've no wish to hear the tidings, how the people's fortunes shift;   25
     What your daily doings are;
Who are wedded, born, divided; if your lives beat slow or swift.

---

1 tranter: a tranter is a carrier.   *6 leads:* the lead coverings of roofs.   *9 stillicide:* the dripping of water.   *10 bane:* poison.   *16 mid:* may.   *17 hold the manse in fee:* have title to my house.   *22 charlock:* a kind of weed.   *23 grinterns:* compartments of a granary.

Curious not the least are we if our intents you make or mar,
>If you quire to our old tune,
If the City stage still passes, if the weirs still roar afar." 30

—Thus, with very gods' composure, freed those crosses late and soon
>Which, in life, the Trine allow
(Why, none witteth), and ignoring all that haps beneath the moon.

William Dewy, Tranter Reuben, Farmer Ledlow late at plough,
>Robert's kin, and John's, and Ned's, 35
And the Squire, and Lady Susan, murmur mildly to me now.

1898

30 weins . . . afar: the reference is to the noisy turbulence of streams diverted by dams.   *32 trine:* trinity.

QUESTIONS

1   The poet implies that death was his friends' greatest achievement. Is he suggesting that they are better off dead because they were failures?
2   These people are dead, yet "still abide," the poet imagines. Is he suggesting that their sense of triumph might be achieved before death? Would it come through complete indifference? Does the poet himself feel complete indifference?

TRACT

William Carlos Williams

I will teach you my townspeople
how to perform a funeral—
for you have it over a troop
of artists—
unless one should scour the world— 5
you have the ground sense necessary.
See! the hearse leads.
I begin with a design for a hearse.
For Christ's sake not black—
nor white either—and not polished! 10
Let it be weathered—like a farm wagon—
with gilt wheels (this could be
applied fresh at small expense)
or no wheels at all:
a rough dray to drag over the ground. 15

Knock the glass out!
My God—glass, my townspeople!
For what purpose? Is it for the dead
to look out or for us to see
how well he is housed or to see   20
the flowers or the lack of them—
or what?
To keep the rain and snow from him?
He will have a heavier rain soon:
pebbles and dirt and what not.   25
Let there be no glass—
and no upholstery phew!
and no little brass rollers
and small easy wheels on the bottom—
my townspeople what are you thinking of?   30

A rough plain hearse then
with gilt wheels and no top at all.
On this the coffin lies
by its own weight.
                    No wreaths please—   35
especially no hot house flowers.
Some common memento is better,
something he prized and is known by:
his old clothes—a few books perhaps—
God knows what! You realize   40
how we are about these things
my townspeople—
something will be found—anything
even flowers if he had come to that.
So much for the hearse.   45

For heaven's sake though see to the driver!
Take off the silk hat! In fact
that's no place at all for him—
up there unceremoniously
dragging our friend out to his own dignity!   50
Bring him down—bring him down!
Low and inconspicuous! I'd not have him ride.
on the wagon at all—damn him—
the undertaker's understrapper!
Let him hold the reins   55
and walk at the side
and inconspicuously too!

Then briefly as to yourselves:
Walk behind—as they do in France,
seventh class, or if you ride   60
Hell take curtains! Go with some show
of inconvenience; sit openly—
to the weather as to grief.
Or do you think you can shut grief in?
What—from us? We who have perhaps   65
nothing to lose? Share with us
share with us—it will be money
in your pockets.
        Go now
I think you are ready.   70
            1917

QUESTIONS

1 Why does the poet want the hearse to be weathered? How would the effect of a
  weathered vehicle differ from that of one painted entirely in black or white? If the
  poet does not want the vehicle painted, why should he suggest gilt wheels?
2 The poet explains why he does not want glass in the hearse. Does he object to
  upholstery for the same reason? Why does he find "small easy wheels" almost
  unthinkable?
3 Is the poet being snobbish in calling the driver the "undertaker's understrapper"?
  What is his point in using a snobbish phrase with such vehemence?
4 Explain the phrase, "We who have perhaps / nothing to lose?" Nothing to lose by
  what? What is the tone of the phrase, "money in your pockets"?
5 What is the general attitude toward death that the poet is objecting to?

PONDY WOODS

Robert Penn Warren

The buzzards over Pondy Woods
Achieve the blue tense altitudes,
Black figments that the woods release,
Obscenity in form and grace,
Drifting high through the pure sunshine   5
Till the sun in gold decline.

Big Jim Todd was a slick black buck
Laying low in the mud and muck

Of Pondy Woods when the sun went down
In gold, and the buzzards tilted down 10
A windless vortex to the black-gum trees
To sit along the quiet boughs,
Devout and swollen, at their ease.

By the buzzard roost Big Jim Todd
Listened for hoofs on the corduroy road 15
Or for the foul and sucking sound
A man's foot makes on the marshy ground.
Past midnight, when the moccasin
Slipped from the log and, trailing in
Its obscured waters, broke 20
The dark algae, one lean bird spoke.

"Nigger, you went this afternoon
For your Saturday spree at the Blue Goose saloon,
So you've got on your Sunday clothes,
On your big splay feet got patent-leather shoes. 25
But a buzzard can smell the thing you've done;
The posse will get you—run, nigger, run—
There's a fellow behind you with a big shot-gun.

Nigger, nigger, you'll sweat cold sweat
In your patent-leather shoes and Sunday clothes 30
When down your track the steeljacket goes
Mean and whimpering over the wheat.

"Nigger, your breed ain't metaphysical."
The buzzard coughed. His words fell
In the darkness, mystic and ambrosial. 35
"But we maintain our ancient rite,
Eat gods by day and prophesy by night.

We swing against the sky and wait;
You seize the hour, more passionate
Than strong, and strive with time to die— 40
With Time, the beaked tribe's astute ally.

"The Jew-boy died. The Syrian vulture swung
Remotely above the cross whereon he hung
From dinner-time to supper-time, and all
The people gathered there watched him until 45
The lean brown chest no longer stirred,
Then idly watched the slow majestic bird

That in the last sun above the twilit hill
Gleamed for a moment at the height and slid
Down the hot wind and in the darkness hid.   50
Nigger, regard the circumstance of breath:
'Non omnis moriar,' the poet saith.''

Pedantic, the bird clacked its gray beak,
With a Tennessee accent to the classic phrase;
Jim understood, and was about to speak,   55
But the buzzard drooped one wing and filmed the eyes.

At dawn unto the Sabbath wheat he came,
That gave to the dew its faithless yellow flame
From kindly loam in recollection of
The fires that in the brutal rock once strove.   60
To the ripe wheat fields he came at dawn.
Northward the printed smoke stood quiet above
The distant cabins of Squiggtown.
A train's far whistle blew and drifted away
Coldly; lucid and thin the morning lay   65
Along the farms, and here no sound
Touched the sweet earth miraculously stilled.
Then down the damp and sudden wood there belled
The musical white-throated hound.

In Pondy Woods in the August drouth   70
Lurks fever and the cottonmouth.
And buzzards over Pondy Woods
Achieve the blue tense altitudes,

Drifting high in the pure sunshine
Till the sun in gold decline;   75
Then golden and hieratic through
The night their eyes burn two by two.

                              1928

52 'Non omnis moriar': "I shall not wholly die." The poet is Horace.

QUESTIONS

1 The plight of Big Jim Todd evidently represents man's inability to cope with the
   mystery of death. How does the creation of the bizarre talking buzzards help the
   poet express his feelings about the problem?
2 Why are there such notable shifts in style?
3 What is the tone of the ninth stanza?

AFTER APPLE-PICKING

Robert Frost

My long two-pointed ladder's sticking through a tree
Toward heaven still,
And there's a barrel that I didn't fill
Beside it, and there may be two or three
Apples I didn't pick upon some bough.   5
But I am done with apple-picking now.
Essence of winter sleep is on the night,
The scent of apples: I am drowsing off.
I cannot rub the strangeness from my sight
I got from looking through a pane of glass   10
I skimmed this morning from the drinking trough
And held against the world of hoary grass.
It melted, and I let it fall and break.
But I was well
Upon my way to sleep before it fell,   15
And I could tell
What form my dreaming was about to take.
Magnified apples appear and disappear,
Stem end and blossom end,
And every fleck of russet showing clear.   20
My instep arch not only keeps the ache,
It keeps the pressure of a ladder-round.
I feel the ladder sway as the boughs bend.
And I keep hearing from the cellar bin
The rumbling sound   25
Of load on load of apples coming in.
For I have had too much
Of apple-picking: I am overtired
Of the great harvest I myself desired.
There were ten thousand thousand fruit to touch,   30
Cherish in hand, lift down, and not let fall.
For all
That struck the earth,
No matter if not bruised or spiked with stubble,
Went surely to the cider-apple heap   35
As of no worth.
One can see what will trouble
This sleep of mine, whatever sleep it is.
Were he not gone,

The woodchuck could say whether it's like his   40
Long sleep, as I describe its coming on,
Or just some human sleep.

1930

QUESTIONS

1   How do we know that the poet is not talking just about the experience of apple-picking and ordinary drowsiness? How would you "translate" the following lines: "There were ten thousand thousand fruit to touch, / Cherish in hand, lift down, and not let fall"?
2   Pick out the words or phrases in this poem that suggest a sense of the ideal.
3   Why does the poet use such an ordinary experience as apple-picking to symbolize all of his aspirations and achievements?
4   What is the point of the last four lines?

IN THE TREE HOUSE AT NIGHT

James Dickey

And now the green household is dark.
The half-moon completely is shining
On the earth-lighted tops of the trees.
To be dead, a house must be still.
The floor and the walls wave me slowly;   5
I am deep in them over my head.
The needles and pine cones about me

Are full of small birds at their roundest,
Their fists without mercy gripping
Hard down through the tree to the roots   10
To sing back at light when they feel it.
We lie here like angels in bodies,
My brothers and I, one dead,
The other asleep from much living.

In mid-air huddled beside me.   15
Dark climbed to us here as we climbed
Up the nails I have hammered all day
Through the sprained, comic rungs of the ladder
Of broom handles, crate slats, and laths

Foot by foot up the trunk to the branches　　　　　　20
Where we came out at last over lakes

Of leaves, of fields disencumbered of earth
That move with the moves of the spirit.
Each nail that sustains us I set here;
Each nail in the house is now steadied　　　　　　25
By my dead brother's huge, freckled hand.
Through the years, he has pointed his hammer
Up into these limbs, and told us

That we must ascend, and all lie here.
Step after step he has brought me,　　　　　　30
Embracing the trunk as his body,
Shaking its limbs with my heartbeat,
Till the pine cones danced without wind
And fell from the branches like apples.
In the arm-slender forks of our dwelling　　　　　　35

I breathe my live brother's light hair.
The blanket around us becomes
As solid as stone, and it sways.
With all my heart, I close
The blue, timeless eye of my mind.　　　　　　40
Wind springs, as my dead brother smiles
And touches the tree at the root;

A shudder of joy runs up
The trunk; the needles tingle;
One bird uncontrollably cries.　　　　　　45
The wind changes round, and I stir
Within another's life. Whose life?
Who is dead? Whose presence is living?
When may I fall strangely to earth,

Who am nailed to this branch by a spirit?　　　　　　50
Can two bodies make up a third?
To sing, must I feel the world's light?
My green, graceful bones fill the air
With sleeping birds. Alone, alone
And with them I move gently.　　　　　　55
I move at the heart of the world.

1962

QUESTIONS

1 What reasons can you find for supposing that the recollections of the tree house symbolize a desire for death?
2 A tree offers an escape from earth, yet is rooted in earth. How does the poet exploit this fact?

THE FAR FIELD

Theodore Roethke

I

I dream of journeys repeatedly:
Of flying like a bat deep into a narrowing tunnel,
Of driving alone, without luggage, out a long peninsula,
The road lined with snow-laden second growth,
A fine dry snow ticking the windshield,   5
Alternate snow and sleet, no on-coming traffic,
And no lights behind, in the blurred side-mirror,
The road changing from glazed tarface to a rubble of stone,
Ending at last in a hopeless sand-rut,
Where the car stalls,   10
Churning in a snowdrift
Until the headlights darken.

II

At the field's end, in the corner missed by the mower,
Where the turf drops off into a grass-hidden culvert,
Haunt of the cat-bird, nesting-place of the field-mouse,   15
Not too far away from the ever-changing flower-dump,
Among the tin cans, tires, rusted pipes, broken machinery,—
One learned of the eternal;
And in the shrunken face of a dead rat, eaten by rain and ground-beetles
(I found it lying among the rubble of an old coal bin)   20
And the tom-cat, caught near the pheasant-run,
Its entrails strewn over the half-grown flowers,
Blasted to death by the night watchman.

I suffered for birds, for young rabbits caught in the mower,
My grief was not excessive.   25
For to come upon warblers in early May
Was to forget time and death:
How they filled the oriole's elm, a twittering restless cloud, all one morning,

And I watched and watched till my eyes blurred from the bird shapes—
Cape May, Blackburnian, Cerulean,—   30
Moving, elusive as fish, fearless,
Hanging, bunched like young fruit, bending the end branches,
Still for a moment,
Then pitching away in half-flight,
Lighter than finches,   35
While the wrens bickered and sang in the half-green hedgerows,
And the flicker drummed from his dead tree in the chicken yard.
—Or to lie naked in sand,
In the silted shallows of a slow river,
Fingering a shell,   40
Thinking:
Once I was something like this, mindless,
Or perhaps with another mind, less peculiar;
Or to sink down to the hips in a mossy quagmire;
Or, with skinny knees, to sit astride a wet log,   45
Believing:
I'll return again,
As a snake or a raucous bird,
Or, with luck, as a lion.

I learned not to fear infinity,   50
The far field, the windy cliffs of forever,
The dying of time in the white light of tomorrow.
The wheel turning away from itself,
The sprawl of the wave,
The on-coming water.   55

III
The river turns on itself,
The tree retreats into its own shadow.
I feel a weightless change, a moving forward
As of water quickening before a narrowing channel
When banks converge, and the wide river whitens;   60
Or when two rivers combine, the blue glacial torrent
And the yellowish-green from the mountainy upland,—
At first a swift rippling between rocks,
Then a long running over flat stones
Before descending to the alluvial plain,   65
To the clay banks, and the wild grapes hanging from the elmtrees,
The slightly trembling water
Dropping a fine yellow silt where the sun stays;
And the crabs bask near the edge,
The weedy edge, alive with small snakes and bloodsuckers,—   70

I have come to a still, but not a deep center,
A point outside the glittering current;
My eyes stare at the bottom of a river.
At the irregular stones, iridescent sandgrains,
My mind moves in more than one place,   75
In a country half-land, half-water.

I am renewed by death, thought of my death,
The dry scent of a dying garden in September,
The wind fanning the ash of a low fire.
What I love is near at hand,   80
Always, in earth and air.

IV
The lost self changes,
Turning toward the sea,
A sea shape turning around,—
An old man with his feet before the fire,   85
In robes of green, in garments of adieu.

A man faced with his own immensity
Wakes all the waves, all their loose wandering fire.
The murmur of the absolute, the why
Of being born fails on his naked ears.   90
His spirit moves like monumental wind
That gentles on a sunny blue plateau.
He is the end of things, the final man.

All finite things reveal infinitude:
The mountain with its singular bright shade   95
Like the blue shine on freshly frozen snow,
The after-light upon ice-burdened pines;
Odor of basswood on a mountain-slope,
A scent beloved of bees;
Silence of water above a sunken tree: 100
The pure serene of memory in one man,—
A ripple widening from a single stone
Winding around the waters of the world.

1962

QUESTIONS

1   Can you distinguish the turns of thought indicated by the section divisions in this
    poem? Does the last section recall the first?

2 Why is the speaker renewed by the thought of his death? Is it something he looks forward to that inspires him?

3 Would you describe the speaker as a mystic?

TOPICS FOR COMPOSITION

1 Write an essay on the subject of coping with the fear of death, using one or more of the preceding poems for illustration or support.

2 Analyze the use of the analogy between death and sleep in one or more of the poems in this unit.

3 Write an essay on the topic "Love of Nature and the Question of Death," using one or more of the following poems for illustration: "To Autumn," "After Apple-Picking," "Hurt Hawks" (see Part Two).

4 Defend the opinion that people can live good and happy lives without believing in life after death.

5 Defend the opinion that traditional moral ideals are meaningless without belief in an afterlife.

6 In recent years there has been considerable protest against current funeral practices. Following William Carlos Williams's example, write on the subject of what is or is not appropriate at funerals.

7 Write an analysis of the handling of tone in any one of the poems of this section.

8 Write an essay on the topic, "The Poetic Idea of Heaven."

9 Write an analysis of the use of imagery in any of the poems in this unit.

10 Suppose that Hardy's "friends beyond" discovered that they had to resume their earthly roles awhile longer. Would they be inclined to behave differently? Present your speculations in an essay, along with a "moral," if one occurs to you.

11 Drawing any inspiration you can from James Dickey's poem, write a descriptive piece entitled "The World of the Tree House at Night."

 # INDEX OF AUTHORS AND TITLES

INDEX OF FIRST LINES OF POETRY